889 BEA

AN INTRODUCTION TO
MODERN GREEK LITERATURE

City and Islington Sixth Form College
283-309 Goswell Road
London
EC1 7LA
020 7520 0652

CITY AND ISLINGTON
COLLEGE

This book is due for return on or before the date last stamped below.
You may renew by telephone. Please quote the Barcode No.
May not be renewed if required by another reader.

Fine: 5p per day

D0322298

SA011096

An Introduction to Modern Greek Literature

SECOND EDITION
REVISED AND EXPANDED

RODERICK BEATON

Koraes Professor of Modern Greek and Byzantine History,
Language, and Literature
King's College London

CLARENDON PRESS · OXFORD

Oxford University Press, Great Clarendon Street, Oxford OX2 6DP

Oxford New York

Athens Auckland Bangkok Bogotá Buenos Aires Calcutta
Cape Town Chennai Dar es Salaam Delhi Florence Hong Kong Istanbul
Karachi Kuala Lumpur Madrid Melbourne Mexico City Mumbai
Nairobi Paris São Paulo Singapore Taipei Tokyo Toronto Warsaw

and associated companies in Berlin Ibadan

Oxford is a trade mark of Oxford University Press

Published in the United States
by Oxford University Press Inc., New York

© Roderick Beaton 1994, 1999

First published 1994

First published in Clarendon Paperback 1999

All rights reserved. No part of this publication may be reproduced,
stored in a retrieval system, or transmitted, in any form or by any means,
without the prior permission in writing of Oxford University Press.
Within the UK, exceptions are allowed in respect of any fair dealing for the
purpose of research or private study, or criticism or review, as permitted
under the Copyright, Designs and Patents Act, 1988, or in the case of
reprographic reproduction in accordance with the terms of the licences
issued by the Copyright Licensing Agency. Enquiries concerning
reproduction outside these terms and in other countries should be
sent to the Rights Department, Oxford University Press,
at the address above

This book is sold subject to the condition that it shall not, by way
of trade or otherwise, be lent, re-sold, hired out or otherwise circulated
without the publisher's prior consent in any form of binding or cover
other than that in which it is published and without a similar condition
including this condition being imposed on the subsequent purchaser

British Library Cataloguing in Publication Data
Data available

Library of Congress Cataloging in Publication Data
Beaton, Roderick
An introduction to modern Greek literature / Roderick Beaton.
Includes bibliographies and indexes.
1. Greek literature, Modern—20th century—History and criticism.
2. Greek literature, Modern—19th century—History and criticism.
I. Title.
PA522.B43 1994   889.09—dc20   93–2640
ISBN 0–19–815974–9

3 5 7 9 10 8 6 4

Printed in Great Britain
on acid-free paper by
Bookcraft Ltd.,
Midsomer Norton, Somerset

SAO1196
889 BEA

FOR MY FATHER

FOREWORD

Preface to the second edition

This book in its original form was written between 1990 and 1992, and published in May 1994. When a Greek translation was commissioned a year later, I undertook a thorough overhaul of the text, correcting such errors as had slipped through the net and updating the bibliographical references. This second edition in English incorporates all the new and revised material written for the Greek edition (most substantially in the Introduction and Chapter 5), and also includes many additional bibliographical references, updated, so far as has proved practicable, to the end of 1997. The chronological period covered by the book (from the early nineteenth century to 1992) remains unchanged.

New debts of the kind listed in the original preface (that is, to graduate students whose work I have known professionally and from whom I have learnt while working on the book) should be recorded to: David Connolly, Aglaia Giannakopoulou, Georgia Gotsi, Anthony Hirst, Kerstin Jentsch-Mancor, Philothei Kolitsi, Maria Margaronis, Jocelyn Pye, George Vassiadis, and Sophia Voulgari.

I am also particularly grateful to Dr Haris Vlavianos, who as commissioning editor for Nefeli, Athens, was instrumental in seeing the Greek edition of this book through press and in the process first encouraged me to update and expand it, and also to the Greek translators Evangelia Zurgu and Marianna Spanaki, with whom it was a pleasure to work closely. In addition, I am grateful to Dr David Ricks for a number of specific suggestions.

As before, responsibility for all remaining omissions and deficiencies, as well as for the views expressed, are mine alone.

King's College London   R.B.
January 1998

Preface

THIS book is not a conventional history of Modern Greek literature, but neither does it aim to replace literary history with any specific radical programme. It starts out from the belief that literary works, or texts, do not exist in a vacuum, and that a full and rewarding understanding of any one work of literature presupposes, ideally, a knowledge of the historical circumstances in which it was written and has since been read, as well as of other works which come before and after it. English-speaking readers have for many years now had access to some of the high points of Modern Greek writing, through translations of the Nobel laureates Seferis and Elytis, of Cavafy and Kazantzakis; and a growing English-language bibliography on the subject now exists. Systematic reference books, the histories of Modern Greek literature by K. Th. Dimaras and by Linos Politis, have also appeared in English; indeed the latter was commissioned by Oxford University Press and appeared only twenty years ago. But Dimaras' history effectively ends with the expulsion of the Greeks from Anatolia in 1922, while Politis gives fairly scant treatment to developments since the Second World War.

There are three reasons why a new approach to the subject is now needed. First, the period since 1960 has seen an unprecedented output of creative literature of all kinds in Greece, but especially of prose fiction, as well as the appearance of vibrant new trends which have also had an effect on the way in which many writers of the past are now being read. Secondly, none of the older histories treats the relationship of literary texts with history, and with other literary texts, sufficiently to give the non-Greek reader an adequate sense of these complex inter-relationships. And thirdly, the growing population of students throughout the English-speaking world, both at school and university, for whom Modern Greek literature forms a significant part of the curriculum, adds to the impetus to provide the kind of overview from which they can find their bearings in the subject.

However this is neither a textbook nor a reference book. My aim here has been to provide a fairly detailed but readable introduction to the subject, highlighting those writers and works, which either now or in the past have enjoyed critical and/or popular acclaim, and placing the emphasis on the relationships that link one work with another and with its historical context. In the process I have frequently proposed readings of particular works, or tried to highlight features which I believe may have been overlooked or which merit further study. In all of these matters there inevitably enters an element of subjective judgement for which I make no apology. No reading of an individual work, and still less any attempt to draw together some of the lineaments of many different works over a period of almost two centuries, can claim to be definitive. I also make no claims to be exhaustive, and the decision on what to omit has often had to be finely balanced. The most glaring of my omissions (of Greek literature before 1821 and of all dramatic works) are explained, if not excused, in the Introduction.

What follows is by no means a recitation of facts, although there are many facts and I have striven to make them as accurate as possible. Essentially this book offers a reading of those facts, with which the reader is invited to engage. If the result is to stimulate non-specialists to delve further into the works themselves, and specialists to respond with different readings of their own, then this book will have well served its purpose.

This book has benefited immeasurably from many hours of tutorials and seminars, spread over many years, with both undergraduate and postgraduate students, at King's College London, and before that at the University of Birmingham, as well as at other places where I have been given the opportunity to lecture and to meet students. The annual 'Greek Weekend', organized by the Standing Committee on Modern Greek in the Universities (SCOMGIU) since 1984, and the SCOMGIU Research Colloquia, held annually since 1988, have each afforded a particularly valuable forum for the exchange of views and ideas. The debts heaped up are too numerous to list, but I should make it clear from the outset that much of my own thinking about Modern Greek literature has taken shape through continuous dialogue with students and colleagues. Specific debts are acknowledged in the notes and in the References at the end of the book. To many whose postgraduate work in Modern Greek studies at British universities I have known, supervised, or examined, I am conscious of a debt that is not always quantifiable or easily identified in retrospect. Excluding those whose theses have already resulted in a publication cited in the References, I would like to record such debts to: Erifilli Bayia, Eleni Calligas, Michalis Chryssanthopoulos, Katerina Krikos-Davis, Sarah Ekdawi, Dionysis Kapsalis, David Landsman, Elli Philokyprou, Jonathan Sherman, Athanassia Sourbati, Alexandra Thalassis, Karen Rhoads van Dyck, Athina Voyatzoglou, Christopher Williams, and Helen Yannakakis.

Thanks are also due, finally, to Virginia Llewellyn Smith, then an Editor at Oxford University Press, who first encouraged me to write a book on this subject, and to Dr Peter Mackridge, who carefully read the whole book, in an earlier draft, and alerted me to many pitfalls. For whatever inaccuracies or deficiencies remain, I am of course solely responsible.

King's College London   R.B.
October 1992

Contents

Contents

How to Use this Book

THIS book is addressed equally to the specialist and the non-specialist reader. In the nature of things, however, there comes a time when the needs of different readers will diverge, and the purpose of this note is to signal the divergences. Specifically addressed to the *specialist*, or at least to the reader with some previous acquaintance with the subject, are the notes, which contain guidance on further reading, in the form of 'author–date' references, and where necessary explain or justify statements in the text which might be thought controversial; the full list of bibliographical References at the end of the book; and the Index of Greek Titles. The Introduction, which sets out the ground rules for what follows, and explains how this book differs from other treatments of the subject, may also be either skimmed or skipped altogether by the reader who is approaching Modern Greek literature for the first time. Specifically addressed to this latter reader, on the other hand, is the Guide to Translations at the end of the book.

No knowledge of Greek is assumed, and all quotations from Greek literary works are given both in the original language and in my own translation. Other quotations from Greek are given in translation only in the text, with the original Greek appearing in the notes. In the text, the titles of Greek works are given in translated form; for each work cited the notes will contain either an 'author–date' reference to a modern edition (the Greek title can then be found in the list of References) or, if no such edition exists or if the work is merely mentioned rather than discussed, the Greek title without further bibliographical information. The References at the end of the book give full bibliographical information on all sources, both primary and secondary, mentioned in the notes. They are *not* intended as a full, or even as a representative, bibliography of the subject. For a full English language bibliography see Philippides 1990 (currently being updated).

Finally, it should be said that there is no satisfactory system for representing the Modern Greek language in the roman alphabet. To a large extent, modern computer typesetting has made it unnecessary to transliterate from the Greek alphabet; but transliteration is still necessary for proper names (especially those of writers) and has been preferred for names of periodicals and publishing houses. In these cases the principle I have adopted has been that, where a Greek name has a well-established form in English, this takes precedence ('Athens', 'Cavafy'; not 'Athina', 'Kavafis'); otherwise transliteration is broadly phonetic but allows some concessions to the *written* form of the Greek.

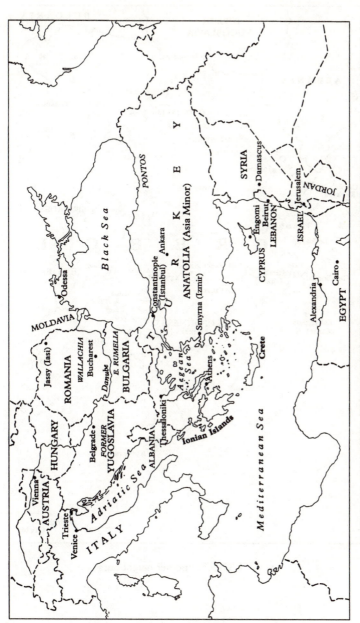

MAP 1. Greece between western Europe and the Middle East

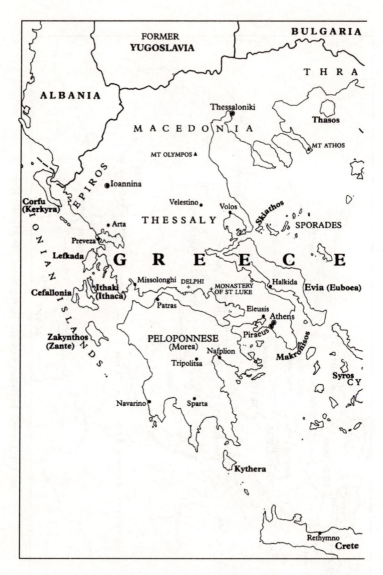

MAP. 2. Greece and her neighbours

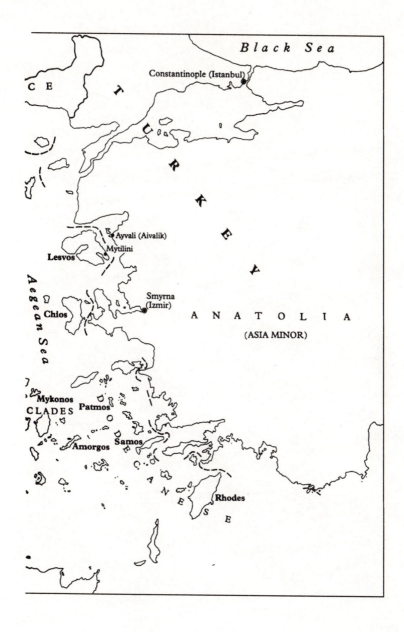

Introduction

This book aims to provide a new overview of Greek poetry and prose fiction since approximately the time that the Greek nation-state came into existence in the 1820s. The purpose of this introductory chapter is, first of all, to set out the reasons why such an overview is necessary and timely, and secondly to explain the perspective, and the self-imposed limitations, which are integral to this particular attempt.

AN 'INTRODUCTION', NOT A 'HISTORY'

It should be declared from the outset that this book has been conceived as a contribution to literary history (as opposed, say, to literary criticism or literary theory). By literary history I mean the whole network of interrelationships through which writings are linked both with one another and with the wider history of the culture of which they form a part. In this sense, literary history is by no means a mere chronicle of names and dates; in particular, it involves critical reading of texts which it may often seek, as criticism does, both to interpret and to evaluate. But interpretation and evaluation, in this book, will always take place against a background of a specific historical *context*, which defines both the production and the reception of the literary work.

However, if the basic thrust of this book is historical, it none the less departs considerably from the established pattern of the traditional *History of Literature*, of the kind that was in vogue throughout Europe at the end of the last century and the early part of this. Such standard works of reference have long been established for all the literatures of Europe. Once upon a time, these *Histories* played an essential role in establishing the 'canon' of literature in the modern vernaculars, and in championing the cause of the vernacular against the cultural hegemony of the classics, particularly Latin. There remains much to argue about in precisely what is 'in' and what is 'out' in the canon of English or French literature since, say, the twelfth century; but the existence of such a canon, as a substantial body of work deserving of both respect and systematic study, is nowhere in doubt. (A hundred years ago, in the days of Hippolyte Taine and Matthew Arnold, the situation was very different.)

As a result, in English, French, German, or Italian literature, the traditional format for the *History of Literature* has tended to be superseded by overviews of particular periods or literary movements. The sheer volume, especially of nineteenth- and twentieth-century literature, and of the scholarship devoted to it, makes comprehensive coverage of the whole span of 'modern' (i.e. vernacular) literature impossible.[1]

In Greece, the history of the country's 'modern' literature has been written approximately thirty times, beginning with Iakovos Rizos Neroulos as early as 1827, and carried on almost half a century later by Alexandros Rizos Rangavis, himself one of the most prolific poets and novelists of his time. Neither of these works understands its subject in anything like the way in which it would come to be defined in the twentieth century.[2] It was only with the histories of D. C. Hesseling in French, and of Ilias Voutieridis in Greek (both published during the 1920s) that the standard pattern began to emerge, clearly to dominate no fewer than twenty-four histories of Modern Greek literature published between 1948 and 1981.[3] Of

---

[1] On this general perspective see in particular Fokkema 1984 and the essays collected in Perkins 1991. A similar dissatisfaction with the traditional scheme of the *History of Literature*, in the field of the Modern Greek studies, has been expressed by Kehayoglou (1980: 60); Lambropoulos, in Alexiou and Lambropoulos 1985: 15–36; Siaflekis 1988; Lambropoulos 1989; Jusdanis 1991; University of Thessaloniki 1994 (contributions by Dimaras, Vitti, Veloudis, Apostolidou, and Beaton).

[2] See, respectively, Neroulos 1870 (1st publd: Geneva, 1827); Rangavis 1877. Neroulos defines his subject, 'letters', as (chiefly) the dissemination of ideas by Greek exponents of the Enlightenment, and sums up the subject matter of his *History* under the headings of Theology and Rhetoric; History; Philology (in the sense of the study of language); Translations; Women Translators and Editors; Travel Writing and Novels (of which the most recent mentioned is Heliodoros' novel or romance of the 4th century AD!); and last of all, Lyric Poetry (see pp. 165–8). Rangavis devoted more than half of his work to scientific, philosophical, theological, even archaeological writing, placing poetry after all this diversity, and touching on the novel only in the closing six pages.

[3] Hesseling 1924 (revision of the Dutch original, published 1920); Voutieridis 1924, 1927. For a critical survey of these histories, together with a further twenty-three histories published between 1948 and 1980, see Kehayoglou 1980. To the *Histories* surveyed by Kechayoglou should be added Tsakonas 1981; 1992; together with two more limited surveys dating from the 1980s, whose approach has more in common with that of the present book: Mitsakis 1985 (which reviews the twentieth century); Meraklis 1987 (dealing with poetry from 1945 to the early 1980s). For an invaluable work of reference which follows a different format but covers the same ground as the traditional *Histories* with factual comprehensiveness, see Mastrodimitris 1997.

these, it is generally acknowledged, three stand out: that by K. Dimaras which appeared in 1948 and inaugurated the proliferation of such histories; that by Linos Politis which was commissioned and first published, in English, by Oxford University Press in 1973; and that by Mario Vitti, first published in Italian in 1971 and updated in Greek as recently as 1987.[4] All of these *Histories* trace the growth and development of modern Greek literature from the emergence into writing of the spoken, or vernacular, form of the Greek language in the late Byzantine period; and together, with appropriate differences of emphasis, they draw and consolidate the main lines of the vernacular canon, clearly distinguishing it at the same time from its classical and Byzantine predecessors.

In Greek, just as in the other literatures of Europe, the traditional format was necessary for as long as it took to establish a 'Modern Greek' canon and to chart the process of its historical emancipation from the learned tradition of Byzantium. This particular battle no longer needs to be fought. It has been won and the fruits of victory exist in the form of valuable works of reference, which at the same time testify in great detail to the perceptions of the Modern Greek literary canon during the formative period from the 1940s to the 1970s. In addition, just as with the other European literatures, the rapid expansion of Modern Greek literary studies, not only in Greek universities but also around the world, has meant that inclusiveness across the whole history of modern Greek literature, from the twelfth century to the 1990s, is scarcely possible any longer within a manageable size. There are practical, as well as fundamental intellectual reasons, for signalling a change.

So this book makes no claims to offer, in the traditional sense, a 'history' of Modern Greek literature. Instead, it seeks to explore, in its historical development, a specific and clearly delineated period of Greek literature which has never been subjected to such treatment before.

AN OVERVIEW FOR THE 1990s

During the same period (1948–81) that saw the proliferation of *Histories of Modern Greek Literature* on the pattern described, a whole series of important changes was under way, changes in which these histories themselves surely played a part. Few readers, I imagine,

---

[4] Dimaras 1974; L. Politis 1973; Vitti 1987.

among those already familiar with the field today, will disagree that these changes have indeed taken place. But as yet we have no overall view of the subject which attempts to place them in perspective.[5]

At the risk of oversimplification, I would summarize these changes as follows: the consolidation and expansion of Modern Greek literary studies to a degree that permits differentiation into distinct periods and professional specialization within them; the ending of the polarized phase of the 'Language Question'; the (consequent?) revival of interest in previously neglected writers who wrote in the formal, or purist, register; and the dynamic developments in new writing, particularly, but not only, in prose fiction, since the 1960s. Taken together, these four changes have transformed the field of Modern Greek literary studies almost beyond recognition, since 1948 when Dimaras' *History* was first published.

Defining the field. The question of when 'Modern Greek' literature begins was aired at a conference in Venice in 1991, conceived and convened by N. M. Panayotakis to debate that very subject. Among several proposals it was suggested, by G. P. Savvidis, that the dividing line between medieval and modern Greek literature could sensibly be drawn at the moment of transition from a manuscript culture to a print culture; that is, with the first appearance of the modern language in print.[6] Such dividing lines can never be entirely clearcut, if only because whatever criterion one adopts, there is almost always a period during which the old and the new co-exist (in the case of manuscript versus print, in the dissemination of texts in Modern Greek, this co-existence covers almost three centuries after the appearance of the first printed texts). Of greater importance, perhaps, than the solutions proposed in Venice, was the fact that the issue came to be addressed at all. The broad sweep of Modern Greek literature, from the twelfth century to the twentieth, covers such a range of linguistic styles, cultural contexts, and modes of production and reception, that it is no longer self-evident that it should invariably be studied as a single continuum. In part this is an inevitable, and not necessarily beneficial, consequence of the

[5] Exceptions in the field of the prose fiction of the last two centuries are the studies by Tziovas (1993a) and Tonnet (1996). Although the latter's declared subject covers a much longer timespan, the greater part of his study is in fact taken up with an overview of Greek fiction from the late 18th century to the 1960s.

[6] Savvidis 1993. See also the contributions to the same volume by: Eideneier, Vitti, S. Alexiou, Kapsomenos (Panayotakis 1993: pp. 42–73).

progressive specialization of academic study in all disciplines. But we also *know* a great deal more than we once did about the earlier periods of 'Modern Greek' literature, and this has enabled us, in turn, to see how they differ from one another.

The term 'medieval Greek' is now increasingly coming to be used to refer to the vernacular language and literature of the period from the twelfth century on, included by most of the standard histories as 'Modern Greek'. Our knowledge of the literary achievements of Crete under Venetian domination and the influence of the Italian Renaissance, between the fourteenth and the seventeenth centuries, and of the complex cultural amalgam that made them possible, has increased immeasurably in the last few years (thanks, in large measure, to the work of Linos Politis, Stylianos Alexiou, and Nikos Panayotakis). The impact of the Enlightenment upon educated Greek circles in the eighteenth century produced a rather different kind of literature again (on which much pioneering work was done by K. Dimaras). Each of these periods of 'Modern Greek literature' is increasingly coming to be studied, in depth, on its own terms.

The period of Greek literature on which I have chosen to concentrate in this book deserves, no less than those earlier periods, to be viewed as a coherent whole. There is more in common between Solomos and Ganas, between Grigorios Palaiologos and Evyenios Aranitsis (in terms of language, aesthetic interests, and the kind of readership addressed) than there is between any one of these and Kaisarios Dapontes in the eighteenth century, Georgios Chortatsis in the sixteenth, or the anonymous authors of the vernacular romances of the fourteenth. This is not, of course, to deny that links exist (those between Solomos and Cretan literature are particularly important): to view a historical period as a coherent whole does not—*and must not*—imply cutting it off from all that has gone before. The revitalization of the legacy of earlier periods is a common phenomenon in literary history. But paradoxically the importance of such revitalization tends to be obscured by an approach which treats cultural history as a continuum. The rediscovery, by writers and readers, of types of literature which flourished before the nineteenth century will often be encountered in this book. One entirely legitimate consequence of concentrating on the literature of only the last two centuries, may well be to clarify our understanding of how, when, and why the precedents of earlier writers in Greek have been invoked, and the role that these have played.

The same, mutatis mutandis, may be said for the folk tradition (comprising oral poetry, legends and wondertales, the shadow-puppet theatre known as Karagiozis), which will frequently be mentioned in the pages that follow as a source on which writers in our period have drawn. But the traditional place assigned to these oral traditions in literary histories, among the historical beginnings, and placed far away in time in the Byzantine period, is a Romantic distortion whose origin can be traced back to the nineteenth-century perspectives of scholars such Spyridon Zambelios (1813–81) and Nikolaos Politis (1852–1921). Through printed collections, through the curriculum of education, and simply as an aspect of life in most parts of the Greek-speaking world, almost all Greek writers of the last two centuries have come directly into contact with this tradition as a strong element of *contemporary* culture.

To sum up, the whole tradition of literary writing in Greek (not just 'Modern Greek'), through Byzantium to Homer and including the oral traditions that have survived into our own time, is an evident and essential resource for Greek writers of the last two centuries. But our much increased knowledge of each of the successive, and overlapping, traditions that comprise these precedents makes it possible, and perhaps essential, to study each of the component parts of this broader 'Modern Greek' literature as a coherent whole.

There are growing signs that in practice this is already happening for the earlier periods of 'Modern Greek' literature.[7] But no such overview, before the first edition of the present book appeared in 1994, existed for the period that is most in demand among students and, judging from what texts are available in English translation, also by the general reader.

In the title of the present book, the term 'Modern Greek' is therefore to be understood, for want of a better term, in a deliberately restricted sense, to refer to Greek literature since the time of national independence.

The Language Question. An issue which has occupied a central position in most accounts of modern Greek literature, as also of

---

[7] See Beaton 1996a (1st edn. 1989) for the medieval romance; Holton 1991 for the Cretan Renaissance. The growing acceptance of linguistic and aesthetic differences, as well as the more obvious geopolitical ones, between 'medieval' and 'Renaissance' Greek literature is also implicit throughout the two volumes of Panayotakis 1993.

other aspects of Greek cultural life, has been that of language. The ancient Greeks divided the world into Hellenes and 'barbarians'—those who did not speak Greek—and since at least the later middle ages it has been primarily with reference to their language that people have defined themselves as Greek. Much attention, both in Greece and abroad, has been devoted to the phenomenon known as the 'Language Question'. Up to the mid-1970s, and going back continuously to the period of the Roman empire, the Greek used in most kinds of writing was formally distinct from the language of speech. The appropriate form of the language to be used in literature, for education, and for official purposes began to be hotly debated in the mid-eighteenth century, as part of the same intellectual process which also laid the foundations for the creation of an independent Greek state, and the debate first came to a head in the early years of the nineteenth century. Throughout most of the period covered by this book the Greek language had no generally recognized standard form. When an official form of the language was first declared, in the Constitution of 1911, it was defined as the formal, archaizing idiom in which the Constitution itself was drawn up, a type of language which had already been decisively rejected by writers of poetry and fiction. The resulting polarization, with rival written forms of the language vying for dominance, is commonly known as 'diglossia', and persisted officially until an Act of the Greek Parliament, passed in April 1976, defined the currently spoken language as the norm.

The long drawn-out process by which the spoken, or 'demotic', language finally won official (if still not universal) acceptance is usually described, emotively, as a 'struggle'. The cause of promoting this form of the language, in the teeth of opposition which was at times even violent, was baptized during the 1890s as 'demoticism' and has proved a rallying call for writers, academics, politicians, and many others at various times in the hundred years since then. More significantly for our purposes, the cause of demoticism has also been a central, although usually tacit, guiding principle underlying the many histories of Modern Greek literature that have appeared since Ilias Voutieridis, in 1924, first published such a history in demotic. Significantly it is only Linos Politis, and only when writing for an English-speaking readership, who makes this explicit: 'history', he writes, 'can be objective only up to a certain point; ... the author is a *demoticist*, and must naturally look at the historical development of literature from that point of view.'[8] The point of view which Politis declares here is no less fundamental to the other most authoritative histories of Modern Greek literature, by Dimaras and Vitti, as well as to almost all of those surveyed by Kehayoglou.[9]

This is important, because it is only since 1976 that it has been possible to write about Modern Greek literature from a standpoint outside the debate about the language. This is not to suggest that all debate has ceased—the reverse is true; but it is only in relatively recent years (since at the earliest the 1960s) that the perception of the modern language as broadly based and indivisible has really taken hold in Greece. It has only quite recently become possible to recognize the formerly embattled linguistic codes of demotic and *katharevousa*, or purist Greek, as concealing a continuous gradation of overlapping *styles* (in the linguistic sense), all of them theoretically available to speakers and writers to deploy in the expected but also, for particular effects, in unexpected contexts. This is the form of the language now known as 'Common' or 'Standard Modern Greek'.[10]

Despite the polarized and polemical nature of the debate, there are ample indications that many, if not most, writers of poetry and fiction since the early nineteenth century have either been conscious of this potential of their language or have unconsciously exploited it in their work. From the perspective of the 1990s it is no longer obvious, as was being claimed as recently as twenty years ago, that the development of Modern Greek literature has been hampered by the absence of a stable or agreed form of the language, in which to work, still less that the 'dead hand' of the purist language, imposed by petty bureaucrats and the prejudices of politicians, has deprived writers of the means of spontaneous expression. All the signs are that many writers since the early 1960s (and in a few cases going even further back) have accepted the challenge of the range of linguistic styles available to them and as a result have been able to obtain effects which would have been unthinkable to the militant theorists, on either side of the debate, who once argued so strenuously for their preferred style to be imposed as the national standard.

---

[8] L. Politis 1973: vi. This sentence was omitted from the (later) Greek version of Politis' *History*, presumably on the grounds that it was superfluous.

[9] Kehayoglou 1980. English and American writers on Modern Greek literature have also tended to express strong support for the demoticist point of view (see e.g. Sherrard 1982; Bien 1972; Fletcher 1984).

[10] See e.g. Babiniotis and Kondos 1967; Mackridge 1985b, esp. 11–14; Holton, Mackridge, and Philippaki-Warburton 1997.

These changes in the last thirty years or so have had a profound effect not only on the way contemporary literature is written and read, but also on the way in which writers and readers see the literature of the past. (It has become a frequent complaint, for example, that schoolchildren in Greece are no longer equipped to read the nineteenth-century classics, written in *katharevousa*.) The changes have also been gradual. As a result, although much literary scholarship on individual writers and movements now assumes, at least implicitly, this changed perspective, there has been little attempt so far at a systematic overview to take account of it.

The changing 'canon'. The literary canon is not something fixed and unalterable, and one of the most fascinating aspects of modern Greek literary studies in recent years has been the visible process of revising the canon; that is, of reviving neglected writers from the past, and revising our perception of past developments, from the changed perspective of the present. And of course these revised perspective are no more stable than the older ones that they have replaced. Literary history changes and has to be re-written as each new generation re-interprets its inheritance from the past. The last thirty years have seen some radical developments in the way Greek writers, critics, and scholars have viewed and interpreted their recent literary history. But there has been no single study in Greek which attempts to draw these many insights and revisions together.

The revisions, and particularly the 'opening up', or extension of the canon of nineteenth-century works, that has taken place in recent years, can plausibly be seen as part of the same process just described: a readjustment of perspective following the end of embattled diglossia. Since the 1960s there has been an ever-increasing interest in the work of the great storytellers of the closing years of the nineteenth century: Vizyinos, Papadiamandis, and Karkavitsas, and since then also in many of their contemporaries. This has been evident in the publication of successive editions, commentaries, critical studies, and doctoral theses in Greece and abroad. Only in the last twenty to thirty years has the full achievement of all three of these writers—and of others of their time—been clearly separated from an evaluation of the form of written Greek in which they wrote. Once the barrier of diglossia is cleared away, all three writers have clearly emerged as consummate stylists, and all three can be seen to explore, through and beyond the 'ethograhic' conventions of the time, an individual vision of the human condition.

Since the 1970s, the canon of nineteenth-century literature has been considerably extended. Roidis' *Pope Joan* has been reappropriated in the name of postmodern parody and knowing self-referentiality. There are signs of renewed interest in one of the most prolific and versatile literary figures of the mid-nineteenth century, who enjoyed great prestige in his lifetime but has been almost totally eclipsed since the early years of this century: Alexandros Rizos Rangavis, whose nineteen volumes of collected works were published in Athens between 1874 and 1889. Rangavis was a Romantic poet who has now been shown to have possessed a sense of humour; the author of more than a dozen novels or novellas, including the first authentic Greek 'who-dun-it'; and one of the first to attempt a history of modern Greek literature. Further back than Rangavis, in prose fiction, we have the phenomenon of a major picaresque novel, published in 1840 and subsequently lost (literally). This was *The Polypath* by Grigorios Palaiologos, whose rediscovery and publication in two modern editions in 1989 sparked off a far-reaching revision of our understanding of the way in which the novel as a genre first developed in modern Greece.

But the extended canon does not stop with the nineteenth century. A phenomenon now taken for granted, to the extent that it scarcely any longer seems surprising, is the slow rise to pre-eminence of Cavafy, over a period of almost a century. A fairly marginal figure in Greece throughout most of his life, and viewed askance by many of the most conspicuous literary figures of the 1930s and 1940s, Cavafy's reputation has gradually gathered momentum, from the time of the first posthumous publication of his collected poems (in Alexandria in 1935), through the growing interest in him by the 'postwar' generation of poets in the 1960s, to the orgy of commemorative publications in and after the fiftieth anniversary of his death in 1983. For many readers today, Cavafy is the 'Number One' poet of modern Greece— a situation which would surely have astonished Palamas and troubled Seferis (who contributed to it), and could not easily be inferred from *any* of the most authoritative *Histories* of Modern Greek literature. Though there are other reasons for his early eclipse and subsequent rise to prominence, it is worth noting that Cavafy had his roots in the Athenian purist tradition of the nineteenth century, and always stood aloof from the linguistic debate in Greece.

Something comparable, although on a less dramatical scale, has happened to the posthumous reputation of K. G. Karyotakis, beginning with the re-issue of his collected poetry and prose in an accessible edition in 1972. Even more surprising—and, again, hard to separate from the new perspective on the Language Question— has been the posthumous success of the Surrealist-inspired writers of the mid-twentieth century, Embirikos and Engonopoulos, as evidenced by successive editions and reprintings of their work since the 1980s, and by the increased attention of writers and scholars. Not least of the ironies of literary history was the phenomenon, when the first two volumes of Embirikos' novel *The Great Eastern* appeared at the end of 1990, of a runaway bestseller, written in elegant pastiche of the katharevousa of the 1890s!

So far, we have seen ways in which the continuing process of revising the canon has reclaimed forgotten ground, or enhanced the reputation of writers whose earlier eclipse may have been due, in part at least, to their stance within the polarized terms of the Language Question in the first half of the twentieth century. The overall effect seems to be one in which gains far exceed losses—and this is in tune with the expanding horizons (and demands) of scholarship within universities as well as (very probably) the proliferation of new publishing houses and literary periodicals in Greece since the mid-1970s. But there have been some losses; or at least, there are certain figures who appear in the standard *Histories* and in the periodical press of half a century ago, and are now less studied, re-edited, or discussed. The most conspicuous examples of this phenomenon are the writings of Makriyannis and Psycharis, whose inclusion within the (demoticist) literary canon was overtly a consequence of their linguistic practice, rather than based on either literary merit or the genre in which they wrote.

The *Memoirs* of Makriyannis, written between the 1830s and the 1850s but not published until 1907, were elevated during the 1930s to the status of 'Bible of demoticism' not because of their subject matter, or the skill or perceptions of their author, but because Makriyannis was self-taught and wrote (or so at least it was believed) directly in the idiom in which he and his contemporaries spoke. The importance that Makriyannis held for those writers who read him with so much admiration is there to be seen, for example, in the later poems of Seferis, in the *Axion Esti* of Elytis, and elsewhere. But there has been no authoritative, scholarly edition of Makriyannis' *Memoirs* in recent years, although reprints of the text established by Vlachoyannis in 1907, with his introduction, have continued to appear.

Somewhat similarly, although for different reasons, Psycharis' fiction has not survived; and even *My Journey* (1888), the only one of his books available in a modern edition, is explicitly (and rightly) valued for its linguistic opinions and the historical importance of their having been expressed in that way and at that time. There has been little discussion, in recent years, of Psycharis as a writer. In line with these perceived developments, discussion of Makriyannis and Psycharis in this book has been postponed until Chapter 6.

Developments in new writing. The process described in the previous section, of extending the canon of earlier works, is not really separate from the production and reception of new writing during the same period (roughly since 1960). Through a complex interaction which it would be difficult, and perhaps not very useful, to disentangle, the practice of contemporary writers plays a part in the changing evaluations of the writers of the past, but is also to some extent shaped by changes in the attitude of readers (and particularly of reviewers) towards those writers of the past. To what extent are new kinds of writing provoked, or at least fuelled, by the new esteem accorded to, for example, Vizyinos, Karyotakis, or Embirikos? Or does greater interest in these precedents result from the *use* made of them by present-day writers?

However one tries to answer these questions, it is clear that the two phenomena are closely linked. New perspectives on the past can certainly be illuminated by an examination of new writing in the present; conversely, current concerns in writing, in order to be understood fully, need to be set alongside the contemporary perspective on the past. For this reason, the work that has been added to the canon in the last thirty years is necessarily part of the subject matter of this book.

Traditional histories of literature were always chary of approaching the historical moment of their own writing. And indeed I am conscious of a degree of 'risk' in seeking, in Chapter 5 of the present book, to present and discuss poetry and prose of the 1980s and early 1990s. But the traditional reason given for this reluctance to approach the present day (that one has to allow a certain temporal distance, in order to comment with sufficient objectivity and authority) is part and parcel of the traditional conception of literary history. Once it is accepted that the preoccupations of new writing have a part to play in our perception of the past as well as of the present, then any claim to 'objectivity' or 'authority' must paradoxically be dependent on our first coming to grips with these preoccupations. Such 'authority' as the present book may ever be able to claim must derive from the degree of accuracy and fulness with which it articulates a set of perceptions implicit in the Greek writing and scholarship of the 1990s.

There is also a practical reason for trying to bring the coverage as close as possible to the time of writing. The 'traditional' histories of Modern Greek literature provide very little information, and even less comment, on the period since the early 1960s.[11] During that period the canon has been very considerably enriched by new writing which in its turn has attracted discussion. Since Dimaras' *History* was first published in 1948, several generations of writers have come and, in some cases, already sadly gone. The poets who transformed the Greek literary scene in the 1930s almost all produced some of their finest work after 1950. A turning point in several senses, as we shall see in Chapter 5, was the seven-year military dictatorship of the 'Colonels', which drew powerful and varied responses from writers, both new and long-established. In the course of covert protest at the suppression of civil liberties (including freedom of expression), the productive and now almost 'establishment' generation of poets, the 'generation of the 1970s' was baptized as early as 1971.

In prose fiction, the new confidence to experiment in the 1960s was carried forward, after a hiatus under the Colonels, to create the impetus for an 'explosion' of literary fiction during the 1980s, when for almost the first time in Greece a large reading public brought rewards to writers and the prestige of prose came to rival that of verse. A conspicuous feature of much of this new writing has been the exploration of a richly allusive linguistic texture, which deliberately draws on many different styles, evoking and sometimes parodying periods of the historical past and more recent perceptions of them. Although this development in recent writing has not been universally admired, it does at least move away from the polarized limitations of diglossia discussed above, to enrich the written language of today in ways that have scarcely been possible since the achievements of Papadiamandis and Cavafy.

These, then, are the four main changes which have contributed to the new perspective on the Greek literature of the last two centuries,

---

[11] Dimaras ends with the 1920s, Politis with the 1960s. Only Vitti's *History* has been updated to include coverage of the 1970s and early 1980s, although by comparison with his treatment of earlier periods this is still relatively restricted.

that will be the subject of this book. It is time, now, to look at that perspective itself, and also at the self-imposed limitations of its treatment here.

PERSPECTIVE AND LIMITATIONS

Looking back from the perspective of the 1990s, one of the first tasks which faces the student of literary history is how to divide up the continuum into more or less coherent units for more detailed study. This periodization is unavoidably a procrustean process, imposing more or less arbitrary boundaries upon the material studied. Conventionally, the boundary lines in Modern Greek literature are marked by 'generations' associated with a particular decade and credited with unusual cohesiveness and power of innovation. According to this traditional scheme, the inaugurators, Solomos, Kalvos, and their contemporaries of the 'Old Athenian School' whose careers began at about the same time as the Greek war of independence in the 1820s, were followed successively by the 'Generation of the 1880s', the 'Generation of the 1930s', and the 'Generation of the 1970s'. On average the forward spurts represented by these literary 'generations' fall half a century apart, and each is followed by a slack period when impetus is apparently lost. Thus the period of inauguration in the early nineteenth century is followed by the more modest achievements of the followers of Solomos in the Ionian islands, and of their contemporaries in Athens, up to the 1870s. After the innovative surge of the 1880s comes a period from about 1910 to 1930, characterized (it is said) by introspection and despair. Again, the forward-looking 1930s are followed by the low-key performance, particularly of poets, of no fewer than two postwar generations before the new departures of the early 1970s. The 'generation of the 1970s', as we shall see in Chapter 5, has undergone considerable changes since it was inaugurated in 1971, but retains much of its vigour, while the new writers and new preoccupations of the 1980s have so far proved relatively resistant to the brand-name of a 'generation'.

This is a simplified account, of course, of the conventional way in which Greek literature tends to be summed up, and indeed these terms, as often as they are invoked, tend also to be qualified by such distancing expressions as 'so-called' or even by outright questioning of their validity. Nonetheless this pattern maintains a dominant position in the historical conceptualization of Greek literature, and in practice is hard to resist altogether.

In the chapters that follow, the period since 1821 has been broken down into constituents of unequal length, and each has been subsumed under a generalizing title which highlights characteristics discernible both in the literature and in the wider history and culture of the time. The criterion for establishing these divisions has been the coincidence of a major political or military event with some detectable shift in the perceptions and interests of writers. It is not assumed that literary developments are the *consequences* of such events; merely that literature is an integral part of general culture and can be expected, among other things, to articulate a response (not necessarily either directly or passively) to the main lines of historical change.

The starting point of 1821 has already been discussed. A convenient terminus after that is afforded by 1881, which at the political level saw territorial expansion and in literature the publication of the three-volume *Poems* of Achillefs Paraschos, generally accepted to be the last representative of the 'Old Athenian School'. It also marks the consolidation of rapid economic and social change in the previous decade, including urbanization, the increased spread of literacy, with the concomitant rise of a more or less modern periodical press.

There would have been a strong case for accepting the military coup of 1909, sometimes described as a 'bourgeois revolution' and surely Greece's counterpart to the Young Turk revolution of the previous year, as another such dividing line. The main reason for not doing so is that it cuts in half the careers of the two most important poets of the time, Palamas and Cavafy, and of the most prolific novelist, Grigorios Xenopoulos. Nonetheless, 1910 saw the publication of the last large-scale work of Palamas, while the following year was (albeit for purely personal, artistic reasons) accepted by Cavafy as a 'watershed' in his career, and also marks the death of Papadiamandis. In any case, the next dividing line has been drawn not, as might have been expected, at 1922 with the decisive defeat of the Greek army in Anatolia, but six years later when the political chaos resulting from that defeat was partially resolved by the return to power of the elder statesman, Eleftherios Venizelos. In literary terms, a similar watershed can be discerned between the suicide of Karyotakis in 1928 and the publication in the following year of Yorgos Theotokas' manifesto for a 'new' national literature, *Free Spirit*.

The period ushered in by that 'manifesto' is so dense with literary innovation and has been so intensively studied, ever since the self-congratulatory phrase 'generation of the 1930s' was coined in 1935, that the longest chapter of the book is devoted to just twenty years up to 1949, when the end of the civil war ushered in a period of cautious recovery and stocktaking of the recent past. After that, the two and a half years of preventive censorship imposed by Greece's military rulers in 1967, and the principled decision by most established writers not to publish under these conditions, provides, for once, a clear dividing line, even although, as we shall see, it bisects the careers of a number of prominent writers.

Finally, the concluding point of the end of 1992 was adopted, somewhat provisionally, because that was the date announced in advance for the completion of the European Single Market and the evolution of the European Community into the European Union, and this date also happened to coincide quite closely with the completion of the book itself in its original form. To what extent that year may be seen as a historical landmark comparable to those already invoked to divide the book into its constituent chapters, is, of course, still too early to determine.

This way of dividing up two centuries of literature turns out not to diverge greatly from that of the standard histories and anthologies. Although the criteria for defining 'periods' of literature differ from the conventional ones, the groupings which result basically confirm the conventional pattern, with more or less radical breaks identified in the 1880s, the 1930s, and the 1970s. It should be questioned, however, to what extent the appearance a 'break' is not really just a consequence of the arrangement of the material. If such 'breaks' at one level of generalization provide useful signposts for finding one's way around the literature of a period, at another they are best regarded with a modicum of suspicion. Although the divisions used are not arbitrary, a rather different picture might nonetheless have emerged had the dividing lines been drawn, according to different criteria, at different points in time. The division of the material into chapters, each with its encapsulating title and historical introduction to the period contained within it, should not be taken as more than a necessary presentational device.

The idea of perspective inevitably involves that of exclusion. From whatever angle we choose to view an object, certain features will always be obscured. This is true even of an 'overview'; and, to move beyond the visual metaphor, writing this book has involved making choices whose consequences cannot be side-stepped. Just as I have tried to make explicit the positive elements of that selection, it will also be necessary to explain, if not to excuse, the negative ones.

The most conspicuous omissions are of Greek literature before 1800, and of drama. The first of these has already been discussed. The omission of drama and almost all theatrical works, whether or not written for the stage, is harder to justify in principle. To have dealt adequately with the subject would either have increased the size of the book beyond its present scope of an 'Introduction', or have led to curtailed treatment of other areas. Faced with that choice, it seemed better to aim at a relatively fuller treatment of the two genres which, all the twentieth-century *Histories* agree, are pre-eminent in the Greek literature of this period, namely poetry and prose fiction. The implied definition of 'literature' in my title is therefore genre-based; and once arrived at, has been rigorously enforced. In extenuation, it may be said that, up to about 1940, and with a small number of conspicuous exceptions, Greek drama lagged well behind poetry and fiction. This is evident in the small number of plays written before 1940 that have been regularly performed and re-issued in new editions. To what extent this may have been due to the practical conditions obtaining in the Greek theatre at that period, to the lack of talent among writers, to the indifference of audiences, or even to the neglect of later writers and critics who may have been looking for something different from what they found, cannot be determined here. In any case, the situation since the 1940s has certainly been different, and I have no doubt that a fuller treatment of post-war Greek literature would have to give an equal place to drama.[12] As a logical consequence of the deliberately restricted definition of 'literature' adopted here, however, I have not attempted to do so.[13]

---

[12] For an informative account in English of Modern Greek theatre, which places the beginning of an 'art theatre' in Greece as late as 1940, see Bacopoulou-Halls 1982. For histories of the theatre before World War II see Laskaris 1938; Sideris 1953; Puchner 1984; 1992; and the essays collected in Constantinides 1996.

[13] As a consequence of this approach, some writers seem to 'disappear off the map' when in fact they have merely extended the lines of their development, already visible in their prose or poetry, into a different genre. This applies particularly to Yorgos Theotokas, Angelos Terzakis, and Margarita Lymberaki, as well as to the dramas of Kazantzakis (in prose and verse) and Sikelianos (in verse), and will at least be noted in what follows.

Another self-imposed limitation concerns the meaning of the term *Greek*. Although the book begins with the creation of the Greek state, not all of the literature discussed in the first two chapters was written within the frontiers of that state. On the other hand, in the twentieth century, an increasing amount of literature in Greek has been produced outside Greece, and some might even wonder whether the 'canon' should not be extended to include writers of Greek origin or background writing in other languages (Jean Moréas, in France, a hundred years ago; Olga Broumas or Stratis Haviaras, in the USA today). A special category is the literature of Cyprus, which has been developing continuously since at least the early twentieth century, and since the independence of the island in 1960 has not only been produced in ever-increasing quantity but has attracted serious attention both in Cyprus itself and in Greece.

A sharp distinction must be drawn, in any case, between emigrant writers, or writers from emigrant families, who make up the 'Diaspora' on the one hand, and writers from parts of the Greek-speaking world outside Greece on the other. Of the latter category, in the second half of the twentieth century, only Cypriot writers remain, and the 1980s saw some intense discussions, in periodicals in Cyprus and Greece, and in Greek universities, about the status and even the name of 'Greek literature of Cyprus' versus 'Cypriot literature'. There are complex sensitivities here, for which comparisons with, for example, the German-language literature of Switzerland or the French-language literature of Belgium may not be fully adequate to deal. A vital issue here must be the extent to which the Greek literature of Cyprus is perceived, in Cyprus and in Greece, as a *national* literature (giving prominence to the political fact of statehood) or as a *regional* tradition within the broader, and not politically determined, boundaries of the Greek-speaking world—which, to complicate matters further, might or might not be additionally extended to include the Diaspora.

These are matters on which no clear consensus has yet emerged. If this seems a poor excuse for excluding the Greek literature of Cyprus, and the literature of the Greek Diaspora, from the present study, I can only suggest that both topics are of sufficient importance to deserve separate treatment, in which these issues would have to be fully addressed.

NEITHER 'MARGINAL' NOR 'MINOR': GREEK LITERATURE IN
EUROPE

Nobody doubts that Greek literature, of any period, belongs to the
European tradition. But the precise nature of the relationship, and
the status of Greek writing in relation to a European 'mainstream',
have been the cause of much anguish on the part of Greek writers
and critics throughout the period discussed in this book, and continue to preoccupy many of those who study the subject in the
English-speaking world today.[14]

One approach to this issue, which has been much, and inconclus-
ively, discussed, is through the broad movements which have generally been distinguished throughout the European literature of the
last two centuries: Neoclassicism, Romanticism, Modernism, and
Postmodernism. (Others could, of course, be added, and will from
time to time be mentioned in the chapters which follow: Symbolism,
Realism, politically committed writing, etc.)

That the Romantic movement of the nineteenth century found its
way to Greece in the nineteenth century is a well-known fact, often
symbolically linked to the footsteps of George Gordon, Lord Byron.
Indeed, we may wonder whether without the particular ferment of
ideas in northern Europe to which we loosely give the name Romanticism, Greece could have become an independent nation at the
time and in the way that it did. The Philhellenes were certainly
Romantics, but so, in interesting respects which have yet to be
studied, was Adamandios Korais, the influential ideologue of the
Greek nation-state. Despite the enormous importance of European
Romanticism in the emergence of the Greek nation and its sense of
identity, until recently the role of Romanticism in Greek literature
has been strangely played down. Conventionally, and in the standard histories, the term 'Greek Romanticism' is restricted to the
minor poetry of the mid-nineteenth century. It is ònly thanks to a
few isolated voices in recent literary criticism—Sonia Ilinskaya in
Ioannina, the late Elizabeth Constantinides in New York—that this
orthodoxy has been explicitly challenged, and it has become possible to place the three Greek poets of stature in the nineteenth

---

[14] Indicative of this preoccupation in its present phase is the series of conference
papers edited by Gregory Jusdanis (1997) under the title *Whither the Neohellenic?* See
also Beaton 1998.

century squarely in the context of the European Romantic movement: Solomos, Kalvos, and Palamas.[15]

This issue is not just a matter of labelling. It reveals a long-
standing set of assumptions about the status of Greek literature in
the wider European context, assumptions which are now beginning
to be challenged. Traditionally, the term 'Greek Romanticism' was
reserved for those who could (more or less) safely be described as
imitators. The obvious candidates to be considered as the leading
Greek Romantic poets tended to be treated apart: to allow that
Solomos or Palamas was a 'Romantic' poet, would be, it was
implied, to invite the charge of imitation, of slavish dependency
which ill becomes a poet of the undoubted stature of these two.

The same caution, or implicit sense of imitation and derivative
status, runs through much of the discussion of other literary 'isms' in
modern Greek studies. Greek Modernism was not true Modernism,
we are told, because it is marked by a powerful quest for national
identity (but so was the Modernism of James Joyce in Ireland, or of
T. S. Eliot in his adopted country of England). Postmodernism, it
was even being argued as late as 1987, was impossible in Greece—
despite all the perfectly obvious evidence to the contrary—because
the ideological preconditions which paved the way for it in the West
had yet to be fulfilled there.[16]

These and many other discussions imply that Greek writers,
living and working on the edge of Europe and on the cultural margin
of the western world, can relate to the dominant culture around
them only passively. The weaker writers imitate; the strong—the
heroes of a national literature—keep their distance from foreign
influences or are impervious to them.

Such a view of literary interrelations ignores much that has by
now become standard in the literary theory of Europe and the USA
since the 1960s (and, curiously, continues to be propounded by
some of those who have been most vociferous in applying to Greek
literature theoretical models current in the 1970s and 1980s). The
horizons of the literary historian have been significantly widened by
such post-1960s concepts as intertextuality and reception theory.
These concepts, the one from French theory, the other from German, provide a theoretical underpinning for a better understanding

---

[15] Ilinskaya 1978; Constantinides 1985. For a new overview of Greek Romanticism
see A. Politis 1993.
[16] Jusdanis 1987a.

of the way in which literary writings interact with one another. Greek writers, perceived in this framework, are no longer the passive receivers of trends, ideas, techniques, which they borrow wholesale from the West. But neither—obviously—do they live and write in a vacuum, isolated from the rest of Europe. Greek writers, like writers anywhere, have been the *readers* of their own and other traditions. Reading, in this sense, is not a passive process. 'Influence' is not something that older or culturally prestigious writers automatically exert; it has to be willed by the writer who is supposedly 'influenced'. And short of literal copying, it is difficult for a writer to be as wholly derivative, as wholly passive, as is suggested by the way the term 'influence' has often been used in older literary studies.

Solomos, Kalvos, and Palamas, viewed from this perspective, become the most highly regarded in Greece today of the poets who in their time engaged most deeply with the ideas, the literary techniques and aspirations, of Romanticism as these were manifested in other parts of Europe. They neither imitated nor rejected what they found: they transformed it. What Wordsworth and Coleridge, in England, did with Kant and Schiller is exactly similar in kind to what Solomos, in Corfu, did with Kant and Schiller; to what Kalvos did with Ugo Foscolo and the political ideals of the Italian *carbonaro* movement; to what Palamas did with Shelley, with Nietzsche, and with many others. What all these Greek writers did with the European literature before them was to read it, select from it, and make something of their own with what they read. The result, I would propose, deserves to be called Greek Romanticism, by which I mean something very different from the conventional label for the minor poetry of the mid-nineteenth century that has become standard in literary history. 'Greek Romanticism', in this sense, refers to the particular interpretations and the particular developments given to aesthetic and cultural ideas that were widely current in Europe, in a specifically Greek context at a particular time.[17]

The case can be advanced, on similar grounds, for 'Greek Modernism' and 'Greek Postmodernism'. In the twentieth century, the Nobel laureates George Seferis and Odysseus Elytis, and several other writers whose careers began in the 1930s, gave their own interpretation and their own—very different—extensions of the legacy of French Symbolism which has come elsewhere in Europe

---

[17] This is argued in more detail, for Solomos, in Beaton 1989a.

to be known as Modernism. And in our own time, the parody of traditional genres, the quizzical re-examination of history and received ideas, the opening of literature towards the realms of dream and fantasy, all of which abound in the Greek poetry and prose fiction of the 1970s and 1980s, surely deserve to be seen as the distinctively Greek component of an international literary dialogue that has been going on for at least thirty years, and is conventionally termed Postmodernism.[18]

The terms 'Greek Romanticism', etc. have not been used in the chapters that follow, since they have not yet become generally accepted in the sense here proposed, and all of them present grave problems of definition. They can, however, and always at the cost of a certain schematization, be related to the subject matter of each chapter in the following way. Almost all of the literature discussed in Chapter 1 (1821–81) constitutes a reading of and a response to the Romantic movement (a response which naturally includes its outright rejection by Roidis no less than the adoption of some of its constituent strands by many other writers). The only significant exception to this would be some of the poetry and satire of the Ionian islands up to about 1880, which may be seen as continuing a Neo-classical tradition established there during the centuries of Venetian rule. The poetry of Kalvos, which is often seen as occupying a position somewhere between Neoclassicism and Romanticism, I would place firmly among the responses to the latter movement.

In the same way, the period which follows, from 1881 to 1928 may be said to embody the culmination and crisis of the Romantic movement which was also taking place at about this time in the rest of Europe, with writers such as Palamas and the early Sikelianos and Kazantzakis taking certain characteristics of Romanticism to their furthest conclusion, while others such as Cavafy, Karyotakis, and most prose writers after about 1900 began to question or to reject the transcendent properties of their art which had been a central pillar of Romanticism.

Keeping to the same level of generalization, we could then define the period covered by the third chapter, from 1929 to the civil war, as the time of Greek responses to the introspection and self-referent-

---

[18] Considerable progress towards defining Greek Modernism and aspects, at least, also of Postmodernism, are made by contributors to Tziovas 1997. See also Layoun 1990 and the essays collected in *Moderno-Metamoderno* 1988. On Postmodernism in prose fiction see also Tziovas 1993: 244–75.

iality of Modernism—a set of responses, once again, that can be seen to be articulated with far greater vigour and variety than could be subsumed under any such term as 'influence' or 'reflection'. After the Second World War in Greece, as during the 1930s and 1940s in other parts of Europe, there is a reaction against some of the broad tenets of Modernism, noticeably with the rise of politically committed poetry and a related return to realism in prose. But already by the 1960s, at the latest, there are signs of renewed experimentation in Greek writing, which are consonant (although again by no means identical) with the conspicuous trends in worldwide literature at this time which have come to be loosely grouped under the rubric of 'Postmodernism'.

In Greek writing from this period onwards we find elements of parody and self-parody, various combinations of the opaque self-referential style of Modernism with more popular or accessible forms, a disposition to undermine accepted values rather than to attack them head-on. Inevitably the label 'magic realism' has come to be attached to some fiction of the 1980s; and the phenomenon of the 'quality bestseller' has transformed the market for fiction in a country where the reading public was for a long time quite restricted. During this 'Postmodern' period, it is clear that Greek writers have been reading the same texts as their peers elsewhere, and have once again been taking up the challenges afforded by new kinds of writing, in their own, by no means uniform, ways.

This attempt to define 'Greek Romanticism,' 'Greek Modernism', and 'Greek Postmodernism' in terms of chronological divisions which are *internal* to Greek literature and history does not wholly resolve the question of the relation of Greek to European literature with which this section began. In rejecting the term 'influence' and its connotations, and ascribing to Greek writers an active role as readers and transformers of the traditions of other parts of Europe, as well as of their own tradition, I hope to have shown that Greek writers have at all times been involved in the broad literary movements of their times, and not merely as consumers or imitators of them. But, of course, the fact of geographical and cultural isolation from Europe has constantly been lamented in Greece itself throughout the last two hundred years; and it is undoubtedly the case that Greek writers have not initiated trends, or created 'isms' of their own that have spread out to engage responses from other languages and cultures.

It is for this reason, as well as for the more obvious geographical and demographic ones, that the terms 'minor', 'peripheral', and 'marginal' have often been applied to Modern Greek literature in recent years, particularly in academic studies abroad. Not surprisingly, many of those who are professionally engaged in the study of this literature have exercised some ingenuity in seeking to claim a higher 'profile' for the object of their studies, particularly in the 'global market-place' of the academic and publishing worlds.

Modern Greek literature, this book contends, is neither marginal nor minor. It is the central and major literature of a worldwide Greek-speaking population which may number some fifteen million people; moreover, it is a constituent part of the literature of modern Europe. European literature includes the work of Modern Greek writers, and readers in the rest of Europe are the poorer if they are unacquainted with it. If Greek writers have not initiated trends which have been taken up and adapted elsewhere, this is not because they are inferior, but because they are still relatively little known.

Greek literature does have particular ideas, preoccupations, and techniques which are its own and which may yet provoke the interest and admiration of writers in other languages. One such, which will be discussed in Chapter 6, is the special power which Greek culture traditionally attributes to language, a cultural resource which twentieth-century writers in Greece have often exploited with extraordinarily impressive results. Another must surely lie in the longevity of Greek, not so much as a spoken medium (all languages are presumed to result from a process of evolution going far back into prehistory), but as a language of *writing*. And that written language, let us not forget, has never lost its central status, at least in the eyes of those who use it, as one of the two primary languages of European Christendom. From the diverse strategies through which Greek writers, in the last two centuries, have faced up to the challenge of that long tradition of writing, the younger literatures of Europe can surely learn.

The Greek literature of the last two centuries, then, is not derivative, and it is not peripheral. It occupies a particular place within the totality of European literature and has, I believe, much to offer not only to Greek-speaking readers but, through translation, to the rest of Europe and the world. We need, simply, to get to know it better.

1. Literature for a New Nation
1821–1881

GREECE was the first of the European nation states to emerge out of the break-up of the multi-national empires of the eighteenth century. From 25 March 1821, the conventional date of the Greek revolt against the ruling Ottoman empire, it took seven years for the new state to win grudging international recognition, and it was not until 1832 that a system of government (monarchy) and stable frontiers were agreed by the Great Powers.

The kingdom that was inaugurated in 1833 under the young King Otho of Bavaria was much smaller than Greece today, and many more Greeks (defined by language and religion) lived outside its borders than within. The northern frontier at this time ran from just south of the town of Arta in Epiros in the west, to the southern end of the bay of Volos in the east, and the only islands included were Evia (Euboea), the Sporades, and the Cyclades. The Ionian islands, to the west of the mainland, had become a British Protectorate in 1815, and remained under British rule until 1864, when the islands were ceded to Greece following the accession of King George I. This was the only territorial gain to be made before the end of the period under discussion, when the large and agriculturally rich province of Thessaly was added to Greece in 1881 by diplomatic moves following the Russian-Turkish war of 1877–8.

The history of the first sixty years of Greek independence is a stormy one. The task of creating the institutions of a nation state more or less overnight was far from easy—and the creation of a national literature during this period was undoubtedly an important component in this process. The first national capital had been established, during the war of independence, at Nafplion in the Peloponnese, the largest town of independent Greece, which possessed a strong fortress. But in 1834 the decision was taken to move the capital to Athens, clearly as part of a broader policy of establishing the modern state, in the eyes of its own citizens and the world, as the heir to the Greek civilization of antiquity, in which a leading role had been played by the city of Athens. The growth of Athens, from little more than a village in 1834 to its present sprawl and population of approximately five million, is one of the most eloquent testimonies to the vigour of the nation state that was founded in the 1820s.

But progress in the direction of an urban way of life, and towards civil and political institutions modelled on those of western Europe, was slow throughout the nineteenth century. The foreign king and his all-powerful advisers, who in addition were Catholics in a country which had liberated itself under the banner of the Orthodox faith, soon came to be deeply resented. Only after a revolt in 1843 were steps taken to restrict the powers of the king through a written constitution (of March 1844), but Otho's reign was eventually brought to an end by renewed civil and military unrest which forced him to leave the country in 1862. A second, and more liberal, constitution was drawn up in 1864, after the accession of King George.

If the kingdom was beset by internal difficulties, its relations with the Great Powers were scarcely easier. Recognition of the new, small state had from the beginning been conditional, and the price paid for this throughout the nineteenth century, in the economic, diplomatic, and even military spheres, was high. Up until the end of the century and beyond, the country was crippled by foreign debt; such territorial gains as Greece made before the end of the nineteenth century were part and parcel of larger diplomatic manœuvres by Britain, France, and Russia rather than the direct result of Greek initiatives, while the same powers consistently held Greek irredentist ambitions in check. In the military sphere the port of Piraeus was blockaded by Britain in 1850, and even occupied by British and French troops in 1854, during the Crimean War. With such externally imposed limits to its self-determination, the Greek state, during its formative stages, was denied the degree of autonomy enjoyed by its larger and longer-established counterparts in Europe. It may be as a result that individuals and institutions during this formative period had little incentive to develop a sense of responsibility for their actions. Be that as it may, a sense of frustration, and a concomitant tendency to resent foreign interference at the same time as inevitably relying on foreign help, is a fundamental facet of nineteenth-century Greek culture whose long shadow extends even into the late twentieth century.

This was the climate in which Greek writers and readers of literature (in the sense defined in the Introduction) lived during the first sixty years of national independence. But before we turn to see how they responded to the challenges of their times, it will be useful to look back to the period immediately before 1821 to see what foundations existed for the writers of independent Greece to build on.

CULTURAL CENTRES BEFORE 1821

Literature, in the sense of written genres, requires a number of basic pre-conditions without which it cannot exist. Most obviously, it requires advanced literacy, not only in those who produce it but also, to an increasing degree as the genres of poetry and fiction have developed since the eighteenth century, in its consumers—the reading public. During the eighteenth century, the Greek reading public was certainly restricted, but by no means negligible, as the number and variety of printed books, published mainly in Venice and Vienna during the century, testifies.

Advanced literacy, and the intellectual interests that tended to accompany it, were however largely restricted to particular social classes, grouped in specific geographical areas; and this fact had important consequences for the development of a national literature after 1821.

The Phanariots.   This group takes its name from the district of Constantinople known as Phanari ('lighthouse') which since the seventeenth century has been the seat of the Ecumenical Patriarchate of the Orthodox Church. To the higher clergy and the bureaucracy which served it were given considerable secular powers and responsibilities after the Ottoman conquest of 1453. In the centuries which followed, the Phanariots, as they came to be called, became not only high-ranking officials of the Church, but often of the Ottoman state as well. In this way a talented and ambitious Greek-speaking bureaucracy came to flourish, and its privileges became the jealously guarded prerogative of powerful families. One of the most prized offices, won by the Phanariots in the early eighteenth century, was that of *hospodar*, or feudal ruler, of the principalities of Moldavia and Wallachia in what is now Romania. It was largely at the courts of these rulers, at Jassy and Bucharest, that the political, philosophical, and literary interests of the Enlightenment in the West were first taken up and discussed in Greek.[1]

[1] On the intellectual interests and achievements of this group see Henderson 1970; K. Dimaras 1983; Angelou 1988a; Kitromilides 1992.

Direct contact with the West was, not surprisingly, via the River Danube and Vienna, and it was here that translations from western languages, as well as original works by Phanariot writers, were mostly published. However, the foreign culture that the Phanariots most admired was French rather than German, and the liberal ideas of Montesquieu, Rousseau, and Voltaire had considerable currency among this élite. The Phanariots as a class were lukewarm (with some notable exceptions) towards the cause of national revolution against the Ottomans that was gathering momentum in other sections of Greek society in the wake of the French Revolution of 1789—and for this they have never been fully forgiven. This did not prevent several of them from becoming active patrons of Greek scholarship, and one of their number, Rigas of Velestino in Thessaly (1757–98),[2] was the first to draw up a 'political constitution' for a new order that might succeed the violent overthrow of the Ottoman empire.[3]

Alongside his political vision, which was firmly rooted in the eighteenth century, Rigas played a distinctive role in the development of a national Greek literature. His rousing call to arms in verse, *Battle Hymn*, was appended to his 'political constitution' of 1797.[4] Its opening lines were imitated by Byron, and are as well known today as the Greek national anthem. If the *Battle Hymn* places Rigas at the head of a tradition of patriotic Greek verse, his other literary works are more securely anchored in the cultivated cosmopolitan world of the Phanariots. His translations of three stories by Rétif de la Bretonne, published in Vienna in 1790, although not the earliest translations of European fiction into Greek, began a short-lived fashion for fiction dealing with contemporary urban life which was taken up two years later with the anonymous original stories, *Results of Love*, and this collection, in its turn, played its part in the emergence of Modern Greek fiction.

These two volumes of short stories of the early 1790s also bear witness to another pastime which seems to have been taken for granted in Phanariot circles, and probably more widely among the well-to-do Greek population of Constantinople. This is the art of lightweight love poetry, which the characters in these stories

[2] Commonly known in Greek as Rigas Velestinlis or Pherraios, from the ancient name of Velestino, Pherai. The latter name was not used by Rigas himself.
[3] Repr. as Rigas 1971a.
[4] Θούριος, frequently reprinted in anthologies.

improvise with astonishing facility, in a wide range of metres, and in a quantity sorely trying to modern sensibilities. A taste for 'popular' urban poetry of this type clearly underlies the more polished achievements of Athanasios Christopoulos (1772–1847), whose single volume of poetry, *Lyrics*, was published in Vienna in 1811, and was revealingly divided into 'Erotic' and 'Bacchic'.[5] Christopoulos has earned a place in the literary canon largely for his overt championship of the spoken form of the language, for which he earned the respect of the 'national' poet Dionysios Solomos.

The Ionian Islands. These were the second distinct centre of learning during the eighteenth century, and consequently also a channel through which western ideas and literary developments later filtered through to independent Greece. Since the thirteenth century the seven islands off the west coast of Greece (from Corfu in the north down to Kythera off the southernmost tip of the Peloponnese) had been under the almost uninterrupted rule of the Republic of Venice. As a result, these islands, and especially their capital Corfu, had the unique distinction of being the only part of the Greek-speaking world never to have undergone a significant period of Ottoman rule. Until 1798 the islands had been ruled as a colony by Venice, and by the eighteenth century a stable political system had evolved, in which the feudal privileges of the landed aristocracy had scarcely changed since the late middle ages, while the Catholic colonial rulers had long since ceased to interfere in the Orthodox religious practices of the inhabitants.

Geographically and politically, the ruling class of the Ionian islands was much closer to Italy, and through Italy to the rest of western and northern Europe, than they were to Constantinople or the Danubian principalities. Throughout the eighteenth century and even well into the nineteenth, it was normal for the sons of the aristocracy of the Ionian islands to study at Italian universities. Men of learning from these islands were usually well versed in ancient Greek language and history, but through the medium of Italian and Latin. It is not therefore surprising that the first major poets of the Ionian islands after Greek independence, Solomos and Kalvos, were both more at home writing in Italian than in their own language.

[5] Christopoulos 1970.

Since the early sixteenth century, Greek printing presses in Venice had been producing not just editions of ancient texts but poetry written in the contemporary vernacular. Most of these literary works had been composed in Crete, which until its conquest by the Ottomans between 1645 and 1669 had also been part of the Venetian empire in the eastern Mediterranean. When Crete fell, large numbers of the aristocracy and the emerging urban middle class (including most of the writers and first readers of this literature) emigrated to the Ionian islands, bringing with them printed books and unpublished manuscripts. Among the latter were manuscripts of the 10,000-line verse romance, *Erotokritos*, by Vitsentzos Kornaros, one of the high points of the literature of the Cretan Renaissance and indeed of all Greek literature. These manuscripts were eventually collated for the first time and printed in Venice in 1713.[6]

If the Ionian islands had provided the essential staging post through which *Erotokritos* and other works of the Cretan Renaissance had had to pass in order to be preserved in print, from about 1700 onwards the islands began to fulfil a similar function in the opposite direction. A significant number of literary works in vernacular Greek, including *Erotokritos*, published in Venice in successive editions up to the mid-nineteenth century, seem to have filtered via the Ionian islands back into the Greek-speaking world, and also, by means of oral recitation and sung performance, throughout the social classes. In this way the poems, and some of the verse dramas, composed in Crete between the fifteenth and the seventeenth centuries, reached a much wider audience than anything composed more recently, until the patriotic poems of Rigas and Solomos received comparable treatment in the early nineteenth century.

During the eighteenth century and much of the nineteenth these texts were usually thought of as 'popular' or even 'vulgar', because they are written in a literary idiom based on the spoken dialect of Crete at the time. More recently they have been recognized as, in many cases, highly sophisticated works of the late Renaissance and re-evaluated accordingly. However, at the time of Greek independence they constituted almost the only 'popular' reading matter that

[6] For *Erotokritos* see the now standard edition by S. Alexiou (Kornaros 1980, 1988). For Cretan drama of the same period, in a bilingual critical edition, see Bancroft-Marcus (forthcoming). On the literature of the Cretan Renaissance in general see Holton 1991.

was available, and as such afforded a valuable foundation for those writers who did not disdain to make use of them.

The writers who drew productively on this older vernacular tradition were, up to the later nineteenth century, almost exclusively those active in the Ionian islands, where the local dialect was still close to that of Crete two centuries before, and where the tradition of public recitations and even dramatic performances of Cretan works was strongest. Anecdotally, the difference between the literary circles of the Ionian islands and the Phanariots can be illustrated in the following way. In Corfu and Zakynthos a vestigial tradition of writing as well as performing verse drama, going back to the sixteenth century in Crete, continues up to the end of the eighteenth century, and these older 'popular' works, and in particular *Erotokritos*, were given a new lease of life in the 1830s by the Zakynthian poet Solomos who deliberately exploited aspects of their language and versification. By contrast, in 1818 the Phanariot writer Dionysios Fotinos published in Vienna his *New Erotokritos*, in which the Cretan poem was rewritten according to the Constantinopolitan sensibilities of the time, in a more learned form of the language, and with the insertion of contemporary ditties of the same sort as adorn the two collections of short stories mentioned earlier![7]

Continued contact between the aristocracy of the Ionian islands and Venice also ensured some degree of continuity in original writing. The *Flowers of Piety*, published in 1708, are a collection of essays by Greek teachers and their pupils in Venice.[8] There is also a succession of enlightened essayists stretching from the late seventeenth century to the late eighteenth; indeed, Evyenios Voulgaris (1716–1806) and Nikiforos Theotokis (1731–1800), both prominent members of the aristocracy of Corfu, played no less a part than their Phanariot counterparts in the transmission of the ideas of the French Enlightenment to the Greek-speaking world. Finally, as already mentioned, there is a thin tradition of original verse drama in the Ionian islands, stretching from just after the heyday of Cretan Renaissance literature in the early seventeenth century to the lively satirical comedy, *Hasis*, by Dimitrios Gouzelis, written in 1790.[9]

[7] *Νέος Ερωτόκριτος*. This work has not been reprinted since the mid-nineteenth century and is something of a rarity. It is not to be confused with the original poem of the same title published by Pandelis Prevelakis in 1985.
[8] Karathanasis 1978.
[9] The religious drama *Evyena* by Theodoros Montseleze was published in Venice in 1646; the anonymous tragedy *Zeno* was written in Zakynthos in 1682–3; in

At the end of the eighteenth century Zakynthos was the home of the first 'revolutionary' poet of the Ionian islands, Andonios Martelaos (1754–1819), who like Rigas in the Danubian principalities was inspired to write patriotic verse by the example of the French Revolution. It was from the same milieu that Ugo Foscolo (1778–1827), whose native language was Greek, went on to establish himself in Italy as a major lyric poet in the neoclassical tradition, writing in Italian. Another poet of the years immediately preceding national independence was Ioannis Vilaras (1771–1823). Often considered a Phanariot because he spent his working life on the fringe of the Greek intelligentsia of the Ottoman empire, as court physician to Ali Pasha of Ioannina, Vilaras' birth and early life place him firmly in the tradition of the Ionian islands. He was born in Kythera, the southernmost of the islands, and his educational background was therefore Italian (he studied at the University of Padua). Vilaras wrote a small amount of poetry, which draws on the rural tradition of oral song as much as it does on the urban Phanariot tradition represented by Christopoulos.[10] Like Christopoulos he owes his position in the literary canon today very largely to his strong championing of the spoken language as a written medium, for which, again like Christopoulos, he earned the admiration of Solomos.

Before the outbreak of the Greek war of independence in 1821 the 'special relationship' of the islands with Venice had already undergone drastic changes. The Venetian Republic came to an end with Napoleon's Italian campaign of 1796–7, and in 1797 the French occupied Corfu. During the Napoleonic wars the islands were subjected to the protection or occupation of several masters, until the capture of Corfu by the British in 1814. From the following year until 1864 they were a British Protectorate, known as the United States of the Ionian Islands, with its own flag. The official language of the Protectorate for the time being remained Italian, as it had been under Venetian rule; the feudal aristocracy retained most of its old privileges; and at least until the middle of the nineteenth century the young men of the nobility still went to Italy to study. It is therefore an irony of history that the first major Greek poet after independence, who has ever since been regarded as the 'national poet' of

---

Cefalonia, Petros Katsaitis wrote two tragedies, *Iphigenia* and *Thyestes*, in 1720 and 1721 respectively. Back in Zakynthos, *The Comedy of the Quack Doctors* (Η κωμωδία των Ψευτογιατρών) was written by Savoyas Rousmelis (or Soumerlis) in 1745.

[10] Vilaras 1995.

Modern Greece, Dionysios Solomos, was throughout his adult life a subject of the British crown.

The Diaspora. The third 'centre' of Greek learning during the eighteenth century is more diffuse, particularly geographically, but still played no less a part than the two already discussed in shaping the Greek cultural horizons of the nineteenth century. Socially this group can be defined as the emergent mercantile middle class. Geographically, the principal common denominator of this class is that it flourished predominantly in commercial centres outside the Ottoman empire. During the eighteenth century there were expatriate Greek communities in Odessa, Amsterdam, Paris, and London, as well as in the (then) cosmopolitan centres of Vienna and Venice, where Greek communities had been established earlier. If we exclude the example of Ugo Foscolo, who was an expatriate for literary rather than for commercial reasons, this group contributed little directly to literature. But the expatriate entrepreneurs were, of all Greeks at this time, the most closely in touch with contemporary western education, and particularly with the social and political changes of the late eighteenth century. And through the founding of the *Filiki Eteria* or Friendly Society in Odessa in 1814, and the activities of powerful pressure groups promoting the Greek cause throughout Europe during the war of independence, this was the group, among educated Greeks of the time, which played by far the largest part in laying the intellectual foundations of the new nation state. It was also the group, by comparison with the Phanariots and the aristocracy of the Ionian islands, which had the most to gain from its success.

Aside from the contribution of the mercantile Diaspora to the establishment of the nation state, the importance of this group to the development of Modern Greek literature is most visible in the single figure of Adamantios Korais (1748–1833). The son of a mercantile family in Smyrna, Korais, after a false start in the commercial world of Amsterdam, studied medicine in Montpellier, then gradually established himself as an intellectual and classical scholar in Paris, where he remained for the rest of his long life. Korais believed in the spread of education as the best means of equipping his fellow countrymen for their future independence, and was also one of the first Greek intellectuals to envisage the emancipation of the Greeks in the form of a nation state, defined in terms which

ultimately derive from J. G. Herder: that is, in terms of its language
and traditions. Korais' writings, directed to this end, are volumi-
nous, especially his letters. During the period of Napoleon's campaigns in the eastern Mediterranean, and again after 1821, Korais
wrote a number of vibrant patriotic poems in the style of Rigas and
Martelaos, which were printed and distributed anonymously or
under a pseudonym. But Korais is best known for his essays and
letters on classical literature, on politics and morality, and on reform
of the Greek language, which were printed in subsidized editions
with a view to wide circulation throughout the Greek-speaking
world. His ideas and influence on this last topic will be discussed
later (in Chapter 6), and his role in the development of Greek prose
fiction later in the present chapter.[11]

THE FIRST ROMANTICS: THE RENEWAL OF GREEK POETRY

Of the three centres of learning described in the previous section, it
was the Ionian islands that were first off the mark in celebrating the
declaration of Greek independence in poetry, with the contrasting
achievements of Dionysios Solomos (1798–1857) and Andreas Kalvos (1792–1869) while the war of independence was being waged on
the mainland.

Solomos, still regarded today as the 'national' poet of Modern
Greece, was born into an aristocratic family of Zakynthos. On
returning from his studies in Italy in 1818 he published the only
collection of his verse to appear during his lifetime, the *Rime Improv-
visate* (Corfu, 1822), a set of poems, as their title indicates, in Italian.
Shortly before this it appears that Solomos had made a conscious
decision to dedicate himself to developing a poetic idiom in Greek.
The magnitude of this task is demonstrated by his surviving autograph manuscripts, which reveal the poet for the rest of his life
drafting poems and commenting on his art in Italian, which of
course had been the language of his education, before painstakingly,
and with infinite revision, recasting most of them into the Greek
verses for which he has been admired by poets and critics since the
mid-nineteenth century.

Solomos' Greek poems of the 1820s are about evenly divided
between lyrical pieces, many of them celebrating the beauty and

---

[11] Most of Korais' writings have been collected by G. Valetas (Korais 1964).

purity of young girls, and playful satires aimed at members of the
poet's immediate circle, both of them drawing on the popular urban
songs of his native island, the *kandades*.[12] But Solomos' fame spread
to newly independent Greece and abroad with the publication in
Paris in 1825—and a few months later on the recently established
printing press at Missolonghi—of his *Hymn to Liberty*, written in
1823.[13] In this poem, in 158 rhyming quatrains, Liberty, personified
as a goddess, is seen to rise again from the bones of the ancient
Hellenes where she had been imprisoned since the end of classical
civilization, and to take a delight, by turns bloodthirsty and tender,
now in the victories of the insurgent Greeks at Tripolitsa and at
Missolonghi, now in the ingenuous hopes newly roused in the
breasts of the young girls of Corinth, and finally in the rituals of
the Orthodox Church. The opening stanzas of this poem, in a
musical setting by Nikolaos Mantzaros, in 1865 became the Greek
national anthem.

Solomos' only other large-scale work to be published in his lifetime was the *Lyrical Poem on the Death of Lord Byron*, written in 1824
and published the following year. In form and style this poem
follows the *Hymn* closely. When news came of Byron's death at
Missolonghi, Solomos is said to have leapt upon the table of the
taverna where he was sitting with friends, and improvised the opening stanza, which refers back to the previous poem:

> Λευθεριά, για λίγο πάψε
> να χτυπάς με το σπαθί·

[12] For many years the standard critical edition has been Solomos 1986 (ed. L.
Politis), of which vol. 1 (first published in 1948) contains all the poems in Greek, and
vol. 2 (first published in 1955) contains prose in both Greek and Italian, and poems in
Italian. To appreciate the nature and magnitude of the difficulties presented by
Solomos' works as they were left at the time of his death, it is essential to refer to
the invaluable research tool, the autograph works in facsimile and transcription, also
edited by Politis (Solomos 1964). An important new departure has been the appearance of a one-volume edition by Stylianos Alexiou (Solomos 1994). Alexiou's edition
is based on a thorough re-examination of the manuscripts, following rigorous methods of textual scholarship, and presents a 'collected' Solomos that is smaller in extent,
but at once more accessible and more intelligible, than has been available in earlier
editions which broadly followed the pattern established by Solomos' first editor,
Iakovos Polylas, in 1859. All quotations from Solomos in this book are taken from
Alexiou's edition (1994), but for the convenience of the reader references are also
given to the Politis edition (1986). Alexiou's edition additionally includes an excellent
and up-to-date 'Selected Bibliography', to which the reader is referred. For the
controversial reception of Alexiou's edition, see S. Alexiou 1997.

[13] Ύμνος εις την Ελευθερίαν (Solomos 1994: 93–122; 1986: i. 71–100).

τώρα σίμωσε και κλάψε
εις του Μπάιρον το κορμί[14]

Liberty, for a while
cease striking with your sabre;
come hither now and weep
upon the body of Lord Byron.

The same period also saw the genesis of two other longer works
which, like many of Solomos' later projects, were never completed.
The prose satire *The Woman of Zakynthos* and the epic/dramatic
poem *Lambros* are both set against a background of violent conflict
between Greeks and Turks. Begun while the war of independence
was still going on, these continued to occupy Solomos after his move
from Zakynthos to the capital of the Ionian islands in Corfu in 1828.[15]

At almost exactly the same time as Solomos was composing his
Hymn to Liberty and the ode on Byron, another Zakynthian poet, at
the other end of Europe, was also celebrating and promoting the
cause of Greek independence, in a poetic style that could hardly have
been more different. Andreas Kalvos was the antithesis of Solomos in
a number of ways. Like Solomos, Kalvos received his education in
Italy; but unlike him he seems to have been largely self-taught (while
Solomos graduated from the University of Pavia), and unlike Solomos, Kalvos remained in western Europe, austerely earning his living
as a private tutor and translator of Protestant religious texts.[16] Like
Solomos, he wrote more in Italian than he did in Greek;[17] but unlike
Solomos, the Greek in which he preferred to write was closer to
the 'learned' than to the spoken form of the language.

Despite these differences, however, the fundamental aims of the
two poets, during the Greek war of independence, were remarkably
similar. Kalvos' output of poetry in Greek is very small, consisting of
two volumes each containing *Odes*, the first published in Geneva in
1824, the second in Paris in 1826.[18] Like the first publication of

---

[14] Εις το θάνατο του Λορδ Μπάιρον (ποίημα λυρικό), st. 1 (Solomos 1994: 123;
1986: i. 101).

[15] *Η γυναίκα της Ζάκυθος* (Solomos 1991), *Ο Λάμπρος* (Solomos 1986: i. 157–
96); respectively Solomos 1994: 481–509; 169–79.

[16] Kalvos contributed the Greek text to an international edition of the *Book of
Common Prayer*, published in London in 1820, and at about same time translated the
Psalms of David (Kalvos 1981). See also Kalvos 1988c.

[17] On Kalvos' surviving works in Italian see Vitti 1960; 1995, esp. pp. 91–117.

[18] The standard critical edition, first published in 1970, is by F. M. Pontani
(Kalvos 1988a). The edition by M. G. Meraklis (Kalvos n.d.) has full notes that are
useful for students, while that by S. Dialismas (Kalvos 1988b) is well produced and

Solomos' *Hymn*, these poems were published in western Europe, and their first editions were accompanied by a French translation. The inclusion, in the second volume, entitled *Lyrics*, of a glossary directed towards the student of the classical language to whom *modern* Greek is unfamiliar, further reveal that these poems of Kalvos, even more than Solomos' *Hymn*, were deliberately addressed to educated Europeans, with the aim of boosting support for the Greek cause abroad.

These twenty highly formal poems, using a unique stanza form invented by Kalvos for the purpose, have a common theme: the war of independence. Kalvos' *Odes* celebrate not only liberty, but many other abstract values which the European Enlightenment saw as exemplified in classical civilization, and which Kalvos strenuously tries to attribute to the Greek insurgents of his own time: patriotism, virtue, courage, and the art of immortalizing these qualities in song. References to the ancient musical instrument, the lyre, abound (indeed the first volume of *Odes* is entitled *The Lyre*), as do allusions to the simple crowns of laurel that were the prizes at ancient Greek athletic contests. These, and many other, classical allusions (Italy is 'Ausonia', England 'Albion', Paris 'the sacred city of the Celts'), and a tendency to apostrophize abstract qualities, are easily recognized as the trappings of European neoclassicism,[19] and as such have usually been an obstacle to twentieth-century readers.

Kalvos' commemoration of the death of Byron, which heads his 1826 volume of *Odes*, substitutes for the spontaneity of Solomos' tribute a strict decorum:

> Ω Βύρων· ω θεσπέσιον
> πνεύμα των Βρεττανίδων,
> τέκνον μουσών και φίλε
> άμοιρε της Ελλάδος
> καλλιστεφάνου. . . .
>
> Χθες τον ουράνιον έτρεχε
> δρόμον ο ήλιος· χύνων
> τας πλέον λαμπράς ακτίνας
> το μέτωπόν σου αντέστραπτεν
> ως αθανάτου.

includes a useful bibliography. Some of the most important studies on Kalvos have been re-issued in a single volume edited by Vayenas (1992), while articles by Mario Vitti have been collected in Vitti 1995. For a full bibliography see Andreiomenos 1993.

[19] For a modern perspective on this phenomenon see Tziovas 1987: 151–93.

Σήμερον κείσαι, ως εύφορος
πολύκλωνος ελαία
από το βίαιον φύσημα
σκληρών ανέμων κείται
εκριζωμένη.[20]

O Byron; o heavenly
spirit of the British Isles,
muses' child and hapless
friend of Hellas
        the finely crowned. . . .

Yesterday the sun
in his heavenly course did running shed
his most resplendent rays
upon your brow, that flashed in answer,
        as though of one immortal.

Today you lie, as an abundant
olive-tree of many branches
by the cruel breath
of harsh winds lies
        uprooted.

But although the formal means to which Kalvos has recourse are at
the opposite end of the spectrum from those of Solomos' poem on
the same subject, both share an extravagance in their use which
paradoxically brings them close together. Kalvos declared in a
lengthy note appended to this volume that his purpose in his poetry
was to 'imitate the movements of the soul', and in this he is surprisingly close to Solomos, who in a somewhat similar note to his *Hymn
to Liberty*, had declared that the 'harmony of the verse' is to be
equated with 'an overflowing of the soul'. It is improbable that either
poet was acquainted with Wordsworth's famous equation of poetry
with 'the spontaneous overflow of powerful feelings', but these
statements by Solomos and Kalvos betray how closely the poetics
of *both* are linked to the contemporary rise of European Romanticism.[21]

[20] Η Βρεταννική Μούσα, η΄, ι΄–ια΄, in Kalvos 1988a: 97.

[21] Kalvos: μιμούμεθα τας κινήσεις της ψυχής (Επισημειώσεις, Kalvos 1988a:
173); Solomos: η αρμονία του στίχου δεν είναι πράγμα όλο μηχανικό, αλλά είναι
ξεχείλισμα της ψυχής (Σημειώσεις του ποιητή, Ύμνος εις την Ελευθερίαν, Solomos 1994: 121; 1986: i. 99); Wordsworth in the 'Preface' to the second edition of
Lyrical Ballads (1800). The context for the comments by both Greek poets is an
explanation/defence of their chosen metrical form, while Wordsworth's preface is also
largely a defence of the form and chosen subject matter of his and Coleridge's poems.

There are other indications, too, that the formal techniques of neoclassicism serve a more serious purpose in Kalvos' poetry than in much of the poetry of the eighteenth-century Europe from which he derived them; a purpose which places him, along with the early Solomos, on the threshold of the Romantic movement. This is evident, first of all, from the title, *Odes*. Kalvos uses the term in a far more precise, and also more far-reaching, sense than is common among his western contemporaries, for whom it meant simply an emotionally charged piece, often in a relatively elaborate verse-form. Kalvos, on the other hand, prefaces *The Lyre* with an epigraph from the ancient lyric poet Pindar, which reminds us that the ode in Greece in the sixth century BC had been a special form of highly elaborated song, specially composed to celebrate the victors in the Olympic Games and other contests. Pindar's odes use mythology to highlight the human virtues that the ancient Greeks sought to promote through the Games, and originally they were sung to the accompaniment of the lyre, during the ceremony when the laurel crowns were given to the victors.[22]

Now it becomes clear why Kalvos' odes are so seemingly over-burdened by allusion to the lyre and the laurel crown, why mytho-logical and other classical allusions are so conspicuous, and abstract qualities extolled. If Pindar sang to celebrate the victory of athletes in the Games, and to extol the moral and physical attributes of the winner, then Kalvos set himself to do the same thing for the victors (as he fervently believed they would be) in the Greek war of inde-pendence, and similarly to extol the ancient virtues he associated with the modern cause.

As 'victory odes' of a rather different sort, and dedicated to a cause even more earnest than that of athletic excellence, Kalvos' poems invoke an ancient model for a far more serious purpose than neoclassical ornamentation. Although twentieth-century attempts to rehabilitate Kalvos have sought to separate his striking moments of lyricism and daring uses of metaphor from what they see as the burden of neoclassical rhetoric,[23] the achievement of the *Odes* in fact depends equally on both. The overall conception of using a classical

[22] Much has been written on alleged Romantic or (neo)classical elements in Kalvos' poetry. For a close analysis of *how* Kalvos employs classical allusions and structural principles drawn from ancient poetry in a single ode, see Perysinakis 1985.

[23] Most notably the essays by Seferis (1981: i. 179–210) and Elytis (1987: 47–112); reprinted in Vayenas 1992: 43–119.

40 LITERATURE FOR A NEW NATION

model in this highly original way is no less daring than the lyrical moments that later poets have singled out and sometimes drawn on themselves. Implicitly, in their overall structure and allusions, the *Odes* both compare and contrast the current war in Greece with the athletic contests for which the ancient Greeks were so much admired in Kalvos' own day; and in this way not just Liberty but poetry itself is claimed by Kalvos as being resurrected, in Solomos' words, 'from the bones of the ancient Hellenes'.[24]

The first steps towards a distinctively 'national' literature for the new Greek nation took place, as we have seen, outside the boundaries of the emergent Greek state. Solomos in fact never set foot in independent Greece; Kalvos' resolve, touchingly announced in a letter prefaced to the second volume of his *Odes* in 1826, to go to join his countrymen in their armed struggle, lasted for only a few months after his arrival in Nafplion later that year.[25] Whatever Kalvos experienced during these months in independent Greece has not been recorded, but he never returned, and he wrote no more poetry either.

But with the establishment of Nafplion as the first national capital during the war of independence, and the spread of relative peace and stability after the battle of Navarino in 1827, a 'cultural vacuum' inevitably began to open up, since none of the centres of learning before independence fell within the boundaries of the new state. This vacuum was filled, and remarkably quickly, by only one of the groups described earlier—the Phanariots of Constantinople and the Danubian principalities. There were good practical reasons for this. After the outbreak of hostilities in 1821 and the execution of the Patriarch Gregory V on Easter Day 1822, it was clear that the privileges of the Greek intellectual élite in the Ottoman empire would never be the same again. In reality, many Phanariot Greeks continued to serve the Ottoman empire throughout the nineteenth century, and many of those who lived and wrote in the Greek kingdom passed back and forth to Constantinople. However, the mainly young Phanariots who flocked to Nafplion and later to Athens to fill

---

[24] See the opening of Solomos' *Hymn to Liberty*, whose second stanza includes the words (addressed to Liberty): Απ' τα κόκκαλα βγαλμένη | των Ελλήνων τα ιερά (Solomos 1994: 93; 1986: i. 71).

[25] Je quitte la France avec regret; mon devoir m'appelle dans ma patrie, pour exposer un cœur de plus au fer des Musulmans... ('Au Général Lafayette', Kalvos 1988a: 174).

the cultural vacuum just described, played such a decisive part in the development of Greek letters during the nineteenth century that the term 'Phanariot' has come to acquire a new and different meaning, when applied to that century. In nineteenth-century Greece the term is almost always applied to the descendants of the eighteenth-century élite of Constantinople and the Danubian principalities who came to constitute the intellectual élite of the Greek kingdom. Conventionally the ascendancy of the 'Phanariots' in this sense is supposed to cover the period 1830–80, and the poets who wrote and published in Athens at this period are known alternatively as the 'Old Athenian' or 'Phanariot' School.

The foundations for this 'school' (and also, as we shall see, for the prose fiction of the period) were laid by three young men, all of them born in Constantinople, and all of them under twenty-five at the time of the battle of Navarino. They were Alexandros Soutsos (1803–63), his brother Panayotis (1806–68), and Alexandros Rizos Rangavis (1809–92). Like the poets of the Ionian islands in the previous decade, Solomos and Kalvos, these three had finished their education abroad (the Soutsos brothers in Paris, Rangavis in Munich). The year 1831 in Nafplion saw the publication of two long poems which initiate the 'full-blooded' phase of the Romantic movement in Greece: *The Wayfarer* by Panayotis Soutsos, which had been written in 1827, and *Dimos and Eleni* by Rangavis.[26] Both are melodramatic works in which a 'Byronic' hero pits his restless spirit against the forces of nature and society to assert his devoted love for an ideal woman, only to lose her through a succession of implausible mishaps and misunderstandings. The plot involves a Byronic frisson—blasphemy in the case of *The Wayfarer*, incest in that of *Dimos and Eleni*—and both end with the death of the main characters from suicide or grief. In these two poems a recognizably imported confection is solidly anchored to the Greek world. The action of *The Wayfarer*, which in form is a verse drama, takes place on the Holy Mountain of Mount Athos, while the characters and situations of *Dimos and Eleni* are drawn from the world of pasha and klefts (brigands) of pre-independence Greece.

[26] *Ο οδοιπόρος* (Soutsos 1915: 83–127); *Δήμος και Ελένη* (Rangavis 1874–89: ii. 109–47). The latter interestingly bears the subtitle, which looks forward to the fragmentary state of Solomos' *Lambros* and other late poems, 'Fragments of a Folk Poem' (Αποσπάσματα δημοτικού ποιήματος).

The juxtaposition of storm imagery and pursuit by Turks with the hero's tender protection of his beloved, in *Dimos and Eleni*, was to reappear in Solomos' unfinished poem of the 1830s, *The Cretan*.

Πλην τ' είν' αυτός ο βρόντος που ο βοριάς μάς φέρνει;
Ταις πέτραις των φαράγκων αστροπελέκι δέρνει;···
Αγάπη μου, ταράττεσαι; ο κρότος σε τρομάζει;
   Αυξάνει, πλησιάζει,
κ' από το δάσος που δεξιά εκτείνετ' απλωμένον,
εν άλογον τινάζεται χρυσοχαλινωμένον,
οπού ανεμοστρόβιλος πως μαστιγόνει μοιάζει.
'Σ ταις πέτραις δεν πατεί, πετά· κ' ο κτύπος των πετάλων
σπίθαις σκορπά και πάταγον αποτελεί μεγάλον.[27]

But what can be this thunder that the north wind brings?
Is it a thunderbolt that whips the rocks in the ravines?...
My love, are you afraid? Does the noise fright you?
   It grows, it nears,
and from the wood that on the right extends
a horse bursts forth with golden bridle,
that like a lashing whirlwind seems.
It does not tread upon the stones but flies; its beating hooves
strike sparks and make a dreadful din.

The Wayfarer and *Dimos and Eleni* seem to have been well regarded throughout much of the nineteenth century; indeed, Soutsos revised his poem no fewer than three times to keep it in line with current tastes, particularly in its language.[28] Neither is ever read today, however, except in extracts in anthologies. But the historical importance of these poems lies not just in the fact that they very largely set the agenda for what is conventionally known as 'Greek Romanticism' (the poetry of Nafplion and Athens from 1830 to about 1880), but also in their relation to Solomos, to whom we now return.

Solomos had publicly declared his admiration for Byron, as we saw, on the occasion of the latter's death in 1824. Throughout most of the following ten years, he seems to have kept up work on a more

---

[27] Rangavis 1974–89: ii. 118. The onomatopoeic effects of the last two lines quoted are impossible to render in translation. Compare the opening of *The Cretan*.

[28] The revised editions were published in, respectively, 1842, 1851, and 1864. Apart from extracts (see L. Politis 1980: iv. 72–83), the text of the first edition, whose language is closest to spoken Greek, is extremely rare. On Soutsos' role in the 'Language Question' see Ch. 6.

ambitious project, an epic–dramatic poem in obviously Byronic mould, entitled *Lambros*. Like all the large-scale projects of Solomos' later years, this poem was never finished.

Although unfinished and unknown outside Solomos' immediate circle during his lifetime, the fragmentary *Lambros* is today far better known than either of the two poems by Soutsos and Rangavis just described. But like them, *Lambros* was projected on a large scale; its affinities to the Romantic movement, particularly of northern Europe, are evident, and its more spectacular ingredients are identical to theirs: incest, the supernatural, ideal love, and suicide. Again like the poems of Soutsos and Rangavis, *Lambros* mixes these ingredients in a specifically Greek historical context: the principal character is a hero of the recent Greek struggles against the Turks.

The similarities among these three poems help to place Solomos' development after the 1820s in perspective. The goal aimed at by all three poets seems to have been the same: to create a 'national' Greek poetry which would stand alongside the most admired achievements of Europe in the early nineteenth century. And it is interesting to see that during the late 1820s no fewer than three poets, all of whom were to make an effective impact on the later development of poetry in Greek, converged on such similar means to attaining this end. Solomos abandoned *Lambros* in about 1834, perhaps recognizing that this particular laurel had now passed beyond his reach. But throughout the 1830s and 1840s, after his move from Zakynthos to the capital of the Ionian islands in Corfu, he tirelessly pursued the goal of a large-scale, 'epic–lyric' composition, which would go beyond the 'Byronic' melodrama of the stillborn *Lambros* and of its more successful counterparts published in Nafplion. In the event the direction taken by Solomos' unfinished poems of the 1830s and 1840s, on which the substance of his reputation rests today, was rather different from that taken by his younger contemporaries in Athens during the same period. But at the beginning of the 1830s, the common ground between the 'national poet' in Corfu and the younger Phanariots of independent Greece was far greater than it has been made to appear by the subsequent course of literary history.

Dating from the time of his move to Corfu in 1828, Solomos embarked on a systematic study of the poetry and ideas of German Romanticism.[29] As a result, in the poems that he drafted

---

[29] See esp. Veloudis 1989.

and re-drafted during the following two decades, he engages more
directly and fundamentally with the preoccupations of contemporary aesthetics and philosophical speculation than any other Greek
poet before Palamas at the turn of the twentieth century. The three
fragmentary poems of Solomos' maturity, *The Cretan*, *The Free
Besieged*, and 'The Shark', have generated a large bibliography,
and have been hailed, ever since the end of the last century, as
flawed or incomplete masterpieces.[30]
All three are in narrative form; and the state of the manuscripts
found after Solomos' death has left almost insurmountable problems in establishing authoritative texts. *The Free Besieged* was the
first to be begun. Originally conceived, in its first draft, as an 'Ode'
on the recapture by the Ottomans of independent Missolonghi in
April 1826, somewhat in the style of Solomos' previous patriotic
poems, by 1833 the raw event had been subsumed, in a very different
second draft of the poem, into a lyrical and expanded exploration of
the paradox of its title. In an evident echo of Schiller, the besieged
citizens of Missolonghi are subjected to a final temptation by the
beauties of nature that surround them in spring, in order for their
souls to achieve true freedom in the renunciation of all earthly
things:

Μάγεμα η φύσις κι' όνειρο στην ομορφιά και χάρη,
η μαύρη πέτρα ολόχρυση και το ξερό χορτάρι·
με χίλιες βρύσες χύνεται, με χίλιες γλώσσες κρένει·
όποιος πεθάνει σήμερα χίλιες φορές πεθαίνει.[31]

Nature an enchanted dream in grace and beauty,
gilding the blackened stone and dried-up weeds,
in a thousand torrents gushes forth, speaks with a thousand tongues;
whoever dies today a thousand times will die.

But Solomos, like many other Greek writers after him, resists and so
modifies the abstract separation between soul and body that he
found in Schiller and the German Romantics. Although neither in

[30] Ο κρητικός. Οι ελεύθεροι πολιορκημένοι. Ο πόρφυρας. The influential series
of essays by Kostis Palamas, dating from the 1880s and 1890s, has been reissued,
with introduction (Palamas 1970). Among many more recent evaluations see, in
particular, L. Politis 1985 and the essays collected in Kapsomenos 1992. The best
introduction to the work of the poet in English is Mackridge 1989, which, however,
includes quotations in Greek only. See also Jenkins 1981; Raizis 1972, both of which
include translated extracts.
[31] Draft B, II, ll. 10–13 (Solomos 1994: 259; 1986: i. 217).

this second draft, nor in the draft that succeeded it a decade later, did Solomos sketch in with any clarity the ending of his poem, on the basis of the fragments that we have it would be fair to say that in this poem there is no 'other' world. In *The Free Besieged* the ideal of absolute freedom is attained only in this world, in the decision of the defenders, suspended as it were between the beauty and vitality of nature in spring on the one hand, and the destructive power of the enemy on the other, to lay down their lives in an act of heroic defiance.

A similar nexus of themes can be observed in *The Cretan* (written about 1833) and 'The Shark' (written 1849). In the first, the hero of the title is discovered, swimming away from a shipwreck on a stormy night, with his fiancée in his arms. Before he can bring the girl to shore, he experiences a vision in which the storm is calmed, and an ethereal female figure rises out of the reflection of the moon on the water. Described as a 'goddess', she 'reads' in his heart the story of his heroic and ultimately futile struggles against the Turks in his native island, before she vanishes to leave behind an indescribably beautiful sound, which all but charms him out of his mortal body in order to follow her. The poem ends with the return to the real world of the storm and the shipwreck, as the Cretan sets the girl down on the shore, only to discover, in the final line of the poem, that she is dead:

Λαλούμενο, πουλί, φωνή, δεν είναι να ταιριάζει,
ίσως δε σώζεται στη γη ήχος που να του μοιάζει·
δεν είναι λόγια· ήχος λεπτός...
μόλις είν' έτσι δυνατός ο Έρωτας και ο Χάρος.

   ·   ·   ·   ·   ·   ·

Με άδραχνε, και μ' έκανε συχνά ν' αναζητήσω
τη σάρκα μου να χωριστώ για να τον ακλουθήσω.
Έπαψε τέλος κι άδειασεν η φύσις κι η ψυχή μου,
που εστέναξε κι εγιόμισεν ευθύς οχ την καλή μου·
και τέλος φθάνω στο γιαλό την αρραβωνιασμένη,
Την απιθώνω με χαρά, κι ήτανε πεθαμένη.[32]

Reed-pipe, bird, singing voice: none can match
that sound, whose like perhaps is gone from earth.
It is not words, but sound as light as air,
Love and Death, I doubt, have scarce such power.

   ·   ·   ·   ·   ·   ·

It seized me; many times it made me yearn
to leave behind my body and to follow.

[32] V, ll. 43–5, 50, 53–8 (Solomos 1994: 229; 1986: i. 205–6).

It ceased; drained empty nature and my soul
that sighing, filled at once with my beloved;
and now at last the shore: I set her down
upon the strand with joy, but she was dead.

In this poem, and in 'The Shark', about the violent death of a British soldier while bathing off Corfu, Solomos again elaborates upon the paradoxical relation of opposites: life and death, body and soul, violence and beauty. No one of these pairs, in Solomos' poetic conception, is complete without the other, but the tragic cost of wholeness, of transcending the divisions on which everyday life and experience are based, is invariably death. This seems to be the meaning of the cryptic and arresting quatrain which, ever since the edition of Polylas, has always been read as the opening of 'The Shark':

Η Κόλαση πάντ' άγρυπνη σου στήθηκε τριγύρου·
αλλά δεν έχει δύναμη πάρεξ μακριά και πέρα,
μακριά 'πό την Παράδεισο, και συ σ' εσέ 'χεις μέρος·
μέσα στα στήθια σου τ' ακούς, Καλέ, να λαχταρίζει;[33]

Hell, ever wakeful, circled you about,
but powerless yet unless far off, beyond
the bounds of Paradise, in which you share,
and—can you feel it?—quivers in your breast.

Like the defenders of Missolonghi in *The Free Besieged*, the soldier, bathing near the shore, is surrounded by the beauties of Nature at its most peaceful and enchanting. But the same Nature that arouses echoes of Paradise within him also harbours the 'tiger of the seas': the shark that will attack and kill him. It is only when the hero is awakened, by the onslaught of the shark, to *both* sides of an ambivalent Nature that is simultaneously both Paradise and Hell, that

'Αστραψε φως κι εγνώρισεν ο νιος τον εαυτό του[34]

In a lightning flash the young man knew himself.

Given this concept of a completeness that depends on the fleeting fusion of opposite forces, it may not be so surprising that formal

---

[33] Alexiou prints these lines, perhaps the most radical of his departures from the textual tradition initiated by Polylas, as the opening of an unfinished poem on the Italian revolution of 1848 (Solomos 1994: 312–13; for reasoning see 280–3; 291–4; for the 'standard' version see Solomos 1986: i 251). Relevant here, however, is the theme of the paradoxical equilibrium of opposites, which is also fundamental to the poem 'The Shark'.

[34] Solomos 1994: 308, line 31; Solomos 1986: i. 255, fragment VII, line 2.

completeness also eluded Solomos in each of these remarkable later poems.[35]

It is tempting, though of course futile, to speculate how the course of Greek literary history might have been different if Solomos had either completed any of these poems to his own satisfaction, or been prepared to publish them even in fragmentary form during his lifetime. As it was, his own near-silence, and the absolute silence of Kalvos after 1826, served to deepen the 'cultural vacuum' which the Phanariots had come to independent Greece in order to fill. The poems of Solomos' maturity were not published until 1859, by which time the interests of poets based in Athens and the readers whom their work reached had taken a rather different direction.

It is a commonplace of Greek literary history to divide the poetry of the period up to about 1880 into parallel 'schools': the 'Phanariot' or 'Old Athenian School', that has already been mentioned, and the 'School of the Ionian Islands'.[36] A recent examination of the evidence suggests that there was little consciousness of separateness among the writers and readers of each group, except on the issue of language, which will be discussed in Chapter 6.[37] The Romanticism which is equally a hallmark of both groups or 'schools', however, never again aspires to the moral and aesthetic 'high ground' of Solomos' poems of the 1830s and 1840s. Instead the early collection of Panayotis Soutsos, *The Guitar*, opts for the innocuous craftsmanship of Gray and Lamartine, which is easily grafted on to the fluent versification, in a wide range of metres and rhyme-schemes, and the absence of thematic innovation or pretensions to seriousness that had characterized Phanariot poetry in the eighteenth century. Lyric poetry of the period, both in Athens and the Ionian islands, is dominated by formal love-poetry and elegies, and by poems on the seasons, especially spring, while longer poems on mainly patriotic themes and either narrative or dramatic in form, appear in both centres of culture.[38]

[35] On the relation of these poems to the 'Romantic fragment' see Lambropoulos 1988: 85–99.

[36] Politis' anthology assigns separate volumes to each (L. Politis 1980). For a useful chronological bibliography of this period, see Savvidis 1981*a*.

[37] See Apostolidou 1988, where some of the older debate on the subject is also discussed and summarized.

[38] Modern anthologies tend to represent the former category at the expense of the latter. Examples of the latter are the 'epic' treatments of the war of independence by

If the lyric poetry of the mid-nineteenth century seems disconcertingly, almost regressively, 'neoclassical' in the formalism of its verse and its restricted thematic range, many of the longer poems of the 1850s and 1860s have in the twentieth century been accused of an artificiality and 'coldness' that accords more with the poetics of eighteenth-century neoclassicism than with the Romantic traits we have observed in Greek poetry in the early years of independence. A parallel is sometimes drawn with the Greek architecture of the period, which produced the varied and sometimes exuberant recreations of classical and classically inspired styles in a large number of villas and public buildings of Athens during the same period. It is worth remembering that the Bavarian architects who inaugurated this style and trained most of the Greek architects who participated in this movement were kith and kin with their counterparts who built the famous gothic castles of Bavaria. The mainspring of Greek 'neoclassicism' of the mid-nineteenth century, it may be suggested, has little to do with the enlightened rationalism of the previous century, but rather derives from the same impetus as led to the emulation of the Gothic middle ages in Germany and England at the same time—namely a 'Romantic' impulse to rediscover the roots (the 'traditions' in Herder's influential formulation) of the nation. In the case of Greece the 'traditions of the people' were exclusively identified at this time with the classical civilization that had ended two thousand years before. As a result, in poetry as in architecture, forms of classical imitation serve a very different function from the neoclassicism of the West during the previous century, which they superficially resemble. Paradoxically, in a Greek context 'neoclassicism' should be understood as the local manifestation of the *Romantic* impulse which in other parts of Europe gave rise to the gothic revival.

In Athens these characteristics can be discerned in the later works of Panayotis Soutsos and Rangavis, and in that of their successors

Alexandros Soutsos: *Hellas at War with the Turks*, 1850 (*Η Τουρκομάχος Ελλάς*); Zalokostas: *Missolonghi* (*Μεσολόγγιον*), which won the first of a series of prestigious annual poetry competitions in 1851; Orfanidis: *St Minas*, 1860 (*'Αγιος Μηνάς*); and in a lighter and subtler vein, the playful re-creation of an ancient myth by Rangavis: *The Voyage of Dionysos*, 1864 (*Διονύσου πλους*). For modern views of these poems see K. Dimaras 1974: 271–88; Vitti 1987: 204–20. On the poem by Rangavis see Vitti 1980: 143–52 and the reassessment by Ricks 1987. On the importance of the annual poetry competitions, which were a significant national event between 1851 and 1877, see Vitti 1987: 220–1 and Moullas 1989.

down to the early 1880s.[39] In the Ionian islands the same can be said
of the work of the followers of Solomos.[40] The only consistent
distinction that can be made between the poetics of the two groups
is in their choice of language, which will be further discussed in
Chapter 6. In Athens, admiration for the ancient classics extends to
the language in which much of the poetry is written, while the poets
of the Ionian islands consistently write in an idiom based on the
spoken Greek of the time, often, as in the case of Solomos, including
elements of the local dialect.

The achievements and limitations of Greek poetry of this period
should not simply be written off. The work of only two poets of the
mid-century has been systematically republished in modern critical
editions: Markoras and Valaoritis.[41] The former is remarkable for
his long poem, first published in Corfu in 1875, *The Oath*, a narrative
poem of the failed Cretan uprising against the Turks in 1866 which
draws extensively on, and in a sense 'completes', Solomos' *The
Cretan*.[42] Valaoritis is the only poet of the mid-nineteenth century
whose reputation has never been fully eclipsed, and this is surely due
to the passionate fervour of his long compositions on patriotic
themes: *Kyra Frosini* (1859), *Athanasis Diakos* (1867), and *Fotinos*
(1879). The first two of these dramatize famous heroic deaths in the
face of Turkish oppression, the third a little-known episode from the
fourteenth-century history of Valaoritis' native island of Lefkada,
under the rule of western 'Franks'.[43] Valaoritis' staunch patriotism
played no less a part in his life than his art. Before the cession of the
Ionian islands he had been elected a deputy to the islands' parliament, where he campaigned vociferously for union with Greece,
and after this was achieved in 1864 he continued his parliamentary
career as a representative of Lefkada in the Greek Parliament in

[39] Notably Yeoryios Zalokostas (1805–58), Theodoros Orfanidis (1817–86), Ioannis Karasoutsas (1824–73), Spyridon Vasiliadis (1844–74), and Achillefs Paraschos
(1838–95).
[40] This applies in particular to Yeoryios Tertsetis (1800–74), Ioulios Typaldos
(1814–83), Iakovos Polylas (1825–96), the shorter poems of Yerasimos Markoras
(1826–1911), Andonios Manousos (1828–1903), all of whom had belonged to the
personal 'circle' of Solomos; and to the shorter poems of Aristotelis Valaoritis
(1824–79).
[41] To these may be added the *Poems* (Ποιήματα) of Andreas Laskaratos (1981),
whose reputation principally rests, however, on his satirical writing in prose.
[42] *Ο όρκος* (Markoras 1988: 53–105).
[43] *Κυρά Φροσύνη. Αθανάσης Διάκος. Φωτεινός.* All three are included in A.
Valaoritis 1981; for the third, with introduction, glossary, etc., see A. Valaoritis 1970.

Athens. Valaoritis' career, together with the fact that his later works were published in Athens, bridges the residual cultural gap between the capital and the Ionian islands, and his fiery grandiloquence inaugurates the final phase of Greek Romanticism before the 1880s.

The other representative of that final, grandiloquent phase was Achillefs Paraschos, whose three-volume collected works appeared in 1881, the year with which this chapter ends. Paraschos, even more than Valaoritis, was acclaimed during his lifetime as the embodiment of the poet's role, and by all accounts his public presence and magnificent reading voice contributed to this reputation. Unlike Valaoritis, however, Paraschos was soon eclipsed by the much more substantial figure of Kostis Palamas, who in addition to dominating Greek poetry for three decades (from about 1890 to 1920), in a series of lectures and articles during the 1890s radically revised the canon of Greek poetry up to that time. And it is Palamas' evaluations which have continued to be accepted, with very little modification, up to the present. It is worth mentioning, however, that one of the most perceptive (and damning) of Greek critics up to this time, Emmanuel Roidis, writing in 1877, singled out only two living poets for praise: Valaoritis and Paraschos.[44]

There is undoubtedly room for some re-evaluation and reinterpretation in this period of Greek poetry, both from a critical and a historical perspective. In the Ionian islands Polylas, although he never published a collection of poetry, has been unduly eclipsed by the very success of his task in editing the posthumous manuscripts of Solomos and presenting them to the world in a form which the critical tools and expertise of a later age have never surpassed.[45] The extent of Polylas' achievement has only been fully appreciated since the materials from which he was working became generally available in 1964. Although Polylas added no verse of his own, and suppressed only variant readings, none the less to a very large extent the 'life and work' of Solomos which since the 1890s have held pride of place in the Modern Greek literary canon, deserve to be seen as the literary creation of his executor. Polylas was also the first to

---

[44] 'On Contemporary Greek Poetry' (Περί συγχρόνου ελληνικής ποιήσεως, Roidis 1986: 160–92).

[45] Alexiou is not the only one to have proposed sometimes quite radical re-editions of Solomos' poems, based on a reading of the manuscripts using modern editorial methods (see e.g. Kehayoglou 1979). The success of Polylas' achievement in 1859 may be gauged by the fact that none of these newer versions has yet found universal acceptance (see indicatively S. Alexiou 1997).

translate Homer into Modern Greek, and was one of the most successful Greek translators of Shakespeare. He was, in addition, one of the very few writers of his generation in the Ionian islands to write prose fiction.[46]

The other literary career which deserves scrutiny is that of Alexandros Rizos Rangavis. The reason for his continued eclipse is undoubtedly the archaizing language in which his later works are written. But in the wake of recent re-evaluations of the work of several prose writers of the century who wrote in the same linguistic style, and of renewed interest today in the prose fiction of the same period, the time may now be ripe for a new look at the poetry—and the poetics—of those who turned away from the exclusive use of the spoken language championed by Solomos. Although there has been no modern edition of Rangavis' collected poetry, and little has been written on it either, except in anthologies and histories of literature, it is clear that Rangavis was an extremely versatile poet, with a large thematic as well as linguistic and formal range, whose long career went through several distinct phases of development which have never been fully explored by criticism. In addition, as we shall see in the next chapter, Rangavis plays an important part in the creation of Modern Greek prose fiction. He was also a prolific translator from Italian and German (he translated Dante's *Inferno* and Tasso's *Gerusalemme Liberata*), and his history of Modern Greek literature that was mentioned in the Introduction makes an authoritative contribution to the perception of the literary canon in the late nineteenth century.[47]

Finally, before leaving the poetry of the period, brief mention must be made of satire, a genre which flourished in both the Ionian islands and Athens alongside the dominant Romanticism in which by its very nature it could not fully share. Satire had been one of the eighteenth-century genres *par excellence* in western and northern Europe, and as such was also practised by the Phanariots and the aristocracy of the Ionian islands at the turn of the nineteenth century. We have already seen that some of Solomos' earliest verse was in this genre; and simultaneously with *Lambros* he also worked on an apocalyptic satirical work in prose, *The Woman of Zakynthos*. The

---

[46] Polylas' *Odyssey* was published in 1875, the *Iliad* in 1890. His Shakespeare translations are *The Tempest* (1855) and *Hamlet* (1890). On the short stories he wrote late in career see n. 83 to the present chapter.

[47] Rangavis 1877; see Introduction.

surviving portions of this work were considered by Polylas as too strong meat for the tastes of the readers to whom he addressed the first collected edition of the poet's work (published in 1859), and so *The Woman of Zakynthos* remained unpublished until 1927.[48] The satirical tradition remained strong in the Ionian islands, both in verse and prose. Andreas Laskaratos (1811–1901) was excommunicated after publishing the prose satire, *The Mysteries of Cefallonia* (1856). Together with another longer prose piece, *Ecce Homo* (1886), this is available in a modern edition.[49] The dominant satirists of the Greek kingdom during the same period were; in verse, Alexandros Soutsos, brother of Panayotis, and in prose Emmanuel Roidis, who like Laskaratos fell foul of the Church, and whom we will meet again as the author of *Pope Joan*.

THE RISE OF FICTION

If the problems facing such writers as Solomos, Kalvos, and Rangavis in creating a 'national' idiom in poetry were intractable enough, those which faced aspirant writers of prose fiction in the early years of Greek independence were more daunting still. Until recently the rise of prose fiction in the first decades of the Greek Kingdom has been conventionally seen in terms of a significant discontinuity, with the new genre effectively imported wholesale from western Europe on the wings of the same Romanticism that is said to have nurtured the 'Old Athenian School' of poetry. According to this long-established view, the precedents available to writers of prose fiction in Greek in the early part of the nineteenth century were even fewer than for poetry,[50] and the dominant 'influence' on the new Greek genre was the romantic historical novel as practised by Walter Scott.[51]

[48] For a modern critical edition of the three main drafts of this work see Solomos 1991.

[49] Laskaratos 1982; 1987. The poet Panayotis Panas (1832–96), also from Cefallonia, published a number of satirical short stories in the Ionian islands between 1868 and the 1880s (see Stavropoulou 1987: 244–58).

[50] For a list of these precedents as perceived up to the 1980s see (in English) Vitti 1988: 5, 9. To these must now be added the Hellenistic novel whose importance (discussed below) was surprisingly not suspected for so long (Tonnet 1994; 1996: 83–102).

[51] This is the view to be found in the standard histories of literature, and in such specialist works on the novel as Sachinis 1981; 1982. Vitti (1987: 259–67) gives prominence to the social criticism of Kalligas in *Thanos Vlekas*, but does not otherwise change the conventional picture.

Since the end of the 1980s, this conventional picture has begun to be radically re-evaluated, with two important results. First, much more is now understood about the forms of prose fiction that circulated in Greek between the seventeenth century and the early nineteenth, which can no longer satisfactorily be labelled 'popular reading matter', and secondly, renewed interest in the texts themselves of the novels published between 1835 and 1850 has revealed a more diverse background and thematic range than had previously been assumed.[52]

The first novel to appear in independent Greece was *Leander* by Panayotis Soutsos, whom we have already met as a poet, published in Nafplion in 1834.[53] But this Romantic epistolary novel, with its evident debt to Goethe and Foscolo, represents only one of a number of more or less simultaneous starts to Greek prose fiction. Nor does it stand quite at the beginning. The earliest known original prose fiction in Greek in modern times is the collection of three short stories, published under the initials I.K. in Vienna in 1792, with the title *Results of Love*.[54] The three are conceived as a contrasting set. Love, as the title implies, is their single, unifying theme. As exemplary tales, each explores a different outcome to the course of love: respectively marriage, suicide, and 'getting over it'. The stories are told simply, in the language, so far as one can tell, of educated urban discourse of the period, and are remarkable for an absence of extraneous narrative detail (extending to details of character and setting that in the nineteenth century would have been considered indispensable), and even of incident. Indeed, the elegance of these tales lies in their formal construction, their single-minded concentration on the theme of love, and the studied ordinariness of the lives they

[52] The catalyst for both these developments seems to have been the rediscovery of the novels of Grigorios Palaiologos, on which see below (see Angelou 1989 and idem in Palaiologos 1989*b*). On so-called 'popular reading matter' before this period (λαϊκά αναγνώσματα) see Angelou 1988*b*, Kehayoglou 1991*a*; 1991*b*. For an anthology of this period see Motsios 1990. For the parallel revival of interest in the texts themselves of the earliest nineteenth-century Greek novels, and the rejection of the earlier characterization of them as 'historical novels', see Vayenas 1994: 187–98 (first published 1988); Angelou 1989; Farinou-Malamatari 1991; Denisi 1990; 1992; and especially 1994; and the essays collected in Vayenas 1997. For an excellent anthology of extracts from the prose fiction of the nineteenth century accompanied by introductory essays and bibliography see Sokolis 1996–7.

[53] P. Soutsos 1996.

[54] I. K. [Ioannis Karatzas] 1989. For the identification of the anonymous author see Eideneier 1996.

represent. An undoubted precedent for the anonymous author was the free translation by Rigas of three love stories from the repertory of Rétif de la Bretonne, which had appeared in Vienna under the title *School for Delicate Lovers* in 1790.[55]

The appearance of these two publications coincides almost exactly, and surely not accidentally, with the reappearance in print of no fewer than four ancient and medieval Greek novels in prose. These editions, which appeared between 1790 and 1793, were all produced by Greek publishers for a Greek readership, not as classical texts for the classroom. And it should not be forgotten that the written language with which the Phanariots of the time were most familiar was ancient Greek. Before the publication of *Results of Love*, the *Aithiopika* of Heliodoros (of the fourth century AD) and the twelfth-century *Ysmini and Ysminias* of Efstathios Makremvolitis had already appeared in print, and were being read by exactly the same Phanariot reading public as was evidently addressed by the new stories.[56] And although the new stories are obviously very different from either of these precedents, so remote in time, the fastidious devotion of the anonymous writer to the theme of love, and the studied absence of extraneous incident, may well represent the aesthetic 'results' of a reading of, in particular, the twelfth-century novel (or romance) *Ysmini and Ysminias*.[57]

If a renewed interest in the ancient novel (together with its one medieval successor in prose) contributed to the first original Greek fiction of the 1790s, the patriot and educator Adamandios Korais, writing in the following decade, was proud to claim prose fiction as a Greek invention. The first of a ten-year series of editions of ancient Greek texts, the *Greek Library*, which had the explicit aim of raising the intellectual level of the enslaved Greeks, was devoted to Heliodoros' *Aithiopika*, published with a long introduction by Korais in 1804. In this introduction Korais notes that although the genre known in his day in France as *roman* had been the creation of the ancient Greeks, no generic term equivalent to 'novel' or 'romance' had ever existed in Greek. The term Korais now proposed was

---

[55] Rigas 1971*b*.

[56] The four are respectively the ancient novels (or romances) of Heliodoros (1790), Longos (1792), and Xenophon of Ephesos (1793), together with the 12th-cent. *Ysmini and Ysminias* by Efstathios Makremvolitis in 1791. See Angelou 1989: 33, where the link with Rigas and the *Results of Love* is suggested but not systematically followed up.

[57] On this text see Beaton 1996: 79–88.

mythistoria, and this was the term in common use throughout the first half of the nineteenth century, before the now-standard variation on it, *mythistorima*, became common.[58]

Moreover, Korais goes on to define the genre to which the term refers; and his definition is closely based on that of Pierre Daniel Huet, whose *Traité de l'origine des romans* of 1670 had been one of the first European attempts to explore the origin of modern fiction in the ancient Greek world. According to Korais, a *mythistoria* (novel) is to be understood, slightly modifying the terms used by Huet, as:

πλαστήν, αλλά πιθανήν ιστορίαν ερωτικών παθημάτων, γραμμένην εντέχνως και δραματικώς, ως επί το πλείστον εις πεζόν λόγον.[59]

a fictional, but plausible story of sufferings in love, written with artistry and dramatically, for the most part in prose.

Although the Modern Greek novel did not exist in 1804, it is significant that Korais' term for its ancient precursor became general among Greek novelists in the decades that followed. What is more, we can reasonably assume that those who gave currency to the term in the first half of the nineteenth century, whether or not they were all directly acquainted with Korais' introduction to the *Aithiopika*, widely disseminated though it was, must also have been aware of this definition, which had first been formulated to describe the *ancient Greek* novel.[60]

In any case, Korais' influential comments on Heliodoros represent a more significant contribution to the course of Greek fiction than does the work of his which has sometimes been hailed as the first Modern Greek novel. This is *Papatrechas*, actually a series of

[58] Korais 1964: A 832–9. The now standard term μυθιστόρημα seems to have gained currency only after 1865, when it is used by Panayotis Soutsos (Koumanoudis 1980). Both μυθιστορία and μυθιστόρημα are used by Neroulos in 1827 (Neroulos 1870: 167). The older term, μυθιστορία, has on occasion been revived in more recent times: for example by Prevelakis in the subtitle to his first novel, *The Chronicle of a Town*, 1938 (*Το χρονικό μιας πολιτείας*) and his trilogy *The Cretan*, 1948–50 (*Ο κρητικός*), and by Embirikos (1980c; 1990–2).

[59] 'Prologue to the edition of the *Aithiopika* of Heliodoros' (Πρόλογος στην έκδοση των Αιθιοπικών του Ηλιοδώρου, Korais 1964: A2, 833). Compare Huet 1966: 4: '...ce que l'on appelle proprement Romans sont des fictions d'aventures amoureuses, écrites en Prose avec art, pour le plaisir & l'instruction des Lecteurs.'

[60] I. Pitsipios actually cited Korais in his announcement (1834) of his novel *The Orphan-Girl of Chios* (*Η ορφανή της Χίου*) which appeared in 1839 (Angelou 1989: 25). The Soutsos brothers, while students, had presented themselves with a formal letter of introduction to Korais in Paris in 1820. Palaiologos also studied in Paris and is likely to have come into contact with Korais' circle (Angelou 1989: 25–6).

fictional letters published as prefaces to successive books of the *Iliad* that appeared between 1811 and 1820. The four letters, which describe the fictional narrator's acquaintance with an astute but unlettered village priest on the island of Chios, have a clearly didactic purpose, and there is no evidence that Korais himself ever saw them as an exercise in the genre which he had earlier defined. (Needless to say, the 'love interest' which, following Huet, Korais had built into his definition of the novel, is totally absent from these didactic pieces.) In any case, it was only after Korais' death that the four prefaces were published together and given the title (after the main character) *Papatrechas.*[61]

And so we return to Nafplion in 1834 and the publication of *Leander*, which as it happens, fits perfectly with Korais' definition of the novel. It is clear, too, from Soutsos' preface that he saw himself as breaking new ground, in fulfilling a need which the new nation was bound to feel sooner or later:

Εις την αναγεννωμένην Ελλάδα τολμώμεν ημείς πρώτοι να δώσωμεν εις το κοινόν τον Λέανδρον. Ευτυχείς, αν εις την οδόν, την οποίαν ενεχαράξαμεν, ιδώμεν μετ' ολίγον άλλους δοκιμωτέρους συγγραφείς μυθιστοριών.[62]

In reborn Greece we are the first to venture to offer *Leander* before the public; happy if ere long we see the way which we have opened up followed by other more worthy writers of novels (*mythistoriai*).

Leander was followed a year later, in 1835, by *The Exile of 1831*, by Panayotis' brother Alexandros, published in the new capital, Athens.[63] The period up to 1850 saw the appearance of at least another ten novels, many of which were published only in serial form, and not all of which survive.

What is most striking about these first novels of Modern Greece is their sheer variety. Panayotis Soutsos sets his novel in the inner world of Romantic sentimentality, and his disclaiming references to Goethe and Foscolo in his preface betray his sources clearly enough. His brother's novel, *The Exile of 1831*, as its title indicates, takes its setting, and in fact much of its action also, from the

---

[61] Korais 1978, first published with this title in 1842. Opinion is still divided on the nature and importance of *Papatrechas*. The claim that it is a novel is put strongly by the text's most recent editor (Angelou in Korais 1978), and more moderately since (Angelou 1989: 30-1; cf. Moschos 1984). For the opposite view see Vitti 1988: 8; Vitti in I.K. 1989: 11.

[62] P. Soutsos 1996: 43. [63] A. Soutsos 1994; 1996.

turbulent political life of the first years of national independence. Two other novels of the same decade focus on episodes of the war that was not long over: the curious and little-known *The Pallikar*, published anonymously in Malta for the London Missionary Society in 1835 and only quite recently shown to be the work of an Englishman, Samuel Sheridan Wilson; and *The Orphan-Girl of Chios* by Iakovos Pitsipios (Athens 1839).[64] Also in 1839 comes *The Poly-path* by Grigorios Palaiologos, a zestful picaresque *tour de force* which takes the reader from Ottoman Constantinople in the 1770s to the Greece of King Otho in which it was published, and concluding with its much-tried hero finally in his sixties reunited with the girl he had loved and lost, and settling down, like Voltaire's Candide, to cultivate his garden.[65] This novel, which seems to have been quite widely read in the nineteenth century, had long been thought lost altogether. Only recently rediscovered, it is one of the small but growing number of Greek novels of this period to have been reprinted in a modern critical edition. Palaiologos himself described this novel as 'a Greek *Gil Blas*'. Following a rather different tack, the same writer published *The Artist* in Constantinople three years later, a novel which is part love romance and part social satire.[66] Satire is more apparent still in the second novel by Pitsipios. *Xouth the Ape, or the Morals of the Century*, published in 1848, which satirizes on the one hand the attitudes of European travellers towards the Greek world, and on the other the pretensions of the arriviste Athenian governing class, so that both stand comically accused of 'aping' manners and morals to which they have no title.[67]

Not surprisingly, most of these writers, who were after all experimenting in a genre without modern precedent in the language, drew in various ways on the example of European novels published during the previous half-century or more. The only unifying strand in all of this is the urge to experiment and, perhaps, to build on the native example of the ancient and medieval Greek novel, which finds echoes in almost all of the novels mentioned.

[64] Respectively: Wilson 1990, (the introduction to this edition, by D. Polemis, sketches the background to this work and the evidence for its curious authorship); Pitsipios 1995*a*.

[65] Palaiologos 1989*a*, esp. 242–4.

[66] Palaiologos 1989*b*. For the reference to the earlier novel, see p. 255.

[67] This novel was twice reprinted in 1995. Pitsipios 1995*a* includes a substantial introduction to the whole of the writer's work, by Dimitris Tziovas (cf. note 64). The text is also available, with a briefer introduction, by Nasos Vayenas (Pitsipios 1995*b*).

It was in the same way, and as part of the same experimental climate, that the historical novel was introduced to Greece. Alexandros Rizos Rangavis, the third of the Phanariot poets whom we encountered earlier, made a slow start in prose fiction.[68] Rangavis' reputation as a novelist was established in 1850 with *The Lord of Morea*. Drawing on the fourteenth-century Greek *Chronicle of Morea* for its plot and (confessedly) on Walter Scott for its treatment of historical material, this novel marks the inauguration of a sub-genre which enjoyed considerable popularity until the early 1880s.[69] During this period historical novels, mostly set during the years of Ottoman domination, were written by Konstandinos Ramfos, Stefanos Xenos, and (in his early years) by Alexandros Papadiamandis, whom we shall meet again in a rather different capacity in the next chapter. Interestingly, Xenos' first novel, *The Devil in Turkey* (1851), was first published in London, in English, and only later in Greek.

But Rangavis was too versatile an artist to confine himself to a single genre, despite the success and influence of *The Lord of Morea*. Only a year later, in 1851, he published *The Notary*, a realistic tale of intrigue, suspense, and romance which, though seemingly less influential, none the less deserves recognition in the company of Collins and Poe among the first ever 'whodunnits'.[70] *The Notary* also has considerable historical significance, since it provides a link between earlier achievements in a realist mode (including some criticism of more or less contemporary mores, such as we found in the pre-independence *Results of Love* and in the two novels of Palaiologos) and the two undoubted high points of Greek fiction before 1880. These are *Thanos Vlekas* by Pavlos Kalligas (1855) and *Pope Joan* by Emmanuel Roidis (1866).

[68] Most of the twenty or so short stories and novels written by Rangavis date from the period 1847–53, although a short story published in 1836 or 1837 (the publication itself is not extant) places Rangavis among the first writers to make tentative beginnings in this genre before the 1880s (see e.g. Sachinis 1982: 30–1; Valetas 1983). Four short stories of this period are reprinted, without adequate introduction or even dates, in Rangavis 1988; and the short novel set in Victorian England, *Gloomymouth*, has been edited, along with a substantial essay, by T. Kayalis (1991).

[69] Repr. as Rangavis 1989. For explicit allusions to Scott in the text and overall conception of the novel, see Sachinis 1982: 42–7. It is not true, however, that the historical novel *dominates* Greek fiction, even in the 1860s, when production in this genre was at its height, although this view has long been commonplace in histories of Greek literature (see Denisi 1990: 61–2 for bibliographical details; 1992 on the rise of the historical novel).

[70] Available in a plain text reprint (Rangavis 1991).

Pavlos Kalligas (1814–96) came originally from Smyrna, but, like most of the Athenian intelligentsia of his generation, had completed his education in western Europe, in this case in Germany. *Thanos Vlekas* is his only novel.[71] The eponymous hero is one of two brothers, at the beginning of the story a small farmer with simple tastes and no ambitions. The other brother, Tasos, as the story unfolds exemplifies all the social and some of the political ills of the age, as he changes roles to suit his own advantage: to bandit to place-seeker to land-grabber. In the nature of things it is the innocent Thanos who pays for his brother's crimes, losing first his land, then his liberty, and finally (and melodramatically) his life. In the course of his enforced wanderings he meets the beautiful Efrosyni (Joy), whose father takes him under his protection and represents the only successful mediator (and mid-point) between good and evil in the story. Before the two can be married, however, Thanos is killed in a vain attempt to prevent a local uprising against his brother's tyrannous stewardship, and the girl, arriving with her father only seconds too late to avert disaster, falls lifeless on his corpse.

This story is told with a good deal of gusto, but in a high-flown rhetorical style, with numerous digressions, that is reminiscent of some of the ancient Greek novels. Kalligas has been praised for the directness with which he bears witness to social ills and for a lack of 'Romantic distortion' in this novel.[72] However, the description of the principal character, for example, clearly draws more closely on literary conventions than on life, and in its idealization of the classical or neoclassical attributes of health, nobility, and cleanliness, partakes of exactly the same kind of 'Romanticism' as we observed in the poetry and the architecture of the period, which revived *classical* forms as part of a *Romantic* quest for the traditions of a people:

Ο Θάνος ήτο νέος ευειδής, περίπου εικοσιτεσσάρων ετών· του σώματός του η ανάπτυξις ήτον εύρυθμος και ευπρεπής, το πρόσωπόν του ευγενές και σεμνόν και οι χαρακτήρες του εν γένει εύγραμμοι, απεικονίζοντες υπό

[71] Among several available reprints see Kalligas 1991 (with introduction by E. N. Horafas).

[72] For *Thanos Vlekas* as 'social realism' see Vitti 1987: 261–3; 1991: 29–36; and the introduction by Horafas to Kalligas 1991. For a (curious) statement of its relation to Romanticism see L. Politis 1973: 148: 'we find the outstanding characters of Thanos and Euphrosyne presented, with no Romantic distortion, as a ray of light in this world of evil and misfortune.'

την γλυκύτητα του ήθους φιλότιμόν τι και αξιοπρεπές. Καθ' όλα είχε τι ανώτερον των ανθρώπων της τάξεώς του, και ηγάπα πολύ την καθαριότητα, ώστε δεν εφαίνετο ότι είναι γεωργός.[73]

Thanos was a good-looking young man, of about 24 years of age; his physical development was well-proportioned and seemly, his face noble and modest, and his features in general well drawn, displaying beneath the sweetness of his manner a certain sense of self-respect and dignity. In all there was something about him which showed him to be superior to persons of his class and he was especially devoted to cleanliness, so that it was not apparent that he was a farmer.

In writing this novel, Kalligas undoubtedly set out to draw public attention to the very real social ills portrayed in the story, in the hope of alleviating them. In this aim, and in some aspects of the novel, he may be compared to Dickens. But there was no such thing in Greece before the 1880s as a professional writer, such as Dickens was; and for all the wealth of incident and speed of narration in *Thanos Vlekas*, the deliberately ornate style, together with the archaizing language which was widely cultivated at the time, have ever since proved a barrier to the kind of mass readership achieved by Dickens at the same period in England.

Pope Joan by Emmanuel Roidis (1836–1904) is the only Greek novel of the nineteenth century to have found a place, albeit a modest one, in the European canon.[74] A maverick work, set both in place and time far from contemporary Greece, and written with consummate disdain for most of the conventions of fiction at the time, *Pope Joan* is one of the few comic masterpieces of Modern Greek literature. Roidis himself was well travelled in western Europe, where like Kalligas he had completed his education; again like Kalligas, he wrote only one novel, although he also wrote literary criticism and, much later in his life, a number of short stories.[75]

Roidis from the start sets out to tease his reader, declaring, after Byron, that he has 'nothing plann'd / Unless it were to be a moment

[73] Kalligas 1991: 68.
[74] The original edition has been photographically reprinted, with a preface by T. Vournas, Roidis' own preface, and extracts from the ensuing controversy (Roidis 1971). A newer edition, with a long introduction by A. Angelou and further supplementary material, is typographically much harder on the eye (Roidis 1988a)! See also Guide to Translations; Georganta 1993.
[75] Roidis' complete works are available as Roidis 1978. For a selection of some of his most important criticism and shorter articles, see Roidis 1986. For a reprint, without introduction, of the short stories see Roidis 1988b.

merry'. The story of *Pope Joan* is culled from the scurillous margin-
alia of medieval history (copiously adduced by Roidis in a long
preface which is part of the novel's teasing game), according to
which the ninth-century Pope John VIII had in fact been a
woman. Around this single 'fact', Roidis weaves his improbable
fiction: from the 'miraculous' birth of the heroine (her mother had
been raped by two Gothic mercenaries on the banks of the Rhine;
her 'father' had already been castrated), to her early miracles; her
romantic involvement with a young monk with whom she shares
many adventures before abandoning him for higher things; her
travels to Byzantine Greece; finally her arrival in Rome, her liaison,
as Pope, with her chamberlain, and her death (in childbirth!) which
brings a miraculous end to a series of plagues which had beset
the city.

All of this is told with the tongue firmly in the cheek, in an elegant
and involved rhetorical style unmatched in Modern Greek, and
punctuated with knowing asides to the reader which quite openly
unmask the illusion of verisimilitude on which all realist fiction is
based. Critics have been divided on the nature and purpose of this
novel (and even on whether it can properly be called a novel at all),
but the authorities of the Greek Church were swift to condemn it,
demanding that the state should impose civil penalties on its
author.[76] This response, and the resulting high-profile controversy
in the Athenian press, undoubtedly helped to establish the novel's
enduring reputation.

For all Roidis' elaborate smokescreen, there can be little doubt
that the contemporary Greek Church, as well as the piety and
hypocrisy of his time, were indeed part of Roidis' target. But the
novel's significance goes well beyond this. First of all, in choosing a
historical subject with the declared aim of showing that times of yore
were every bit as sordid and corrupt as the present, if not more so,
Roidis pours timely cold water over the whole sub-genre of the
historical novel, then at the height of its popularity. What is more,
in the central episodes of his novel, dealing with the romantic
attachment of Joan to the young monk Frumentius, he also plays
on the expectations of the reader used, ever since the *Results of Love*
in 1792, to the conventions of romance. And finally, as has only

---

[76] The text of the Synodical Encyclical of 31 Mar. 1866 is repr. in Angelou 1988*c*:
44–5.

recently begun to be noticed, the whole playful, allusive game with the reader, which subverts the conventions of realistic narrative, looks forward almost a century to the sophisticated self-referentiality and parody in Greek and world-wide fiction in the later twentieth century.[77] These characteristics of *Pope Joan* are apparent in the novel's brief farewell to Frumentius, after Joan has sailed away to become Pope. After some days of bitter reproach and lamentation, he wakes up one morning to see a beautiful shepherdess going past:

θεωρών αυτήν ο Φρουμέντιος τότε κατά πρώτον ησθάνθη ότι πλην της Ιωάννας υπήρχον και άλλαι εις τον κόσμον γυναίκες. Η θεραπεία αυτού ηδύνατο ήδη να θεωρηθή ως ριζική. Ούτω διά του θαύματος του Αγίου γυμνωθείς του ανοήτου πάθους του και άχρηστος ήδη ων ημίν ως ήρως μυθιστορήματος καθίστατο από της στιγμής εκείνης χρησιμώτατον της κοινωνίας μέλος, *λίαν κατάλληλος*, αν έζη σήμερον, να *εξασκήση* οιονδήποτε έντιμον επάγγελμα, να γείνη γραμματοκομιστής, κατάσκοπος, βουλευτής, προικοθήρας ή θεσοδιώκτης, να κρατή τα κατάστιχα Χίου εμπόρου ή τους πόδας αγχονιζομένου καταδίκου. Αλλά κατά την εποχήν εκείνην τα *Κύριε ελέησον* ήσαν η καλλιτέρα τέχνη, και καλώς ποιών έμεινε καλόγερος ως πρότερον ο Φρουμέντιος.[78]

at the sight of her Frumentius then for the first time felt that besides Joan there were other women in the world. His cure could now be considered radical. Thus by the miracle of the Saint stripped of his senseless passion and so already of no further use to us as the hero of a novel, from that moment he could have become a most useful member of society, *highly suitable*, had he lived today, to *practise* any respectable profession whatever, to become a postman, a spy, a member of parliament, a fortune-hunter, or a place-seeker, to hold the ledgers of a Chiot merchant or the feet of a hanged convict. But in those days the best art was that of the *Kyrie eleison*, and Frumentius wisely remained a monk as before.

Two other novels of the period should also be briefly mentioned, as they are conventionally thought of as paving the way for the far-reaching developments in Greek fiction that took place in the 1880s and beyond. One is *Military Life in Greece*, published anonymously in Romania in 1870–1. This clear-sighted, autobiographical account of its subject made little impact at the time, and was only rescued from oblivion after the Second World War.[79] Both this work and

---

[77] See in particular Tziovas 1987: 259–82.
[78] Roidis 1971: 224–5.
[79] Anon. [Harilaos Dimopoulos] 1977. For the identification of the author see Moullas 1997. See also Vitti 1991: 46–9.

Loukis Laras (1879) by Dimitrios Vikelas (1835–1908) tell true stories, and one might therefore quibble about the extent to which either truly belongs to fiction.[80] Both have been singled out in the literary histories of the last fifty years as forerunners of a less rhetorical style and a language closer to the spoken idiom than was normal at the time. *Loukis Laras*, set during the war of independence but before the lifetime of its author, may be considered as one of the last 'historical novels' of the nineteenth century, in which true heroism is shown to lie not in spectacular action but in prudently, and bravely, laying the foundation for future commerce.

Now that some of the characteristics praised in these two works have also been recognized in earlier Greek fiction, notably in the *Results of Love* and the two novels of Grigorios Palaiologos, the historical significance of *Military Life in Greece* and of *Loukis Laras* may be assessed rather differently. These are the first *documentary* novels in Greek; and their deliberate simplification in both style and language reflects this purpose. Modern Greek fiction in its earliest stages (perhaps following the lead given by Korais) was fully conscious of the boundary between fact and fiction. Factual narrative had also flourished in the years following the war of independence, as many of the leading participants wrote memoirs, although many were not published until long afterwards. The most famous example of this type of narrative is the *Memoirs* of Makriyannis, which exercised an influence on literature only after their publication in 1907.[81] For the first time, in the 1870s, the boundary between fact and fiction becomes deliberately blurred, as the anonymous author of *Military Life in Greece* and Vikelas adopt some of the techniques of fiction in order to tell a true story. Such documentary fiction is unknown before this time, but as we shall see, comes to play a major role in Greek fiction in the twentieth century.

Before closing this chapter, mention must be made of fiction in the Ionian islands, or rather the lack of it. All the novels so far discussed were published in the capital of the Greek kingdom (first Nafplion, then Athens), and the efforts to establish a tradition in this genre find scarcely an echo in the other cultural centre of the time,

[80] For a reprint of the 1879 edition with full critical introduction see Vikelas 1991.

[81] Frequently reprinted, see e.g. Makriyannis n.d., which includes Vlachoyannis' introduction to the 1907 edition, together with other comments and the set of contemporary illustrations by Panayotis Zografou and his sons. For bibliography on other memoirs, see Svoronos 1976: 272–4.

that of Corfu and the Ionian islands. Prose there was limited to satire, but unlike the satire of Roidis, the satire of the Ionian islands never adapted itself to the form of the novel or short story. The unfinished prose satire of Dionysios Solomos, *The Woman of Zakynthos*, certainly represents an attempt at prose fiction of a kind, but it is not clear from the surviving fragments what its final form and scope might have been. Andreas Laskaratos and other satirists in prose were writing in a genre older than that of the novel, and seem never to have been tempted to experiment in that direction. Apart from the fragmentary autobiography of Elizabeth Moutzan-Martinengou (1801–32), written shortly before her death but not published until half a century later, and sometimes cited as an early (and rare) example of women's fiction at this time,[82] only Spyridon Zambelios (1815–81), who is better known as a historian and folklorist, wrote a novel. However, his *Cretan Wedding*, a historical novel set in sixteenth-century Crete, was published as far away as Turin, and has never been admired for anything other than its patriotic spirit.[83]

That the writers of the Ionian islands were capable of sustained literary expression in prose is proved, however, by the unique example of *The Basil Plant* by Andonios Matesis. This is a play, written in 1829–30 for performance in an aristocratic milieu in the author's native Zakynthos (and as such, strictly speaking, falls outside the scope of this study). The importance of *The Basil Plant* for the history of Greek fiction lies in the fact that when Matesis published it much later, he added a preface (in the formal language of the time, which is not the language of the text) in which he describes the work as 'a historical novel presented in the form of drama, rather than a comedy'.[84] The play is in fact a social comedy which owes a fair amount to the examples of Beaumarchais and Schiller, dramatizing the clash of ideas between the older generation of the local aristocracy and the values of the Enlightenment, which for reasons of tact

---

[82] Moutzan-Martinengou 1956 (first pub. 1881). On the belated development of fiction in the Ionian islands, see Tziovas 1994.

[83] Zambelios 1989. The few stories of Polylas, which appeared in Estia in 1891–2, late in the author's life, occupy a modest place in the rise of the 'ethographic' or folkloric short story at that time and therefore belong in the context of the next chapter (repr. in Polylas 1988).

[84] This preface is dated 1860, the edition in which it appears, 1859. Τὸ παρόν ὅθεν δύναται μᾶλλον νὰ ὀνομασθῇ ἱστορικὴ μυθιστοριογραφία δραματικῶς παρισταvομένη ἡ κωμῳδία... (Matesis 1973: 1).

Matesis had set a century earlier. *The Basil Plant* can in no sense be regarded as a 'historical novel', but evidently its author thought that he had to attach that label to it if it was to have any chance of being read as a book in the 1860s. As with the poetic fragments of Solomos, which were only published long after they were written, a significant initiative by a writer of the Ionian islands remained without sequel, and it is tempting once again to wonder how the course of Greek fiction might have been different if Matesis' polished comedy, in a prose style based closely on the spoken language of Zakynthos at the time, had been available to be read in Athens when it was written, instead of having to fit rather awkwardly into the subgenre of the historical novel which was then beginning to achieve notable success in Athens.

Be that as it may, it was not until the last years of the century that the Ionian islands produced two novelists of stature: Grigorios Xenopoulos and Konstandinos Theotokis. The first, as we shall see, was at first more successful as a playwright; and it may not be accidental that the novels of the second take as their theme the irreversible decline of the old aristocracy of the islands and the belated emergence there of an entrepreneurial middle class.

2. National Expansion and its Limits: From 'Great Idea' to Aftermath of Disaster 1881–1928

THE annexation of the rich agricultural province of Thessaly in 1881, although the result of Great Power diplomacy rather than of military success, appeared to the Greeks of the time as the first tangible proof that territorial expansion was a realizable goal. The need to extend the geographical frontiers of the new state had been implicit almost from the beginning,[1] and it had been during the deliberations on the first constitution, in 1844, that the classic formulation of the Greek irredentist call had first been made. 'Greece', according to this formulation, did not mean only the kingdom of that name, but included all the Greek-speaking communities of the Ottoman empire as well. The goal of national policy was therefore to 'redeem' those Greeks living beyond the confines of the nation state, and in particular to re-establish Constantinople, the seat of the Ecumenical Patriarchate of the Orthodox Church and once the capital of the Greek-speaking empire of Byzantium, alongside Athens as the twin centres of this wider Hellenism. Ever since 1844, these aspirations have been known simply as the 'Great Idea'.[2]

There is an impressive unanimity of support for the 'Great Idea' throughout Greek cultural life in the nineteenth century, and until the eve of the disastrous defeat of the Greek expeditionary force in

[1] As early as 1830 Korais had written of the need for 'renewed struggles' in order to 'redeem the old boundaries of ancient Hellas' ('Capodistrian Dialogues IV' Καποδιστριακοί διάλογοι Δ', Korais 1964: A2, 791; see also Chaconas 1968: 152), although Korais was always rather vague about where these boundaries were supposed to lie.

[2] The key passage of a speech to the Constituent Assembly by Ioannis Kolettis, later to become prime minister, runs as follows: 'Greece is geographically placed at the centre of Europe, between East and West, her destiny in decline [i.e. the decline of *ancient* Greece] to spread light to the West, but in her rebirth to the East. The former task our forefathers achieved, the latter falls to us. In the spirit of this oath [i.e. to liberate Greece] and of this *great idea* I have consistently seen the nation's representatives gathered here to decide the fate not only of Greece, but of the Greek race' (my emphasis, cited in Beaton 1988b: 95). The most accessible source for the Greek text is K. Dimaras 1982: 406.

Asia Minor in 1922. This is not entirely surprising. The nineteenth century in Europe was the age of the nation state, and territorial expansion, in one way or another, was taken for granted as a legitimate aim for nation states at the time. The linguistic reformer Psycharis, writing in Paris in 1888, was not far out in his sweeping generalization:

Ένα έθνος, για να γίνη έθνος, θέλει δυο πράματα· να μεγαλώσουν τα σύνορά του και να κάμη φιλολογία δική του.[3]

A nation, in order to become a nation, wishes for two things: to enlarge its frontiers and to create its own literature.

The 'Great Idea' was not new, then, in the 1880s. But in the aftermath of the annexation of Thessaly a greater self-confidence and sense of purpose began to be discernible in Greek cultural and political life. This new mood seems to have been maintained in the face of reverses which were scarcely less humiliating than those of the previous period: blockade by the Great Powers in 1886; national bankruptcy in 1893; defeat by Turkey in 1897; friction with Bulgaria over Macedonia from the 1890s until 1913. But despite military setbacks, the Greek state up to 1920 continued to expand, and despite the economic crash of 1893 and the control over Greece's foreign debt imposed by the Great Powers in 1897, the economy was also able to expand during the same period.

Political life was severely shaken up by the intervention of the military in 1909 (the Goudi putsch), a 'bourgeois revolution', as it has been perceived by some in hindsight,[4] whose aftermath brought to power the reforming statesman from Crete, Eleftherios Venizelos. Under Venizelos' premiership Greece embarked in 1912 and 1913 on the two Balkan Wars (the first against Turkey, the second against Bulgaria) which extended Greece's northern frontier to more or less where it stands today, and at the same time also secured Crete (which had been formally independent since 1897) and most of the northern Aegean islands. At the outbreak of the First World War, Greek territory had almost doubled since the 1870s, and the 'dream and hope'[5] of capturing Constantinople seemed more than ever realizable.

Venizelos' policies, throughout a long and varied career, often involved a high degree of risk. His far-sighted but dangerous

[3] Psycharis 1971: 37.   [4] See e.g. Vitti 1987: 354.
[5] Kolettis' words, from the speech quoted in note 2 above.

attempts to push Greece's advantage from the First World War to the utmost, on two crucial occasions proved fatally divisive for the country. During the war itself, Venizelos' attempts to push Greece into alliance with the Entente led to effective partition of the country in 1916, with Venizelos' provisional government in Thessaloniki opposing the official government in Athens. This crisis was resolved only in 1917 with the departure of the king into self-imposed exile. Two years later, in the expectation of territorial gains from the Paris Peace Conference, Venizelos committed troops to the occupation of Smyrna, but failed to carry the electorate with him in the general election of 1920. His successors ordered Greek troops in the enclave around Smyrna on to the offensive, apparently hoping, in the absence of a clear mandate from the Great Powers, to secure Constantinople and western Anatolia for Greece. Given the fast-changing realities of Great Power diplomacy in the years following the armistice, and their own limited resources, the Greek position was by the end of 1921 fatally exposed in both military and political terms.

Following a successful counter-attack by the newly formed army of the Turkish Nationalists under Mustafa Kemal (later known as Atatürk), the Greek forces in Anatolia were routed in the last days of August 1922. In the first week of September the rich and cosmopolitan city of Smyrna was devastated by fire. It is not known how many of the Orthodox Christian population of Anatolia died in the course of these events. Many of those who could, fled to Greece; the remaining survivors were exchanged, under the terms of the Treaty of Lausanne, signed in January 1923, with the Muslim population of northern Greece and Crete. The upshot was that more than a million refugees eventually arrived in Greece, for the most part destitute. These events have been known ever since in Greek as the 'Asia Minor catastrophe' or, simply, as 'the Catastrophe'.

The Asia Minor catastrophe brings to an end the chapter of Greek history which began with the expansionist optimism of the early 1880s, and at the same time sets the scene for the political, social, and cultural life of Greece throughout much of the twentieth century. The chaotic period of the immediate aftermath of the disaster, however, belongs to the present chapter, as some time was to pass before the new social and political realities, and the loss of an overriding ideal that had united most Greeks for more than half a century, could be assimilated and could stimulate new developments in literature and culture.

This period of rapid and painful adjustment lasted from 1922, through the vengeful execution, in November of the same year, of six of the top political and military leaders held responsible for the disaster; the plebiscite replacing the monarchy with a republic in 1924; and a succession of short-lived governments, both civilian and military, until 1928. In that year Venizelos returned to power and inaugurated the process of rebuilding but also of political rivalry between Right and Left, which will set the scene for the next chapter.

By 1928 Greece had acquired frontiers which were substantially those of today (with the exception of the islands of the Dodecanese, which were added in 1947). The exchange of populations between Greece and Turkey (which excluded only the Christian population of Constantinople and the Muslims of western Thrace, who were allowed to stay where they were) was complete. In consequence, the new Greek state that emerged in the 1920s did, as the irredentists of the previous century had dreamed, include almost all the Greeks of the former Ottoman empire. But the circumstances in which this had come about, and the social and economic strains involved in assimilating so many refugees, brought in their train a complete overhaul of the nation's sense of identity. The long process of adjustment to the new reality will be the subject of Chapters 3 and 4.[6]

NEW HORIZONS IN POETRY AND PROSE

The new self-confidence of the early 1880s found literary expression in ways that on the face of it seem contradictory. On the one hand writers, translators, and critics looked outside Greece to Europe, and particularly to France, and presented what they found there to the Greek reading public; on the other, interest began to be directed with a new intensity and sense of purpose towards identifying, defining, and describing those areas of Greek life which were still uncontaminated by European influence. Symptomatic of the first trend are the experiments with the anti-Romantic poetics of the French 'Parnassian' movement, or *Parnasse* (named after an anthology of 1866), by Nikos Kambas (1857–1932), Yorgos Drosinis (1859–1951), and Kostis Palamas (1859–1943), as well as the translation into Greek of Emile Zola's novel *Nana* in 1879, which

---

[6] See further, on the historical and cultural developments of this period, in English, the essays collected in Carabott 1997; Chryssanthopoulos 1997; and, in Greek, Skopetea 1988.

provoked an outcry, and the long and impassioned introduction (published in 1880) urging the case for the realism of life in the raw to which Zola had given the name 'naturalism'.[7]

Symptomatic of the second trend is the evocation of the traditional way of life in the Greek countryside, also in the poetry of Drosinis, as to some extent in that of Palamas, and more evidently in the work of Kostas Krystallis (1868–94), many of whose poems are adaptations of traditional oral folk poetry. This same turn towards traditional Greek life and customs is still more evident in the emergent science of folklore study, which begins with the work of the pioneering folklorist Nikolaos Politis (1852–1921) in the 1870s, and in turn seems to have exercised a formative influence on writers of prose fiction in their choice of subject-matter up to the turn of the century.

Contradictory though these two trends obviously are from a strictly logical point of view, it would be a serious mistake for the literary historian to try to choose between them. Indeed, those writers who did so, looking either exclusively abroad or exclusively to their own 'roots', are the ones who today are regarded as minor or of purely 'historical' interest: the poet Kambas,[8] or writers of 'idyllic' short stories set in the Greek countryside such as Drosinis (in his stories of the 1880s), Christovasilis, and Eftaliotis.[9] All the most significant literary achievements of the 1880s and 1890s take place in the cross-currents set up between these two opposing trends, and the most enduring literary works of this period—the stories of Vizyinos, Papadiamandis, and Karkavitsas, and, a little later, the mature poetry of Palamas—all exploit the possibilities of recent innovations abroad to explore, each in a very different way, the nature of the writers' own indigenous culture.

[7] A[yesilaos] Y[annopoulos] E[pirotis], repr. in Mastrodimitris 1980: 239–63.

[8] Kambas' importance is purely 'historical' in that he introduced the 'Parnasse' to Greece and exercised an acknowledged influence on Palamas. Yorgos Themelis, writing in 1963, interestingly places Kambas alongside Dorros and Randos (1978: 11–12), whose technical innovations in the early 1930s were more obviously fruitful in the hands of others (see Ch. 3).

[9] The names are taken from a partial list of writers whom Eleni Politou-Marmarinou proposes as 'ethographers' proper, in contradistinction to the 'realist or naturalist' writers of the period, in which category all the major names are included (1985: 147 n.). The distinction is a valid one, but in my view is one of degree only. Either the term ηθογραφία (ethography) should be abandoned altogether (as is proposed, for instance, by Milionis 1992), or it should be defined so as to include *all* the realist writers of the period. My own preference is for the second solution, as will become clear later in this chapter.

FOLKLORE AND REALISM IN PROSE (1880–1904)

Much of the cultural ferment of the years around 1880 went on in the periodical press, and especially in the columns of *Estia* (1876–95) and *Rabagas* (1878–89). The first was a sober periodical, aimed at a family readership, and throughout its life an ardent proponent of folklore studies.[10] The widely heeded call for the Greeks to 'know themselves' through the study and literary dissemination of their indigenous popular culture was very largely proclaimed through the columns of *Estia*. *Rabagas* on the other hand declared itself to be a 'politico-satirical newspaper' and it was here that the first, experimental verse of Kambas, Drosinis, and Palamas appeared.[11] Characteristically, it was also in *Rabagas* that the controversial translation of Zola's *Nana* first began to appear in serial form in 1879, before its publication was suspended by the public outcry; and it was from the columns of *Estia* that the authoritative voice of Angelos Vlachos joined in that outcry.[12] Significantly, however, both periodicals throughout their existence continued to publish translations from a wide range of recent foreign literature.

A more positive contribution by *Estia* to the literary developments of the time was the announcement, in 1883, of a new competition for a story whose 'subject will be Greek, that is, will consist either of the description of scenes from the life of the Greek people in any of its historical periods, or of the narration of an episode of Greek history'.[13] The terms of the competition are not quite as groundbreaking as they have usually been assumed, with hindsight, to be. It is not clear from the announcement exactly what kind of work is meant by 'story' (*diegema*): only a *minimum* length is prescribed, and subsequent correspondence in *Estia* reveals some confusion as to whether the term, whose literal meaning is simply 'narrative',

[10] Other new periodicals at this time were *Parnassos* (1877–94) and *Mi Hanesai* (1880–3, thereafter the better-known daily newspaper, *Akropolis*). For a new appraisal of the importance of these developments, see Chryssanthopoulos 1997. On *Estia*, see Papakostas 1982. For a critique of this work, and some far-reaching proposals about the nature of Greek realist prose of the period, see Politou-Marmarinou 1985; cf. Papakostas 1985.

[11] See Politou-Marmarinou 1979.

[12] Politou-Marmarinou 1985: 145.

[13] Η υπόθεσις του διηγήματος έσται ελληνική, τουτέστι θα συνίσταται εις περιγραφήν σκηνών του βίου του ελληνικού λαού εν οιαδήποτε των περιόδων της ιστορίας αυτού ή εις εξιστόρησιν επεισοδίου τινός της ελληνικής ιστορίας. The text of the announcement, from the issue of 15 May 1883, is most readily available in Mastrodimitris 1980: 269–70.

actually meant something different from a novel.[14] In practice most
of the entries received were short, and it is from about this time that
the term used in the announcement came to acquire its modern
sense of 'short story'. Furthermore, the emphasis given in the
announcement to settings drawn from the 'ancient, medieval, or
modern period' accords better with the by now well-established
genre of historical fiction than with the contemporary realism
which is in fact the hallmark of fiction in the 1880s and 1890s.

If the *Estia* competition did not actually set out the ground rules
for the new fiction, its practical effect seems to have been to boost
and to provide a rationale for two innovations which had already
begun to appear on the scene before the competition was
announced: first the short-story form, and secondly the choice of a
traditional, rural setting.[15] The move from the novel (usually serialized) to the short story at this time cannot really be explained; but it
is certainly a fact that the short story as a genre was hardly cultivated
in Greek before the 1880s, while in the following twenty years it
outstrips novels as a proportion of the total prose fiction of the
period. However, the 'folkloric' content, which from 1883 effectively
dominates prose fiction for the next twenty years, and as we have
seen also plays a formative role in poetry during the same period,
merits some further explanation.

To discover and cherish the indigenous traditions of a people is
one of the basic tenets of nineteenth-century nationalism in
Europe, deriving ultimately from the work of Herder and other
German thinkers of the late eighteenth century. In the period up
to the 1870s, as we noted earlier, the native traditions of the Greek
people were thought of primarily as those of the *ancient* Greeks, and
the traditions and traditional way of life that folklorists in other
countries were already assiduously collecting went largely unnoticed. (True, the poets Rangavis, Solomos, and Valaoritis had
recognized the importance of oral traditional songs as a basis for a
new means of expression in verse, but they had had little interest in
the way of life, beliefs, and rituals of those who sang them.)[16]

[14] See Moullas 1980: μστ´–μζ´.
[15] Two 'ethographic' stories by Vikelas appeared in *Estia* as early as 1877 (Moullas
1980: λδ´–λε´), and the first of Vizyinos' short stories set in his native Thrace to be
published, 'My Mother's Sin' (Το αμάρτημα της μητρός μου), appeared in the same
periodical in April 1883, a month before the announcement of the competition.
[16] Valaoritis, by the 1870s, does seem to have been infected by the folkloric
interests of the decade. His unfinished verse drama *Fotinos* (first pub. 1879) in this

Indeed, up to the 1870s the majority of publications about Greek folklore had been the work of foreigners. The significance of traditional oral sources as a factor in the historical continuity linking ancient with modern Greece was first recognized by Spyridon Zambelios, a younger member of the circle of Solomos, in the 1850s, and it was he and the influential historian Konstandinos Paparrigopoulos (whose *History of the Greek Nation* in five volumes was completed in 1876) who first began to rehabilitate the long intervening period of Byzantine history. But even so, it was not until the 1870s that Greek intellectuals, and prominent among them the founding father of Greek folklore study, Nikolaos Politis, began to realize that the products of the traditional, indigenous way of life formed an indispensable link in the chain of cultural continuity that was perceived as stretching back to antiquity.[17] It is not hard to see how such an interest takes its place as part of the new-found self-confidence of Greece in the 1880s, alongside the irredentist ideals which gathered momentum from then until the débâcle of 1922. What is more, a glance through the pages of *Estia* shows that prominent literary writers of the time were also contributing raw materials similar to those of their fiction, in the guise of amateur folklorists.[18]

The common denominator of almost all the fiction published in Greek during the last two decades of the nineteenth century is *the detailed depiction of a small, more or less contemporary, traditional community in its physical setting.* Elsewhere in this book this characteristic, when it re-emerges in later Greek fiction, will be termed for short *folkloric realism*, and this latter term is intended to correspond to, and to interpret, the controversial Greek term *ethography*, which

respect can be seen somewhat schematically as bridging the literary demands of the previous period, in its fourteenth-century setting, which is reminiscent of the historical novel of the time, and its focusing on the life of a poor peasant and his family, with a wealth of 'folkloric' detail (cf. Moullas 1980: λε′).

[17] On Politis' career and achievements see Kyriakidou-Nestoros 1978: 99–110; for a fairly trenchant critique of the nationalist aspirations of Greek folklore study in its emergent phase, together with much useful information and discussion, see Herzfeld 1982. On the relation of folklore study and its attendant aspirations to literature see Beaton 1982–3; on the place of Byzantine history in these developments see Beaton 1988b: 102–5.

[18] Karkavitsas' account (written and published in *Estia* in 1890) of the real village on which the fictionalized account of a village of beggars in his novel *The Beggar* (1896) is based, is well known (and reprinted, in part, in Mastrodimitris 1980: 42–3). Even Vizyinos, whose inclusion under the term 'ethography' is still the subject of debate, was involved for a time in a government project to collect folkloric materials from the Greek population of the Ottoman empire (Moullas: 1980: νζ′–νθ′).

defies either a satisfactory definition or translation into English. The definition of this common denominator is intended to be inclusive, but not restrictive. It describes a characteristic that is common to most of the fiction of the period, but does not imply homogeneity either in the way that the common subject-matter is approached or in the artistic effects achieved.[19]

The stories and novels which share this common denominator have often been termed 'realist', in contrast to an earlier 'Romantic' period of Greek fiction. However, with the single exception of *Pope Joan*, the Greek novel in its emergent phase had always been broadly realist in its aspirations. What is new in the 1880s is not the representation of 'reality' in fiction (that had been taken for granted since at least the time of Korais' definition in 1804), but the particular 'reality' selected by writers, with a remarkable degree of consensus, to be represented. Nor is the depiction of contemporary communities at this time especially motivated by a desire for verisimilitude. Some writers, such as Drosinis, notoriously sentimentalize their material; the more seriously regarded among them (who are often, misleadingly, detached from the label of 'folkloric realism' altogether for just this reason) go out of their way to emphasize the harsher and more brutal aspects of the lives they depict. In any case, as we shall see, a shared common denominator of 'folkloric realism' could become for some writers a springboard for explorations that go far beyond the bounds of either folklore or realism, narrowly understood.

It is probable that this consensus was as much the result of the editorial policy of *Estia* and the expectations of readers of this and other periodicals as of the inclinations of individual writers. But at the same time there is a wide diversity in the ways in which writers actually exploited this common ground for their own artistic ends.

[19] On the significance of the term ethography (ηθογραφία) and the complex debate surrounding it see especially Vitti 1987: 290–303; 1991 *passim*, but esp. 143–80; Politou-Marmarinou 1985: 146–8 n. 42; Baloumis [1990]; Milionis 1992; Mackridge 1992*a*. According to the interpretation of ethography advanced here, the term includes, in addition to the examples mentioned in the following paragraphs, the four stories of Vizyinos set in Thrace, all of Papadiamandis' stories and novels from 1887 onwards (including those set in Athens), and all of Karkavitsas' stories and novels. Vizyinos' first story, 'Between Piraeus and Naples' (Μεταξύ Πειραιώς και Νεαπόλεως, pub. 1883), and Papadiamandis' novella *Christos Milionis* (1885) can be seen, schematically, as 'transitional'; Vizyinos' 'The Consequences of the Old Story' (Αι συνέπειαι της παλαιάς ιστορίας, 1884), is not, it may be suggested, as foreign to the conventions of ethography, as defined here, as is often supposed.

These encompass the bucolic idyll of Drosinis' 'Chrysoula' (which won the *Estia* competition in 1883); the fickle unmasking of the conventions of fairytale in Vizyinos' 'The Only Journey of His Life' (1884); the brutal 'naturalism' of Papadiamandis' first short story 'The Christmas Loaf' (1887) and of Karkavitsas' novel *The Beggar* (1896); the equation of the traditional male code of honour, by the poet Palamas, with his own aesthetic ideal of beauty, in his single significant incursion into this genre, 'Death of a Hero' (1891);[20] the gentle mockery of the heroic simpleton in Ioannis Kondylakis' *The Big-Foot* (1892)[21]—to name but a few examples. Indeed, as we shall see, the three major writers who exploited this trend, Vizyinos, Papadiamandis, and Karkavitsas, far from representing a new-found realism in Greek fiction, were actually the most experimental (after Roidis) in questioning and challenging the conventions on which realist narrative is based.

Vizyinos. This is particularly evident in the six stories by G. M. Vizyinos (1849–96), all but one of which were published in *Estia* between April 1883 and December 1884.[22] Vizyinos, like most Greek writers of fiction up to this time, had travelled widely abroad, and had studied philosophy and psychology in Germany. Two of his stories, uncharacteristically for the period, are set outside Greece; the remainder are set in the writer's native Thrace, which at the time was a province of the Ottoman empire.

Vizyinos' stories build to some extent on the suspense narrative pioneered in Greek by Rangavis in *The Notary*, as well as on his reading abroad. With the exception of the first to be written, 'Between Piraeus and Naples', the very titles of Vizyinos' stories invoke a mystery: 'My Mother's Sin', 'Who was my Brother's Killer?', 'The Consequences of the Old Story', 'The Only Journey of his Life', 'Selim the Muscovite' (the name, part Russian, part Turkish, of the principal character, which seems therefore a contradiction in terms). All six are told in the first person, and the stories

[20] Θάνατος παλληκαριού (Palamas n.d.: iv. 11–39). 'Mitros Roumeliotis, without being fully conscious of the fact, worshipped only one god: Beauty, the sacred Beauty of youth and health, whose temple is the human body' (Ο Μήτρος ο Ρουμελιώτης, χωρίς καλά-καλά να το νιώθη, μονάχα ένα θεόν ελάτρευε: την Εμορφιά, την άγια την Εμορφιά της λεβεντιάς και της υγείας, πόχει εκκλησιά της το κορμί, p. 19).

[21] Ο πατούχας, several times reprinted.

[22] There are two modern editions, each with substantial introduction: Vizyinos 1980 (Moullas) and Vizyinos 1991 (Athanasopoulos). See also Guide to Translations.

are resolved, not so much by the solution of the mystery, as by the reversal of the character–narrator's expectations, in which the trusting reader, too, is often implicated.[23]

But the deployment of suspense, like the vivid evocation, in four of the stories, of the setting of his own childhood, is for Vizyinos only the means to an end. With their devious twists of plot but straightforward, urbane manner of narration these stories lead the reader into a series of labyrinths where nothing is what it seems. In two stories a boy is brought up as a girl; in another the elusive heroine is described in terms as much boyish as feminine; the bulwark of nationality is challenged by the story of Selim the Muscovite, the Turk who would rather be a Russian because his treatment at the hands of the traditional enemy of his country has been so much kinder than that he had received from his own people. The nature of guilt is questioned in three stories. Did 'My Mother's Sin' lie in the accidental killing of her child, or in the conscious wish that another of her children should die in expiation? Was 'My Brother's Killer' the man who pulled the trigger in ignorance, or the man who saved his own skin by knowingly sending another in his place? And is the guilt carried over from the 'Old Story' (of making love to a washerwoman) as heinous as its 'Consequences' (the hero cannot bring himself to consummate his love with the woman he loves and she goes mad)? These are psychological suspense-stories not just in what they reveal to the reader about the characters, but in what is revealed within them to the characters themselves, and in the disturbing way in which the reader too is sucked into the labyrinth of ambiguities by Vizyinos' consummate skill in playing with the conventions of realist narrative.

Papadiamandis. The conventions of realism are also challenged by the stories of Alexandros Papadiamandis (1851–1911). The son of a village priest on the small island of Skiathos, Papadiamandis had none of the cosmopolitan advantages of most prose writers before him. He left the University of Athens without taking a degree, and for most of his life supported himself by translating fiction for the burgeoning newspaper and periodical market, and by writing.

[23] The most important book-length studies in Greek of Vizyinos are by Athanasopoulos (1992) and Chryssanthopoulos (1994). For studies in English see: M. Alexiou 1993; 1995; Chryssanthopoulos 1988; Peckham 1995; 1996; Barbeito 1995; Syrimis 1995.

Papadiamandis is Greece's first fully professional writer, in the sense that he wrote for a living.

Not surprisingly, therefore, his career as a writer shows a marked sensitivity to the demands of the periodicals and their readers. Between 1879 and 1884 Papadiamandis published no fewer than three historical novels in the once-popular mould established by Rangavis in 1850. All three were serialized in periodicals, but none was reissued in book form in Papadiamandis' lifetime.[24] Then, in what may have been an attempt to follow the precepts of the 1883 *Estia* competition to the letter, he produced the novella *Christos Milionis*, which draws its theme from a ballad about Greek brigands in conflict with the Turks in mainland Greece a century before. Later in his life Papadiamandis seems to have disowned this work,[25] but with hindsight it can be read as a revealing, and somewhat laborious, hybrid in which the conventions of the romantic historical novel are crossed with those of the emergent folkloric short story.[26]

Papadiamandis' career as one of the foremost of all Modern Greek writers of fiction begins in 1887 with the terse little story 'The Christmas Loaf', in which a mother mistakenly poisons her son instead of her daughter-in-law.[27] Like many of its successors this is a seasonal story, of a kind demanded by periodical editors,[28] and set in Papadiamandis' native island of Skiathos. 'The Christmas Loaf' was followed by more than two hundred stories both short and long, the longest of them, *Guardian of the Plague Ships* (1893), *The Murderess* (1903), and *Rosy Shores* (1907) being described as novels on their first (serial) publication.

Of these the most successful undoubtedly is *The Murderess*, dubbed by Papadiamandis himself as a 'social novel'.[29] The

---

[24] For the standard critical edition of all Papadiamandis' works, see Papadiamandis 1981–8; among anthologies of the short stories, Papadiamandis 1974 (ed. Moullas) stands out for its introduction. Book-length critical studies (in Greek) include Triantafyllopoulos 1981; Kehayoglou 1984; Lorentzatos 1986; Farinou-Malamatari 1987; Elytis 1989; Angelopoulos et al. 1991; Kollyvas 1991. See, in English: Constantinides 1988; Ricks 1992; Mackridge 1992a; Tziovas 1993b.

[25] Χρῆστος Μηλιόνης, 1885 (Papadiamandis 1981–8: ii. 11–76). He also disowned the earlier novel, *The Gypsy Girl* (Η γυφτοπούλα; see Moullas 1974: λα'–λβ'.)

[26] On this work see Beaton 1982–3: 117–19.

[27] Το Χριστόψωμο (Papadiamandis 1981–8: ii. 77–81).

[28] A similar phenomenon can be seen in Britain earlier in the century, e.g. in the *Christmas Stories* of Charles Dickens.

[29] Η φόνισσα. The only critical edition is to be found in Papadiamandis 1981–8: iii. 417–520. Although never published in book form in its author's lifetime, *The Murderess* has often been reprinted: see Papadiamandis 1988.

murderess of the title is an elderly woman whose reflections on the lot of women in the traditional community she lives in, juxtaposed with the troubled history of her own family, lead her into a series of murders of infant girls, which she sees as acts of mercy. The heroine, Frangoyannou, is eventually found out and pursued, and is drowned in the sea just as she was making her way to a hermitage to confess her sins—as the narrator puts it, 'midway between divine and human justice'.[30] This story is told with consummate skill, particularly in the first part, which consists of the long series of reveries in which Frangoyannou's sense of reality is progressively and inexorably inverted until the point where, in an echo of *Macbeth*, 'nothing is but what is not'. Reflecting on the funerals of infant girls that she had attended in the past, she muses:

'Όταν επέστρεφεν εις την νεκρώσιμον οικίαν η γραία Χαδούλα, διά να παρευρεθή την εσπέραν εις την *παρηγοριάν*,—παρηγορίαν καμμίαν δεν εύρισκε να είπη, μόνον ήτο χαρωπή όλη κι εμακάριζε το αθώον βρέφος και τους γονείς του. Και η λύπη ήτο χαρά, και η θανή ήτο ζωή, και όλα ήσαν άλλα εξ άλλων.

—Α! ιδού . . . Κανέν πράγμα δεν είναι ακριβώς ό,τι φαίνεται, αλλά παν άλλο—μάλλον το εναντίον.[31]

When old Hadoula returned to the house of death, to be present in the evening at the funeral meal [lit. 'consolation']—she could find no word of consolation to speak, instead she was all smiles and blessed the innocent infant and its parents. And sadness was joy, and death was life, and everything was mixed up.

'Ah! behold . . . Nothing is precisely what it appears to be, but something completely different—rather the opposite.'

Papadiamandis' handling of the issues of crime and punishment, of the individual and society, and of the human and the divine order, is so carefully balanced that the novel can be read simultaneously as an indictment of the social and economic burdens placed on women in traditional Greek society, as a Dostoevskian exploration of the psychology of the killer, and as a Miltonic attempt to 'justify the ways of God to men'.

Papadiamandis' stories are 'realistic' in the sense that romantic love and heroic ideals are constantly being brought down to earth. For example, in 'Eros–Hero' (1897) a young man who discovers that he

---

[30] . . . εις το ήμισυ του δρόμου μεταξύ της θείας και της ανθρωπίνης δικαιοσύνης (Papadiamandis 1981–8: iii. 520).

[31] Papadiamandis 1981–8: iii. 446.

has been jilted realizes, in the course of a phantasmagoric chain of
thoughts, that true heroism lies in *not* taking the opportunity for
vengeance that presents itself, but in accepting his lot instead.[32] And
in many stories the life of the small, traditional community of Skiathos
is presented with much devotion to the details of its poverty, isolation,
and the harshness of winter there. But Papadiamandis, at least in the
stories which are the most read today, goes well beyond the realistic
portrait of a community. Many of the stories do not narrate series of
events in a sequence of cause and effect but present juxtapositions of
characters, of tableaux, of apparently unrelated incidents whose connection the reader is compelled to tease out for himself. Critics have
often noticed a 'poetic' or a 'lyrical' quality in Papadiamandis' prose
(he has been especially admired in later times by poets),[33] and this
quality has often been linked to the pervasive themes of unfulfilled
longing and nostalgia in the stories, and to their author's staunch
commitment to the beliefs and rituals of the Greek Orthodox Church.

What Papadiamandis achieves in his stories, particularly those
which stretch the conventions of nineteenth-century realism close to
the limit,[34] is to present a world 'in the round', but a world none the
less incomplete. Pointers to an inscrutable Providence that lies
beyond are the numerous churches, icons, and rituals which play
such an important part both in the life of the community and in the
stories. And the pathos of unfulfilled love and the nostalgia for lost
innocence that are also encountered so often in the stories can be
understood in the same way. Papadiamandis exploits the techniques
of realist fiction to interpret what is ordinarily thought of as 'reality'
as being pitifully incomplete, a fallen world where nostalgia and
deprivation, suffering and faith, are the pointers to a very different
'reality' which could never be represented 'realistically'.[35]

[32] Ἔρως–Ἤρως (Papadiamandis 1981–8: iii. 165–82).

[33] Seferis conceded (seemingly grudgingly, no doubt because of Papadiamandis'
use of the formal language, *katharevousa*) that Papadiamandis was the greatest
Modern Greek prose-writer (Seferis 1981: i. 253–4). See also the essay by Elytis
(1989).

[34] Classic examples (and very different from each other) are 'The Black-
Kerchiefed Woman', 1891 (Η Μαυρομαντηλού), 'All Around the Lake', 1892
(Ολόγυρα στη λίμνη), and 'Our Lady of the Sweet Kiss', 1894 (Η
Γλυκοφιλούσα). See, respectively, Papadiamandis 1981–8: ii. 153–68; ii. 379–400;
iii. 71–88. All three are discussed by Farinou-Malamatari (1987); on the first see also
Beaton 1989b: 258–9; and Mackridge 1992a: 160–5.

[35] A key text which gives support to this reading of Papadiamandis' later fiction as a
whole is the story 'Dream upon the Wave', 1900 (Όνειρο στο κύμα, Papadiamandis
1981–8: iii. 261–73). On this story see Tziovas 1993a: 237–8; 1993b.

Karkavitsas. Folkloric realism was also more a means than an end in the work of Andreas Karkavitsas (1866–1922). By profession a doctor, first in the navy, later in the army, Karkavitsas had the opportunity to observe many different traditional communities at close quarters. Between 1886 and 1904 he published a large number of short stories, many of which were also published in collected form soon afterwards,[36] and three novels: *The Fair Maid* (1890), *The Beggar* (1896), and *The Archaeologist* (1904).[37]

The Fair Maid, the only one of the three to draw directly on Karkavitsas' own childhood in the province of Eleia in the north-west Peloponnese, has been described as 'a graphic, true, and accurately drawn picture of life in the Greek countryside, in which the writer simply presents manners, customs, and beliefs, without looking any further'.[38] But all is not so straightforward in this tale of a young girl's romantic attachment to a flamboyant cart-driver and marriage, against her will, to a mean, middle-aged grocer on the make. A different approach to the novel has persuasively shown how the inexorable process by which the 'fair maid' Anthi is transformed into 'the pragmatic spouse, the wife of Nikolos Pikopoulos',[39] duplicates in miniature the contemporary decline of the traditional way of life exemplified by the 'fair maid' and the cart-drivers, before the spread of commerce and the arrival of the railway.[40] According to this reading the gentle but detached sympathy of the novel's third-person narrator conceals a searing indictment of the arrival of new social and economic values which not only triumph over the romantic spontaneity of Anthi and her young cart-driver, but actually transform the heroine into a different person, as she becomes, in spite of herself, fully assimilated into her new role. This partly

---

[36] Collections of Karkavitsas' stories first appeared in 1892, 1899, and 1900 and have been frequently reprinted since. There are also several editions of the complete works (see Vitti 1987: 491).

[37] For the first of these, see Karkavitsas 1994; for the second, see Mastrodimitris 1980, both with introduction and useful supplementary material. There is no modern critical edition of *The Archaeologist* (Ο αρχαιολόγος). The translation of the title, *The Fair Maid,* deserves explanation: the quaintness of the English rendering is already present in the Greek. 'Λυγερή' literally means 'slim girl'; but the word belongs almost exclusively to the folk tradition, where its connotations are exactly those of 'fair maid' or 'pretty maid' in English balladry.

[38] Sachinis 1975: 159.

[39] ... η θετική σύζυγος, η γυναίκα του Νικολού Πικοπούλου (Karkavitsas 1994: 183).

[40] See Politi 1981.

allegorical dimension to *The Fair Maid* anticipates *The Archaeologist*, while the implied indictment of contemporary social changes looks forward to *The Beggar*. But the latter novel is also anticipated by the specific *tour de force* with which *The Fair Maid* ends. It is not just the juggernaut of social and economic change that crushes the heroine's romantic instincts and brings about a complete change in her personality. When she becomes pregnant with her first child, it is Nature (with capital letter), described as 'all-powerful' and a 'goddess', that imperceptibly but inexorably brings about her transformation:

Η αφομοίωσις επήλθε πλήρης. Ό,τι δεν κατώρθωσαν αι θερμαί συμβουλαί της κυράς Παναγιώταινας και αι αδιάκοποι προσπάθειαι της Φρόσως, κατώρθωσε μόνη της η Φύσις. Η Φύσις, η παντοδύναμος θεά, η οποία μικρόν κατά μικρόν κατά μικρόν παρήλλαξε το σώμα και προδιέθεσε την ψυχήν της Ανθής εις πλήρη συνεννόησιν μετά της ψυχής του Διβριώτου.[41]

The assimilation was now complete. All that had not been achieved by the warm counsels of Kyra Panayotena, and the ceaseless efforts of Froso, was achieved by Nature all by herself. By Nature, that all-powerful goddess, who little by little brought about a change in Anthi's body and predisposed her soul towards complete mutual understanding with the soul of Divriotis [her husband].

'Assimilation' is the part-ironic title of the final chapter, and in this way Karkavitsas implies that just as Nature determines the feelings and thoughts of Anthi as a wife and mother, so the romantic dreams of the 'fair maid' that the narrator has presented to us with such sympathy must equally have been determined by Nature.

This reading of *The Fair Maid* brings us close to the 'naturalism' of Emile Zola, a method of writing fiction based on the belief that human actions are determined by natural forces over which we have no control. This theorem is much more evident in Karkavitsas' second and most successful novel, *The Beggar*. The world of this novel is more ostensibly nasty than that of *The Fair Maid*, and a further effect of raw immediacy is achieved by casting the whole narration in the spoken language, with a strong admixture of rural vocabulary. The story, and its organization into five long chapters,

---

[41] Karkavitsas 1994: 182–3; cf. 171: '. . . it was however a sign that Nature, the all-powerful, was working to set it [sc. the marital harmony of the couple] right in the future' (. . . ήτο όμως σημείον ότι η Φύσις, η παντοδύναμος, εργάζετο να κατορθώση αυτήν εις το μέλλον).

have a watertight construction that heightens the sense of a relentless progression from causes to their effects which no act of human will or spark of human decency (even if it existed, which it doesn't in the novel) would have the power to alter.

The beggar of the title, Kostas Tziritis or Tziritokostas, as he is usually called, is a professional, possessed of almost superhuman cunning and strength. But although able, by these means, to manipulate the lives of all the other characters for his own ends, he himself did not have the power to choose his profession or to develop his natural talents in any other way. Tziritokostas is the product of a mountain village so poor that the inhabitants have long turned to beggary and deception as a way of life, training their children from infancy to assume the most horrific deformities and to develop their cunning and endurance to the utmost. The beggar, for all his disturbing superhuman qualities, is at the same time doubly a victim, of Nature and of society.

The other characters in the novel, as presented, have almost no powers of self-determination at all. The action of the story is set in a village at the foot of Mount Olympos in Thessaly, close to the then frontier between Greece and the Ottoman empire. The plight of the local peasants, landless serfs whose conditions have paradoxically worsened since the annexation of Thessaly to Greece, is vividly presented. Destitute though they are, Tziritokostas plays on their indolent, greedy, and superstitious nature to rob them of the little that they possess. The catastrophe (in the Aristotelian sense) is brought about by the presence in the village of a customs official, himself presented as the hapless though far from amiable victim of the corrupt system of patronage that obtains in the civil service. This official, who of course is as corrupt as his masters, gratuitously attacks the beggar, and the spectacular revenge of the latter culminates in the burning down of the mansion of the absentee landlord and the eviction of the villagers, who are held responsible, from their homes. The final chapter has the sardonic title 'Justice', and ends, after the triumph of Tziritokostas, with a sinister echo of the closing pages of the earlier novel:

Η κοιλάδα πρόθυμη εδέχθηκε τον ζητιάνο στους υγρούς και μαλθακούς κρυψώνες της, όπως δέχεται τόσα κακούργα ερπετά και παράσιτα.

Ο άνθρωπος πολλές φορές δεν βρίσκει της υπάρξεώς τους τον σκοπό. Και όμως τα κρατεί στους κόρφους της η Φύσις, θεότης αδιάφορη, ανεπηρέαστη, ίση δείχνοντας αγάπη και στου Κάη τους καρπούς και στα πρωτοτόκια του 'Αβελ.[42]

The vale willingly received the beggar into its soft damp hiding-places, as it receives so many evil serpents and parasites. Man is often at a loss to explain the existence of these things. But Nature, an indifferent, impartial deity, holds them to her bosom, showing equal love for the fruits of Cain and the first-born of Abel.

It is clear that in this novel Karkavitsas has exploited the common interest of writers and readers in folklore for ends which go far beyond realistic description. First of all, in drawing attention to the existence of the village of beggars, to the plight of the Thessalian serfs under Greek rule, and to the effects of corruption in the civil service, the novel shows an evident zeal for social reform; and to this end it successfully borrows from satire the element of exaggeration. Secondly, it adapts the ideas of Zola to a Greek context and explores the consequences of doing so—one of which is to create not a picture but an *interpretation* of reality. And thirdly, the novel's 'naturalism' goes beyond Zola in elevating Nature into an Olympian deity, frequently described in itself as breath-takingly beautiful, but in its very majesty and beauty coldly indifferent to the concerns of its human playthings. It has even been proposed that in this respect Karkavitsas harks back not so much to Zola as to the moral world of the *Iliad*.[43]

Karkavitsas' final novel is universally acknowledged as a failure. *The Archaeologist* follows the folkloric precepts of the time, but daringly breaks altogether with the conventions of realism. In this allegory of Greece's relations with its past and with its foreign neighbours, couched in the form of a folk-tale, the balance between realist conventions and a desire to transcend them is finally lost. The novel remains an important testimony, however, to the artistic aims of the generation of writers who are so often grouped under the 'realist' label. *The Archaeologist* takes to its logical (and unsustainable) conclusion the underlying impetus of the whole movement in Greek fiction that has been discussed in this section: namely, to draw on the resource of indigenous folklore in order to buttress an emerging national identity and establish a literary tradition unambiguously linked to that identity. It may not be so much because of its technical imperfections (the difficulty of bridging the gap

---

[42] Mastrodimitris 1980: 224.   [43] See Wyatt 1988.

between the expectations built into the folk-tale form and the subject-matter) that *The Archaeologist* fails, as because, quite simply, it gave the game away.[44]

PALAMAS

Of all the writers active around the turn of the century who aspired to achieve a synthesis of indigenous tradition with contemporary artistic developments elsewhere in Europe, far and away the most influential was Kostis Palamas (1859–1943).[45] Palamas made his début as a poet, as we have seen, among the group of poets of the early 1880s who espoused the austere formal perfection of the French Parnassian movement. But Palamas, throughout his long writing life, was no adherent of any one 'school' or 'movement'.

From the French Parnassian poets he learned the importance of form, and from his early sonnets and *Iambs and Anapaests* (1897) until the late collections with such uncompromising titles as *Penta-syllables, Poems of Fourteen Lines, The Cycle of Quatrains*, his pre-occupation with form never left him. But we have already seen Palamas, alongside Drosinis, turning towards native Greek folk poetry. This is evident in the early collections *Songs of my Homeland* (1886), *Homelands*, and Palamas' first long poem, which draws on traditional oral poetry to give form to an expressly nationalist mes-sage, *Greetings of the Sunborn Maiden* (1900), together with the 'folkloric' short story 'Death of a Hero'.[46] Indeed, it was during the same formative period (approximately the last fifteen years of the century) that Palamas embarked on the series of critical articles

---

[44] On this novel see (in English) Wyatt 1985; Politi 1988.

[45] References in the notes which follow are to the 16-volume edition of Palamas' 'collected' works (Palamas n.d.), which falls far short of today's standards for a critical edition, despite the subsequent addition of an index volume (Palamas 1984). Plans for a truly complete, critical edition of Palamas, that were announced by the Kostis Palamas Foundation at a conference held in Athens in 1993 to mark the fiftieth anniversary of the poet's death, run to almost fifty volumes and are unlikely to be realized in the near future. There remains a pressing need for a uniform edition of Palamas' major works, with critical introduction, bibliography, line numbering, and glossary.

[46] See, respectively: Ἴαμβοι καὶ ἀνάπαιστοι (Palamas n.d.: i. 325–71). Οἱ πεντασύλλαβι, 1910 (Palamas n.d.: vii. 451–517). Τὰ δεκατετράστιχα, 1919 (Pala-mas n.d.: vii. 319–431). Ὁ κύκλος των τετράστιχων, 1929 (Palamas n.d.: ix. 249–78). Τραγούδια τῆς πατρίδος μου (Palamas n.d.: i. 13–175). Πατρίδες (Palamas n.d.: iii. 13–40). Οἱ χαιρετισμοί τῆς ἡλιογέννητης (Palamas n.d.: iii. 253–83). On the short story see n. 20 of the present chapter.

and lectures on his predecessors which decisively shaped the whole canon of nineteenth-century Greek literature up to our own day.[47] Before embarking on his large-scale poetic compositions of the first decade of the new century, Palamas more than any other of his contemporaries had immersed himself in all the available 'traditions' of his country and consciously taken stock of them.

Meanwhile, in the last two decades of the nineteenth century in France, the lead had been taken by the group of poets known as *Symbolistes*. The French Symbolism of this time is actually a highly diverse phenomenon, but two principles which are common to this group are adapted by Greek poets in the early years of the twentieth century: first that the aim of poetry is to draw the mind and emotions of the reader, by indirect suggestion, towards a higher plane of transcendent 'ideas'; and secondly, that the poet himself, glimpsing this higher plane 'through a glass darkly', sees his immediate environment as a place of melancholy and despair. These principles, and particularly the second, make a strong appearance in Greek poetry at the very end of the nineteenth century.[48] Although Palamas declared that he had never belonged to this movement, it is clear from his poetry, and in particular from the collection *The Inert Life*,[49] that the Symbolist concepts of the transcendent idea and of poetry

[47] See Apostolidou 1992.

[48] Notably in the work of Lorentzos Mavilis (1860–1912), Konstandinos Hatzopoulos (1868–1920), Ioannis Gryparis (1870–1942), and Lambros Porfyras (1879–1932), although not all of these writers can simply be labelled as 'Symbolists'. The austere perfectionism of Mavilis' sonnets (repr. in Mavilis 1990) owes at least as much to Parnassianism, while Gryparis' brief career in poetry shows a clear development from the 'Parnassian' sonnets of 'Scarabs' and 'Terracottas' to the more evidently Symbolist 'Elegies' (published together in 1919; see Gryparis 1967), with their strong resemblances to some of the early poems of Cavafy. 'The Ivy' (Ο κισσός) may be compared to Cavafy's 'Walls' (Τείχη); 'Vestals' (Εστιάδες) to Cavafy's 'Waiting for the Barbarians' (Περιμένοντας τους βαρβάρους).

[49] This wayward translation of the title *Η ασάλευτη ζωή*, usually rendered as *Life Immovable* (Phoutrides: see Guide to Translations) or *Motionless Life* (Fletcher 1984), is also an attempt at interpretation of a title whose precise significance has not been adequately considered. The title is to be understood as deliberately oxymoronic, and the definite article as distinguishing a *particular* sort of life. Cognates of the verb σαλεύω, which denotes motion on the spot rather than from place to place, abound in Palamas' poetry, to the extent that one could reasonably suggest that this verb connotes a fundamental characteristic of life itself as perceived by Palamas. The life which is *without* this kind of motion is therefore contrasted to life in general; and it is this kind of life, the life of the transcendent *idea*, that provides the unifying theme for the volume. Corroboration of this interpretation can be found in the passage of *The Emperor's Reed-Pipe*, Canto VII, describing the Acropolis of Athens, and the life of the ancient monuments there as μια ασάλευτη ζωή (Palamas n.d.: v. 90).

as a means of approaching it through indirect suggestion had taken their place alongside Palamas' other artistic and aesthetic interests.

Other ideas from abroad also had a role to play in the formation of Palamas as a poet. The first account of the philosophy of Nietzsche to appear in Greek was published in 1898, and we have the evidence of Palamas himself that at about the same time he and others avidly discussed what he called the 'enchanting philosophy of Nietzsche'.[50] Palamas' direct knowledge of Nietzsche's work was probably fairly limited, but the concepts of the Superman and of the Death of the Idols play a central role in his long poem *The Dodecalogue of the Gypsy*. Another component of the matrix of ideas from which Palamas created his poetry is Socialism. It is characteristic of the poet's eager receptivity to new ideas that he should have toyed, in several poems and essays, with the possibility that the hope for the future lies not with Nietzsche's Superman but with the untamed vigour of the proletariat. But although Marxist readings have been offered for the *Dodecalogue*, a more sober reading of all Palamas' scattered references to the subject makes it clear that Palamas was no more minded to throw in his lot with this party or movement than with any other.[51]

Palamas himself, for all his cosmopolitan interests, travelled little during his long life, and never left Greece. The child of middle-class parents, he was born in Patras but was orphaned very young and brought up by relatives in Missolonghi. Critics have made much of the trauma of the poet's early years, which is often adduced to account for the vein of morbid self-pity which runs through much of the poetry, and contrasts strikingly with the energy, vitality, and optimism which are no less characteristic of the work of Palamas' middle years. His life was otherwise outwardly uneventful: after a precarious career in journalism, he served as Secretary to the University of Athens from 1897 until his retirement in 1928. In his later years he was at least twice a candidate for the Nobel Prize for literature, but without success. Palamas died in Athens during the famine of the second winter of the Axis occupation, in 1943.[52]

[50]   Palamas n.d.: x. 452–3; cited and discussed in Eklund 1972: 21.

[51]   The evidence is well presented and discussed by Eklund 1972: 39–51; and placed in the context of the period by Gounelas 1984: 209–18. For Marxist interpretations see Zachariadis 1945 (who was at the time the leader of the Greek Communist Party) and Thomson 1969.

[52]   There are two informative general accounts of Palamas' life and work in English, well illustrated with translated quotations: Maskaleris 1972, and Fletcher 1984.

Although Palamas continued writing and publishing into his eighties, his reputation most securely rests on three volumes of poetry which were all published during the first decade of the twentieth century. *The Inert Life* (1904) includes much of the poetry that Palamas had already published, but its nucleus is the 'trilogy' (as Palamas later termed it) made up of the poems 'The Palm-Tree', 'A Hundred Voices', and 'Man of Ascra', all written during the period 1900–4.[53] This was followed by Palamas' most complex work, the *The Dodecalogue of the Gypsy*, which first appeared in its entirety in 1907, although it is clear that much of it had been written at the same time as the new poems of *The Inert Life*.[54] The third and longest of these volumes is, like the *Dodecalogue*, epic in scope: *The Emperor's Reed-Pipe*, which appeared in 1910, although once again it seems that much of it had been written during the earlier part of the decade.[55]

All these poems seem to have been written at much the same time, so it would be unwise to seek in them for signs of progression.[56] Rather they must be read as complementary expressions of a multifaceted poetic personality. The principal components of this poetic personality have already been outlined; and the major achievement of this group of poems of Palamas' maturity is that each in a different way seeks to create a synthesis out of these diverse and often incompatible elements.[57]

---

[53] Φοινικιά, dated 1900 (Palamas n.d.: iii. 127–39), Εκατό φωνές, dated 'January 1902' (Palamas n.d.: iii. 141–76), Ασκραίος, dated 1903–4 (Palamas n.d.: iii. 203–22). For Palamas' comments on the central 'trilogy' in this collection see n.d.: x. 523.

[54] *Ο Δωδεκάλογος του Γύφτου* (Palamas n.d.: iii. 285–450).

[55] Η φλογέρα του Βασιλιά, Palamas n.d.: v. 11–147; for a parallel-text edition in one volume see Guide to Translations. On the dating of the poem see Fletcher 1984: 167–8. Once again the translation of a title requires some justification, as this poem has been published in English as *The King's Flute* and is always so called in the English bibliography. The word φλογέρα however does not refer to a flute (αυλός), but to the primitive reed-pipe made and played by Greek shepherds. The *primitiveness* of this instrument, and its integral connection with the folk tradition, is essential for an understanding of its role in the poem. Βασιλιάς, although the common meaning of the word today is 'king', is in context quite clearly the demotic form of the Byzantine imperial title Βασιλεύς, and in the poem is applied to the emperor Basil II. The oxymoronic juxtaposition of the imperial title with the humblest of musical instruments has certainly escaped the poem's English translators and commentators, and has not apparently been explicitly remarked on by Greek critics either. As with *H ασάλευτη ζωή*, the title is to be understood as an understated oxymoron, and this rhetorical figure in turn has a bearing on the interpretation of both poems.

[56] Only the 'trilogy' which makes up most of the new part of *The Inert Life* is clearly dated, and within these three poems *is* a sequential progression. Otherwise, Palamas worked concurrently on all three projects between 1899 and 1907.

[57] On this aspect of Palamas see in particular K. Dimaras 1989.

Palamas' poetry proceeds by way of juxtaposition. In *The Inert Life*, 'The Palm-Tree' juxtaposes the 'voice' of a group of small flowers growing at the foot of a giant palm-tree with the distant crown of leaves that overshadows them, and through this literal juxtaposition hints at others more metaphysical: between man and the divine, between the poet and his art. Out of the doubts and anxieties provoked by this irreconcilable juxtaposition and the inability of the tormented flowers to comprehend the nature of the palm-tree above them, is born:

> Νέο τραγούδι αφάνταστο που δεν ειπώθη,
> ήχος που τίποτ' από μέσα του δε λείπει[58]
>
> A new and unimaginable song never before sung,
> a sound that will include everything.

This is of course the poem itself, and these lines allude to Palamas' ambition for art in general. The flowers, at the end of the poem, accept that they will die in obscurity, but leaving behind a radiance that will 'clothe' and 'adorn' the transcendent, awesome palm-tree:

> και θά ειναι η σκέψη μας κι ο λόγος μας η ρίμα[59]
>
> it will be our thought and our speech and rhyme.

The hundred short poems of the 'Hundred Voices', written two years later, are grouped into sections called 'Nights', and are easily understood as representing a 'dark night of the soul'. A counterbalance to their unrelieved gloom is provided by their formal diversity and epigrammatic style. The final poem is a more explicit counterpart to the reading of 'The Palm-Tree' offered here: the poet dies at the end of a life of suffering but when the hand of Death comes to take him:

> πύρινα γράμματ' άσβηστα θα ιδή γραμμένα απάνου μου:
> "Ω Μούσα, Ιδέα, σ' αγάπησα!"[60]
>
> it will see written in letters of fire above me:
> 'O Muse and Idea, I have loved you!'

Finally in *The Inert Life*, 'Man of Ascra' is the dramatic monologue of the ghost of Hesiod of Ascra, a modern *Works and Days* which begins and ends with the ancient poet handing on his spirit to his worthy successor, Palamas.

---

[58] Palamas n.d.: iii. 137, stanza 4.   [59] Palamas n.d.: iii. 139.
[60] Palamas n.d.: iii. 176.

Out of the juxtaposition of irreconcilably diverse elements comes art which transcends division by creating something new and different that contains all those elements. This is the significance of Palamas' epigraph to the *Dodecalogue of the Gypsy*, from Plato's *Phaedo*: 'Make music, and work.'[61] The hero and the speaker of this poem, the unnamed Gypsy, is the representative of a people traditionally seen as restless wanderers, spontaneously rejecting the 'idols' of civilization that Nietzsche had cast down. This figure, more symbolic than real (as Palamas is at pains to reassure us in his preface), is juxtaposed in the poem with Greek culture at a turning-point in its history, on the eve of the fall of Constantinople to the Turks. And by giving him prophetic powers, Palamas is able to pit the spontaneous fervour of his Gypsy against each in turn of the 'idols' of Greek civilization of his day: love, religion, fatherland, and particularly the relics of the ancient past.

But although the presence of Nietzsche is pervasive in this poem, Palamas' radicalism is directed elsewhere. In the later books of the poem the Gypsy finds a violin that had belonged to a holy hermit, and is then inspired, through the music of the violin, to re-create anew the idols that he had previously cast down. The problematic figure of the Superman in Nietzsche's thought is subtly but decisively transformed in the last two books into a Super-*Artist*, whose birth is foretold in an inserted tale in Book XI. Here the artist of the future, with power to achieve the ultimate synthesis that (perhaps) eludes the Gypsy/Palamas himself, is figuratively introduced as the product of the union of a fairy-tale prince and princess. He is called Adakrytos (Tearless), she Ayelasti (Laughterless). It is hinted that these two respectively represent Art and Science, the synthesis of which will in the final book be celebrated as a 'Third Olympos'. In the special place it reserves for Art, and in its technique of lyrical suggestivity, this long poem owes much to Symbolism, although its frequently declamatory style and sheer scale are diametrically opposed to the poetics of the French movement. The twelve books and the universal claims of the subject-matter invoke the epic genre, and to describe it as a 'Symbolist epic', although not something that Palamas ever did, is to draw attention to a further synthesis of extremes underlying the very form of the poem.

---

[61] Μουσικὴν ποίει, καὶ ἐργάζου.

The Emperor's Reed-Pipe is also epic in scale, but for all its length it lacks the universalism of the previous poem. On the eve of the recapture of Constantinople from the Latins in 1261, the soon-to-be-victorious Byzantine army, in the opening canto of the poem, discovers the tomb of the long-dead emperor Basil II (reigned 976–1025). Known as the 'Bulgar-Slayer' for his victories in Bulgaria, Basil had also extended the territory of the Byzantine empire to the furthest limits ever reached during the middle ages. The juxtaposition of these two historical events (the reign of Basil and the reconquest from the Latin crusaders two and a half centuries later) has an obvious relevance to fears and aspirations in Greece during the first decade of the twentieth century: relations with Bulgaria were tense over rival Bulgarian claims in Macedonia; and the 'Great Idea' of another Greek reconquest of Constantinople, this time from the Turks, seemed at this time closer than ever to being realized.

But the poem goes well beyond merely juxtaposing historical memories. Following a real historical source, Palamas describes how the skeleton of Basil was found in the thirteenth century, with a crude shepherd's pipe thrust between its jaws. Such a musical instrument, in the hands of Palamas, can do great things. This one becomes the mouthpiece for the whole of the rest of the poem, as the incongruously humble instrument proclaims to the astonished onlookers the greatness of the emperor whose tomb it now graces. And, although the whole of Basil's career is present in the poem, the poem does not describe directly any of his deeds in battle; but focuses instead on another (real) event: Basil's pilgrimage to Athens to pray at the Church of the Virgin Mary, which had once been the Parthenon.

The progress of the emperor's army through Greece is lavishly described, but the heart of the poem is Basil's long prayer to the Virgin, who is also both Athena, to whom the Parthenon had been dedicated, and Aphrodite, goddess of love. The prayer begins in Canto IX and in Canto XI turns to fiery prophecy of the future. Much of the poem is taken up with the juxtaposition and attempted synthesis of the ancient monuments and the living present, of pagan belief and Christianity, of Athens and Constantinople (the 'twin centres' of Hellenism for the nineteenth century), of the classical and Byzantine heritages. The synthesis at which the poem aims is not only thematic. All this is achieved in an 'epic' style, now lyrical now declamatory, that draws consciously both on contemporary oral poetry and on stylistic devices found in Byzantine poetry, particularly that written in the vernacular and in the same fifteen-syllable metre. In form and style as well as in theme the poem attempts to draw together the most important strands, as Palamas sees them, of Greek culture through the ages: the ancient world (epic), Byzantium (metre, many features of style), and modern oral tradition (metre, language, features of style).

If for modern readers this seems a long-winded and overburdened way of achieving the imaginative synthesis of different epochs of the Greek past, which Sikelianos would achieve much more economically in 'In the Monastery of St Luke' in 1935 and Seferis in 'Engomi' in 1955, it is none the less worth noting that *The Emperor's Reed-Pipe* is the first poem in Greek literature to attempt such a synthesis.[62] Moreover, Palamas brings about this synthesis in a way which is very much his own. Just as in the *Dodecalogue* it was the discovery of the dead hermit's violin that enabled the Gypsy to resurrect the 'idols' and make an entirely new music for the future, so here another musical instrument actually takes over the role of narrator. The words of the reed-pipe, like the songs of the Gypsy, clearly 'aspire to the condition of music', and 'music' for Palamas, as for the ancient Greeks, means 'the service of the Muses', that is, Art in its most abstract and ideal sense.[63] The voice that in this poem weaves together ancient, Byzantine, and the traditional oral culture of Modern Greece is not produced directly by any human agency. It is by means of a simple reed-pipe, made by shepherds long ago and left in the mouth of a dead emperor, that the accumulated traditions of the Greek people 'make music' for the future.

---

[62] Precedents for such a treatment can perhaps be found in stories by Papadiamandis which link an ancient site or deity with a later church and/or popular superstition: see e.g. 'The Looser of Spells' (Η Φαρμακολύτρια) and 'Beneath the Royal Oak' (Υπό την βασιλικήν δρυν), in, respectively, Papadiamandis 1981–8: iii. 304–14 and iii. 327–31; and the discussion by Ricks (1992). However, a recent close reading (Hirst 1998) has thrown into question the whole idea of pagan-Christian synthesis in *The Emperor's Reed-Pipe*. The first articulation of that synthesis in Greek poetry would then have to be dated to the subsequent decade, to the 'Consciousness' poems of Sikelianos (see nn. 101, 103 below).

[63] The assertion that 'all art constantly aspires towards the condition of music' belongs to Walter Pater, and finds close echoes in the statements of French Symbolist poets in the last two decades of the nineteenth century. Palamas much later (in 1926) offered as a definition of poetry: 'It is language/discourse on the point of turning into song' (Είναι ο λόγος που πάει να γίνη τραγούδι, Palamas n.d.: viii. 171).

CAVAFY

If the most productive period of Palamas' writing life can be said to end in 1910 with the publication of *The Emperor's Reed-Pipe*, it was not until a year later, in 1911, that his close contemporary Konstandinos Kavafis, better known in English as C. P. Cavafy, reached his 'maturity' as a poet (on his own admission and in the opinion of many critics). This is worth pointing out, since Palamas is generally thought of as belonging to the thought-world of the nineteenth century, while Cavafy stands unassailed today as the first, and in the opinion of many also the foremost, of the Greek poets of the twentieth century. But the truth is that only four years separated Cavafy (1863–1933) from Palamas (1859–1943). And although the environments in which the two poets grew up were very different, none the less the intellectual climate with which they both had to come to terms in their early years was the same. In order to place Cavafy (whose work is much better known today than that of Palamas) in historical perspective, it will be useful to explore further parallels and contrasts between the two near-contemporaries.

Both poets lost their fathers early, and as a result spent much of their childhood in an environment very different from that of the family home: Palamas with his relatives in Missolonghi, Cavafy in Liverpool and London. Both were reluctant travellers in later life: Palamas rarely leaving Athens, Cavafy equally sedentary in his native Alexandria. But here of course comes the greatest contrast between them: Palamas lived and worked in the national capital of a Greek state with strong aspirations to expand its frontiers; Cavafy in the expatriate Greek mercantile community of Alexandria, on the periphery of a Greek-speaking world that had expanded centuries ago and knew no frontiers.[64]

Palamas' work, published in Athens, had an immediate impact; contemporary and younger poets could not ignore it. Cavafy's poetry, on the other hand, was mostly published privately in Alexandria and, despite a favourable review by Xenopoulos as early as 1904, was not widely known in Athens before the 1920s.[65] His

---

[64] For a useful account of the historical background of the Greek community in Alexandria see Kitroeff 1983.

[65] In his lifetime Cavafy published only two slim pamphlets, in 1904 and 1910, and a collection in 1917, all of them in Alexandria. Most of his poems circulated in privately printed and bound folders which he distributed among friends and kept

collected poems were not published until 1935 (in Alexandria), two years after the poet's death. The response by poets and critics to Palamas' work was therefore immediate, while the response to Cavafy's was delayed until the 1920s and 1930s, by which time Cavafy had already been 'discovered' by E. M. Forster when he visited Alexandria in 1917, and was beginning to acquire the international reputation he has enjoyed ever since (and which eluded Palamas).[66] Both poets drew in their early years on the legacy of nineteenth-century Athenian poetry and of French Symbolism, and both were capable of exploiting a deep vein of self-pity in their poems. Both had also learnt the lesson of the French Parnassian movement to see the poem as a finely crafted, impersonal artefact, and both placed great emphasis on formal perfection. For both poets the aesthetic qualities of the work of art were paramount: for Palamas the goal and justification of the suffering poet was to 'make music', in which the imperfections and oppositions of real life would be subsumed; in Cavafy's poems 'Art' is invested with the power to transform the imperfections of experience into a perfect aesthetic object.

Both Palamas and Cavafy, late in their respective careers, described their poetry as being of three kinds. Palamas in his 'Poetics' identifies what he calls the 'three lyricisms': of the 'we', of the 'I', and of the 'all', corresponding to the national, the personal, and the universal.[67] Cavafy, too, divided his poems into three kinds: erotic, historical, and philosophical.[68] The 'philosophical' category is as difficult to isolate in Cavafy's poetry as the 'universal' in that of Palamas; both can best be seen as tendencies present in poems which also have a more immediate reference, either personal or national. But there are more significant parallels to be drawn between Cavafy's 'erotic' poems and Palamas' 'lyricism of the "I"', and between Cavafy's historical poems and Palamas' 'lyricism of the "we"'.

under close control. For an analysis of Cavafy's idiosyncratic publishing habits see Savvidis 1966, together with important revisions by Hirst (1995). For the currently standard editions see n. 72.

[66] Forster's two justly admired essays on Cavafy (one in *Pharos in Pharillon*, first pub. 1923; the other in *Two Cheers for Democracy*, pub. 1951) are reprinted in Forster *et al.* 1983: 13–18, 40–5.

[67] Palamas n.d.: x. 498–534. The sections on the three 'lyricisms' are dated 1920. Palamas' *Poetics* (*Η ποιητική μου*) was first published in 1933.

[68] Unsigned note attributed to the poet, cited by Savvidis (1966: 209; cf. 269–70; Hirst 1995).

Palamas' personal and introspective style gives expression to feelings of unspecified guilt and personal inadequacy which conform to the role of the *poète maudit* common among the French Symbolists. Cavafy's poems which are similarly personal in subject-matter testify to very similar feelings, which in his case are 'explained' to some degree by the poet's self-confessed homosexuality. But both poets present themselves as outcasts from society; both are haunted (particularly in their early years) by images of old age; and for both the outlet is to be found in their art. Palamas' 'lyricism of the "we" ' clearly enough refers to the element of nationalism in his poetry, and to the attempt to identify and create a synthesis of the Greek tradition past and present that was particularly evident in *The Emperor's Reed-Pipe*. Cavafy never attempted a composition on that scale and his allusions to contemporary military and political realities were invariably so discreet as to pass virtually unnoticed.[69] But in all Cavafy's poems set in the ancient world, there is an underlying attempt to identify and define, behind his own place and time, a 'Hellenic' past, different though it is from the traditions of the Greek past and present that Palamas wove together into a synthesis.

The past that Cavafy re-creates in his historical poetry is that of the Near East during the centuries between the conquests of Alexander the Great and the fall of Constantinople to the Turks in 1453. He has little interest in the oral folk traditions of the Greek peasantry, and even less in the physical landscape of Greece. He has little to say about the conquerors, such as Basil the Bulgar-Slayer (except when things go wrong for them).[70] His Byzantine emperors

---

[69] It was not until 1941 that Seferis, transplanted to Cavafy's world of Egypt by the Axis invasion of Greece, realized that some of Cavafy's poems set in ancient times, that had been written at the time of the Greek débâcle in Anatolia, drew an implicit parallel between an ancient and a modern disaster (Seferis 1981: i. 324–63). The conclusions Seferis drew from this about Cavafy's method of treating history lead, I believe, away from Cavafy's poetics and towards Seferis' own, and for this reason I have elsewhere argued against this reading (Beaton 1983). However, there is no reason to doubt that poems such as 'Those who Fought for the Achaean League', 1922 (Ὑπέρ τῆς Ἀχαϊκῆς Συμπολιτείας πολεμήσαντες), and 'Darius', 1917 (Ο Δαρείος), do allude indirectly to the great events of that time. Similarly, although Tsirkas' reading of Cavafy as a crypto-socialist (1958; 1971) has generally been discredited, this should not exclude the possibility that particular poems do allude to the contemporary events and situations that Tsirkas says they do.

[70] See e.g. 'The Footsteps' (Τα βήματα) and 'Manuel Comnenos' (Μανουήλ Κομνηνός, Cavafy 1991: i. 44; i. 51).

are forced by poverty to wear artificial crown jewels,[71] and in general he prefers to present historical events as seen from the point of view of the losers. The characters that populate the world of Cavafy's historical poems are almost never Greeks from Greece; they inhabit the cosmopolitan cities of the eastern Mediterranean and more often than not their racial or cultural background is described as mixed. It is certainly not in racial or territorial terms that Cavafy sees the Greek world as being defined. Hellenism, 'to be Greek', for Cavafy consists in a knowledge of the Greek language and in subscribing to a set of values, primarily aesthetic, which in the course of centuries have spread far beyond the bounds of classical or modern Greece. If Cavafy's historical poems are poles apart from Palamas' 'nationalist' poetry in the version of the Greek past which they lay before the reader, Cavafy none the less shares with Palamas the attempt to explore through the medium of poetry the historical precedents for the culture to which he belonged, and by doing so to define that culture for the present.[72]

What crucially separates Cavafy from his predecessors in the nineteenth century, and indeed from most of his contemporaries in the early twentieth, is neither his subject-matter nor his beliefs about his art, but an ironic detachment, a sense of the fallibility of human beings and the *relativity* of values, even of those he holds most dear, coupled with a disconcerting sense of humour. Cavafy's

---

[71] 'Of Coloured Glass' (Από υαλί χρωματιστό) describes the coronation of the impoverished emperor John Cantacuzene in 1347 (Cavafy 1991: ii. 50).

[72] The standard edition of the 154 poems that Cavafy at the time of his death had endorsed as his poetic 'canon' was established by G. P. Savvidis in 1963 (= Cavafy 1991). Seventy-two poems, not rejected by the poet but according to his idiosyncratic habits not passed as fit for publication either, appeared in 1968 (the so-called 'unpublished poems', Cavafy 1993). 'Rejected' and 'unfinished' poems have also been published (Cavafy 1983; 1994). A considerable amount of unpublished material, including personal notes and drafts of poems, remains in an archive in Athens. There is an exceptionally large bibliography on Cavafy, a substantial portion of it in English. My primary concern here has been to place a well-known poet in his historical context, and so I have not dealt with the remarkable reception of the poetry by generations of (mostly later) critics. For book-length studies in English the reader is referred to: Bien 1964, Liddell 1974, M. Alexiou 1983, Jusdanis 1987*b*, Robinson 1988; Anton 1995; Keeley 1996*a*. Particular emphases have been given by: Malanos 1933 (psychological), Seferis 1981: i. 324–63 (parallels with T. S. Eliot, written 1947), Tsirkas 1958; 1971 (Marxist), Ilinskaya 1983 (realist), Dallas 1974; 1984 (history, particularly the period of the 'Second Sophistic'), Vayenas 1979*a* (irony), and Beaton 1987*a* (parallels with Proust). The collected studies of the poet by G. P. Savvidis (1985; 1987) also contain much of interest. See also Pieris 1992.

own (tongue-in-cheek) description of his poetry, which he provided for a correspondent of a French newspaper towards the end of his life, has never been surpassed, and derives additional force from an element of parody, both of self and of the language and expectations of literary criticism, provided by the context:

Cavafy in my opinion is an ultra-modern poet, a poet of future generations. In addition to his historical, psychological, and philosophical worth, the fastidiousness of his style, which at times verges on the laconic, his measured enthusiasm, which arouses mental excitement, his correct syntax, the consequence of an aristocratic disposition, his subtle irony, are elements that generations of the future will enjoy even more . . .[73]

Cavafy's poetry, particularly from 1911 onwards, is spare, with every word weighed carefully; disarmingly close to prose until its highly subtle verse-patterns are examined. Whether the subject-matter is historical or drawn from the low life of contemporary Alexandria, it focuses almost invariably on a human individual and his perceptions; perceptions which the course of the poem will expose in all their vulnerability and partiality. A Syrian student with a Greek name, coming to Alexandria to study in the late fourth century AD, at a time when the old Greco-Roman religion still survived alongside the new official religion of Christianity, declares himself able to make the most of the pagan fleshpots with impunity, because he has, at bottom, an 'ascetic soul':

> Το σώμα μου στες ηδονές θα δώσω,
> στες απολαύσεις τες ονειρεμένες,
> στες τολμηρότερες ερωτικές επιθυμίες,
> στες λάγνες του αίματός μου ορμές, χωρίς
> κανένα φόβο, γιατί όταν θέλω—
> και θάχω θέλησι, δυναμωμένος
> ως θάμαι με θεωρία και μελέτη—
> στες κρίσιμες στιγμές θα ξαναβρίσκω
> το πνεύμα μου, σαν πριν, ασκητικό.[74]

---

[73] Cavafy selon mon avis est un poète ultra-moderne, un poète des générations futures. En complément de sa valeur historique, psychologique, et philosophique, la sobriété de son style impeccable, qui touche parfois au laconisme, son enthousiasme pondéré qui entraîne à l'émotion cérébrale, sa phrase correcte, résultat d'un naturel aristocratique, sa légère ironie, sont des éléments que goûteront encore plus les générations de l'avenir... (Cavafy 1963: 82–4).

[74] Τα επικίνδυνα (Cavafy 1991: i. 50).

My body I shall give to pleasure,
to dreamed-of delights,
the wildest erotic fancies,
voluptuous impulses of the blood, without
the slightest fear, because when I will—
and I shall have the will, armed well
as I shall be with contemplation and with study—
at crucial moments I shall regain
my spirit, as it was before, ascetic.

The poem makes no overt comment. We are not told whether this young man is deluding himself, or boldly turning his mixed cultural and religious background to advantage; nor do we learn how things turned out for him. The title, however, affords a different perspective which the character cannot be expected to share: these are 'Dangerous Things'.

In another poem, 'Darius', written in May 1917, on the eve of Greece's entry into the First World War, a court poet whose name, Phernazes, sounds more Persian than Greek, is writing an epic about his patron's purported ancestor, Darius the Great of Persia, when he is interrupted by news that war has broken out. We know from a number of details inserted into the poem that we are in the kingdom of Parthia in Anatolia, about the year 74 BC, on the eve of its crushing defeat by the Romans. A parallel can be drawn between this situation and that of Greece at the time when the poem was written, and between Cavafy, writing a poem set in the remote past at a time when his nation was in danger, and the fictional poet within the poem. But the main impact of the poem derives from its matter-of-fact account of Phernazes' thoughts as disaster looms: never mind the fate of kingdoms, what of his hopes for a professional triumph with his new poem, now that no one will have time to be bothered with 'poems in Greek'? The poem exploits the pathos of Phernazes' pettiness of mind when all is in turmoil around him; but at the end the partial, limited viewpoint of the individual character about to be swept away on the tide of history, seems to be vindicated. The poem ends with Phernazes' thoughts reverting to the poem he is working on:

'Όμως μες σ' όλη του την ταραχή και το κακό,
επίμονα κ' η ποιητική ιδέα πάει κ' έρχεται—
το πιθανότερο είναι, βέβαια, υπεροψίαν και μέθην·
υπεροψίαν και μέθην θα είχεν ο Δαρείος.[75]

[75] Ο Δαρείος (Cavafy 1991: ii. 24–5).

> But in the midst of all his anxious turmoil,
> insistently the poetic idea comes and goes—
> the most plausible solution is, of course, arrogance and intoxication;
> arrogance and intoxication would have been Darius' mood.

For all his all-too-human limitations, Phernazes is surely on to something here. Because, although unimaginable to him in 74 BC, the 'poetic idea' did survive the demise of his Anatolian kingdom; two thousand years later people still do have time for 'poems in Greek', since here (with another war looming) is Cavafy writing one!

It is surely Cavafy's sense of 'relativity', of the unbridgeable gulf that separates the perceptions of the individual from the 'reality' of his surroundings, as well as from those of other individuals, that has constituted a large part of his appeal to twentieth-century sensibilities. And here, at the risk of being over-schematic, we might also locate the final contrast between Cavafy and Palamas. Where Palamas in his poetry had juxtaposed heterogeneous elements in pursuit of an overarching synthesis, achieved through the medium of art, Cavafy's art is constructed like a prism, to break up the light of experience into contrasting and apparently irreconcilable colours and shades. The completeness that, in many of Cavafy's poems, art can confer on imperfect experience is, to continue the metaphor, the completeness of the spectrum, not of the pure white light.[76]

URBAN FICTION: REALISM, SYMBOLISM, SOCIALISM

If prose fiction during the early decades of the twentieth century produced no writers of the stature of Vizyinos, Papadiamandis, and Karkavitsas to rival the poetic giants Palamas and Cavafy, there is none the less a great deal of it. It is also marked by a new diversity, which runs parallel to the diverse interests and achievements of the poets of the period.

The convergence of interest among writers of fiction, during the last two decades of the nineteenth century, in the folkloric background of small Greek communities in their physical setting gave, as we saw, a distinctive character to the short stories and novels of that

---

[76] The metaphor conceals an allusion to the English poet Robert Browning, who once wrote: 'I only make men and women speak—give you truth broken into prismatic hues, and fear the pure white light' (*Letters*, ii. 182). The allusion is not gratuitous: Cavafy was well versed in nineteenth-century English poetry and his poetic method has many affinities with that of Browning.

period. Prose fiction in the early years of the twentieth century presents a much more varied picture. Although, as we shall see, the folkloric realism of the earlier period provided a basic training-ground for all the writers that will be discussed in this section, and was not decisively abandoned by serious writers until 1920, the major shift that defines the fiction of the early twentieth century is away from the rural setting and into the towns.

This is by no means merely a matter of local colour. An interest in urban society is a sign of, and in turn fuels, a concern for the way in which social relations are *changing*, and indeed an interest in a more complex set of social relations than is to be found in village life. Papadiamandis had described *The Murderess* as a 'social novel', but the society he depicts in that novel is presented as largely static and timeless. Indeed, for all the harshness and, often, cruelty of the village life from which they derived their subject-matter, the writers of that period are without exception sceptical, if not downright antagonistic, towards innovation deriving from Europeanized, urban institutions. In the work of Papadiamandis' successors, by contrast, it is the new and developing face of Greek society which provides the focus of interest for writers and their readers. From looking over the shoulder of the folklorist at the ageless past, the novelist now looks over the shoulder of the social historian or even of the political activist, at the changing realities of the present and (often) at further, more drastic change to come.

Very broadly the writers of fiction during the first three decades of the twentieth century may be divided into three main categories: those who describe contemporary urban (mainly Athenian) life on a broad canvas without implying any prescriptive programme for reform; those who focus on the inner world of the individual and consciously adapt the techniques of Symbolist poetry; and lastly (from a chronological point of view) those whose portrayal of society is overtly or implicitly directed by a particular vision of the future (the 'ideological' novel). Needless to say, in practice these three categories are by no means clear-cut, and there is some overlap between them and the folkloric realism of the earlier period.

Urban Realism. Fiction which seeks to represent the experience of urban life may not have been so much under-represented in nineteenth-century Greece as neglected by subsequent readers and scholars. As we have seen, the first writers of prose fiction in

Greek, going back at least as far as the *Results of Love* in 1792, were not strangers in their work to the urban environment—and it is notable that most of them had themselves started out from urban centres (Constantinople, Smyrna, Syros) and had studied in university cities abroad. But even during the 1880s and 1890s, when as we have seen, the preferred scene of action, for writers, publishers, and readers alike, was the rural community, urban life was not ignored as a subject by writers. The Athenian short stories of Papadiamandis have only recently begun to be valued in their own right, and not merely as an inferior appendage to his main work set in Skiathos,[77] and writers of short stories and 'sketches', such as Emmanuel Lykoudis (1849–1925) and Michael Mitsakis (1863–1916), who directed a 'camera's eye' at the crowded streets of Athens during these same decades, have recently been rescued from the obscurity in which they had languished for many years, with new editions of selections from their work. Ioannis Kondylakis (1861–1920), whose best-known work exploits the 'folkloric' setting of the writer's native place, in this case Crete, published in 1894 the first large-scale, panoramic novel of life in the Greek capital (whose title declares an immediate allegiance to Victor Hugo), *Les Misérables of Athens*.[78]

It may be that these, together with the first novels of Grigorios Xenopoulos (1867–1951), represent a minority 'opposition' to the dominant folkloric realism of the time, and should be seen as the neglected forerunners of an urban tradition that only came fully into its own in the first decade of the twentieth century. On the other hand, the (justified) excitement at the rediscovery and reassessment of these neglected texts should not obscure the adherence of most of them to the dominant 'folkloric' model of the period, as that was defined above. The focus in them is frequently on a community rather than on an individual, and descriptive details of setting and social behaviour are no less prominent than in the rural ethography of the time. It would not be unreasonable to suggest, then, that the urban fiction of the last two decades of the nineteenth century gives a distinctive 'twist' to folkloric realism without fundamentally

---

[77] See Kotzias 1992.
[78] Respectively: Lykoudis 1990; M. Mitsakis 1988; Kondylakis 1980. The importance and sophistication of this body of writing are argued, with reference to Mitsakis, by Gotsi (1996*a*) and on a wider canvas by Voutouris (1995: 109–98) and Gotsi (1996*b*).

challenging its preoccupation with social groups and with individuals, either representative or 'picturesque', whose fates are presented as the inescapable consequences of their social and physical
environment. The same could also be said, despite its subtitle 'An
Athenian Novel', for *The Wax Doll*, the posthumously published
work of Konstantinos Christomanos, who after many years in the
service of the Empress Elizabeth of Austria returned to Athens and
left behind this rather lushly written novel which appeared as late as
1911.[79]

Although Ioannis Kondylakis is chiefly remembered for his earlier
'folkloric' stories set in his native Crete, Xenopoulos went on during
the next forty years, after his literary debut in 1888, to write as many
novels (mostly in the form of serials in newspapers and periodicals—
only twenty were published in book form during his lifetime) and
literally hundreds of short stories, as well as a great many stage-plays,
almost all of them set in the urban environment. Xenopoulos came
from Zakynthos in the Ionian islands, and it is significant that it was
not until the last years of the nineteenth century that these islands,
with their local aristocracy and long-standing links to western Europe, produced a writer who devoted his efforts to prose fiction. It is
no less significant that when they finally did so, the writer was one
who professed himself indifferent to the folkloric preoccupations
that had dominated Athenian cultural life in the 1880s, and who
based his fiction instead on the exploration of a more complex urban
society, such as had grown up in Athens in the preceding fifty years,
but had a much longer tradition in his native islands.

Xenopoulos' first novels, set in Athens, were written in his early
twenties and draw on his experiences of student life in the capital.
Thereafter he drew equally on the urban life of Athens and of
Zakynthos in his novels (and also in his plays), drawing characters
from all social classes and weaving around them plots more or less
romantic and melodramatic. Xenopoulos acknowledged Balzac,
Dickens, Zola, and Daudet as his masters,[80] but the greatest of
these was surely Balzac. The vast tapestry of social life and manners,
the exclusively urban settings, and the consummate manipulation of
the reader's expectations in plots devised with mathematical precision, all combine to make Xenopoulos' large fictional canvas a
comédie humaine of Greece at the turn of the century.

---

[79] Christomanos 1988.   [80] Cited by Sachinis (1975: 245).

Like Papadiamandis, Xenopoulos was a writer by profession, and like him has also been criticized for sloppiness and repetition in consequence. But while Papadiamandis has been rehabilitated by recent criticism and scholarship, and his best work separated from his juvenilia and ephemera, it seems that in Xenopoulos' case long-standing popularity has stood in the way of critical re-evaluation. However, since 1984 his novels have begun being reissued in paper-back, and this may be a prelude to renewed critical interest.[81] It may be suggested, however, that Xenopoulos' exploration of social issues in an urban context, his sheer professionalism as a story-teller, and his modest acceptance of the novel as first and foremost a medium of entertainment, place him closer to the upsurge in the novel that has taken place in Greece since the 1960s than to much of the fiction of the intervening years.

Symbolism and the Inner World of the Individual. The inner world of a central character is by no means unknown territory to Greek fiction before the end of the nineteenth century. The action of the *Results of Love* (1792) and of the first Modern Greek novel, *Leander* (1834), as we have seen, takes place largely there; and part of the achievement of Papadiamandis lies in the subtlety with which he could convey the thoughts and state of mind of a character on the page. But in the first two of these examples the characters are representative of a type and a social class, rather than presented with the particularity of the individual; while Papadiamandis' char-acters, when they are presented from within, are certainly indi-viduals, but are always seen simultaneously as part of a social and physical environment.

The attempt to explore the psychological or spiritual state and *subjective* perceptions of the individual is generally accepted as a characteristic of Modernism, a movement which, as we shall see, has had its adherents in Greece in the 1930s and since. A significant precursor of this aspect of Modernism in Greek fiction is Konstandinos Hatzopoulos (1868–1920), who was also one of the

---

[81] Aside from occasional special issues of periodicals, the only recent monograph on Xenopoulos is Trovas 1984. For a scholarly analysis of the prologues to the novels see Farinou-Malamatari 1990. After the novelist's death his complete works were issued in a uniform format (Xenopoulos 1958–71). Most of the novels and plays have now been issued separately, in a new series, by the Athens publisher Vlassis.

leading exponents, in poetry, of the French Symbolist tradition in Greece.[82]

Hatzopoulos, like most of the prose-writers of his generation, began by publishing stories in the folkloric mode, but is principally remembered for the two novels: *The Manor by the Riverside* (1909) and *Autumn* (1917).[83] The first of these tells the story of three orphaned girls growing up in their father's derelict manor-house, listlessly incapable of interacting with the hostile world outside, until they gradually become physically and emotionally derelict themselves. The rural setting still owes something to folkloric realism,[84] while the suspicion and distrust between social classes that blocks any happier outcome to the story looks forward at the same time to the socialist novel. But the real achievement of Hatzopoulos here has been to convey the shifting moods and perceptions of the three central characters, with a powerful overall evocation of helpless passivity and boredom.

Boredom is still more in evidence in *Autumn*, a love-story without beginning or end, and so elliptical and understated as to leave the reader knowing more about the weather than about the lives of the characters. The setting is a seaside town in autumn, and the reader is left with a predominant impression of a vague and mysteriously frustrated yearning by the characters to be able to express themselves fully and to lead full lives. The evocation of the season in the title implicitly stands for the wasting-away, implicit in the Greek word for 'autumn', not only of the individual lives described but also of the middle-class society to which they seem to belong.[85]

These two novels, and particularly the second, later became the precedents for more radical innovations in the genre. But at the time when they were written, such external impulses as contributed to

[82] For a collected edition of the poetry, with introduction, see Hatzopoulos 1992. See also n. 48 above, and more generally, Débaisieux 1995.

[83] Respectively: Hatzopoulos 1986; 1990 (both with critical introductions). Hatzopoulos also published two long stories which are sometimes referred to as novels: 'Love in the Village', 1910 (Αγάπη στο χωριό) which curiously applies this writer's idiosyncratic, almost telegraphic, mode to the village setting beloved of the previous generation of folkloric realists, and the urban satire 'Superman', 1911 (Υπεράνθρωπος).

[84] Indeed, Hatzopoulos himself subtitled the novel (perhaps ironically): Ηθογραφία.

[85] This symbolic function of autumn is also common to much of the poetry of this period that has links to French Symbolism, including the poetry of Hatzopoulos himself.

them derive in about equal measure from Symbolist poetry and from the Scandinavian theatre and novel.[86]

The 'Ideological' Novel. An overriding interest in social conditions, conflicts, and change does not necessarily imply that the writer has a particular view of how society might or should change. By the 'ideological' novel (and short story) is meant a type of fiction in which the writer either explicitly or implicitly indicates that he holds such a view, whether or not that view is actually propounded in his fiction. Ideological in this sense are the three novels of the politician, patriot, and diarist Ion Dragoumis (1878–1920) published between 1907 and 1911, the first of which, *Blood of Martyrs and Heroes*, tells in rousing terms of the Greek struggles in Macedonia; and the most successful Greek children's novel of all time, *In the Time of the Bulgar-Slayer* (1911), by Penelope Delta (1874–1941). This novel, which appeared only a year after Palamas' *The Emperor's Reed-Pipe*, re-traverses some of the same ground in an entirely different mode, but obviously shares with that poem a concern to strengthen Greek morale in the continuing duel with Bulgaria over the future of Macedonia. But the most important development in the direction of the 'ideological' novel at this time is the rise of a socialist consciousness in fiction.

Socialist ideas had been discussed in Greek intellectual circles since the late 1880s, although it was not until 1918 that the Socialist Labour Party (soon to transform itself into the Communist Party of Greece, or KKE) was founded. We have already noted the impact of socialist thinking on Palamas, and the early interest in the plight of the urban poor in Kondylakis' *Les Misérables of Athens* (1894), as well as in many of the novels and stories of Xenopoulos.[87] A socialist perception of individual and class relations plays a more fundamental part, as we also saw, in two of Hatzopoulos' novels, but really comes into its own in Greek fiction in the four novels of Konstandinos Theotokis (1872–1923), who was a friend of Hatzopoulos and shared many of his ideas.

---

[86] Plays by Ibsen had been performed by the newly formed New Stage company in Athens between 1901 and 1905, and made a significant impression on Palamas among others. Hatzopoulos' interest in the novels of Knut Hamsun and J. G. Geijerstam is well attested.

[87] See in particular *Rich and Poor*, 1919 (Πλούσιοι και φτωχοί, Xenopoulos 1958–71: ii. 9–317).

The scion of an illustrious aristocratic family of Corfu, Theotokis studied in Germany, and between his return to Greece in 1896 (to fight in the successful Cretan revolt of that year) and his last foreign visit in 1908 he became a committed socialist, finally even giving up his landed property in Corfu. His literary career, like that of most of his contemporaries, began in the folkloric tradition (although he had previously published a novel in French), and his early short stories are marked by an unflinching portrayal of brutality and human degradation that builds on the precedent of Karkavitsas in *The Beggar* and anticipates the later novels of Myrivilis and Kazantzakis. The four novels are very different from one another, and although the author's socialist commitment is evident in various ways, the implication that human beings *could* order their society differently serves to heighten the tragedy of lives which the author leaves without interference to run their 'natural' course in the real world of Corfu in the early years of the century. The four also effectively straddle the divide between the folkloric, rural tradition and the new urban novel. The second and third are set in the world of the village, the first and last in the town.

The two novels which exploit the folkloric setting that had dominated at the end of the nineteenth century, and with which that tradition is generally considered to end, are *Condemned* (1919) and *The Life and Death of the 'Hangman'* (1920).[88] Each is built around an exemplary central character, and this rather unpromising 'recipe' is saved in each case by the wealth of realistic detail with which the central portraits are adorned. Tourkoyannos in *Condemned* was particularly admired by writers of the 1930s, who recognized his generic resemblance to Dostoevsky's *Idiot*; the old man nicknamed the 'Hangman' (*Karavelas*) in the novel named after him, by contrast, exemplifies all that is cruel and perverse in human nature. But what gives point to this grisly tale is the subtle way in which the character's instinctive potential for evil is deliberately worked on by his fellow villagers, and particularly by the two relatively wealthy brothers who cunningly play on his miserly nature to deprive him of his property and finally even of his life. The description of the brothers and their family in the early chapters of the book implies that the unhealthy, sweaty Argyris, who is the brains of the family but may not have much longer to live, represents capitalism, while

[88] Respectively: Theotokis 1979 (critical edn.); 1990 (reprt.)

the happy-go-lucky Yannis, who is much stronger than he knows, stands for the proletariat. In the novel the model of society represented by the brothers successfully destroys its primitive victim, the peasant branded with the nickname 'Hangman'. But the only person that 'Karavelas' ever hangs is himself.

Theotokis' first urban novel, *Honour and Price* (1912), a compact story about a young penniless aristocrat and the hard-working daughter of a working-class family, is essentially a rehearsal for the much larger novel that occupied him for a decade before it was published in 1922: *Slaves in their Chains*.[89] The titles of both Theotokis' urban novels prepare the reader for a *roman à thèse*, but this is only really true of the first. *Slaves in their Chains* stands, alongside the Zakynthian novels of Xenopoulos, as the belated fictional expression of a society that had undergone rapid change since the islands became part of Greece in 1864, and which in 1922 was fast disappearing. It may not be accidental that the genre of the novel, whose rise is traditionally associated with the rise of the middle class in Europe, was slow to emerge in the Ionian islands, and reached its most developed form in the work of an aristocrat who had espoused the cause of socialism, and who, from a socialist standpoint, charted the decline of the old ruling class to the benefit of the rapacious *nouveaux riches*.

In fact, for all its socialist commitment, *Slaves in their Chains* offers little comfort for the idealist. The character in the story who shares the author's beliefs, Alkis Sozomenos, despite his name which means literally 'being saved' or 'saving himself', is not in the event saved but dies of tuberculosis and a broken heart, after the aristocratic girl he loves has been forced to sacrifice her love for him in a vain attempt to maintain the fortunes of her family. And the feckless pride of the various members of that family, the Ofiomachi (or 'Dragonslayers'), is presented in the novel with sympathy and nostalgia. The decline of the old aristocracy is charted with a sharp eye for detail, but the novel betrays a very aristocratic disdain for the rising middle class, represented by the whinging money-lender and the self-made doctor who ends by stealing the heroine from the idealistic socialist hero, a lover from one of her brothers, and estates and money from the family, and finally gains political influence through pandering to a corrupt party machine.

---

[89] Respectively: Theotokis 1978; 1981.

This novel is also remarkable for its conscious elegance of style (an 'aristocratic' trait?) and structure. Alongside direct speech and racy description it contains many elaborate sentences of Proustian length, and for the first time in Greek exploits the technique of the 'leitmotiv' or repeated phrase which triggers particular associations. This is especially effective in a scene where a character plays a piece on the piano and another listens, while the reader is given mainly the thoughts of the listener. A few pages later the player plays the piece again, and the *thoughts* of the listener are repeated word for word, just as the notes of the music would have been.[90] The same stylistic technique, on a larger scale, sets the seal on the structure of the novel: all the events narrated take place during the space of a year. The opening scene and the closing scene are almost identical, describing Alkis Sozomenos' illness, with the difference that in the opening scene he recovers while in the closing scene he dies. But not only are the situations closely parallel, even the *words* of the final scene are wherever possible identical to those of the opening.

These technical innovations alone would be sufficient to rank *Slaves in their Chains* as one of the formative Greek novels of the twentieth century (the same innovations were taken up and developed later by Kosmas Politis in particular). But in its panoramic view of a whole society in a time of change, and its large cast of characters, it also looks forward to the urban novels of the 1930s and later (particularly Theotokas' *Argo*), while the character and fortunes of the socialist hero, Alkis Sozomenos, together with the parallel case of Popos Dagatoras in Xenopoulos' *Rich and Poor* (1919), established a character-role which would be taken up again and again in Greek fiction in the twentieth century: that of the young socialist whose beliefs find no outlet in action and who becomes finally the victim of society and his own human weakness. Variations on this character-role reappear in such diverse places as Kosmas Politis' *Gyri* (1944), the post-war stories and novels of Dimitris Hatzis and Menelaos Loudemis, in Tsirkas' trilogy *Drifting Cities* (1960–5), and Maro Douka's *Fool's Gold* (1979).

With the founding of the Socialist Labour Party in 1918, and its transformation into the Communist Party of Greece in 1924, an explicitly socialist perspective becomes more common in fiction during the 1920s. This is evident in the stories and novels of Kostas

[90] Theotokis 1981: 242–5.

Paroritis (1878–1931) and Petros Pikros (1900–56), the latter a pseudonym which translates another literary pseudonym, *Gorky* ('bitter'), into Greek. Paroritis began publishing fictional vignettes of the harsher aspects of life in small communities in the periodical *Noumas* from its inception in 1903, and in 1910 published his first novel, *Before the Mast*, in which the author's later socialist commitment is for the first time explicit.[91] In the 1920s Paroritis wrote regularly (under a pseudonym) for the Communist newspaper *Rizospastis* and published two more novels with an overtly socialist perspective. Pikros' collection of short stories, *Down and Outs* (1922), and the novel *Keep Your Trap Shut* (1927) use the techniques of realism to portray, uniquely in Greek fiction, the urban subculture of hashish dens, brothels, and prisons that gave rise to the music and lyrics of the Greek equivalent of the blues, *rebetika*.[92] Although the same age as Yorgos Seferis, whose literary début in 1931 is traditionally taken as one of the landmarks inaugurating the 'generation of the thirties', Pikros' writing career hardly extends beyond the 1920s.[93]

A more complex case is that of Demosthenis Voutyras (1871–1958). Long relegated to the company of the 'socialist realist' writers just mentioned, and often subjected to some of the same charges as used to be levelled against Papadiamandis (charges of carelessness, of writing too much, and of breaking all the 'rules'), Voutyras has been one of the more surprising rediscoveries of the 1990s. His rich and varied output, mainly of stories but including a few short novels, long out of print, has become accessible once more in a scholarly collected edition, and one commentator has credited him with being the first to introduce the Modernist short story into Greece, as well as being the first Greek writer of the 'fantastic'.[94]

This survey of Greek fiction up to 1928 should not end without a brief mention of two new departures of the 1920s, which might perhaps be grouped together under the heading 'escapism'. Both,

---

[91] *Στο άλμπουρο*. Paroritis' early short stories have been reprinted with an informative introduction on the author's career (Paroritis 1982).

[92] *Χαμένα κορμιά*. *Τουμπεκί*. On the significance of the title of the second (from Athenian street slang) see Pikros 1979: 9–12.

[93] During the 1930s Pikros published a historical novel and a book for children; Paroritis died at the beginning of the decade.

[94] Voutyras 1994–5. For this opinion see Tonnet 1996: 176–80; cf. S. Alexiou 1990, and the special issue of the periodical *Diavazo* dedicated to Voutyras (no. 298, Nov. 1992). On the fiction of this period see also Baloumis 1996.

however, have important sequels in the following period. Fotis
Kondoglou (1897–1965) is the first of the refugees, uprooted by
the Asia Minor catastrophe of 1922, to establish a literary career in
his new homeland. His first novel, *Pedro Cazas* (1923), makes a
decisive break with the exclusively Greek settings and preoccupations of fiction since Roidis' *Pope Joan* half a century before.[95] *Pedro
Cazas* is a spooky tale of treasure-hunters and buccaneers on the
high seas, its characters are Spanish and Portuguese, not Greek, and
Kondoglou makes explicit his admiration for Defoe and other foreign writers of adventure stories.

Kondoglou's escapism has its serious side, however, and is not so
remote from the realities of his time and place as might appear. The
whole of his large output (mostly of short stories) is made up either
of adventure stories set in distant lands, or of nostalgic evocations of
the simple life of the peasants of his native Anatolia, described not so
much with realism as with the religious colouring of an earthly
paradise. Religion plays an important role in Kondoglou's work
(he was also a highly regarded painter, and in that medium did
much to revive the traditional art of icon-painting), and he frequently
insisted on the fundamentals of Orthodoxy as a system of practical
belief and worship that had been exemplifed by the rural communities of his childhood. Although he is often likened to Papadiamandis, whose religious outlook he shared, Kondoglou strips
human nature down to its primitive essentials, whether for good (as
in his Anatolian peasants) or for evil (as in his buccaneers and other
representatives of western culture in his adventure stories); and this
is far removed from Papadiamandis' vision of the vagaries of human
nature and a merciful but unknowable Providence.

Escapism takes a different route in the novels of Thrasos Kastanakis (1901–67). Born in Constantinople, Kastanakis lived for most
of his life in Paris. His first novel was published a year after *Pedro
Cazas*, in 1924, and was followed by many more in the inter-war
years.[96] Although he gave to a trilogy the title *Greek Soil*, Kastanakis'
lasting contribution was to lift the Greek novel out of the exclusively
Greek setting to which both folkloric and urban fiction had become
indissolubly attached, and to entice his readers into contemporary
settings outside Greece. Kastanakis was not an innovative writer in
terms of technique, but in the cosmopolitan settings of his novels he

[95] Kondoglou 1967: v. 5–79.   [96] *The Princes*, 1924 (Οι πρίγκιπες).

reminded his readers (who included the writers of the 1930s and beyond) that Greece was part of a larger social and political world, in which Greeks had a part to play. And this widened horizon will be taken up again, to a limited degree during the 1930s and more confidently from the early 1960s onwards.

THE SUCCESSORS OF PALAMAS IN POETRY

The expression 'under the heavy shadow of Palamas', coined by the historian of Modern Greek literature K. Th. Dimaras, has become something of a cliché. Under this shadow Dimaras (writing in the 1940s) grouped all the writers of poetry and prose of Palamas' generation and younger. The characterization is therefore somewhat sweeping, and it also implies that Palamas continued to occupy the dominant position in letters that he won for himself between about 1890 and 1910, beyond the first decade of the century. In fact there is little to connect the developments in fiction we have just been considering with the pre-eminence of Palamas, and the parallels between Palamas and Cavafy that we looked at in the section before make more sense as parallel responses to a common intellectual climate than as the direct response of the one poet to the work of the other.

But when we come to the poets who began to publish in the first and second decades of the twentieth century the position is rather different. This generation was by no means uniformly cowed by the towering presence of Palamas, as Dimaras' phrase implies, but produced no fewer than four poets of major stature, each of whom implicitly challenged the synthesis achieved by Palamas by extracting one or more of the elements from the whole and testing it, as it were, to destruction. For Sikelianos that element was the unity of the Greek past with the present; for Varnalis as (for a time) for Kazantzakis it was the hint that the creative forces that would build the future were to be found in the proletariat; for Kazantzakis it was the idea of the poem as all-inclusive synthesis; while Karyotakis drew both on the Symbolist legacy of Palamas and his contemporaries and on the vein of introspective despair cultivated by Palamas, to shape a poetic career that culminated in suicide. The first three—Sikelianos, Varnalis, and Kazantzakis—further shared with Palamas the conviction that the poet has a role in society as a prophet, while the careers of Sikelianos and Karyotakis, and to some extent of the other two as well, exemplify the late-nineteenth-century concept, also shared by Cavafy, of the artist's life as itself a work of art.[97]

Angelos Sikelianos (1884–1951). Sikelianos was born and grew up on the Ionian island of Lefkada, and may be regarded as the last (fairly distant) heir to the separate intellectual and artistic tradition of those islands. His debts to that tradition are made explicit in his verse tributes addressed to Mavilis (killed in the First Balkan War of 1912) and Valaoritis, as well as in an early poem which venerates simultaneously both Solomos and the folk tradition.[98] The visionary Romanticism of Solomos, and the way in which that poet had used the oral folk tradition almost a century before, are clearly acknowledged in the title of Sikelianos' first volume, the long poem *Visionary* (1909).[99] But more than anything *Visionary* recalls Palamas, whose *Dodecalogue of the Gypsy* had been published two years before, and to which it fairly evidently is a response.

Sikelianos' poem is entirely in the first person, but the voice of the poet here has affinities with the voice of Palamas' Gypsy, who also had visionary powers, and like him celebrates the wholeness and freedom of the inspired individual. In its length (almost a hundred pages in the standard edition) and in the breathless abandon of a verse-form which, though highly rhythmical, anticipates free verse in its disregard for the number of syllables in a line, it also follows the precedent of Palamas' poem. But here the resemblances end. The whole intellectual apparatus that governs the structure and much of

---

[97] Vitti tellingly groups together Cavafy, Sikelianos, Kazantzakis, and Varnalis as the Greek variations on the European 'Decadent' movement, under the slogan: 'my poetry is myself' (Vitti 1987: 331). Although Cavafy certainly shares this characteristic (also usefully underscored by Robinson 1988: 2–6), he none the less belongs to an earlier generation and is best, in my opinion, treated separately. Conversely, I see no reason not to include Karyotakis (and indeed most of the 'minor' poets of his generation) under the same heading. As we shall see, the careers of many of these poets, and especially that of Karyotakis himself, reveal a disturbing cross-over between art and life which is very much in tune with the 'Decadence' of a slightly earlier period in northern Europe.

[98] The first two were included by Sikelianos in his collected works to which he gave the title *Lyrical Life* (Λυρικός βίος), see Sikelianos 1965: ii. 68–74. The last was originally published in 1904 and only included posthumously in *Lyrical Life* (1965: vi. 55).

[99] Αλαφροΐσκιωτος (Sikelianos 1965: i. 83–169). The word belongs to the folk tradition, where it means 'having a faint shadow', and hence 'with second sight', 'with visionary powers'. Since its use by Solomos in the third draft of *The Free Besieged*, it has also acquired a degree of currency, with this meaning, in literature.

the content of the *Dodecalogue* is absent from Sikelianos' poem, and the distance that separates Palamas the poet from his mouthpiece the Gypsy has been annulled. Sikelianos has no interest in the synthesis of intellectual ideas through lyrical expression: *Visionary* proclaims that lyrical expression by itself is quite enough, and the sheer exuberance of the poem, with its unabashed celebration of the poet himself in instinctive harmony with his native land, amply demonstrates just now far it was possible for Sikelianos to go in this direction.

Between 1909 and 1925 Sikelianos published many short poems in a variety of strict metrical forms (including the sonnet), of which the most famous are 'Thalero', 'Pan', and 'Yannis Keats', Sikelianos' 'tribute' to the English poet.[100] In all these poems the possibilites for rich sound-patterning are taken to an extreme unprecedented in Greek poetry; in subject-matter these poems are devoted principally to commemorating literary figures of an earlier generation and to evoking the spirit of ancient Greece through the vivid depiction of the contemporary landscape.

The ancient world also plays a prominent role in the long poems which Sikelianos published during the same period. These are the four 'Consciousness' poems ('Consciousness of my Land; of my Race; of Woman; of Faith') published between 1915 and 1917, and collectively known, together with the later 'Consciousness of Personal Creativity', as *Prologue to Life*.[101] These poems build upon the exuberance, the nature-worship, and the reverence for ancient Greece of *Visionary*, and also extend its metrical tendencies towards free verse. Characteristic of Sikelianos' enthusiastic optimism in these poems is an enormous complexity of syntax, particularly in extended similes, in which a single sentence may extend to almost fifty lines.[102]

During the same decade, which in terms of volume was the most productive of his career, Sikelianos wrote two more long poems. *Mother of God* (written 1917) is a convoluted and lyrically ornate lament for his sister (who had been married to the brother of Isadora

---

[100] On this poem and Sikelianos' relation to English poetry see Savvidis 1981*b* and Ricks 1988; 1989: 65–74.

[101] *Πρόλογος στη ζωή*. The five poems or sections make up the whole of Sikelianos 1965: iii. The fifth poem was added in 1946, in the first edition of *Lyrical Life*.

[102] See e.g. Sikelianos 1965: iii. 21–2, 75–6 for extended similes; 102–4 for a sentence of 49 lines and a single main verb (which occurs in line 131 of the poem)!

Duncan), while *Easter of the Hellenes* represents Sikelianos' first, and never completed, attempt at a synthesis of ancient paganism, Christianity, and Romantic Pantheism.[103] The terms of this attempted synthesis recall Palamas, but *Easter of the Hellenes* lacks the historical sense of different periods of Greek culture that distinguishes Palamas' poems on this theme. It is the underlying unity and ahistorical contemporaneity of apparently diverse religious experience that interests the more mystical and intuitive Sikelianos. In Sikelianos' poetry 'all time', in T. S. Eliot's words, 'is eternally present'.

During the 1920s Sikelianos' efforts were temporarily diverted away from his art to the attempt to realize some of his ideals in the real world. What he called the 'Delphic Idea' was celebrated in a long poem of 1927, and explained in the preface to his collected poems, *Lyrical Life*, as:

the holy yearning for the establishment of a spiritual Centre which would draw together all the World, from which . . . on the one hand would flow an enlightening of the conditions for a general educational and moral equilibrium of peoples, and on the other the intensive cultivation of a spiritual climate, thanks to which these same peoples would spontaneously contribute to and cooperate in the miracle and the wonder of a bottomless Spiritual Unity.[104]

The practical form that these universalist ideas took was the organization, together with his American wife Eva Palmer, of the spectacular international festivals held at the ancient religious sanctuary of Delphi in 1927 and again in 1930. These went far beyond the ambitions of the arts festivals that have become familiar throughout

---

[103] Μήτηρ Θεού (Sikelianos 1965: iv. 9–41). Πάσχα των Ελλήνων (Sikelianos 1965: iv. 45–141). The title of the latter poem means more than simply 'Easter of the *Greeks*' as it is translated in the English editions of Politis' and Dimaras' histories. In context the juxtaposition of the Christian festival and the term Έλληνες invokes the medieval sense of that word, meaning 'pagans', as well as its modern (and also ancient) meaning of 'Greeks'. The understated oxymoronic figure of this title closely follows the practice of Palamas (see nn. 49 and 55 above). Christianity, which is notably lacking from Sikelianos' early poetry, makes its first appearance, after the death of his sister, in 1917, in the fourth of the 'Consciousness' poems: 'Consciousness of Faith' (Η συνείδηση της πίστης), and is still more evident in *Mother of God*.
[104] η ιερή λαχτάρα για την ίδρυση μιας Κοσμικά συνθετικής πνευματικής Εστίας, από την οποία . . . από τό 'να μέρος ν' απορρέει η διαφώτιση των όρων για μια γενική εκπαιδευτική και ηθική ισορρόπηση των λαών, κι από το άλλο η εντατική καλλιέργεια ενός κλίματος πνευματικού, χάρις στο οποίο αυτοί οι ίδιοι λαοί να συμμετέχουνε αυθόρμητα και να συμπράττουνε στο θαύμα και το χάρμα της απύθμενης Πνευματικής Ενότητας (Sikelianos 1965: i. 41).

Europe since the Second World War, or indeed those of the Cultural Centre at Delphi which was founded in the early 1980s. As well as staging ancient drama in its original setting, Sikelianos and his wife attempted to re-create the full religious atmosphere and associated spectacles of an ancient Greek festival: games were held in the stadium (although the participants were not naked as in ancient times), and an attempt was made to restore the ancient dramas to their context as part of a religious ritual, drawing on the Byzantine and modern folk traditions, as well as classical precedents, for music, dance, and costume.[105]

The financial failure of the festivals, and the ensuing separation from his wife, put a brake on Sikelianos' efforts to cross the boundary between art and life, and also drew to a close the first and longer phase of his career as a poet. Although he held true to his mystical and universalist ideas all his life, Sikelianos after 1930 adopted a new and distinct style in his poetry, one which belongs, albeit idiosyncratically, with the work of his younger contemporaries of that period. Discussion of Sikelianos' late poetry will be postponed until the next chapter.

Kostas Varnalis (1884–1974). Varnalis was in his earlier years a more faithful follower of Palamas than any other of this group of poets. He was born in Eastern Rumelia, in what is now Bulgaria, and studied at Athens University before becoming a schoolteacher by profession. The culmination of his early career was the long poem *Pilgrim* which he dashed off in the enthusiasm of a nine-month sabbatical visit to France in 1919, and which was published in the same year. In this poem the temporarily exiled poet celebrates his native land, its culture through the ages, and its living folk tradition. The synthesis of ancient, Byzantine, and modern folk culture that Palamas had pioneered, together with the more particular synthesis of pagan, Christian, and popular religious sentiments that Sikelianos had begun to articulate two years before, is evident in the following lines:

Πού πάμε; Ακούω πάσ' άνοιξη τ' αηδόνι
όλβια ζήση στο πάθος του να βρίσκει.

---

[105] The performance of *Prometheus Bound* at Delphi in 1927 was even filmed, an event alluded to in Karyotakis' poem 'Delphic Festival' (Δελφική Εορτή), in Karyotakis 1972: 108.

Δεν έχει χτες και σήμερα. Η Δωδώνη
κι ο 'Αγιος Τάφος βαθιά μας όρθιος μνήσκει.[106]

Where are we going? I hear each spring the nightingale
in his passion finding blessèd life.
There is no yesterday and no today. Dodona's oracle
and the Holy Sepulchre erect within us keeps its [sic] place.

And the stanza concludes with a resoundingly Palamic statement
(also echoed by Sikelianos in *Visionary*) that 'we are not beings, | we
are Ideas, that live in conflict'.[107]

The same visit to France, in the immediate aftermath of the First
World War, also produced in Varnalis a profound change of heart
that determined the course of the remainder of his long life. He
returned to Greece at the end of 1919 a committed Marxist, and
from that time onward turned his back on the world of non-material
'Ideas' and on the cultural unity of ancient and modern Greece,
setting himself the task of adapting his poetic expression to the task
of proclaiming materialism and the dictatorship of the proletariat.

Reading the poem *Pilgrim* with hindsight, it is possible to see some
continuity between the heady prophet of an idealism embodied in
the land and peasantry of Greece, and the morose banter alternating
with strident optimism that in his later works heralds the coming of
the new order. The earlier poem had already seen the poet subsumed in the mass of his people, with whose voice he claims the
authority to speak,[108] and already shows the lyrical and declamatory
powers that Varnalis would dedicate to his new purpose to be fully
developed in 1919.

Only three years after *Pilgrim*, in 1922, Varnalis published a long
work, *The Burning Light*.[109] This is revolutionary in form as well as in

---

[106] Sect. X, ll. 57–60 (Varnalis 1988: 59). The effect of synthesis is further heightened by the choice of vocabulary: όλβιος is a Homeric word revived only in very
limited contexts in the modern language, while πάθος in the same line means both
'suffering' and, with a capital letter, the Passion of Christ. In ll. 67–8 the ancient
language and the Christian doctrine of the Resurrection are linked to the 'resurrection' of nature in spring.

[107] 'Οχι όντα, | είμαστε Ιδέες, που ζούνε πολεμώντα (X. 63–4). Compare Sikelia-
nos' *Visionary* (sect. I, 1. 119): 'We are idols and shadows' (Είδωλα είμαστε και
ίσκιοι), which is, moreover, directly translated from Sophocles' *Ajax*.

[108] See in particular sect. V, ll. 30–2; sect. XI, ll. 15–16 (Varnalis 1988).

[109] Varnalis 1989. Varnalis made some revisions to the text of *The Burning Light* for
a second edition published in Athens in 1933 (the first edition had appeared in
Alexandria), and it is this later version which has been reprinted ever since.

content: of its three parts the first is in prose, while the second and third are in verse. The first part, in prose, is the 'Monologue of Momos'. Momos in ancient mythology was the personification of blame, and here represents the native wit of the common man. The 'monologue' in fact takes the form of a dialogue in the mind of Momos, in which he shares the stage with Prometheus, nailed to a rock by Zeus as a punishment for helping mankind, and with Jesus nailed to the Cross. The dialogue exploits the similarities between the pagan story of Prometheus and the Christian story of Jesus, in the manner of Palamas and Sikelianos. But while they, and indeed the earlier Varnalis, had sought a synthesis of the pagan and the Christian, the ancient and the modern, Varnalis in a witty display of logic in which his alter ego, Momos, holds all the cards, exposes the gods of both religions as nothing more than figments of the human imagination. What has the appearance of dialogue is in reality no such thing: neither the pagan gods nor the Christian God has any existence outside the mind of the human speaker, Momos. In this way the synthesis of the past becomes a way of *liberating* the present from its pervasive and (for Varnalis) pernicious legacy.[110] Man, in the guise of Momos, is left at the end of the first part of *The Burning Light* free to pursue his own destiny in the remainder of the work.

This he does not do immediately, however. The second part of *The Burning Light*, in verse this time, is a lyrical intermezzo in which the poet reverts to an idiom closer to that of his early work. Before the strident third part, Varnalis places four 'laments', as he terms them: lyrical, even nostalgic, farewells to the twin faiths of the classical scholar and the Orthodox Christian. Then, in the third part, comes the biting satire of 'Aristea and the Monkey', the former being a high-class prostitute who represents in turn the ruling class, the Church, and the kind of idealist concept of 'Art' that Varnalis had earlier shared with his contemporaries, the second a burlesque representation of the bourgeois intellectuals who defer to such institutions. This is followed by a section subtitled 'The Leader',

---

[110] Even this inversion of Palamas' goal does not represent a complete break with the poetics and thought-world of Palamas. The Gypsy, in the *Dodecalogue*, had followed a comparable course to Momos in casting down the idols on which contemporary Greek culture was based, and there are strong similarities of 'character' and outlook between Palamas' Gypsy and Varnalis' Momos. The essential difference between the two works lies in the final part of each, where for Palamas' vision of a 'third Olympos' Varnalis substitutes the coming of the new materialist order.

who is presented as crucially different from the old gods of the first part in that (like the poet in *Pilgrim*) he is not one but many, he exists as the voice of the masses. Again like the people in *Pilgrim*, the Leader lives in and for strife, and instead of the soothing comforts of religion he offers each man only a dagger. Finally, the People reply to the Leader, marching into the future and celebrating (all with capital letters) such abstractions as Man, Logos, Art, Imagination, Language, Existence, in response to the leader's call for 'Friendship of all Mankind'.

The Burning Light is the first fully fledged Marxist work of literature to be produced in Greek, and in its formal and stylistic variety, as well as in the variety of responses its different parts seek to arouse in the reader, it represents a fully conscious attempt to tackle problems of expression which have preoccupied politically committed writers throughout much of the twentieth century. Given an overriding materialist belief in social change, what role does an art-form with mainly bourgeois precedents have to play in the communist movement? What balance is to be struck between undermining the old order by satire and proclaiming the new in the form of propaganda? How far can poetry go in the direction of propaganda and still lay claim to the privileges of an art-form? Conversely, how far is it legitimate for the Marxist to mourn the passing of bourgeois culture and the values and intellectual horizons with which the writer would have grown up? And above all, how are the poetics of a non-communist culture to be adapted to the needs of a new society? These are all questions with which Varnalis was the first Greek writer to grapple fully; and the solutions he proposed in *The Burning Light* established the matrix within which later poets like Ritsos, Vrettakos, and Anagnostakis, together with prose-writers like Hatzis, Hakkas, and Alexandrou, would later have to operate in order to find solutions of their own.

The Burning Light was followed by a collection of poems, *Slaves Besieged* (1927), whose title deliberately alludes to the *Free Besieged* of Solomos (as well as, in all probability, to the novel *Slaves in their Chains* by Theotokis); and it is principally on these two collections, together with the satirical prose piece, *The True Apology of Socrates* (1933), that Varnalis' reputation rests today. Although he continued to write after 1927, he never abandoned traditional metres and, unlike his Marxist successor Yannis Ritsos, never experimented with the Modernist poetics of the generation who began to publish

after 1930. In his adherence (albeit an experimental one) to traditional forms and to the role of the poet as prophet with a 'message' to
convey, he became more and more isolated from later developments
of Greek poetry after 1930.[111]

Nikos Kazantzakis (1883–1957). Although older (if only by a few
months) than either Sikelianos or Varnalis, Kazantzakis was a relatively slow developer among this group of writers. Kazantzakis is
principally known today for the seven novels that he wrote late in
life, in the 1940s and 1950s, but these represent a late extension to a
literary career which until then had been primarily in drama and
poetry, and will be considered in their context in the next two
chapters.

Kazantzakis was a writer of truly vast ambitions. Critics both
favourably and negatively disposed have been wont to take at face
value statements which place him in the company of 'The great
teachers: Homer, Dante, Bergson',[112] or which claim such culturally
diverse mentors as Christ, Buddha, Lenin, Nietzsche, and a Greek
workman called George Zorbas. Kazantzakis' intellectual and spiritual debts to these and other teachers have been fully explored by
criticism, notably in a series of studies by Peter Bien;[113] but less
attention has been paid to placing Kazantzakis in his historical
context in *Greek* literature, which is after all where he belongs, for
all the mutual disdain that for much of his life kept him at a distance
from his fellow countrymen.

Kazantzakis' early writing, and his many recorded statements
about his writing, reveal an abiding passion for synthesis,[114] which
immediately places him in the company of Palamas. No less in line
with Palamas' views is Kazantzakis' enthusiasm for the 'peaks' of
world literature, and ambition to rival them with his own work. The
juxtaposition of the ideas of Nietzsche, aesthetic idealism, a strong
sense of the national culture with its roots in the folk tradition, and
an admiration for the potential vitality of the proletariat which at the

---

[111] For an excellent critical edition of *Slaves Besieged* see Varnalis 1990.
[112] Bien 1989a: 40.
[113] See, most recently, Bien 1989a; 1989b. See also Friar 1958; Prevelakis 1961.
[114] Well documented in Bien 1989a. See in particular the unpublished letter
describing the conclusion of the *Odyssey* as 'an organic synthesis (. . . synthesis, not
obliteration) of all antinomies' (p. 198), and Bien's more general statements of
Kazantzakis' intellectual method (1989a: 48, 62).

same time remains distinct from political commitment to socialism, are all common to Palamas' major poems of the first decade of the century, and to much of Kazantzakis' writing.

Kazantzakis of course adds further ingredients: Buddhism, Bergsonian vitalism, Leninist communism (he also flirted for a time with the fascism of Mussolini and Franco), the religious mysticism of Sikelianos. But this in a sense only raises the hurdles in a course already established by Palamas. Kazantzakis' synthesis will be yet grander, more universal, and less Hellenocentric than that of the sedentary Palamas.

The links between Kazantzakis and his contemporary Sikelianos are more direct and better documented. During 1914 and 1915 the two became close friends, and made long walking expeditions together on Mount Athos and in the Peloponnese. It seems to be from this time that Kazantzakis acquired the intense and always ambivalent interest in spirituality and asceticism which in the early 1920s led him to study Buddhism. There is no reason to doubt the contribution of Sikelianos' idiosyncratic, ebullient mysticism here, and it was during the visit to Mount Athos with Sikelianos that Kazantzakis first formulated a doctrine that he would enunciate again and again throughout his career: that the goal of human life is the 'transubstantiation of matter into spirit'.[115]

The intellectual backbone of this idea is generally taken to be Henri Bergson's theory of the *élan vital*. Since Kazantzakis had studied under Bergson in Paris in 1908, and is credited with introducing Bergson's philosophy into Greece in a lecture delivered in 1912, one need not doubt this. But the progression from matter to spirit is not far removed from the progression from the visible world to that of the invisible idea, which was central to the poetics of the French Symbolists, and plays a part, as we have seen, in the poetry of Palamas and many of his contemporaries, as well as of Sikelianos and of the young Varnalis. No less important than Bergson for Kazantzakis' formulation of his doctrine is Sikelianos, who at precisely the time of his friendship with Kazantzakis was beginning to elaborate on the theme of the soul's redemption or deliverance—a favourite Kazantzakian word from then on.[116]

---

[115] Cited in Friar 1958: xxiii–xxiv; cf. Bien 1989a: 40–1.

[116] Λύτρωση. See in particular 'Heracles' (Ηρακλής), ll. 103–11 (Sikelianos 1965: iii. 49), which must have been written at about this time (pub. 1915), and the slightly later first section of 'Consciousness of Faith': ll 86–7, 103–6 (first pub. 1917). A poem of 1937, 'The Suicide of Atzesivano, Disciple of Buddha' (H

Kazantzakis' career affords parallels, too, with that of Varnalis. Although Kazantzakis was never an orthodox Marxist, the abruptness of his volte-face, from one end of the ideological spectrum to the other, invites comparison with the contemporary Marxist poet. Varnalis' conversion from the uncompromising patriotic idealism of *Pilgrim* occurred in France in 1919; Kazantzakis, after a decade of nationalist fervour culminating in his work with Greek refugees from Bolshevism in the Caucasus, seems first to have proposed becoming a communist in Paris at the end of 1920,[117] and wrote his 'meta-communist' Credo, known in English as *The Saviours of God: Spiritual Exercises*, in 1922–3. Furthermore it was the figure of Lenin and the rhetoric of redemption of a corrupt world by violent action that appealed to both men, more than the economic philosophy of Marx and Engels; and in the work of both it is possible to see revolutionary communism in the context of other, more or less drastic, contemporary expressions of disenchantment with a social and national life that was falling progressively short of the grand ideals harboured by Palamas and his successors. Characteristically, in *The Saviours of God*, Kazantzakis describes his version of the dictatorship of the proletariat in terms which owe little to the economics of Marx but share much of the rhetoric and aspirations of Palamas and Varnalis:

Σήμερα ο Θεός είναι αργάτης, αγριεμένος από τον κάματο, από την οργή κι από την πείνα. Μυρίζει καπνό, κρασί κι ιδρώτα. Βλαστημάει, πεινάει, γεννάει παιδιά, δεν μπορεί να κοιμηθεί, φωνάζει στ' ανώγια και στα κατώγια της γης και φοβερίζει.[118]

Today God is a worker, made savage by toil, by rage and hunger. He smells of smoke, wine, and sweat. He swears, hungers, begets children, he cannot sleep, his cry rings out through the upper and the lower reaches of the earth with menace.

Kazantzakis' literary career began in 1906 with the publication of the novel *Serpent and Lily* and the writing of the first of many plays, *Day is Breaking* (performed 1907).[119] The novel draws heavily on

αυτοκτονία του Ατζεσιβάνο (μαθητή του Βούδα), Sikelianos 1965: v. 40) develops the same theme, although here it is likely that the Buddhist reference owes something in turn to Kazantzakis' immersion in Buddhism in the early 1920s.

[117] Bien 1989*a*: xix, 55.
[118] Kazantzakis 1971: 76.
[119] *Όφις και κρίνο. Ξημερώνει.*

the aesthetic excesses of the *fin de siècle* in much of the rest of Europe and failed to establish a place in the rapid development of Greek fiction at this time; while the play is heavily indebted to Ibsen, whose work had a considerable impact in Athens in the first years of the century. Then in 1909 came another play written for the stage, *The Master Builder*, whose title in Greek alludes in the first place not to Ibsen's play of the same name but to the narrative ballad in the Greek folk tradition about a wife walled up in the foundations of a bridge. In this play Kazantzakis took the first step in the direction of the folkloric realism whose vogue was then coming to an end, a step that after thirty years would find its sequel in his novels of the 1940s. But *The Master Builder* was rejected for performance, and most of Kazantzakis' subsequent dramas were not written for the stage.

Throughout the greater part of his life Kazantzakis supported himself by journalism, much of it describing his far-flung travels, and by translating several of the world's classics into Modern Greek. In 1920, after Venizelos' defeat in the election of November, he left Greece disillusioned, and with the exception of a period of nearly a decade before and during the Second World War, the greater part of his life from then on was spent abroad. His Credo, *Saviours of God*, was written in Vienna and Berlin in 1922–3, with some revision in 1928. But the work that, then and later, Kazantzakis regarded as his *magnum opus* was the epic poem entitled in Greek, simply and boldly, *Odyssey*, and in its English translation *The Odyssey: A Modern Sequel*.[120] The writing of this enormous work, through successive drafts, took fourteen years, from 1925 until its publication in 1938. Although its late publication places this work in the 1930s, in conception and execution it belongs to the 1920s, and in many respects looks back to the 'epic' syntheses of Palamas in the first decade of the century, rather than forward to any other development in Greek poetry after 1930.

Billed in the Prologue, in language and style which strongly echo the folk tradition, as a 'song', this *Odyssey* spans twenty-four books (like Homer's). With a carefully contrived (and declared) total number of 33,333 lines, of seventeen syllables each, Kazantzakis' *Odyssey* must surely lay claim to being the largest poem ever composed. Its language is a recondite treasury of the attested oral speech of the Greek regions, so comprehensive as to require a glossary for

---

[120] Kazantzakis 1960.

the benefit of the poem's urban readers, and its unusual metre represents a compromise between the fifteen-syllable metre of traditional Greek folk poetry and nineteenth-century attempts to adapt the hexameter of Homer to modern metrics.[121] (The same metre was also used by Kazantzakis in his translations into Modern Greek of the *Iliad* and the *Odyssey*, in collaboration with the classical scholar Yannis Kakridis.) The poem is narrative in form, interspersed with long speeches or inner monologues.

The story begins where Homer's *Odyssey* leaves off, with Odysseus finding his native Ithaca too small to hold him after all his adventures experienced on the way there, and turning his back on his responsibilities to his family and people, in order to set out for pastures new. His travels take him at first through a Greek landscape and a social world familiar as the Late Aegean Bronze Age as recreated in the contemporary restorations of the Palace of Minos at Knossos. At Sparta he pauses long enough to elope with Helen, before beginning a southward pilgrimage that will take him, by way of the archaeologically attested destruction of Knossos in Crete, through ancient Egypt to the source of the Nile. In Africa, on the equator, he leads his followers in building an ideal city which is no sooner built than it is destroyed by earthquake. But, at this midpoint of the epic, Kazantzakis' Odysseus has already realized the pointlessness of action, and for the remainder of the poem the scene moves inwards, to the consciousness of the hero as he continues an increasingly dreamlike progress southwards, to die many books later adrift on an iceberg headed, with some geographical licence, for the South Pole. In the monologue of the final books, all actions, all beliefs, and all opposing forces are brought together in the mind of the hero, who has by now experienced everything and is at last ready to face the void. In this way the poem achieves its final, dizzying synthesis, in which human experience only achieves its long-sought completion at the moment of being consumed in its opposite, absolute Nothingness.

For Kazantzakis after the completion of such an *Odyssey*, as for Sikelianos after the Delphic Festivals and for Varnalis after *Slaves*

[121] For an imitation of the hexameter which turns out to be a seventeen-syllable accented metre (though with a different accentual pattern from that of Kazantzakis' poem) see Th. Orfanidis, *Chios Enslaved*, 1858 (*Χίος δούλη*), extract in L. Politis 1980: 126–7.

Besieged, there was nowhere further to go in the same direction. The legacy of Palamas had finally ended in hypertrophy.

Karyotakis and the Later Symbolists.   The poets we have just been considering were all born within a few months of each other in the mid-1880s; and their most striking common characteristic is their unquestioning acceptance of the mantle of prophet. Each in his own way conceived of poetry as a medium with a *message*, and for this reason all of them (in the works considered in this chapter) became progressively isolated from the mainstream of twentieth-century poetics, which in Greece as elsewhere has tended to conform to the dictum of Archibald MacLeish (in 'Ars Poetica') that 'A poem should not mean/But be'. Palamas had managed to bestride even this dichotomy, since in addition to being a poet-prophet with a message he was also a Symbolist. Palamas' successors who were born in the following decade, the 1890s, made a decisive break with the vatic role and chose instead to look back beyond Palamas directly to the French Symbolists, on whom he and others of his generation had drawn for their poetics.

Traditionally this generation of poets is associated with the pessimism and disorientation experienced by the whole country after the failure of the 'Great Idea'. However, most of these poets had already established their characteristic themes and styles before 1922. If anything the new direction taken by the poetry of this generation (and also, interestingly, of Palamas himself after 1910) betrays a loss of interest in the 'Great Idea', which can perhaps be traced back as far as the 'bourgeois revolution' of Goudi in 1909. Even before military defeat ruled it out as a reality, territorial expansion had already begun to lose its hold on the imagination of poets as an ideal worthy of the highest aspirations.[122] Instead these poets, like the novelists of the same time who turned their attention to the inner state and experiences of the individual, turned to the legacy of French Symbolism and to the melancholy, introspective side of Palamas. For all of them the lives they find themselves leading

---

[122] The exceptions, of course, are Sikelianos, Varnalis, and Kazantzakis. But it is worth noting that the last two of these rebelled in extreme form against their former beliefs *before* the disaster of 1922: Varnalis in 1919 and Kazantzakis at the end of 1920. Sikelianos' position is more ambivalent, as he never underwent such an extreme conversion, but after 1917 the nationalist optimism of the four 'Consciousness' poems becomes redirected simultaneously inwards to religious experience and outwards to religious universals which transcend national boundaries.

have already been shorn of ideals, and the poet's task is to lament this loss, in this way either affirming the existence of such ideals in an unattainable, transcendent sphere, or scornfully reviling the society whose perverse banality has destroyed them.[123] The first solution is more or less present in the work of many of the minor writers of this generation, whose debt to Palamas is also the greatest. Kostas Ouranis (1890–1953) evokes the same landscape— the lagoon of Missolonghi—as Palamas had done in his *Sorrows of the Lagoon* (1912).[124] Napoleon Lapathiotis (1889–1944) repeats in a poem entitled 'De Profundis', published in 1939, the same onto-logical anxiety as Palamas' little flowers grouped beneath the shadow of a palm-tree (in the poem 'The Palm-Tree' of 1900):

Λυπήσου με, Θε μου, στο δρόμο που πήρα,
χωρίς ώς το τέλος να ξέρω πώς,
χωρίς να 'χω μάθει, με μια τέτοια μοίρα,
ποιο κρίμα με δένει και ποιος σκοπός.[125]

Pity me, my God, on the road I've taken,
without until its ending knowing how,
without discovering, with such a fate,
to what sin and what purpose I am bound.

Similar sentiments, and a similar attention to craftsmanship within traditional metres and rhyme-schemes, can be found in the work of many contemporaries in the 1920s and 1930s.[126] Not untypical of what one anthologist has called the *sotto voce* of this group is the rueful recognition of his own limitations by one of the more extrovert of their number, Romos Filyras (1888–1942), in a poem of the early 1930s:

ό, τι δεν είπα στη ζωή μου θα πασχίζω
σ' ένα μονότονο σκοπό ν' αθανατίζω.[127]

---

[123] An anthology of the poetry of this group, by the poet Manolis Anagnostakis, is indicatively entitled *Sotto Voce* (Χαμηλή φωνή, Anagnostakis 1990). For a re-evaluation of the work of these poets see Philokyprou 1991.

[124] Οι καημοί της λιμνοθάλασσας.

[125] Εκ Βαθέων (Korfis 1985: 128–9). Note that σκοπός also means 'tune', 'melody', which implies a degree of self-reference in the poem.

[126] For a full discussion of the work of this group of poets, which includes Tellos Agras (1899–1944), Mitsos Papanikolaou (1900–43), I. M. Panayotopoulos (1901–82), and Maria Polydouri (1902–30), as well as Filyras, Lapathiotis, and Karyotakis, see Philokyprou 1991.

[127] Korfis 1992: 43. (Note the recurrence of the term σκοπός, with its double reference to purpose and, by way of melody, to the poet's art, in this and the previous extract.) It is indicative that the poems of Filyras' later years, from which this (untitled) poem comes, remained uncollected until 1992.

all that in my life I never said I'll try
to make immortal to a dreary tune.

The second solution, to turn with biting sarcasm on the society
that has banished the ideals whose absence the poet also laments, is
the distinctive province of K.G. Karyotakis (1896–1928). During his
short life Karyotakis published three collections of poems, the last of
them characteristically entitled *Elegies and Satires* (1927).[128] Karyotakis' 'elegies' express something of the same existential anxiety as
we observed in Palamas' 'The Palm-Tree' and the poem of
Lapathiotis just quoted:

> Ποια θέληση θεού μάς κυβερνάει,
> ποια μοίρα τραγική κρατάει το νήμα
> των άδειων ημερών που τώρα ζούμε
> σαν από μια κακή, παλιά συνήθεια;[129]

> What will of god holds us in thrall,
> what tragic fate holds firm the thread
> of the empty days we live through now
> as though out of some old bad habit?

The collective plural is shared with Palamas, as is the question
articulated in the first two lines of this extract. The third and fourth
lines, however, introduce a new theme into Greek poetry: the boredom that we have seen the characters of Hatzopoulos' novel,
Autumn, struggling against. The struggle against fate and habit
will reappear in the poetry of the 1930s, particularly that of Seferis.
But the self-laceration with which this poem ends, and in particular
the idea that boredom and despair are not just the consequences of
the loss of ideals but actually a punishment for the 'original sin' of
losing them, hark back to Baudelaire. By the time the poem ends we
discover that the 'we' who speak are actually the dead, who find
themselves no wiser or better employed than the living, but to make
matters worse are ignored by them:

> Είναι κάτι φριχτές ανταποδόσεις.
> Είναι στον ουρανό μια σιδερένια,
> μια μεγάλη πυγμή, που δε συντρίβει,
> μα τιμωρεί, κι αδιάκοπα πιέζει.

---

[128] *Ελεγεία και σάτιρες* (Karyotakis 1972: 61–135).
[129] Karyotakis 1972: 88 (the poem has no title).

There are some terrifying retributions.
There is in heaven an iron-mailed,
a giant fist, that does not crush,
but metes out punishment with unrelenting pressure.

The speaker in this poem is recognizable as the type of the *poète maudit* whom we have already encountered in French Symbolism from Baudelaire onwards, and in some of the poetry of Palamas. The possibility that the universe is governed by actively hostile forces had been considered in Palamas' poem 'The Palm-Tree' referred to earlier, where the flowers in the shadow of the tree at one point see the branches above them as swords poised to destroy them. But whereas the morbid fears of Palamas' little flowers are balanced within a larger synthesis, Karyotakis in this poem (and many others) is categorical. Rejecting synthesis, he draws a single element of the legacy of Palamas to its logical—and finally self-destructive—conclusion.

By contrast with the *Elegies*, Karyotakis' *Satires* bring him closer also to Cavafy, with whom he shared a sceptical vantage-point towards all received values and opinions. But if an ironic detachment from those around them, and a self-mocking attitude to their own values and aspirations, are common to both Cavafy and Karyotakis, there is also an important difference between them. Where Cavafy is characteristically ironic, with a fundamental compassion for human weakness, Karyotakis' irony more commonly has an edge of sarcasm that betrays contempt for himself and his fellow men. An 'ode' which brilliantly parodies the language and versification of Andreas Kalvos pours scorn on the ideals of liberty and selfless nobility that Kalvos had exalted in his odes of a century earlier, dedicated to the struggle for Greek independence.[130] One of Karyotakis' most famous satires has the revealing title 'Ideal Suicides', and with dispassionate attention to detail reveals the preparations of the would-be suicides of the title as nothing but an empty gesture, since at the last moment they are 'convinced deep down they'll put it off'.[131] The poem is double-edged in a manner reminiscent of Cavafy, since it does not tell us whether this 'conviction' is followed by a change of heart. The 'ideal suicide' may be the one who

---

[130] Εις Ανδρέαν Κάλβον (Karyotakis 1972: 99–101).
[131] πως θ' αναβάλουν βέβαιοι κατά βάθος, from the poem Ιδανικοί αυτόχειρες, l. 20 (Karyotakis 1972: 114).

constantly puts off the deed. But (again reading the poem with the benefit of hindsight), it may be that the realization that even his own death will be no more than a bogus and self-deluding gesture is presented as the hallmark of the true, the 'ideal' suicide. As, once again, with Cavafy, even his own art is not immune to Karyotakis' satire. In an evident allusion to Palamas' claims for the power of poetry, which that poet had often described as 'song' or 'music', Karyotakis retorts with a terse four-line poem entitled 'Critique':

> Δεν είναι πια τραγούδι αυτό, δεν είναι αχός
> ανθρώπινος. Ακούγεται να φτάνει
> σαν τελευταία κραυγή, στα βάθη της νυχτός,
> κάποιου πόχει πεθάνει.[132]

> This isn't a song any more, it is no human
> noise. Its sound arrives
> as though it were the final cry, at dead of night,
> of someone who has died.

Karyotakis shot himself, in the provincial town of Preveza, on 21 July 1928. This act not only completed, in a spectacular fashion, the identification between the artist and his art that had been a goal of most of his older contemporaries; it also, more schematically, represents an extreme instance of the poetic cul-de-sac into which we have seen the legacy of Palamas leading his successors in the late 1920s.

[132] Κριτική, from *Elegies* (Karyotakis 1972: 77).

3. *In Search of a New National Identity 1929–1949*

SINCE the founding of the Greek state, political and cultural life in Greece had often been riven by sharply polarized divisions. But until the collapse of the irredentist dream in 1922 these divisions had been about means rather than about ends. The seeds of a more fundamental, and traumatic, division were sown in the National Schism of 1915–17, when the opposing views of King Constantine I and his prime minister, Venizelos, over Greece's entry into the First World War also brought to the surface deeper divisions about the kind of nation that Greece was or should be, and about how it ought to be governed. The ensuing instability of the monarchy throughout the period covered by this chapter is only a symptom of a more fundamental disunity, this time about ends rather than means, that continued well beyond the end of the Second World War, up to the early 1970s.

Put at its simplest, this was the period when the fundamental split in Greek society and intellectual life changed character, so as to reflect the main political split throughout the developed world in the twentieth century, into Left and Right. The reasons for this shift, however, were as much internal to Greek politics and society as they were the consequence of international developments. The collapse of the 'Great Idea' necessitated a complete rethink of what it meant to be a Greek and a citizen of the Greek state, and at the same time brought with it political instability and unprecedented economic and social difficulties over the assimilation of refugees. By the same period, as we saw in the last chapter, socialist ideas had been gaining ground in Greece, and 1918 had seen the foundation of the Socialist Labour Party, which two years after the disaster of 1922 changed its name to Communist Party of Greece (KKE). From that time on, the possibility of social reorganization along the lines established in Russia after the 1917 Revolution, whether as an aim to be promoted or as a fate to be feared, was never far from the political horizon.

Economically, as recent studies have begun to show,[1] Greece survived the international slump of the early 1930s with considerable success, adapting quickly to the requirements of a self-sufficient economy after the collapse of the international money markets. This shift from an internationalist economic perspective in the late 1920s to a workable assessment of Greece's potential to 'go it alone' by the mid-1930s, as we shall see later, is closely shadowed by the changing perspective of literary writers during the same period. Politically, however, in Greece as in much of the rest of Europe, the split into Left and Right led to extremes on both sides, and finally to fragmentation. In 1936, as also later in 1967, an authoritarian government of the Right compelled obedience in the name of an ill-defined nationalism, and justified its actions by invoking Communism as a threat to the integrity of the nation. The Greek Communist Party has throughout its existence been scarcely less authoritarian either in its own internal organization or in its political programme; but its intellectual basis has always been relatively clear and consistent. The middle ground between these extremes (to which, in Greece as elsewhere, such labels as 'liberalism', 'humanism', and 'pluralism' have often been attached) failed politically in the 1930s, as again in the 1960s, largely because the divisions ran so deep that no political party, however moderate or broadly based, could for long command the loyalty of all sections of society, or even of its own members. This failure led, in the 1930s, as again in the late 1960s, to right-wing military rule, while in the 1940s the same liberal forces failed, at the end of the Second World War, to prevent polarization between Left and Right leading to outright civil war.

The main events which define the history of the period are these. The government of Venizelos, restored in 1928, failed to win an outright majority in the election of 1932, thus ushering in a renewed period of political instability which culminated in the return of the monarchy (after a rigged ballot) in 1935 and the slide into military rule under the premiership of Ioannis Metaxas, who assumed dictatorial powers on 4 August 1936. Metaxas' rule was in many respects modelled on that of Mussolini and Hitler, but ill-judged Italian aggression in 1940 had the effect of bringing Greece into the Second World War on the Allied side. Metaxas' famous one-word reply to an Italian

---

[1] This subject and the relevant bibliography are well covered by Mazower 1991. See also (in Greek): Liakos 1993.

ultimatum, 'No', briefly united all Greeks in defence of their country, and Greek forces successfully beat back the Italian invaders into Albania during the winter of 1940-1. Then followed Hitler's invasion of Greece in the spring of 1941 and the start of the Axis occupation of the country which lasted until October 1944.

Metaxas had already died before Hitler invaded; the Greek government was hastily evacuated via Crete to Egypt, and diplomatic exchanges during the war, concerning the future of the country, were carried on in Cairo and London. In the meantime, by 1943, most of the active resistance to the Axis occupiers, concentrated in the mountains of central Greece, was in the hands of the political party whose leadership, since it had been driven underground by Metaxas and was therefore not included in the post-Metaxas government in exile, had had perforce to stay at home: namely the Communists. Rivalry between resistance groups inside Greece erupted into violence as early as 1943; in 1944 the return of the government from its exile in Egypt, coupled with British pressure to uphold the monarchy, brought divisions about the future government of Greece to a head. Civil war erupted in the streets of Athens in December 1944. After the failure of a series of compromises, and the return of King George in September 1946, the final round of the civil war was fought in the mountains of mainland Greece between 1947 and 1949.

One might suppose from all this that the literature produced under these conditions would be highly political. In fact, most of it is not, at least in the narrow sense; but the common denominator underlying almost all of the literary production discussed in this chapter is undoubtedly the quest for a new conceptual order. Indeed, the political developments just outlined could be described as the external, large-scale manifestations of the same underlying quest. Only a small number of writers during this period were, for all or part of their careers, committed to the Left. The opposite extreme, represented politically by the quasi-fascism of Metaxas, finds no literary adherents. The majority of writers can be placed at various (often shifting) points along the intermediate spectrum. But to approach the literature of a period through the perceived political beliefs of writers, as has been done in one serious study of the decade of the 1930s,[2] is to adopt far too crude an approach. More fundamentally,

---

[2] Tsakonas 1989.

writers on the Left already possessed a more or less coherent conceptual framework against which to interpret the world around them; their task was to relate the world that they saw to the framework. On the other hand, all those writers who were not *committed* to the Left, and who represented the great majority for most of this period, faced the larger task of creating a new conceptual framework that would be capable of replacing the old one that had rested on the 'Great Idea', and capable at the same time of offering a fully modern alternative to the Marxist model. It is in this context that the exuberant variety of literary experiment that characterizes the decade of the 1930s in Greece, and that has proved formative for later generations as well, can best be understood.

A MANIFESTO FOR A NEW AGE: THEOTOKAS' *FREE SPIRIT*

Just over a year after the suicide of Karyotakis, a young graduate of the Athens University Law School published (under a pseudonym) a pamphlet entitled *Free Spirit*.[3] The author turned out to be Yorgos Theotokas (1905–66), who went on to establish himself during the following three decades as one of the leading novelists and playwrights of the self-styled 'generation of the thirties'. This term was first coined by the group of innovative poets and novelists who collaborated to produce the literary periodical *Ta Nea Grammata* (1935–44), but has since been extended to cover almost all the diverse forms of literary experiment that began during this decade. Although none of the new departures that were to mark the decade had yet been clearly taken, and only a few of the writers who were to prove influential later were as yet known to Theotokas, none the less in hindsight *Free Spirit* can be seen as a manifesto for much of what actually followed.

The tone of *Free Spirit* is youthful and enthusiastic; the judgements it offers are sweeping and uncompromising. In this pamphlet Theotokas lines up the reasons for the failure, as he sees it, of all Greek literature during the past century: provincialism and isolation from Europe; the absence in Greece of a liberal philosophical tradition; and the polarization of ideologies in his own time. More specifically he attacks the fiction of the previous fifty years for its emphasis on the community rather than on the individual; for what

---

[3] Theotokas 1973, originally published under the pseudonym Orestes Digenes.

he sees as its slavish realism; and for its narrowly local focus,[4] while in poetry he lumps together Cavafy and Karyotakis, regarding the work of both as dead ends. Interspersed with this radical clearing of the ground, Theotokas offers a number of prescriptions for the future. There is nothing wrong, he insists, with writers learning aspects of their craft and adapting ideas from the rest of Europe; what is wrong is that they have given nothing back. Where, in an earlier period of innovation, Psycharis had linked a burgeoning national literature with the imperatives of an expanding nation state, Theotokas implies instead an analogy with diplomacy: 'A literature acquires international significance when it begins to exert an influence, without of course ever ceasing to be influenced itself.'[5]

A repeated plea in the essay is for intellectual freedom. Theotokas puts forward a reasoned proposal for a new intellectual approach to the problems of the age; and this, as was argued in the previous section, did indeed turn out to be a vital ingredient of much of the literature that followed. His standpoint is indicated succinctly by one of the characters in his first novel *Argo*: 'All theories contain a dose of truth.'[6] In the field of fiction, Theotokas calls for a new urban novel capable of reflecting the complexity, the technological developments, and the international dimension of contemporary city life—a programme which, as we shall see, was never fully effected during his lifetime. In literature generally, *Free Spirit* claims a role for art and the artist which is strongly imbued with the spirit of nineteenth-century Romanticism. The artist is a favoured being, with privileged access to a daemonic force whose power he must control by virtue of his art, in order not to be destroyed by it. Higher than economic or social utility stands the goal of artistic creativity.[7] Essentially the inheritance of the generation of Palamas and Cavafy, although the young Theotokas would probably not have been willing to admit it, this view of the nature of art and the role of the artist

---

[4] See esp. Theotokas 1973: 53. This is how Theotokas interprets the problematic and by this time well-established term ηθογραφία, which he invariably uses pejoratively. The third chapter of *Free Spirit* is entitled Η ηθογραφία.

[5] Μια λογοτεχνία αποχτά διεθνή σημασία όταν αρχίσει και να επιδρά, χωρίς βέβαια να πάψει ποτέ να επιδράται (Theotokas 1973: 37).

[6] Όλες οι θεωρίες περιέχουν μια δόση αλήθειας (Theotokas n. d. (1): i. 312).

[7] The terms δαιμόνιο, δημιουργία, τέχνη recur frequently throughout *Free Spirit* and also in Theotokas' fiction, of which a central theme is the relation between the artist and society.

remains central to most Greek writing throughout the period covered by this chapter.

THE NEW FICTION (1929–1936)

Although no area of literature escapes censure in *Free Spirit*, the main thrust of Theotokas' 1929 manifesto was directed towards the creation of a new type of fiction. The years between Venizelos' return to power in 1928 and the beginning of the Metaxas dictatorship in 1936 saw the first appearance in print of more than a dozen novelists and short-story writers, and a productivity in these genres unmatched in earlier years. Few, if any, of these writers consciously followed Theotokas' prescriptions; but all, in their different ways, seem to have risen to the same challenge, to 'make it new', as he had urged in his manifesto.

The writers who published a first novel during this period can be divided into three groups. At the heart of each group is a coterie of individuals who worked closely together and shared common aims, aims which were often picked up and adapted, or even shared independently, by other writers beyond the confines of the group. The first of these to appear was the so-called 'Aeolian School' of novelists, all of whom had been directly involved in the violent uprooting of the Greek population of Anatolia in 1922, and which saw fiction as a way of communicating and preserving experiences of historical significance. The second group, some of whom had also been displaced from Anatolia, shared the broadly realist aims of the first, but made a point of looking forward to the future rather than back to the past. Some of this group were associated with the periodical *Ta Nea Grammata*, founded in 1935, and their novels and stories share a predominantly urban and contemporary setting. Many deal, explicitly or implicitly, with social and/or ideological issues and most carry a heavy burden of ideas. Finally, in sharp distinction to both of these groups, are the writers centred upon Thessaloniki and the periodical *Makedonikes Imeres*, founded in 1932. These writers turned their backs on the direct representation of reality, and gave nuances of their own to the introspective experiments that had characterized the Modernism of the previous decade in other parts of Europe.

Fiction as Testimony: The 'Aeolian School'.   The desire to preserve and perpetuate a personal recollection of events whose significance touches the entire nation has surfaced at crucial times of Greek history. In the wake of the war of independence in the 1820s, many leading participants wrote personal 'memoirs' of their experiences. The factual nature and historical content of these narratives has traditionally placed them outside the literary canon (with the interesting exception of the *Memoirs* of Makriyannis which, as we shall see in Chapter 6, were considered to be 'literary' because they were written in the spoken language). However, in Chapter 2 we noticed some convergence between this extra-literary genre and fiction in two works, generally considered to be novels, of the 1870s. In a comparable way, beginning as late as the mid-1960s, we find a systematic drive to record and publish oral testimonies of ordinary people caught up in two world wars and in the Asia Minor débâcle of the early 1920s.[8] In the immediate aftermath of these events, however, the preservation of such testimonies fell almost exclusively to literary writers.

The three writers who make up this group all made their earliest appearance in print with narratives based very closely on events; and all of these débuts actually pre-date Theotokas' manifesto for a new generation. However, this group only fully established itself at national level with the publication of *A Prisoner's Story* by Stratis Doukas (published in 1929, the same year as *Free Spirit*), and with the expanded editions, published in Athens, of two novels whose earliest versions had first been published in 1923–4 in a provincial periodical in Mytilini: *Life in the Tomb* by Stratis Myrivilis (1930) and *Number 31328* by Ilias Venezis (1931).

Doukas and Venezis were themselves refugees from Ayvali, modern Aivalik on the west coast of Turkey; Myrivilis was a native of Lesvos (Mytilini), part of Greece since 1912 but only a few sea-miles distant. Together with Fotis Kondoglou, also from Ayvali, they lived and wrote during the remainder of the 1920s in Mytilini.[9] Their common geographical origin in the north-eastern Aegean earned for all four of them the sobriquet, the 'Aeolian School'. Although the commitment of the first three to the raw realism of actual experience in their early writings sharply distinguishes them from the escapism of Kondoglou, they further share with him a reverence for the traditions of Greek rural life, and a corresponding resistance to the

---

[8] See Papademetriou 1975–9; Mourelos 1980–2; Hatzipateras and Fafaliou 1988. See further: Sokolis 1993.

[9] On Kondoglou see Ch. 2.

new, relatively westernized urban culture in which they found themselves after 1930. In this way, this group is sharply distinguished from the 'urban realists' that make up the second group.

The distinct achievement of *A Prisoner's Story* by Stratis Doukas (1895–1983) is the complete effacement of its author (who never again achieved the success of this book).[10] Only a brief epilogue supplies the information that Doukas, visiting a refugee settlement in northern Greece in 1928, had heard of an escapee from Turkey who had survived by pretending to be a Turk, and persuaded him to tell his story. This is the story that Doukas retells, in the first person. A footnote to the 1980 edition adds the further curious detail that, for greater immediacy, Doukas *dictated* the story orally, from his own *written* notes of the original oral testimony that he had heard! But the result is not quite oral history. Doukas does not reproduce the linguistic idiom of his informant (which, he tells us, was heavily influenced by Turkish) and on at least one occasion he alters the story for reasons which, he archly tells us, his informant 'wouldn't have understood'.[11]

In the resulting brief, matter-of-fact narrative, events are apparently allowed to speak for themselves. Although the end of the story is never in doubt, the constant terror of the fugitive that he might betray his alien race and religion by talking in his sleep or not knowing how to behave in a mosque, is powerfully communicated to the reader. Through its artful avoidance of any overtly literary technique, *A Prisoner's Story* aspires to speak with the anonymous voice of a people, and by the 1950s had come to acquire the status of an exemplary text. In the 1930s, however, its exemplary status was at first restricted to the 'Aeolian School' from which it came.

A similar aim, to 'tell it as it really was', is apparent in the earliest fiction of Stratis Myrivilis (pseudonym of Efstratios Stamatopoulos, 1892–1969). A native of Lesvos, Myrivilis volunteered for service in the Balkan wars of 1912–13, again on the Macedonian front in the

[10] Doukas 1980. He was the author of several other books and, interestingly, one of the editors of the periodical *To Trito Mati*, associated with the third group of prose-writers of the 1930s (see Korfis 1988).
[11] Doukas 1980: 67. In Doukas' narrative, the narrator's friend, who also tries to survive by disguising himself as a Turk, is found out and hanged (presumably in order to intensify the considerable sense of threat to the narrator which the text re-creates). However, in his epilogue Doukas relates how he read the finished version back to his original informant, together with his friend who in reality had also escaped and was somewhat offended to hear of his fictional fate.

First World War, and in Anatolia in the campaign of 1921–2. His first short stories, published in Mytilini as early as 1913, draw upon the 'folkloric realism' whose day was then coming to an end, and particularly on the vivid portrayal of brutality in Karkavitsas' *The Beggar* and in the early stories of Theotokis. Myrivilis directs the apparently dispassionate eye of the folklorist, not towards the traditional life of a settled community, but towards the communities of soldiers who fought in the campaigns that he himself lived through. His own diary of his experiences in Macedonia in 1917–18 formed the basis of the first version of his novel *Life in the Tomb*, published in Lesvos in 1924.[12] Rewritten and much expanded, the novel first attracted critical attention when it appeared in Athens in 1930, a year after *A Prisoner's Story* by Doukas, and ever since has been one of the top best sellers in Greek fiction.[13]

Life in the Tomb, like Myrivilis' early stories, gives a new extension to the tradition of 'folkloric realism' devoted to the life of small communities, that had developed in the 1880s and 1890s. Its episodic structure also harks back to the preferred form of the short story that dominated at that period, as a rich cast of diverse characters is brought to life and then, for the most part, either forgotten or relegated to the background. But, although based on real experience, *Life in the Tomb* is no more the unmediated transcription of events than is Doukas' book. Myrivilis' own experiences and thoughts are distanced by being presented as the diary of a fictional sergeant; and the book (even in its earliest version) begins with the discovery, after the war, of the notebooks of this sergeant who, we learn, had been accidentally killed by his own side at the start of the decisive battle in 1918.

In this way the reader knows from the beginning that the character whose thoughts he is reading is doomed, and that as the book nears its end so does the life in which he is privileged to share. This structural device adds greatly to the central discovery that the narrator makes in the course of his diaries: that once the superficial trappings of civilization have been stripped away—and in particular the bombast of wartime propaganda and conventional notions of

---

[12] This version, inaccessible for many years, has been reprinted (Myrivilis 1991).

[13] For the first edition of the expanded text, see Myrivilis 1993; Myrivilis introduced many changes, between this edition and the now standard seventh edition, regularly reprinted (Myrivilis 1955), on which see Boudouris 1983; Lykourgou 1993.

heroism—life is a matter of flesh and blood, not of ideas or metaphysics:

Ο πόνος του κορμιού! Δεν υπάρχει τίποτ' άλλο που να κάνει πιο δυστυχισμένη την ψυχή και το πνέμα. 'Ολ' αυτά είνε κορμί. Και σαν πονά το κορμί όλα πάνε κατά διαβόλου. Ο κόσμος είνε ωραίος, κι ο άθρωπος είνε καλόκαρδος, μεγαλόψυχος ή ευτυχισμένος, κι όλα τα καλά πράματα έχουν αξία, μονάχα σαν είνε γερό το κορμί. Η πλάση υπάρχει μόνο μέσο του κορμιού.[14]

Bodily pain! Nothing else can cause so much misery to the soul and the spirit. The body is all. And when the body is in pain everything goes to the devil. The world is beautiful, man is kind-hearted, generous, or happy, and all good things have value, only while the body is sound. The universe exists only through the body.

Moreover, the narrator only comes to recognize the full potency of life as a force within himself and others, through the presence of death; and this revelation takes many forms: in the orgiastic 'return to nature' of the chapter 'In the Forest'; in the narrator's rapturous discovery of a single poppy flowering on the rim of his trench; in the tenderness of his feelings for the fiancée back in Lesvos for whom he is notionally writing these diaries. *Life in the Tomb* has usually been read as an 'anti-war' book, but paradoxically it is the experience of war which brings the narrator, and vicariously the reader too, to this revelation which is presented in intensely positive terms. This is the significance of the book's title, a quotation from the Orthodox liturgical lamentations for Good Friday, in which Christ is represented as the 'life' laid in the tomb in order to be resurrected. Myrivilis' novel, no less than the Good Friday hymn, glorifies life. But the life that is celebrated in Myrivilis' novel is neither spiritual nor immortal; by contrast it is the intense experience of the flesh, driven by and responding to powerful natural forces.

In *Life in the Tomb*, there is a great difference between the passionate introspection of the narrator, whose discoveries about his own nature and the nature of the war in which he is engaged go far beyond realistic 'testimony', and the matter-of-fact detachment

[14] Myrivilis 1993: 222. In addition to minor linguistic alterations, the 1955 edition adds ερωτεμένος before ευτυχισμένος, and an entirely new sentence to conclude the paragraph: 'The equilibrium of the former depends on the equilibrium of the latter' (Η ισορροπία της κρατιέται από την ισορροπία του), Myrivilis 1955: 168.

with which the actions and the fates of all of the other characters are seen. The gulf separating these two distinct literary techniques is bridged by the novel's language, which draws seemingly inexhaustibly on the full resources of the vernacular. The result is linguistically much richer than the direct speech of the characters which it also includes, and to that extent is not a 'realistic' representation of the language of the trenches; nor does it necessarily describe things or experiences with especial precision. But the exuberance of the book's language (particularly in the edition of 1930) produces a similar effect to the artful re-creation of oral testimony by Doukas in *A Prisoner's Story*: observer and observed are subsumed by a linguistic form which seems to give voice to the raw experience of events.

Myrivilis, along with the other members of the 'Aeolian School', moved to Athens at the end of the 1920s, and it was there, for the first time in direct contact with a wider circle of his contemporaries, that he wrote and published his second novel, *The Schoolmistress with the Golden Eyes* (1933).[15] Despite its disarming title and outwardly idyllic setting in peacetime Lesvos, this novel too is a testimony to the nature and in particular to the after-effects of war and violence. Its fictional nature and structure are more evident than was the case with *Life in the Tomb*, but in this novel too, Myrivilis combines a fictional exploration of the themes of violence and sexuality with a powerful urge to testify to the experience of war and its crippling aftermath, in a way that transcends the purely individual lives of the characters he creates.

The third member of this group of novelists is Elias Venezis (pseudonym of E. Mellos, 1904–73). Venezis' first novel, *Number 31328*, in its earliest version was published in Mytilini in serial form in 1924, following on immediately from the first version of Myrivilis' *Life in the Tomb*. It won widespread acclaim, again like Myrivilis' novel, only with its publication in expanded form in Athens in 1931. Like Myrivilis, Venezis in this novel tells his own story; like Doukas, he tells of the fate of the Anatolian Greeks in the months following the disaster of August and September 1922, with a minimum of overt literary or fictional technique.

Venezis was only 18 at the time of these events. Rounded up by the victorious Turks, the young men of his town were force-marched

---

[15] Myrivilis 1956.

into the interior of Anatolia to work in labour camps. Thousands were killed in random acts of violence, or in reprisal for atrocities that had often been committed by others (it was only by accident that Venezis himself was spared this fate); many more died as a result of the conditions they had to endure. The single aim for those who survived long enough was to achieve the protection afforded by a Red Cross number.

Prisoners with numbers had to be accounted for, and, once agreement for the compulsory exchange of populations was reached in January 1923, would be shipped to Greece under the supervision of the Red Cross. It is a measure of the effects of such experiences on the human individual that the narrator of the story, like many thousands of others, should have found such relief in exchanging his identity for the inhuman anonymity of the number that gives the book its title.

Like Doukas and Myrivilis, Venezis in his own way seeks literary means to enable facts to speak for themselves.[16] And like them, he also believed that the experiences he had lived through had betrayed how shallow were the foundations of 'civilization' as he and his contemporaries knew it. As also for Myrivilis, included in this indictment were most inherited abstract ideas; and Venezis, in the preface to the second edition of *Number 31328*, written in 1945, echoes Myrivilis' narrator in *Life in the Tomb* on the primacy of physical pain:

Έχουν να λένε πως κανένας πόνος δεν μπορεί να είναι ισοδύναμος με τον ηθικό πόνο. Αυτά τα λένε οι σοφοί και τα βιβλία. Όμως αν βγεις στα τρίστρατα και ρωτήσεις τους μάρτυρες, αυτούς που τα κορμιά τους βασανίστηκαν ενώ πάνω τους σαλάγιζε ο θάνατος... θα μάθεις πως τίποτα, τίποτα δεν υπάρχει πιο βαθύ και πιο ιερό από ένα σώμα που βασανίζεται.

Το βιβλίο τούτο είναι ένα αφιέρωμα σ' αυτόν τον πόνο.[17]

There are those who say that no suffering can equal moral suffering. That's what wise men and books tell you. But if you go out on the highways and byways and ask the witnesses [the Greek word also means 'martyrs'], the people whose bodies have been tortured while death thundered over them

---

[16] Like them he also made a number of revisions to the text of the book in subsequent editions up to the 1950s. The second edition of 1945 contains a new prologue, and by the time of the fifth edition (Venezis n.d.), chapter-headings in the form of quotations from the Psalms have been silently added. See also, in English, Karanikas 1969.

[17] Repr. in Venezis n.d.: 13.

... you'll find out that nothing, nothing exists more profound and more holy than a body in pain.
This book is dedicated to that suffering.

The reality that Venezis had glimpsed also exposed the limitations and in particular the artificiality of his chosen medium, literature. A new form of expression was required; and in Venezis' case this was achieved in part by the same sort of unadorned directness of narrative that had been perfected by Doukas, but also by a constant thread of ironic juxtaposition between the raw reality he describes and the established conventions and clichés of literature. The famous opening sentence of the novel (which anticipates the use of the same device in English by Raymond Chandler) well illustrates this:

1922. Η Ανατολή γλυκύτατη πάντα—για σονέτο, κάτι τέτοιο.[18]

1922. The East was as sweet as ever—right for a sonnet, that sort of thing.

Like Myrivilis, Venezis also went on to write a second novel dealing with the aftermath of these events, in which established fictional conventions are more overtly present. This was ironically entitled *Tranquillity*, and tells of the settlement of refugees from Anatolia in Attica, and the hostility they encountered from the native population. But *Tranquillity* was not published until 1939.[19]

Urban Realism. The group of writers to be introduced under this heading shared with the previous one a desire to capture the essence of the historical moment at which they lived. Urban these writers certainly were, both in background and, in later life, by choice; and their fiction sets out to explore, by means of narrative, the changes that were taking place in urban society by the early 1930s. The principal setting for the novels and stories of this group is a city or large town, usually Athens, but part of the action, in many cases, also takes place in foreign settings. All in various ways can be considered 'social novels', whether lamenting the decline of a traditional class or inveighing against its survival. Adjustment in the wake of the Asia Minor disaster, often reflected in the changing fortunes of a family over a period of time, is an ever-present theme, but

---

[18] Venezis n.d.: 17. Compare Raymond Chandler, 'Pearls are a Nuisance': 'It was a nice late April morning, if you care for that sort of thing.'
[19] See Venezis 1971.

presented in a very different way from the raw directness sought by the writers of the first group. In all these works of fiction, the time of the main action is close to, if not identical with, the time of writing; and all of their writers comment, more or less explicitly, on the recent and current changes in Greek urban life and mores.[20] To these ends they worked (in most cases throughout their careers) within the confines of realist fiction.

Indeed, technically they are on the whole less innovative than the first group, in that the innovations of their work lie more in their choice of subject-matter and in their explicit concern to air ideological issues in their fiction, than in the way in which they exploited the resources of language and literary convention. Despite this, they do not seem to have regarded themselves as realists. The work of the true creative artist, Theotokas had proclaimed in *Free Spirit*, 'is not an objective observation of external conditions, an arid reproduction of forms and a setting out of facts, as the Greek realists have believed literature to be'.[21] His fellow novelist Angelos Terzakis, in an essay on realism in 1934, was much more radical in theory than either he or Theotokas ever was in practice, declaring: ' "Reality" is an invention of the nineteenth century.'[22] Of this group only Kosmas Politis followed through the implications of such statements, in seeking to represent inner states of mind which go beyond the experience of 'reality' that a reader might be expected to share. In this respect Politis represents a special case, with a foot in the non-realist camp as well.

The resistance of this group to what they saw as the limitations of realism can be explained by the anxiety of these writers, clearly

---

[20] Under this heading can be grouped the first novels of Kosmas Politis: *Lemon Grove*, 1930 (*Λεμονοδάσος*); Angelos Terzakis: *Prisoners*, 1932 (*Δεσμῶτες*); M. Karagatsis: *Colonel Lyapkin*, 1933 (*Ο συνταγματάρχης Λιάπκιν*); Theotokas himself (*Argo*, 1933/36); Thanasis Petsalis: the trilogy *Strong and Weak Generations*, 1933–5 (*Γερές και αδύναμες γενεές*); Loukis Akritas: *Young Man with Excellent Credentials*, 1935 (*Νέος με καλάς συστάσεις*); and of the women writers Elli Alexiou: *Third Christian School for Girls*, 1934 (*Τρίτον Χριστιανικόν Παρθεναγωγείον*); Lilika Nakou (on whom see, in English, Tannen 1983): *Delinquents*, 1935 (*Παραστρατημένοι*); and Tatiana Stavrou: *The First Roots*, 1936 (*Οι πρώτες ρίζες*). To this sizeable collection of first novels should be added the short stories and later novels of the same writers up to the first years of the Metaxas dictatorship, and the continuing production of Thrasos Kastanakis, whose career, as we saw in Ch. 2, began in the previous decade. See further: Sokolis 1993.

[21] Theotokas 1973: 43.

[22] Cited in Vitti 1979: 237.

articulated by Theotokas in *Free Spirit*, to distance themselves from their predecessors. The folkloric realism of an earlier generation (which in some respects, as we saw, actually transcended the conventions of realism in remarkable ways) they dismissed as 'photographic'; while the unwary reader of *Free Spirit* might never have suspected the existence of the urban novels described in the previous chapter.[23] One may suspect that the real objection to Papadiamandis and Xenopoulos, on the part of this group of writers, lay not so much in their realism as in the fact that they wrote successfully for a wide readership. The writers of this group claimed a higher purpose, and were mostly indifferent to the lure of the market-place.

Something of the range, and also of the limitations, of this group can be seen in Theotokas' first novel, and in the three novels of M. Karagatsis (pseudonym of Dimitrios Rodopoulos, 1909–60), published during the 1930s. *Argo* by Theotokas was planned as an ambitious project, in the three-volume format that had been common in much of Europe (although not in Greece) during the nineteenth century. In the event, only the generously constructed first volume (published in 1933) keeps to this grand, if somewhat anachronistic programme. By contrast with the leisurely sweep of the prologue to the first volume, in which the fortunes of a contemporary Athenian family are linked through history and legend with the last days of the Byzantine empire, the pace in the shorter second volume becomes breathless, the narrative more succinct, and the novel reaches its conclusion within the much reduced compass of this second volume (published in 1936).[24]

Argo has no central character, but a focus is given to this panorama of Athenian life in the 1920s by the three brothers Notaras, whose contrasting fates invite comparison with Dostoevsky's *Brothers Karamazov*, as well as by the students' union whose mythological name gives the novel its title. Among the large cast of characters whose lives intertwine in the novel, two stand out: the hardbitten but fundamentally idealistic socialist politician Pavlos Skinas, whose dreams of power are shattered by the intrusion of

---

[23] Indeed, the veteran Grigorios Xenopoulos commented huffily on *Free Spirit*, 'I do not believe that any worthwhile writer will be expunged from the book of the living, because he fails to win the recognition of Orestes Digenes [Theotokas' pseudonym in this essay]' (cited in Theotokas 1973: 77).

[24] Theotokas n.d. (I). See (in English) Doulis 1975; Tziovas 1988*a*.

real history into the story as Venizelos is returned to office; and Damianos Frantzis, a young man whose education by a fanatical Orthodox priest sets him on the path, after 1922 and the shattering of his ideals, of an equally fanatical commitment to Communism. The ambitions of this character, too, are thwarted when the novel's fiction abuts against real history: Frantzis dies in a futile attempt to assassinate Mussolini. Both of these fictional characters, Skinas and Frantzis, are displaced persons whose formative years had been spent in Constantinople, and this background they share with Theotokas himself. Finally, although the author remains studiously aloof from his creations, whose actions and whose feelings he narrates with dispassionate omniscience, his own point of view is clearly represented by his fictional *alter ego* in the novel, the relatively minor character Lambros Christidis, whose philosophy of life forms the 'interlude' with which the first volume ends.[25]

Argo is by no means a social documentary, however. The social world it depicts is largely confined to the governing élite (university, politics, the arts); and Theotokas' presentation of those worlds is far from neutral. With the exception of two 'anchor' characters (Christidis, who has already been mentioned, and the stolidly reliable but uncomprehending leader of the students' union), all the main characters are driven by a thirst for power or achievement, which here and elsewhere Theotokas termed the *daemon*. The allusion to Jason's mythological quest for the Golden Fleece adumbrates the common quest in which the principal characters of the novel are engaged. This quest (which as we shall see is shared with the contemporary long poem of Yorgos Seferis, entitled *Novel*) takes a variety of forms, but all involve the attainment of an ideal that is finally revealed as unattainable. As the author's mouthpiece puts it at the end of the first volume, anticipating the novel's conclusion:

Αλίμονο! το ιδανικό το έργο δε θα το φτιάσουμε ποτέ. Μήτε θα βρούμε την ιδανική γυναίκα. Μήτε θα πραγματοποιήσουμε την ποίηση στη ζωή μας. Μήτε τις ιδέες. Μήτε ο διπλανός μας θα καταλάβει ποτέ τι ζητούμε. Αυτά όλα είτανε παιδιαρίσματα, εφηβικοί ρεμβασμοί. Δεν υπάρχει πουθενά το Χρυσόμαλλο Δέρας. Μα υπάρχει το ταξίδι της Αργώς.[26]

---

[25] Although the terms in which the novel operates are wholly secular, it is noteworthy that the two components of this character's name allude to the Christian story of redemption: *Lambros* echoes *Lambri*, the popular term for Easter, while the presence of 'Christ' in *Christidis* is evident enough.

[26] Theotokas n.d. (I): i. 310.

Alas! the ideal work will always elude us. The ideal woman too. Nor will we ever realize the poetry in our lives. Nor the ideas either. Nor will our neighbour ever comprehend what it is that we seek. All these are childish hopes, adolescent dreams. There is no Golden Fleece. But there *is* the voyage of the Argo.

Both volumes of the novel end with the same word, which appears with increasing frequency in the closing pages and hints at the most that the Greek intellectual of the time could hope to achieve: a state of tranquillity.[27]

Even this consolation is denied to the protagonists in the first three novels of Karagatsis. In contrast to Theotokas' panoramic *Argo*, each of these novels follows the fortunes of a single character. The protagonist in each case has an exotic background: the eponymous heroes of *Colonel Lyapkin* (1933) and *Jungermann* (1938) are respectively a White Russian and a German/Finn, while the heroine of the novella *Chimaera* (1936) comes from Rouen.[28] The internal lives of these characters are exotic too, as they wrestle in vain against the huge biological forces that, for Karagatsis, ineluctably determine human action and character.

Lyapkin, displaced after the Russian civil war to a farm school on the malarial plain outside Larisa, becomes a drunkard and his past catches up with him when it emerges that he had murdered his wife over an affair of honour. After a phantasmagoric series of visions he drowns himself. Marina, the young French heroine of *Chimaera*, is swept off her feet and marries a Greek sea captain for love. Her idyll turns to tragic melodrama as she becomes part of the family in the port of Syra (Syros), and fails, after much effort, to resist sexual temptation while her husband is away on a long voyage. Through an inexorable chain of circumstances her indiscretion brings death and shame upon the family and Marina, like Lyapkin, ends by drowning herself. Finally, Jungermann, in the novel named after him, wins fame and fortune as a businessman in Piraeus, but deep down is driven by his obsession for a young girl who is separated from him by a series of mishaps ending in her death.

---

[27] Γαλήνη. The word is used similarly in Seferis' poem *Novel* (*Μυθιστόρημα*) of 1935, and in 1939 provided the (ironic) title for Venezis' second novel (1971).

[28] See, respectively, Karagatsis 1976, 1978, the latter published together with the short sequel, *The Last of Jungermann*, 1941 (*Τα στερνά του Γιούγκερμαν*). *Chimaera* was revised and reissued in 1953 as a full-length novel with the title *The Great Chimaera* (*Η μεγάλη χίμαιρα*), which ever since has superseded the original shorter version.

By contrast with the dispassionate detachment of Theotokas, Karagatsis' manner of narration verges upon the hysterical. But the despair which Karagatsis' characters are forced to face, however melodramatic the circumstances in which they do so, is similar in kind to the disillusion that confronted the seekers after a modern Golden Fleece in Theotokas' *Argo*. Karagatsis' characters, like those of Theotokas, are driven by a force which they barely understand and cannot control, towards a fulfilment that their surroundings deny them. And these surroundings are above all Greece and the Greek society of the 1930s. Karagatsis' choice of foreigners as his protagonists should not blind us to the fact that his novels are fundamentally about Greece.[29] Later Karagatsis referred to these three novels as a trilogy with the common title *Acclimatization under Phoebus*, but the successes and the failures of his characters in becoming assimilated in Greece do not of course reflect any real social issue of the time: there was no significant foreign element in Greek society to be assimilated. What is more fundamentally 'acclimatized' in these novels is firstly the imported ideals which the characters fail fully to realize in a Greek context, secondly the theory of biological determinism which their careers embody, and finally something of the literary style in which their stories are narrated. The underlying theme of Karagatsis' novels of the 1930s is the explosive interpenetration of traditional Greek and relatively new foreign ways of thought.

The somewhat extreme example of Karagatsis also serves to highlight another general characteristic of this group of novelists, namely their close and deliberate relation to other European fiction. A 'European dimension' had indeed been a major component of Theotokas' prescription for a new literature in *Free Spirit*. Many writers of this group allude implicitly to the work of Balzac, Zola, Dostoevsky, Hamsun, and Gide in particular, or employ techniques that seem to have been learnt from them.[30]

Realism Rejected: The Modernists. The writers who make up this group were no less involved with literary developments in the rest of

---

[29] This is specifically recognized by one account of his work which implicitly places him close to the folkloric realism (ηθογραφία) of the late nineteenth century: 'Karagatsis has given us in one large synthesis a huge picture of the manners (ήθη) of our country during the period 1919–1930' (Tsakonas 1989: 69).

[30] These and other European connections of the Greek novel during the decade of the 1930s are documented more fully and discussed by Mackridge 1985a.

Europe, but their adherence was to the more recent and radical trends of European writing, with which many of them came into contact as students in France or Italy in the 1920s. The geographical nucleus of this group was Thessaloniki, which at the time was fast emerging into its present role as 'second city' of Greece. Here explicitly Modernist issues were first discussed in the periodical *Makedonikes Imeres* (founded 1932), before being taken up in the capital (in *To Trito Mati*, founded 1935). The foreign writers whose work was translated and discussed in these periodicals included Edouard Dujardin (generally credited with the invention, in 1887, of the technique of 'interior monologue'), James Joyce, Stefan Zweig, and Rainer Maria Rilke.

In Thessaloniki itself a fairly close-knit group of writers emerged, and rapidly (and predictably) became known as the 'School of Thessaloniki'. The principal members of this group were the short-story writer Alkiviadis Yannopoulos (1896–1981), who in the previous decade, under the name of Alc Gian, had made a minor contribution to the Italian Futurist movement; Yeoryios Delios (1897–1980), for whom the novelist's task is equated with the 'mysterious and quiet interior drama of the writer in search of the unity of his own self';[31] the indefatigably experimental Stelios Xefloudas (1901–84); and, the only one of this group to achieve (eventually) a secure reputation beyond the confines of his own immediate circle, Nikos Gavriil Pentzikis (1908–92). Strong affinities with this group are shared by another provincial writer, the maverick Yannis Skarimbas (1893–1984) from Halkida, and by Yannis Beratis (1904–68), the only Athenian in this company, the importance of whose first novel, *Diaspora* (1930), has only recently begun to be recognized.[32] More distant affinities with this group can be seen in the unfinished novel of Yorgos Seferis, *Six Nights on the Acropolis*, the first draft of which was written in 1927–8, and which shares with Xefloudas' first book the format of a diary.[33]

[31] Delios 1939: 68 (from one of a series of lectures on the 'contemporary [European] novel', first published in *Makedonikes Imeres* in 1937).

[32] The work of this group of writers, together with that of Melpo Axioti, up to 1944, is the subject of a doctoral thesis in English (Yannakaki 1990). This is the first study to be devoted to close readings of a number of works by the group, which are analysed from a positive standpoint. Vitti (1979) discusses only Xefloudas, Pentzikis, Skarimbas, and Yannopoulos, while Tsakonas (1989) omits all but Skarimbas and Axioti and omits *Makedonikes Imeres* and *To Trito Mati* from his section on periodicals. See also Mackridge 1997.

[33] Seferis 1974; cf. Charalambidou 1997.

The 'action' of these novels and stories takes place neither in the traditional rural environment favoured by the first group of writers, nor in the changing world of the city that was represented in the work of the second group, but on the printed page. In most of them the place of the traditional plot or story is taken by the seemingly uncontrolled thought-processes of the principal character. Although the technical innovation of 'interior monologue' is often taken as the hallmark of this group of writers,[34] this device was actually little used during the 1930s (the monologues with which these novels abound and of which in some cases they consist are usually imagined as being *written* rather than spoken). In any case, more important than the technical means employed is the explicit resistance of all these writers to the traditional conventions of fictional narrative. Narrative is seen by this group not as a means through which terrible events can speak for themselves, nor as a forum for airing contemporary social and philosophical questions, but as the attempt to construct an alternative reality out of nothing more substantial than the words on the page.

Xefloudas' first two novels are explicitly *about* the difficulties faced by a fictional *alter ego* in writing a novel, while his subsequent fictions attempt to put into practice the lessons learnt in the first two. The narrator of Beratis' first novel, *Diaspora*, traverses lurid landscapes of the imagination:

για να βρω τη λέξη, να βρω την απαραίτητη μικρή σταγονίτσα που μού 'λειπε και που όμως αυτή και μόνη θά 'κανε το ποτήρι να ξεχειλίσει, για να μπορέσω να πω ήσυχος πια "τετέλεσται" κι εγώ, για να μπορέσω να κλείσω τα μάτια μου και να χαθώ πανευδαίμων πια στη σιωπή και το κενό του αχρώμου απείρου.[35]

in order to find the *word*, to find the necessary tiny droplet I lacked but which would be enough to make my cup run over, so that in peace at last I too could say 'It is finished', so that I could close my eyes and abandon myself blissfully at last to the silence and the void of bland infinity.

The quest of the principal character in the first novel by Nikos Gavriil Pentzikis, *Andreas Dimakoudis*, published in 1935 under the

[34] See e.g. Vitti 1979: 272–8; 1987: 387–9. Interest in this technique in Greek literary criticism goes back to the early 1930s (Mike and Gana 1988); see Peri 1994; Kakavoulia 1997. For a full study of selected novels of this group, and the significance of self-referential techniques in them, see Yannakaki 1990.

[35] Beratis 1980: 22 (note the biblical echoes, in a text which has nothing to do with Christian belief or practice).

pseudonym of Stavrakios Kosmas, is fundamentally similar, although very differently expressed.[36] Dimakoudis is a student in a foreign university town which although it is not named appears to be based on Strasbourg. He falls in love with a French girl but needlessly insults her, and then resorts to ever more bizarre means in the vain hope of winning back what has now taken on the proportions of an ideal love. Insinuating himself into her room in disguise as a pot plant, he is predictably turned away and drowns himself in despair. Much of the narrative consists of the thoughts of this character and his inner quest for an ideal which is plainly at odds with the external reality in which he has to live. Dimakoudis' attempt to reach his ideal by creating his own reality, although defeated at the end of the story, is also the attempt of his creator Pentzikis, and indeed of the other writers in this group as well:

Ένιωσε τότε την προσπάθεια του κάθε ήρωα που κάνει να υπάρχουν όσα έχει στο νου του, δαπανώντας τον εαυτό του.
Είπε ότι γι' αυτόν υπήρχαν όλα, το σπίτι, η θρησκεία, και η πατρίδα. Θα έμενε χωρίς καμιάν άλλη σκέψη να τα συλλογιέται, ίσαμε που θα νύχτωνε, ακίνητος στην καρέκλα, ώστε να λάβουν ζωή όσα ήθελε να τον πλησιάσουν σαν υπάρξεις.[37]

Then he experienced the attempt of every hero (*or*: character in a story) who makes all that is in his mind exist, by expending himself.
He declared that for him all these things existed: home, religion, his native land. He would empty his mind of all other thoughts so as to think of them, until nightfall, motionless in his chair, so as to give life to all those things that he wanted to come close to him as if they really existed.

Among this group of writers, and indeed in his generation in Greece, Yannis Skarimbas stands out as a comic writer—and it is probably relevant here that he was also an accomplished performer of the traditional shadow-puppet plays whose hero is the starving trickster Karagiozis. The narrator of Skarimbas' first novel, *The Divine Goat* (1933), is a tramp who speaks French and knows about Einstein, whose language and behaviour offend against both social and literary norms, in a way that closely anticipates the influential creations of Samuel Beckett: Murphy and Molloy. *Mariambas* (1935) is a tall tale of small-town life whose hero is a tragicomic Harlequin or Pierrot, a social misfit whose most disquieting faculty is the sympathetic imitation of those around him. Even his

---

[36] Pentzikis 1977.   [37] Pentzikis 1977: 56.

very existence turns out to be a (failed) piece of imitation, as Mariambas had in fact changed identities with a chance acquaintance, Pittakos, whose name suggests both the letter in which the ruse is revealed, and also, by a near-pun, the quality of a parrot.[38] Madness and suicide frequently lie in wait for the characters of Skarimbas' fiction; indeed, *Figaro's Solo* (1938) reads like the product of a deranged mind, and in later editions of this novel Skarimbas added an epilogue confirming that the narrator had in fact been confined to a lunatic asylum![39]

POETRY OF THE 1930S

The decade heralded by Theotokas' 1929 'manifesto', *Free Spirit*, was no less productive and innovative in verse than it was in prose. The poetry of the 1930s was not marked by the turn that affected prose fiction after 1936, so that the whole of the decade until Greece's entry into the Second World War can be considered as a unity. This section will also include poetry written up to 1940 but published later. This is not to suggest, however, that the poetic achievements of this decade were uniform. The criticism of the time, following Theotokas' lead, made a sharp distinction between the pessimistic legacy of Karyotakis on the one hand, and those poets who were seen to be striking out in new, more optimistic directions. Since 'optimism' represented a break with the immediate past, such an outlook tended to be associated with technical innovations deriving from European Modernism and described by the Greek term *protoporia* which roughly translates the French *avant-garde*. The most clearly marked division in the Greek poetry of the 1930s that is discernible in hindsight, however, is that between poetry in formal metres and poetry written in free verse. The story of Greek poetry during this period is the story of the progressive dominance of free verse through the course of the decade. In 1930, despite some notable pioneers, verse which had no regular pattern of rhyme or metre was still an oddity; by 1940 there was no significant poet writing who had not at some time in his career published poetry in the new form.

[38] In medieval Greek πιττάκιον means a 'letter'; in the ancient language ψιττακός means a 'parrot'.

[39] Respectively (reprinted in critical editions with afterword by K. Kostiou): Skarimbas 1993; 1992*a*; 1992*b*. For critical discussion see also the essays collected in Kostiou 1994.

As we shall see, there is a broad coherence between the continued use of traditional verse-forms and the thematic legacy of Karyotakis and late Symbolism, while the adoption of new verse-forms (free verse or the prose poem) tends to go hand in hand with new thematic horizons. But the new themes and new means of expression can only very subjectively be termed 'optimistic'; and in reality this label could only be credibly applied to Elytis and Embirikos, who wrote in free verse, and to Sikelianos, who at this period of his career used exclusively traditional forms. In other words, the majority of poets experimenting with the new form of free verse were not really 'optimistic' in their outlook, while the continued use of traditional metres was not in itself incompatible with an 'optimistic' presentation of themes, as the example of Sikelianos shows.

The Legacy of Late Symbolism and Karyotakis.   Although the decade of the 1930s is remarkable for the number and diversity of first publications by younger writers, several contemporaries of Karyotakis continued to write and publish throughout the period.[40] Kazantzakis' *Odyssey*, published in 1938, also represents a survival from an earlier period. The only other major poet of the previous generation who continued writing and publishing during the thirties was Angelos Sikelianos.

Sikelianos had been the first poet writing in Greek to dispense altogether with both rhyme and formal metre, in the series of long poems published between 1915 and 1917 to which he later gave the title *Prologue to Life*.[41] Thereafter he used free verse only sparingly, in a handful of later poems which were probably written during the Second World War. During the 1930s, when so many of his younger contemporaries were in their own ways extending a path that he himself had opened up, Sikelianos consistently used a variety of regular metres. The collections which were later entitled *Voyage to the Dead II*, *Orphics*, and *Desires*, were written in whole or in part during this period, and make predominant use of the unrhymed eleven-syllable line which is the inheritance, via Sikelianos' Ionian

---

[40] Notably these include Kostas Varnalis, Nikos Kazantzakis and the 'post-Symbolists' listed in Ch. 2, n. 126. This latter group also includes Skarimbas, who wrote poetry in formal metres during the 1930s (see Philokyprou 1991). See also Steryopoulos 1967; Vayenas 1991.
[41] These poems are discussed in Ch. 2.

island predecessors, of Italian poetry.[42] In many of these poems
Sikelianos takes up once again, this time on a small to middle-
sized canvas, the main themes of the long poem *Easter of the Hellenes*
which he now definitively abandoned.[43] As happens with much of
Cavafy's poetry (which again is based upon formal patterns,
although flexibly employed), the reader is often scarcely aware
that he is reading verse; and yet the regular rhythm underlying the
lines unobtrusively lends authority, and at times an incantatory
quality, to Sikelianos' characteristically heightened diction. But by
comparison with Sikelianos' poems written before the collapse of
the Delphic Festivals in 1927 and 1930, these are restrained and
concentrated. Although their subject-matter is still elevated, many
also include a new realism, and some of the best known use a
straightforward narrative style of presentation that contrasts with
the more heady lyricism of the earlier Sikelianos.

In the poems later collected under the title *Orphics*, in particular,
Sikelianos gives a new lease of life to the attempted synthesis of all
periods of Greek culture that he had begun in *Prologue to Life* and
continued in the unfinished *Easter of the Hellenes*. But now the grand
scale inherited from Palamas has been abandoned, and Sikelianos'
blend of mysticism (which is entirely alien to Palamas) with realism
superimposes past and future on the present in a way that would
have been inconceivable for Palamas. In 'Sacred Way' (1935), a
realistic narrative of an encounter with a gypsy leading two bears
on the road that leads to the ancient sanctuary of Demeter at Eleusis
'initiates' the poet-narrator into an ancient religious perception
which brings with it a promise of deliverance in the future.[44]
Another poem of the same year, 'In the Monastery of St Luke',
describes, again realistically, the traditional celebration of the Resurrection; but in the manner of its description the dead Christ is
superimposed on the pagan Adonis, and at the height of the ceremony a young man appears on the threshold of the church, whom
everyone thought had been killed in the war.[45] In these and other
poems Sikelianos gives a more mystical extension to the earlier
efforts of Palamas to create a synthesis of ancient, medieval, and
modern in his poetry.

[42] Νέκυια Β'. Ορφικά. 'Ιμεροι (Sikelianos 1965: v).
[43] Πάσχα των Ελλήνων (Sikelianos 1965: iv. 43–141).
[44] Ιερά Οδός (Sikelianos 1965: v. 41–5).
[45] Στ' 'Οσιου Λουκά το μοναστήρι (Sikelianos 1965: v. 46–8).

Sikelianos' use of traditional metres during the 1930s is therefore quite untypical of that decade. Significantly it was a *return* to formal metres by a poet who had already made the leap into free verse; and to this extent Sikelianos anticipated the development of many younger poets who used free verse early in their careers, before turning to explore the more formal properties of their medium in later works.

A number of poets who began to publish during the 1930s, and who later went on to use free verse, began by writing in traditional forms, and in the work of most of them the debt both to later French Symbolism and to Karyotakis is evident. Not all of these are minor poets: the list includes two of the leading figures in Greek poetry between the 1930s and the 1980s: Yorgos Seferis and Yannis Ritsos. In addition, the early collections of the Marxist/Christian poet Nikiforos Vrettakos (1912–91)[46] and of the introspective poet of Thessaloniki, G. Vafopoulos (1904–96)[47] also use traditional metres, although these poets, like Seferis and Ritsos, later turned to free verse. Only Nikos Kavvadias (1910–74), whose poems were inspired by a life at sea, as well as by the unconventional, biting wit of Karyotakis and Baudelaire, never abandoned the verse-forms that had been standard in the 1920s. Kavvadias' three slim collections, widely spaced in time, are very different from one another in themes and style, but absolutely consistent in the verse-forms they use.[48]

It is in the company of the late Symbolists that one of the most highly regarded and influential of all Greek writers of the twentieth century makes his first appearance in print: Yorgos Seferis (pseudonym of Yorgos Seferiadis, 1900–71). Seferis at this time was a close friend of Yorgos Theotokas. Like Theotokas, Seferis had been

---

[46] See the collections *Beneath Shadows and Lights*, 1929 (*Κάτω από σκιες και φώτα*), *Descending to the Silence of the Ages*, 1933 (*Κατεβαίνοντας στη σιγή των αιώνων*). Free verse makes its first appearance in Vrettakos' work in some (only) of the poems of *The Grimaces of Man*, 1935 (*Οι γκριμάτσες του ανθρώπου*). For a representative selection of Vrettakos' poetry, in two volumes, see Vrettakos 1981.

[47] *The Roses of Myrtale*, 1931 (*Τα ρόδα της Μυρτάλης*), containing poems written between 1924 and 1931. Vafopoulos' second collection, *Offering*, 1938 (*Προσφορά*), uses some elements of free verse, although the rhythm remains predominantly regular. For the complete poems see Vafopoulos 1990.

[48] *Μαραμπού* (1933), *Πούσι* (1947), *Τραβέρσο* (1975). For a complete bilingual edition see Kavvadias 1987. See also Korfis 1991.

brought up in a cosmopolitan city of the Ottoman empire before the disaster of 1922, in his case Smyrna; and he shared many of the attitudes and aspirations expressed by Theotokas in *Free Spirit*. Even before that pamphlet had been written, Seferis had worked on the draft of a novel, *Six Nights on the Acropolis*, between 1926 and 1928, a project which had tried to put some, at least, of Theotokas' ideas into practice. But the novel was never finished to Seferis' satisfaction, and was not published until 1974, three years after the poet's death.

Seferis had studied Law in Athens and Paris; and in 1926 embarked on a distinguished career in his country's diplomatic service that was crowned by his posting as Ambassador to London from 1957 to 1962. His first volume of poems, *Turning-Point* (1931), is often cited as representing a 'turning-point' in Greek poetry, and as ushering in the new experimental decade of the 1930s.[49] In fact Seferis' literary début faces both ways: the Greek title also means a 'stanza' or 'verse', and the collection betrays Seferis' debt to such later French Symbolists as Valéry and to Karyotakis in Greek, in its technical mastery of traditional verse-forms which are stretched almost to breaking-point but never quite violated or abandoned. Also developed from late French Symbolism are the semantic density of many of these poems, and an elliptical obscurity which is almost without precedent in Greek.[50]

Although Seferis later largely abandoned the formal verse of his first collection and of its successor *The Cistern* (1932) these two short early collections already show many of the thematic preoccupations of the later Seferis fully formed. In these poems we already find the central role of love, linked to a troubled attempt to define the place of the past (both memory and tradition) within the present time—and this latter preoccupation is central not just to the work of Seferis but to the whole period of Greek cultural history that is the subject of this chapter. At the same time these poems testify to the technical

[49] Στροφή (Seferis 1972: 7–32). The collected poems of Seferis in Greek have been published in successive editions, which from the eighth edition onwards (Seferis 1972) include all the verse that Seferis published in his lifetime. For a biographical study in French, see Kohler 1985. For bibliography, see Daskalopoulos 1979; 1986.

[50] Precedents for semantic density of this kind can be found in Palamas (notably *The Palm-Tree*), and in Karyotakis. Obscurity, although of a different kind, is a characteristic of the early Sikelianos (most notoriously in *Mother of God*) and of all the poetry of Papatsonis.

mastery of traditional forms by a poet who is best known for his later achievements in free verse.[51]

The other major poet whose career began with traditional verse-forms is the prolific Marxist poet Yannis Ritsos (1909–90). Ritsos, in his youth a victim of tuberculosis and of the tangible decay of his middle-class family's fortunes, had good grounds for recognizing, in his own experience, symptoms of the withering-away of the bourgeoisie that Marx had predicted. His lifelong adherence to the Greek Communist Party began in his twenties, and in 1934 he published his first volume of poetry, *Tractors*.[52] Ritsos draws in about equal measure, in these early poems, on his predecessors Varnalis and Karyotakis. The sometimes strident praise of the achievements of the USSR, couched in appropriately upbeat rhythms, extends the more overtly programmatic elements in the poetry of Ritsos' fellow Marxist Varnalis. In much of this poetry powerful enthusiasm for the subject, coupled with a rare fluency in the composition of traditional verse, explicitly challenges any attempt to draw a distinction between poetry and propaganda. It is not merely that Ritsos deploys the armoury of the largely 'bourgeois' poetic tradition acquired from his predecessors for a specific political purpose: if he had, his poetry could have been dismissed— or admired—as propaganda pure and simple. Ritsos' target in his early poetry is not just the bourgeois culture from which he has been obliged, willy-nilly, to learn his craft as a poet; but the attitude, dominant within that culture, which seeks to separate 'Art' from any utilitarian and especially political purpose.

This is the significance of the provocative title *Tractors* (which vehicles are only mentioned in passing in the poems themselves). And many of the poems, with their repeated invocations to 'Muses' and 'Poets' (with capital letters) pour scorn on traditional attitudes to art, while at the same time appropriating the techniques and prestige of the very same art in order to direct them to new and different ends. In the self-mockery of many of these poems, Ritsos draws on the satirical mode of Karyotakis more than on that of

---

[51] The most important of these early poems in 'Erotikos Logos', written 1929–30 and included in *Turning-Point* (Seferis 1972: 26–32). For contrasting analyses of this poem in English see Capri-Karka 1982: 178–84 and Beaton 1991: 76–9.

[52] *Τρακτέρ* (Ritsos 1989–90: i. 7–60). Although the Greek could be either singular or plural, it is clear from the text, as well as from citations of this collection in Greek, that the title is to be understood in the plural.

Varnalis; and throughout his later work he also cultivates a style of
introspective self-pity whose expression is grounded in the elegies of
Karyotakis and in their more distant precursors in Palamas' 'lyricism of "I"'.

But Ritsos' most original achievement, before he regularly turned
to free verse, was to transform the lessons learnt from Varnalis and
Karyotakis into something uniquely his own, in the long poem
Epitaphios, written in 1936 and circulated clandestinely the same
year.[53] The poem is the first of many dramatic monologues by
Ritsos, in which a speaker and a setting are introduced by a brief
'stage direction' in prose, while the rest of the poem consists exclusively of the speaker's words. In this poem the speaker is the mother
of a young tobacco worker, shot down by police during a demonstration in Thessaloniki in May 1936. The mother's lament for her
dead son, supposedly delivered even before the demonstration has
dispersed around her, moves from pity and grief to a steadfast
affirmation of belief in the cause for which her son has died, as at
the end of the poem she sees her son resurrected in the other young
men around her who will carry on the struggle. The figure of the
grieving mother here owes something to Varnalis' poems depicting
the Virgin Mary, while the unremittingly painful focus on the
bereaved mother's feelings owes something to Karyotakis.

But the real achievement of this poem lies in its choice of metrical
form: in this poem Ritsos uses the fifteen-syllable metre of traditional oral poetry, the form in which *actual* laments are still composed by mourners in Greek villages even today. In this way Ritsos
has found a mode of poetic expression exactly suitable to represent
the social class of his speaker, but which also links that speaker to the
'fountain-head' of Modern Greek poetry, and at the same time of
national consciousness, in the oral tradition. The significance of the
form of *Epitaphios* goes even beyond this. In the Greek oral tradition
there exists a type of song sung by the women of a village or community on Good Friday, as the Epitaphios, a bier with the effigy of
the dead Christ, covered with flowers, is carried through the streets.
This 'Good Friday Lament', as the song is called, retells the story
of the crucifixion with the Virgin Mary as the central character,
portrayed as a distraught mother trying everything to save her son
and at the last being comforted only by Jesus' admonition from the

---

[53] Επιτάφιος (Ritsos 1989–90: i. 161–82); also published separately.

Cross to await the Resurrection. These songs are known throughout Greece, and Ritsos has strikingly inserted *his* modern and secular lament of a grieving mother in springtime into this older tradition. It is this silent appeal to tradition that lends force to the mother's faith, at the end, in the 'Resurrection' of her son in a new—secular and political—sense. The poem derives its effect very largely from its appropriation of a traditional form, which implies a constant series of parallels and contrasts between the mother of the contemporary tobacco worker and the mother of Jesus in the realization of the Gospel story in the Greek oral tradition.

'Free Spirit' and Free Verse. Theotokas in 1929 had not been very specific about the new poetry that he hoped would emerge in the coming decade. Some of his remarks are worth quoting here, however, because the goal of freedom from past habits of thought and established means of expression that he marks out, was clearly shared in the event by many of the poets who began publishing during the 1930s. Theotokas writes:

if tomorrow we have the strength to create lyricism we'll [have to] change direction. Because the direction we've been going in up till now has reached its end. . . . I imagine the future poets of Greece as very different from those poets you've known up till now. . . . An aesthetics is created spontaneously out of the air that we breathe. This 'prosaic and materialistic' century conceals in its unexplored soul much more poetry than our teachers suppose. But someone has to take the trouble to discover it. The time is ripe for daring pioneers.[54]

One way to achieve these goals, although not specifically foreseen by Theotokas, was to break free of the traditional conventions governing the form of poetic expression. A forerunner of this freedom had been the 'prose poem', a form which in France goes back to Baudelaire, and in Greece had been tried by Karyotakis, who never otherwise abandoned formal verse; by Seferis just before he took the

---

[54] Κι αυτό σημαίνει πως αν έχουμε τη δύναμη να κάνουμε λυρισμό θα αλλάξουμε δρόμο. Γιατί ο δρόμος που περπατήσαμε ως σήμερα έφτασε στο τέλος του. . . . Μα φαντάζουμαι κάποτε τους αυριανούς ποιητές της Ελλάδας πολύ διαφορετικούς από τους ποιητές που γνωρίσατε ως σήμερα . . . Μια αισθητική μορφώνεται αυθόρμητα μέσ' στον αέρα που αναπνέουμε. Αυτός ο "πεζός και υλιστικός" αιώνας κρύβει μέσ' στην ανεξερεύνητη ψυχή του πολύ περισσότερη ποίηση από ό,τι νομίζουν οι δάσκαλοί μας. Αλλά πρέπει κάποιος να λάβει τον κόπο να την ανακαλύψει. Είναι η ώρα κατάλληλη για τολμηρούς σκαπανείς (Theotokas 1973: 69–70). On the subject of this section see, in greater detail, the essays collected in Vayenas 1996.

definitive step from formal to free verse in the early 1930s; and by a number of younger writers during the 1930s as an alternative to free verse. But in Greek, as in other European languages at about the same time, it was not by turning to a different medium, prose, that poets found a way out of the impasse that they perceived around them, but by developing a new form of verse which combined the freedom of prose with the visual appearance and many residual effects of verse. For one Greek poet of the period explicitly, and for many others, one must suppose, implicitly, the freedom afforded by free verse was only a symptom of a more fundamental revolution:

μα το συφλογικό κείνο ρυθμό
που μ' ακολουθάει
πώς να καταγράψω
μια που καίει τους ιάμβους
και της λύρας τις νότες
σαν νά 'ταν όλα
στης φωτιάς τη φριχτή μανία
αφιερωμένα.[55]

but that rhythm dressed in fire
that follows me
how can I write it down
when it sets fire to iambs
and the notes of the lyre [i.e. conventional lyrical expression]
as though everything
were dedicated to
the terrible raging of the fire.

The first Greek poet to use free verse systematically was, as we have seen, Sikelianos, whose visionary quest to break the bounds of conventional perceptions and expression in his poems of 1915–17 has already been described. Another mystical poet, T. K. Papatsonis (1895–1974), began publishing poems with characteristically long lines and a ponderous, deliberately prosaic rhythm, as early as 1920; and most of his output, which belongs to the 1930s and 1940s, is in this form.[56] Papatsonis' part-Italian background helps to account

---

[55] Nikolaos Kalas 1983: 29. The extract is from the poem 'Reading History Books' (Διαβάζοντας βιβλία ιστορίας) first published under the name of Nikitas Randos in 1933.
[56] Papatsonis' earliest poem to adopt this form was 'Beata Beatrix', published in 1920. Papatsonis' collected poems from 1914 to 1934 were published under the title *Selection* (Εκλογή) in 1934 (expanded and reprinted as Papatsonis 1962). For an introduction to Papatsonis' work in English, which argues the case for treating

for an important element in his poetry which has tended to estrange Greek readers and critics; namely his conspicuous use of the Catholic tradition. His poems abound with quotations from the Latin Mass; among poets the medieval Dante is an explicit presence, the contemporary Claudel an implicit one. Papatsonis is almost as allusive as T. S. Eliot (whom he was the first to translate into Greek), and his dry, fastidious style makes few concessions to the reader. In its central theme, however, of transcendent love and its discovery or rediscovery through tradition, Papatsonis' work quietly complements the more flamboyant visions of Sikelianos and also anticipates aspects of the later work of Seferis.

But despite the significant precedents of Sikelianos and Papatsonis, the impetus which within a decade would transform Greek poetry, making free verse no longer a rarity but the norm, did not begin until the eve of the 1930s. Thereafter, collections of poetry in free verse were published in rapid succession. Anastasios Drivas published his first poems in free verse in 1929,[57] but it is generally now agreed that the first 'blow' in this campaign was struck by the enigmatic Theodoros Dorros, with a provocative, though at the time little-known volume published in Paris in 1930.[58] The *Poems* of Nikitas Randos (again relatively neglected until the 1980s) followed in 1933,[59] while in the same year the Italian-educated Yorgos Sarandaris began publishing short poems in free verse which, initially at least, drew to a considerable extent on the example of Ungaretti.[60] A year later, in 1934, Papatsonis published his first collection, most of it in free verse, of poems written and published during the

Papatsonis as a poet of the 1930s and 1940s, rather than of the 1920s as is common in histories of Modern Greek literature, see Myrsiades 1974.

[57] Drivas (1899–1942) published two collections of verse during the 1930s. See Argyriou 1979: Introduction, 113–18; Anthology, 34–49.

[58] Dorros 1981. Little is known about Dorros' biography. The name, which is presumed to be a pseudonym, is slang for 'noise, rumpus'. In addition to being, along with Drivas, one of the first 'Modernist' poets in Greek, Dorros is also sometimes seen as a precursor of Greek Surrealism (see Vayenas 1984: 13 n.; Tsakonas 1988: 31–6, Vayenas 1994: 63–89).

[59] Pseudonym of Nikolaos Kalamaris (b. 1907), who also published under a number of different names and later became associated with the Greek Surrealists. The *Poems* (Ποιήματα) of 1933 have been reissued under the pseudonym of Nikolaos Kalas (Kalas 1983). Subsequent poems, originally published under the name of Randos, have been reissued as Kalas 1977.

[60] Sarandaris (1908–41) wrote his first poems in Italian and French before turning to writing in Greek in 1933. His large output was only collected after his death, and is now available in a five-volume edition (Sarandaris 1987).

previous twenty years. Then in 1935 Yorgos Seferis published his first volume in free verse, *Novel*, which for the first time absorbs lessons learnt from T. S. Eliot, James Joyce, and Theotokas.[61] The same year saw the publication of Palamas' last collection and the first collected edition of Cavafy's poems; of the first free-verse poems of Nikiforos Vrettakos and Yannis Ritsos;[62] of the Surrealist prose poems, allegedly the product of 'automatic writing', *Blast-Furnace*, by Andreas Embirikos;[63] and of the first poems of Odysseas Elytis in the newly founded periodical *Ta Nea Grammata*. Thereafter Ritsos published his first volume in free verse, *My Sister's Song*, in 1937,[64] and went on to use free verse predominantly, although not exclusively, throughout his career, while G. Vafopoulos turned to free verse in a collection published in 1938.[65] Finally, 1938 also saw the first collection by the second major Greek Surrealist poet, Nikos Engonopoulos.[66]

The quest for something new, to be discovered or created both in and through poetry, runs through the work of all of these poets that was written during the 1930s. Not surprisingly this quest, for a new sense of identity and for new expressive means, takes many forms. Something of the range of possibilities opened up, for poets of this generation, by the new medium of free verse can be seen from the work of three of them: Seferis, Embirikos, and Elytis.

The idea of the quest or voyage of discovery (at one point even called a 'pilgrimage') is most fully articulated by Seferis in the twenty-four short poems or sections that comprise the volume *Novel*. A parallel reading of this volume alongside an essay on contemporary Greek identity, written three years later, suggests that the many references in these fragmentary poems to 'voyaging' and 'waiting' allude to the urgent attempt of the contemporary Greek to come to terms with the past of his culture, both ancient and recent. The deliberately disjointed structure of the poems, with their frequent changes of

---

[61] Μυθιστόρημα, usually known as *Mythistorema* in English. On the title see Seferis' own note on the poem and Beaton 1987*b*: 135–6; 1991: 89–90.

[62] Vrettakos 1981: i. 31–59; Ritsos' first poems in free verse were published under a pseudonym in *Ta Nea Grammata*. On the details of Ritsos' 'progress towards free verse' see Kokoris 1991.

[63] Embirikos 1980*a*.

[64] Το τραγούδι της αδερφής μου (Ritsos 1989–90: i. 183–212).

[65] See Vafopoulos 1990: 105–35.

[66] *Do Not Speak to the Driver* (Μην ομιλείτε εις τον οδηγόν, Engonopoulos 1977: i. 7–63).

speaking voice and abrupt and unexplained shifts of scene, as well as the new-found technical solution of free verse, owe something to Seferis' discovery of the poetry of T. S. Eliot at the end of 1931. But *Novel* is more than a Greek 'Waste Land': it is also a Greek *Ulysses*. Its twenty-four sections recall, although not obtrusively, the twenty-four books of the *Iliad* and the *Odyssey*, and the constant references to travelling, particularly by sea, reinforce the impression that what we are reading is the 'odyssey' of contemporary Greece.

This 'odyssey' (rather like Joyce's in *Ulysses*, although obviously using very different means) is above all a voyage into the past, and an attempt to come to terms, in the modern world, with a long historical and cultural tradition, a resource of enormous potential richness, but also, in the unassimilated form which the disjointed juxtapositions of the poems mimic so well, a burden and a danger. *Novel* ends with its speakers frustrated in their search for supernatural guidance or revelation, but finding 'tranquillity' in leading the lives 'given them to live' and in the knowledge that when they die they too will have something to hand on to future generations. 'Tradition', in the sense of the handing on of acquired knowledge and experience, has undergone in these poems a serious rupture, but is finally vindicated. The jarring modern world, unable to assimilate the past or to make sense of the present (often represented in Seferis' poetry by the music of the phonograph), is brought, by the skin of its teeth in these poems, into an organic relationship with a past order built up out of centuries of accumulated experience:

> Οι ελιές με τις ρυτίδες των γονιών μας
> τα βράχια με τη γνώση των γονιών μας
> και το αίμα του αδερφού μας ζωντανό στο χώμα
> ήτανε μια γερή χαρά μια πλούσια τάξη
> για τις ψυχές που γνώριζαν την προσευχή τους.[67]

> The olive-trees with the wrinkles of our forefathers
> the stones with the knowledge of our forefathers
> and our brother's blood spilt living on the ground
> were a potent joy a rich order
> for souls who knew how to call to them in prayer.

The metaphor of the voyage is carried over from *Novel* into the first of three collections to which Seferis gave the title *Log-Book*. The poems which make up *Log-Book I* (1940) are the product of the years

---

[67] *Novel (Mythistorema)* sect. 17, ll. 7–11 (Seferis 1972: 64).

of the Metaxas dictatorship, and many of them make cryptic allusions to the lack of political freedom at the time, and to the shadow of war which was already looming.[68] A poem of 1936, 'In the Manner of G.S.', includes the famous image of Greece as a ship travelling, while her people fail to realize it and are left behind.[69] That the voyage is unlikely to be a happy one, however, is indicated not in the poem at all but in the date-line at the end which, characteristically for Seferis, adds something to the whole poem: 'Steamship Aulis, waiting to sail. Summer 1936'. Aulis in ancient mythology had been the port at which the Greek fleet was becalmed on its way to fight the Trojan War, and where the king's daughter, Iphigenia, had had to be sacrificed in order for the ships to set sail. The bloody consequences of that sacrifice are retold in Aeschylus' tragedy *Agamemnon*, which is quoted in the poem.[70] Greece, 'waiting to set sail' in the midst of the political crisis of the summer of 1936, may be condemned to re-enact once again the ancient cycle of violence and vengeance that, ever since Homer and Aeschylus, has been irrevocably part of the Greeks' inheritance.

The weight of the past, and increasingly also the threat of an ominous future, that are such central components of Seferis' poetry of the 1930s, are boldly shrugged off by the other two poets to be considered here, Andreas Embirikos (1901–75) and Odysseus Elytis (pseudonym of O. Alepoudelis, 1911–96), in their poems of the same period. While Seferis had spent his apprenticeship in the company of the French Symbolists, of ancient Greek literature, and latterly of T. S. Eliot, Embirikos had committed himself to the principles set out in the two manifestos of the French Surrealist Movement (by André Breton, in 1924 and 1929), while Elytis had also found himself more at home with the Surrealists, but particularly with the poetry of Paul Eluard, part of whose name is even subsumed into Elytis' pseudonym.[71]

[68] Ημερολόγιο καταστρώματος Α' (Seferis 1972: 153–87).

[69] Με τον τρόπο του Γ.Σ. (Seferis 1972: 99–101). First published in the collection *Book of Exercises* (Τετράδιο γυμνασμάτων), which appeared in Mar. 1940, only a month before *Log-Book I*.

[70] l. 35.

[71] The components of Elytis' pseudonym have been persuasively linked by G. P. Savvidis to the elements Eluard, *élite*, and the Greek word αλήτης, used by Homer to describe Odysseus disguised as a beggar and still current in slang with the sense of 'lout' or 'tramp' (Savvidis 1980). Additional resonances are proposed by Kimon Friar (1990: 3–4).

The principles and practice of Surrealism were abruptly introduced to Greece by Embirikos' first published volume, *Blast-Furnace*. Surrealism in France had been closely associated with the psychology of Freud, and one of its avowed principles was to facilitate the free expression of the unconscious, liberated from all conventional taboos, artistic as well as ethical. In keeping with the Surrealist refusal to separate art from life, Embirikos was also a practising psychoanalyst. The sixty-three short prose poems that make up *Blast-Furnace* were written between 1928 and 1934, and are supposed to be the product of the technique which the Surrealists called 'automatic writing', in which the unconscious is allowed to unfold with the unmediated spontaneity of dreams.[72] The resulting texts are to a large extent literally incomprehensible, although one sympathetic close reading has shown that through the absurd and seemingly random juxtapositions of these texts certain key concepts emerge (perhaps like recurring motifs in dreams) and that in their unorthodox way many of these poems convey the sense of a change of state from inhibition to freedom.[73] The freedom claimed in these poems, and increasingly in Embirikos' later works, takes many forms: sexual, linguistic (in the aggressive mixture of linguistic styles normally kept rigidly separate in usage at this time), formal (in the absence of any verse-form), freedom even from all constraints of place and time. The space in which all Embirikos' writings are situated is the inner space of the mind which the poet sees as infinite.

This space is more clearly delineated in Embirikos' second collection, *Inner Land*, which may be a deliberate response to the Greek title of T. S. Eliot's *The Waste Land*.[74] The poems of this collection were written between 1934 and 1937, although publication was delayed (the first of many instances of the notoriously delayed publication of Embirikos' works) until 1945. Here the form is usually recognizable as verse, often with a pronounced rhythm, and many, though by no means all, of these poems have a logical and formal coherence that suggests an artistic control of the medium that Embirikos seems to have eschewed in his first collection.

---

[72] Embirikos 1980a. On the chronology of these poems, and of Embirikos' work generally, see Yatromanolakis 1983: 40–1, who also quotes Embirikos' own explanation and defence of automatic writing (pp. 28–9). For the response of poets and critics to this work, and to Surrealism generally, see e.g. Vitti 1979: 127–58; Argyriou 1983; Tsakonas 1988; Trivizas 1996.

[73] Yatromanolakis 1983: 66–75.

[74] First translated by Papatsonis (1933) and more famously by Seferis (1936).

Here, more clearly than in *Blast-Furnace*, Embirikos' most characteristic images can be seen to dominate: the sea voyage, the lighthouse, the gleam of light reflected from a hard, bright surface. The voyage into the *Inner Land* of the individual unconscious is at the same time, for Embirikos, the way towards mystical union with the whole human race and even with the universe, as is hinted in the second half of the short poem, 'The Gleam':

Κανείς από μας δεν στέκει ποτέ στα βήματά του
Καθένας πορεύεται και απομακρύνεται προς τα
  κρησφύγετα της οπτασίας του
Η γη που τα σκεπάζει είναι στα σπλάχνα μας
Οι πόθοι μας συναγελάζονται
Τα μαλλιά τους αναμιγνύονται
Τα στόματά τους φιλιούνται
Τα χέρια τους μας σφίγγουν
Και η σφιγξ μάς συνθλίβει επί του στήθους της
Στην στίλβουσα σιωπή του φάρου.[75]

Not one of us stands firmly in his own footsteps
Each of us goes forward into the distance towards
  the secret hiding-places of his visions
The earth that covers them is in our hearts
Our desires flock together
Their hair becomes entwined
Their mouths exchange kisses
Their hands clasp us tightly
And the sphinx [a pun on 'to clasp tightly']
  crushes us upon her breast
In the gleaming silence of the lighthouse.

The shock waves set up, particularly by Embirikos' first collection, took some time to die down; and by the time they did, as we shall see later, the legacy of Surrealism had been assimilated by many writers of the younger generation. One reason for this lasting effect of the Surrealist experiment in Greece—which contrasts with its more evanescent reign in France—may be that Embirikos and his fellow Surrealist, the painter and poet Nikos Engonopoulos (1910–85), used the theoretical principles of Surrealism to draw upon and emphasize traits already present in the Greek literary tradition. As this is of some significance for later developments, it will be worth pausing here to substantiate this claim.

[75] Η στιλβηδών (Embirikos 1980b: 82).

In an article written shortly after his first two collections of poetry, Embirikos describes how the discovery of the Surrealist manifesto by André Breton had shown him the way to achieve a kind of writing that he had *already* conceived, but had been unable to put into practice. The tale, as he tells it, bears striking affinities with Seferis' account of his chance discovery of a poem by T. S. Eliot in a bookshop in Oxford Street.[76] But more revealing still is Embirikos describing how he was driven by an 'almost organic compulsion' to discover 'a more immediate and fuller means of expression'. Inspiration came while watching a waterfall, which gave him the idea of a poem which would reproduce the *process* of the water cascading,[77] rather than merely describe it: a poem made up of 'whatever elements were present within the flow of its becoming'.[78] Although the means found, and the characteristically non-Greek imagery of a Swiss waterfall, are distinctively Embirikos' own, the avowed aim here can be linked with the quest for new and 'more direct' ways of expression which is common to most of Embirikos' generation in Greece.

Even the solutions found by the Surrealists can sometimes be seen to draw as much on the work of earlier Greek poets as on the programmatic claims of Surrealism. The 'inner land' sought by Embirikos in the collection of that name is not so different from the world of fantasy and imagination which Cavafy often juxtaposes provocatively with the real world. The following brief poem from *Inner Land* seems deliberately to reaffirm, in Embirikos' vocabulary, the wry disdain for externals and the introspective preference of Cavafy in his poem 'Morning Sea':

EMBIRIKOS:

Είναι τα βλέφαρά μου διάφανες αυλαίες
'Οταν τ' ανοίγω βλέπω εμπρός μου ό,τι κι αν τύχη
'Οταν τα κλείνω βλέπω εμπρός μου ό,τι ποθώ.[79]

My eyelids are transparent theatre-curtains
When I open them I see before me whatever happens to be there
When I close them I see before me whatever I desire.

[76] Seferis 1981: ii. 9–12.
[77] Embirikos here uses the German word *Prozess* transliterated into Greek.
[78] The article, whose title Αμούρ-Αμούρ puns on the French word for love and the Amur river in Siberia, was written in 1939, and is published as a prologue to the volume of Embirikos' prose-writings which appeared in 1960, *Writings, or Personal Mythology* (*Γραπτά, ή προσωπική μυθολογία*, Embirikos 1980c). For the opening passage cited, see 1980c: 9–10.
[79] Πουλιά του Προύθου (written 1935), no. 16 (Embirikos 1980b: 56).

CAVAFY:

Εδώ ας σταθώ. Κι ας γελασθώ πως βλέπω αυτά
(τα είδ' αλήθεια μια στιγμή σαν πρωτοστάθηκα)·
κι όχι κ' εδώ τες φαντασίες μου,
τες αναμνήσεις μου, τα ινδάλματα της ηδονής.[80]

Here let me stand. Let me delude myself I see these things
(I saw them truly for a moment when I stopped at first);
and not here too my fantasies,
my memories, the ideal images of sensual pleasure.

It is also remarkable that the brief extract from Breton's *Surrealist Manifesto* chosen by both Embirikos and Engonopoulos to be the epigraph of their first volumes not only proclaims the Greek poets' affiliation to the Surrealist movement but also happens to echo an earlier passage of Palamas, which, of course, has nothing to do with Surrealism. The epigraph from Breton which both poets prefix to their first collections is this:

la voix surréaliste, celle qui continue à prêcher à la veille de la mort et au-dessus des orages . . .

The passage by Palamas which Breton, obviously unknowingly, echoes here comes from the long poem *The Dodecalogue of the Gypsy* (1907). The speaker is the gypsy, whose self-proclaimed freedom from all social and ethical allegiances forms the subject-matter of the greater part of the poem, and in itself anticipates the Surrealist quest of Embirikos' and Engonopoulos' later writings:

> Κ' ένα χάλασμα μού φτάνει
> για να γύρω χρυσοπλέκοντας
> των ονείρων το στεφάνι·...
> ζίζικας τραγουδιστής!
>
> Κ' εγώ μέσα στο τρικύμισμα
> και στη χλαλοή του κόσμου
> κάτι γνώριζα που αρπάζοντας
> με ξεχώριζε και με είχεν
> αποπάνω απ' το τρικύμισμα
> κι απ' τη χλαλοή του κόσμου... [my emphasis][81]

And a ruin will suffice
where I may stoop to weave a golden

---

[80] 'Morning Sea' (Θάλασσα του πρωιού, Cavafy 1991: i. 56, stanza 2).
[81] Canto I (Palamas n.d.: iii. 313–14).

crown of dreams; . . .
a singing cicada!

And I amid the tempest
and in the tumult of the world
something saw that seized me
and made me stand apart
above the tempest
and the tumult of the world . . . [my emphasis]

Whether consciously chosen or not, this declaration of intent by the two Greek poets who fully espoused the cause of Surrealism simultaneously provides a context within Greek poetry for their radical experiments, and so opens the way for a definition of Greek Surrealism, a phenomenon both longer-lasting and more closely integrated with the older tradition of poetry in the language than was its counterpart in France.

Odysseas Elytis (1911–96) was closely associated with the Surrealists Embirikos and Engonopoulos during the 1930s, but unlike them never subscribed fully to the principles of the *Surrealist Manifesto*. The distance that would later separate Elytis from that movement, however, is minimal in his poems written during the 1930s.[82] Elytis' early verse shares with that of Embirikos an irrepressible thirst for the freedom of the individual psyche, but Elytis stops short of the programmatic challenge to intelligibility of Embirikos' *Blast-Furnace*; and although his second collection owes an evident debt, in form and sometimes in vocabulary, to Embirikos' *Inner Land*, Elytis' lyricism is quite different from the measured intensity or the humorous incongruities of that collection.

Elytis eschews the juxtaposition of different types of language that lends an effect at once of gravity and parody to the poetry of the Surrealists. By contrast Elytis' effervescent language and unrestrained flow of images directly imitate the spontaneity and intimacy with the forms and processes of nature that was also the goal of his Surrealist contemporaries. While Embirikos writes, in *Inner Land*, of the great ocean liner that will set out on the voyage of liberation of

---

[82] There has never been a collected edition of Elytis' poetry in Greek, although there is now one in English translation (see Guide to Translations). Elytis' first two collections were published respectively in 1940 and 1943 and have been regularly reprinted since. For bibliography see Vitti 1977 (to 1971); Daskalopoulos 1993 (to 1992).

the inner man, and Engonopoulos wistfully conjures up glimpses of a Utopia just over the frontier in Albania(!), Elytis right from the start *celebrates* a liberation and a communion with nature that are already fully established. The celebratory character of Elytis' early poems, and their pervasive interpenetration of body, soul, and the landscape of the Aegean islands, have long been recognized. Physical health and vigour play a prominent part in these poems, to the point that they have even been linked to the quasi-fascist propaganda of the Metaxas regime under which most of them were written. But Elytis' emphasis on the body and its well-being probably has at least as much in common with the same emphasis placed by the novelists Myrivilis and Venezis on the body and its suffering, at the start of the decade; and with these writers of fiction Elytis also seems to share the desire to create, through an exuberant language, the illusion of intense experience spontaneously finding expression.

With the sea and islands playing such a large role in the natural imagery of these poems, it is not surprising that we should sometimes find in them the idea of the voyage or quest, also used by Seferis and Embirikos. In the following extract from an untitled poem of Elytis' second collection, *Sun the First*, Elytis seems to be giving his own answer to the anxious doubts expressed by Seferis in the poem 'In the Manner of G.S.'. Elytis is not 'wounded', as Seferis was in that poem, by the Greek landscape, and if Greece, as Seferis had it, was travelling, then Elytis, at least, is not going to be left behind. The extract, in its final two lines, also seems to represent Elytis' response to another contemporary, this time Embirikos, with his desire to capture the process of the waterfall 'in the flow of its becoming':

> Είπα τον έρωτα την υγεία του ρόδου την αχτίδα
> Που μονάχη ολόισα βρίσκει την καρδιά
> Την Ελλάδα που με σιγουριά πατάει στη θάλασσα
> Την Ελλάδα που με ταξιδεύει πάντοτε
> Σε γυμνά χιονόδοξα βουνά.
>
> Δίνω το χέρι στη δικαιοσύνη
> Διάφανη κρήνη κορυφαία πηγή
> Ο ουρανός μου είναι βαθύς κι ανάλλαχτος
> Ό,τι αγαπώ γεννιέται αδιάκοπα
> Ό,τι αγαπώ βρίσκεται στην αρχή του πάντα.[83]

[83] *Sun the First*, sect. III (Elytis 1971: 14). The poem may have been written in 1940, although the whole collection was put together during the Axis occupation, in 1942 (see Vitti 1984: 102–3; 180 n. 3).

> I spoke of love of the health of the rose the sun's ray
> Which all by itself finds its way to the heart
> Of Greece that treads with assurance on the sea
> Of Greece that takes me travelling always
> To naked mountains crowned with snow.
>
> I give my hand to justice
> Translucent spring supreme source
> My sky is profound and unchanging
> Whatever I love is ceaselessly born
> Whatever I love is always beginning.

By the time that this poem was published, in 1942, the decade of peace and, in literature, of innovation and reorientation, that was the 1930s had already been brought to an abrupt end. How novelists and poets responded to military defeat and occupation, and made their own contributions to their country's struggle for survival, will be the subject of the following sections.

FICTION UNDER DICTATORSHIP AND OCCUPATION (1936–1944)

It is generally accepted that the character of Greek fiction changed abruptly in or just after 1936, when rule by military decree was introduced by Metaxas. According to an influential view, this was the result of a regressive move by writers, a pre-emptive response to the new authoritarian climate and more particularly to new laws of censorship (which banned, for instance, Myrivilis' *Life in the Tomb*).[84] It may be suggested, however, that the new fiction was driven less by a refusal to face up to an unwelcome reality than by increased urgency in the attempt to create, through literature, a new conceptual order, distinct from the outmoded expansionism of the 'Great Idea' but also from Communism. In this attempt, there is no reason to suppose that writers of fiction, few of whom at this time belonged to the Left, which was being persecuted by Metaxas, were fundamentally at odds with the regime. Rather, as was suggested at the beginning of this chapter, the political upheavals of the 1930s can themselves be seen as the product of a similar quest for a stable new ideology in the world of real politics. Certainly, as recent studies have suggested, the attempt to create and establish a new national identity, which is a common

---

[84] Vitti 1979: 351–8.

denominator of much of the fiction of this period, develops naturally enough out of the critical and ideological debates that had been current throughout the 1930s.[85] The change in perspective that comes about in fiction at this time, which also brings fiction closer to poetry in this respect, might more usefully be seen not as a simple response to political change, but as a more fundamental reflection of the change in *economic* perspective that marked the first half of the decade of the 1930s. The quest for stable resources in the historical past and present-day landscape of the country, that comes to dominate fiction in the late 1930s, runs exactly parallel with the adjustment of economic and wider cultural horizons mentioned at the beginning of this chapter, as Greece tried to adjust to the international financial crisis by moving towards economic self-sufficiency.[86]

The simplest way to understand the developments of Greek fiction during the Metaxas dictatorship and the war which followed is in terms of a convergence of the three distinct groups or trends discussed earlier in this chapter. This is not to suggest uniformity; but the distinctions that were fairly clear-cut in the new fiction before 1936 now become blurred, and it is possible, at least with the benefit of hindsight, to discern a common artistic aim underlying much of the fiction of this later period. The most important development is that the fundamental aim of the 'Aeolian School' of writers—to find a collective voice in which the experience of a community or the whole Greek people can 'speak'—is now consciously or unconsciously adopted by almost all writers of fiction. However, as the traumatic events that gave focus to the first books of these writers recede into the distance, the vital experience to be captured comes more and more to be situated in the past.

This is what happens in the later novels and stories of Myrivilis and Venezis, which are set in the rural villages of the authors' childhood before the upheavals of 1922; but also now in the work of 'urban' writers from the second group, such as Kosmas Politis and Theotokas, who published novels drawing on their experiences, respectively in Smyrna and Constantinople, in the early years of the century,[87] and of new writers such as Pandelis Prevelakis and

---

[85] See Tziovas 1989a; A. Thalassis 1991; Dimadis 1991.

[86] See Mazower 1991.

[87] On Politis' *Eroica* (1937) see below; Theotokas' *Leonis* (1940) is a 'portrait of the artist as a young man' set in Constantinople. The uncensored version of this novel, with its original title, *Flags in the Sun* (Σημαίες στον ήλιο) was published in 1985.

Melpo Axioti, whose first novels, as we shall see, are set in provincial towns, again at the time of the writers' childhood. Sometimes, and increasingly in the 1940s, this turn towards the past is further extended into the historical past. This is classically the case with Angelos Terzakis, whose *Princess Ysabeau* (1938; revised 1945) revisits the 'nationalist' struggles of the Greeks of the Peloponnese against western crusaders in the thirteenth century, that had been the subject of the first Greek historical novel, *The Lord of Morea*, by Rangavis in 1850.[88] The past traditions of his own country even come to occupy a new and central place in the writings of Pentzikis, who with his second novel, completed in 1938 but not published until 1944, returns from his wanderings in Europe to exploit the setting, both present and past, of his native city of Thessaloniki.[89]

Although the effects of this new convergence are most strikingly evident in the novels written, and in some cases also published, under the Axis occupation of 1941–4, some of its most sophisticated products date from the first years of the Metaxas dictatorship. Two new writers who appeared at this time extend the search for a 'communal' voice, begun by Doukas, Myrivilis, and Venezis, in new directions. The first novel of the Cretan writer Pandelis Prevelakis (1909–86), *The Chronicle of a Town* (1938), is a panoramic tableau of the author's native town of Rethymno in decline around the time of the Asia Minor disaster.[90] In defiance of its title, this is a 'chronicle' in which time stands still: there is no plot and no central characters. Indeed, the protagonist is the town, and a large cast of vividly drawn characters and narrated episodes drawn from their lives are subsidiary to the 'still life' depicting the town of Rethymno in decline. Much emphasis is placed on the traditional arts and crafts, and especially the skill of the icon painters for which Prevelakis (who for many years held a Chair in Fine Art) had a professional admiration.

The technique of the novel deliberately imitates the art of these painters, who are seen as at once naive and the guardians of a hallowed tradition. The conventions of the genre are stretched as far as they will go in the direction of a different medium (visual art)

---

[88] *Η πριγκιπέσσα Ιζαμπώ*. First published in serial form in 1937–8, the novel was considerably rewritten before its appearance in book form in 1945.
[89] Pentzikis 1987.   [90] Prevelakis 1976.

and a different tradition (folk narrative). To this end the language and style of the unseen narrator are very different from those of the Professor of Fine Art, or indeed from those of Prevelakis' other books. The narrator of *The Chronicle of a Town* speaks entirely in the idiom, forged out of centuries of oral tradition, of the unsophisticated people he describes (and it is here that Prevelakis' debt to Kondoglou and Myrivilis is most evident). The difference between Prevelakis and his predecessors of the 'Aeolian School' is that this novel represents the attempt to find a means of direct expression, not for *events*, but for a *place*.

The same year, 1938, saw the publication of another first novel, which in quite a different way also tries to order contemporary experience through the language and the perceptions of oral tradition. *Difficult Nights* by Melpo Axioti (1905–73) in many respects belongs with the Modernist trend of the decade.[91] Drawing on the writer's own experience of growing up in a well-to-do family on the island of Mykonos, it presents the outside world through the eyes of a young girl for whom adult, and particularly 'bourgeois' male, society makes no sense. In the fragmented sequence of experiences and perceptions that make up the narrative, no clear plot emerges, although there is an evident progression through about ten years of the narrator's life. The alienated heroine takes refuge in her inner world (and here the novel comes closest to the 'School of Thessaloniki'), but also increasingly in the *voices* of the peasants of her island. A large proportion of the novel consists of the direct speech of these characters, and here the novel's language, and the traditional perceptions of these speakers, seem to offer to the narrator the coherence and the sense of community that she lacks in her own life.

In these two novels, the legacy of the 'Aeolian School' converges with that of the Modernists centred upon Thessaloniki, but also with the more distant legacy of the 'folkloric realism' that had dominated Greek fiction in the last decades of the nineteenth century. It is not so much in their style that these novels look back to the preoccupations of the 1880s with traditional communities, but rather in the renewed focus on the community rather than the individual, and in their insistence on the concept of 'tradition'. For these and other writers of the time, 'tradition' did not just mean local colour. As Prevelakis' narrator puts it in *The Chronicle of a Town*:

[91] Axioti 1981. For a full-length study of this novel see Kakavoulia 1992; cf. 1997.

'Όμως εκείνος που ξαστοχά τις τέχνες και τις συνήθειες της περασμένης ζωής, ξαστοχά την ίδια τη ζωή, πούναι καμωμένη από τον αγώνα των ανθρώπων και τα μεράκια τους.[92]

But he who ignores the arts and customs of the life of the past, ignores life itself, which is fashioned out of human struggle and vibrant yearning.

The turn towards tradition as a validating force in the present, which we have already seen as an important element in the poetry of Seferis after 1935, comes to dominate Greek fiction in the years up to the end of the Second World War.[93] Predominantly it draws on the rural settings and the life of small communities that had earlier marked the fiction of the late nineteenth century. Under the conditions of the Axis occupation, the appeal to traditional values and a traditional, communal way of life had especial immediacy when thousands of Athenians were dying of hunger in the streets. The model of western urban life had doubly failed, as it had come to be exemplified by the German conquerors and by the starvation of the Greek urban population.

The appeal to tradition is by no means confined to nostalgia for rural life and its values, however. In addition to the novels of Prevelakis and Axioti, the first years of the Metaxas regime also produced two highly innovative novels by writers who had already established themselves in the earlier part of the decade: Kosmas Politis and Nikos Gavriil Pentzikis.

Eroica (1937) is the third novel of Kosmas Politis (pseudonym of Paris (Paraskevas) Taveloudis, 1888–1974).[94] Politis' previous two novels had been set in well-to-do Athenian society, their theme the impossible quest for ideal, pure love in the new world of *bain mixte* and Einsteinian relativity. *Eroica* turns to the past: the action of the novel is set about thirty years before, in a fictional town which

---

[92] Prevelakis 1976: 131.

[93] The preoccupation with tradition goes hand in hand, even before 1936, with radical innovations and departures. Two of the new periodicals which did most to support new and experimental writing, *Ta Nea Grammata* (1935–44) and the more radical *To Trito Mati* (1935–6) also were at pains to identify and promote strands of the older literary tradition, with which to underpin the new writing. *Ta Nea Grammata* devoted special issues to Palamas and the minor figure of Periklis Yannopoulos, an idealist nationalist who had committed suicide in a spectacular manner in 1907. *To Trito Mati*, in a sense unexpectedly, promoted the popular tradition and especially the *Memoirs* of the unlettered General Makriyannis (discussed in Ch. 6).

[94] K. Politis 1982. Serialized in *Ta Nea Grammata* in 1937, first published in book form in 1938.

combines characteristics of Politis' home town of Smyrna and of Patras where he now worked as a bank manager. The story tells of a group of boys in early adolescence, whose heroic world of make-believe is devastatingly transformed by their first brush with death and with their own emerging sexuality. The theme of elusive, ideal love, carried over from the earlier novels, is again hauntingly present, but is now juxtaposed with another ideal: the innocence of the heroic code. The boys in their games play at being firemen, dressing up like the real firemen of Smyrna, with helmets like those of ancient warriors. Subtly, the novel weaves a parallel between these young warrior-heroes and the heroes of the *Iliad*, and when one of their number dies, his close friend organizes an athletic contest in the railway goods yard, as part re-enactment and part parody of the funeral games for Patroclos in the *Iliad*. With humour as well as nostalgia, the novel looks back to a heroic 'golden age', not only of the contemporary individual, but, through the Homeric parallel, also of Greek culture and indeed of the whole of European literature.

Politis in *Eroica* goes further than in his previous novels in the direction of Modernist experiment. Although the conventions of realism are never quite broken, the perspective in *Eroica* jumps without warning from that of the boys to that of the narrator remembering the events years afterwards, and the identity of the narrator is only revealed half-way through. By contrast the second novel of Nikos Gavril Pentzikis, *The Dead Man and the Resurrection* (written in 1938 although not published until 1944), belongs uncompromisingly to the Modernist camp.[95] Like other novels and short stories of the 'School of Thessaloniki', this novel is *about* its author's efforts to write. Provocatively, it begins with no fewer than three different attempts to begin a novel. Supposedly the novel will be about a young man who (like the hero of Pentzikis' first novel, *Andreas Dimakoudis*) commits suicide out of unrequited love. But the writer within the novel is unable to concentrate; he cannot be bothered writing a conventional novel; what he wants, instead, is to create a 'form'.[96] The story of the young man becomes more and more disjointed; in any case he is not a real young man, we are

---

[95] Pentzikis 1987. For an introduction to Pentzikis' work, in English, see Thaniel 1983. On this novel see Yannakaki 1991.
[96] Επιθυμούσε ένα σχήμα (Pentzikis 1987: 7).

reminded: he is the hero of a novel. About half-way through the novel the hero commits suicide and the narrator begins to take a more serious interest in his task, the unconventional one of resurrecting his hero from the dead.

Through a long monologue the narrator struggles to achieve this impossible feat. At the moment of exhaustion, he goes to turn out the light in his room, and his eye falls on the inscription on the light bulb: 'OSRAM 25 × 220 volts.'[97] The conjunction of the bulb as a source of light, of its shape suggesting the bulb from which a plant grows, and of the maker's name stamped on it, is sufficient to spark off a chain reaction which recklessly fills the last third of the book. In a *tour de force* probably without precedent in European fiction, the narrator is inspired to create, godlike, a whole new world in which his hero is resurrected; and this world is created by *naming* its constituent parts. The naming is applied mainly to the physical landscape of Greece, and the language used is drawn from the Orthodox religion and (as in Myrivilis, Prevelakis, and Axioti) from the oral tradition. The novel ends with the narrator hymning the praises of his native city, Thessaloniki, and telling finally this parable of what Pentzikis has been trying to do throughout the novel:

Τότε θυμήθηκα τη διήγηση από ένα όνειρο που είχε δει επανειλημμένα η γιαγιά μου, η μητέρα της μητέρας μου, πως στο πατρικό μας σπίτι από κάτω ήταν εκκλησία θαμμένη. Της παρουσιάζονταν Σεβάσμια μορφή, που έδινε την εντολή να γκρεμίσουμε το σπίτι και να σκάψουμε, να βρούμε από κάτω την Εκκλησία.[98]

Then I remembered my grandmother, my mother's mother, telling of a recurring dream she'd had, that beneath our paternal home a church lay buried. An Angelic form appeared to her, each time bidding us demolish the house and dig to find, underneath, the Church.

The novelist is drawn back through the generations of his family to the voice of his grandmother, the voice, that is, of tradition. Knocking down the house sounds exactly like what Pentzikis has done to the conventions of the novel genre in the first part of *The Dead Man and the Resurrection*. What is resurrected in the novel is a religious awareness (the Church of the parable) which has been preserved in religious texts and kept alive through the oral tradition passed on from generation to generation.

Pentzikis' *The Dead Man and the Resurrection*, although not an easy book to read, is surely the most radical of all the novels and stories of this period which seek some sort of salvation in the traditions of the past. Much better known, however, are the wartime evocations of traditional life in Anatolia and the Aegean before the disaster of 1922 in the novella by Myrivilis, *Vasilis Arvanitis*, and the novel *Aeolian Earth* by Ilias Venezis, both published, under conditions of censorship, in 1943.[99] Myrivilis' short novel is a compact and vividly narrated essay on a theme which had also occupied Politis in *Eroica*, namely heroism in its traditional Greek guise. Set in Myrivilis' native Lesvos in the first decade of the century, it depicts the career of futile self-assertion which raises a young villager to the pinnacle of his fellow villagers' esteem, until overweening pride brings him, quite literally, to a fall. As the career of Vasilis unfolds, the narrative implicitly alludes to the classical Greek concept of the tragic hero, to Nietzsche's concept of the Superman, and to traditional songs and tales which have defined the popular concept of heroic masculinity in Greek communities since the middle ages. The story is told from the point of view of an admiring narrator who, however, rarely intervenes to comment on what he narrates. It is the view of this narrator that the heroic career of Vasilis, although motiveless and futile in its effects, was none the less pleasing in the sight of God. The novel itself, however, teasingly leaves the reader to make up his own mind.

Of all the novels which make up this group, none has been as widely read and acclaimed as *The Life and Times of Alexis Zorbas* by Nikos Kazantzakis, better known in English as *Zorba the Greek*.[100] With this novel, written mostly in the winter of 1941/2 and completed the following year, under the Axis occupation, although not published until 1946, Kazantzakis at the age of 58 made his second

---

[99] Myrivilis 1971; Venezis 1969. Like *Life in the Tomb*, Myrivilis' novella had had a long gestation. First published as a short story as early as 1934, it appeared again in revised form in the short-story collection, *The Blue Book* (*Το γαλάζιο βιβλίο*) in 1939. The charge of escapism into an idealized past that is sometimes levelled against these texts is only justifiable, and that partly, in the case of Venezis' novel. A similar idealizing tendency is discernible in Myrivilis' last novel, *The Mermaid Madonna*, 1949 (*Η Παναγιά η Γοργόνα*).

[100] Kazantzakis 1969; see also Guide to Translations.

début in Greek literature, after the dead end of his *Odyssey*, described in the previous chapter, and effectively his first on the international literary stage. *Zorbas* was the first of seven novels (if we count the autobiographical *Report to Greco*) that Kazantzakis wrote in his final years.[101] Like other Greek fiction of the Metaxas years and the Occupation, most of these are set in the past, either in an earlier period of the author's life or in the historical past; and all of them are set in the small, rural communities favoured by the 'folkloric realism' of the late nineteenth century and its contemporary successors. If Kazantzakis' novels contain a higher than average dose of philosophical and religious speculation, such ideas had already found a home in Greek fiction in the work of urban novelists such as Theotokas, Karagatsis, and Kosmas Politis in the early 1930s.

This is worth emphasizing, because Kazantzakis' English-speaking readers have inevitably, given the lack of translations of the work of his peers, had to read his novels in isolation. In Greece, on the other hand, Kazantzakis' determination to reach an audience beyond what he saw as the narrow horizons of his own country, as well as his provocative success, have led readers and professional critics to view him with a somewhat jaundiced eye, and, more crucially, to set his work apart from its real context in Greek literature. In fact, for all Kazantzakis' professed disdain both for the novel as a genre, and for its contemporary practitioners in Greece, it is quite arbitrary to separate this new, late phase of Kazantzakis' career from the creation by the end of the 1930s of a tradition in fiction which looks back to the concerns of the period when Kazantzakis himself had been growing up.

Zorbas has many features in common with this tradition, such as its setting more than twenty years before the time when it was written, against the background of a rural community drawn from the life of the author's native region, in this case Crete. Indeed, it is clear that, in a number of specific instances in *Zorbas*, Kazantzakis has drawn directly on the example of his fellow Cretan Prevelakis in *The Chronicle of a Town*.[102] Like other writers of this tradition, and

---

[101] For a readable and authoritative discussion of five of the novels see Bien 1989b.

[102] The character of the retired prostitute, Madame Hortense, in Kazantzakis' novel is elaborated directly from one of the vignettes of local Cretan life in *The Chronicle of a Town*. In addition the word πολιτεία, on which see below, is common to the Greek title of both novels although used in different senses: *Βίος και πολιτεία του Αλέξη Ζορμπά* and *Το χρονικό μιας πολιτείας*.

like the best of their predecessors at the end of the nineteenth century, Kazantzakis exploits a traditional Greek background for purposes that transcend it. Discussion of the novel has chiefly centred on its philosophical ideas, and on the larger-than-life character of Zorbas, whose peasant wisdom and vitality, honed by hard experience, wean his timid employer, the narrator of the novel, away from his books and abstract lucubrations.

The hero of the novel, Alexis Zorbas, is loosely based on a real workman, George Zorbas, with whom Kazantzakis in 1915, like the narrator of the novel, had opened a lignite mine (although the real mine had been not in Crete but in the Peloponnese). Into this character Kazantzakis has crammed many of the attributes and qualities he saw inhering in the traditional Greek peasant. The primitive practices, and something of the raw brutality, of traditional Cretan life are also highlighted in the novel. It should be mentioned that the folkloric element in this novel is more obviously distorted by the author's intellectual preoccupations than happens in any other Greek novel of this period, although the tendency is endemic to fiction of this type.[103] But Kazantzakis in this novel also takes up the common search for tradition in unexpectedly subtle ways. The tale of the workman Zorbas, the narrator tells us in a preface omitted from the English translation, is to be a kind of saint's life in the popular tradition (*synaxarion*). Such tales, often entitled *The Life and Times of . . .*, had throughout the middle ages and beyond been the principal form of prose narrative in Greek. A *synaxarion* was in part the life story of a remarkable man or woman; it was also an exemplar of the good life, and at the same time represented an important strand of popular, traditional narrative in the Greek-speaking world. To present his novel, through its title and some elements of its form, as a modern *synaxarion* is at once to claim the status of a modern, secular saint for its hero, Zorbas, and at the same time to reclaim for the purpose a Greek narrative tradition much older than that of the modern novel.

The novel's appeal to tradition does not even end there. It has not, so far as I know, been noticed that its opening words: 'I first met him

---

[103] It is likely that other writers who incorporate elements of folklore into their novels and stories at this period also drew on written sources, sometimes from outside the Greek world, as well as on their own experience (Prevelakis in *The Sun of Death* is a case in point, discussed in Ch. 4). For distortions of the ethnographic record by Kazantzakis see A. Thalassis 1991.

in Piraeus. I had gone down to the harbour . . .' are a close echo of the famous opening sentence of Plato's *Republic*: 'I went down yesterday to Piraeus.'[104] Once this resemblance has been spotted, it becomes clear why Kazantzakis dropped his original title for the book, *The Synaxarion of Zorbas*, in favour of a title which kept the saint's life formula (*Life and Times*) but now included the word *politeia*, which in Plato's *Republic* is the term used to describe the ideal state. Plato had introduced his philosophical dialogue, as he often did, with a realistic narrative of daily life. In precisely the same way, Kazantzakis echoes Plato's words in order to introduce a narrative, the whole novel, which is also intended as a modern equivalent of the Platonic dialogue. Thus warned, we should not be too surprised at the interminable discussions of ultimate things between Zorbas and his 'Boss' who tells the story. The novel is, as well as a modern saint's life, also a modern Platonic dialogue. And like many of the dialogues of Plato, it ends without either side conclusively winning the argument. In this way, in *The Life and Times of Alexis Zorbas*, Kazantzakis succeeds in weaving together elements of the literary, philosophical, religious, and popular traditions of the Greek language since ancient times. Read like this *Zorbas* becomes more formally and technically accomplished, and even more experimental, than most critics have allowed it to be who have seen only a conventionally 'realist' novel which doesn't however manage to be very 'realistic'. Although the strategy of reclaiming past Greek tradition is common to most fiction written at this time, and is deeply rooted in the intellectual anxieties of the 1930s, it must be acknowledged that Kazantzakis' method of pursuing it is highly individual. Finally, it may be timely to recall that in *Zorbas* the search for tradition, characteristic of the late 1930s and early 1940s, approximates more closely than in any other work of fiction to the synthesis of the past pursued by Palamas in the early years of the century.

POETS AT WAR: THE 'GENERATION OF THE THIRTIES'

Given the importance attached by prose writers, from the late 1930s onwards, to the recovery of tradition, it is not surprising to find the same preoccupation figuring largely in the poetry of the war years.

---

[104] Τον πρωτογνώρισα στον Πειραιά. Είχα κατέβει στο λιμάνι . . . (Kazantzakis). Κατέβην χθὲς εἰς Πειραιᾶ (Plato).

This holds true of those poets whose careers had begun during the previous decade; but during the first half of the 1940s there is a marked difference in outlook between the older generation and the new poets who began writing and/or publishing during that decade. Schematically, the poetry of the older group during this time can be seen as a development and in some cases as a culmination of directions established by the same poets during the 1930s, a development moreover which has close links to the prose fiction of the period. By contrast the poets whose careers were beginning at this time, although they continued to use the free verse of the 1930s and to draw quite extensively on stylistic and thematic precedents in the work of Seferis and Embirikos in particular, almost without exception turned their backs on this common project, and, as we shall see in the next section, came to occupy a decisive position in shaping the course of Greek poetry after the war.

We have already noted the important place afforded to tradition in the poetry of Sikelianos and Seferis during the 1930s, and also in one case even in the poetry of Ritsos. During the first half of the 1940s, however, this preoccupation came to assume even greater importance in the work of those poets who had founded their careers in the previous decade, even finding a place in some unlikely quarters, as well as in the expected ones. In poetry, as in prose fiction, this 'squaring up' to the past of Greek culture takes on many different guises and produced highly diversified results. It is also often more evident in the case of poetry than in that of prose, that this culling of tradition is not motivated by escapism or evasion of the grim realities of the present. Significantly, it is often the very same things that in poetry have been praised as a 'coming down to earth' that have been criticized in prose fiction as avoidance of contemporary reality (evocation of the Greek landscape, turning to the folk tradition, drawing parallels from the past). This may have come about because critics have been more used to reading verse metaphorically than they have prose. Be that as it may, the poetry of this generation during the war and its immediate aftermath looks to the resources stored up in various aspects of the Greek past for a promise of deliverance from present evils.

The veteran Angelos Sikelianos, in the summer of 1942, clandestinely circulated handwritten copies of five poems written during the first winter of the Axis occupation, with the title *Akritika*, which refers to the legendary popular hero of Byzantium, Digenes Akrites, whose exploits had been celebrated in oral song through eight centuries. In these and other poems written during the war Sikelianos continued to draw on the resource of ancient myth, often combining pagan and Christian myths so that together they would offer a message of hope for a country in defeat. In 'Dionysos in the Cradle', Mother Night gives birth to a divine infant who is at once' the pagan Dionysos and Christ. If the poet and his people can protect the helpless child from the wolves that threaten it during the long night (of the occupation, the poem implies), the light will return and the dead will be resurrected by His call.[105]

Tradition, and particularly the dangerous effects of alienation from its resources, is also a unifying theme in the short collection of wartime poems by Yorgos Seferis which he published in 1944 under the title *Log-Book II*. Unlike Sikelianos, who endured the hardships of the occupation and had to run the gauntlet of Nazi censorship, Seferis, as a senior civil servant, had been evacuated to Egypt along with the Greek government. The war years were years of exile for Seferis, and the personal hardships to which his wartime poems bear witness stem from the feeling of being cut off from his country and from its traditions. This sense of dangerous isolation is most strikingly captured in the poem from this collection, 'Stratis Thalassinos among the Agapanthi', written at the furthest point of Seferis' exile, during his posting to South Africa in early 1942.[106]

Stratis Thalassinos is a familiar *alter ego* for Seferis, appearing in several earlier poems. The two parts of his name suggest the idea of travelling, the one by land, the other by sea. Exiled to the southern hemisphere, the traveller acutely misses the familiar components of the Greek landscape that, throughout Seferis' poetry, guarantee the continued and fructifying presence of the past. In an alien landscape, in which the flowering agapanthus lilies belong to a different culture, the poet sees himself bound upon a journey like that of Odysseus, a journey which can only reach its goal with the help of the dead. But the voices of the past reach the poet only disjointedly: the poem ends (like Eliot's *The Waste Land*) with a series of fragments quoted or paraphrased from older texts: in this case from Homer, Aeschylus, and Solomos, interspersed with the despairing cry: 'Help us!'

---

[105] Διόνυσος επί λίκνω (Sikelianos 1965: v. 151–4).
[106] Ο Στράτης Θαλασσινός ανάμεσα στους αγάπανθους (Seferis 1972: 203–6).

Tradition is also invoked, in a different way again, in the long poem, published in 1945, in which Odysseas Elytis came to terms with his traumatic experience of fighting as a second lieutenant in the Albanian campaign during the first winter of the war. Entitled *Heroic and Elegiac Song for the Lost Second Lieutenant of Albania*, this poem marks a turning-point in Elytis' career.[107] The unbounded optimism and carefree celebration of freedom that had character-ized his earlier poetry would be tempered, throughout the rest of his *œuvre*, by an acute awareness of the threat of destruction and violent death. The means by which Elytis was to contain this striking juxtaposition of opposites in his later poetry are not fully developed in the *Heroic and Elegiac Song*, but it has long been recognized that this poem signals the beginning of a remarkable development which finds fulfilment in the poems Elytis wrote between 1950 and the early 1970s. The hero of the *Heroic and Elegiac Song* is killed in the snows of Albania but, like the heroes of Ritsos' poem *Epitaphios* and of Pentzikis' novel *The Dead Man and the Resurrection*, is imagin-atively resurrected. In this case the resurrection is effected by nature, as the snows melt and the grass grows up through the dead man's bones: although the individual is lost, the life that he repre-sents is renewed by the forces of nature, and the poem ends by (once again) celebrating the creative power of nature. Like Ritsos and Pentzikis, Elytis is able to bring about imaginatively what is impos-sible literally, by drawing on the permanence of the landscape and the age-old tradition of the spring resurrection.

Tradition again plays an evidently central role in another long poem, this time by Yannis Ritsos, written just after the end of the war.[108] *Romiosini* is one of the best-known poems of the prolific Ritsos, thanks in part, no doubt, to the highly successful musical arrangement of sections of it by the popular composer Mikis Theo-dorakis in 1966. The title, which defies exact translation, refers to the contemporary and historical experience of the Greek-speaking people, perceived not as history or mythology but as popular culture. In a weighty free verse which never strays too far from the characteristic rhythm of traditional oral poetry, *Romiosini* vividly depicts the Greek people and their historical struggles against

---

[107] Elytis 1981.
[108] *Ρωμιοσύνη* (Ritsos 1989–90: ii. 59–72). Written 1945–7 but not published, for political reasons, until 1954, in the volume *Vigil* (*Αγρύπνια*).

foreign invaders as the extension of the rugged, uncompromising landscape in which they live. The poem melds the unkempt figures of peasants and guerrilla fighters together with the rocks, olive trees, and light, and allusively places the Communist partisans of the war and the civil war in the tradition of older popular heroes—the *akrites* who fought against the Arabs in the middle ages, the klefts who raided the Turks during the period of Ottoman rule, the insurgents of 1821 who fought for national independence. In this way the poem claims the weight of tradition for a partisan cause, but more interestingly, and subtly, transcends the bitter divisions of the time when it was written, by presenting the Greek people, as a whole, throughout its history, as indissolubly bound to the struggle to preserve its territory and its integrity.

In all the poems discussed so far the appeal to tradition, in some form or other, is clearly evident, and no less evidently linked to a search for salvation that is both individual and communal or national. More surprising, and less obvious, are the strategies adopted by Surrealist poets who might have been expected, true to the principles of the French Surrealist movement, to turn their backs on the past and in particular the specifically Greek past. In fact, as we have already noted, the Greek Surrealists were not as indifferent to the literary precedents afforded by their own culture as they outwardly chose to appear. (A stinging attack on the movement by no less a person than Sikelianos in 1944 only serves to highlight the substantial common ground in practice between the libertarian, universalist visions of Sikelianos and the libertarian, universalist visions of those he attacked as anti-Greek and anti-poetic.)[109] But Surrealism during the Second World War went on to forge new (and as it turned out durable) links with some of the same constituent elements of the Greek tradition as are also prominent in more 'orthodox' writing of the time.

This development is at its most striking in the long poem that Nikos Engonopoulos published in 1944. Very different from either of Engonopoulos' two previous collections of explicitly Surrealist poetry, this was *Bolívar* (1944), a hymn of praise to the South American revolutionary Simon Bolívar (the stress on his name is

---

[109] Sikelianos 1983: 124–5. This fact is wryly noted in a posthumously published poem of Embirikos, probably written during the 1960s: 'Meeting of Minds, or Angelos Sikelianos is One of Us' (Μέθεξις ή Ο Ἀγγελος Σικελιανός είναι δικός μας, Embirikos 1984: 107–8).

displaced in Greek, presumably following French pronunciation), which moreover carries the subtitle *A Greek Poem*.[110] Far horizons had already been a prominent feature of Greek Surrealism, and earlier poems by Engonopoulos had opened up new poetic territory in Albania and South America. But *Bolivár* goes further, and, under Nazi censorship, established a tradition which would prove productive again during the regime of the Colonels. By drawing on South American parallels, topical allusions are displaced under a thin disguise. Indeed, apart from ecstatic invocations to its hero, the disguise is thin enough in this poem, which in the name of Bolivár rolls together an incantatory list of names and events in Greek history. Many of the allusions, although evidently Greek, are also obscure, to the point that the standard edition contains nine pages of notes, provided by the poet some years after the poem's first publication. But the distant Bolivár is triumphantly naturalized amid the greater and lesser heroes of modern Greek history and the folk tradition. At one point he is described in terms that link him very closely with such explorations in fiction of the nature of the traditional Greek hero as Myrivilis' *Vasilis Arvanitis* and Kazantzakis' *Zorbas*. Bolivár is described as

> ηττημένος και νικητής μαζί, ήρωας τροπαιούχος κι'
> εξιλαστήριο θύμα.[111]
> vanquished and victor both together, triumphant
> hero and sacrificial victim.

The meeting of a hero-saviour drawn from the resources of Greek history and oral tradition with the broader quest of the Surrealists for freedom in a global sense is an uneasy one in *Bolivár*, and it may be significant that Engonopoulos never returned to this mode.

Of all Greek poets the most resistant, throughout his career, to any reliance on the history and traditions of his country was Andreas Embirikos. Embirikos was the most thoroughgoing of the Greek writers who since the 1930s have been attracted to the lessons of French Surrealism. Much of his later work, after *Inner Land*, is difficult even to classify in terms of genre, and the erratic pattern of its publication has until recently made it impossible to chart its

---

[110] *Μπολιβάρ, ένα ελληνικό ποίημα* (Engonopoulos 1977: ii. 7–33). On this writer, often marginalized before the 1980s, see the book-length studies by Zamarou (1993), and Philokyprou (1996).
[111] Engonopoulos 1977: ii. 17.

184 IN SEARCH OF A NEW NATIONAL IDENTITY

development. Most of this work, which belongs to the post-war period, will be discussed later, but Embirikos' wartime production, even though formally it is in prose and none of it was published at the time, gains from being placed in this context. It was at this time that Embirikos began to cultivate the form of prose narrative alongside that of verse and the prose poem, and that ancient Greek mythology makes its only sustained appearance in his work.

The final years of the war gave rise to four prose narratives, each of which gives an unexpected twist to an ancient myth.[112] Possibly the earliest of these, *Argo, or the Voyage of a Balloon*, was finished in September 1944, although it was not published until much later.[113] *Argo* is much the longest of the four and could, just, be termed a novella. The story has little overtly to do with ancient mythology. Starting from the landfall reached by Engonopoulos in *Bolivár* (which is even mentioned in the text), *Argo* tells of the launching of an international team of balloonists in Bogotá in 1906, five years after Embirikos' birth. As the balloon, named after Jason's ship, heads off on its journey of no return towards the equator, the passionate love-making of a patrician girl with a half-caste South American Indian is perfectly consummated when the girl's father shoots both lovers dead at the exact moment of orgasm. Watching from the balloon, the raunchy Russian admiral Vladimir Vyerkhoy mutters to himself:

Ο μέγας Παν δεν πέθανε! Ο μέγας Πάνας δεν πεθαίνει![114]

The great god Pan is not dead! The great god Pan does not die!

For all its exoticism, this modern voyage of discovery is, as its title implies, a continuation of the mythical voyage of the Argo in search of the Golden Fleece. And the goal of the voyage is also, in this story, presented in terms of ancient mythology: in the spontaneity and unity of the natural world of the instincts presided over by the pagan god Pan.

Of the shorter stories, 'Oedipus Rex' does for the Oedipus myth what Cavafy in his poem 'Ithaca' had done for that of Odysseus. The

---

[112] On the date of these see Yatromanolakis 1983: 125–6, where the texts are also analysed. Some of the readings of Embirikos' later texts in this and the following chapter are expanded in Beaton 1992.

[113] An expurgated version appeared during Embirikos' lifetime, in the periodical *Pali* in 1964–5. It was first published in full in 1980 (Embirikos 1980*d*).

[114] Embirikos 1980*d*: 85.

tragedy of Oedipus, according to this version of the story, was brought about by dark forces within himself, puritanical Furies whom the narrator of the story, an uninhibited shepherd in the service of Pan and of Freud, simply slays, although too late to save his master Oedipus.[115] 'Neoptolemos I, King of the Hellenes' comes nearest of all Embirikos' writings to taking on the burden of three thousand years of Greek history.[116] The narrator is a modern psychiatric case who celebrates his 'cure' at the hands of Embirikos himself by announcing his intention of claiming the Greek throne in succession to Achilles. The story, like many of Embirikos' pieces, heralds a new dawn of imagination and liberty. But the attempt to reclaim the past as a necessary step towards that goal, an attempt which in various ways commands the serious attention of almost all the Greek writers of the time, is overlaid in this story by a fatal, if ambiguous, layer of irony: the speaker is mad. Finally 'The Return of Odysseus' has only a very tenuous connection with the story of the *Odyssey*.[117] Its theme is actually the creation of a 'New Jerusalem' by the Mormon founders of Salt Lake City. The allusion to the *Odyssey* serves only to claim a Greek mythological foundation for an imaginary new world, whose other foundation is biblical. In this highly idiosyncratic way, Embirikos can be seen to be trying to build a future imaginative order on foundations at once pagan-Hellenic and Christian; and this attempt places even Embirikos squarely in the company of his non-Surrealist contemporaries.

In all the work that emerged from this group of poets during and immediately after the Second World War, that we have looked at so far, an imaginative response to the real conditions of the time is couched more or less obliquely and approached by way of the traditions of the past. The oblique approach, and even obscurity, had been theoretically defended by some of the same poets during the previous decade, Seferis arguing (after T. S. Eliot) that poetry in the modern world had to be 'difficult', the Surrealists and those close to them seeking liberation from the restrictions of rationally controlled expression. But obscurity in modern Greek poetry reaches its apogee during the war years. It is tempting to link this phenomenon with the conditions of censorship to which poets who

[115] Οιδίπους Ρεξ. Notice the use in Greek of the *Latin* title of Sophocles' play (Embirikos 1980c: 145–52).

[116] Νεοπτόλεμος ο Α΄, Βασιλεύς των Ελλήνων (Embirikos 1980c: 153–61).

[117] Η επιστροφή του Οδυσσέως (Embirikos 1980c: 195–202).

attempted to publish their work during those years were subjected. These conditions certainly militated in favour of an indirect approach to such central themes as freedom and future regeneration. Thus for example Sikelianos' poems, although several were circulated without the approval of the censor, speak almost exclusively in parables; and we have already noted the diversionary tactic devised by Engonopoulos in drawing on the exotic background of South America in *Bolivár*.

Two poets who had already been noted for their obscurity in the years before the war excel themselves in this direction in long poems written at the end of the conflict. The poems are *Ursa Minor* (1944) by T. K. Papatsonis and *'Thrush'* by Yorgos Seferis (1947). In neither case can the notorious obscurity of the poem be directly attributed to the effects of censorship, but both poems take indirectness of expression to an extreme which can reasonably be seen as the inheritance of the period when freedom of speech had been denied. The poems are linked in a more important way too: while both draw, as we might expect by now, on mythology as the foundation-stone of post-war reconciliation, first Papatsonis and then Seferis present this reconciliation in terms of love reborn out of conflict.

Ursa Minor[118] (The Little Bear) takes its name from the constellation as which, according to mythology, the nymph Kallisto was immortalized, after a jealous Artemis had turned her into a bear. The name of the nymph, which only appears in the seventh and last section of the poem, signifies the ultimate degree of beauty. Beauty, according to the first part of the poem, had been the quarry that the poet himself and his contemporaries had vainly hunted (like the goddess Artemis) for years. Only now, face to face with defeat, starvation, and violent death, does the poet see what a delusion the post-Symbolist hunt for the ineffable had been. Instead, he now sees his former quarry translated to the stars, as a cosmic force of love. Kallisto, representing beauty, is conflated with Aphrodite, goddess of love and also (as the planet Venus) the evening star:

ήρθε η εσπέρα με τις δικές της μελιχρότητες
με τις δικές της δροσιές και τα δικά της ρεύματα

[118] Papatsonis 1962: 123–60. The standard edition contains the brief prose piece, also published in 1944, 'Chronicle of Slavery and Endurance' (Χρονικό της σκλαβιάς και της καρτερίας), which serves as the author's commentary on the poem (1962: 163–6).

ήρθε το πρώτο δυσδιάκριτο άστρο
η περηάνεια του Αρκτούρου η μύτη του
επουράνιου χαρταετού
και μας τα κόμισε όλα χωρίς φειδώ
ό, τι σιγόγνεθε ο πόνος οι μακρόσυρτες ώρες
τα μισερά πράματα ό, τι εικόνιζε μαύρο
η έλλειψη η στέρηση η απουσία
πώς μεμιάς όλα καταλυθήκαν στη μισοσκοτισμένη
είσοδό σου τη μισολανθάνουσα κι' εσπερινή
καθώς έφτασες με τα τόσα δώρα[119]

evening came with its own honeyed tones
its own cool breaths and breezes all its own
came the first barely distinguishable star
the pride of Arcturus the tip of the heavenly kite
and brought us everything in abundance
all that had been quietly spun on the spindle of pain
    the long-drawn hours
the crippled things all that was painted in black
by lack by deprivation by absence
how all at once all these things were dissolved by your twilit
entrance half unseen at eventide
as you came with so many gifts

Later Kallisto/Aphrodite is addressed as 'the great magnet of the
world',[120] and the poem throughout adopts the vocabulary of New-
tonian physics, in order to present love as the guiding power behind
the laws of gravity which govern the universe.[121] It is this divine,
cosmic force that the poet addresses at the close of the poem, when
he compares his people to the runner from Marathon who brought
the news to the Athenians of their victory over the Persians in 490
BC:

"βασιλεύει" σου λέμε "από σήμερα η αγάπη"
"βασιλεύει από σήμερα η αγάπη"
μαραθωνοδρόμοι σού το φωνάζουμε

---

[119] *Ursa Minor*, II: 'Faith and Hope' (Πίστη κι'ελπίδα, Papatsonis 1962: 135).
[120] είσαι ο μεγάλος μαγνήτης του κόσμου (Papatsonis 1962: 157).
[121] In this Papatsonis gives a modern extension to the mystical principle enun-
ciated by one of his abiding mentors, Dante, whose cosmology consistently incorporated the known facts about the physical universe into a Christian framework,
famously concluding that it is 'l'amor che move il sol e l' altre stelle'. Dante's guide
Beatrice is also alluded to in other poems of Papatsonis, and it has been suggested that
this semi-divine female figure has also been rolled up into the composite visionary
embodiment of love and beauty in *Ursa Minor* (Myrsiades 1974: 62–89).

που φτάξανε τρεχάτοι στο κατώφλι
της ζωής...[122]
'from today' we tell you 'love reigns supreme'
'from today love reigns supreme'
we proclaim the news to you like Marathon runners
arriving breathless at the threshold
of life...

It is once again by allusion to the past that a Greek poet, during the
Second World War, points to regeneration and reconciliation. But
the particular form that this takes in Papatsonis' poem—the
inauguration of the reign of love—is very much his own.[123]

All of the characteristics of Greek poetry of the Second World War
that have been discussed so far are drawn together in the long poem
that Yorgos Seferis wrote in the immediate aftermath of the war, in
the summer and autumn of 1946, and published the following year:
'Thrush'.[124] This is probably the most obscure and allusive poem of
a famously obscure and allusive poet; like other poems of the period
it draws on the Greek landscape (the setting of the house on the
island of Poros where the poem was written) and on the traditions of
the past (the stories of Odysseus, of the children of Oedipus, and of
the birth of the goddess Aphrodite). Unlike earlier poems it also
reflects, in its second part, on the causes of the recent conflict. These
the poem locates in a catastrophic failure of communication on the
part of the pre-war generation, who are presented as either obsessed
with the past or crassly indifferent to it, and whose voices within the
poem fade out before the mechanical, inhuman voice of mass communication, the radio. Like Papatsonis in Ursa Minor Seferis concludes his poem by proclaiming the rebirth, out of the ruins of war,
of Aphrodite and the new reign of love:

η καρδιά του Σκορπιού βασίλεψε,
ο τύραννος μέσα απ' τον άνθρωπο έχει φύγει,

---

[122] Ursa Minor, VII: 'Gravitational Forces' (Οι έλξεις, Papatsonis 1962: 160).

[123] One could expand on the parallels and precedents for this poem. The most
striking parallel is with Embirikos, whose prose texts of the period and later prophecy
of a 'New Jerusalem' of sexual liberation extend the gratification of the Freudian libido
into the realm of mysticism. Some elements of Papatsonis' 'reign of love' can also be
traced back to earlier poems of Sikelianos, notably 'Sacred Way' (1935) in which a
conflation of ancient myths again centres (although in quite a different way) on a bear.

[124] On the genesis of this poem see Vayenas 1979b: 247–97; Keeley 1996b. For
discussions see Argyriou 1961 and, in English: Thaniel 1977; Capri-Karka 1982: 299–
320; 1985: 151–68; Beaton 1991: 110–17; and 1996b.

κι όλες οι κόρες του πόντου, Νηρηίδες, Γραίες
τρέχουν στα λαμπυρίσματα της αναδυομένης·
όποιος ποτέ του δεν αγάπησε θ' αγαπήσει,
στο φώς...¹²⁵

the heart of Scorpio has set,
the tyrant has fled from the heart of man,
and all the nymphs of the deep, Nereids, Graeae
flock to the twinkling light of Venus rising;
whoever has never loved shall love,
in the light...

Much has been written on Seferis' poem, a good deal less on
Papatsonis', and almost nothing at all on the links between
them.¹²⁶ Seferis' poem marks a turning-point in that poet's career:
the first unambiguous appearance of a mystical (although not yet a
Christian) dimension in his poetry, and the first and clearest statement that love, in an all-inclusive sense, may be the goal of the quest
marked out in his poetry of the previous decade. Both of these
crucial ingredients of Seferis' later poetry can be traced back to
Papatsonis and in particular to *Ursa Minor*.

There are other, smaller, indications that a reading of Papatsonis'
poem can help to elucidate the dense and complex '*Thrush*'. Both
poems refer in their titles and in their opening sections to small
creatures which are hunted. In *Ursa Minor* the small bear is understood to be the nymph representing beauty metamorphosed, and is
hunted in a dual sense—by her enemy Artemis and by poets who
seek in vain to capture her. In '*Thrush*' the hunting of small birds is a
metaphor for the war.¹²⁷ In both poems the allusion of the title is
complex: Ursa Minor is at once a hunted animal, a nymph representing beauty, a constellation, and an avatar of the goddess of love;
while the '*Thrush*' in Seferis' poem is literally a bird but in fact the
name of a boat sunk in the war (another victim), and later in the
poem is conflated with the ship that took Odysseus to the underworld in order to find his way home. Both poems conclude with
references to the constellations and their metaphorical associations,
as well as to the mythological birth of Aphrodite. And a curious and

¹²⁵ '*Thrush*' ("Κίχλη"), III, ll. 70–5 (Seferis 1972: 228–9). Line 74 is a close
translation from the Latin hymn to Venus (Aphrodite): 'cras amet qui numquam
amavit.'
¹²⁶ See Vayenas 1979b: 290–1; Beaton 1996b.
¹²⁷ See '*Thrush*', I, ll. 3–9 (Seferis 1972: 219).

unexplained reference to 'those who struck the voluntary Marathon runner' in the last part of *'Thrush'* is surely a direct allusion to the lines from the closing section of *Ursa Minor* quoted above.[128]

Finally, both poems bear close comparison with the undated prose poem of Embirikos, which belongs almost certainly to the war years, 'Venus'.[129] This poem is in the form of a prayer, simultaneously to the planet in the sky and the goddess (Venus/Aphrodite) whose name it bears. The names of the constellations, which also appear prominently in the poems by Papatsonis and Seferis, serve as a refrain throughout.[130] In all of these poems of the older generation written during or just after the Second World War the recovery of tradition crystallizes upon faith or hope in the rebirth of love.

POETS AT WAR: NEW VOICES

There is little trace of the optimism or affirmation in the face of adversity that we saw in the wartime poetry of the older generation, in the work of those poets (most, but not all, of whom belong to a younger generation) who began writing during the Axis occupation and publishing towards its end. Confronted, at a formative stage of their careers, with the ordeals of defeat and occupation, the horizons of these poets were inevitably shaped by the political polarization that was already part of the experience of the occupation, as well as by the violence and repression of those years. As a result, these poets have no visions of hope to offer. Images of violence and death pervade their work; and poetry itself no longer claims the redemptive power that it does in the work of their elders. As the poet faces up to his own powerlessness in the face of events, the status and value of his art are called into question.

The writers who began to publish during and immediately after the war were of varying ages and backgrounds. In literary terms all,

---

[128] 'And those who left the wrestling-ground to take up their bows | and struck the voluntary Marathon runner' (Κι αυτούς που αφήσαν την παλαίστρα για να πάρουν τα δοξάρια | και χτύπησαν το θεληματικό μαραθωνοδρόμο, *'Thrush'*, III. 42). The word θεληματικός, which is also rare in Seferis, occurs in the prologue to *Ursa Minor* in a comparable context: 'for this I admire you | that voluntarily you shed your blood...' (για τούτο σε θαυμάζω | ματώνεις θεληματικά..., Papatsonis 1962: 127); cf. Beaton 1996b.

[129] Αφροδίτη (Embirikos 1980c: 95–7).

[130] 'Behold Sagittarius, Capricorn, Sirius, Orion' (Ιδού ο Τοξότης, ο Αιγόκερως, ο Σείριος, ο Ωρίων).

on their first appearance, find something to echo in the poetry of
Seferis; in this way a visibly 'Seferian' stamp is set upon virtually all
Greek poetry written since the Second World War. In other respects,
their affiliations differ considerably. Many are linked more or less
closely with Surrealism (although after the end of the thirties the
term Surrealism itself becomes increasingly anachronistic). Others,
such as Takis Sinopoulos and G. Themelis, began by following very
closely in the footsteps of Seferis. On a rather different tack, many
poets during this time responded to events with a new-found directness and realism, testifying, in the same way as novelists had done
after the Asia Minor disaster, to the sufferings they had witnessed, in
a voice more communal than private, more extrovert than introvert.
The work of mainly, but not exclusively, socialist writers, this new
kind of poetry is usually described as either 'political' poetry or
'social' poetry.[131] It often seeks to address a wider audience, and in
so doing restores to poetic language something of the communicative function that had all but disappeared after the Modernist
experiments of the 1930s.

The Legacy of Surrealism.   Poets with a background in Surrealism,
such as Nikos Gatsos, D. P. Papaditsas, Miltos Sahtouris, Eleni
Vakalo, and Nanos Valaoritis, draw on the well-established Surrealist resources of dreams and the irrational. But in these writers'
poems of the 1940s the liberating dreams of the earlier Surrealists
have become nightmares; the free association of ideas and images
is diverted inexorably into morbid obsession; the power of the
irrational once sought by Surrealism as a goal now comes to be
seen as a terrifying reality under the conditions of occupation and
civil war.

Among the writers just named, Gatsos, Sahtouris, and Valaoritis
tellingly adapt into Greek the example of the Spanish poet Federico
Garcia Lorca, in marrying the illogicality of the unconscious cultivated by Surrealism to the equally illogical associations traditional
in Greek folk poetry and tales. The result is an appeal to tradition
rather different in character from that made by the pre-war generation. The single collection by Nikos Gatsos (1915–92), *Amorgos*
(1943), alludes in its title, for no apparent reason, to an Aegean

---

[131] Respectively by Maronitis 1976: 14–15, and Meraklis 1986: 233. For annotated
anthology, see Argyriou 1982.

island.[132] The language of the poems, like that of Elytis, is rich with terms drawn from traditional rural life; one even uses the traditional fifteen-syllable metre. Gatsos in 1943 does not altogether forsake the hope for a new life that so informs the work of his elders at this time. But unlike them he invests that hope in voyages of discovery beyond the bounds of the traditional Greek world:

Παιδιά ίσως η μνήμη των προγόνων να είναι βαθύτερη παρηγοριά και πιο πολύτιμη συντροφιά από μια χούφτα ροδόσταμο και το μεθύσι της ομορφιάς... Καληνύχτα λοιπόν βλέπω σωρούς πεφτάστερα να σας λικνίζουν τα όνειρα μα εγώ κρατώ στα δάχτυλά μου τη μουσική για μια καλύτερη μέρα. Οι ταξιδιώτες των Ινδιών ξέρουνε περισσότερα να σας πουν απ' τους Βυζαντινούς χρονογράφους.[133]

Children, it may be that the memory of our ancestors is a deeper comfort and a more precious companion than a fistful of rose-water and the intoxication of beauty.... Good-night then, I can see heaps of shooting stars to rock your dreams to sleep but in my fingertips I hold the music of a better day. The travellers to the Indies have more to tell you than the Byzantine chroniclers.

The most consistent explorer of the nightmare inner world, in which the Surrealist exploration of the unconscious and the traditional world of Greek folk poetry meet, is Miltos Sahtouris (b. 1919). Sahtouris' nightmare is meticulously cultivated throughout a poetic career spanning almost half a century, and reflects and comments in grotesque fashion on the atrocities of the poet's formative years. Unlike Gatsos, Sahtouris offers no hint of a way out, but obsessively elaborates on the themes of mutilation, violent metamorphosis, and enclosure. The traditional 'open-air' world of folk poetry, instead of affording an alternative, is itself reinterpreted as part of the nightmare. The poet may be looked on by others as a saviour, but he has no power to save: all he can give is 'his songs, in this terrifying darkness'.[134]

---

[132] Gatsos 1987. The first six untitled poems may be thought of as comprising a (precarious) unity. 'Death and the Knight (1513)' (Ο Ιππότης και ο Θάνατος, 1513) and 'Elegy' (Ελεγείο), which conclude the volume, are clearly self-contained poems.

[133] Gatsos 1987: 22–3. This route to future salvation is also shared by the Surrealists of the older generation: Engonopoulos (in *Bolívar*) and Embirikos in *Argo* and other prose pieces of the time which draw on a 'New World' setting.

[134] κι έν' άσπρο πουλί, από πάνω, θ' απαγγέλει μέσα | σ' ένα τρομακτικό τώρα σκοτάδι, τα τραγούδια μου. From the poem 'The Poet', 1962 (Ο ποιητής, Sahtouris 1977: 201).

The feeling of impotence articulated in this and other poems of Sahtouris is shared by other poets whose early work is indebted to Surrealism. Nanos Valaoritis (b. 1921), in a youthful long poem published in 1944, warns against precisely the kind of prophetic promises being made then and later by poets of the older generation,[135] while D. P. Papaditsas echoes Sahtouris in refusing the traditional mantle of the poet-prophet.[136]

The Legacy of Seferis. Other poets, whose early work links them particularly closely with Seferis, place themselves in different ways within the same territory. G. Themelis (1900–76), who by birth belongs to the previous generation, did not begin to publish poetry until the war years. The keynote of much post-war Greek poetry, not only by Themelis himself, was sounded in a poem published in 1945:

> Πώς να το πω δεν ξέρω
> Καμιά γλώσσα δε μιλιέται
> Σιωπή από βυθισμένα άστρα
> Ερημιά ουρανού μέσα σε κάθε φωνή
>
> Έχω μια κρυφή ελπίδα
> Να συναντήσω κάπου τη θάλασσα.[137]

> I don't know how to say it
> There's no language spoken
> A silence of sunken stars
> A desert of sky in every voice
>
> I have a secret hope
> somewhere to come upon the sea.

The same dilemma haunts the poetry of another follower of Seferis during the early part of his career, Takis Sinopoulos (1917–81). Sinopoulos' first poems vividly evoke what he called, in the opening phrase of his first published poem, a 'landscape of death' and, in the title of two early collections, a 'no man's land'.[138] This desolate landscape, which in the early poems owes an evident debt to Eliot's *The Waste Land* by way of Seferis, is peopled by the ghosts of the poet's friends and acquaintances killed in the war and civil war,

[135] 'The Lesson of Daybreak', 1944 (Το μάθημα της χαραυγής, N. Valaoritis 1983: 9–16, esp. 15–16).
[136] See in particular the 4th section of *The Adventure (Η περιπέτεια)*, Part A, dated 1951–3 (Papaditsas 1978: 56).
[137] 'Cymothoe' (Κυμοθόη, Themelis 1969–70: i. 29).
[138] Μεταίχμιο (Sinopoulos 1976: 20).

sometimes conflated with mythical figures. It is characteristic of Sinopoulos (and also of his generation's relation to the previous one) that Elpenor, the impressionable young companion of Odysseus in the *Odyssey*, is taken over from Seferis and Ezra Pound, but moves for the first time to centre stage in Sinopoulos' poem named after him.[139] By contrast with Seferis' haughty treatment of this unfortunate and all too ordinary young man whose fate was passingly described by Homer, Sinopoulos' poetry as a whole is implicitly dedicated to the ordinary and uncomprehending victims of a conflict which is anything but heroic.[140]

'Social' Poetry. Sinopoulos, at least in his early poems, confronts the realities of his time through the Seferian prism of mythical archetypes. In the work of the 'social' or 'political' poets of the time, the same 'landscape of death' is described and evoked with an immediacy and 'realism' which at the time mark a significant innovation in twentieth-century Greek poetry. This directness is the most radical answer to the question put by Themelis, and had already, by 1945, begun to be articulated by a group of young poets, mostly of the Left, who had begun writing during the occupation.[141] Manolis Anagnostakis (b. 1925) published his first collection in 1945, Aris Alexandrou (pseudonym of A. Vasiliadis, 1922–78) and Tasos Livaditis (1922–88) in 1946. These poets, along with many others of whom Titos Patrikios (b. 1928) stands out with a first collection published as late as 1954,[142] had all been involved in the resistance, and all four of those just named suffered imprisonment, during and after the civil war, because of their left-wing sympathies.[143]

Anagnostakis in his early poems both sets the tone and takes to extreme the terse, unadorned presentation of a grim reality that is characteristic of these poets. A poem from his first collection *Seasons*

---

[139] Sinopoulos 1976: 11–12.

[140] See Savvidis 1990.

[141] The group solidarity often expressed in the work of these poets, and the emphasis on the victims of defeat, are not necessarily to be equated with adherence to the communist 'party line'. Alexandrou, for instance, often speaks out in his poems against the authoritarianism of the party itself, while Th. D. Frangopoulos expresses similar attitudes on behalf of ordinary people of the other side.

[142] See Patrikios 1990; cf. Ricks 1996.

[143] Maronitis 1976: 28–30; see also the special issues of the periodical *Diavazo* devoted to Alexandrou (no. 212, Mar. 1989) and to Livaditis (no. 228, Dec. 1989).

(1945) tells of the death of a comrade, whose name and the date of his death become the title of the poem: 'Haris 1944'. These lines form the centre of the poem:

Μια μέρα μάς σφύριξε κάποιος στ' αφτί: "Πέθανε ο Χάρης"
"Σκοτώθηκε" ή κάτι τέτοιο. Λέξεις που τις ακούμε κάθε μέρα.
Κανείς δεν τον είδε. Ήταν σούρουπο. Θά 'χε σφιγμένα
    τα χέρια όπως πάντα
Στα μάτια του χαράχτηκεν άσβηστα η χαρά της καινούριας
    ζωής μας
Μα όλα αυτά ήταν απλά κι ο καιρός είναι λίγος. Κανείς δεν
    προφταίνει.[144]

One day someone hissed in our ears: 'Haris is dead'
'Killed', something like that. Words we're used to hearing
    every day.
No one had seen him. It was dusk. He'd have had his fists
    clenched as he always did
Etched indelibly in his eyes the joy [in Greek a near-pun on the name
    Haris] of our new life
But all these things happened very simply and time is short.
No one has enough time.

Beyond the bald, breathless tone of the narration lies a deep distrust of the poet's very medium, which runs through almost all the poetry of this generation irrespective of the poets' political and literary affiliations. For Anagnostakis, words are inadequate, the message of death reduced to a commonplace in the face of events whose very 'simplicity' makes them more terrible still. There is simply no time to contemplate the event—not even, or especially not, for the poet.

In the face of such calamities, and faced with his own impotence to change anything in the practical and social terms which for these poets are the ones that count, the poet himself becomes a devalued figure. As Alexandrou ruefully concedes, in a brief poem written in a prison camp in 1951, the only weapon in the poet's armoury is the words he doesn't write at all, the ordinary spoken language that he shares with the people around him:

Η μόνη ξιφολόγχη μου
είταν το κρυφοκοίταγμα του φεγγαριού απ' τα σύννεφα.
Ίσως γι' αυτό δεν έγραψα ποτέ

[144] Χάρης 1944, from the collection *Seasons* (*Εποχές*, Anagnostakis 1985: 37–8), cf. Ricks 1995–6.

στίχους τελεσίδικους σαν άντερα χυμένα
ίσως γι' αυτό εγκαταλείπουν ένας-ένας τα χαρτιά μου
και τους ακούω στις κουβέντες όσων δε με έχουνε διαβάσει.[145]

The only bayonet I had
was the moon peeping between the clouds.
Perhaps that's why I never wrote
verses as decisive as dangling entrails
perhaps that's why one by one they abandon my papers
and I hear them in the conversation of people who've
never read me.

[145] 'Poetics 3' (Ποιητική 3), from the collection *Bankrupt Line*, 1952 ('*Άγοιη γραμμή*, Alexandrou 1978: 60).

4. The Aftermath of War and Civil War
1949–1967

DESPITE the determination of the older generation of poets and novelists, during the years of occupation and the slide into civil war, to see the present trials of their country as the darkness before the dawn of a new period of reconciliation, the 1940s in reality proved to be a decade of disintegration unprecedented in Greece in modern times. The most visible consequence of the civil war of the late 1940s was the intense and continued political polarization, whose origin was described in the previous chapter. Between 1947 and 1974, when the Communist Party was outlawed, the face-off between the victorious Right and the obstinate rump of the Left which, particularly in intellectual circles, refused to lie down and admit defeat, reflected in miniature the stalemate in Europe as a whole throughout the cold war.

Indeed, the Greek civil war has often been seen in retrospect as the first skirmish of the cold war, with the government side receiving military and economic backing first from Britain and then, after 1947, from the US, and the communists counting on similar backing from Greece's newly communist neighbours to the north and from the Soviet Union. In the event Soviet backing for the Left proved very limited, while US determination to halt the spread of communism was in its first flush and as yet untarnished by experiences in Korea and Vietnam. These were probably the most decisive factors that prevented Greece from being absorbed into the eastern bloc for the duration of the cold war.

The victory of the Right in 1949 was in any case a pyrrhic one, and the scars of the conflict, in which some 80,000 Greeks were killed and 700,000 lost their homes,[1] were clearly visible in many aspects of Greek public life until at least the mid-1980s. Although parliamentary government survived the conflict, many communists and sympathizers continued to be held in prison camps on Aegean islands throughout the 1950s; while the persecution of known or

---

[1] Figures in Clogg 1986: 164. On the history of the civil war, see also (in English): Close 1993; 1995; Hondros 1983; Mazower 1993.

suspected leftist sympathizers, and very often of their families as well, had not completely ceased by the early 1960s, and reached new heights once again under the seven-year military rule of the Colonels from 1967 to 1974.

Some relief from this polarization was afforded, during the 1950s, by the final phase of British colonial rule in Cyprus. Left and Right in Greece were temporarily united in the face of a flat refusal by the British government, delivered in 1953, ever to countenance cession of the island, with its predominantly Greek-speaking, Orthodox population, to Greece. In the late 1950s violence broke out in Cyprus, while in Greece the British policy of emphasizing the rights and needs of the Turkish-speaking Muslim minority of Cypriots was deeply resented. After much bitterness a settlement was reached in 1959, in which a leading role had been played by the poet and diplomat Yorgos Seferis. According to this settlement, Cyprus became an independent state under the presidency of Archbishop Makarios. Thus the only territorial gain made by Greece in the wake of the Second World War was the islands of the Dodecanese, ceded by Italy in 1947 after a thirty-five-year colonial occupation.

The 1950s and 1960s were a time of unprecedented economic advance, with the foundations being laid for the mass tourism which since the 1970s has played such a key role in the Greek economy. But despite the orderly hand-over of power from the Centre-Right party of Konstandinos Karamanlis to the Centre-Left party of George Papandreou following the general election of 1963, the twin spectres of the communist plot and of illegal, ultra-right-wing activities within the establishment continued to haunt national life during much of the 1960s. The second of these spectres, for which the Greek term 'para-state' was coined, was seen at work in the murders of a left-wing member of parliament in Thessaloniki in 1963 and of a left-wing student in Athens in 1965, acts which seem at the very least to have been condoned by members of the security forces. The other spectre (of the communist plot) was most nearly realized in allegations of a conspiracy within the army in 1965, over which the prime minister's son (and later prime minister) Andreas Papandreou was all but brought to trial. And it was again on the excuse of forestalling a communist plot that a group of army colonels, led by George Papadopoulos, seized power on 21 April 1967, a few weeks before a general election was due to take place, in which victory for Papandreou's Centre-Left party had been widely predicted.

POETRY: THE POST-WAR GENERATION

The most admired achievements of this first post-war period, viewed as a whole, are still considered to have been the mature work of poets who had broken new ground in the thirties: Seferis, Elytis, Embirikos, Engonopoulos, and Ritsos. At the same time, the 'new voices' that had begun to make themselves heard at the end of the war include a probably unprecedented number of poets, many of whom have since died or retired from the scene without ever either matching the achievements of their elders or overcoming in their work the stunting experience of the violent decade in which their careers began. Criticism has been slow to grapple with the poetry of this generation, and there has been a marked reluctance among poets themselves to seek or to award laurels.[2] These poets have voluntarily shunned the high ground occupied by their predecessors—a principled stand which none the less helps to explain the generalized perception of their work as 'elegiac' and 'minor'.[3]

Although it seems unlikely that any of the poets of this latter group will be seen to command the stature of a Seferis or an Elytis, none the less it is not quite true, as has been suggested, that after the barnstorming of the 1930s there were 'no new lands left to conquer' for the generation that came after.[4] As we shall see, there are specific areas of new ground that were broken by poets of this generation. And since the innovations of the younger generation also left their mark on the later achievements of the older poets who overshadowed them, it will be timely to consider the post-war generation first.

During the decades following the civil war these poets and others continued to grapple with the overwhelming legacy of their

[2] One of the first critical studies which singled out three poets from this group, by the influential academic critic D. N. Maronitis, articulates a view which seems to have been commonly held in the early 1970s: 'The reading public is less concerned by now with poets' personalities, and more concerned with their poems. It recognizes mature poems, not mature poets' (1976: 14). A similar note is struck in other critical studies of poets of this period, e.g. Themelis 1978; Anagnostaki 1980; Meraklis 1987; Vitti 1987: 422–3. For anthologies of this and the subsequent 'generations', see, respectively: Argyriou 1982; Evangelou 1994.

[3] See the comments of G. P. Savvidis and Alexis Ziras, and the ensuing discussion, recorded in Skartsis 1982: 23–54.

[4] 'For the writers of the first post-war generation there was no revolution left that had not already happened' (Vitti 1987: 424).

formative years. None decisively and unambiguously leaves behind the 'landscape of death' delineated by Sinopoulos. Remaining within this restricted zone, the poets of this generation explore contrasting strategies. One is towards more open and public utterance, and this is broadly the strategy of the 'social' poets of the Left. Another, more surprisingly, is to breathe new life into the 'post-Symbolist' poetry of the 1920s and 1930s with its interiorized melancholy and its respect for traditional poetic forms. This legacy of the low-key successors of Palamas lives on into the 1950s and 1960s, most notably in the work of Kostas Steryopoulos (b. 1926), who has also done much to rehabilitate this whole group,[5] and in the highly individual, if in some respects anachronistic, poetry of Aris Diktaios (1919–80), which unusually owes almost equal debts to his fellow Cretan Kazantzakis and to Rilke.[6]

A final strategy is to move away from communication and indeed from any direct reference to the outside world at all. In the work of many poets of the 1950s and 1960s a hermetic, almost secretive poetry develops. This new hermeticism is clearly a development of the Modernist experiments of the 1930s which culminated in the notorious obscurity of the wartime poems of that generation discussed in the previous chapter. But the sense of liberation that accompanied these experiments has gone; and common to all these newer strategies is the continuing doubt that poetry itself has a positive role to play. For the 'social' poets, poetry remains inferior to action. For the others, poetry becomes the opaque, intransitive medium through which poets reach out tentatively towards something else. Characteristically that 'something else' is either the objective solidity of *things*, or a new religious awareness which often draws on the Orthodox tradition although its perceptions are not necessarily Christian.

Among the 'social' poets, the lucid irony of Cavafy, with his humane sympathy for the losers in the battles of history, proved a productive model. Distinctively new poetry which at the same time alludes to the style and subject-matter of Cavafy had first been written by Seferis in 1941, and becomes a feature of some of Seferis' later poetry. But during the later 1950s and the 1960s Anagnostakis and Alexandrou, in particular, make effective use of Cavafian

---

[5] For a sympathetic retrospect on the earlier group see Steryopoulos 1967. For his own collected poems see Steryopoulos 1988.

[6] See Diktaios 1974.

allusion in circumstances and in the interests of a cause quite distinct from those of Cavafy himself.[7]

A quest for the solid reliability of objects runs through the later poetry of Eleni Vakalo (b. 1921), from a background in Surrealism, and of G. Themelis whose early work, as we saw, was closely linked with Seferis. The austerity of Vakalo comes close to a kind of poetic asceticism; her style has justly been described as tactile rather than visual.[8] By the time of her long poem *Genealogy* (1971) her spare, elliptical style has eschewed not just communication in any conventional sense (as Surrealism also did) but almost all of the unbridled subjectivity which gave Surrealism its vitality.[9]

By comparison Themelis is relatively open, in a series of collections which, like those of Vakalo, seek the 'life of things' in a paradoxically abstract way. A recurring preoccupation in Themelis' poetry is with mirrors, and the solid reality he seeks is constantly being displaced as 'reality' turns out to be composed of endless mirror-images. In a poem entitled simply 'Things' (1968), everything together, whether real or reflected, calls out in vain for a resurrection, while the Cross turns out to be empty and sacrifice 'in vain'.[10]

The spiritual or religious solution hinted at by the unfulfilled plea of Themelis' 'Things' for a resurrection assumes greater importance in the later work of three poets whose names have been linked, with varying degrees of plausibility, with the legacy of Surrealism: D. P. Papaditsas (1922–87), Ektor Kaknavatos (b. 1920), and Nikos Karouzos (1926–90).

Papaditsas in 1964 published a poem in eleven short sections entitled *In Patmos*.[11] The title alludes to the biblical Apocalypse, written by St John the Divine in the island of Patmos, where a famous monastery was founded in his name in the eleventh century. There is an entirely new sense of a religious quest in this poem, which also adopts a new religious vocabulary. This, and much of Papaditsas' poetry of the 1960s, has all the spare austerity of Vakalo;

---

[7] The publication, in 1963, of the first critical edition of Cavafy's poems, to mark the thirtieth anniversary of the poet's death, may have added further impetus to the rediscovery of Cavafy by poets of this period.

[8] Anagnostaki 1980: 9.

[9] First published in a bilingual edition, with translation by Paul Merchant, reprinted in Vakalo 1990.

[10] Τα πράγματα, the concluding poem of the collection *Exodus*, 1968 (Έξοδος, Themelis 1969–70: ii. 200–3).

[11] Εν Πάτμω (Papaditsas 1978: 7–22).

but Papaditsas will not be content with the 'life of things'. Even the solid objects of Vakalo's and Themelis' poetry are transient and untrustworthy for Papaditsas. As the poet wrote in 1972:

The poet immersed in the primeval birth and death of things . . . not surprisingly is nostalgic for lost unity or imaginatively opens windows on the unknown to gain light and air, windows on god and fate. That's to say he resorts to a religious sense, which is the equivalent of a lost faith.[12]

The search for an elusive faith takes a different form in the poetry of Ektor Kaknavatos. A teacher of mathematics, Kaknavatos is probably the first Greek poet to have grappled with the cosmology of post-Einsteinian physics (and surely the first to name an artificial computer language, in a poem of 1964).[13] Kaknavatos is more unusual still among his contemporaries in that his first poems, published in 1943, make no direct reference at all to the conditions of that time. Instead their titles allude to the two abiding preoccupations of his later work, music and science, and one of them, 'Fuga' (meaning perhaps both 'fugue' and 'flight'), is in effect a series of passionate prayers to the ancient Asiatic goddess of love, Astarte, that anticipates aspects of Papatsonis' long poem of 1944, *Ursa Minor*.[14] Kaknavatos' intense but always abstract quest involves the dissolution of the familiar world and—something which he shares with a number of his contemporaries—a determined attempt to dissolve the conceptual frontier that separates the self from what it perceives. Drawing on the surrealist practice of collapsing boundaries in the interests of greater freedom, Kaknavatos' poetry seeks the primeval unifying strands that knit together the entire cosmos, animate and inanimate, present and past.[15]

Of all the poets of this generation perhaps the most difficult to categorize is Nikos Karouzos. A supporter of the Left during the

---

[12] Ο ποιητής διαποτισμένος από την πανάρχαιη γέννηση και το θάνατο των πραγμάτων . . . δεν είναι παράδοξο που νοσταλγεί τη χαμένη ενότητα ή ανοίγει με την ενόρασή του παράθυρα του αγνώστου για να κερδίσει φως και αέρα, παράθυρα του θεού και της μοίρας. Καταφεύγει δηλαδή σ' αυτό που λέμε θρησκευτικότητα, ισοδύναμο μιας χαμένης πίστης (Papaditsas 1974: 104).

[13] 'thought from the Algol age' (η σκέψη από τη γενιά του αλγόλ), from *Scale of Hardness*, 1964 (*Η κλίμακα του λίθου*, Kaknavatos 1990: i. 67).

[14] Kaknavatos 1990: i. 17–26; on Papatsonis' poem see Ch. 3.

[15] Strands or fibres (ίνες) are a recurring motif. Sometimes this quest for primeval principles ('principia' as he at one point calls them, after Newton, see 1990: i. 119) comes close to that articulated by Seferis, particularly in his early poem *Novel* (*Μυθιστόρημα*). See e.g. Kaknavatos 1990: i. 65, 182.

civil war and for long afterwards, Karouzos avoided the overt commitment and the open, public style of so many of his socialist
contemporaries. In his last decade he repudiated Marxism altogether: 'Capitalism made a brute of man, Marxism made a brute
of the truth.'[16] His relationship to Surrealism is also somewhat
unclear, and has provoked uneasy or ambivalent comments.[17] Karouzos has variously been described as a religious or a philosophical
poet;[18] but although he frequently alludes to the Orthodox tradition, what he seems so often to be seeking is not so much transcend-
ence as a wordless immersion in the totality of real things.[19]

Although Karouzos elected to tread an increasingly lonely road
from the late 1960s onwards, in the early part of his career he is
notable for a more positive, if characteristically humble, faith in the
poet's own art than most of his contemporaries. Karouzos' definition of poetry, which dates from 1955, is unusually positive, and also,
in its religious metaphor, partakes of precisely the kind of difficulty
that is the hallmark of his poetry:

Η ποίηση είναι λόγος εν μέθη, καθώς ο πρωτεύων άνθρωπος είναι
χρόνος εν Χριστώ. Γι' αυτό και οι λέξεις ομοιάζουν με κλυδωνιζόμενα
πράγματα και τα νοήματα χάνονται στο βάθος της φωνής ατελείωτα.[20]

Poetry is logos [or 'words' or 'discourse'] in intoxication, just as the excellent man is time in Christ. That's why words resemble things in tumult and
meanings are lost in the depths of the voice without end.

Even this somewhat tortuous faith, however, seems to elude Karouzos in his later poetry. His 1979 collection *Possibilities and Use of
Speech*, for example, describes his art in terms that closely echo the

[16] Cited in Pilidis 1991: 41.
[17] See e.g. Themelis 1978: 234; Aranitsis in Karouzos 1981: 9. To compound the
uncertainty, Aranitsis illustrates his anthology of Karouzos' work with reproductions
of paintings by Dalí. There is nothing to indicate, however, whether the poet
approved of this.
[18] Themelis 1978: 231–40; Meraklis 1987: 111–13; Pilidis 1991: 16 and *passim*.
Meraklis draws attention to the *erotic* element in Karouzos' religious awareness,
something which can be paralleled in Papatsonis, Kaknavatos, and even Seferis,
and goes back, in Greek poetry, at least as far as the early poems of Sikelianos.
[19] See in particular Karouzos 1986: 50, from the poem 'The Evil of the Day':
Ενυπάρχει στη μέγιστη φωτιά κ' η δική μου σπίθα. | Δώρα πολύτιμα δώρα που 'χει
τραγουδήσει ο πιο άθεος θεός ο αθωότερος. (In the supreme fire my own spark
coexists. | Rich gifts; gifts that have been sung by the most godless god the most
innocent of them all.) It is only since the poet's death that a collected edition of his
work has been published (Karouzos 1994).
[20] Cited in Themelis 1978: 281.

'social' poets of the post-war decades, as 'mementoes of horror' and 'forged banknotes':

Γιατί η γλώσσα είν' η αχόρταγη
μοιχαλίδα του Πραγματικού
με αρίφνητα ψέματα προσπαθώντας
να περισώσει το γάμο της.[21]

Because language is an insatiable
adulteress of the Real
trying with a thousand lies
to save her marriage.

Karouzos' poetry pays homage, in different ways, to Papadiamandis and Cavafy, and develops a dense and often alliterative style. In the later poetry the moon is a dominant image; when the sun appears its light is characteristically refracted, diffused, or broken up.

For all the activity of the new poets who emerged during and after the Second World War, there can be no question but that the poetic 'high ground' until at least the 1970s continued to be occupied by poets who had embarked on their writing careers in the heady days of the 1930s. Of these poets Seferis, Ritsos, and Elytis are by no means indifferent to the experiments of their younger peers, but they, together with the Surrealist poets of the 1930s, Embirikos and Engonopoulos, retain and extend, in the face of the post-war trauma, their faith in the redemptive power of their art.

Seferis. After heralding the reconciliation of conflict and the birth of love in the long poem '*Thrush*' (1947), Seferis published no more poetry for almost a decade. A few poems of the late 1940s which allude to the civil war seemingly failed to satisfy the poet and were published only posthumously.[22] Seferis' next collection, like

---

[21] Karouzos 1979: 22 (ενθύμια φρίκης: the closing words of the poem Διερώτηση για να μην κάθομαι άεργος), 25 (κάλπικα χαρτονομίσματα). The quotation in the text is from the same poem: 'Clay Figurine' (Πήλινο αγαλματίδιο). In poems of the 1980s Karouzos meditates on Fredric Jameson's term, the 'prison house of language', which becomes το αχανές | δεσμωτήριο της γλώσσας (Karouzos 1986: 11), and even 'an indecency perpetrated upon Being' (η γλώσσα είναι ασέλγεια πάνω στο Είναι, Karouzos 1986: 52).

[22] The only reference to these momentous events in a poem published by Seferis himself comes in the closing lines of '*Thrush*', where, writing before the final round of the conflict, Seferis had prophesied or called for reconciliation; cf. Vitti 1989: 231–2. On the posthumous poems relating to the civil war (published in Seferis 1976) see Beaton 1991: 54–7.

'*Thrush*', again has a topical basis, and again imaginatively seeks the resolution of a conflict that would not, in reality, be averted. The poems of *Log-Book III* (1955) are dedicated 'to the people of Cyprus, in memory and love', and most were the fruit of two autumn visits to Cyprus in 1953 and 1954, when tension was rising over the future of the island.[23]

After the war Seferis had been posted first to the Turkish capital Ankara, and then by way of London to Beirut, from where he made his visits to Cyprus. While in Turkey he had had the opportunity to revisit his childhood haunts on the coast near Smyrna, and had seen how all but the merest traces of the Greek community, in which he himself had grown up, had been obliterated. At the same time his travels in Turkey and the Middle East opened his eyes to the wider historical perception of Hellenism that had been championed by Cavafy from the peripheral vantage-point of Alexandria. Cyprus, which Seferis visited for the first time in 1953, seems to have been almost literally a 'revelation' for him. Here, far from the boundaries of the Greek state which he served and whose shortcomings he knew only too well, the kind of rural, Greek-speaking, Orthodox Christian community that he had known as a child, and since lost irrecoverably, still existed. And Seferis also, as a diplomat, was not slow to perceive the very real threat that hung over that community, as Britain seemed determined to maintain colonial rule while momentum was gathering among the Greek-speaking population for union with Greece.

This is the significance that Cyprus held for Seferis: a link with the past and a hope for the future of a Greek language and culture which transcended national boundaries. The landscape and people of Cyprus figure largely in the poems, as do historical allusions to the island's turbulent medieval past, often presented with an ironic detachment which pays evident homage to Cavafy. As one might expect from Seferis, a wealth of ancient allusions adds historical depth and literary complexity to the poems. These allusions no longer hark back to the primitive myths or stories of the ancients behind the literary texts that have come down to us (the 'primordial drama' of his poem of 1935, *Novel*) but to the literary texts themselves. The archetypal Odysseus never again appears in a poem of Seferis after '*Thrush*'. Instead, the ancient allusions in *Log-Book III*

[23] On these poems, see in English, Krikos-Davis 1994.

are to specific works, most memorably to two ancient tragedies which have a 'happy' ending: the *Persians* of Aeschylus and the *Helen* of Euripides. At the same time Christian texts also begin to occupy a significant place in Seferis' complex web of literary allusion.

Against this very different landscape, and with the new political and historical perceptions of the mid-fifties, Seferis ends the collection with a poem that carries forward the visionary synthesis achieved at the end of '*Thrush*'. The earlier poem had ended with the Odysseus-figure regaining his home, the 'light' in which Aphrodite, goddess of love, is at the same time reborn. According to legend, the birth of Aphrodite out of the sea had taken place off the coast of Cyprus. In the poem 'Engomi', named after an archaeological site in Cyprus, Seferis depicts the rising of a visionary figure not from the sea but from the land, and specifically from the local labourers working on the site under the eye of the foreign archaeologist. This 'goddess' is at once sensuous and spiritual, a conflation of the ancient goddess of love with the Virgin Mary as depicted in Orthodox iconography, and of both, together, with the ideal female form that has been elusively sought in much Modern Greek literature, ever since the 'moon-clad woman' in Solomos' poem *The Cretan*. In this way Seferis achieves, within the unprecedented economy of only fifty-four lines, and in his own distinctive manner, the synthesis of different epochs of Greek culture that had first been proposed by Palamas on the large canvas of *The Emperor's Reed-Pipe*, and had been extended by Sikelianos in *Easter of the Hellenes*.

None the less the poem does not end on this note of affirmation. In this poem, as in '*Thrush*', the visionary moment is followed by a return to earth, and at the end of 'Engomi' we recognize the same real world which inhibited the younger poets of the time from similar achievements of the imagination:

Ο κόσμος
ξαναγινόταν όπως ήταν, ο δικός μας
με τον καιρό και με το χώμα

.   .   .   .

κι όλα στεγνώσαν μονομιάς στην πλατωσιά του κάμπου
στης πέτρας την απόγνωση στη δύναμη τη φαγωμένη
στον άδειο τόπο με το λιγοστό χορτάρι και τ' αγκάθια

όπου γλιστρούσε ξέγνοιαστο ένα φίδι,
όπου ζοδεύουνε πολύ καιρό για να πεθάνουν.²⁴

    The world
became once more as it had been, our own
with time and earth

· · · · · · · · · ·

everything all at once dried out in the expanse of the plain
in the desolation of stone in the eroded strength
in the empty land with the sparse grass and thorns
where a snake slid by untroubled,
where a lot of time is taken up in dying.

Seferis was almost alone among Greek writers in giving such
prominence in his work to the fate of Cyprus.²⁵ In his final collection, *Three Secret Poems* (1966), he abandons altogether the allusive
commentary on contemporary history that had characterized his
three *Log-Books* and had also set up a productive legacy for post-
war 'social' poets of the younger generation. Seferis' final collection,
which has been much translated but little studied, marks a return to
the interiority of his own first poems, but interestingly also shows
Seferis, as an 'elder statesman' among poets, going forward hand in
hand with many of the younger poets around him.²⁶

The *Three Secret Poems*, as their title implies, share the hermeticism which by the 1960s had become a common denominator of
most poetry of the younger generation that was not politically committed. Taken together with a number of essays by Seferis written at

²⁴ 'Εγκωμη, ll. 45–7, 50–4 (Seferis 1972: 268–9). The phrase το λιγοστό χορτάρι
alludes to the famous epigraph of Solomos on the massacre of Psara in 1824, and so
hints at violence to come, while the 'thorns' and 'snake' point, respectively, to the
Crucifixion and the Fall. For the significance of the enigmatic final image of the
snake, compare the (later) novel by Seferis' friend Theotokas, *The Bells*, discussed
below. See also: Savvidis 1961: 404–5; Kehayoglou 1991c; Krikos-Davis 1994:
147–58.
²⁵ Rodis Roufos, a fellow diplomat, published his novel about Cyprus in the 1950s,
The Age of Bronze (Η χάλκινη εποχή), in 1960 (as a reply to Durrell's *Bitter Lemons*),
and Ritsos wrote poems about the island, both in the late 1950s and after the invasion
of 1974. In the 1950s Ritsos' perspective is much simpler than Seferis', and his
programmatic solidarity with the Greek-Cypriot guerrillas brings him perilously
close to the viewpoint of the extreme Right, who were promoting the cause of union
with Greece in terms very similar to his (see the dramatic monologue of the EOKA
fighter G. Afxendiou, 'Farewell' (Αποχαιρετισμός), written and published in 1957.
The people of Cyprus became once again the subject of a poem by Ritsos in 'Hymn
and Lament for Cyprus' ('Υμνος και θρήνος για την Κύπρο), an 'occasional' poem
on the Turkish invasion of the island in 1974.
²⁶ *Τρία κρυφά ποιήματα* (Seferis 1972: 275–306).

the same time, and with his translations of the biblical *Song of Songs* and the *Apocalypse* into Modern Greek, they bear witness to a much increased religious and philosophical awareness, which is common to many of his younger contemporaries. The *Three Secret Poems* are a modern *Apocalypse*, and their starting-point was a visit in 1955 to Patmos, where the *Apocalypse*, or *Book of Revelation*, had been written. But instead of *revealing*, Seferis' poems tease the reader with their title and the concise, distilled, hermetic brevity of their twenty-eight sections. In these poems the philosophy of Heraclitus, Christianity, ancient and Renaissance drama, and modern folk customs are all juxtaposed, and interwoven with allusions to Dante and the *Four Quartets* of T. S. Eliot. The cryptic style and the attempt to reach beyond poetic language towards a profound truth about the universe are shared with poems of the 1950s and 1960s by Themelis, Papaditsas, Kaknavatos, and Karouzos. Papaditsas' own poetic variation on the biblical *Apocalypse*, *In Patmos*, had appeared in 1964; and all of the last three poets mentioned share a strong interest in Heraclitus and other 'pre-Socratic' philosophers, who flourished in the sixth and fifth centuries BC, when the formal distinction between philosophy and poetry had not yet been fully made.

The discovery that

"Κατά βάθος είμαι ζήτημα φωτός"

'Fundamentally I am a matter of light'

echoes such statements as those of Themelis in 1959:

Είμαστε από φως, δεν μας αγγίζει ο θάνατος

We are made of light, death cannot touch us

and Kaknavatos in 1964:

πώς λοιπόν μπορεί να μην είσαι φώς;[27]

so how can you be anything other than light?

The *Three Secret Poems* offer at best a harsh deliverance, and are pervaded by images of random violence which have much in common with the poetry of the post-war generation. The point of noting

---

[27] Respectively: Seferis 1972: 280; Themelis 1969–70: ii. 21; Kaknavatos 1991: i. 78 (the whole section of the Kaknavatos poem, and other parts of the same collection, contain other pre-echoes of the *Three Secret Poems*).

these similarities is not, of course, to diminish the achievement of Seferis' last collection, but rather to place it in its historical context. All of the poets mentioned here themselves acknowledge, explicitly or implicitly, earlier debts to Seferis. To read the *Three Secret Poems* alongside other poetry of the 1960s is to reveal a poetic transaction too complex to be adequately described as 'influence'.

Seferis' 'revelation' in the *Three Secret Poems* is both bleak and cryptic. But the final poem of the three, 'Summer Solstice', is the only poem by Seferis which ends on an unqualified note of affirmation, and it is this that marks out the *Three Secret Poems* from other hermetic poetry of the period, and indeed in Seferis' work as a whole. The penultimate section of 'Summer Solstice' looks forward to:

Αναστάσιμη ωδίνη[28]
A birth-pang of resurrection

and the last section envisages the final conflagration, which is both the biblical end of the world and the catastrophe imagined by Heraclitus when the sun 'oversteps his measure' and the balance of forces, both natural and moral, that constitutes the visible world is destroyed. After the conflagration:

φώναξε τα παιδιά να μαζέψουν τη στάχτη
και να τη σπείρουν.
'Ο,τι πέρασε πέρασε σωστά.

Κι εκείνα ακόμη που δεν πέρασαν
πρέπει να καούν
τούτο το μεσημέρι που καρφώθηκε ο ήλιος
στην καρδιά του εκατόφυλλου ρόδου.[29]

call the children to gather the ashes
and sow them.
Whatever has passed has passed rightly.

And all things more which have not passed
must burn
this noontide when the sun has stood still
at the heart of the centifoliate rose.

Elytis. The Orthodox tradition and religious language during the same period come to occupy an important place in the *magnum opus* of Odysseas Elytis, *The Axion Esti* (1959). Elytis, more clearly than

[28] 'Summer Solstice' (Θερινό ηλιοστάσι), XIII, l. 12 (Seferis 1972: 305).
[29] 'Summer Solstice', XIV, ll. 12–17 (Seferis 1972: 306).

any of the poets so far discussed, enlists the language and the expressive forms of a centuries-old religious tradition for a purpose which is in no conventional sense religious. The title refers to a Byzantine hymn: 'Worthy is...'. But the starting-point for the poem, which was some fourteen years in the writing, was Elytis' abrupt confrontation with war and violent death on the Albanian front in 1940. In the poem he wrote in the immediate aftermath of these events, discussed in the previous chapter, he had drawn, for the first time in his poetry, on the mythical archetype of the spring resurrection. In *The Axion Esti*, a poem whose liturgical precedents are clearly proclaimed by its title, Elytis confronts the national experience of war, defeat, and occupation in terms of Christ's Passion. The equivalent in this poem to the Christian Resurrection is the triumph of poetic language, as the poet finally creates a better world by exultantly naming its parts and declaring them 'worthy'.

The Axion Esti is a long poem on a scale relatively rare in twentieth-century poetry, running to eighty-eight pages.[30] Its component units are all short however; each one is constructed according to a strict formal pattern and the arrangement of the whole is governed by a complex arithmetical scheme based on the numbers three and seven. In what amounts to a clear break with his Surrealist past, Elytis after publishing this poem declared his conviction that 'it is possible for modern experience to pass into its classical period, not with a return to the constraints of the past, but with the creation of new constraints, which the poet himself imposes in order to overcome them and so achieve once more a solid construction'.[31] Elytis' new kind of 'classicism' amounts to more, however, than formal experiment. It is justified by the attempt to produce a poetry in which 'technique becomes also part of the content'.[32] If poetic language is to prevail over the forces of violence and destruction (which is what happens in *The Axion Esti*) then that language has to be both resonant with the formal patterns that have claimed

[30] Elytis 1970.
[31] είναι δυνατόν η μοντέρνα εμπειρία να περάσει στην κλασική της περίοδο, όχι με την επιστροφή της στους περιορισμούς των παλαιών, αλλά με την δημιουργία νέων περιορισμών, που θέτει ο ίδιος ο ποιητής για να τους υπερνικήσει και να επιτύχει έτσι, ακόμη μια φορά, ένα στερεό οικοδόμημα (from a previously unpublished note by the poet on *The Axion Esti*, cited by Vitti 1984: 234; cf. Vitti 1979: 151). For the full text see Kehayoglou 1995.
[32] η τεχνική να γίνεται κι αυτή μέρος του περιεχομένου (cited by Vitti 1984: 234–5; cf. Kehayoglou 1995).

redemptive power in the past, and also 'solidly constructed', in Elytis' metaphor, so as to bear the weight of the redemptive role that the poem demands.

Both Elytis' highly individual, lyrical style and the continued boldness of his juxtapositions and imaginative leaps, which derive from his earlier association with Surrealism, have tended to set his post-war poetry apart. But *The Axion Esti*, like Seferis' poems of the same decade, actually continues and refines the culling of tradition as a basis for future redemption that we identified as a common project of poets and novelists of the 'thirties' generation during the Second World War. By his own route, Elytis traverses the same terrain as Ritsos in *Romiosini* and Seferis in poems from *Novel* (1935) to *Log-Book III* (1955), in summoning up resources from the Greek past with which imaginatively to confront the realities of the present. With Ritsos' *Romiosini* the poem shares the evocation of the Greek people throughout their history, embedded in the harsh landscape that they fight to preserve, and of the foreign conquerors throughout that history, whose ways and whose laws 'didn't gel with' the ancient land.[33] The principal traditional 'resources' on which this poem calls, in addition to the Orthodox, Byzantine tradition, are the forces of nature, as visible in the Greek landscape, and the folk tradition; and both of these are of course common ground for Seferis and Ritsos as well as Elytis. Although the ancient world plays only a small part in the poem, the often-quoted lines about the modern language in which the poem is written are close to the spirit of Seferis:

Τη γλώσσα μού έδωσαν ελληνική·
το σπίτι φτωχικό στις αμμουδιές του Ομήρου.[34]

Greek the language that was given me;
the poor man's house on Homer's shores.

These lines, and the whole section from which they come, have especial significance in a poem which as it unfolds proclaims the victory of poetic language itself. This early section of *The Axion Esti* places the poet's language in a historical relation not only to Homer, but also to Christian hymnography, to folk songs celebrating Greek independence from the Turks, and to the 'national poet' Solomos.

[33] 'The Passion', VII (Τα Πάθη, Ζ΄, Elytis 1970: 42). Compare the opening lines of Ritsos' *Romiosini*.
[34] 'The Passion', II (Τα Πάθη, Β΄, Elytis 1970: 28).

The poetic language that will prevail in *The Axion Esti* is not, in the words of T. S. Eliot echoed by Seferis, 'the words of one man only'.[35] It is the historical depth of the Greek-language tradition that makes possible the audacious bid for power and authority by poetic language in this poem. Vindicated by the power of the language at his command to recreate the pure world of his own youthful imagination, the poet at the end of the central section, 'The Passion', sets off for a new land:

Σε χώρα μακρινή και αναμάρτητη τώρα πορεύομαι.
Τώρα μ' ακολουθούν ανάλαφρα πλάσματα
με τους ιριδισμούς του πόλου στα μαλλιά
και το πράο στο δέρμα χρυσάφισμα.[36]

To a distant and sinless land I now fare forward.
Now in my train come ethereal creatures
with polar iridescence in their hair
and gentle gilding on their skin.

The poet is a Christ-figure, hailed with cries of Hosanna and credited with victory over death; at the same time he is also the prehistoric 'Prince of the Lilies', the lithe, hieratically depicted young man painted on a mural in the Minoan palace of Knossos, close to Elytis' birthplace in Heraklion.[37] In *The Axion Esti* the national and personal trauma of the Second World War has been transfigured by the agency of poetic language and its declared alliance with the free, creative forces of nature. As a synthesis of the Greek historical experience of different periods, and of history with religion, it stands alongside Seferis' last two collections and especially the poem 'Engomi' as a worthy successor to the long poems of Palamas, and especially to Sikelianos' abortive *Easter of the Hellenes*.

Almost at the same time as *The Axion Esti* Elytis produced another much shorter collection, *Six and One Regrets for the Sky* (1960).[38] The contrast with the large-scale work has been much noticed. Where *The Axion Esti* stands out as a spectacular affirmation at a time when most poets were squaring up to the experience of defeat

---

[35] From 'The Dry Salvages'; cf. Seferis 1981: ii. 246 and discussion by Beaton 1991: 84, 124.
[36] 'The Passion', XVII (Τα Πάθη, IZ', Elytis 1970: 69).
[37] Πρίγκιπας των Κρίνων (Elytis 1970: 70) translates the name given by 20th-cent. archaeologists to this mural in its restored form.
[38] Elytis 1979.

of various kinds, these shorter poems of Elytis are in their own way as inward-looking and as hermetic as the *Three Secret Poems* of Seferis and much other poetry of the 1960s. With these two volumes published at the turn of the decade, Elytis established the twin paths that would mark out his later work: a lyricism of the grand sweep encompassing both public and private utterance, and what has aptly been termed an 'interior lyricism' of greater depth.[39] In this alternating emphasis on the extrovert and the intimate, of the small canvas with the large, Elytis can be compared, once again, to the lyricists *par excellence* of an earlier period, Palamas and Sikelianos.[40]

Embirikos and Engonopoulos.   Elytis' later work would scarcely have been possible without his earlier apprenticeship to Surrealism. But the Surrealist crusade to liberate the anarchic forces of the unconscious becomes tempered in Elytis' work by the poet's fascination with the formal qualities of poetic language, whose discipline, particularly in *The Axion Esti*, brings with it power. By way of contrast, Andreas Embirikos, always the most committed of Greek Surrealists, had made some concessions to the demands of poetic form in his second collection *Inner Land*, written before the Second World War. But Embirikos' indefatigable quest for the wholesale liberation of the Freudian unconscious continues after the war with an apparent indifference to form. This strategy, which is diametrically opposed to that of Elytis (although as we shall see it has a not dissimilar goal), has the paradoxical consequence of creating a *new* literary form which collapses the traditional distinction between verse and prose, between poetry and fiction.

It is not especially helpful to describe Embirikos' work after the war as 'Surrealist', although he himself continued in his role as spokesman for the movement in Greece.[41] Rather Embirikos belongs in the company of such idiosyncratic geniuses as Luis Buñuel and Salvador Dalí, whose peculiar flair for capturing the irrational in their chosen medium went on developing long after Surrealism as a movement had broken up. A further difficulty in approaching Embirikos' post-war work arises out of the long delay in the publication of most of it. Embirikos' two collections of poetry,

---

[39] Maronitis 1980: 103, 107, 115–16.
[40] This is also pointed out by Maronitis (1980: 107–8).
[41] See e.g. the radio interview on the subject in 1960, quoted by Yatromanolakis (1983: 28–9).

one in verse and one in prose, which were mainly composed after the war, appeared only posthumously, while the eight volumes of his novel *The Great Eastern* only appeared in print between 1990 and 1992, and other prose works apparently remain unpublished because, as Embirikos coyly put it some years before his death, of 'their unbridled freedom of expression'.[42]

It might well be questioned whether Embirikos' later work, the great preponderance of which is in the medium of prose, should be considered under the heading of poetry at all. But criticism continues to describe the author of what is surely the longest novel ever written in Greek as a poet, and to describe his shorter prose pieces as poems—indeed it is difficult to know what else to call them. To attempt to divide up the *œuvre* under the separate headings of poetry and fiction would be to ignore what is probably Embirikos' most important single contribution to Greek literature, namely his rigorous assault on the concept of genre and on the formal constraints which usually go with it. A further reason for considering Embirikos' late work together, and under the heading of poetry, is that the crusading optimism which runs through all of it, and its quasi-religious quest for salvation by means of the written word, place it inextricably alongside the post-war poetry of the dominant figures from the 1930s.

Formally recognizable verse, in the style of *Inner Land*, appears only in the collection *Today as Tomorrow and as Yesterday* (1984). More critical attention, however, has been given to the generically indefinable short pieces of prose, many of which were published in periodicals during the 1960s, and which were collected, again posthumously, under the title *Oktana* (1980). However defined in terms of genre, these texts in their own way maintain the affirmation of the worth and even power of the poet's art in the face of recent traumatic experiences. 'The Road' (written 1964), although apparently in prose, makes greater use of traditional metre than much *verse* published in Greek after the mid-1930s, and even surreptitiously introduces some rhyme. The road of the title is life itself, as it passes through every corner of the earth, traversing in its course some violent episodes of modern Greek history. The end of the road of course is death, but that is not how the text ends:

---

[42] In an interview of 1967 entitled 'I Fight for the Freedom of Love' (Μάχομαι διά την ελευθερίαν του έρωτα). Cited by Yatromanolakis (1990: 288).

Και ο δρόμος εξακολουθεί, σκληρός, σκληρότερος παρά ποτέ,
σκυρόστρωτος ή με άσφαλτο ντυμένος, και μαλακώνει μόνο, όποια και
αν είναι η χώρα, όποιο και αν είναι το τοπίον, κάτω από σέλας αγλαόν
αθανασίας, μόνο στα βήματα των ποιητών εκείνων, που οι ψυχές των ένα
με τα κορμιά των είναι, των ποιητών εκείνων των ακραιφνών και των
αχράντων, καθώς και των αδελφών αυτών Αγίων Πάντων.[43]

And the road continues, a hard road, harder than ever, metalled or asphalt-
coated, and softens only, whatever the country, whatever the place, beneath
the resplendent radiance of immortality, only to the tread of those poets
whose soul is one with their body, of those poets who are pure and spotless,
as also of their brothers the Blessed Saints.

'The Road', and others of the disparate poems which make up
this collection, in different ways open up a new terrain, a new world
of freedom, which for Embirikos means primarily the abolition of
sexual taboos. Many of these taboos are of course enshrined in
language, and in the conventions of 'decent usage'. Simply by
naming and describing sexual practices, Embirikos is already
enabled, in his writing, to break taboos, and the language of *Oktana*
is characterized by a sexual directness which at the same time,
however, is combined with the fervour of the mystic and the
authority of the prophet. Embirikos in this way joins other poets
of the time in appropriating biblical language for his own poetic
purposes.

The keynote of this collection is struck in the piece which also
introduces and explains the title: 'Not Brasilia but Oktana', dated
1965. This was the time when the new capital of Brazil was being
created out of nothing in the midst of the Amazon jungle. The New
World had exercised a fascination for Embirikos at least since the
time of his novella *Argo, or the Voyage of a Balloon*, written in 1944;
and the Utopian project undertaken by the Brazilian government
offered a real-life parallel to the 'New Jerusalem' that Embirikos was
by this time attempting to create in his writing. 'Not Brasilia but
Oktana' is in the form of an incantation, defining the nature of the
new ecumenical paradise, whose (invented) name is also the title of
the collection:

Οκτάνα θα πη ανά πάσαν στιγμήν ποίησις, όμως όχι ως μέσον εκφράσεως
μόνον, μα ακόμη ως λειτουργία του πνεύματος διηνεκής.[44]

---

[43] Ο δρόμος (Embirikos 1980e: 17–18).
[44] 'Οχι Μπραζίλια μα Οκτάνα (Embirikos 1980e: 77).

Oktana means poetry at every moment, but not only as a means of expression, but also as a function of the spirit in perpetuity.[45]

Oktana is to be a Garden of Eden without original sin, in which everything is possible, everything is permitted.[46] This Utopian vision has less to do with Surrealism than with the 'liberated' attitudes of the 1960s in America and western Europe, and it is no coincidence that it was the elderly Embirikos, rather than any representative of the younger generation, who first welcomed American 'beat' poetry to Greece.[47]

By the time that *Oktana* appeared in book form, in 1980, the 'beat' generation was a thing of the past, and the reality of the new capital of Brazil had failed to live up to its much publicized expectations. Embirikos' idealism remains, however, not least because of his use of language. The name 'Oktana' refers to nothing real; unlike the Brazilian capital it is not a real place, but a Utopia. The freedom Embirikos envisages is only possible in the realm of language. In its turn, that freedom demands not only new genres in which to find expression, but even new words and a new language. Much of Embirikos' later work is actually about words and how they mean.[48] The final poem of the collection, 'The Robinsons' Island', actually declares the need to 'create new words (new vessels for the old meanings)'—and with examples of this new, unintelligible language, the freedom of which Embirikos dreams is most nearly achieved in the closing pages of *Oktana*.[49]

[45] The following nuances escape translation: ποίησις may be understood in its ancient Greek sense of 'making', 'creation', while λειτουργία (function) in an ecclesiastical context means 'liturgy'.

[46] See esp. Embirikos 1980e: 78: 'Oktana means Paradise on earth, Eden here on earth, without original sin, beyond all sense of evil, with freedom in every circumstance everywhere even for incest' (Οκτάνα θα πη επί γης Παράδεισος, επί της γης Εδέμ, χωρίς προπατορικόν αμάρτημα, πέραν πάσης εννοίας κακού, με ελευθέραν εις πάσαν περίπτωσιν παντού και την αιμομιξίαν).

[47] Most obviously in the prose poem from *Oktana* entitled (in English): 'Beat, Beat, Beatitude and Glory' (1963), with an epigraph from Jack Kerouac.

[48] See in particular 'The Words' (Αι λέξεις, Embirikos 1980e: 9) and Kehayoglou 1987.

[49] Οι λέξεις έχασαν και αυτές τα ηχητικά των περιγράμματα, και τώρα μοιάζουν με πηλό, απ' τον οποίον ο ερημίτης πλάθει νέες λέξεις (νέα δοχεία των ιδίων παλαιών εννοιών)... Whether the reference of the (plural) title is to Defoe's hero or to *Swiss Family Robinson*, the hermit is alone upon his island: Η νήσος των Ροβινσώνων (Embirikos 1980e: 92–5). The poem, which is undated, was probably written at about the same time as 'Not Brasilia but Oktana' (Yatromanolakis 1983: 188–9).

But this is not the end of the story. In 1990 the first two volumes of Embirikos' *magnum opus*, *The Great Eastern*, were published. This work, written between 1945 and the early 1970s, is almost as cavalier with the conventions of the novel as the poems of *Oktana* were with those of poetry. In the novel, the New World is again the destination, and the steamship of the title is the floating paradise of sexual licence that conveys its passengers and crew thither. The cosmopolitan passenger list includes Jules Verne, and the episodic and inexorably repetitive narration of the sexual gyrations of the characters aboard is couched in the formally polished style and archaic language into which Verne, along with other European 'classics', was translated in Greek in the late nineteenth century.[50] At one level *The Great Eastern* is a gigantic parody, but the purpose of this obsessively sexual narrative is evidently serious. The great god Pan, symbol of sexual licence in Embirikos' earlier voyage in prose, *Argo*, is here seen to be triumphant on a scale unmatched in any other work by Embirikos.

But *The Great Eastern* transcends the charge of pornography (it certainly does not escape it!) just as *Oktana* has outlived the 'beat' generation and the brave new world of Brasilia. In its language and in the incidents that make up its plot, the novel works consistently by means of ironic juxtaposition. The effect often seems calculated to shock: the elevated archaic style of the narrative is regularly sprinkled with all the most 'taboo' words in the Greek language, and often as much as a paragraph will be given over to the inarticulate sounds of pleasure which at crucial moments replace language altogether. The novel's plot, in so far as it has one, makes similar play between the reader's expectations of how characters such as those described might be expected to behave (especially in 1867, when the action is supposed to take place) and the things they actually do. This results in a sophisticated comedy reminiscent of Cavafy (who had also praised hedonism in terms both sexually explicit and frequently ironic).

Sex, in the gentle and curiously innocent atmosphere of Embirikos' fantasy liner, acquires mystical significance, as the heights of sexual pleasure, by whatever means reached, bring about the total immersion of the individual in the cosmos.

[50] I am grateful to Mr George Lemos for the observation that the language of *The Great Eastern* is not so much that of Papadiamandis and Vizyinos, as of Greek translations of Verne and other 'classics' of the period, on which several generations of readers were brought up.

Έχει τον όλβον του Θεού, μέσα στην αιωνίαν δόνησιν της Ενεργείας εν ηδονή διαβιών και εν εκστάσει υπάρχων στον κόσμον τούτον τον παντοτινόν, στον κόσμον τον ανέσπερον, όπου το "Εγώ," διά τον πλήρη άνθρωπον, σημαίνει "Εκείνος," και ο εκάστοτε και εκασταχού "Εκείνος" σημαίνει πάλι Εγώ— *εγώ* που είμαι εν Θεώ και συνεπώς Θεός, εν Ηδονή και Κραδασμώ και εις τους αιώνας των αιώνων . . . [51]

He [then] enjoys the bliss of God, in the eternal vibration of Energy, passing his life in pleasure and experiencing ecstasy in this world, the eternal, never-setting world, in which the word 'I', for the complete human being, means 'He', and 'He' whenever and wherever he might be, again means 'I'—*I* who am in God and consequently am God, in Pleasure and in Arousal world without end . . .

In this way the idiosyncratic affirmation of the exotic Utopia, Oktana, and of the floating garden of delights that is *The Great Eastern*, comes to echo the quasi-religious affirmation of Seferis and Elytis at about the same time, as well as the more tentative, low-key quest of some younger poets. It is especially interesting to notice how Embirikos' borrowing of religious terminology here, in order to define the ideal state of sexual pleasure, echoes Karouzos' borrowing of the same terminology in the attempt to define his concept of poetry, quoted earlier.

The exotic voyage reappears in the poetry that another Surrealist of the older generation, Nikos Engonopoulos, published during the 1950s before turning almost entirely to painting.[52] For Engonopoulos, as also for Embirikos, 'Surrealism is the legitimation of desire'.[53] After the wartime bravura of *Bolivár: A Greek Poem*, Engonopoulos returned to the more intimate scale of his earlier poems, seeking through his art for a liberation both more catholic and more personal than that offered by his South American/Greek revolutionary hero. Less opaque than Engonopoulos' pre-war poems, his poetry of this period joins with Seferis, with Embirikos (in *The Great Eastern*), and with 'social' poets like Anagnostakis and Alexandrou in objectifying hope or desire through ironic distancing and more or less explicit allusion to the example of Cavafy.[54] But an abiding

[51] Embirikos 1990–2: ii. 196.
[52] Engonopoulos published four volumes of poetry between 1946 and 1957, included in the standard two-volume edition of his work (Engonopoulos 1977). His last published work, *In the Vale of Roses* (Στην κοιλάδα με τους ροδώνες), appeared separately in 1978.
[53] Engonopoulos 1981: 28.
[54] See esp. the poem 'For Rent' (Ενοικιάζεται), published in 1957 (Engonopoulos 1977: ii. 186–9).

image of Engonopoulos' later poetry is the voyage through mist and rain, a voyage which, like that of Embirikos' transatlantic liner, has no real goal other than the space it opens up in which desire can be fulfilled in language: a voyage, quite literally, out of this world. In a prose poem provocatively entitled 'Reality', the poet is compared to the captain of such a ship, taken for granted by all, except in time of danger when they turn to him:

Αυτός, που δεν έχει τη χαρά κι' όμως τηνέ γνωρίζει, που δεν είν' ελεύθερος κι' όμως την ποθεί την Ελευθερία, αυτός που βασανίζεται κι' όμως ελπίζει.[55]

He who is not joyful but yet knows joy, who is not free but yet desires Freedom, he who suffers and yet hopes.

The emphasis on suffering and hope here signal a retreat from the heady affirmation of Elytis' *The Axion Esti* and the later works of Embirikos, and remind us instead of the 'social' or 'political' poetry which by this time had become largely the prerogative of the Left, defeated in the civil war. The doyen of this latter group, and the last of our 'survivors' from the 1930s who went on to produce their most characteristic work after the war, is Yannis Ritsos.

Ritsos. Ritsos' post-war career is divided by periods of imprisonment, first during the civil war, and then during the regime of the Colonels. Between his release from prison in 1952 and his second release, after three years of prison-camp and house arrest, in 1970, Ritsos produced much of the poetry on which his worldwide reputation now rests.[56] Faced with the political and personal consequences of the defeat of the Left in 1949, Ritsos for much of this period found himself in a position comparable to that of other poets of his generation who had seen their hard-won wartime faith and hope in a better future go up in smoke in the reality of civil war. Further blows to Ritsos and many of his fellow poets of the Left were undoubtedly dealt by the volte-face in the Soviet Union after the death of Stalin and the Soviet suppression of the Hungarian uprising in 1956. Not surprisingly, the self-questioning and some of the solutions that Ritsos explored during this time have something in common with the conversational commentary and communal

[55] Πραγματικότης (Engonopoulos 1977: ii. 147–9 (p. 148)).
[56] See e.g. Dialismas 1984: 43–4; and Keeley in the introduction to his 1991 translations (see Guide to Translations).

lament characteristic of the 'social' poets of the post-war generation; but there are strong links to the more fundamentally affirmative solutions being worked out at the same time by his contemporaries. Ritsos' poems of this period fall into two main categories: the very short and the relatively long. Short poems, of which the two volumes of *Testimonies*, written between 1957 and 1965, are perhaps the most characteristic, draw at once on the 'testimonies' of 'social' poets of the time, as their title implies, and also on the legacy of Surrealism, in particular in the unexplained juxtaposition of images and in the low-key interiority which contrasts noticeably with Ritsos' more 'public' poems. Long poems, beginning with 'The Moonlight Sonata' (1956), develop the form of the dramatic monologue with greater consistency than is found in the work of any other Greek poet, including Cavafy. Formally Ritsos' dramatic monologues are unusual in that they are framed by prose 'stage directions' of a paragraph or more.

This form is adopted in all but two of the sixteen dramatic monologues written between 1956 and 1972 and collected in the volume *Fourth Dimension* (1972).[57] 'The Moonlight Sonata' (1956) introduces an elderly woman in black, who talks with obsessive yearning to a young man who seems impatient to leave her decaying house with its grand piano no longer used, and lit only by the 'pitiless moonlight'. The youth clearly belongs to the future, and the woman's monologue is punctuated by the phrase 'Let me come with you.' It seems unlikely that the speaker ever will leave the decaying surroundings that her words conjure up, and which clearly derive both from Ritsos' personal, childhood experience of the dissolution of a middle-class home and from Marx's prediction of the 'withering-away' of the bourgeoisie. But the poem ends ambiguously, and poetry itself occupies an ambiguous position between the old 'bourgeois' world that includes the woman, the piano, and Beethoven's sonata from which it takes its title, and the new 'city with its callused hands, the city of wage labour' in which the young man is apparently at home.[58] Significantly the narrative frame ends by telling us that all the time the radio has been playing, and there then follow three bars of the 'Moonlight Sonata'. In this way the last

---

[57] *Τέταρτη διάσταση* (Ritsos 1989–90, vi). A seventeenth monologue, 'Phaedra', written in 1974–5, was added to the sixth and subsequent editions.

[58] την πολιτεία με τα ροζιασμένα χέρια της την πολιτεία του μεροκάματου (Η σονάτα του σεληνόφωτος, Ritsos 1989–90: vi. 52).

'word' is given to Beethoven, and it has been suggested that the particular bars were chosen because they also contain the direction *misterioso*.[59] Here, as elsewhere in Ritsos' work of this period, the redemptive, renewing power of art is hinted at.

Most of the dramatic monologues in *Fourth Dimension* were written during the 1960s, and more than half are devoted to ancient myth and legend. Characteristically, in his poems of the 1960s which refer to the ancient world, Ritsos will adopt a technique indebted about equally to the examples of Seferis and Cavafy: Cavafy, in that a familiar story is viewed from an unfamiliar perspective, engaging the reader's sympathy for the unheroic, the losers, the ordinary people caught up in great events; Seferis, in the clearly implied parallel between the historical or mythical events narrated and present-day realities. 'Philoctetes' (written 1963–5) is another monologue in which the younger generation confronts the old. But this time it is the young man who does the talking, and his silent interlocutor, we are told at the end, regains his youth and vigour from the young man's words. The scenario alludes to Sophocles' play of the same title: the elderly Philoctetes has withdrawn from the Trojan War, but the Greeks need his weapons in order to win. In Ritsos' reworking of the confrontation between the young Neoptolemos, who has been sent to fetch the weapons, and the older Philoctetes, both men have instinctively come to realize the futility of the war in which they are engaged. The young man resignedly accepts the role of warrior and hero which he has no choice but to play. But he can see beyond the petty hatreds that motivate the leaders to the futility of the whole expedition and the transience of the values which he is obliged to serve. Of this recognition he says:

Κ' ήταν σα μια ευτυχία η γνώση αυτή μια άφεση,
μια κατευναστική παραδοχή, μια αδρανής ευφροσύνη
απ' την αφή του αιώνιου και του τίποτα...
μια ελάχιστη δικαίωση,
κι' όλος ο φόβος, αναρίθμητος κι' άγνωστος, διαλύονταν πέρα,
ένα βαθύ, ιλαρύ σύννεφο στη μυθική απεραντοσύνη.[60]

And this knowledge was a kind of happiness; an absolution,
a soothing acceptance, a passive joyfulness
from the touch of the eternal and of the void...
                                                    a tiny vindication,

---

[59] This is the persuasive suggestion of Peter Bien (1990–1).
[60] Ο Φιλοκτήτης (Ritsos 1989–90: vi. 260).

and all the fear, boundless and unknown, dissolved into the
distance,
a profound, laughing cloud in the endlessness of myth.

The young man will play his part, as history requires, in winning the
Trojan War for the Greeks. But he wants Philoctetes' weapons for a
different purpose. It is not the weapons (the leaders, we are told, are
interested only in weapons, not in the men who bear them) but
Philoctetes himself that the young man wants:

'Όμως εσύ είσαι τα όπλα σου, τα τίμια κερδισμένα
με τη δουλειά, τη φιλία και τη θυσία, δοσμένα απ' το χέρι
εκείνου που στραγγάλισε την Επτακέφαλον, εκείνου που σκότωσε
τον φύλακα του 'Άδη. Και τό 'δες
με τα ίδια σου τα μάτια και τό 'ζησες: κληρονομιά σου
και τέλειο όπλο σου. Αυτό νικάει μονάχα....[61]

But *you* are your weapons, that you won so honourably
with so much work, friendship, and sacrifice, given by the hand
of him who strangled the Seven-Headed Beast, of him who killed
the guardian of Hades. And you saw
with your own eyes; you lived these things: your inheritance
and your perfect armoury. This alone will conquer. . . .

According to the story Philoctetes' weapons had been the gift of the
demigod Heracles, who had killed the seven-headed Hydra and
Cerberus, the guardian of the Underworld. Described in this way,
what the young man is enlisting, in a cause which far transcends that
of any war between states, is the inherited wisdom of past generations, and the power of honest labour to take on the real enemies of
all mankind: death, and the many-headed monster whose title here
implies a pun on Capitalism.

'Philoctetes', like most of Ritsos' poems of this period, whether or
not they allude explicitly to political matters, is nothing if not a
Marxist poem. Attempts have been made, particularly by his translators into English, to represent Ritsos as 'not really' or at least as
'not only' a political poet.[62] This view has provided a valuable
corrective to the tendency in Greece, during most of the poet's
lifetime, to respond primarily to the politics. But the peculiar tension which gives to much of Ritsos' poetry its vitality derives from
the interplay between nostalgic respect for the old order, in which

---

[61] Ritsos 1989–90: vi. 261.
[62] See Keeley 1983: 149–79; Friar 1989, esp. 446.

his own art of poetry is inescapably rooted, and a commitment to the vision of a revolutionary future. In this way Ritsos succeeds to the mantle of Varnalis, the first Greek Marxist poet, in his works of the 1920s which had laid the foundations for an aesthetically viable *Marxist* poetics.[63]

On the other hand, the fact that Ritsos' vision of an ideal future is integrally bound up with a specific political programme does not differentiate it *in kind* from the affirmations of his contemporaries. Ritsos' poetry of this productive period goes far beyond the 'testimonies' of the defeated Left, just as that of Seferis, Elytis, and Embirikos transcends the self-imposed limitations of these poets' younger peers. No less than these three, Ritsos mobilized all the resources of his art in the service of a powerful and consistent affirmation. The nature and content of that affirmation are as distinctive of Ritsos as for example Embirikos' allegiance to Freud is of that poet's post-war achievement. While there is always the danger that affirmation will topple over into propaganda, that danger is not confined to poetry with a political dimension: Embirikos has been accused of 'preaching', and Elytis of blatant self-advertisement. Ritsos is not alone among his contemporaries in seeking through poetry to articulate a vision of a better world. And in the poetry of this period of his life, at any rate, that better world is no more realizable by political means than are the corresponding Utopian or mystical solutions sought by Seferis, Elytis, Embirikos, or Engonopoulos.

POETRY AND MUSIC

One final innovation, in a very different direction from those so far discussed, needs to be mentioned before we leave the poetry of this period, and this is the appearance at the end of the 1950s of the phenomenon that has become known since as 'popular art song'. It has been a commonplace of Greek poetry since at least the time of Palamas for the poet to describe his work in terms of *song*. In general, as has often been noted, the conventional if somewhat tenuous insistence of modern European poetry on its origins in an oral/aural medium has been very strongly emphasized in Greek poetry

---

[63] Among older studies of the poet, that by Prevelakis (1981) stands out. For a full bibliography, including English translations, see Makrynikola 1993.

since Solomos. Not only has oral folk poetry played a more formative role in the growth and development of a national literature in Greece than was usually the case in western Europe, but for historical and cultural reasons that oral tradition has continued to play a vigorous part in social and cultural life at least into the second half of the twentieth century.[64] We have often seen how this oral tradition has provided a bulwark for writing poets, not least because it provides a ready bank of allusions that Greek readers of any background can be relied upon to pick up. Generally, however, when a Greek poet refers to his work as a 'song' we can be confident that he is exploiting a well-worn analogy between his own sophisticated written medium and the more direct, extrovert lyricism of the oral tradition. The idea that his poem might literally be *sung* and achieve fame as a popular song, although not alien to Solomos, is far removed from the expectations of Palamas or any of his successors down to the 1950s who continued to draw on this analogy.[65]

The initiative which radically changed this situation for most of the 1960s and 1970s was taken not by poets but by composers. In the late 1950s Manos Hatzidakis and Mikis Theodorakis, drawing together the fruits of a Conservatory training with their practical knowledge of Orthodox church music, and in particular of the Turkish-influenced and socially ostracized music of the urban poor, known as *rebetika*, launched what turned out to be a new and highly successful genre of popular song. The classic instrument of the new style was the bouzouki, which now began to emerge from its long-term associations with the criminal urban underworld and the poorer margins of society. Modified by the addition of a fourth string, which allowed the playing of European chords, and brought to new heights of virtuosity in the hands of Manolis Hiotis and Kostas Papadopoulos, the bouzouki and these musicians in particular were taken up enthusiastically by Hatzidakis and Theodorakis. The resulting idiom, with its catchy melodies, 'modal' scales, and unusual rhythms, often interspersed by dazzling solo improvizations on the bouzouki, has ever since been recognizable the world

---

[64] See e.g. Eideneier 1985; Tziovas 1989b.

[65] Solomos' *Hymn to Liberty* was set to music by Nikolaos Mantzaros, as a cantata in something of the style of Schubert, from which the present-day Greek National Anthem derives. Poems of Palamas and Sikelianos were incorporated into symphonic works by Manolis Kalomiris (1883–1962) in the first half of the century—but this, again, was by no means 'popular' music.

over as 'Greek' music, and after nearly forty years has lost little of its
extraordinarily broad appeal in Greece.

The relevance of this digression here lies in the choice and nature
of the lyrics which these composers chose to set to music. Often
these were not the products of conventional song-writers (an active
and productive guild in Greece since the late nineteenth century)
but of established poets who deliberately took on this rather different mantle. The doyen of the new song-writers of the 1960s and
1970s was Nikos Gatsos, whom we encountered earlier as the author
of the Surrealist-inspired volume of poetry, *Amorgos*, during the
Second World War. Gatsos never published another volume of
poetry, and all of his later output was instead destined for
musical settings by Hatzidakis, Theodorakis, and many other composers who have followed in their footsteps. Although only *Amorgos*
has found an honourable place in literary histories or university
courses, it is now recognized that Gatsos' 'songs' represent a poetic
achievement in a different genre, but not inferior to his 'literary'
poetry.[66] In this way the oral traditional poetry which Gatsos in
Amorgos and Sahtouris among others had drawn into the rarefied
ambit of Surrealism now comes full circle. In the songs of Gatsos,
and of many others who followed him, notably Manos Eleftheriou
and K. Ch. Myris, the meld of the Surrealist irrational with echoes of
traditional folk poetry is returned to a popular oral/aural medium.
And as a consequence, certain of the achievements of a post-war
poetry remarkable for its hermeticism and refusal of communication
have paradoxically gained something approaching universal currency among Greek-speakers.

This remarkable appeal to a wider audience through the medium
of 'popular art song' has not been confined, either, to poets who
have been prepared to make the leap into the formal and generic
restraints of song-writing.[67] Theodorakis' settings of sections from
Elytis' *The Axion Esti* as a 'folk oratorio' in 1959 (recorded in 1964),
and from Ritsos' *Romiosini* in 1966, have clearly been crucial in
bringing the work of these poets to a wider audience, and indeed

[66] Some of these lyrics have been collected in Gatsos 1992; cf. Lignadis (1983) who
devotes a chapter to the songs, but irritatingly fails to give chronological details or
discography. The case for considering Gatsos' songs alongside his more 'respectable'
output is strongly put by Manos Hatzidakis (1988: 126–37).
[67] The most distinguished case is Odysseas Elytis, who provided lyrics for Theodorakis' song-cycles *Archipelago* (1959) and *Little Cyclades* (1963), as well as allowing
previously published poems to be set to music (see Theodorakis 1987: 61, 87–94).

in shaping the perceptions of readers of the poems themselves. One of Theodorakis' earliest successes came in 1961, with the recording of four early poems of Seferis in musical settings.[68] Although the poet was not best pleased, the first of these in particular has ever since occupied a cherished place in the popular repertoire, and undoubtedly provided the catalyst that turned the poet's funeral, in 1971, into a spontaneous (and rare) public demonstration against the regime of the Colonels. As we shall see, during the years of military dictatorship 'popular art song' and the close relationship between poets and musicians, and between poetry and music, had a significant part to play.

POST-WAR FICTION: VERSIONS OF THE PAST

In fiction there is not such a clear-cut division between generations as we observed in the case of poetry. Up till about 1960 there was little attempt by novelists and short story writers to break new ground, either thematically or in terms of technique. Even such inveterate Modernist pioneers of non- or anti-realist fiction before the war as Stelios Xefloudas, Melpo Axioti, and, in the most extreme case, Yannis Beratis, reverted to representational techniques and topical subject-matter. By and large, 'new' writers of the younger generation, no less than their elders, in the immediate aftermath of the war and civil war either continued or revived modes of realist writing established in the 1930s, which underwent more radical transformation only in the 1960s.[69]

Retrospect on the 1930s. In order to pick up the threads of post-war developments in Greek fiction we have to go back before the nominal starting-point for this chapter, to 1946. *Straw Hats* by Margarita Lymberaki (b. 1919), published in that year, may be seen as the first of a sporadic group of novels that appeared during the following ten years, which begin to look back at the intellectual and social world of the 1930s as something complete and ended.[70] At the same time, in

[68] Under the collective title *Epiphany* (Ἐπιφάνια), frequently reissued on record and cassette.
[69] An invaluable and informative reference book on the *younger* generation of prose writers during this period is Sokolis 1988–90.
[70] Lymberaki 1974 (cf. Guide to Translations). *Straw Hats* was Lymberaki's second novel. The first (Lymberaki 1994) was originally published in 1945 under the author's maiden name, Margarita Karapanou. Confusingly, Lymberaki's

its narrative style, and particularly in a drily epigrammatic humour
that is scarcely found in earlier Greek fiction, it looks forward to the
lighter, more allusive touch that characterizes new writing in Greek
from the early 1960s onwards, and, as we shall see, anticipates
techniques that will become standard in the novels and stories of
the late 1970s and the 1980s.

Straw Hats tells the story of three girls growing from adolescence
to womanhood during three successive summers, on a farm just
outside Athens. The eldest, Maria, marries Marios and has children. The middle one, Infanta, has too indomitable a spirit for her
suitor and chooses a lonely dedication to art and beauty. Katerina,
the youngest, who is also the narrator, rejects an offer of marriage
from the sympathetic young English Jew who lives nearby, as she has
fallen in love with a seafaring cousin, Andreas, whom she has never
met and who only really exists in the novel that his father is weaving
out of the diaries and letters that record his adventurous life.

The action of *Straw Hats* is set exclusively during the 1930s.[71]
Although Katerina looks back on the period of the story from the
distance of an unspecified 'now', we are told nothing about the fate
of the characters after the end of the third summer. This distance is
important because the writer and her first readers could only have
been highly conscious of the events that separated them, in 1946,
from the summers of the previous decade. Because of the way the
story is constructed, it is always summer in the world of the book. In
this way the implied contrast is heightened between the time of the
story and the time when the novel was published. Although the
coming war is never hinted at directly in the novel, this implied
contrast with what came later is especially strong in the portrayal
of the English Jews, David and his mother, and is reinforced by
reference to Andreas' activities in illegally repatriating Jews to Pales-
tine. In hinting, in this understated way, at the fate of the Jews under
the Nazis (as well as in its lyrically evocative style), the novel invites

daughter, whose first novel was published in 1976 (see below), also publishes under
this latter name.

[71] The novelist and critic Alexandros Kotzias cannot be right to conclude that the
three summers of the story are to be understood as the summers of the German
occupation (in Argyriou *et al.* 1977: 65), although his remark highlights a fascinating
indeterminacy in the temporal distance that separates the story from the moment of
its supposed narration. Kotzias' comment also emphasizes a characteristic which this
novel shares with the next one to be discussed, namely the unexpected (and surely
eloquent) *absence* of reference to recent traumas.

comparison with the later and better-known work of Giorgio Bassani, *The Garden of the Finzi Contini*.

The setting of *Straw Hats* is neither the purely urban and often over-intellectualized world of Athenian fiction of the 1930s, nor is it precisely the idyllic confluence of childhood and tradition sought after in so much Greek writing of the late 1930s and early 1940s. Instead it occupies the boundary between the two. The narrator's family is well-to-do; the girls are not starved of professional and intellectual contacts or of 'serious' conversation. But at the same time, on the outer fringes of the city, they are close to the life of the farm and especially to a landscape which is often described as if the urban sprawl of Athens was on a different planet, and not just down the road.

Lymberaki draws on the backward glance of much recent fiction, and particularly on its often fervent evocation of nature and tradition. This is particularly evident in the treatment of the shadowy character Andreas, the seafaring cousin who never appears. Andreas is described with all the panoply of the traditional Greek hero, as he had been re-created in Politis' *Eroica* (1937), in the hero of Myrivilis' *Vasilis Arvanitis* (1943), and others. Lymberaki, however, subtly (and sympathetically) exposes this representative of a heroic tradition as the product of the unreliable art of narration, of dreams and fantasy. He is first mentioned to Katerina by his father in the context of the enigmatic remark:

Καμιά φορά νιώθει κανείς την ανάγκη να την προεκτείνει τη ζωή, ε;[72]
Sometimes you feel the need to extend your life, don't you?

There is no clue as to whether this remark alludes to the physiological relationship of a parent to a child, or to the literal travels of the son, or to the activity of the father as the writer of a novel which will both extend his experience and, as art, will outlive him. Later we are told that the son, Andreas, 'has told lies ever since a child',[73] so that the idol of Katerina's dreams is doubly a product of the novelist's own art of story-telling: Andreas' unreliable reminiscences are retold to Katerina (and to us) by his novelist- father. What Katerina falls in love with at the end of *Straw Hats* is an ideal constructed by the art of narrative, a character built only out of words and of 'such stuff as dreams are made on'. (The narrative sequence near the end

---

[72] Lymberaki 1974: 252.   [73] Lymberaki 1974: 291.

of the novel, in which Andreas actually appears and invites the heroine to elope with him, is revealed in an understated *coup de théâtre* as a dream.)

Without abandoning realist conventions, *Straw Hats* ends with the narrator falling in love with her own art of story-telling, and so gently reflects on the very conventions on which the novel itself depends.[74] In this way *Straw Hats* draws very closely on the fiction of the immediately preceding period in its evocation of a vanished era and the attempt to recover, through the character and deeds of Andreas, a vibrant tradition. But at the same time as it participates in this kind of writing, *Straw Hats* also pronounces its epitaph: the lost world of the past in the story is the very time and place where the nostalgic fiction of the thirties had taken shape; and the rediscovery of tradition that in these novels gives a promise of future vitality and regeneration is gently laid bare as none other than the process of making fiction.[75]

In this last respect *Straw Hats* anticipates by some distance the style and preoccupations of Greek fiction in the 1970s and 1980s. Indeed, it is significant that it was not reprinted until 1964, while between 1974 and 1995 it was reprinted no fewer than thirty times. Another novel which affords an unusual and innovative retrospect on the 1930s—and which also, like *Straw Hats*, remained without sequel for many years—is again by a woman writer: *Contre-Temps* by Mimika Kranaki (b. 1922), first published in 1947.[76] The story follows the fortunes of a rather spoilt young girl of a well-to-do family, from an idyllic summer holiday in the 1930s, through her studies at the Athens Conservatoire and then in Paris. Everything happens to her *à contretemps*, as her hopes and desires are always fatally out of step with the real world around her. Marriage to her childhood sweetheart leads quickly to disillusion; determining to

---

[74] The parallels with *Aeolian Earth* by Venezis are particularly striking. Set on a farm in Anatolia in the years leading up to 1914, that novel made no mention of the catastrophe of 1922 (although these events are foreshadowed directly in a way that does not happen in *Straw Hats*). The atmosphere of nostalgia and the narrative technique of evocation is common to both novels, as are the setting on a farm (for which the same word υποστατικό, with its possibly metaphysical connotations, is used) and the benignly patriarchal role of the grandfather, who in both novels has himself built the family house and enjoys an almost magical rapport with nature.

[75] On the narrative technique of this novel and its self-referential character, see Farinou-Malamatari 1988.

[76] Kranaki 1982.

return to the fellow student she had earlier rejected, she finds him dead.

The narrative is in the third person throughout, but obsessively follows the inner thoughts and preoccupations of the heroine, Kyveli. The first part of the novel, with its idyllic rural scenes from childhood in the 1930s, shares a nostalgic evocation of the past with *Straw Hats* and its immediate predecessors. But then the war comes, and Kranaki's approach to recent momentous events invites comparison with that of Lymberaki in *Straw Hats*. We are told in passing that there are German soldiers in the streets, that Kyveli has to get home before the curfew, later that the Germans have gone. Returning to her childhood haunts, she finds the house has been commandeered by the People's Army. The casual way in which the war comes and goes in the background to the personal quest of the heroine provokes a sense of shock in a novel written at this time, and is surely the most remarkable achievement of *Contre-Temps*.

It is not just the heroine, with her single-minded quest for fulfilment in music (which she achieves) and in an ideal love (which eludes her), who is out of tune with her times. The kind of novel that narrates such a quest, characteristic of both Greek fiction and poetry during the 1930s, is fundamentally at odds with the world in which, in 1947, it seeks to be read. As the heroine herself puts it, everything in the world:

γίνεται *à contre-temps*. Δεν ξέρω αν καταλαβαίνεις. Όπως στη μουσική. Να, έρχεται άδοξα στην αδύνατη στιγμή, όταν δεν το ζητάς ακόμα ή δεν το ζητάς πια, κι έτσι πλέκεται, μια ατέλειωτη, αξεδιάλυτη παρεξήγηση.[77]

happens *à contretemps*. I don't know if you understand. Like in music. There, it pops up at a moment of weakness, when you don't want it yet or don't want it any more, and creates an endless, inextricable web of misunderstanding.

This is certainly the story of the fictional Kyveli's life. But the continuation of this passage shows how fundamental the analogy of music is for the novel as well:

Αυτό, άλλωστε, είναι και το μεταφυσικό νόημα της τζαζ. Οι αντιχρονισμοί, που αποτελούν τη ρυθμική της βάση, καθώς κι οι διαφωνίες, στο αρμονικό επίπεδο, είναι ακριβώς η έκφραση αυτής της αλυσίδας των απωθήσεων και των πόθων που δεν μπορούν να συγχρονιστούν.[78]

---

[77] Kranaki 1982: 150.   [78] Ibid. 151.

You know, that's the metaphysical meaning of jazz. The syncopations that make up its basic rhythms, like the discords at the harmonic level, are precisely the expression of this chain of hates and loves that can never be synchronized.

Jazz provides the analogy for a new way of writing, adequate to represent the 'lack of fit' between inner and outer worlds, between private emotions and great events—between, even, the vanished world of the 1930s and the post-war world in which this conversation takes place.[79] And in this way *Contre-Temps* is not merely a retrospective novel, but like *Straw Hats* anticipates later departures in Greek fiction.

It may be indicative that after the publication of these two novels both of these innovative women writers went to live for many years in France, where they also wrote and published in French. In Greece the novels which for many years most authoritatively set the seal on the decade of the 1930s come chronologically after *Straw Hats* and *Contre-Temps*, but unlike them are the work of veteran novelists from that decade, and formally and technically represent their authors' fullest development in the direction of urban realism.

Without a God (1951) by Angelos Terzakis and *The Yellow File* (1956) by M. Karagatsis have both been proposed as their authors' finest work.[80] Both are long novels, with a large cast of characters, written in an entirely realist mode (which is not to say that the events they chronicle are always very realistic!). The action of *Without a God* takes place during the 1930s and ends on the eve of the Second World War; *The Yellow File* is more obviously an autopsy on the pre-war world, as the action is split between the life and deeds of the main character, who died in mysterious circumstances in 1938, and the activities of the post-war narrator who opens the file and unravels the case.

The principal character of Terzakis' novel, the improbably named Michalis Paradisis, is presented as the impotent product and victim

[79] The analogy with jazz itself, and particularly the presence, in a novel, of dialogues about 'metaphysical meanings', are themselves grounded in the pre-war period. Similar analogies between jazz and the discordancy of modern life had been drawn by T. S. Eliot and, in a manner closer to Kranaki's, by Jean-Paul Sartre in the closing pages of *La Nausée* (1938); while an overtly philosophical 'content' in the novel is a hallmark of 1930s urban realism in Greece.

[80] Terzakis 1989; Karagatsis 1980. See the respective volumes of the series *Τετράδια Ευθύνης*: on Terzakis no. 4 (1977), e.g. p. 33; on Karagatsis see no. 14 (1981), e.g. p. 152.

of his times. Born in 1897, the year of a crushing defeat for the Greeks at the hands of the Turks, in common with a whole generation he sees active service in the First World War and in Anatolia, to return after the catastrophe of 1922 'emptied of everything that had filled him before', and unable to believe in anything.[81] Like many *novelists* of that generation in the late 1930s, Paradisis seeks renewal in a return to nature and the humble people of an Aegean island paradise, where he 'cultivates his garden' to almost miraculous effect.[82] Unsatisfied with the lonely innocence of his achievement, however, he returns to the city, where he takes it upon himself, for no very clear reason, to bring up his orphaned nephew and niece and rather ineffectually to work for the radical reform of society, first through the Communist Party, later through his association with an anarchic arms dealer. In both of these causes Paradisis becomes the sacrificial victim as the children bring about his death and the world about him slides towards total war. The unhappy conclusion of this novel is summed up by the character himself near the end:

Το δραματικό χαρακτηριστικό του καιρού μας, λέω, είναι ότι για πρώτη φορά στα ιστορημένα και στ' ανιστόρητα ίσως χρόνια, πασχίζει να ζήσει δίχως θεό.[83]

The dramatic characteristic of our age, I believe, is that for the first time in all the years of history and perhaps of prehistory as well, it strives to live without a god.

There is an interesting parallel to be drawn between the vain sacrifice of Paradisis in this novel and that of Manolios in Kazantzakis' *Christ Recrucified*, written shortly before *Without a God* but not published until three years later. But unlike Kazantzakis, Terzakis presents this theme not as a perennial pattern in human experience, but as the specific experience of a generation in Greek urban life.[84]

---

[81] Αδειανός απ' όλα όσα τον είχανε γεμίσει πριν... Απλούστατα, δεν πίστευε πια σε τίποτα... (Terzakis 1989: 33).

[82] There are parallels here with the fictional grandfathers in *Aeolian Earth* by Venezis and *Straw Hats* by Lymberaki, but also with the return to nature and tradition that is characteristic of Greek fiction in the late 1930s and early 1940s, including Terzakis' previous novel, *Voyage with the Evening Star* (on which see below). The garden-paradise in Greek literature goes back at least to Papadiamandis in his 1893 short story, 'The Black-Kerchiefed Woman'.

[83] Terzakis 1989: 393.

[84] On Kazantzakis' novel see below. It should be noted that both characters have symbolic names: Manolios is the popular form of Emmanuel, while the symbolism of Paradisis as a character's name is obtrusive.

Paradisis, we are told early on in the novel, 'had the feeling that he belonged to a generation that had been sacrificed',[85] and later on another character warns him that revolutions do not feed on their children, as the saying goes, but on the fathers. The unappealing future represented by the children for whom Paradisis is willing to give up so much, apparently needs to devour its parents.[86] In this way the 'thirties generation' is seen as doubly a victim—sacrificed by its elders in the futile wars of its youth, sacrificing itself to the voracious and ungrateful spirit of the age that will succeed.

A brighter and more vigorous picture of the same period in Greek urban life is presented by Karagatsis in *The Yellow File*, although the verdict it implicitly pronounces on the demise of the pre-war world is not very different. Karagatsis in the 1930s had published novels and stories in which characters of exceptional qualities were hounded and finally destroyed by the biological urges that drove them. *The Yellow File* is the story of a *fictional* novelist of the 1930s who plans a novel that will prove just this theory of biological and materialist determinism. Like Karagatsis himself at this period, the fictional Manos Tasakos echoes the claim of Emile Zola that the novelist is a kind of scientist, dispassionately experimenting with his material. But in the novel, Tasakos carries his experiment into real life, as he imperceptibly weaves the real people around him into a sinister plot which will prove his theory and become the 'plot' of his novel. The final victim of his plot, however, is Tasakos himself, when the girl who had been his principal victim reads the contents of the yellow file and shoots him fatally. The novel for which he had ruthlessly sacrificed his own and others' happiness is short-circuited, and the flaw in Tasakos' whole theoretical proposition is revealed by his dying act of writing a bogus suicide note, so as to save the girl whom after all he loves

ώς το αναπότρεπτο, το δίκαιο θάνατο που μού 'δωσε το χέρι σου.[87]

unto this ineluctable, just death by your hand.

Karagatsis in this novel reflects on his own earlier work, which, like the 'satanically' driven decade in which he produced it, he now

[85] Είχε την αίσθηση πως ανήκει σε μια γενιά θυσιασμένη (Terzakis 1989: 33).
[86] Terzakis 1989: 276–7 and *passim*.
[87] Karagatsis 1980: ii. 110.

sees as a closed circle.[88] From his own particular perspective, Karagatsis looks back on the world of Manos Tasakos and pronounces its epitaph. The circle is not quite closed however. Although Tasakos is dead and his novel unfinishable,[89] it is now possible after the lapse of ten years for Karagatsis to make a different novel out of Tasakos' failure, in a new bright world where industrial capitalism promises happiness for the future.[90]

Fictional Testimonies. In the same year that saw the publication of Lymberaki's critical retrospect on the 1930s, Yannis Beratis published two books which chronicle some of the events from the war and occupation that had been provocatively omitted or hurried over in the novels we have just been considering: *The Broad River* and *Itinerary of '43*.[91] The first, with its vivid and unadorned personal chronicle of life at the front during the Albanian campaign in the winter of 1940, won wide acclaim for its author, a success which until the 1980s eclipsed his other two novels. As early as 1930, as we saw in the previous chapter, Beratis had written the esoteric fantasy *Diaspora*, one of the earliest and most radical of the Modernist experiments of that decade, and as we shall see he was ready to participate again in the van of a new surge of experimental fiction in the early 1960s with his final novella *Whirlwind* (1961).[92] Together with *Itinerary of '43*, which contains a similarly unvarnished account of Beratis' experiences serving with the right-wing partisan group EDES, in the mountains of Epiros, *The Broad River* both satisfied a

---

[88] 'Satanic' and its cognates abound throughout the text, and come thick and fast in the chapter, entitled 'The Death of Satan', in which Maria narrates how she killed Tasakos. There she describes him as Satan, and herself and her circle as 'children of Lucifer' (ii. 101; cf. 105–6). The idiosyncratic doctor and novelist in the novel, Christos Nezeritis (whose unusual surname sounds suspiciously like Nazareth), has written a much talked-of novel, *The Indomitable Lucifer*.

[89] Nezeritis declares that Tasakos never would have finished the novel (ii. 136), given that the experiment had proved almost exactly the opposite of its author's conviction (ii. 140).

[90] In the post-war scenes in the novel some prominence is given to the industrial success of the young Miltos Rousis, the son of one of the principal pre-war characters in the story, who is even aided by the son of Jungermann (the hero of another novel of Karagatsis from the 1930s). The idealistic enthusiasm of the young industrialist is commented on by Nezeritis near the end of the novel (ii. 138). Karagatsis carries over into this novel from *Jungermann* (1938) the narrative idiosyncrasy of quoting balance sheets and the facts and figures of industrial enterprises.

[91] Respectively: Beratis 1992; 1976, both first published 1946. On the first, see Farinou-Malamatari 1994.

[92] See Beratis 1980.

need and gave a new lease of life to the kind of literary testimony that, as we have seen, has a long history in Greek literature. Beratis' two 'testimonies' of 1946 apply the lessons of Doukas, Myrivilis, and Venezis to more recent events, but in doing so they by no means merely repeat what the earlier writers had done. For Beratis, as for the older writers, the line between fiction and fact was to be blurred, and the techniques of the former mobilized in the service of the direct representation of the latter. As we saw, Doukas, Myrivilis, and Venezis had each developed a distinct strategy for bringing about this kind of effect. Beratis' strategy is not identical to any one of theirs, and is most clearly revealed in the original title for *Itinerary of '43*, namely *Document*. The literary testimonies of the First World War and the catastrophe of 1922 had given a central place to the language and style of *oral* testimony. Beratis for the first time writes what today we would call a *documentary* novel (and indeed *The Broad River* raises the same uncertainties about its true genre as does more recent English and American 'faction').

Although the narrator and his personal opinions are consistently effaced in favour of the narrative of what he experienced, we are none the less given a good many factual details about him which make it clear that he is to be understood not as the Everyman of his time that Doukas' and Myrivilis' narrators seem to be, but as the author himself without disguise. Nor, for all their factual detail of events, can either of Beratis' 'testimonies' be read as history: the events described are not chosen for their historical significance but simply because the author happened to be there; and the rigorous exclusion of any comment or evaluation becomes even more striking if one tries to read the books as historical accounts. Finally, as in the case of the earlier 'testimonies' we have already examined, *The Broad River* apparently gives a voice to unmediated experience by means that are themselves literary.

The title may allude to a line of a poem by Seferis from 1935:

Λυπούμαι γιατί άφησα να περάσει ένα πλατύ ποτάμι μέσα
από τα δάχτυλά μου[93]

It grieves me that I have let a broad river slip between my
fingers,

---

[93] *Novel* (Μυθιστόρημα), sect. 18 (Seferis 1972: 65.)

and in this way the whole book becomes tacitly an epitaph on the preceding decade. The subtitle of the first part, *Symphony*, points up not only the underlying structure of the whole narrative, in 'movements' of differing 'tempi', but also more fundamentally its theme: the 'harmony' of the many disparate individual voices that it harnesses together, and the 'accord' or 'agreement' (the other meaning of the word in Greek) of a whole nation of previously uncoordinated individuals in the face of an external threat. At various points of the narrative, too, the conscientious build-up of realistic details sometimes conceals a purpose that goes beyond realism. This happens for example in the description of the narrator's first acquaintance with a battle-seasoned Cretan lieutenant-colonel on a hilltop in the front line. Although no detail is out of keeping with a realistic description, the whole passage conjures up a cumulative picture of the traditional Greek hero of folklore and historical legend:

Αν και καθιστός, φαινόταν πως θά' ταν τεράστιος όταν θα σηκωθεί
...' Ηταν καθιστός...με τό 'να πόδι πάνω στ' άλλο...Είχε ρίξει πάνω
του, χωρίς να φορέσει τα μανίκια, τη μανδύα του...Τα μάτια του ήταν
γαλάζια, γκρίζα—πάντως ανοιχτόχρωμα, και κοιτούσαν έμμονα, αλλά με
πραότητα και καλοσύνη, πράμα που σε ξάφνιζε απότομα μέσα σ' όλη
αυτή την τραχιά και σχεδόν πρωτόγονη εμφάνιση.[94]

Although seated, he seemed as though he would be enormous when he stood up. He was seated... with one leg crossed over the other... He wore his greatcoat thrown over his shoulders, leaving his arms free... His eyes were light blue, grey—at any rate pale, and their gaze was unwavering, but also gentle and kind, something that took you all at once by surprise in the midst of all his harsh and almost primitive appearance.

Following Beratis' lead, 'documentary' or lightly fictionalized accounts of events in the war and the civil war became the dominant form of expression among new writers who emerged during the following decade. On the right of the political spectrum the first novels of Rodis Roufos, Th. D. Frangopoulos, Nikos Kasdaglis, and Alexandros Kotzias all conform to this pattern, as do the first novel and many of the short stories of Dimitris Hatzis and (although with a stronger element of fiction and fantasy) the novels of Menelaos Loudemis on the Marxist side.[95] Of older writers only the Cypriot

[94] Beratis 1973: 226–7.
[95] Many of these writers, together with Beratis and Tsirkas, are discussed, in relation to the testimony to real events, by Mackridge (1988).

Loukis Akritas (1909–65) and Yorgos Theotokas attempted to chronicle the national experience of wartime, although neither approaches the austere 'documentary' form of Beratis.[96] Interestingly, Theotokas in *Sacred Way* (1950) concludes his narrative with the defeat of the Greek army and the arrival of the Germans in Athens in April 1941. Later he said of this book, 'I thought then that I had exhausted my subject and had nothing more to add.'[97] It was not for another twelve years that Theotokas found himself able to follow the careers of his fictional characters through the occupation to the end of the civil war, in a sequel. The second volume of *Invalids and Travellers* (1964) is a rare monument in Greek fiction, in which the full technical range, and also the burden of ideas, of the urban novel of the 1930s are brought somewhat uneasily to bear on the very events that had intervened to make this kind of novel obsolete.[98]

Before 1960 there is a noticeable reluctance, on the part of writers who sought to record the traumas of war and civil war, to indulge in any overt experiment in the *form* of their fiction. An exception to this is the second novel of Margarita Lymberaki, whom we have already met as the author of *Straw Hats*. *The Other Alexander* (1950) marks a significant break with the critique of realism from within that we identified in the earlier novel, and also, in its later (and better-known) stage adaptation, heralds Lymberaki's move into the theatre for most of her subsequent career.[99] *The Other Alexander* juxtaposes the legitimate and the illegitimate children of a father who owns a mine. The legitimate family own and run the mine; the illegitimate ones, who have the same names, belong to the work-force. The children grow up with a fascinated blend of love and hatred for their opposite numbers, until tensions over the running of the mine spill over into violence and the half-brothers and half-sisters take a series of terrible revenges on one another. All this, it emerges only casually as the novel progresses, is coming to a head at the same time as the nation itself is being torn apart in the fratricidal conflict of the civil

---

[96] On Theotokas see below. Akritas' novel *Men-at-Arms* (Αρματωμένοι) was published in 1947.

[97] Theotokas 1967.

[98] Ασθενείς και οδοιπόροι is now the title of a two-volume novel, of which volume i bears the title Ιερά Οδός (Theotokas 1967).

[99] Lymberaki 1979. The stage version, which is probably better known today, was first published in French in 1957, and in Greek in 1963.

war, on which the book provides the earliest commentary in fiction.[100] The juxtapositions are presented in such a way as deliberately to confuse the reader, to whom the relationships only gradually become clear, and who is unlikely at first to realize in each case that the same name refers to different people on opposite sides of the social and economic divide. In addition to bringing an indirect narrative technique to bear on these events, the novel also comments on them in a way that the more direct 'testimonies' of the time do not. A running theme throughout the novel is the yearning for 'wholeness' of individuals who can never be 'complete' because they also see themselves reflected in another person whom they can neither annihilate nor assimilate. This incompleteness is seen in the novel, beyond the fictional scenario of this curious family and the explicit reference to the civil war of the late 1940s, as an unavoidable fact of nature. One of the (legitimate) brothers says to Alexander, the hero:

Άκου, Αλέξανδρε, την πληρότητα δεν τη φτάνει ποτέ κανείς, ούτε η φύση τη φτάνει... Πληρότητα δεν υπάρχει. Υπάρχει μόνο η κίνηση και η αλλαγή. Οι μεταμορφώσεις των σωμάτων, η καταστροφή που φέρνει την ανανέωση, κι όλο το μυστικό είναι να συνταυτιστείς μ' αυτή την κίνηση και τον κύκλο, να βοηθήσεις τη φύση. Νομίζουμε πως ικανοποιούμε τα πάθη μας πολεμώντας ο ένας τον άλλον, όμως μόνο τη φύση ικανοποιούμε...[101]

Listen, Alexander, no one ever manages to be complete, not even nature can do it.... There's no such thing as completeness. There's only motion and change. The changing shape of bodies, the destruction that brings renewal—the whole secret is to identify yourself with this motion and this circle, to give nature a helping hand. We think that by fighting among ourselves we're satisfying our passions, but we're only satisfying nature...

Not only does this novel attempt, only a year after the end of the civil war, to place recent events in a more fundamental context, it also, in its allegorical mode and in its questioning of the nature of individual identity, anticipates the freer literary experiments of the 1960s.

[100] The same year also saw the publication of *Pyramid 67 (Η πυραμίδα 67)* by Renos Apostolidis, which approaches the same contemporary subject matter by the means of direct and vivid testimony (cf. Tziovas 1993: 203–6).
[101] Lymberaki 1979: 66–7. Later in the novel this 'balance' in nature is linked explicitly to the philosophy of Heraclitus (1979: 109).

Apart from *The Other Alexander*, it was not until the 1960s that a degree of overt literary experiment became acceptable in the fictional representation of wartime experience. This development is most evident in the best-known novel of this period by Tatiana Gritsi-Milliex (b. 1920), *Behold a Pale Horse* (1963), and in the trilogy of Stratis Tsirkas (pseudonym of Yannis Hatziandreas, 1911–80) known collectively as *Drifting Cities* (1960–5).[102]

Unlike the majority of wartime 'testimonies' published in the late 1940s and the 1950s, these and other technically more complex treatments of the subject during the 1960s are written from the point of the view of the Left. The title of *Drifting Cities* alludes to a poem of Seferis written during his service in the Middle East during the war, and the setting of each of the novels is one of these cities in wartime: Jerusalem, Cairo, and Alexandria. The central character of the trilogy is Manos Simonidis, a Marxist Hamlet whose finer feelings and probing intellect constantly conspire to frustrate his theoretical commitment to action. In the cosmopolitan melting-pot of the Middle East between 1942 and 1944 Manos' allegiance to his ideals is severely tested as he tries to steer a course between the hardline, narrow-minded ideologue who is his immediate Party boss, and his contacts with displaced Europeans whose cultural and intellectual horizons evoke his love and admiration, but whose fundamental frivolity finally appals him.

The three novels are urban and panoramic, with large casts of characters, on a scale scarcely attempted in Greek fiction since Theotokas' curtailed *Argo* of the 1930s. In addition to their ambitious scale, they are formally innovative in two ways: in their handling of point of view, and in their treatment of time. Each of the three novels is divided among three narrative viewpoints. Manos, as the focal point linking all three, always tells his own story in the first person. But this is interspersed with the stories of other major characters, told from an omniscient third-person point of view; and in two of the three books a third narrative viewpoint is that of a 'split personality' who addresses herself (in *The Club*) and himself (in *The Bat*) in the *second* person, a rare device in realist fiction. As a

---

[102] Gritsi-Milliex 1990. This writer has been aptly praised for 'often applying the techniques of the French *new novel* to social purposes that are all too often lacking in French literature' (Robinson 1989: 1131). For Tsirkas' trilogy see Tsirkas 1980–1. The three novels are *The Club* (Η λέσχη), *Ariagni* (Αριάγνη), and *The Bat* (Η νυχτερίδα).

result, in two of the three books, the three points of view which succeed one another throughout the novel correspond to the three grammatical persons, while in the middle book of the trilogy there are again three points of view, of which one (Manos') is in the first person and the other two in the third. The effect gained is partly one of universality (all grammatical persons and a wide variety of intimate points of view are there) and partly of the instability and fragmented nature of the social and political reality described, which is further implied by the title of the trilogy. Like Lawrence Durrell, whose *Alexandria Quartet* had just previously traversed some of the same ground, and like Cavafy, to whom Durrell was also explicitly indebted, Tsirkas in his trilogy set himself the task of portraying the essential *relativity* of human experience and perception.

This sense of relativity also extends to the treatment of time in the trilogy. As a Marxist, Tsirkas had a great respect for the process of history, and his novel faithfully, and with much accuracy of detail, builds up a picture of the events during the Second World War which, it is clearly implied, made the subsequent civil war in Greece inevitable. But from his fellow Egyptian-Greek Cavafy, Tsirkas has acquired a much broader view of the history of Hellenism and of the whole region, while from Seferis, whom he quotes in the title of the trilogy, he has also adopted an interest in myth as the proof of a cyclical or repetitive pattern in history. This last preoccupation is not easily reconciled with a Marxist, teleological conception, and is overtly associated in the novels with the (mainly English) upper-class characters whom Manos admires but finally rejects. More fundamentally, however, this cyclical concept of history is also enshrined in the basic structure of the three novels, each of which is built around a myth which its plot in some way re-enacts. *The Club*, set in Jerusalem, re-enacts the story of the biblical fall, and the overtly mythological character is the primitive sensualist Adam. *Ariagni*, the second novel, is a modern tale of the labyrinth and Ariadne/Ariagni's thread, while the bewildering metamorphoses that take up much of the plot in *The Bat*, set in Alexandria, turn out to be the work of a sinister modern Proteus. The counterpoint between history as cause-and-effect, and history as cyclical pattern, adds further to the 'relativity' explored in Tsirkas' trilogy, and to the new technical subtlety which he brings to his theme.

Other 'testimonies' written during the 1960s, this time not about the war years but about the experience of the civil war and its aftermath, are also stylistically more self-conscious. The short story or novella *The Descent of the Nine* (1963) by Thanasis Valtinos (b. 1932) uses the language and the oral style of a simple villager to chronicle the final agonies of a small unit being 'mopped up' at the end of the civil war,[103] while the chronicle of the life of political prisoners on the island of Makronisos, *Plague*, by Andreas Frangias (b. 1923), narrates horrific and bizarre happenings in a deliberately deadpan style, and conveys a sense of communal experience by its determined avoidance of proper names.[104] Both these cases show a reversion to a traditional or older manner of story-telling which, in context, must be seen as a conscious choice, motivated by both political and literary ends.

The revival and sophisticated refinement of the style of oral testimony by Valtinos, and to some extent also by Frangias, is more evident still in what is probably the best-selling Greek novel of the decade: *Bloodied Earth* (1962) by Dido Sotiriou, which had been reprinted fifty-five times up to 1992.[105] This novel looks back beyond more recent disasters to the exodus of the Greek population from Anatolia in 1922–3, and retells in literary form the testimony of a real informant who had lived through the Turkish labour camps of the 1914–18 war, the Anatolian campaign of the Greek army in 1921–2, and the subsequent expulsion of the Greek population. In many respects this novel represents a return to the practice of Stratis Doukas in 1929, but with two significant differences: first Sotiriou keeps much more of the linguistic idiom of her Anatolian Greek informant, with its liberal sprinkling of Turkish, which Doukas had mentioned but toned down in *A Prisoner's Story*; and secondly she adds a political gloss which is absent from all the pre-war accounts of these events.

The narrator (who is given the fictional identity of Manolis Axiotis) learns from a comrade-in-arms, while serving in the Greek army shortly before the rout of 1922, that his sufferings have been due to the machinations of international capital.[106] In this way, although

[103] Valtinos 1984.
[104] Frangias 1987. First published in 1972, although the book was apparently completed by the time of the Colonels' coup in 1967.
[105] Sotiriou 1983. This figure corresponds to a total number of copies somewhere between 110,000 and 165,000 (see the editor's note to the 26th edn.).
[106] See in particular Sotiriou 1983: 273–4, where the *later* interpretation of these events by the Greek Communist Party is rather improbably given at the time of the events, in 1922 (before the founding of the KKE).

the story ends with the narrator swimming to the safety of the Greek islands, the novel implicitly looks forward to subsequent events, in which the survivors from Anatolia would play a significant part in the development of the Greek Left. More radically, it retrospectively (and anachronistically) claims the defeat in Anatolia as the first defeat of the Greek rural proletariat at the hands of international capital, and so presents the sufferings of ordinary Greeks in the First World War and its aftermath as a precursor to the sufferings inflicted in the Second World War and the civil war which followed.

Folkloric Realism Comes to Town.   *Bloodied Earth*, in looking further into the past than other 'testimonies' of the time, and in its detailed re-creation of the world of Greek peasants in Anatolia, stands midway between this kind of fiction and the 'folkloric realism' which, as we saw, underwent a vigorous revival in the search for salvation through tradition that became a hallmark of Greek writing shortly before and during the Second World War. To see how these pre-occupations of the early 1940s developed after the end of the war, it will again be necessary to go back to 1946, and the novel *Voyage with the Evening Star* by Angelos Terzakis.[107] Terzakis had begun his career in the thirties with long novels of urban, middle-class life— a form to which, as we saw, he was to revert in *Without a God*. The post-war *Voyage* transposes an urban character into the depths of the Greek countryside, where he is enabled to 'come through' his personal crisis thanks to the presence of nature and the dangerous re-enactment of a story from traditional Greek folklore. This story-pattern, and still more the rather lush manner of its telling (exceptional in the work of Terzakis), bring us close to the novels and stories of the late 1930s and early 1940s which had sought redemption through the recovery of tradition. Terzakis draws closely on his immediate predecessors and like them gives a new lease of life to the legacy of the 'folkloric realism' of the late nineteenth century. But *Voyage with the Evening Star* signals an important shift in this remarkably hard-wearing sub-genre, in that for the first time the principal character, like the author himself, comes from and returns to the *urban* environment.

By no means all the post-war writers who continued to exploit the resources of 'folkloric realism' did so from this angle. The early

[107] Terzakis 1985.

stories of Nikos Kasdaglis (b. 1928), for example, collected in the
volume *Squalls* (1952), and the novels of adventure by Yannis Manglis depict traditional life on the islands of the Dodecanese without
ulterior motive (although Manglis, like Loudemis, constructs his
stories with an evident left-wing slant).[108] Together these novels and
stories provide the background for one of the most admired of all
Greek novels to draw on the tradition of 'folkloric realism', *Christ
Recrucified* by Kazantzakis (written in 1949 but not published until
1954). The setting of this novel is a remote Greek village in Anatolia
on the eve of the 1922 disaster, but on to the 'folkloric' representation of the life of this village Kazantzakis has grafted his troubled
perception, gained outside Greece, of the Christian story not as the
promise of divine redemption but as a tragic pattern ever-present in
human life. According to this pattern, man's longing for a divinity
who does not exist is in constant conflict with the imperatives of his
material life.

This conflict Kazantzakis dramatizes within the confines of a
traditional Greek community. Inventing a plausible, and fictionally
necessary, addition to the canons of Greek folklore, Kazantzakis sets
his traditional villagers to re-enact the events of the Passion as an
improvised drama. The chief characters in the story become wholly
identified with their roles, but other members of the community too,
whether they know it or not, find themselves constrained by the
momentum of events into acting out parts dictated by the Passion
story. The village elders unwittingly re-enact the role of the Phari-
sees, the village priest corresponds to Caiaphas, and the Turkish
landlord, an irascible pederast who becomes exasperated by the
antics of his Greek subjects, presumably never knows how closely
his words and actions echo those of Pontius Pilate. In all these
details the story of the novel repeats the pattern of the Passion
story. But of course the villagers do not, this time, simply act out
their ritual drama. Instead the drama takes over their lives, and in a
spectacular inversion of the Christian calendar, the story of the
novel begins at Easter and culminates on Christmas Eve
when Manolios, the Christ-figure, is murdered by the priest in
church. There is no resurrection, and the novel ends with the
realization that this pattern of events has been and will be repeated
again and again—'in vain'.

<hr>

[108] On Manglis see, in English, Hionides 1975.

244 THE AFTERMATH OF WAR AND CIVIL WAR

All this is done without ever violating the established conventions of 'folkloric realism'. On the other hand, in common with the best of the pioneering stories and novels in this sub-genre written in the late nineteenth century, and their successors in the late 1930s and 1940s, *Christ Recrucified* at the same time reaches beyond the bounds of realism. The novel is not only a modern parable of man's inability to grasp the means of his own salvation; it also provides an implicit and sustained allusion to the events of the Greek civil war. These events of course took place long after the fictional events narrated, but it was during the final stages of that conflict, and hard on the heels of his efforts to write about the civil war directly in *The Fratricides*, that Kazantzakis wrote this novel. In *Christ Recrucified*, the chain of events which brings about the disastrous inversion of the Christian story is set in motion by the arrival outside the village of a group of refugees who have lost their homes in a Turkish massacre. Refused aid by the village elders, the refugees set up camp on the mountain nearby. Manolios and his disciples try to help them, and this is why they are condemned by their own people. The conflict between the destitute and desperate Greeks on the mountain and the well-to-do village elders below eventually erupts into armed skirmishes in which both sides are finally the losers. In this way the civil war between the haves in the cities and the have-nots in the mountains of mainland Greece is also hinted to be just the latest realization of the same fundamental and irresolvable conflict as underlies the main story in the novel.[109]

'Folkloric realism' again provides the point of departure for the trilogy by Pandelis Prevelakis, *Roads to Creativity*, the first novel of which, *The Sun of Death* (1959), draws in different ways on the use made of this traditional resource both by Kazantzakis and by Terzakis in *Voyage with the Evening Star*.[110] *The Sun of Death*, even more obviously than Terzakis' *Voyage with the Evening Star*, is a *Bildungsroman*. Moreover, as the first work in a trilogy, it not only returns the young hero to the urban environment from which he started out, but, in its two sequels, follows his fortunes there, thus integrating

---

[109] See further Bien 1989b: 31–44.
[110] Οι δρόμοι της δημιουργίας. For the first volume, discussed here, see Prevelakis n.d. The other two volumes, *The Medusa's Head* (Η κεφαλή της Μέδουσας) and *The Bread of Angels* (Ο άρτος των αγγέλων), were published in 1963 and 1966 respectively.

the 'folkloric realism' of the first novel into a whole work which in conception and style has much in common with the 'urban realism' of the 1930s. The adolescent hero, Yorgakis, orphaned during the First World War, is adopted by his aunt Rousaki. The novel is set in Crete, and Yorgakis up till this time had lived in town. Now Rousaki takes him to her mountain village, and the description of the journey from one life to the other, seen through the boy's eyes and realized with a visual skill which is one of the hallmarks of Prevelakis' writing, is simultaneously a progression into the literary world of 'folkloric realism'.

The remainder of *The Sun of Death* takes place in Rousaki's village, and ends with her death as she sacrifices herself to protect Yorgakis from a family blood feud. In the detailed descriptions of the landscape and people, and in Rousaki's initiation of the hero into the traditional lore of a community little touched by the outside world, Prevelakis' novel follows quite closely the precedents of Terzakis and indeed of older 'folkloric realism'. But the culling of tradition is to be only a part of the young Yorgakis' 'sentimental education'. Rousaki as the representative of tradition is paired in the novel with an intruder from the cynical modern world outside. This is Loizos Damolinos, a Cretan who has studied abroad, been successful in business, and has now withdrawn to his country house, having been accused of supplying German submarines (and thus indirectly causing the death of Yorgakis' father, among others). Damolinos, like the hero himself, is an outsider both to the community and to the conventions of 'folkloric realism'. Where Rousaki had shown the hero the constellations and given them names from the imaginative world of traditional fairy-tales, Damolinos teaches him their scientific names. Where Rousaki teaches him a homely piety, Damolinos seeks to release in him, much to the former's alarm, 'the spirit of poetic creativity'.[111] And the whole exercise turns out be justified, beyond the confines of this first book, as the first stage of Yorgakis' growth to become a writer and, eventually, to write this very novel. Yorgakis, in order to become a writer, has to be initiated equally into the mainsprings of his own tradition and into the wider, alienated 'spirit of the age' in which he will grow to maturity.

The shift of the 'folkloric' perspective from a rural to an urban setting, of which the first hints were discernible in the handling of

[111] Η αποστολή η δική μου, είπε, είναι να ξυπνήσω την ψυχή σου στην ποιητική δημιουργία (Prevelakis n.d.: 319).

this traditional base by Terzakis and Prevelakis, is completed in the novels and stories which draw on this resource during the 1960s. Now the focus is again on the urban individual, seen this time not against the background of a traditional, rural community, but rather as part of the urban community itself, typically the small-town or city neighbourhood. The transition comes about in the early part of the decade, in novels which at first share something of the attempt of Dido Sotiriou to recapture the lost Anatolian past. In the last completed novel of Kosmas Politis, *In the Hatzifrangou Quarter* (1963), and in the first of a series of novels by Maria Iordanidou (1897–1989), *Loxandra* (1963), we are taken back, as we were in *Bloodied Earth*, to the world east of the Aegean before the 1922 catastrophe.[112] Politis' novel brings panoramically to life a working-class Greek neighbourhood of cosmopolitan Smyrna in the first years of the century; Iordanidou does the same thing for Constantinople at the same period. A tradition of writing about largely *rural* communities has now moved into the cities, but significantly without becoming *urban fiction* in the sense that Theotokas had understood the term in his 1929 manifesto, *Free Spirit*. These are novels of ordinary people in their social and physical environment; the focus is on the group, the family, the environment itself, rather than on individuals who rise above their background or find themselves plunged into a new and strange world (as happens, for example, in the novels of Theotokas, Karagatsis, and Politis himself in the 1930s, and in Tsirkas' *Drifting Cities*).

This shift is especially important because it helps to provide a context for the work of a number of writers who appeared in the early 1960s. Kostas Tachtsis (1927–88) is best known for the novel, *The Third Wedding* (1962), and a number of short stories.[113] The settings of these are exclusively urban, but Tachtsis' forte is the vivid portrayal of 'traditional' characters in an environment which more or less shapes their destinies. *The Third Wedding* is a tale of two mothers, who constantly fall victim to the stereotypes that determine their own behaviour and that of their families. The story is told with a panache and lightness of touch which place it alongside much of the fiction of younger writers at this time; but this novel is motivated by a profounder sense of comedy, that is very rare in

[112] K. Politis 1988. Iordanidou 1980.
[113] Respectively: Tachtsis 1974a; 1974b. See, in English, Mackridge 1991; Robinson 1997a; 1997b; cf. Mitropoulos 1993.

Greek literature, and invites comparison with such distant precursors as Roidis and Cavafy.

Comedy, although in a more understated and more sombre way, is also the keynote of the short prose pieces of Yorgos Ioannou (1927–85). The first collection of these, *For a Sense of Self-Respect*, appeared in 1964. Beginning as very brief 'prose writings', as Ioannou himself preferred to call them, these elusive and atmospheric pieces, mostly set in the writer's native Thessaloniki, develop by the time of his third collection, *The Only Inheritance* (1974), into fully-fledged short stories.[114] Characteristically, the viewpoint is that of an adolescent boy, and many of the pieces draw on the period of the author's own adolescence during the war. Taken together, Ioannou's stories provide a rueful commentary on the waywardness of human nature, and employ a method of ironic juxtaposition for comic effect, which seems to draw on the example of Cavafy. Another characteristic of these stories, their intense compression and the use of abrupt, dramatic transitions, further draws on the legacy of traditional oral songs and tales, of which Ioannou also edited collections.

The early stories and novels of Menis Koumandareas (b. 1933) share a number of features with the urban inheritors of 'folkloric realism' just mentioned. Like Ioannou, Koumandareas during the 1960s wrote mainly short stories (his first collection, *The Pinball Machines*, appeared in 1962), and as with Ioannou and Tachtsis the focus of these stories is the small world of the urban neighbourhood.[115] Although this focus ostensibly widens out in later novels, such as *The Handsome Captain* (1982), which relates, in painful detail, the ramifications of a case brought before the Supreme Court, a basic preoccupation of Koumandareas' fiction remains the claustrophobic effect of the social environment on the individual.

Other writers during the 1960s also drew on the traditional portrayal of the small community in new ways that were particularly associated with the political left. Dimitris Hatzis (1913–81) had begun his career with the somewhat strident commitment to a proletarian future of his novel, *Fire* (1946), but is most highly regarded today for the more low-key stories, with their muted sympathy for the victims of an unjust society, and based on his native town of Ioannina,

---

[114] Respectively: Ioannou 1973; 1974. See also 1980 and Guide to Translations.
[115] Koumandareas 1986.

that he wrote during the 1950s and 1960s while living in enforced exile in eastern Europe. Marios Hakkas (1931–72), who died of cancer at the age of 41, drew on his experiences in the poorer suburbs of Athens, again as the material for short stories.[116]

The Historical Novel. Before ending this survey of the diverse ways in which writers in the two decades following the civil war sought to re-create and to come to terms with the past in their fiction, mention should be made of the historical novel. Terzakis, before trying his hand at the folkloric realism that underlies his novel of 1946, *Voyage with the Evening Star*, had been one of the first of his generation to revive the historical novel, which had been relatively neglected since the early 1880s, in *The Princess Ysabeau*.[117] Other writers, who like Terzakis had established reputations for 'urban' fiction in the 1930s, followed this lead during and after the war: M. Karagatsis in the trilogy *The Kodjabashi of Kastropyrgo* (1941–7), and Thanasis Petsalis, in *The Maurolykos Family* (1947–8), the success of which set the seal on this writer's later career in the historical novel.[118] Similar subject-matter, and the similarly broad canvas of the family 'saga', were also taken up by Prevelakis in his trilogy *The Cretan* (1948–50), which paints a broad picture of the previous hundred years' history of his native island.

Probably the best-known historical novels of this period are those of Kazantzakis: *Freedom and Death, God's Pauper: St Francis of Assisi*, and *The Last Temptation*. The first of these, *Freedom and Death*, shadows the second volume of Prevelakis' trilogy *The Cretan* in taking for its theme one of the last of the nineteenth-century revolts in Crete against Ottoman rule. The main difference from Prevelakis lies in the fact that the failed uprising of 1889 falls within Kazantzakis' own lifetime; and this novel falls somewhere between the historical novel proper and the novel of reminiscence of the author's childhood, which, as we saw earlier, had become elevated and refined to a high degree during the Metaxas dictatorship and the occupation. There are good reasons for supposing that the example of Prevelakis' *The Chronicle of a Town* had played some part in Kazantzakis' first 'mature' novel, *Zorba the Greek*, and a precedent

[116] See respectively: Hatzis 1974 (and Guide to Translations); Hakkas 1986.
[117] See n. 88 to Ch. 3.
[118] On the trilogy and Petsalis' conception of the historical novel see Pikramenou-Varfi 1986.

for the setting of *God's Pauper* in medieval Italy can also be found in
Prevelakis' second novel, *The Death of De' Medici* (1939).

That said, Kazantzakis' three historical novels of the early 1950s
stand apart from their peers in their strongly metaphysical orienta-
tion, and in their implied critique of the Greek nationalist fervour
embodied by the protagonist in *Freedom and Death*, Captain Michalis. While the later two novels ignore specifically Greek concerns
altogether, St Francis and Jesus preaching a gentleness and tolerance that are not easily reconciled with the Greek nationalist cause,
what is admired in *Freedom and Death* is not finally the struggle of the
Cretans, for which the hero dies at the end, but the absolute dedication to *any* cause, which inspires human beings to self-assertion and
self-sacrifice on a superhuman scale.

POST-WAR FICTION: NEW HORIZONS (1960–1967)

The economic revival in which Karagatsis had expressed such faith
in *The Yellow File* may well, if one takes a determinist view of literary
history, have been a significant factor in the resurgence of literary
fiction during the early 1960s. We have already seen that it is predominantly during this decade that new stances *vis-à-vis* the past
and tradition were beginning to develop, for example in the more
technically experimental treatment of recent history by Gritsi-
Milliex and Tsirkas, and in the growth, out of the 'folkloric' tradition,
of a new way of writing about local urban communities. At the same
time new preoccupations, both thematic and stylistic, begin to
appear, and are associated with an exuberance and a self-confidence
little seen in the immediate post-war years. This new writing has
little directly to say about economic and social changes, particularly
in urban life, in the early 1960s. Indirectly, however, a deep and
challenging scepticism may be discerned, and it may be timely to
begin with a group of novels and short stories which question, in a
partly allegorical mode, the basis of the new prosperity.

Viewed from this perspective, the decade begins with *The Dam*
(1961) by Spyros Plaskovitis (b. 1917).[119] An unnamed country
has come to depend on a gigantic dam, which improbably sweeps
in a great arc many miles long from the mountains to the sea. The
dam is the work of a previous generation, no one now knows the

[119] Plaskovitis 1977.

specifications to which it was built or its tolerance to the water pressure inexorably building up behind it. An élite corps has the duty of guarding and inspecting the dam, and of conducting running repairs. Despite the efforts of these professionals to paper over the cracks, word reaches the capital that the dam may be unsafe. The central character of the novel is the engineer whose mission it is to investigate and report. Most of the action takes place in the run-down town which huddles at the foot of the giant wall of concrete, as the engineer goes about his task and oppressive rain builds up the pressures on the dam to crisis level. The dam does not give way, but the engineer detects something more sinister still: water is starting to well up out of the ground below the dam. Unable finally either to find the weak spot in the dam and propose a remedy, or to provide the reassurance that all around him really crave, the engineer makes the radical proposal that the dam should be destroyed. For this he is pilloried by all sides, as everyone's life in this country is affected in some way by the dam.

There are several characteristics of this fable that distinguish it sharply from earlier Greek fiction, but which it also shares with other novels and short stories of the same period. The first of these is the element of the fantastic (although realistically *described*, the dam belongs to the world of fantasy, not of reality). Closely related to this is the non-Greek setting, although the characters, their speech, and their traits are more homely than exotic. Most important of all is the theme. Although it is one of the strengths of the book that the evidently symbolic nature of the dam is never precisely defined, there are sufficient indications that the story is to be read as at least in part an allegory, and that that allegory is to be understood both politically and more 'globally'. Within its context of Greece at the end of the 1950s, the dam hints clearly enough at the capitalist system, an inherited, man-made construct whose real strength to hold back the pent-up momentum of the working-class nobody knows but which almost everyone, regardless of class, has a vested interest in preserving. But the novel's allegory surely goes further than this. Although it might be anachronistic to read *The Dam* as a 'green' novel, its more fundamental theme appears to be man's dangerous attempt to impose his will on nature. The perfect scheme turns out to have a fatal flaw, and this underlying theme of *The Dam*, which might be summed up as 'Nature's revenge', is also the principal theme of the trilogy of 'novellas' with which the prolific career of Vasilis Vasilikos (b. 1934) began (*The Plant, The Well, The Angel*, 1961),[120] and of the short stories of Andonis Samarakis (b. 1919), and in particular of the novel whose title is *The Flaw* (1965).

All of these books are also marked by a throw-away humour, a lightness of touch, and a knowingly ironic stance with which the narrator implies complicity with the reader in telling a tall story which means rather more than it says, or more than its characters could possibly understand. In Vasilikos' trilogy, Nature takes its revenge in contrasting ways, all of them grounded in everyday reality which rapidly takes off into the realm of the fantastic. Topical allusion is most evident in the first novella, *The Plant*. 'In the beginning was Chaos',[121] the tale begins, and goes on to tell, in a parody of the biblical Genesis, of the creation of a modern apartment block in Thessaloniki. On the top floor, in the month of April, an unnamed student of botany grows a pot plant that he has stolen form the veranda of a girl he had seen in the street and timidly followed home. The plant takes over the room, then the family flat, then its tendrils get into the lift shaft and stop the lift working; finally it succeeds in its blind inexorable quest for the natural earth below the foundations, the concrete starts to crack, and the electricity and water fail. The residents find out the cause of all the trouble and demand the plant's destruction.

The Well is a sinister tale, set in the island of Thasos, which parodies some of the conventions of 'folkloric realism', and hints at the fear of global destruction which was at its height in the year of the Cuban crisis, when it was published.[122] *The Angel* is a parodic narrative of military service transposed to outer space, where the reluctant conscripts are the recently dead, and have to be kitted out with wings and turned into angels to fight against Satan in a cause that means little to them, but whose rhetoric is that of cold-war militarism.

---

[120] *Το φύλλο, Το πηγάδι, T' αγγέλιασμα*, published together with *The Photographs*, 1964 (*Οι φωτογραφίες*), as Vasilikos 1987; see also Vasilikos 1994.

[121] Στην αρχή ήταν το χάος (Vasilikos 1987: 9).

[122] The possible consequences of nuclear war are also developed, with a black humour that owes something to Surrealism, by Nanos Valaoritis in some of the short prose pieces written at this time and published much later (N. Valaoritis 1981). The 'Yaroslavs' who appear in some of these texts are a super-race of cannibals who thrive on nuclear fall-out and are allergic to the colour green (see 1981: 18–21); cf. Voulgari 1997.

Where Vasilikos makes extensive use of parody and of the fantastic, Samarakis employs a deadpan style whose light irony is often at the expense of his characters. In one of his most successful short stories, 'New Year's Eve', it is the reader who is duped, as a straightforward account of a stroll through the backstreets of Athens turns out half-way through to be narrated from the point of view of a stray horse.[123] *The Flaw*, like Plaskovitis' *The Dam*, is set in an unnamed country whose daily life, however, seems very much like that of Greece.[124] Published in 1965, the novel achieved new fame two years later when the Colonels seized power and imposed upon Greece a regime identical in many of its most petty details to that in force in the imaginary country of the novel.

The story is told from the alternating point of view of two secret policemen, who are charged with escorting a political suspect from their provincial town to the capital. A fiendish and foolproof plan has been devised to break the suspect: be nice to him for twenty-four hours, by which time his basic human instincts will drive him to reciprocate and share his secrets with his captors. The flaw of course turns out to be that it is one of the secret policemen who cracks first; *his* basic human instincts triumph over his training, so that in the end it is one of his tormentors who tries to help the suspect escape.

In all of these novels the focus has moved beyond the physical frontiers of Greece, and all of them address anxieties which were common to much of the western world at that time. Hard on the heels of these novels and stories, in 1966 came the last novel of Yorgos Theotokas, which confronts the same anxieties from the perspective of the older generation. *The Bells* has nothing of the humour or lightness of touch that tempers the underlying seriousness of the books just discussed.[125] The advocate of a more or less 'westernized' literature for Greece in the polemical essay *Free Spirit* which had begun his career in 1929, Theotokas by 1966 had grown deeply sceptical of the rationalist, technocratic values of the western world which he saw as taking over Greece as well.

The hero of Theotokas' last novel is a top-level banker who has been entrusted by the Greek government with a complex economic mission on which the nation's future depends. The flaw in this particular plan is, at one level, as in the other stories, simple

---

[123] Οδός Σταδίου, παραμονή Πρωτοχρονιάς (Samarakis 1973: 76–81).
[124] Samarakis 1970.   [125] Theotokas n.d. (2).

human frailty. Filomatis, the banker and lifelong workaholic, falls victim to mental illness, experiences bizarre hallucinations, goes missing, and finally is found dead from a fall not far from the summit of Mount Sinai. But the mental breakdown of his hero offers a route for the veteran realist Theotokas to enter the world of allegorical fantasy opened up by such younger writers as Plaskovitis and Vasilikos. Against backgrounds which are mostly far from Greece—in New York, Paris, Stockholm, finally Mount Sinai—the demented banker finds himself locked in dialogue with a mysterious *alter ego*, Doctor Snak. The subject of this dialogue, and of the hallucinations which accompany it, is the violent destruction of civilizations. The question 'Who is Doctor Snak?' becomes the title of one of the book's chapters; and clearly the answer belongs in the same domain of symbolism or allegory as do similar questions about Plaskovitis' dam or Vasilikos' plant. Theotokas no more provides a categorical answer than do these younger writers, but Snak is evidently a harbinger of the downfall of a civilization that has become too clever for its own good. He is certainly presented in the novel as something more than the psychiatric symptom of the banker's divided self. Filomatis dies in a vain attempt to reach the place where Moses had received the Ten Commandments. The novel ends, in a striking elaboration of the closing lines of Seferis' poem 'Engomi', with the description of a large snake sunning itself on the slopes of Mount Sinai, and the implication that the snake, Doctor Snak, and the serpent in the Garden of Eden are all manifestations of the same evil in the world.[126]

None of the novels and stories of the 1960s so far discussed departs significantly from the conventions of literary realism, although they employ them in new ways. But the same period also saw a resurgence of the kind of formal experiments in prose fiction that had begun in Greece in the 1930s, and largely disappeared in the years since the Second World War. One factor influencing this development is undoubtedly the interest aroused by the French *nouveau roman* of

---

[126] On the reception of this novel, its place in Theotokas' *œuvre*, and in particular the identity of Doctor Snak see Farinou 1977. On the last point my reading differs slightly from hers in that I see the elusive Snak as *both* a projection of something within the banker himself *and* a manifestation of the devil. The novel is about the discovery of the 'devil within', and this reading is also consistent with Seferis' 'Engomi', with which it shares its basic preoccupations.

the 1950s, which set its face firmly against traditional notions of character and plot. But the non- or anti-realist fiction that springs up with renewed vigour in Greece in the 1960s is first and foremost a continuation and development of Greek experimental writing from the 1930s. A few of these writers have since described their work published during the 1960s as 'post-modern'.[127]

The range and quantity of experimental writing at this period are perhaps more impressive than many of its results considered individually. The surrealist technique of 'automatic writing' re-emerges briefly in the third novel of Yannis Beratis, *Whirlwind* (1961),[128] an inconsequential tale which moves through an imaginary landscape with no other guide than the author's imagination and a sense of intrigue and menace which may distantly reflect experiences of the civil war. A style closer to the monologues *about* writing of Stelios Xefloudas and Nikos Gavriil Pentzikis (in *The Dead Man and the Resurrection*) is adopted by Nikos Kachtitsis (1926–70) in *The Balcony* (1964), except that here the monologue belongs to a fictional character who gradually succumbs to paranoia about a shameful wartime secret which is never fully revealed. Set in an unnamed African colony, and based on Kachtitsis' experience in Cameroon, *The Balcony* follows the inner progress of a single character into his own 'heart of darkness'.[129]

In these novels the setting is again either imaginary or far from Greece. In the prose of E. H. Gonatas (b. 1924) and Yorgos Heimonas (b. 1939), setting is dispensed with altogether, as we find ourselves in the ill-defined no man's land between poetry and fiction opened up by the surrealist Andreas Embirikos. Heimonas, in eight short prose texts published between 1960 and 1985, embeds fragments of the speeches, thoughts, and narratives of different speakers in his texts, to achieve a polyphonic effect reminiscent of Melpo Axioti's use of different voices embedded in the heroine's monologue in *Difficult Nights*. Heimonas goes about as far as it is possible to go in detaching language from any identifiable referent. Where his texts refer to a 'world' at all, it is to the world of dreams, and also of ritual, to which the haunting, incantatory

---

[127] Notably Nanos Valaoritis and Yorgos Heimonas. The term was certainly not current in Greece, however, before about 1980, and its usefulness will be discussed in the context of Greek literature after 1974.

[128] Or so at least its author claimed (Beratis 1980: xii).

[129] Kachtitsis 1985. On Kachtitsis' life and work see Thaniel 1981.

quality of his language also contributes. At stake in Heimonas' writing seems to be the identity, or even the concept, of the individual self. The equivalent of the narrative voice in these texts is split into many overlapping roles, as individual 'characters' are either grotesquely transformed, killed, or merged into other 'characters'. The sense of violent dissolution present in these texts, and indeed some of their imagery, is reminiscent of Seferis, particularly in his *Three Secret Poems* of 1966. At the end of this violent apocalypse, there lies a vision which has a strong basis in Orthodox theology:

Θα έρθει που τα σώματα των ανθρώπων θα συνενωθούν. Το ένα θα κολλά στο άλλο κι ό,τι είναι από άνθρωπο θα στερεωθεί. Θα δημιουργηθεί ένα πελώριο σώμα κοινό. Θα εμφανιστεί ένα καινούριο δέρμα κι ένα πλατύ καινούριο πουκάμισο δέρματος. Ωκεανός από δέρμα θα σκεπάσει τα ενωμένα σώματα των ανθρώπων. Θα σκεπαστούν εκείνα τα φριχτά ενώματα.[130]

There will come a time when the bodies of mankind will be united together. The one will stick to the other and whatever is made of man will have a sure foundation. There will be created an immense common body. A new skin will appear and a broad new shirt of skin. An ocean of skin will cover the united bodies of mankind, covering those frightful joins.

Heimonas' rejection of the western world and its values is more extreme than any of those so far discussed, and of course this is only one among many finely entangled strands that make up his writing. The world of his fiction bears similarities with the demented experience of Theotokas' protagonist in *The Bells* (although even insanity in Theotokas' novel follows a more rational course than is found in any of Heimonas' texts!). Heimonas, in other words, takes to its limit the fundamental anxiety and/or critique of the western world that we have identified as the hallmark of the new Greek fiction in the 1960s.

This same anxiety, and as trenchant a rejection of western rationality and its works, find their monumental expression in the *chef-d'œuvre* of Nikos Gavriil Pentzikis, *The Novel of Mrs Ersi* (1966).[131] Pentzikis we have already met as one of the most far-reaching experimental writers of fiction in the 1930s, whose second novel, *The Dead Man and the Resurrection*, had effectively declared an

[130] *The Builders* (Οι χτίστες, Heimonas 1979: 59); cf. Maronitis 1986.
[131] Pentzikis 1992.

unbridgeable gulf between the kind of realist fiction traditional in the West and the Greek experience and tradition. Pentzikis returns to the attack in *The Novel of Mrs Ersi*, which again derives much of its technique and some of its preoccupations from European Modernism, while the main thrust of the novel is seemingly to reactivate narrative traditions and spiritual perceptions which are, by contrast, the inheritance of eastern Orthodoxy. Pentzikis has here moved well beyond his second novel, and in doing so has remained in step with the concerns of the principal *poets* of his generation, in seeking the roots of a Greek culture that is no longer particularly *local*. The Hellenistic and Byzantine novel, the eleventh-century history of Michael Psellos, Homer, the 1922 novella of Yorgos Drosinis from which the heroine and her husband are quite explicitly borrowed, as well as a strong (Orthodox) religious element running through the entire novel, all work together to place *The Novel of Mrs Ersi* in a larger and more sophisticated context than that of the Greek folklore to which it also makes significant allusion.

At the heart of Pentzikis' novel (in which geometry, number, and time play an obsessive part) is an unprecedented resolution of the 'eternal triangle'. At the beginning the narrator admires from a distance, and tries to re-create in a third-person narrative, the summer holiday of a newly married couple, Pavlos and Ersi.[132] The unnamed narrator admires Ersi from afar, but when Pavlos suddenly dies, his dreams come true in an unexpected way. Ersi comes to him to retrace the steps of her former happiness with her husband. In a daring series of metaphors the narrator becomes first the needle and thread in his heroine's hand as she 'weaves' the tapestry of her past life, and then, when the needle pricks her finger and draws blood, he is finally transformed into the husband himself as the couple set off by train on their honeymoon, 'weaving' in and out of tunnels on their way to the idyllic seashore where we first met them.

---

[132] The names and the 'story', in so far as there is one, of Pavlos Rodanos and his wife are taken, quite explicitly, from Drosinis' *Ersi* (1922). The same first names had also been used by Kosmas Politis for the principal characters of his second novel, *Hecate*, 1933 (see K. Politis 1985), where the mythological connotations of the names Ersi/Herse and Hecate are explored. An allusion to these connotations is also found in Pentzikis' novel (1992: 124–6, 340), which probably draws as much on the bizarre metaphysical speculations of Politis (whose novel is never mentioned) as on the more down-to-earth *Ersi* of Drosinis (which appears frequently in the text).

It takes more than four hundred pages for this daring 'osmosis of persons'[133] to be completed, and the novel's extraordinarily rich texture also encompasses a playful digressiveness which has as much in common with *Tristram Shandy* and Joyce's *Ulysses* as with any Byzantine text. The significance of *The Novel of Mrs Ersi* was well summed up by Yorgos Seferis, whose sympathetic, if somewhat impatient, reading of the novel was published in 1967, and helped to find a place for Pentzikis in the mainstream of Greek literature: 'The whole book of *Mrs Herse* [*sic*] is a splintering of the ego, of place and time.'[134]

These words were written only months before the Colonels' seizure of power on 21 April 1967. By then, Greek fiction had undergone almost as profound a renewal as it had in the early 1930s. With the initiative now largely, but not exclusively, in the hands of a younger generation of writers, the foundations of the new-found competence and confidence of Greek writers of fiction that has marked the period since 1974 had been well and truly laid.

---

[133] The phrase is Ezra Pound's (*Cantos*, XXIX), and helps to underscore certain congruities between European Modernism and the Byzantine/Orthodox tradition which Pentzikis seeks to reactivate in his writing.

[134] Seferis 1973: 79 (reprinted in Seferis 1992: 193–236) Seferis consistently spells the heroine's name in its ancient Greek way, with the rough breathing, as had Drosinis and Politis (but only the first edition of *Hecate*), while Pentzikis 'modernizes' the spelling. For a brief discussion of this novel in English, in the context of Pentzikis' work as a whole, see Thaniel 1983 (esp. 54–61).

5. From Military Dictatorship to the European Union
1967–1992

THE period of the Colonels' junta, from 1967 to 1974, marks a significant transition from the polarized divisions of the period of Greek history that goes back to the Asia Minor disaster of 1922, to a new phase whose foundations, we can now see in retrospect, were quietly being laid in the 1960s. In the short term, the rule of the Colonels brought back much of the rhetoric and most of the repressive measures that had been used earlier by Metaxas, and against the Left during the civil war. In the first years of the Colonels' rule, laws of censorship were so strict that many writers of literature refused to publish in Greece at all.

Resistance to a regime that was both repressive and petty united many writers of different political persuasions, and a concerted effort to beat censorship by overt compliance and covert mockery resulted in the publication of the 'protest' volume *Eighteen Texts* in 1970. In the following the year the funeral of the poet Yorgos Seferis unexpectedly became the occasion for a massive, and peaceful, show of popular rejection of the regime. By 1973 Colonel George Papadopoulos, who had regularly been described in foreign press reports as the 'strong man' of the regime, had declared himself president, and in the face of mounting student unrest and international unease at the Colonels' dictatorial methods, was beginning to promise some limited reforms. He was pre-empted however by the students, who for three days in November 1973 barricaded themselves inside the Athens Polytechnic and began broadcasting from a pirate radio station inside, calling on the citizens of Athens to join with them in overthrowing the junta. The outcome is well known: on the night of 16–17 November tanks and troops were deployed alongside armed police to evict the students. In the violent events of that night thirty-four students were killed, and over a thousand injured.

Events were now sliding out of control. A week after the violence at the Polytechnic, a military coup ousted Papadopoulos, but it quickly emerged that the new move had been engineered by even more hardline elements within the army. The new regime, in a desperate bid for popular legitimation, began to stir up Greek nationalist sentiment against the fragile constitutional settlement in Cyprus. In the summer of 1974 a coup in Cyprus by Greek army officers from the mainland gave the opportunity to Turkey, as one of the guarantor powers of the island's independence, to send troops to Cyprus. After several weeks of bitter fighting, in tandem with fruitless international negotiations, the Turkish army consolidated its hold on the northern part of Cyprus, imposing the *de facto* partition between Greek-Cypriot and Turkish-Cypriot communities which remains in force today. Overwhelmed by a turn of events which they had apparently been unable to foresee and now could not control, the military regime turned back from the brink of war with Turkey, and handed over to a civilian administration on 23 July 1974.

The period since 1974 invites both comparison and contrast with the years before the Colonels. In the political sphere, the creation of two new major parties defined more by the personality of their founder-leaders than by any political programme, continued a long-established (and by many lamented) tradition in Greek politics. The New Democracy party of Konstandinos Karamanlis, which governed from 1974 to 1981, and the Panhellenic Socialist Movement (PASOK) of Andreas Papandreou, which governed from 1981 to 1989, are both hard to separate from the personality and influence of their charismatic founders. Although the parties, created in 1974, were new, it is worth remarking that their leaders were not: Karamanlis had been prime minister from 1955 to 1963, and Andreas Papandreou had served in the government of his father, George Papandreou, between 1963 and 1965. An additional legacy from the past was the continuation, and even, in the 1980s, the wholesale extension, of traditional patron–client relationships in politics and public services. The second PASOK government, from 1985 to 1989, was particularly marred by scandals and financial abuses which soured the atmosphere of public life at the end of the 1980s and left behind a continuing legacy of cynicism and mistrust into the 1990s.

But the contrasts with the earlier period are even greater. Between 1974 and 1992, Greece twice saw an orderly handover of power from one major party to another following a general election. True, the 'hung' parliaments of 1989–90 were messy and the victory of New Democracy under Konstandinos Mitsotakis in 1990 a narrow one, but neither in 1981 nor in 1990 was there any real threat either of intervention by the military or of ballot-rigging to frustrate the democratic process; and this was in striking contrast to most earlier elections in modern Greek history.[1]

Other more fundamental changes, whose roots go back at least to the 1960s, can also be seen in the period since the Colonels. After the legal recognition of political parties of the far Left in 1974, the Communist Party stabilized its share of the popular vote in free elections at around 10 per cent, and the Right–Left polarization which had built up since 1922 and reached a peak in the civil war ceased to dominate national life. Other preoccupations rose to dominance: on the domestic front, with economic prosperity; and in external affairs, with negotiating a place for Greece in the international community which involved more participation and less dependence on foreign powers. The architect of Greece's entry into the European Community (effected in two stages in 1981 and 1988) was Konstandinos Karamanlis, who as far back as 1962 had signed a treaty of association with the EEC. Despite much confusion during the 1970s and early 1980s about the consequences and advisability of Greece's entry, it had become clear by the end of the 1980s that membership had brought both considerable economic benefits, and a concomitant loosening of Greece's traditional client status *vis-à-vis* a single dominant power.

In the period from 1947 to 1974 this role had fallen to the USA, as an inevitable consequence of that country's decisive contribution to the victory of the Right in the civil war. Although the extent of American involvement in Greece during this period has sometimes been exaggerated, and claims that the Central Intelligence Agency masterminded the 1967 coup remain unsubstantiated, it is clear that throughout that period Greece was a front-line state in the cold-war confrontation between NATO and the Warsaw Pact. It is in this context that the guarded toleration of the Colonels' regime shown by most western European countries, and still more the open approval shown by successive American administrations,[2] need to be understood. Seen in this light, and from the perspective of the

---

[1] See Clogg 1987.
[2] Clogg 1986: 193; see also McDonald 1982; Woodhouse 1985.

1990s, Greece in 1973–4 was the first 'buffer' or client state in eastern Europe to shake off an undemocratic regime imposed and
maintained in power by the dynamics of the cold war.

While it would be naïve to underestimate the continued American
role in Greece after 1974, or to overplay Greece's participation as an
equal partner in the European Community after 1981, there was
certainly a new and growing internationalism in Greek cultural
perceptions after the early 1960s. This new perspective increasingly
displaced the old antagonisms of the cold war, and at the same time
gave a radically new direction to the 'search for identity' which had
marked the traumatic period from the 1920s to the 1940s, as we saw
in the previous two chapters. An indication of this can be seen in the
political sphere. After Greek hopes of territorial gains in Cyprus had
been frustrated by the terms of the island's independence signed in
1959, and had been briefly and disastrously revived by the Colonels'
adventure in 1974, it was finally clear that Greek influence in the
world would not in future be increased by territorial expansion.

At the same time (and highlighted by the regressive line taken by
the Colonels) perceptions of 'Hellenism', or what it means to be
Greek, were beginning to change. The poet Yorgos Seferis revealingly discovered, while touring the Byzantine monasteries of the
interior of Anatolia in 1950, that 'the whole of Greece, from many
points of view, is a *frontier*'.[3] Hellenism from this time on becomes
less territorial, and less a matter of purely *national* identity. Seferis
was not alone in seeing the Greeks of the post-war period as the
inheritors of the traditions of eastern Orthodoxy, reaching far
beyond national or geographical boundaries. At about the same
time it began to be appreciated that, through emigration, Greek
culture had been effectively spread around the world. In the post-
war period, long-established Greek communities abroad (in the
USA for example) began to take on a distinctive 'ethnic' character
within their countries of adoption.

Both these new perceptions have played a significant part in the
'internationalization' of the Greek sense of identity in the years since
the Colonels' junta. A new awareness of the inheritance of eastern
Orthodoxy has led to a strong revivalist movement, both at a popular level and in intellectual circles, asserting the primacy of spiritual
values and social attitudes associated with the Orthodox Church.

[3] Seferis 1981: ii. 88.

Interestingly this 'New Orthodoxy', as it has been called since the 1970s, is diametrically and implacably opposed to Greek integration into western Europe, and especially to assimilation of the material values of the West. This tension between looking eastwards and looking westwards represents a deeper ambivalence about Greece's place in the world than its cold-war manifestation in the split between Right and Left, between allegiance to Washington and allegiance to Moscow.

Finally, the ending of the cold war, in Greece as elsewhere, has produced, at least temporarily, a return to older anxieties that were particularly manifest in the wave of nationalist sentiment, at both popular and official levels, which greeted international recognition of the 'Former Yugoslav Republic of Macedonia' in 1992. At the end of the period surveyed by this chapter, it remained to be seen whether the internationalist momentum described here would continue, within the European Union which came into being in that year.

LITERATURE UNDER MILITARY DICTATORSHIP (1967–1974)

The most direct consequence of the *coup d'état* of 21 April 1967 for Greek literature was the introduction of preventive censorship, which remained in force for the first two and a half years of the seven-year rule of the Colonels. By contrast with the early 1940s, when writers took an evident pride in submitting to the censor's office poems, stories, and novels which in a covert way sought the seeds of future victory, the majority of established writers in 1967 made up their minds not to publish at all under these conditions. In part, this difference in tactic was probably due to the nature of the enemy: in the 1940s the forces of oppression were external and powerful; in the late 1960s they were internal, and despite their firm grip on the country, the bombastic rhetoric and naïve puritanism of the junior army officers who had taken over was often not taken entirely seriously. In addition, except during the closing stages of the regime, opposition to it was by no means universal.

A few writers, who had already chosen to distance themselves from politics, did publish under preventive censorship—notably the poets Karouzos and Themelis.[4] Others, such as Elytis, published

---

[4] Karouzos' volume *Acts of Mourning* (Πενθήματα) was published in Feb. 1969, the first volume of Themelis' *Poems* in Oct., both before the lifting of preventive censorship in Nov. of that year.

their work abroad. In March 1969 Yorgos Seferis, now a Nobel laureate and retired from the diplomatic service, broke with the habits of a lifetime of government service to issue a public statement, via the BBC, condemning the regime and its suppression of individual and artistic freedom.[5] Finally, in November of the same year, preventive censorship was lifted, but only to be replaced by a Press Law which made editors, publishers, and authors legally responsible for censoring their own work in conformity with the 'Revolution of 21 April'. One of the best-known provisions of this Press Law was the stipulation that a title or headline must correspond exactly to the content of what followed it.

Writers quickly began to respond in a way that has left its mark on much Greek writing since.[6] In July 1970 the Kedros publishing house brought out a volume of new writing whose title, *Eighteen Texts*, conformed impeccably to the letter of the law, in matching the book's contents, but at the same time neatly subverted its spirit, in giving no clue as to what the book was *about*.[7] *Eighteen Texts* is the first of several collaborative publications of the early 1970s, in which writers clearly found, as well as safety in numbers, a common purpose, despite the variety of their ages, backgrounds, artistic aims, and political allegiances, in using their art to combat the perceived threat of imposed self-censorship.

Pride of place in the collection is given to a poem by Seferis, 'The Cats of St Nicholas', which had been written in draft fifteen years before, and allusively refers to the corrosive effects of evil in the body politic and to the indifference of those who stand by.[8] Apart from Seferis, all the other contributors are listed alphabetically on the plain front cover of the book. As well as poetry and fiction by (mainly) established figures of the post-war generation, *Eighteen Texts* includes essays by two leading critics, Alexandros Argyriou and D. N. Maronitis, and two personal reminiscences (by Nora Anagnostaki and the novelist Nikos Kasdaglis).[9] Several of the short stories develop an 'alibi' first exploited by Engonopoulos in

[5] The text appears in *Νέα κείμενα 2* (Kedros 1972: 15–16).
[6] This subject has been explored in depth by van Dyck (1997: 12–56).
[7] Kedros 1970.
[8] Οι γάτες τ' Άϊ Νικόλα (Seferis 1972: 271–3).
[9] The volume also includes poems by Sinopoulos, Anagnostakis, and Lina Kasdagli, and short stories or excerpts from longer prose fiction by Kay Cicellis, Takis Koufopoulos, Spyros Plaskovitis, Alexandros Kotzias, Rodis Roufos, Yorgos Heimonas, Th. Frangopoulos, Stratis Tsirkas, Thanasis Valtinos, and Menis Koumandareas.

264 FROM DICTATORSHIP TO THE EUROPEAN UNION

his wartime poem about Bolívar, and share a setting in the South American country of 'Boliguay'—which unsurprisingly is in the grip of military dictatorship.

The undeclared themes of most of the pieces in the collection are censorship and repression. In an understated short story by Kay Cicellis, the small talk between a taxi-driver and his passenger establishes a mutual, tacit understanding of all that cannot be said. In one of the most memorable of the eighteen texts, Thanasis Valtinos appropriates the regime's favourite metaphor, of Greece as a patient in need of plaster, to produce a tale of a hapless victim coated in plaster from head to foot. As the patient discovers, too late, that the doctor who is treating him is the same man as had caused his injury, the plaster finally reaches his mouth to deprive him simultaneously of both speech and breath. In a different genre Maronitis meditates on a poem by Cavafy that had presented the dilemma of a poet in the face of the larger forces of history.[10]

Despite (or perhaps because of) its unpromising title, *Eighteen Texts* was reprinted five times in little over a year, and was followed by two uniform volumes, *New Texts* and *New Texts 2*. The later volumes continue broadly the same strategy as the first, although the scope is widened still further to include many more writers (only Plaskovitis and Roufos appear in all three), and even essays on political theory and economics.

One of the most striking features of the *Eighteen Texts*, in view of the book's seemingly influential role, is the absence of any new *writers*. With the exception of Seferis, the elder statesman among them, all belong to the generation which began publishing between the Second World War and 1960, and the book includes no writers under the age of 30. *New Texts 2* includes the work of only two writers born after 1940, one of whom, Lefteris Poulios, is now recognized as one of the leading poets of the 1970s. If the *Eighteen Texts* established a strategy whereby writers could beat the censors at their own game, this initiative is noticeably the work of the older generation of established writers, and indeed is carried out under the protection of the oldest of them all, Seferis.

However, by the time that *New Texts 2* appeared in 1972, the existence of a new 'generation of the seventies', at least in poetry,

[10] 'Arrogance and Intoxication' (Ὑπεροψία καὶ μέθη, Kedros 1970: 135–54). The poem by Cavafy, 'Darius', is discussed in Ch. 2.

had already begun to be asserted.[11] The first concerted appearances of this 'generation' in public seem to have been inspired by the collective format and blamelessly uninformative title of the *Eighteen Texts*, and bear similarly bland, catch-all titles.[12] *Six Poets*, which appeared in 1971, presents new work by a group of poets most of whom were still little known and whose publishing careers, under different circumstances, would presumably have developed during the second half of the 1960s.[13] If *Six Poets* is to be read as a protest volume, the protest it embodies is more ecumenical and less political than that of the older generation in *Eighteen Texts* and its sequels. The same can be said of a number of individual volumes of poetry published at the same time by completely new (and younger) writers, who together with the 'six poets' have since been recognized as forming the backbone of the new 'generation' of the 1970s: *The Chronometer* by Yannis Kondos (b. 1943), *Tolls* by Jenny Mastoraki (b. 1949), both in 1972, followed in the next three years by *Field of Mars* by Nasos Vayenas (b. 1945) and *Albeit Pleasing* by Rea Galanaki (b. 1947).[14] The same writers, together with others, also took part in further collective publications of verse: the huge compilations entitled *Deposition '73* and *Deposition '74*, published in the respective years.[15]

The poets just named are the first Greek poets systematically to demystify and domesticate myth, and to explore, in a way which is not merely defensive, the contemporary meeting of traditional Greek culture, including language, with the internationalism of pop culture and the electronic age. None of these poets tries to recover or reconstruct the traditions of the past as earlier generations of Greek poets had done, but neither are they oblivious to the myths, history, traditions, and language that lie behind them. Instead they see their own heritage as a vast store of bric-à-brac waiting to be put to some sort of use, and therefore as not different in

[11] On the origin of the term (in a review of Poulios by Steriadis in 1970) see Maronitis 1987: 232–3 and van Dyck 1997: 61–8. For an overview and anthology of this 'generation' see Papayeoryiou 1989; Panayotou 1979, vol. i; Ziras 1979.

[12] *Six Poets* (1971); *Anti-Anthology* (Iatropoulos 1971); *The New Generation* (Bekatoros and Florakis 1971).

[13] Only Anghelaki-Rooke, of the six, had published a volume before 1967. Potamitis' first volume was published in that year, while Isaia and Poulios each published a first volume (despite preventive censorship) in 1969, and Steriadis in 1970.

[14] Vayenas 1974; Galanaki 1975. Galanaki belongs here since the poems included in that volume had been written, and many of them had been published, in the early 1970s.

[15] Boukoumanis 1973; 1974.

kind from all the other cultural artefacts and sense-impressions of modern life. The Greek poets of the early 1970s eschew all assumptions of a hierarchy of values, and build their poetry to a large extent out of juxtapositions which are striking, epigrammatic, often parodic, but which characteristically resist resolution or synthesis.

This kind of juxtaposition, and this new way of traversing the much-travelled territory of ancient myth, are evident in two short poems of 1972, the first by Yannis Kondos, the second by Jenny Mastoraki:

Ο μίτος της Αριάδνης
Χιλιάδες πεινασμένοι μινώταυροι
περάσανε μπροστά μας με φωτιές
γυρεύοντας ένα λαβύρινθο να ξαποστάσουν.

('Οσο για την Αριάδνη κοιμάται
πλάι στο τηλέφωνο και περιμένει.)[16]

Ariadne's Thread

Thousands of hungry minotaurs
passed before us breathing fire
looking for a labyrinth to shelter in.

(As for Ariadne she's asleep
waiting by the telephone.)

Ο Δούρειος 'Ιππος τότε είπε
όχι, δε θα δεχτώ δημοσιογράφους,
κι είπαν γιατί, κι είπε
πως δεν ήξερε τίποτε για το φονικό.
Κι ύστερα, εκείνος
έτρωγε πάντα ελαφρά τα βράδια
και μικρός
είχε δουλέψει ένα φεγγάρι
αλογάκι σε λούνα παρκ.[17]

The Wooden Horse at that point said
no, I refuse to see the press,
and why, they said, and he said
that he didn't know a thing about the murder.
What's more he always
ate very lightly in the evening
and in his younger days
had earned his living once
as a toy horse at the fun-fair.

[16] G. Kondos 1983: 55.
[17] Mastoraki 1972: 11. The poem is untitled. Cf. van Dyck 1996.

Kondos has since emerged as the master of the short epigram (and elsewhere has made explicit his debt to the satire of Kostas Karyotakis).[18] The early poems of most of the other poets mentioned are generally short, and also, like the examples quoted, in a free verse in which an understated iambic rhythm is discernible.[19]

The only poet of the group to write at length is Katerina Anghelaki-Rooke (b. 1939), who also stands out from the other poets mentioned in that her career had already begun before 1967, and for the strongly personal affirmation of a poetry grounded in the physicality of the female body. However, the new strategy for handling hallowed myths, which dominates the poetry of the younger generation throughout the early 1970s, can be traced back to Anghelaki-Rooke's first collection. Here, 'Iphigenia's Refusal' retells the story of the sacrifice of Agamemnon's daughter: in defiance of the myth, the victim refuses to die as she declares the cause to be unworthy, and this long, lyrical poem ends with the epigrammatic epilogue:

Έκπληκτοι οι στρατιωτικοί
ανέβαλλαν τον πόλεμο
και την Ελένη βρήκαν ταπεινή
να ετοιμάζει το δείπνο.[20]

Astonished the military men
put off the war
and found Helen
humbly preparing dinner.

Anghelaki-Rooke has, however, held aloof from the other most conspicuous innovation which was evident in the new poetry of the early 1970s, namely its assimilation of the technological and pop cultures that were increasingly becoming an international currency at the time. We have already seen the mythological Ariadne's thread upstaged by the telephone, and the early poetry of Kondos and Mastoraki is full of such allusions to the technological realities of modern life. Two of the 'six poets', Lefteris Poulios (b. 1944) and Vasilis Steriadis (b. 1947), take this trend further, each in a different way.

[18] G. Kondos 1982: 145–6.
[19] On this see also Maronitis 1987: 243.
[20] Η άρνηση της Ιφιγένειας, from the collection *Wolves and Clouds* (*Λύκοι και σύννεφα*, Anghelaki-Rooke 1971: 33–8).

Poulios echoes the American 'beat generation' in hitting out at the consumer society in a brash, often violent language which is presented as itself the product of that society. Poulios differs significantly from the American poets, however, in that the culture that he simultaneously has absorbed and scorns is that of a foreign power which was widely seen, at the time, as condoning the restriction of freedom in his country. This is why the notorious poem 'American Bar in Athens', which was included in the 1971 volume *Six Poets*, is not, as has been claimed, merely a rewriting of Allen Ginsberg's 'A Supermarket in California' and Pound's 'A Pact' (both of them poems by younger poets about the dominant position occupied by Walt Whitman).[21] Poulios' truculent dialogue is between himself and *his* illustrious predecessor, Kostis Palamas, and the setting is an *American* bar (this part of the title is even in English). As a result the poem represents not merely a classic illustration of the neurosis that Harold Bloom had just at that time identified and named as 'the anxiety of influence', but also of the unwilling and unavoidable absorption of a dominant, alien culture. The 'alienation' which plays such a large part in the American, and to some extent also western European, popular culture in the 1960s takes on a different meaning when that culture is transposed to Greece under military rule in the early 1970s.

Steriadis' first two volumes, published under the dictatorship, have been likened to comic strips, in their technique of laying a series of unrelated images end to end in a way that frustrates the reader's every attempt to make sense of them.[22] As the poet himself puts it, in the first of two poems entitled, for no particular reason, 'July':

> Στο κάτω κάτω είμαι ανισόρροπος. Η ψυχή μου ενίοτε
> καίγεται σ᾽ ένα μικρό λυχνάρι, όπως άλλωστε όλων σαν
> εμένα. Ουδεμία σχέση με το λυχνάρι του Αλαντίν
> τους εξήγησα και τους γύρισα την πλάτη στο καινούριο
> ρεστωράν για να γίνη ατμόσφαιρα-ταμπαρατούμπαρα.[23]

> Fundamentally I'm unbalanced. At times my soul
> burns in a little lamp, just like everybody else's

---

[21] Αμέρικαν Μπαρ στην Αθήνα (Poulios 1982: 21–2). See Christianopoulos 1975 and discussion by van Dyck 1997: 78–9.

[22] *Mr Ivo*, 1970 (*Ο κ. 'Ιβο*) and *The Private Plane*, 1971 (*Το ιδιωτικό αεροπλάνο*). For a discussion of Steriadis' poetry see van Dyck 1997: 83–99.

[23] *Six Poets*, 1971: 94 (also printed the same year in *The Private Plane*, 14).

who's like me. No connection with Aladdin's lamp
I explained to them and turned my back on them in the new
restaurant so as to set up an atmosphere of hullabaloo.

In many respects this short poem, published in 1971, can be read in
retrospect as a 'blueprint' for much of the poetry of the younger
generation during the 1970s. The place of the Aladdin's lamp of
myth and magic is usurped by the more modest 'little lamp' of the
poet, who is neither more nor less than an individual, and whose aim
is not to find or create equilibrium, but to set up an 'atmosphere of
hullabaloo'. 'The little lamp' could well stand as the title of an
anthology of the poetry of the decade that followed its publication.

Not all the new poetry that appeared in Greece after the lifting of
preventive censorship at the end of 1969 followed in the footsteps of
either the *Eighteen Texts* of the older generation or the *Six Poets* and
the other anthologies of their younger contemporaries. The later
years of the Colonels' rule saw a resurgence of the 'popular art song'
which married words by established poets to musical structures that
derived simultaneously from the long-despised music of the urban
poor and from the music of the Greek Church. The music of
Theodorakis, a declared leftist, was banned throughout the seven
years of the dictatorship; and indeed preventive censorship of sound
recording was not formally lifted until the end of the 1970s.[24] Both
Theodorakis and Hatzidakis, the dominant figures in this new
musical idiom during the 1960s, continued to produce records and
to give concerts abroad. Meanwhile, within Greece new music was
presented to audiences in small, expensive *boîtes* in the Plaka district
of Athens, and, from the start of the 1970s, issued with huge success
on records whose subtle subversion had eluded the vigilance of the
censors.

In musical terms an innovation at this time was the incorporation
of traditional rural folk-music into a modern popular idiom. This
development is especially associated with three composers who

---

[24] After 1974 the purpose of such censorship was no longer chiefly political. But
even after the restoration of civilian government, songs of the partisans in the Second
World War and the civil war, which underwent a revival in live performance, could not
at first be released on record. The principal purpose of this restriction (which predates
the Colonels' take-over) was to excise all public reference to the illegal use of drugs,
which up to 1936 had formed a conspicuous part of the urban subculture in Greece.
Several scholarly reissues of pre-1936 recordings in this genre bear evident witness to
the intervention of the censor's office.

appeared during the early 1970s—Yannis Markopoulos, Christodoulos Halaris, and Eleni Karaindrou—and with the music of these years by Stavros Xarhakos, who had already established a reputation before the coup. Markopoulos' *boîte* in Plaka became a notorious place of pilgrimage for intellectual opponents of the regime, and his music of that period is characterized by an unassimilated blend of the traditional with brash sound-effects and experiments taken from the imported pop culture. In many ways Markopoulos' music runs parallel, in a different art-form, to the protest poetry of Lefteris Poulios. This blend of native folk and foreign pop idioms took further political point from the fact that the military rulers had from the first appropriated 'authentic' folk-music as their own, and at moments of crisis or solemnity the national radio would play traditional music and dances long associated with national resistance against the Turks. It was this musical tradition that Markopoulos used in such unexpected ways, as the basis for an idiom that is often witty or shocking, but could also be highly imaginative and deeply lyrical.

The 'popular art music' of the early seventies, with a basis in the old rural traditions, only rarely used lyrics by established poets. Some lyrics are traditional or based on traditional folk-poetry, but most of the best-known songs of these composers use lyrics by Nikos Gatsos (whom we have already encountered as a Surrealist poet in the 1940s and as a successful songwriter in the 1960s), and the new poets Manos Eleftheriou and K. Ch. Myris (pseudonym of the critic and essayist G. Yeorgousopoulos). The lyrics of such 'classic' recordings of the early 1970s as *Chroniko* (Markopoulos/Myris, 1972), *Thiteia* (Markopoulos/Eleftheriou, 1973), *Syllogi* (Xarhakos/Gatsos, 1973), *I Megali Agrypnia* (Karaindrou/Myris, 1974), and *Drosoulites* (Halaris/Gatsos, 1976), draw allusively on the style, language, and well-known stories of the folk tradition, but bring to them an epigrammatic incisiveness and a compelling 'logic' of the absurd. In this way the 'marriage' of Surrealism with the folk tradition, that we noted in the poetry of the 1940s, attains the self-confidence and wins the authority to reach out to a mass audience.

At the same time, and in a distinctly more idiosyncratic way, the composer and songwriter Dionysis Savvopoulos rose to the status of a cult figure through his own unique blend of an imported American idiom and traditional Greek music. Savvopoulos stands in a similar relation to Bob Dylan as Poulios does to Allen Ginsberg.

Savvopoulos could scarcely have created words, music, and public image together as he did without the example of Dylan before him, but he is no more an uncritical imitator than is Poulios—and it is worth noting that Savvopoulos' influence and standing continued unabated throughout the later 1970s and the 1980s. In a justly famous song issued on record at the end of the dictatorship, Savvopoulos compares himself to the comic hero of the traditional shadow-puppet theatre, Karagiozis:

> κείνο που με τρώει κείνο που με σώζει
> είναι που ονειρεύομαι σαν τον Καραγκιόζη
> φίλους και εχτρούς στις φρικτές μου πλάτες
> όμορφα να σήκωνα σαν να 'ταν επιβάτες[25]
>
> what torments me and what saves me
> is that I can dream like Karagiozis
> friend and foe I'd carry beautifully
> on my ugly rump like passengers.

The anarchic and irrepressible Karagiozis, as his name implies, is a cultural hybrid, adapted by Greek players and audiences from the Turkish shadow-puppet character Karagöz (Black-Eyes), and made peculiarly their own. Savvopoulos here presents himself and his songs as hybrid in the same way, and so as empowered, like Karagiozis, to dream his way out of an impasse where 'love is flawed and can't protect us', and death, in traditional anthropomorphic guise as the cruel but slightly comical Charos, lies in wait 'with slavering jaws'.[26]

The potential afforded by song did not escape the two veteran poets of the 1930s who were still active at this period: Yannis Ritsos and Odysseas Elytis. The early years of the dictatorship, in particular, were immensely productive for both poets, and as we saw, Ritsos produced some of his best poetry in the period up to 1970. In the later years of the dictatorship Ritsos wrote several song cycles, of which the best known, with music by Mikis Theodorakis, is the *Eighteen Short Songs of the Bitter Fatherland*, recorded and ready for issue during the brief 'thaw' in 1973, and finally released on record within days of the Colonels' fall from power in July 1974.[27] Elytis,

---

[25] Savvopoulos 1983: 80.
[26] See in particular the lines: τρύπια η αγάπη μας και δεν μας προστατεύει, and μας κοιτάει ο χάρος και του τρέχουνε τα σάλια...
[27] Δεκαοχτώ λιανοτράγουδα της πικρής πατρίδας (Ritsos 1989-90: x. 153-60).

who in the 1960s had written songs specially for musical settings, returned to the form in the early 1970s with the briefly lyrical and highly condensed sequences *The Sun the Very Sun* (1971) and *The Rs of Love* (1972), although neither seems to have been seriously intended for music. These 'songs', however, represent only a small part of Elytis' remarkable output during these years. To the same period belong some of his most admired and lyrically condensed pieces, collected in the volumes *The Light Tree* (1971), *The Monogram* (1971), and *The Half-Siblings* (1974),[28] and also (although they were published only much later and in reverse order) his two large-scale compositions which continue and develop the exterior, public voice of *The Axion Esti*. These are *The Little Sailor* (written 1970–4 and published in 1985) and *Maria Nefeli* (written between 1968 and shortly after 1974, published in 1978).

Both of these later long poems follow the precedent of *The Axion Esti* in their complex organization into constituent parts which contrast formally and thematically. In both, the affirmation of the earlier poem is repeated and tempered, but with a new didactic element added which, although its epigrammatic expression recalls the newer poetry of the time, suggests a fundamental difference from it.[29] *Maria Nefeli*, however, does open up a new international dimension in Elytis' poetry, which has closer links with the strategies of Poulios, Steriadis, and some of the younger poets. The young girl who is one of the principal speakers in the poem, and who gives it its title, is supposed to reflect the revolutionary climate of her generation that found expression in the turbulent *événements* of Paris in the spring of 1968, and for the first time in Elytis' poetry the principles of collage and violent juxtaposition are extended to include phrases and quotations from other languages, to such an extent as to give the poem a literally polyglot character.

Between them the young Maria Nefeli and her interlocutor (the poet?) simultaneously deplore and celebrate a new world in which the 'time to be born, and a time to die' of Ecclesiastes have been

---

[28] *Το φωτόδεντρο. Το μονόγραμμα. Το ετεροθαλή.*

[29] See e.g. the aphorisms which conclude each of the main sections of *Maria Nefeli*, and (among many others) the memorable statement near the end of *The Little Sailor*: 'Learn to pronounce reality correctly' (Μάθε να προφέρεις σωστά την πραγματικότητα, Elytis 1985: 118).

replaced by the easy exchanges of the 'time of spare parts' from which even language is not exempt:

> Μιξοευρωπαϊστί τα πάντα λέγονται
> γίνονται ξεγίνονται
> μ' ευκολίες με δόσεις.
> Καιρός των ανταλλακτικών:
> σπάει λάστιχο—βάζεις λάστιχο
> χάνεις Jimmy—βρίσκεις Bob.
> C'est très pratique που 'λεγε κι η Annette
> η ωραία σερβιτόρισσα του Tahiti.[30]

> Everything can be said in eurospeak
> can be made and unmade
> facilities or instalments are available.
> A time of spare parts:
> bust a tyre—replace a tyre
> lose Jimmy—find Bob.
> C'est très pratique as Annette used to say
> the beautiful waitress in the 'Tahiti'.

In May 1987 the critic D. N. Maronitis hazarded the opinion that the innovations of the new generation that emerged in the early 1970s had been taken over and surpassed by the late poetry of their more experienced elders from the 'generation of the thirties', Elytis and Ritsos—fathers, as he figuratively puts it, who like the mythical Kronos have devoured their children.[31] If this is true of Elytis, the case must rest very largely on the polyglot evocation of contemporary youth culture in *Maria Nefeli*. As far as Ritsos is concerned, it is true that a strongly erotic element which enters his writing during the 1980s, and his shift into prose during the same decade, are evidence of a *rapprochement* with the poetics of the younger generation, but the relative importance of these late developments within Ritsos' work as a whole still seems uncertain. Some of Ritsos' best-known reworkings of ancient myth and history are to be found in the poems written in prison and under house arrest on Aegean islands between May 1967 and June 1969 and published in the three sequences *Stones, Repetitions, Railings* (1972). Ritsos' deft and individual handling of this material, however, does not differ significantly from that of the mostly earlier poems of *Fourth*

---

[30] 'Pax San Tropezana' (Elytis 1978: 54).
[31] Maronitis 1987: 246.

Dimension,[32] and on closer examination seems quite different from what is termed here the 'domestication' or 'demystification' of myth in the poetry of the younger generation. Ritsos, in poems such as 'Penelope's Despair', 'The Real Reason', and most of the others in the three series that comprise *Repetitions*, inverts the myth by bringing out a meaning which is the opposite of the conventional one,[33] while Anghelaki-Rooke, Kondos, Mastoraki, and Galanaki *subvert* the myths they use by bringing them down to earth and so questioning whether they have any intrinsic meaning at all.

There are, then, quite marked contrasts to be observed between the poetry of Elytis or Ritsos during the dictatorship and the poetics of the emerging generation of the time. In contrast to the situation between 1945 and 1967, to which Maronitis' metaphor of the fathers devouring their children might more convincingly be applied, it is by no means certain that the most important of the late work of Elytis and Ritsos has much to do with the innovations of the 'generation of the seventies'. It would still be wisest to treat this suggestion with the caution with which Maronitis himself concludes: 'For the present such a hypothesis remains unproven.'[34]

So far the discussion has dealt almost exclusively with poetry, although we noted that writers of fiction were in the majority among the contributors to the *Eighteen Texts*. The relative absence of new fiction during the years of dictatorship is all the more surprising in that poetry, and more particularly song, played a visible role in resistance to the regime, and it was during this period that the main lines of Greek poetry for the following fifteen years were laid down. By contrast, the lifting of preventive censorship, and of the self-imposed ban on publication by many established writers, at the end of 1969, did not at once pave the way for a new 'generation' or even for new kinds of writing in the field of prose fiction. The later years of the dictatorship saw the delayed appearance of the novel *Plague* by Frangias, which had been completed before 1967, and several collections of short stories by established writers of the previous decade, many of which had been written, and quite a few

---

[32] See Ch. 4.

[33] Η απόγνωση της Πηνελόπης (1968). Η πραγματική αιτία (1969). Originally published in the volume *Stones, Repetitions, Railings*, 1972 (*Πέτρες, Επαναλήψεις, Κιγκλίδωμα*). See, respectively, Ritsos 1989–90: x. 69, 89.

[34] See n. 31 above.

published in periodicals, before 1967. The best-known examples are the collection *Small Change* (1972) by Kostas Tachtsis, and *The Passport* (1973) by Andonis Samarakis, while *Barbed Wire* (1975) by Spyros Plaskovitis collects stories written while the author was imprisoned under the dictatorship.[35]

There is little sign at this time of the new directions and the new self-confidence that would come to dominate Greek fiction, and the novel in particular, in the late 1970s and 1980s. Indeed, the years of dictatorship are particularly notable, in the field of prose fiction, for a series of published discussions among established writers who agree, more or less, on the impasse that their genre had reached in Greece. In 1972 the translator Nick Germanacos convened a tape-recorded discussion with Thanasis Valtinos, Stratis Tsirkas, and Yorgos Ioannou which was published in English in the following year;[36] while in the short-lived but influential periodical *Synecheia*, which took over the mantle of the *Eighteen Texts* and its successors during 1973, another four writers (again including Tsirkas) and the critic Alexandros Argyriou went over much of the same ground in Greek.[37] Four years later, with the dictatorship now over, some of the same group returned to debate a fuller obituary on post-war Greek fiction in the newly established periodical *Diavazo*.[38]

In all three discussions there is broad agreement that the Greek novel lags behind Greek poetry. All the participants are particularly conscious of the limitations of the *urban* novel so far,[39] but there is also a shared sense of frustration that the not inconsiderable achievements of their predecessors in the genre have failed to find an adequate critical response at home or recognition abroad through translation.[40] These failings are attributed, throughout the three discussions, to a number of causes: the limited urbanization of Greek

---

[35] Respectively: Tachtsis 1974*b*; Samarakis 1973; Plaskovitis 1976.

[36] Germanacos 1973.

[37] Argyriou *et al.* 1973.

[38] Argyriou *et al.* 1977.

[39] See in particular Germanacos: 'It seems to me that very few Greek novelists have successfully tackled the current urban realities of Greece. Not the "neighborhood", which, in a sense, is little more than an extension of the rural landscape, but the realities of the megalopolis with all that that entails. No one has yet written the great urban novel set in the Athens of the endless apartment blocks, traffic jams, affluence, sexual emancipation, and all the pressures as well as the liberations of mid-century bourgeois life' (Germanacos 1973: 282–3).

[40] On the first of these points see, in particular, Kouloufakos in Argyriou *et al.* 1973: 178; on the second see Germanacos 1973: 270–2.

society by the early 1970s; the lack of a stable language; the lack of continuity with previous generations; foreign influence; a tendency towards lyricism and autobiography which is difficult to shake off in a culture that had for so long given precedence to poetry over prose. But by far the greatest prominence is given to political causes, which is hardly surprising given the highly politicized nature of the post-war generation in Greece and the conditions under which two of the three discussions took place. As these writers see it, the novelist has a duty and a responsibility faithfully to convey the reality of his time and place, and Greece has been ill served by so many writers of fiction who since the late 1930s have turned away from political realities. As Alexandros Kotzias trenchantly put it, Greek writers themselves cannot grasp these realities clearly or in their entirety.[41]

The remedy that seems to be proposed is one that quite explicitly looks backward to the 'poetics' of most Greek fiction since the Second World War. As the poet and critic A. Ziras sums up the 1977 discussion:

I conclude with the view that the younger writers of fiction no longer have the craft that their elders had, they may no longer give such importance to cultivating their expression, but they compensate for this by their more consistent engagement towards the political significance of their everyday experiences...[42]

In other words the future lies not with the craft of fiction but with political *engagement*. Although a political awareness is far from lacking in the new novels and stories that had already begun to appear by the time that this discussion took place, on the contrary, as we shall see, the future of Greek fiction was in reality to lie in a new sophistication of craftsmanship, and in a new and more self-confident exploitation of the resources offered by tradition, both Greek and foreign.

'THE LITTLE LAMP': POETRY OF THE LATE 1970s AND 1980s

The title of a brief article which appeared at the end of 1988 sums up a development that would have surprised the writers of fiction

---

[41] See Kotzias in Argyriou *et al.* 1973: 173: 'it's true that we don't even know the Greek reality very well ourselves.' Notice also the emphasis given by the writers interviewed by Germanacos to the factual and autobiographical basis of their own work, and their declared reluctance to *invent* anything which would not be true.

[42] Ziras in Argyriou *et al.* 1977: 83.

whose discussions during the previous decade we have just been considering: 'The Hour of Prose Fiction, Or the Exhaustion of Poetry.'[43] In this article Dimitris Tziovas chronicles the shift in emphasis on the part of the leading literary publishing houses away from poetry lists towards new fiction, and suggests that the enormous boom both in the production and in the reading of fiction during that period took place at the expense of the more traditionally established genre of poetry.

Although it would be premature to try to guess how influential this trend will turn out to be in future, some of the developments *within* poetry during this period seem at first sight to point in the same direction. There is little sign since 1974 of younger poets claiming the 'high ground' that still, at the start of the 1990s, appeared as the distinctive prerogative of those veterans of the 1930s generation, Elytis and Ritsos: the latter in his posthumously published swansong, *Late, Very Late at Night*, the former in the *Oxopetra Elegies* (both published in 1991).[44] Instead, the poetics summed up in Steriadis' phrase of 1971, 'the little lamp', with its paradoxically aggressive modesty and its epigrammatic juxtapositions of tradition with modernity, Greek with foreign, can be seen to predominate.

One noticeable change that has followed the return to civilian government in 1974, and the concomitant relaxation of the constraints against which the younger poets of the late 1960s and early 1970s were writing, has been the attenuation and final dissolution of the *collective* enterprise which had been such a feature of poetry under the dictatorship. This is not to say that poets no longer collaborate in joint publications or anthologies,[45] but the poetry of the 1980s has come to be dominated by what one anthologist has termed 'private vision'. The attempt has even been made to define yet another post-war 'generation' of poets, the 'generation of the 1980s', on the basis of this characteristic; but what Ilias Kefalas terms 'over-protection of personal life' can also be observed as a developing feature in much of the more recent poetry of the 'Six Poets' and their contemporaries.[46]

[43] Tziovas 1988.
[44] Respectively Ritsos 1991; Elytis 1991.
[45] Continuing examples of this trend in the 1990s are the slim collaborative volumes: Layios *et al.* 1991; 1993; but the nature of these collaborations is very different from that of the *Six Poets* during the dictatorship, grounded, as it evidently is, in a shared interest in poetic form (on which see below).
[46] ... υπερπροστασία της προσωπικής ζωής (original emphasis) (Kefalas 1989: 20).

The collections *Tales of the Deep* by Jenny Mastoraki (1983) and *Hers* (1985) by Maria Laina, both by this time veterans of the '1970s generation' fairly evidently carve out an inner space or territory: a terrifying subconscious inheritance in the case of Mastoraki, a rigorously Spartan equivalent of Virginia Woolf's 'room of one's own' in the poems of Laina. Although the approach is very different, the territory explored by these collections is not far removed in kind from the inner landscape of an elusive autobiography explored by Dionysis Kapsalis, whose first collection appeared in 1978,[47] or the characteristically epigrammatic (and perhaps also ironic) acceptance by Haris Vlavianos (who first appeared with a collection in 1983) that:

Στην ποίηση τίποτα δεν είναι αληθινό
εκτός από τις υπερβολές του εγώ.[48]

In poetry nothing is true
except the excesses of the self.

As regards the '1970s generation' it may even be symptomatic of this trend that the National Poetry Prize was won in 1993 by Maria Laina and in 1994 by Michalis Ganas, both of whom embarked on their careers during the dictatorship, but whose names were not conspicuous in the collective endeavours of that time. Laina, in her collections up to 1985, has been noted for a sparsity of style and utterance bordering almost on the naive: it is only with the later collection *Rosy Fear*, which takes us beyond the chronological limits of this chapter, that she has allowed a richer, more lyrical element to appear in her work.[49] Ganas, by contrast, is one of the few poets of this generation to have built strongly upon the traditional links between literary poetry in Greece and the traditional or oral folk poetry. In the hands of Ganas the imagery and even some of the formal characteristics of the oral tradition become a vivid resource once again for the poet in the 1980s and 1990s, and by being used in this way take on, in turn, a new lease of life.[50] In a more sombre manner, the resources of traditional oral poetry, and also of late

[47] See Kapsalis 1982; 1986.
[48] Vlavianos 1991: 20, from the poem 'The Triumph of the End' (Ο θρίαμβος του τέλους), part 6.
[49] Laina 1993.
[50] See Ganas 1989 and (although just beyond the time-limit for this chapter) 1993; and on this writer, in English, Ricks 1997.

medieval vernacular narratives in verse, are also revitalized by Jenny Mastoraki in her most recent volume.[51]

But perhaps the most surprising development in Greek poetry since 1980 has to do with poetic form. By 1980, free verse had been the accepted, almost the natural, means of expression for a poet to use, for almost half a century. Deviations from this norm during the post-war period are sufficiently systematic as, in hindsight, to have proved the rule. Forms other than free verse appear only when they are exploited for one of two well-defined purposes: either they are used by poets who normally wrote in free verse but who wished in a particular poem to draw attention to the use of 'traditional' form, often with a satirical aim (this applies to the later rhymed poems of Seferis, for instance); or in lyrics intended to be set to music. Almost all of the poetry of the younger generation throughout the 1970s is in free verse. The other possible recourse for a poet, throughout the half-century of free verse, was to turn to prose, or to mix prose, in some way, with verse. Both of these solutions had been tried extensively by Embirikos during and after the 1940s: respectively in the texts later published in the collections *Writings, or Personal Mythology* and *Oktana*, and in his works of fiction, *Argo* and *The Great Eastern*.[52] In this Embirikos had been followed, as was discovered much later, by Ritsos, the first of whose short novels, published in 1982, had been written forty years earlier, and became, in its definitive edition of 1983, the first of the nine volumes which make up the *Iconostasis of Anonymous Saints*.[53] Almost the only other poet before 1980 to make the leap into prose on a comparable scale was Aris Alexandrou, whose novel *The Box*, to be discussed in the next section, was published in 1974.

The picture since 1980 has been significantly different. The hybrid prose-poem reappeared during that decade, in collections by Rea Galanaki and Jenny Mastoraki.[54] Nasos Vayenas, in a volume teasingly subtitled 'an essay on poetry' also adopted the formal medium of prose for what one might suppose are really poems; Yannis Kondos, in a volume of 1985, adopted a more narrative style of prose; while Kostis Gimosoulis established his versatility

[51]   Mastoraki 1989 (see especially the opening of the poem on p. 60, in traditional fifteen-syllable rhythm, and Savvidis 1989).
[52]   Respectively: Embirikos 1980c; 1980e; 1980d; 1990–2 (on all of which see ch. 4).
[53]   Ritsos 1983; see also Guide to Translations.
[54]   Galanaki 1980; Mastoraki 1983.

during the 1980s with several volumes of both verse and prose fiction.[55] Others have, if not abandoned verse for prose media, chosen to establish parallel careers in prose. This has been the case with Rea Galanaki, whom we shall meet again as a novelist in the next section; with Maria Laina who has written successfully for the stage;[56] and more recently by Yorgos Kakoulidis.[57]

At first sight this phenomenon might seem to confirm the trend noted by Tziovas in the article with which this section began: a movement, on the part of poets themselves, away from verse towards prose. Though there were undoubtedly social and publishing pressures at work during this period to reinforce such a trend, as we shall see in the next section, the evidence suggests that the truth is more complex. The turn by some poets towards prose in the 1980s can better be understood as part of a larger phenomenon: a renewed questioning of received poetic forms.

That such a questioning has taken place is convincingly demonstrated in one of the few essays to appear, so far, which approaches the poetry of the last twenty years with scholarly rigour.[58] With ample illustration from the work of a dozen poets, mostly of the generation that began to publish at the end of the 1970s or during the 1980s, Evripidis Garantoudis reveals the renewed preoccupation with form in the work of writers whose medium remains for the most part free verse, but who increasingly approach or incorporate elements of more formal, traditional metrical patterns. Though Garantoudis does not make this point, the return of form has been no less an element of English-language poetry since the 1970s, and it would not be surprising if, after half a century of almost unchallenged rule, the reign of free verse in Greece, too, were coming to an end.

One of the most controversial aspects of this new poetic quest concerns a minority of poets who have reacted against free verse in a direction exactly the opposite of those who have explored prose as

<hr/>

[55] See, respectively: Vayenas 1982; G. Kontos 1985; Gimosoulis 1983; 1986. On this issue, from the perspective of the time, see also Maronitis 1987: 230–46.

[56] The 'theatrical monologue', *The Clown* (*Ο κλόουν*), was published in 1985. The three-act play, *Reality is Always Here* (*Η πραγματικότητα είναι πάντα εδώ*, 1990) has been performed by the Theatro Technis in Athens.

[57] *Φαλαμπέλα* (1995). Although this work falls outside the chronological scope of this chapter, its appearance nonetheless confirms the more general trend discussed here.

[58] Garantoudis 1993.

an alternative. At least three poets of the younger generation, in the late 1980s, turned their attention to writing in a variety of strict, and mostly traditional, metres with rhyme: Dionysis Kapsalis, Yorgos Koropoulis, and Ilias Layios. Curiously, Garantoudis dismisses this group under the heading, 'The return to traditional form without the experience of free verse'.[59] Factually this is untrue: the formal versatility of these poets includes both free and freed verse, as is evidenced by their collections published before the volume on which Garantoudis is commenting here.[60] But the more substantive issue raised by the extreme position taken by these poets is whether it is possible, at the end of the twentieth century, to achieve more than a pastiche of an earlier era, by reverting to formal patterns that had been decisively rejected fifty years ago.

The significance of *Three-Way Crossroads*, a volume in small format containing three 'traditional' ballads, has probably been exaggerated—not least because its collaborative format, already mentioned, might be taken to imply a 'manifesto'. The serious case for the revival of form has been put by the critic Aris Berlis:

It is impossible for a reader who has an adequate acquaintance with the texts of our poetic tradition to confuse a sonnet by Kapsalis with a sonnet by Mavilis, a stanzaic poem by Koropoulis with an 'equivalent' poem by Tellos Agras. . . . Our contemporary sonneteers do not imitate—they *repeat* . . . or they *parody* . . . forms that have been centuries in the making and which there is no guarantee have been exhausted (author's emphases).[61]

If it were indeed a case of imitation or pastiche, then the phenomenon would be of only passing interest. However, Berlis reminds us, 'repetition' is not identical to imitation, nor 'parody' to pastiche. To write in a forgotten style, as Hans Robert Jauss pointed out long ago, is not an 'automatic return'.[62] To write in the 1990s, actually

---

[59] Η ανάκληση του παραδοσιακού ρυθμού δίχως την εμπειρία του ελεύθερου στίχου (Garantoudis 1993: 135–7).

[60] Layios *et al.* 1991.

[61] Είναι αδύνατον αναγνώστης που δεν έχει ελλιπή σχέση με τα κείμενα της ποιητικής μας παράδοσης να μπερδέψει ένα σονέτο του Καψάλη με ένα σονέτο του Μαβίλη, ένα στροφικό ποίημα του Κοροπούλη με ένα "αντίστοιχο" ποίημα του Τέλλου Άγρα... Οι σύγχρονοι σονετογράφοι μας δεν μιμούνται— επαναλαμβάνουν...ή παρωδούν ... φόρμες που έθρεψαν πολλούς αιώνες και τίποτα δεν μας εγγυάται πως εξαντλήθηκαν (Berlis 1992).

[62] 'One can line up the examples of how a new literary form can reopen access to forgotten literature. These include the so-called "renaissances"—so-called, because the word's meaning gives rise to the appearance of an automatic return, and often prevents one from recognizing that literary tradition can not transmit itself alone.

ignorant of the free-verse tradition in Greek, or without some experience of writing it, would be as unpromising a start as for a poet in the 1930s to have begun writing free verse without ever having read a sonnet or attempted to write in traditional metres. As we saw in Chapter 3, the poets who were the first in the 1930s to establish the reign of free verse had in most cases already published verse in more-or-less traditional forms. The challenge to which 'traditional' poetry in the 1990s must respond is to offer or imply an answer to the question: what is the *significance* of writing and publishing a sonnet at the end of the twentieth century? Garantoudis argues that the radical shift in worldview, which brought about the rejection of old poetic forms and the introduction of free verse in Europe in the 1920s and in Greece in the 1930s, has surely not been reversed.[63] But it may be a mistake to insist too readily on literary forms as simple reflectors of *Zeitgeist* or worldview. The rise of free verse in the 1930s can be seen in terms of dissatisfaction with then-established forms of *expression*; not necessarily of a more fundamental concept of a 'lost centre'.[64] It is perfectly possible, in the same way, to see a contemporary dissatisfaction with a mode of expression which has become firmly established—and indeed Garantoudis' own analysis, already mentioned, valuably serves to confirm this.

A rather different—and disturbing—perspective on the way literary modes of expression may take part in the wider historical process is suggested by the fact that once again, in the era of the new Balkan Wars, poets pit their skills against the traditional and formal demands of the sonnet, at a time when the issues of national identity and territory have come to be restated, throughout much of the region, in terms so reminiscent of 1912, when the master of the

That is, a literary past can return only when a new reception draws it back into the present, whether an altered aesthetic wilfully reaches back to reappropriate the past, or an unexpected light falls back on forgotten literature from the new moment of literary evolution, allowing something to be found that one previously could not have sought in it' (Jauss 1982: 35; first published in German 1970). This principle is well illustrated in practice by Vayenas' volume of 'odes' (1992), whose title and publication in the year of the 200th anniversary of the birth of Andreas Kalvos clearly establish a relation between these poems of the 1990s, in which a rough-hewn freed verse is implicitly contrasted with the formalism of Kalvos in the 1820s, and in which strict rhymes appear in the prologue and epilogue.

[63] Garantoudis 1992.

[64] Garantoudis uses this term in the passage referred to in the previous note. It derives from the celebrated essay of that title by Zisimos Lorentzatos (1961). On the rise of free verse in Greek, and its relation to traditional forms in the first half of the twentieth century, see the essays collected in Vayenas 1996.

Greek sonnet, Lorentzos Mavilis, lost his life fighting as a volunteer in Epiros.

Such thoughts can only be speculative. But if it is true that the dominant development in Greek poetry in the latter part of the period covered by this chapter was a renewed anxiety about form, underlying all the various departures discussed here, and not simply the 'exhaustion' of poetry before the onslaught of prose fiction, then it can at least be concluded that in Greece poetry, whose very existence has always been inseparable from the formal properties of language, is neither dead nor moribund, but very much alive.

Other indications might be adduced towards the same conclusion. The late poems of Elytis and Ritsos have already been mentioned; and in both cases were publishing 'events' of the early 1990s, powerful proof of the continued interest, on the part of readers, in the work of these established masters. The 1980s also saw the publication of new collections, and often also of collected volumes, by several poets whose reputations had been established during the 1940s and 1950s, most of whom continued, in the period after the dictatorship, to plough their own distinctive furrow.[65] At the younger end of the spectrum, encouraging signs must surely be the large number of slim poetry volumes published since the late 1980s in a uniform series under the imprint of the Kastaniotis publishing house, and the appearance in 1993 of the substantial journal *Piisi* (*Poetry*) which by 1998 had published eleven issues of approximately 150 pages each, bringing together new poetry, translations, and essays on poetics.

THE 'EXPLOSION' OF FICTION

While a largely new group of poets emerged to be hurriedly baptised as the 'generation of the seventies' under the conditions of military rule, there was, as we have seen, no comparable development at the time in prose fiction.[66] What emerged only slowly during the latter

[65] See respectively: Dallas 1990; Dimoula 1990*a*; 1990*b*; 1990*c*; Dimoulas 1986; Kaknavatos 1990; Karouzos 1994; Livaditis 1978; 1987; 1988; Patrikios 1990; Sachtouris 1980; 1986; 1990; Sinopoulos 1980; Steryopoulos 1988; 1992; Vakalo 1995.

[66] The anthology of this generation by G. Panayotou (1979) bravely includes a second volume devoted to prose fiction, but the nature of the material has largely vitiated the anthologist's task. Several writers included had already begun publishing during the 1960s (e.g. Katerina Plassara), while others such as Yatromanolakis and Drakondaidis had not yet produced the work for which they are now best known.

half of the seventies was not so much a new generation of writers—
perhaps a majority of the innovators were already established—but
an undoubtedly new style of writing. Recent political history, and in
particular the violent events of the Athens Polytechnic that heralded
the downfall of the dictatorship in the following year, evidently
provide a jumping-off point for this new fiction. *The Box* (1974) by
Aris Alexandrou is an allegorical tale of the civil war, while no fewer
than three innovative novels published between 1976 and 1979
dramatize the events of the Polytechnic: *The Rite* (1976) by Margarita Lymberaki, *Usurped Authority* (1979) by Alexandros Kotzias
(1926–92), and *Fool's Gold* (1979) by Maro Douka (b. 1947),
while the first novel by Lymberaki's daughter Margarita Karapanou
(b. 1946), *Cassandra and the Wolf* (1977), also owes much to the
recent experience of censorship and the 'usurped authority' of the
Colonels. The same events are revisited, from a later perspective, by
Nikos Kasdaglis in *The Bowstring* (1985).

Alexandrou we have already met as a poet of the post-war generation; Lymberaki and Kotzias had first appeared as novelists
during the same period; only Douka and Karapanou belong to the
younger generation. Although at some level most of these novels
fulfil the now well-established demand (repeated in the debates of
the early 1970s) that Greek fiction should bear witness to recent
events, they all conspicuously shun the goal of objective authenticity
that was such a hallmark of the fictional 'testimonies' of the Asia
Minor disaster in the 1920s and of the Second World War in the
1940s and 1950s. These novels are not just, or even not primarily,
about events: they are about the way in which particular individuals
see these events *and then narrate them.* The narrative which makes up
The Box is supposedly written down on sheets of paper supplied to
the narrator in prison, on which he confesses everything he knows
about a bizarre secret mission of which he is the sole survivor,
frequently contradicting himself and, in his excruciating search for
literal exactitude, progressively revealing how the austere demands
of service to a cause have emptied language of any reliable meaning,
just as the box that he and his comrades have been conveying at such
sacrifice turns out at the end of the story to be empty. *The Rite*, which
draws heavily on Lymberaki's background, since 1950, as a play-

More significant still are the omissions: Alexandrou, although older, is a significant
newcomer to *prose* in the 1970s; and Karapanou is also left out, presumably because
recognition of her work was limited until the publication of her second novel in 1985.

wright, horribly distorts the events of the Athens Polytechnic, as experienced by various participants, so as to present them as the enactment of a primitive blood-rite.

Kotzias' practice of presenting events through the eyes of a particularly unsavoury character (which goes back to his first novel of 1953)[67] reaches a new sophistication in *Usurped Authority*. In this novel the events are seen through the prism of an informer called Katsandonis, who happens once in his life to have chanced upon the classic nineteenth-century novel that dramatizes the life of the revolutionary hero of the same name. There is a constant ironic interplay in the novel between the heroic style and antiquated language of the hero's literary *alter ego*, and the squalid personality and language of the character himself.

Kasdaglis, like Kotzias, had begun his career in the aftermath of the occupation and civil war, and his novels and short stories published since 1952 cover a markedly wide range of subject matter, from the 'folkloric realism' of his first short stories, to the very different kinds of horror encountered in *Tonsured* (1959), about the life of contemporary conscripts in the Greek army, and *Maria Visits the Metropolis of the Waters* (1982) which is Kasdaglis' homage to Hiroshima.[68] All of this writing remains true to the broadly 'neorealist' perspective that was dominant in the immediate post-war era. Kasdaglis has little interest in the technical pyrotechnics that characterize Kotzias' later fiction. The focus in *The Bowstring* is not on the events of the Polytechnic, with which it begins, but on the relentless inner destruction of its main characters' lives, which follows many years afterwards. More shocking than the events played out on the public stage, in this novel's portrayal, is the death of an infant from meningitis while the doctor's telephone has been taken over by his wife, gossiping with her friends. *The Bowstring* is a novel impatient of the history which fuelled its predecessors. Not the least of its achievements is the grim, but always humane humour with which it confronts its often tragic subject-matter.

In *Fool's Gold*, by Maro Douka, the same events are seen through the very different perspective of a girl student who begins university in the wake of the coup of 1967, but the girl's perceptions of these events and the interlocking stories of her family and friends are skilfully filtered through the highly subjective frame of her later

---

[67] *Siege* (Πλιορκία)
[68] Κεκαρμένοι. Η Μαρία περιηγείται τη Μητρόπολη των Νερών.

reminiscences. Towards the end of the novel Myrsini, the narrator, admits that her recollections may not always be accurate, and contrasts the elaborate tissue of the whole novel with the factual but finally empty answers demanded by a questionnaire on her life-history with which the novel both begins and ends. In a less realistic mode, Cassandra in Karapanou's first-person novel, is again a girl growing up, but this girl, somewhat like her mythical counterpart, operates a terrifying and self-centred logic of her own which almost literally makes a nonsense of the world around her. A similar strategy is also followed by another novelist, Nikos Houliaras (b. 1940), in his first novel, *Lousias* (1979), a tale, like Faulkner's *The Sound and The Fury*, 'told by an idiot', whose own simple logic reveals an underside of absurdity to the familiar world of provincial post-war Greece.[69]

The exploration of different points of view and the limits of subjectivity are not of course new in Greek fiction, and it is interesting to note a renewed interest at this time in two earlier pioneers in this area who had previously been relatively ignored. The short stories of G. M. Vizyinos from the 1880s were reprinted in two modern editions; and the complete works of Melpo Axioti, who died in 1973, have been collected in a uniform edition, significantly under the co-editorship of Maro Douka. We have also noted already the increased interest in Lymberaki's novel of 1946, *Straw Hats*, which had anticipated some of these developments, and the exploration of partial points of view, in novels of the 1960s, by Stratis Tsirkas and Tatiana Gritsi-Milliex.

But these are only some of the ingredients that go to make up the heady mixture that is Greek fiction in the 1980s. Not only have more novels, many by young or previously little-known writers, met with critical acclaim than perhaps ever before, but the readership for novels, and particularly for new novels, has increased spectacularly. A further innovation, compared to any period before 1974, is that more than half the novels produced in Greece during this period have been the work of women writers, a trend continued in one of the most successful novels to have been published just after the chronological limit of this chapter, *And with the Wolf Light they Return* by Zyranna Zatelli (1993; with translations into French, Dutch, and German).

[69] Houliaras 1979.

It is difficult to tell to what extent these developments have been 'market-led'; but certainly since the late 1970s or early 1980s there has been a visible demand for 'quality fiction' in Greece, and, almost for the first time in Greek publishing history, the financial rewards for novelists have been substantial. These facts in themselves deserve some comment.

In the final decades of the nineteenth century, as we saw, a 'market' existed for fiction in magazines and newspapers, but it is significant that the first Greek writer ever to subsist on the earnings from his work, Alexandros Papadiamandis, never published a *book* in his lifetime. Later, significant book sales (as evidenced by reprintings) seem to have been restricted to novels dealing closely with recent history, of which the most successful of all has probably been Myrivilis' *Life in the Tomb*.[70] Among other novelists of the 1930s, only Karagatsis seems to have enjoyed a relatively wide readership. The state of the fiction market in 1972 was aptly summarized by Stratis Tsirkas: 'Once [a novel] was regarded as a best-seller if it sold three thousand copies. Today, a book that sells a thousand copies covers its costs and leaves a pittance to the publisher and author.'[71] By contrast, *Achilles' Fiancée* (1987) by Alki Zei (b. 1923), the first novel for adults by a writer who had already achieved an international reputation for children's fiction, sold over 100,000 copies in the first three years.

None the less, it remains true that the highest sales today are usually the prerogative of novels whose subject-matter is recent Greek history. The success of *Achilles' Fiancée*, which chronicles the experience of the defeated Left from the end of the war to the dictatorship of the Colonels, and includes a vivid and rare account of the Greek communist exiles in Tashkent in the 1950s, has been spectacular even by the standards of the decade; and the unadorned testimony to the traumas of the 1940s reached an unprecedented readership in the international success of the novel *Eleni* by Nicholas Gage (Gatzoyannis), first published in English and translated into Greek by Alexandros Kotzias (1983), and within Greece of the oral-style testimonies, from the side of the Left, of Chronis Missios.[72]

---

[70] The 26th printing, in 1989, brought the total copies since 1930 to 118,000 (publisher's note). Now in its 30th printing (1995).

[71] Germanacos 1973: 270–1.

[72] See Missios 1985.

Among the many novels of the 1980s which have met with critical acclaim and, in varying degrees, popular success, are *History* (1982) by Yoryis Yatromanolakis (b. 1940), *The Seventh Garment* (1983) by Evyenia Fakinou (b. 1945), and *The Life of Ismail Ferik Pasha* (1989) by Rea Galanaki. These three novels share with others of the decade a technical competence and assurance which builds on but surpasses the new departures of the 1960s. They have been singled out here because they each, in their different ways, confront questions which run right through Greek literature in modern times: namely, the relation of the Greek present to the historical past, of modern writing to the Greek tradition, and of both to a dominant foreign culture or cultures.

All three deal with the Greek past: *History* covers local events in a Cretan village at the end of the 1920s; *The Seventh Garment* concerns the experience of three generations whose memories manage to cover all the major historical events from 1824 to the dictatorship of the Colonels; while *Ferik Pasha* is a fictional biography set in Crete and Egypt and ending with the failed Cretan insurrection of 1866. All three approach their subject-matter through the prism of earlier Greek literature: *History* has an epigraph from Herodotos, the first historian, and melds the credulous narration of wonders in the fifth century BC with the folkloric attention to detail of the fictional chroniclers of local rural life in Greece at the end of the nineteenth century. *The Seventh Garment* juxtaposes a traditional oral style of narrative with the brash speech of contemporary Athens, and follows the poets Sikelianos, Seferis, and Sinopoulos in elaborating a fictional ritual for communication with the dead. *Ferik Pasha* also concludes with a ritual act of communication with the dead, and in so doing comments directly on poems by Seferis and, more distantly, on Sikelianos[73] and on Homer.

The confrontation between the Greek experience and tradition on the one hand and a dominant foreign culture on the other is, as we shall see, one of the principal themes of *Ferik Pasha*. In *The Seventh Garment* this theme is evident in the language and mentality of the youngest of the book's three narrators, Roula, who works as a typist in an Athens office, while *History* throughout the entire novel juxtaposes the associative, homoeopathic 'logic' of its principal characters with the corrupt rationality of the law enforcers and

[73] See the allusion to the 'Easter of the Hellenes' (Galanaki 1989: 146).

more distantly of government, so as to present the rationality of an educated reader of the 1980s as an alien way of thinking.

In all three novels (as in many others of the decade) there are also signs of a new relationship to contemporary foreign writing. These writers seem finally to have exorcized the inferiority complex, or the anxious looking over the shoulder at European achievements in the novel, that had characterized Greek fiction ever since the time of Theotokas' manifesto *Free Spirit* in 1929. The new Greek novel of the 1980s is grounded in the fictional techniques of allusion, parody, the *rapprochement* between realism and the fantastic, and between realistic story-telling and Modernist experiments—techniques which by the end of the 1980s had established a world-wide, but not especially western-European currency, in the work of such writers as Thomas Pynchon, Milan Kundera, Salman Rushdie, and the South American successors to Jorge Luis Borges.[74] It may be that in the late 1970s and the 1980s Greek fiction again reached the productive equilibrium between inward-looking and outward-looking that we identified in the somewhat comparable 'explosion of fiction' exactly a century before.

History (published in English with the title *History of a Vendetta*) by Yoryis Yatromanolakis is the story of a vengeance killing which supposedly took place in a Cretan village in 1928. The murderer has the family name Dikaios (Just), while his victim's family, who will exact vengeance in their turn after the end of the main story, bears the name Zervos (Left, with some of the connotations of 'sinister'). The story is told in the third person, in an abstemiously factual way, although the facts that we are given are, like many of Herodotos' tall stories, scarcely compatible with the commonsense, logical manner of their narration. Already on the first page, which describes the murder, we learn that:

Ο νόμος της βαρύτητας που, *καθώς λένε*, κρατεί στη θέση τους τα πράγματα, τα ζώα και τους ανθρώπους, καταλύθηκε, έτσι ώστε δημιουργήθηκε ανάμεσα στο χώμα και στα γόνατα του πυροβοληµένου ένα κενό που ίσως έφτανε τα δύο μέτρα, ίσως όμως και περισσότερα. [my emphasis][75]

---

[74] Many Greek novels of the 1980s, including the three discussed here, practise what is often rather vaguely known as 'magic realism', while these three in particular exemplify the category of postmodern fiction that Linda Hutcheon has termed 'historiographic metafiction' (1988: 87–123; cf. G. Thalassis 1992) and the essays collected in *Moderno-Metamoderno* 1988.

[75] Yatromanolakis 1982: 9.

The law of gravity which, *so they say*, keeps things in their place, animals and people, was set at nought, so that there was formed between the ground and the knees of the victim a gap of perhaps as much as two metres, perhaps even more. [my emphasis]

The murderer, in order to escape justice, must go through a kind of ritual initiation in which, in hiding in the wild, he must imitate in turn each of a series of animals for a prescribed number of days. But despite these and a series of other bizarre precautions he is caught and dies in prison, leaving his son as the next victim in the inexorably cyclical pattern of this *History*.[76]

In contrast to the firmly dispassionate narrative voice which dominates *History*, *The Seventh Garment* is presented as a series of monologues by three women: an elderly mother, her spinster daughter who lives with her, and her granddaughter Roula. The mother is a survivor of the Asia Minor disaster whose wanderings in search of her first, lost, daughter repeat the myth of Demeter and Persephone. In her youth, while passing near a remote village in Thessaly called Rizes (Roots), she had had a vision of her dead husband, and so remained in the village, where she went on to learn the secrets of the oldest inhabitant, a woman known simply as Vavo (Granny), who had suffered a very similar fate during the Greek war of independence, almost exactly a century before. (In the myth, Demeter had been consoled in her search for Persephone by an old woman with the ancient form of this name, Baubo.) Through the families of these two women and their later fortunes all the major traumas of post-independence Greece are brought into the compass of this short novel, but the principal action concerns the ambiguous initiation of the brashly urban Roula into the fraying mythical world of the older women which draws its life from the past. As in the poetry of Seferis, the service of the past, and the enactment of rituals which enable the past to fructify the present, demand a sacrifice of living blood. But the novel ends with a neat balance between the centrifugal Roula heading for the bus back to civilization and declaring 'I'm not spending another night here ... and going raving bonkers',[77] and the centripetal guardianship of the past by the older

---

[76] For sophisticated readings of this novel, from somewhat differing perspectives, see Maronitis 1986; 261–82; G. Thalassis 1992: 61–94.

[77] 'Άλλη νύχτα εδώ δεν κάθομαι ... 'Οχι και να τρελαθούμε κιόλας (Fakinou 1983: 128).

women. The confrontation between tradition and modernity is left
unresolved.

We have already encountered Rea Galanaki, author of *The Life of
Ismail Ferik Pasha*, as a poet who began writing during the dictatorship, before turning increasingly to prose.[78] The novel is based on
the life of a real historical person: the commander of the Egyptian
army which was sent in 1866 to quell the Cretan revolt of that year
against Ottoman rule. The novel is woven around two further
historical facts: that Ferik had himself been born a Cretan
Christian, and sold as a slave in Egypt after an Ottoman reprisal
raid on his village; and that Ferik had a brother, Andonis, who in
1866 was active in organizing and supporting the Cretan revolt from
Greece.

The early life of the hero is relatively briefly told in the third
person in the first half of the book, from his hiding in a cave on the
Lasithi plain (there are indications that this is the same as the cave in
which mythology places the birth of Zeus), his captivity and his
upbringing in Egypt, to his achievement of wealth and rank and
his formative friendship with Ibrahim, who becomes Regent of
Egypt. The second part shifts into the first person, in order to
chronicle the nine months of Ferik's stay in Crete in 1866–7, leading
up to his death on the Lasithi plain where he had been born. With a
remarkable blend of austerely factual narrative and lyricism, this
novel elaborates in a way unprecedented in Greek literature upon
Borges' 'Theme of the Traitor and the Hero'.[79] These two characteristics of the style, as well as this theme, are signalled at the close
of the first chapter, where Ferik as a child watches the destruction of
his village by the victorious Ottomans:

Τράβηξε το βλέμμα του από τις φλόγες και κοίταξε τη γη μπροστά στα
πόδια του. Βράχια και λίγο ξερό χώμα. Ο Χασάν πασάς, κατακτητής του
ορπέδιου και γαμπρός του αντιβασιλέα της Αιγύπτου Μωχάμετ 'Αλη,
διέσχιζε το ξερό χώμα επιστρέφοντας στον Χάνδακα νικητής. Το
μέγεθος αλόγου και αναβάτη δεν ξεπερνούσε το περίγραμμα της
πεταλούδας που πετά. Είδε το άλογο ν' αφηνιάζει και να ρίχνει καταγής
τον ιππέα. Το αγόρι σήκωσε τον σκοτωμένο ιππέα πιάνοντάς τον

[78] Following her last volume of poetry to date (1980), which is in the medium of
prose, Galanaki had published two volumes of shorter fiction before this novel, in
1982 and 1986.
[79] See J. L. Borges, *Labyrinths* (Harmondsworth: Penguin Books, 1979), 102–5;
see also Maronitis 1992: 225–36; Yannakaki 1994; Calotychos 1997.

προσεκτικά από τα φτερά των κόκκινων ρούχων, κι αμέσως τον πέταξε πέρα φοβισμένο· το πρόσωπο του κατακτητή έμοιαζε στο δικό του.[80]

He withdrew his gaze from the flames and looked at the ground in front of his feet. Rocks and a little dry earth. Hasan Pasha, conqueror of the plateau and son-in-law of the Regent of Egypt, Mohamet Ali, was making his victorious way across the dry earth, returning to Handakas. The size of the horse and rider was not greater than the outline of a butterfly in flight. He saw the horse stumble and throw the horseman to the ground. The boy picked up the dead horseman, holding him carefully by the wings of his red robes, and at once threw him away in fear; the face of the conqueror resembled his own.

Ferik grows up with two identities, two pasts, two religions, even perhaps two genders, as the military man chronicles his nine months' agony, in Crete, to give birth to his true self. At the end of the story, after he has returned to the wreck of his childhood home and raised the ghosts of his family, the novel reveals that these identities are irreconcilable: there is no single, true self for him to recover, just as he realizes, in allusion to the world-wide literature of exile from Homer and Dante to T. S. Eliot and Seferis:

Το μυαλό του έλαμψε ξαφνικά και κατανόησε ότι δεν υπάρχει, ούτε και υπήρξε, κάτι τόσο αθώο ώστε να χαθεί. Άρα, πως δεν υπάρχει, ούτε και ποτέ υπήρξε, επιστροφή.[81]

His mind was lit up by a flash and he understood that there is not, and never has been, anything so innocent as to be lost. Therefore, that there is not, and never has been, such a thing as return.

This novel's rejection of the very idea of identity as single and undivided grows, in part, out of the exploration of subjectivity in earlier Greek novels, particularly in the 1970s and 1980s. But for the first time it applies these insights to the Greek historical past. It is not only Ferik whose identity is simultaneously that of conqueror and conquered, who is at once as indigenously Greek as Zeus born in the cave above Lasithi or Sikelianos' *Easter of the Hellenes*, and at the same time the product of an *Ottoman* past, which the claims of national identity reject with the scorn and shame heaped upon

---

[80] Galanaki 1989: 18–19.

[81] Galanaki 1989: 197 (from the Epilogue which reverts to the third-person narrative of the first part of the novel). There is probably an allusion in the first sentence quoted to the end of Solomos' poem 'The Shark' (see Ch. 1): 'In a flash of light the young man knew himself' ('Αστραψε φως και εγνώρισεν ο νιος τον εαυτό του), in the moment before death.

Ferik by the ghosts of his family. At this level, *Ferik Pasha* can be read as a parable of Greek identity as it has been forged over the past two hundred years: of the impossibility of return to a glorious past, and almost the first acceptance, in literature, that the heritage of Greece today includes its history as a province of the Ottoman empire.[82]

The novel ends with three incompatible versions of the death of the hero. Either he was poisoned by the Turks who suspected him of treason, or he was shot down by the Greeks. Either way, one half of his double self kills the other. The third version, which is presented more as a meditation on Ferik's fate than as narrative fact, has him rejecting both his pasts and killing himself with the bronze knife that has accompanied him as a kind of talisman throughout his life, and which he had found as a child in the depths of the Lasithi cave—that is, with the archaeological link back to his most distant possible ancestors.[83]

Writing in the same article on the rise of prose fiction at the expense of poetry as was quoted earlier, Dimitris Tziovas notes the new demand for 'easy reading', and observes that the recipe for success demands a length of 170–200 pages.[84] All three of the novels just discussed fulfil this requirement. None could be described as 'easy reading', but all show a respect (whether or not tinged with parody)

---

[82] The exploration of the divided or double self which defies the imposed categories of religion, nationality, and gender is taken up by Galanaki, after just over a century, from the short stories of Vizyinos discussed in Ch. 2. It is conspicuous that two of these stories, in particular, present a central Turkish character not only in a sympathetic light, but as in some way the counterpart or *alter ego* of a Christian one: Kiamil in 'Who was my Brother's Killer?' and Selim the Muscovite, in the story of that name. Although there had been increasing signs of a belated interest in Greece's Ottoman past, particularly among young people during the late 1970s and 1980s, this had largely been confined to music, the Karagiozis shadow-puppet theatre, and antiques. The complex, and new, *rapprochement* with that past which is worked out by Galanaki is not followed by other contemporary writers who draw their subject-matter from the centuries of Ottoman rule, as can be seen for example in the conventional nationalism which informs the sensitively written historical novel by another poet, *Of Epirotes and Turks*, 1990 (Ἀπειρωτάν καὶ Τούρκων) by Ismini Kapandai. Cf. the regressively nationalistic *Castle of Memory*, 1993 (Τὸ κάστρο τῆς μνήμης) by Aris Fakinos, whose novels, also written in French, have been well received in France.

[83] For an extended discussion of this novel see Sourbati 1992; cf. Calotychos 1997.

[84] Some of the same points are made in a round-table discussion which took place the previous year, and which marks a striking contrast with the gloomier discussions of the previous decade (Yatromanolakis *et al.* 1987).

for the tastes and expectations of readers of *stories*, which is in marked contrast to their Modernist predecessors such as Axioti and Pentzikis. Perhaps more directly indicative of these tastes and expectations as they were being formed during the 1980s are the slighter novels of Petros Tatsopoulos and Yannis Xanthoulis with their contemporary urban settings and colloquial language, and spiced with a new sexual frankness.[85] Since there has never been a well-established tradition of popular or 'middle-brow' fiction in Greece,[86] it is difficult to tell whether some of these novels modestly aim to fill this gap, or (perhaps at the same time) set out to parody the conventions of foreign mass-market fiction. A case in point is Tatsopoulos' exuberant tale of petty drug abuse and bungled crime in modern Athens, *The Heart of the Beast* (1988). There are many allusions in this book to English and American crime fiction, but what is one to make of a scene in which one character pours a can of petrol over another and slowly smokes a cigarette in an enclosed space, threatening to set his victim alight unless he reveals all?[87] Has the author failed to take into account the inflammable properties of petrol vapour? Or is the sophisticated reader meant to smile and recognize that this kind of popular realism is all a game? Finally, although the short novel certainly became an established and commercially successful form during the 1980s, the turn of the decade saw a surge in the publication of significantly longer novels.[88]

Whatever the future of Greek poetry, Greek fiction by the early 1990s has transformed itself from the doldrums revealed in the public discussions of the 1970s, and in ways that were almost

[85] See e.g. Yannis Xanthoulis, *The Dead Liqueur*, 1987 (*Το πεθαμένο λικέρ*), and Tatsopoulos 1988.

[86] Not to be confused of course with the popular (λαϊκό) novel, on which see Kassis 1983.

[87] Tatsopoulos 1988: 226–32.

[88] Among these must be numbered: *Achilles' Fiancée*, 1987 (*Η αρραβωνιαστικιά του Αχιλλέα*), which has already been mentioned; *From the Other Side of Time*, 1988 (*Από την άλλη όχθη του Χρόνου*) by Tatiana Gritsi-Milliex; *The Great Square*, 1987 (*Η μεγάλη πλατεία*) by Nikos Bakolas; *Dyed Red Hair*, 1989 (*Βαμμένα κόκκινα μαλλιά*) a first novel by the successful playwright Kostas Mourselas, and *Africa*, 1988 (*Αφρική*), the first novel of Evyenios Aranitsis. Interestingly the first four are by older writers who had begun publishing in the 1950s and 1960s, and several have been best-sellers. *Achilles' Fiancée* (350 pp.) has already been discussed. Mourselas' novel (493 pp.) was reprinted seven times and sold 35,000 copies in the first year. Gritsi-Milliex's novel (363 pp.) had gone into a second edition within a year and Bakolas' *The Great Square* (553 pp.) had been reprinted five times by 1990. The trend continues beyond 1992, as can be seen in the (rare) international success of Zatelli 1993 (667 pp.).

entirely unforeseeable then.[89] In addition to reaching out in a confident and unabashed way to contemporary world-wide developments in the novel, Greek writers have rediscovered and drawn creatively on neglected parts of their own narrative tradition: most notably the parody of Roidis and the exploration of subjectivity by Vizyinos more than a century ago.[90] Whatever the verdict of later generations on the remarkable 'explosion of fiction' in the 1980s, the signs are that a more substantial, and seemingly a more sophisticated, reading public for the novel existed in Greece in the early 1990s than ever before.

[89] Two group-interviews with novelists, one representing the generation which began publishing before 1967, the other among writers whose careers began in the late 1970s and early 1980s, converge on the distance that now separates writers from their predecessors of the 1930s (see, respectively, *Dendro* 1992: 9–13; *Dendro* 1991). Indicatively, Tatsopoulos in the latter interview declares, 'What relation could I possibly have to the language of Myrivilis?' (23). Later in the discussion E. Aranitsis says, 'I consider the prose generation of the thirties insignificant.' The only exceptions proposed by his interlocutors are Kosmas Politis, Beratis, and ('perhaps') Karagatsis (41).

[90] There is now a need for a full-scale study of Greek fiction since 1974. For studies based on close readings of particular texts see G. Thalassis 1992; Sourbati 1992, the latter of whom makes a convincing case for the leading role of women writers during the period.

6. *Literature and Language: The 'Language Question'*

LITERATURE is nothing if not language, and in a Greek context language, the raw material of literature, has not been something that writers or readers could take for granted. On the eve of Greek independence, in the second half of the eighteenth century, the need for a written 'standard' (in the sense in which the term is used in modern linguistics) came to be recognized and debated in intellectual circles. This was the beginning of the notorious 'Language Question', which reached a climax in the polarization and even violence of the first years of the twentieth century, and has still not entirely died down despite reforming legislation in the 1970s and 1980s.

The 'Language Question' has primarily been a debate about the correct or desirable form of the *written* language, although both in theory and in practice it has not left the spoken language untouched. An enormous amount has been written on this 'question' since the late eighteenth century, nearly all of it prescriptive. Contributors to the theoretical debate have unceasingly rehearsed the arguments of their predecessors, often in order to debunk them and to proceed to prescriptive formulae of their own. As a result, the contours of the debate have become consolidated into a well-trodden path. Although the story tends to be told piecemeal and there is no single, authoritative history of the debate from the late eighteenth century to the late twentieth, the historical contest of argument and counter-argument can be followed clearly enough in all its minutiae.

What is more difficult to determine is how these prescriptive formulae, and the often topical and personal rhetoric with which they are barbed, interact, if at all, with the realities of developing written usage. The complex history of the Modern Greek language as actually written during the last two centuries, or indeed going back to the earliest known texts of the twelfth century, has usually been studied for the evidence it offers for the development of the *spoken* language.[1]

---

[1] See e.g. Browning 1983. A useful exception, although outdated in important respects, is the 'Historical Introduction' to Manolis Triandafyllidis' *Modern Greek Grammar* (1938), which is generously illustrated with samples of written usage going back to late antiquity. Cf. Horrocks 1997.

But written, and particularly literary, usage has a history of its own, and it will be necessary, in addition to summarizing the theoretical debate about the language, to trace the main lines of development in written Greek during the period covered by this book.

The linguistic situation which obtained in the Greek-speaking world at the birth of the Greek nation state was certainly complex, but not necessarily as different from that of other emerging states as is often made out. The modern language was (and is) the direct and sole descendant of the language spoken and written in the Greek peninsula and the islands of the eastern Mediterranean in antiquity (so far as is known, from at least *c*.1300 BC). In this, its relation to an ancient language of learning is closely comparable to the relation between the modern Romance languages (epecially Italian) and Latin. Spoken Greek in the early nineteenth century, so far as we can tell, was divided into dialects, mostly on a geographical basis, but there seems also to have been an 'educated' spoken dialect, influenced by written usage, among the eighteenth-century élites of Constantinople and the Ionian islands. Very few of these dialects had diverged far enough to be mutually incomprehensible. (Today only the dialects of Cyprus, of the small Greek-speaking communities of southern Italy, and of the descendants of refugees from the Pontos region of northern Anatolia are not fully comprehensible to a native speaker brought up in Athens.) Before the emergence of a state, with its capital city, none of these geographically dispersed dialects had any claims to predominate, except for that of the élite which, however, is not fully separable from the written language. After independence, the dialects of the Peloponnese became the spoken language of Athens, and hence rose to dominance in the new state, but since many of the educated élite of the first generation came from Constantinople, they brought with them and in time grafted on to the Peloponnesian dialects many of the written traits which marked their speech. Here too an instructive parallel may be drawn with Italy, where dialect differences in modern times have been much greater than in the Greek-speaking world, but this has not prevented the emergence of a standard language which is identical to no one spoken dialect.

So much, briefly, for the spoken language, which at the turn of the nineteenth century was usually called not 'Greek' (a term reserved for the ancient language) but 'Romaic'.[2] But Greek has also been continuously *written* since antiquity, and herein lies the root of the 'Language Question'. Between the second century BC (the time of the translation of the Septuagint) and the first half of the eighteenth century, the normal medium for writing in Greek was either the Attic dialect, as it had been refined in written form in Athens during the high point of classical civilization in the fifth century BC, or the simpler Common Dialect, or *Koine*, that had become a lingua franca for native speakers of many different languages around the eastern Mediterranean following the conquests of Alexander the Great in the late fourth century BC. Attic is the language of classical tragedy, of Plato, Xenophon, Aristophanes, and classical oratory. Koine is best known as the language into which the Old Testament was translated and in which the New Testament was written. Both of these, by the early middle ages, were already obsolete as spoken languages, and both together provided sometimes mutually contradictory models for writing throughout the middle ages and beyond.

In the meantime, the spoken language had not stood still, but there are few direct traces of its development throughout much of the middle ages. The vernacular (that is, a written dialect based more or less closely on current speech) only began to appear in texts of the twelfth century, but for several hundreds of years was used for quite restricted purposes, almost exclusively those that today we would call literary. The scale of this vernacular writing increased between the fourteenth century and the seventeenth, although still largely restricted to verse. These early attempts at writing in the Modern Greek vernacular are far from homogeneous, and none of them achieved the cultural status accorded to a Chrétien de Troyes, a Dante, or a Chaucer in the West. A contributory factor here must surely be the fragmentation of the Greek-speaking world as the Byzantine empire (with Greek as its language of culture and religion) broke up between the thirteenth and the fifteenth centuries, to be succeeded by that of the Ottoman Turks. Only the written

---

[2] Korais, for instance, is consistent in restricting the meaning of Ἑλληνική to Ancient Greek. Indicatively, there is no agreement at this period on how the *word* 'Romaic' (from 'Romios' (Ρωμιός), the popular self-designation of the Greeks under the Ottoman empire) is to be written (see the citations from the period collected by Papazoglou 1991: 16–20).

vernacular of the island of Crete, as it had been shaped for literary purposes between the late fourteenth century and the fall of the island to the Ottomans in 1669, ever achieved a degree of recognition as a literary medium, but this was already considered outdated and geographically restricted by the time of national independence.

By the eighteenth century the evolution of the written language had reached an impasse. The twin models of ancient Attic and ancient Koine continued to maintain a powerful presence, but were becoming increasingly obsolete as the 'modern' rather than classical or theological thinking of the Enlightenment began to make an impact among the learned élites of the Danubian principalities and the Ionian islands. In the West there already existed well-established written vernaculars which had been laying down traditions of their own, alongside Latin, for hundreds of years: no special dilemma confronted Rousseau or Locke. But in the Greek-speaking world the dilemma could not be avoided. The customary written language was precluded from reaching a wide readership; if an alternative was to be used, there was no clearly established set of precedents which writers could follow.

By the time of Greek independence in 1821 there were essentially three theoretical solutions to this problem 'on the table', and each had its already vociferous adherents. According to these, the national (written) language should be (*a*) based on the traditional written language, although there is some vagueness as to what this really means; (*b*) a transcription of the spoken language, or (*c*) some form of more or less planned convergence between the two. By the end of the nineteenth century, the debate had essentially developed into a polarized contest between the spoken language (now called 'demotic', in preference to the older term 'Romaic') and its adherents ('demoticists') on the one hand, and the advocates of a form of compromise (*katharevousa*) on the other. But this situation did not come about at once, and these terms, which are now widely used to refer to the whole course of the debate, would not become generally current until late in the nineteenth century.[3]

---

[3] The term δημοτική is first applied to a form of the language by Panayotis Kodrikas in 1818, where its meaning is very different from that which it came to acquire later. The earliest use of καθαρεύουσα has been traced back to 1796, although the term is not regularly used until late in the 19th century (cf. Koumanoudis 1980).

THE 'LANGUAGE QUESTION' IN THEORY: THE MAIN LINES OF
THE DEBATE

Discussion of the language in the eighteenth century is generally a
subsidiary strand in the network of abstract writing, ranging from
the philosophical to the political, that grew up in the Greek-speaking
world as a response to the Enlightenment. The most radical thinkers, from the point of view of language, were those who dared to
propose that western philosophy was at least a match for that of the
ancient Greeks, and that this modern philosophy had managed
successfully to find expression in the modern languages of Europe.
Such views were proposed among the intellectual élite of the Danubian principalities (described in Chapter I) during the second half of
the century, and paved the way for a number of writers to seek a
means of written expression that would be more comprehensible to
their less educated contemporaries than 'correct' in terms of the
ancient language. The most outspoken of these was Dimitrios
Katartzis (c.1730–1807), who between 1783 and 1791, at the Phanariot court of Bucharest, set out a series of educational reforms
including the then revolutionary proposal that Ancient Greek
should be taught through the medium of Modern Greek. By
means of translations, both from Ancient Greek and from the modern languages of the West, 'learning could be made common to the
whole people, to whom [Ancient] Greek is an enduring barrier, just
as Latin was in Europe for hundreds of years'.[4] Katartzis even wrote
one of the earliest grammars of Modern Greek (Romaic), as it was
spoken in Constantinople in the late eighteenth century, in which he
tried to draw a clear distinction between the ancient language and its
modern descendant.[5] Katartzis was the first to propose such a
programme of reform, but his call went almost entirely unheeded.
His many works remained unpublished at his death, by which time
he himself had abandoned the attempt to write in the idiom he had
proposed, perhaps in response to the increased conservatism among
his aristocratic patrons in the aftermath of the French Revolution.[6]

[4] να γένουν η μάθησες κοιναίς εις όλο το έθνος, εις το οποίο είν' αΐδιο
πρόσκομμα η ελληνική, καθώς ήταν εκατοσταίς χρόνια η λατινική στην Ευρώπη
(Katartzis 1970: 21, written 1783).
[5] Katartzis 1970: 217–61 (dated Jan. 1788). For the principles defining the subject
of the Grammar, see pp. 217–22.
[6] Katartzis' surviving works were not published in full until 1970. On his career and
importance see K. Dimaras 1983: 177–243 (essay first published 1974).

After the politer debates of the eighteenth century, the characteristically embattled contours of the 'Language Question' proper begin to emerge in the work of the expatriate classical scholar Adamandios Korais (1748–1833), whose trenchant and voluminously argued views on education, language, and the nation state, formulated in Paris, were widely disseminated in the Greek-speaking world through subsidized editions and pseudonymous pamphlets. A doctor by professional training, Korais was one of the first to advocate the nineteenth-century model of the nation state for independent Greece, although with the proviso that nationhood could not be achieved until a sufficient level of education had been reached—which Korais estimated would take a century and a half. Unlike Katartzis, Korais found a wide readership for his ideas, and exercised an influence on the debate which reaches far into the twentieth century.

Korais was a far from systematic thinker, and his views on language are scattered throughout letters, prefaces, and polemical pamphlets that he wrote between 1804 and the eve of his death in 1833. Twentieth-century commentators have not been slow to point up the contradictions between statements made at different times and in different contexts.[7] Essentially, Korais' contribution to the debate lies in the elaboration of three principles: first, that the language of the ancients is the key to a storehouse of learning to which their descendants must gain access in order to claim the right of national self-determination;[8] secondly, that the modern (written) language must be consistent with the grammar and intuitions of *today's* (spoken) language; and thirdly, that the way to square this circle is to take the modern (spoken) language as the basis, and *so far as practicable* to 'correct' it in order to minimize those elements which differentiate it most obviously from its ancient predecessor.[9] Despite what came to be preached in his name later in the century, Korais did not advocate a return to Ancient Greek (he rather

---

[7] See e.g. Bien 1972; Moschonas 1981.

[8] This idea runs through all Korais' writings. It is perhaps most succinctly summarized in the 'Extempore Thoughts II' (Στοχασμοί αυτοσχέδιοι Β΄) of 1807 (Korais 1964: A857).

[9] These ideas are first set out clearly in the letter to A. Vasiliou that was published in 1804 as the preface to Heliodoros' novel of the 4th century AD, the *Aithiopika* (Στοχασμοί αυτοσχέδιοι· επιστολή προς Αλέξανδρον Βασιλείου, Korais 1964: A832–56). It was in the same preface that Korais proposed his influential definition of the novel, that was discussed in Ch. I.

wistfully conceded that this was impossible). Although the 'correction' of the language that he proposed was later to be invoked in the name of *katharevousa* (literally: '[language] in the process of purification'), Korais himself never used this term,[10] and his arguments in some respects anticipate those of later *demoticists* no less than of those 'purifiers' who ostensibly were his followers. Korais seems to have been the first to declare, as the demoticists were later to do, the identity between language and nation, and to insist that a speaker's mother tongue is his inalienable democratic right.[11] The chief forms which the process of 'purification' of the mother tongue was to take were, first, the replacement of all foreign loan words by Greek equivalents; secondly, the restoration of ancient spelling; and thirdly the revival of ancient words that had long gone out of use, together with the coinage of new words from ancient roots.

This 'middle way', as Korais termed it, between the extremes of reviving the ancient language or of transcribing speech was fiercely attacked in the two decades following its first formulation in 1804. Indeed, the principal consequence of Korais' attempt at compromise was to bring to a head the divisions that had been largely latent in the later eighteenth century. For some of his opponents, Korais went too far in cautiously accepting that the written language should be based on the spoken; for others, he did not go far enough. But both sides were united in rejecting Korais' prescriptive compromise as artificial. The only alternative was to argue that no such compromise was necessary because a normative basis for contemporary written usage already existed. The attempt to identify such a basis, however, led in contradictory directions and only served to highlight the twin gulfs between spoken and written usage, and between the modern language and the ancient, that Korais had sought to bridge. The alternatives to Korais' prescriptive formula that emerged in these twenty years were mutually exclusive, and so the agenda was set for the linguistic divisions of the next hundred and fifty years.

On the one side, from within the learned élite of Constantinople and the Danubian principalities, came the objections of Neophytos

---

[10] The preferred terms for his own procedure are 'embellishment' (καλλωπισμός) and 'correction' (διόρθωσις).

[11] See Chaconas 1968: 58 (from Ἄτακτα Β΄). The form of language which Korais proposed to 'embellish and correct' is that which 'we imbibed with our mother's milk' (Korais 1964: A850). This language is shared throughout 'the nation with democratic equality'. Correction must take the form not of 'the tyrant's decree' but of 'brotherly advice' (A854).

Doukas (1780–1845), a cleric, teacher, and outspoken advocate of the ancient language. Doukas took exception to the spoken elements of the language endorsed by Korais, which he haughtily attributed to 'the notorious philanthropy of the philosophers towards the women of the vegetable market'.[12] A more reasoned case was made by the talented civil servant and diplomat Panayotis Kodrikas (1762–1827), who like Korais lived for much of his life in Paris.[13] In practice, as we shall see in the next section, Kodrikas shared much of Korais' theoretical ground, but vigorously opposed his presumption to legislate in matters of language, insisting instead that an adequate medium for writing already existed: in the 'style of the Great Church'.[14]

Others, though, had already begun using similar arguments to reach a diametrically opposite conclusion: that a perfectly good form of the language existed in spoken usage, and all that was needed was to acquire the habit of writing it. Even before Korais' widely disseminated views had begun to fuel the debate, the Phanariot poet Athanasios Christopoulos had proposed that the spoken dialect of Constantinople should form the basis of the written language, and had tried to reconcile this radical solution with the prestige of the ancient language by arguing that this dialect actually *was* the 'fifth dialect of Ancient Greek'. But the purest antithesis to Kodrikas' identification of the language of the Church as the basis for the written language comes in the work of another poet, Ioannis Vilaras, who like Korais was a doctor by profession and shared his liberal ideas. Vilaras in 1814 published, in Corfu, a treatise called *The Romaic Tongue*, in which he sets out principles for transcribing the spoken language and establishing it as the accepted medium for writing. Vilaras was one of only very few reformers, at any time in Greek history, to propose drastic changes in the traditional orthography of the written language. His system is strictly phonetic, and dispenses not only with the smooth and rough breathing marks over initial vowels (which are not functional in the modern language) but also with the accents denoting stress (which are). The result is a written language which is visually differentiated from Ancient

---

[12] In Triandafyllidis 1938: 377.

[13] For Kodrikas' career see Daskalakis 1966: 25–42; Angelou in Kodrikas 1991. Between them, these two volumes reprint a large part of Kodrikas' writings.

[14] Γενικόν ύφος της κοινής Διαλέκτου Ημείς ονομάζομεν...το ύφος της Μεγάλης Εκκλησίας (Daskalakis 1966: 503).

Greek, and indeed from almost all written usage before or since. In Vilaras' system Modern (spoken) Greek asserts its identity as a modern language (something which Korais had also been prepared to concede), but goes much further in claiming its own distinct orthography based on faithfulness to the spoken word.

One of the few reactions against Korais which is still regularly read and commented upon today is again by a poet, and again takes the side of the 'language of the people', that is, demotic: the 'Dialogue' of Dionysios Solomos. By the time it was written (1824–5), the war of independence had already diverted attention away from theory to more practical matters. Like much of Solomos' poetry, this work was left unfinished and was published only posthumously in 1859.[15] Solomos' contribution to the 'Language Question' has been widely praised, since the late nineteenth century, as an early manifesto for the use of the spoken language in writing, and to that extent as a precursor of later demoticism. It can also be read as the character-istic response of the Ionian islands both to the expatriate Korais and to Phanariots such as Kodrikas—indeed, Solomos does not make a clear distinction between them. Like Vilaras before him, Solomos had been educated through the medium of Italian, not Ancient Greek, and the resulting difference of outlook is characteristic of the aristocracy of the Ionian islands in the first half of the nineteenth century.[16]

Solomos, as we know from his career as a poet, was acutely conscious of the need to establish a contemporary written form of his native language, but he distrusted equally the 'Common Dialect' upheld in Phanariot circles, which for him was tainted with subser-vience to the Turks, and the reforms of Korais, which were in addition artificial. The Poet, who is Solomos' spokesman in the 'Dialogue', declares to his interlocutor, the Pedant: 'I give you notice that your dominion in Greece is at an end with the dominion of the Turks. It's at an end, and maybe you'll curse the hour of the Revolution.'[17] And the language of Korais, he insists, 'is not spoken,

---

[15] Citations here refer to Solomos 1994: 505–51; see alternatively Solomos 1986: ii. 9–30.

[16] The 'Dialogue', significantly, is one of only two prose works that Solomos wrote in his native language, while his letters and many of the first drafts of his poems were written in Italian (see Mackridge 1994).

[17] Σας δίνω όμως την είδηση ότι ετέλειωσε το βασίλειόν σας εις την Ελλάδα με των Τουρκών το βασίλειο. Ετέλειωσε, και ίσως αναθεματίστε την ώρα της Επαναστάσεως (Solomos 1994: 548; 1986: ii. 24).

has never been spoken, and never will be spoken'.[18] Although in the Ionian islands at this time many of the functions of a written language were fulfilled by Italian, Solomos obviously could not propose the language of his own education as the national language of his countrymen. Instead, he drew on the example of the Italians, in proposing that the spoken 'language of the people' should provide the basis for the contemporary written language, and in this he enlisted the support of Dante, whose defence of spoken Italian as a written language, *De Vulgari Eloquentia*, dates from the early fourteenth century. 'All the wise nations have settled after all for writing in the language of the people',[19] the Poet declares in the 'Dialogue', and goes on to offer the much-quoted advice: 'first submit to the language of the people, and, if you are able, master it.'[20]

Solomos is the most explicit, among the early contributors to the debate, in invoking the model of the western European vernaculars. But in doing so he does not assume that the written language will therefore be identical to the 'language of the people'. A telling point in the dialogue comes when the Poet has to admit that the writer cannot always 'follow the people':

PEDANT: In what circumstances does the poet not follow the phrases of the people?
POET: In a great many; but even in those his phrases must be to some degree analogous to those which do exist.[21]

Here, inevitably, the element of prescription returns to the debate. The difference from Korais is that Solomos does not propose changing either the grammar or the vocabulary of the spoken language: he demonstrates, for instance, the absurdity of rewriting the first line of Dante's *Divine Comedy* so as to conform to the rules of Latin.[22] But he does accept that new norms will have to be created on the principle of analogy, and this principle, although not the

[18] οι δικοί μας θέλουν να γράφουμε μία γλώσσα, η οποία μήτε ομιλιέται, μήτε άλλες φορές ομιλήθηκε, μήτε θέλει ποτέ ομιληθή (Solomos 1994: 534; 1986: ii, 13).
[19] Ησύχησαν τέλος πάντων γράφοντας τη γλώσσα του λαού τους τα σοφά έθνη (Solomos 1994: 533; 1986: ii. 13).
[20] υποτάξου πρώτα στη γλώσσα του λαού, και, αν είσαι αρκετός, κυρίεψέ την (Solomos 1994: 543; 1986: ii. 20).
[21] ΣΟΦΟΛΟΓΙΟΤΑΤΟΣ : Εις ποιες περίστασες ο ποιητής δεν ακολουθάει στες φράσες του τον λαό;
ΠΟΙΗΤΗΣ : Εις πολλές· όμως και εις αυτές πρέπει οι φράσες του να έχουν κάποιαν αναλογία με τες άλλες οπού υπάρχουν (Solomos 1994: 543; 1986: ii. 20).
[22] Solomos 1994: 539; 1986: ii. 17.

manner of its practical application, was also shared both by Korais and, later, by Psycharis for the demoticists.

So far all the solutions proposed in opposition to Korais' prescriptions for the language had necessarily been themselves to some degree prescriptive, and all are strongly dogmatic. But the 'Language Question', in the wake of Korais' proposed reforms, also provoked its share of satire. The play *Korakistika, or Correction of the Romaic Tongue* was published in Vienna in 1813. Its author was Iakovakis Rizos Neroulos (1778–1849), whom we encountered in the Introduction as the first to write a history of Modern Greek literature. Like the later *Babel* by Dimitrios Hatzi-Aslan Vyzandios (1836), this play exploits the comic effects which result when the prescriptive formulae aimed at standardizing the written language are applied to ordinary speech.[23] *Korakistika*, which puns on Korais' name and the common word for a kind of children's *argot* which is supposed to be incomprehensible to adults, takes as its butt Korais' proposed 'corrections' to the spoken language (and actually invents many more). In the play, a zealot of the new language chokes in the attempt to order a cabbage salad, for which the supposedly corrected word contains thirty letters, and is cured by being induced to utter its everyday equivalent.[24]

Babel, or the Regional Corruption of the Greek Language tackles a weak point in the case for the spoken language that had been rather unsatisfactorily dealt with in the serious debate: the existence of regional dialects.[25] To the dialects of seven different regions that are spoken by characters in the play is added an eighth, the language of the pedant who, like the zealot in *Korakistika*, has created a new dialect all his own in the attempt to replace common words with

[23] Neroulos' play is reprinted, with a substantial introduction and much other material of the period relating to the 'Language Question', in Vilaras *et al.* 1981: 8–62. For *Babel* see Vyzandios 1972.
[24] Ελαδιοξιδιολατολαχανοκαρύκευμα, for λαχανοσαλάτα, as the author's footnote tells us (Vilaras *et al.* 1981: 51–2).
[25] It was axiomatic both for Korais and his conservative opponents, as for the later 'purists', that no single common form of spoken Greek existed. This was one of the reasons for Korais' proposed 'corrections'; and on these grounds Kodrikas had rejected even the speech of the educated élite of Constantinople. Solomos, like many later demoticists, simply brushes the issue aside, but the passage of the 'Dialogue' in which he does so invites the suspicion that he had a very limited knowledge of the dialects spoken in other parts of the Greek-speaking world (Solomos 1994: 545–6; 1986: ii. 21–2).

ancient equivalents. The scene is set in Nafplion (then the Greek capital) in 1827, on the day that news is brought of the decisive victory over the Turks in the battle of Navarino. A group of Greeks in a *taverna* celebrate their now assured freedom, but mutual misunderstandings lead to violence and they are all taken off to jail, before returning to the same *taverna* to celebrate all over again, in a potentially endless cycle. In both plays the inadequacy of particular kinds of language is pointed up by repeated reference to eating and defecating: in *Babel*, the brawl breaks out when an accusation of stealing sheep is understood as a charge of eating excrement; a good deal of the humour in *Korakistika* is scatological; and crucial scenes in both plays involve (unsuccessful) attempts to order food.

The first fifty years of Greek independence saw a slackening of the theoretical debate. An exchange of fire in the 1850s, between the veteran Romantic poet Panayotis Soutsos and the classical scholar and university professor Konstandinos Asopios, is chiefly notably for the extent of the common ground uniting the contestants: both agree that Korais' reforms of the spoken language had proved inadequate and vie with one another in claiming the credit for introducing more drastic substitutions of ancient elements of the language. Soutsos even claimed, as apparent justification for this procedure, that the language of the simple shepherds he met on Parnassos actually *was* Ancient Greek, and to prove his point quotes not the shepherds he actually heard, but Theocritus describing similar people in similar places in the third century BC! In this vein Soutsos was able to declare that 'The language of the ancient Greeks and ourselves will be one and the same; their Grammar and ours will be one and same,' and the subtitle of his *New School of the Written Language* announces a project that Korais had conceded was impossible: *The Resurrection of the Ancient Greek Language Understood by All.*[26] The principal difference between Soutsos and his more soberly academic rival Asopios lies in how much further

---

[26] *Νέα σχολή της γραφομένης γλώσσης· Ανάστασις της αρχαίας ελληνικής γλώσσης εννοουμένης υπό πάντων*, 1853. The sentence quoted is from p. 5: Η γλώσσα των αρχαίων Ελλήνων και ημών των νεωτέρων έσεται μία και η αυτή· η Γραμματική εκείνων και ημών έσεται μία και η αυτή (cited and discussed by Tziovas 1986: 96). See also the extract reprinted by Panayotopoulos *et al.* 1956: 47–55. Soutsos' programme was not wholly new: something similar underlies the attacks on Korais by, for example, Doukas in the first decades of the 19th century. But it only now gathered momentum and came to be fully acknowledged as a goal for the nation.

Korais' reforms could and should be taken. But despite Soutsos' enthusiasm, and the quaint delight of his rival Asopios at the delusion of some western classical scholars that the modern language was already no different from the ancient, both reformers seem to be agreed on the piecemeal *method* of Korais: 'the correction, enrichment, and embellishment of the [modern] language.'[27]

The only serious dissent from these views came from the rival centre of Greek culture that had not yet been incorporated into the Greek state, namely the Ionian islands, where, as we saw, Solomos' 'Dialogue' belatedly appeared in 1859. Although the text itself does not seem to have been widely known before that,[28] Solomos' opinions on the language were well aired among the circle of younger poets and writers in Corfu who looked up to him in his later years. One of these, Andonios Manousos, in 1850 edited the first collection of Greek folk-songs to be published in the Greek-speaking world (1850), and prefaced it with a lively dialogue between himself and the 'windbag' who speaks in the corrected language of Korais, on the propriety of publishing the 'overflowing of the soul' of the unlettered people.[29] It is clear from the peroration of this brief dialogue (which consists of an extended quotation from Vilaras' *Romaic Tongue*) that the more radical proposals of Vilaras had not fallen on deaf ears in the Ionian islands.

It was also in the Ionian islands that the next extended defence of the spoken language as the language of writing appeared in the form of two tracts by Nikolaos Konemenos, published in 1873 and 1875. A minor poet who divided his time between Corfu, Patras, and Athens, and in this way was one of the first to bridge the cultural divide that still separated the Ionian islands from the Greek Kingdom, Konemenos' contributions were a timely reminder that a separate consensus in Athens and another in Corfu did not amount to a solution to the 'Language Question'. The 'Question' itself, he declared, is really simple: his proposal is that the national language

[27] Τα Σούτσεια, ήτοι ο Κύριος Παναγιώτης Σούτσος εν γραμματικοίς, εν φιλολόγοις, εν σχολάρχαις και εν ποιηταίς εξεταζόμενος, published anonymously. For a substantial abstract, see Panayatopoulos *et al.* 1956: 56–86. The sentence quoted appears on p. 72: προς διόρθωσιν, πλουτισμόν και καλλωπισμόν της γλώσσης.

[28] On the manuscript and its publication see Coutelle 1990: 69–81.

[29] The phrase ξεχείλισμα της ψυχής, with which the Editor describes the oral songs of his collection, is taken from Solomos' notes to the 'Hymn to Liberty' (see Ch. 1 n. 21). See Manousos 1969: 3.

should be that commonly spoken, whose deficiencies should be made up by quarrying the ancient language as necessary, 'but not to excess, as the pedants do today'.[30] He is responsive to the claims of usage, arguing for instance against Vilaras' orthographic reforms on these grounds, but with the rider that since usage is a matter of convention, there is no inherent reason why they could not have been adopted.[31] In addition, Konemenos also proposed what was to become a central plank in the demoticist movement that would gain momentum in the next decade: the identity of the language of speech and of writing, although he is, tellingly, also prepared to compromise and accept a degree of 'correction' to the spoken language.[32]

The theoretical debate came to a head in the 1880s, as part of the period of literary renewal and new-found self-confidence that was discussed in Chapter 2. Provocation came in the form of the publication, in 1882, of the collected *Linguistic Observations Concerning the Modern Greek Language* by Konstandinos Kondos. There are two hundred of these 'observations', and together with an introduction and an index they take up almost six hundred pages. With nit-picking thoroughness Kondos dissects dilemmas that had emerged to face the followers of Korais as they attempted to write in an appropriately 'corrected' language. Kondos' method was to extend almost to their limits the revisionist prescriptions of Soutsos and Asopios, whereby the balance of Korais' pragmatic compromise became progressively tipped towards ancient (written) precedents at the expense of modern (spoken) ones. Kondos' 'observations' unwittingly exposed, in the starkest terms yet, a central weakness in Korais' prescriptive programme, namely that where compromise was not predicated on usage there could be no final arbiter of what was 'correct'. Since, however, even Kondos did not advocate *replacing* the entire system of (spoken) Modern Greek with that of the ancient language, but operated, like his predecessors, piecemeal, and generally at the level of the individual word, the prescriptive programme reached the point of theoretical impasse. If every

---

[30] Konemenos' choice of language is defined as η κοινή, η ομιλούμενη, which he further describes as γλώσσα ζωντανή. For the whole of the passage summarized here see 1873: 4–5.

[31] Konemenos 1873: 48–50.

[32] On the identity of writing and speech see Konemenos 1873: 12; cf. Tziovas 1986: 123–4. Konemenos' proposals for compromise, expressed in language very similar to that of Korais (μέσος όρος, where Korais had proposed a μέση οδός) and in content very similar to some of his, are put forward on pp. 58–65.

separate constituent of an utterance in Modern Greek was to be replaced by the equivalent constituent in Ancient Greek, the result would not be a well-formed sentence, nor even a fully comprehensible one, in either language.

Several more or less simultaneous responses to this impasse were formulated in the 1880s. First into print (although anonymously and from the safe distance of a publishing house in Trieste) was Dimitrios Vernardakis, who had held the Chair of History and Philology at the University of Athens since 1861, and resigned amid the ensuing controversy. The formidably entitled *Pseudo-Atticism Censured, or A Refutation of K. S. Kondos' Linguistic Observations Concerning the Modern Greek Language*, which appeared in 1884, is a point-by-point reply, and is scarcely shorter than the volume it attacks. Essentially, Vernardakis argued for a return to the pragmatism of Korais, from whose controlling reins, as he puts it, the written language had escaped altogether since the 1850s and 1860s.[33]

The next year Emmanuel Roidis, the veteran stylist in *katharevousa*, announced a forthcoming analysis of 'what ought to be done' in the language.[34] When Roidis' study finally appeared, under the title *The Idols*, in 1893, it surprisingly supported the cause of the spoken language, although in this, as in everything else that he wrote, Roidis expressed himself in elegant *katharevousa*.[35] But the single event that launched the new phase of the 'Language Question' and contributed, in all probability, more than any other to the intensification of the theoretical debate at the turn of the twentieth century, was the appearance of the book *My Journey* by Psycharis in 1888.

Psycharis himself was a Greek of the 'Diaspora'. Born in 1854 in Odessa, he was educated in Constantinople and Paris, and settled permanently in the latter city at the age of 20. Trained as a classical scholar, he went on to hold a series of academic appointments, culminating in a Chair at the Ecole des Langues Orientales Vivantes (from 1904). In French he published an important series of articles on the historical linguistics of Greek in the medieval period, as well as a number of novels. These he signed Jean Psichari. When he wrote in Greek he signed himself with his surname alone, explaining that his Christian name had undergone too many transformations in his early life for him to feel comfortable with any of the colloquial

[33] Vernardakis 1884: 2.   [34] Angelou in Psycharis 1971: 18.
[35] *Τα είδωλα*, 1893 (Roidis 1978: iv. 93–363).

Greek equivalents for Jean/Ioannis/Vanya.[36] This in itself is a significant index of Psycharis' cosmopolitan background: it was as an outsider that he entered the debate on the language, and this fact undoubtedly coloured both the manner in which he did so, and the reactions he provoked in Greece.[37]

My Journey is the highly stylized account of a visit to Constantinople, Chios, and Athens in 1886. The book has often been called a novel, but although Psycharis did go on to write fiction, both in French and Greek, this book contains no indication as to its genre and employs only the most cursory of narrative pretexts. Interwoven with an itinerary that starts in Paris and ends with the narrator's horrified flight from the hotbed of linguistic archaism that he finds in Athens (it seems to have been Psycharis' first visit to the capital of independent Greece) is a passionate and rhetorical defence of the spoken language as the sole and necessary medium for writing in Greek. The book also contains as nit-picking a set of observations on the shortcomings of specific 'corrected' words and forms as can be found in the exchanges of Kondos and Vernardakis.

Many of the arguments put forward (in trenchant and flamboyant terms, it must be said) are not in themselves new. Psycharis takes exception to the phenomena of 'loan-translation', whereby fixed collocations or clichés in other languages are literally translated into *katharevousa*, and hypercorrection (where non-existent ancient forms are produced by analogy).[38] A large part of the book is devoted to phonology, a subject which also dominated Psycharis' linguistic research; and he was one of the few contributors to the debate to accept unequivocally that the phonological system of Greek had changed fundamentally since ancient times.[39] In his

[36] See the introduction to *My Journey* by Alkis Angelou (Psycharis 1971: 11).

[37] For a series of modern assessments of Psycharis' multifaceted career see the essays collected in Holton 1988.

[38] See, respectively, Psycharis 1971: 70–5, 105–11. These phenomena are not, of course, confined to Greek, and loan-translation has played a significant part in the development of all modern European languages.

[39] The contemporary revival or coinage of words and forms, written according to the phonological system of the *ancient* language, but pronounced in the modern way, involved violation of *both* ancient and modern phonology. Psycharis illustrates this phenomenon in the chapter entitled Συμβιβασμός, an aptly chosen word which becomes the object of his scorn. Historically speaking Psycharis is quite correct: in Ancient Greek the written characters would have had the phonemic value /mb/, while in the development of the modern spoken language, such juxtapositions are regularly resolved into /b/, written μπ, or /v/, written β (1971: 145–7; on the different pronunciation of Ancient Greek, see 193–7).

emphasis on change rather than on static continuity or regressive 'correction', Psycharis drew crucially on the theory of the contemporary 'Neogrammarians'. To that extent his was the first contribution to the debate to be founded on a central tenet of modern linguistics, namely the principle that progressive and systematic change is integral to all living languages. Psycharis' commitment to demotic does not therefore imply any weakening of the link between the ancient language and the modern that had assumed such importance in Greece throughout the nineteenth century. According to Psycharis' system, it was paradoxically only by demonstrating that the language has *changed* since ancient times that the moderns could convincingly demonstrate that the ancient language still lives—in its modern descendant.

The other, related, tenet which Psycharis took from the Neogrammarians was that a living language is a coherent system, and this led him to the most controversial element of his linguistic programme. Nominally, the *Grammar* of spoken (demotic) Greek that he several times announced but never completed, would be descriptive. In a phrase reminiscent of Solomos' 'Dialogue', he advises the grammarian: 'your job is first to accept the [linguistic] forms of the people; the duty of grammar is to explain them.'[40] But, as Solomos also knew, it could not be so simple: the language of the people was not a written language. In his preface Psycharis admits the prescriptive agenda that he will himself try to follow in the language of the book:

I write in the *common* language of the people; when our demotic language doesn't have a word that we need, I take a word from Ancient Greek and try, as far as possible, to adapt it to the grammar of the people. . . . I have tried to write [this language] regularly, to respect its laws, to be attentive to its phonology, morphology, to the forms and syntax of demotic grammar. [author's emphasis][41]

Where Korais and his followers had increasingly sought to make the modern (spoken) language look, in its written form, as much like

---

[40] Η δουλειά σας είναι πρώτα να παραδέχεστε τους τύπους του λαού· της γραμματικής χρέος είναι να τους ξηγήση (Psycharis 1971: 175).

[41] Γράφω την *κοινή* γλώσσα του λαού· όταν η δημοτική μας γλώσσα δεν έχει μια λέξη που μας χρειάζεται, παίρνω τη λέξη από την αρχαία και προσπαθώ, όσο είναι δυνατό, να την ταιριάξω με τη γραμματική του λαού... Προσπάθησα να τη γράψω κανονικά, να φυλάξω τους νόμους της, να προσέξω στη φωνολογία, στη μορφολογία, στο τυπικό και στη σύνταξη της δημοτικής γραμματικής (Psycharis 1971: 38).

Ancient Greek as possible, Psycharis proposed to make his borrow-
ings from Ancient Greek conform, wherever he could, to the system
of the spoken language. In practice Psycharis quickly found himself
obliged to *systematize* the spoken language, with results scarcely less
prescriptive than the proposals of Korais, and incidentally no less
dependent on the ancient language as a means of making good the
deficiencies of the modern. The language of Psycharis, as was to be
pointed out both by purists and by less radical supporters of demotic, in the earlier words of Solomos, 'is not spoken, has never been
spoken, and never will be spoken'.

The next few years saw a flood of publications (most, but not all of
them, now written in demotic) in broad support of Psycharis' theoretical position. The poet and editor of Solomos' posthumous
collected works, Iakovos Polylas in the Ionian islands, and the novelist and critic Emmanuel Roidis in Athens both produced book-
length treatises in which they argued for demotic, particularly as the
language of literature.[42] In the same decade, the 1890s, the cause
was taken up by the poet Kostis Palamas, the journalist Vlasis
Gavriilidis, the translator Alexandros Pallis, the historian and
short-story writer Argyris Eftaliotis, and even by the foreign Byzantine scholars Karl Krumbacher and Karl Dieterich, and the linguist
A. Thumb. By 1893 the growing movement in favour of the spoken
language had been christened with the term 'demoticism'.

But Psycharis' book also aroused fierce opposition. The most
sustained, but also one of the more moderate, counter-arguments
was mounted by a fellow classical scholar, also trained in contemporary linguistics: Yeoryos Hatzidakis (1848–1941), who had
already entered the debate in the same year as Vernardakis, with a
defence of Kondos' *Linguistic Observations*. German-trained, Hatzidakis was appointed to the Chair of Linguistics at the University of
Athens in 1881, a post which he held for many years. Hatzidakis'
response to Psycharis is set out at length in a series of articles he
wrote in Greek between 1890 and 1895, and in a long pamphlet
which he published in French in 1907.[43] Hatzidakis sought to place
the whole question in its historical and social context. While he did
not dissent from Psycharis' (and others') identification of nation
and language, he insisted, as Kodrikas had done before him, that

---

[42] Polylas, *Our Literary Language* (Η φιλολογική μας γλώσσα) 1892 (Polylas 1959:
246–305); for Roidis see n. 35.
[43] Collected in G. Hatzidakis 1901: 236–537; 1907.

different forms of the language are appropriate to speaking and to writing, and therefore resisted one of the most widespread tendencies of the demoticists, namely to ignore or to minimize this difference.[44] Again like Kodrikas, Hatzidakis based much of his argument on the continued existence of Greek as a *written* language throughout antiquity and the middle ages. The *katharevousa* of his own day, he insists, is merely the contemporary manifestation of this continuing tradition; if those who write the language choose to express themselves in a 'more demotic *katharevousa*', then he as a linguist will have no reason to object, but will merely record the new stage in the linguistic history of the nation.[45] But what Hatzidakis objected to in Psycharis is precisely what Kodrikas had objected to in Korais: the prescriptive interference of the expatriate who rides roughshod over centuries of written usage.[46]

It was in the course of the immediate controversy over Psycharis' book that another term entered the debate, one which has remained current ever since: *diglossia*. Today this is the term used by linguists to define a special form of bilingualism, in which two distinct forms of the same language are used side by side in the same community for different purposes, and this model has often been applied to modern Greece.[47] When it was first used in Greece at the end of the 1880s, 'diglossia' referred to the historical split between written and spoken Greek that goes back, as we saw, to the beginning of the Christian era. But in a modern context, the perpetuation of this split was seen as something to be avoided.[48] Ironically, it was Psycharis' intervention in the debate that established diglossia, both as word and as reality, in its full modern sense in Greece. Different styles or dialects had long existed for speech and writing, but with the advent

[44] On nation and language see 1901: 242; on speech and writing see 1901: 284–5.

[45] G. Hatzidakis 1901: 296.

[46] Among the conclusions reached in the first part of Hatzidakis' 1907 pamphlet are: 'Qu'il y a en usage chez nous, depuis déjà deux mille ans, une langue écrite, simple, vraiment nationale, connue, qui plaît et qui, depuis un siècle, a commencé à devenir aussi la langue du commerce journalier.... Qu'une habitude si vieille, enracinée si profondément dans l'âme de la nation... ne peut d'aucune façon être abolie par une ordonnance' (1907: 59–60).

[47] See e.g. Householder 1962; M. Alexiou 1982.

[48] Apart from an isolated occurrence in 1830, the term 'diglossia' became current for the first time in the debate surrounding Psycharis' *Journey*. The term is first used, in the sense defined here, by Roidis in his review of Psycharis' book (Roidis 1978: iii. 299–327 (p. 300); cf. his 1893 essay *The Idols*, Roidis 1978: iv (p. 358), and Koumanoudis 1980 *ad loc.*) and by G. Hatzidakis in 1890 (1901: 238 ff.).

of demoticism and the sharpened conflict between rival *written* forms of the language, the way was paved for diglossia to become institutionalized, not just as a separation between spoken usage and written, but as a formal division within written usage, as happened between 1911 and 1976, when the appropriate contexts for the (written) use of demotic and *katharevousa* were legally and institutionally sanctioned.

By the first years of the twentieth century the thunderous rhetoric injected by Psycharis into the debate was finding a responsive echo in newspaper columns and university lecture halls. In 1901 Gavriilidis' newspaper, *Acropolis*, began publishing Alexandros Pallis' translation of the Gospels into the modern language, including elements of demotic. The publication provoked a public outcry, which culminated in several days of violent demonstrations by university students, led by many of their professors. Newspaper offices and public buildings were attacked, until at the height of the disturbances, on 8 November, police opened fire on a mass demonstration outside Athens University, leaving eight people dead.[49] Two years later, at the end of 1903, the staging of Aeschylus' *Oresteia* in a demotic translation provoked further clashes. Why, one might well ask, should an abstract debate spill over into violent action, and on such a scale? The answer lies in the close conceptual link between language and nation that can be traced back to Korais. This standard article of faith for nineteenth-century Greece had been restated in characteristically pugnacious terms by Psycharis in the preface to *My Journey*: 'Language and fatherland are one and the same. To fight for the fatherland or for the national language is one and the same struggle.'[50] The same rhetoric appears no less vigorously among the most implacable opponents of demotic, during the decade when tension was rising between Greece and Bulgaria over the two countries' rival claims to Macedonia, which was still part of the crumbling Ottoman empire. Characteristically, G. Mistriotis, one of the university professors who figured prominently in the disturbances of 1901 and 1903, justified his inflammatory stance by declaring:

---

[49] For an account and analysis of these events in English, see Carabott 1993.

[50] Γλώσσα και πατρίδα είναι το ίδιο. Να πολεμά κανείς για την πατρίδα του ή για την εθνική τη γλώσσα, ένας είναι ο αγώνας (Psycharis 1971: 37).

316 LITERATURE AND LANGUAGE

Many peoples have been enslaved but have not laid down their language. The Greek people risks losing its very existence for the sake of a few individuals who call themselves demoticists.... I do not know if these people are paid in money or in kind, but I can give my assurance that the enemies of the Greek nation and the vulgarizers [i.e. demoticists]... are reaching the same results.

The Bulgarians are trying to detach from mother Greece her dearest daughter [i.e. Macedonia], while those who call themselves demoticists are taking a hatchet to the mother herself.
... Had I not spoken out I would have been committing a crime against the Nation and its History...[51]

At this time, as these quotations demonstrate, both demoticism and the conservative reaction to it were equally predicated upon nationalism and irredentism. For the demoticists, the dead hand of the ancient language was a barrier to the fulfilment of nationalist goals, and some empirical support for this view came from the disputed area of Macedonia itself, where slavophone children were being taught to read and write in *katharevousa*, but could hardly *speak* Greek at all.[52] On the other hand, the purists saw any weakening of the link between the modern language and its illustrious ancestor as a potentially fatal slippage in the fight to assert the nation's identity, and more particularly to fulfil its irredentist ambitions. The rhetoric, and much of the serious thinking too, that underpinned these ambitions, was framed in terms of historical continuity: if the Modern Greek language were to be neither the prestigious idiom of classical Athens nor the timeless written language of the Byzantine Church and State with its capital at Constantinople, on which irredentist eyes were keenly trained at this time, then, the purists believed, the foundations both of the present state and of its future aspirations would be swept away.

---

[51] Πολλοί λαοί εδουλώθησαν αλλά δεν απέβαλον την γλώσσαν αυτών. Το ελληνικόν όμως γένος κινδυνεύει να απολέση και αυτήν την ύπαρξίν του ένεκα ολίγων ανθρώπων οίτινες ονομάζουσιν εαυτούς δημοτικιστάς.... Δεν γνωρίζω εάν ούτοι λαμβάνωσιν αμοιβάς εις νομίσματα, ή εις είδη, αλλά δύναμαι να βεβαιώσω ακριβώς ότι οι πολέμιοι του ελληνικού έθνους και οι χυδαϊσταί... εις τα αυτά αποτελέσματα φθάνουσιν.

Οι μεν Βούλγαροι πειρώνται ίνα αποσπάσωσι από της μητρός Ελλάδος την προσφιλεστέραν αυτής θυγατέρα, οι δε καλούμενοι χυδαϊσταί φέρουσι τον πέλεκυν κατ' αυτής της μητρός.
... Εάν εσιώπων ήθελον διαπράξει έγκλημα προς το Έθνος και την Ιστορίαν αυτού (A. Dimaras 1974: ii. 38).

[52] Moschonas 1975: κδ'.

Meanwhile the demoticist movement that had sprung up in the wake of Psycharis' *Journey* continued to gain momentum. In 1903 the periodical *Noumas* began publication, which was to continue until 1922. *Noumas* was founded to promote the ideals of demoticism, but quickly also established itself as the leading literary periodical of its day. It was in the columns of *Noumas*, too, that the first cracks began to appear in the fabric of demoticism itself, as cautious reformers headed by Palamas began increasingly to distance themselves from the all-or-nothing systematization of Psycharis and followers such as the fellow expatriate Alexandros Pallis, who earned themselves the disparaging title of 'Hairies' (*Malliari*), on account of their allegedly bohemian appearance.

Probably the last of the general, quasi-philosophical treatments of the subject came in 1908, in the little book *Language and Life* by the demoticist E. Yanidis.[53] Although less polemical than Psycharis or Solomos before him, Yanidis brought to the subject a humour and a restraint more reminiscent of Konemenos. But he also shared with the purists the aspiration to promote a form of the language that would be common to all, and he used much the same arguments in favour of demotic as Hatzidakis had brought forward in favour of *katharevousa*.[54] But he rejected Hatzidakis' conclusions, repeated in print the previous year, by insisting that it is *katharevousa*, not demotic, that lacks rules and stable forms. Thus far Yanidis merely echoes moderate conservatives such as Vernardakis and Hatzidakis, but he goes on to insist: 'True literature . . . will never be given to us by an artificial language.'[55] Yanidis neatly sums up the terms of the debate as they had become established throughout the nineteenth century; and also, inadvertently, points to the same impasse as had become apparent in the wake of Kondos' compendious *Observations* in 1882: is demotic really any less 'artificial' than *katharevousa* as a written language?

From this time on the debate began to move on to other ground, becoming less philosophical, and at the same time increasingly political. The political dimension had already begun to emerge clearly in the violent events of the first years of the century, but what is interesting, in hindsight, about the clashes of that time and

[53] Yanidis 1969.
[54] See esp. 1969: 43–4.
[55] Τη λογοτεχνία την αληθινή ... η τεχνητή γλώσσα δε θα μας τη δώσει ποτέ (Yanidis 1969: 113).

the rhetoric which accompanied them is the almost complete unanimity of political aims underlying both camps: as in other spheres of Greek political life, the divisions were then about means, not ends. A foretaste of the later, and rather different, political polarization of the 'Language Question' comes in the proto-socialist manifesto, *Our Social Question*, published by G. Skliros in 1907, and particularly in the debate that it provoked in the columns of *Noumas* during the following two years.[56] For the first time the issue of the 'language of the people' became linked to the political claims of those same people,[57] and at the same time the seeds were sown for a further division in the demoticist camp, which was to come to a head in the late 1920s: between those who saw linguistic reform as part and parcel of social reform, and those who did not.

During the same years the 'Language Question' was also becoming politicized in a more practical way. Many of the leading demoticists were now turning their attention to education. A private girls' secondary school in Volos, founded by Alexandros Delmouzos in 1908, was a far-sighted educational experiment for its time, and its programme included systematic teaching of and in demotic. Although the scheme ended in farce three years later, a more broadly based plan, in 1910, to open an Experimental School in Athens led to the foundation of what was to be a highly influential pressure group during the next decade and a half: the Educational Society, of which Delmouzos was a leading member, together with Dimitrios Glinos, later the leading Marxist exponent of demoticism, and Manolis Triandafyllidis, whose demotic *Grammar* of 1941 has still not been fully superseded today. In the context of literature, it should also be mentioned that the Educational Society included among its members the young Nikos Kazantzakis.

The most conspicuous consequence of the success of the demoticists at this time was actually a negative one. The 'Language Question' for the first time entered Parliament in the debates on

---

[56] *To κοινωνικόν μας ζήτημα.* The main texts have been collected, with introduction and commentary, in Stavridi-Patrikiou 1976.

[57] The debate in the years leading up to Greek independence had also had a political colouring, when many of those who advocated the spoken language were sympathetic to the social ideals embodied in the French Revolution, while their opponents were often politically and socially conservative. This aspect of the debate has been highlighted by Moschonas in his studies both of the early period and of the twentieth century, although his approach tends to exaggerate social and political factors (Moschonas 1975; 1981).

the new Constitution which followed the 'bourgeois revolution' of 1909. When the Constitution appeared in 1911, it included the first legal attempt in Greece to define and impose an official language:

The official language of the State is that in which the political system and the texts of Greek legislation are drawn up; any interference which deviates from this is forbidden.[58]

But in fact the official attitude to the 'Language Question' during the first Liberal government of Eleftherios Venizelos (1910–20) was ambivalent. It was not long before members of the Educational Society were being invited to write textbooks in demotic for use in primary schools. By 1917 demotic had been officially introduced into the earliest years of primary education, and members of the Educational Society even served in government for a time. Nevertheless, it was something of a Pyrrhic victory. The educational reforms authorized by the Venizelos government were restricted to the 7–12 age group, and even this limited success brought with it practical responsibilities undreamed of in the heady days of Psycharis' *Journey*. Opposition to the Educational Society came from both sides: from the teaching profession whose own education had of course been firmly grounded in *katharevousa*, but also from Psycharis who bitterly denounced the compromises that were, in effect, the price of success.[59]

Every supporter of demotic, including Psycharis, had recognized the necessity of supplementing the spoken language with resources drawn from Ancient Greek. But as reformulated by Triandafyllidis, now Superior Supervisor of Public Education, in 1919, this principle is hard to separate from the 'compromise' so vociferously denounced by Psycharis in *My Journey*, or even from the 'middle way' of Korais a century before:

the demotic *that we write, based* always on the popular language *and its literary tradition*, simultaneously avoids linguistic elements that are truly incompatible with the linguistic and socio-linguistic sensibility of the

[58] Επίσημος γλώσσα του Κράτους είναι εκείνη, εις την οποίαν συντάσσονται το πολίτευμα και της ελληνικής νομοθεσίας τα κείμενα· πάσα προς παραφθοράν ταύτης επέμβασις απαγορεύεται (A. Dimaras 1974: ii. 307).

[59] The first of a series of intemperate attacks by Psycharis on the aims and personalities of the Educational Society, with the provocative title Πάμε σκολειό, is reprinted in part by A. Dimaras (1974: ii. 75–7); for discussion see Sherman 1988.

modern urban population, and *both takes from Ancient Greek and retains from katharevousa*, whatever is truly needed or is viable ... [my emphases].[60]

The reforms were put into reverse, in any case, after Venizelos' defeat in the general election of 1920. From then on demotic kept a toe-hold, of varying extent, in primary education and, bucking the trend, also in Greece's second university, which opened in Thessaloniki in 1926. But it was not only Venizelos' electoral defeat that set decisive limits to the aspirations of the Educational Society. The language of the demotic textbooks for primary schools was scarcely less an artificial language than *katharevousa*, and the attempt to impose a linguistic standard based on the spoken language had led to exactly the same impasse as *katharevousa* had already reached: there was no agreed ultimate authority on which written usage could be based.

Now that the 'Language Question' had found a place in the Constitution and in the political programme of governments, the political nature of the debate was firmly established. Then in the mid-1920s, the basis of party politics in Greece began to change, as we saw in Chapter 3, towards an alignment of Left and Right. The Socialist Labour Party of Greece, founded in 1918, changed its name to Communist Party of Greece (KKE) in 1924. It was not until 1927, however, that it adopted as its 'official' language the form of Greek most obviously associated with those whose interests it set out to promote. Significantly, the adoption of demotic by the communists coincided with the attempt by Glinos, who became a member of the Party at just this time, to reform the Educational Society along clearly Marxist/Socialist lines. Reform of education, Glinos argued, should not stop at promoting the language of the people, but should promote the political interests of the 'popular classes: the workers, farm labourers, the petty bourgeoisie'.[61] Glinos and his supporters won the constitutional debate within the Educational Society in 1927, but the Society itself was wound up two years later.

---

[60] η δημοτική που γράφομε, στηριγμένη πάντοτε στην κοινή μας λαϊκή γλώσσα και τη φιλολογική της παράδοση, και τα γλωσσικά στοιχεία αποφεύγει όσα αληθινά δεν μπορεί να συμβιβαστούν με το γλωσσικό και γλωσσοκοινωνικό αίσθημα των σύγχρονων αστικών πληθυσμών, και από τ' αρχαία παίρνει και από την καθαρεύουσα διατηρεί ό,τι αληθινά χρειάζεται ή είναι βιώσιμο... (cited in Moschonas 1975: λα').
[61] A. Dimaras 1974: ii. 152.

From this time until the mid-1970s, the tendency continued for the *written* use of the spoken language to be understood (and often intended) as a signal of left-wing political allegiance, while adherence to the loosely defined conventions of *katharevousa* maintained its older connotations of political conservatism, now increasingly equated with the Right and with the preservation of the established order. During the dictatorship of Metaxas (1936–41) an attempt was made to break the perceived link between demoticism and the political Left, which only serves to show how firmly established that link had already become. Metaxas himself, although politically of the far Right, favoured demotic and took advantage of his dictatorial powers to do for demotic what none of his more liberally minded predecessors had thought to do for either demotic or *katharevousa*. He commissioned a state-backed, 'official' grammar of demotic, and picked one of the leading former members of the Educational Society and now Professor of Linguistics at the University of Thessaloniki, Manolis Triandafyllidis, to do the job. Triandafyllidis' grammar did not appear until 1941, by which time Metaxas and his dictatorship were both dead, and Greece was under occupation by German and Italian forces. It was some time, therefore, before the impact of Metaxas' intervention in the 'Language Question' could be measured, but for all the evidence of its authoritarian conception (the 1941 edition included Metaxas' own preface) Triandafyllidis' grammar has undoubtedly provided an important reference point both for subsequent theoretical debate and for written usage, particularly in education.

In the same year as Triandafyllidis' grammar of demotic appeared, there also occurred one of the most bizarre episodes in the history of the 'Language Question', which brought out into the open some deep-seated prejudices among the intellectual élite that had hardly changed, at least in Athens, since the days of Mistriotis and the riots of the first years of the century. The classical scholar and professor at the University of Athens, Yannis Kakridis (later known for his translations of the *Iliad* and the *Odyssey* into Modern Greek, in collaboration with Nikos Kazantzakis) republished the text of a lecture which he had given some years before at the University of Thessaloniki (where, exceptionally, demotic had prevailed since the University's foundation). Not only was the lecture printed in demotic, it was also published without the traditional accents and breathing marks that Vilaras, in the early nineteenth century, had unsuccessfully sought to abolish. Kakridis' offence seems to have escaped the notice of his colleagues when it was first committed in 1936. But under the conditions of the first months of national defeat and the Axis occupation, the Faculty of Arts of the University of Athens denounced the publication, calling on the Principal of the University to 'restore order' to the School and punish Kakridis.

The so-called 'Trial of the Accents' dragged on for six months, throughout the first winter and spring of the occupation, when people in Athens were dying of starvation by the thousand. The upshot was that Kakridis was briefly suspended from his post. The action of the university authorities, and particularly the letter of denunciation from the Dean of the Faculty of Arts, have to be seen as an intellectual response to the conditions of defeat and occupation. It is against that background (which naturally is not explicitly stated) that Kakridis' publication was described as 'an act detrimental to the nation', 'dangerous', 'destructive', and the perpetrator himself as a man 'known for his left-wing linguistic theories'.[62] The association of demotic with the political Left was clearly ingrained by this time, but so was the assumption that any deviation from the conservative linguistic norm amounted to a renunciation of national identity. Mistriotis in 1903 had accused the demoticists of selling out the national heritage to Bulgarian claims in Macedonia. Underlying the 'Trial of the Accents' is precisely the same fear that a dilution of *katharevousa* (especially by a scholar trained in the ancient language) would imply a weakened resolve for the restoration of national sovereignty. Significantly, Kakridis' accusers claimed that his linguistic practice paved the way for the replacement of the traditional Greek orthography by the Latin alphabet, something which has never been seriously considered in Greece, but which, under the conditions of German and Italian occupation, must have seemed a real enough threat.

Political polarization of the 'Language Question' between Left and Right reached its peak during the decade of the 1940s. As early as 1944 the main communist-dominated resistance organization had tabled a plan for educational reform, stipulating that the 'common Demotic language' should be used throughout education, and

---

[62] Memorandum from the Dean of the Faculty of Arts to the Principal of the University of Athens, dated 27 Nov. 1941. Extracts are reprinted in A. Dimaras 1974: ii. 193–7.

calling for a reformed orthography.[63] Not surprisingly, during the civil war and its aftermath there was little theoretical discussion of how the language should be written. Both sides adhered in theory to the somewhat artificial poles of *katharevousa* and demotic, although as we shall see this polarization itself was beginning to become obsolete. But on neither side was there much interest in redefining what was meant by the particular form of the written language that had come to be espoused as an article of political faith.

In the 1960s the debate was reopened, although in a somewhat half-hearted way, in the periodical *Epoches*. This was the time when George Papandreou's Centre-Left party briefly came to power and for the first time introduced Triandafyllidis' grammar of demotic into schools. Against the background of increased sanction for demotic in the classroom, the linguist and classical scholar A. Tsopanakis proposed a number of systematic but minor modifications which would result in what he called the 'third demotic' (after those of Psycharis and of the Educational Society).[64] Like most of the proposals of his predecessors since Korais, Tsopanakis' reforms were intended as a compromise between a theoretical precedent (in this case Triandafyllidis' grammar) and the usage of the time, and like them they fall between the same two stools; the search for a practical compromise winds up in a series of prescriptions based neither on usage nor on precedent. The controversy that Tsopanakis aroused was muted by comparison with the rhetorical fireworks of earlier times, and is chiefly memorable for the first appearance, in the context of the debate, of the counter-proposal that a decade later would form the basis for an official 'solution' to the 'Language Question'. This was the view that the 'question' itself no longer existed. This view amounts to a denial of the artificially imposed and maintained state of diglossia. The Modern Greek language, it began to be argued, is one and indivisible, and merely awaits increased standardization through usage.[65]

[63] A. Dimaras 1974: ii. 205–6.

[64] Tsopanakis (1966) never explains the term, but this is how it was understood by his critics (see L. Politis 1966: 529).

[65] See L. Politis 1966; Vlachos 1967. The same view underlies the *Synchronic Grammar* of G. Babiniotis and P. Kondos, also published in 1967. The brief introduction to that book (in *katharevousa*!) echoes the terminology of Tsopanakis, in invoking a 'third koine' (after the 'Prehistoric' [*sic*] and the Alexandrian). By the 'third koine' is meant the contemporary 'speech of educated people', which, the writers argue, has drawn in practice on both demotic and *katharevousa*. In a different context

This 'solution' was delayed, however, for a decade by the intervention of the Colonels from 1967 to 1974. The military rulers reversed the educational changes of the 1960s, and both in theory and practice became the last to revive the nineteenth-century arguments for the maintenance of *katharevousa* as an official, written language. The contorted utterances of the leaders and spokesmen of the regime were a byword at the time, but the military men were also not shy of entering the theoretical debate. In 1973 a book-length pamphlet appeared under the blankly dispassionate imprint of the 'Armed Forces Headquarters', entitled *National Language*. Believed to have been the work of the then Commander-in-Chief of the Armed Forces, Odysseus Angelis, this is one of the more curious documents to have been generated by the debate.[66] Its arguments are largely drawn from those of Hatzidakis more than half a century before, with an occasional sprinkling of the headier nationalist rhetoric that had surfaced in the speeches of Mistriotis in the first decade of the century, and in the denunciations directed against Kakridis in 1941. Those who advocate the 'abolition' of *katharevousa* and its replacement by demotic are accused of a 'national crime', and there is an obligatory excursus on communism,[67] but the main thrust of the argument is that demotic has no rules, while *katharevousa* is backed up by both the prestige and the precedent of the ancient language, described somewhat lyrically as an 'inexhaustible source'.[68] Had it not been for the anxious discussions of the mid-1960s about the most suitable form of demotic to be taught in schools, one might have been forgiven for thinking that this argument had long become obsolete. In fact, although the text denies it, the prescription of the Armed Forces HQ marks the final assertion of a more or less formal state of diglossia.[69]

With the fall of the Colonels' regime in 1974, several things happened that speeded an end to the polarization of the previous

George Seferis had declared, as early as 1937, that 'as far as literature is concerned, [the 'Language Question'] doesn't exist' (Seferis 1981: i. 65; cf. i. 259), and, as we shall see in the next section, literary writers from the late 1930s were often prepared to transgress the notional boundaries marked out by diglossia.

[66] Armed Forces HQ 1973. On the likely authorship see Moschonas 1975: ρια'.
[67] Armed Forces HQ 1973: 137, 152–4.
[68] Armed Forces HQ 1973: 111.
[69] See pp. 135–7, where the barbed comments of French and British linguists (Mirambel, Browning) are quite wittily turned back on their authors, with examples of di- or even triglossia in English and French!

ninety years. The removal of the legal ban on communist organiza-
tions and political parties of the far left helped to remove the political
stigma from the forms of the written language associated, respectively, with Left and Right. A new constitution in 1975 made no
mention of an official language. But the crucial step, which at least
officially ended diglossia at a stroke, was the passing by Parliament
of an Education Act in April 1976. Generally cited ever since as a
victory for demotic, the relevant clauses of the Act stipulate that:

1. The language of instruction, the object of instruction, and the language of
textbooks in all classes of General Education is from the school year 1976–
1977 Modern Greek.
2. Modern Greek is understood to mean the language shaped by the Greek
People and by classic writers as a Panhellenic organ of expression; that is:
Demotic, codified, without local peculiarities and extremes.[70]

The 'official' solution was therefore a compromise, and to this
extent is closer to the spirit of Korais, the founding father of *katharevousa*, than to the uncompromising demoticism of Psycharis. The
second clause effectively begs some of the crucial questions that
have dogged the whole debate. It is not clear, from the parallel
references to the 'people' and to 'writers', to what extent the written
language and the spoken are supposed to coincide. The status
accorded to writers implies recognition of a *written* tradition: but
given the parallel existence of demotic and *katharevousa* as written
languages since at least the end of the 1880s, this implies a choice.
Who, after all, are the 'classic' writers, and in particular how far back

---

[70] 1. Γλώσσα διδασκαλίας, αντικείμενον διδασκαλίας και γλώσσα των
διδακτικών βιβλίων εις όλας τας βαθμίδας της Γενικής Εκπαιδεύσεως είναι από
του σχολικού έτους 1976-1977 η Νεοελληνική. 2. Ως Νεοελληνική γλώσσα νοείται
η διαμορφωθείσα εις πανελλήνιον εκφραστικόν όργανον υπό του Ελληνικού Λαού
και των δοκίμων συγγραφέων του 'Εθνους Δημοτική, συντεταγμένη, άνευ
ιδιωματισμών και ακροτήτων (cited and discussed by Landsman 1989: 171). On
the range of meaning of the term ιδιωματισμός, translated here as 'local peculiarity',
see Landsman 1989: 174. It is interesting to note that much of the phraseology of the
1976 Act was borrowed from its predecessor passed in 1964: 'Article 5.1. Demotic,
codified and without local peculiarities, as it has been shaped by the Greek People and
by classic writers of the nation as a Panhellenic organ of expression, is [to be] used
freely in writing and in speech . . . throughout the educational system' (A. Dimaras
1974: ii. 270; also cited by Moschonas 1975: ρι'). In 1964, however, *katharevousa* was
still to be taught in parallel with demotic (see articles 5.2–5.3). It should also be noted
that the 1964 legislation was enacted by a government of the Centre-Left, which had
ousted Karamanlis' right-wing party from power in the general election of the previous year. The 1976 Act was passed by a *right-wing* government under the premiership of Karamanlis.

do they go? Similarly, it had been a demand of the demoticists since Psycharis that demotic should be codified, and a running jibe by their opponents that it never had been. How was this to be achieved now? Finally, the terms 'local peculiarities' and 'extremes' offer little help in defining what is to be excluded, and none at all in determining the mechanism for their exclusion.

The conclusion is inescapable that the 'solution' of 1976 shares something of the prescriptive character of most solutions to the 'Language Question' that had been proposed over time. If the 'question' ended formally with the Education Act of that year, there was ample evidence ten years later that a 'language *problem*', less acute but serious none the less, had taken its place.[71] Subsequent legislation has taken reform further. In 1982 Parliament sanctioned (and codified) a simplified orthographic system, abolishing the (functionally redundant) breathing marks and rationalizing the traditional three different stress marks (which are not functionally differentiated) into one. This is the system, known as the monotonic or 'single-accent' system, that is used in quotations from Greek throughout this book. A further Act of Parliament in 1985 established demotic as the language of the lawcourts and legal documents.

Discussion since 1976 has centred on the issue that was left crucially unresolved in the relevant Act of Parliament. What is meant by 'demotic'? And, given the highly prescriptive character of the debate in all its phases, this question usually shades indistinguishably into the related one: what *should be* meant by 'demotic'? The best answer to this question has been given by those linguists who have attempted a synchronic description of the Modern Greek language in its present phase. Yeoryos Babiniotis has attempted to define and describe what he calls 'Common Modern Greek', in terms of an evolving convergence between linguistic styles.[72] Peter Mackridge, in his study of this language in English, uses the term 'Standard Modern Greek', which he defines as 'the language normally written and spoken today by moderately educated Greeks in the

---

[71] This was the view of almost all those linguists and public figures who took part in a debate in 1985, organized by the Communist Party of the Interior, entitled, 'Is There a Language Question Today?' (Dimosios Dialogos 1988). Three years later, in a recorded discussion which took place at the end of 1988, the novelist Alexandros Kotzias declared that there was no 'language problem', but there *was* a 'language crisis'! (Kotzias *et al.* 1989: 4).

[72] Babiniotis 1979*a*; 1979*b*.

urban centres'.[73] Mackridge's book includes a brief section on written styles, whose partially overlapping and partially differentiated relationship with spoken styles is aptly documented. Such solidly descriptive work has not, however, set the newly christened 'language problem' or 'language crisis' to rest. The veteran demoticist Emmanuel Kriaras, writing in 1985, condemned the wholesale 'demoticizing' of forms which properly belong to a formal and archaic register, but at the same time upbraided those contemporary writers whose linguistic 'acrobatics' violate the 'spirit' of demotic and lead to a kind of demotic, or even 'neo-*katharevousa*', that is purely their own.[74] A frequently reiterated fear since the 1980s is that the influx of foreign words and even grammatical forms, now mainly from (American) English, is putting the integrity of the Greek language at risk. Even such a theoretically descriptive linguist as Babiniotis has played a large part in campaigns since the early 1980s to protect the language from degeneration,[75] and contemporary usage, both in writing and in the mass media, has been the subject both of close scrutiny and of strongly negative rhetoric.[76]

In many respects the terms of the debate in the 1980s and early 1990s seem depressingly little changed since the time of Korais. A large issue, now as then, is the relation between the modern language and Ancient Greek, and this issue was both complicated and exacerbated throughout the 1980s by the contiguous debate about the place of the ancient language in the school curriculum. Another is the absence of a stable and fully standardized written form of the language, which raises the attendant question of the acceptable limits of standardization. Yet another is resistance to intrusion from other, culturally dominant languages. Remarkably constant, throughout nearly two hundred years of debate, seems to be a powerful centripetal impetus towards prescriptive standardization,

[73] Mackridge 1985b: 12; cf. Joseph and Warburton 1987: 2: 'In this description of Modern Greek, the primary focus is what may be termed the *emerging standard language*' [my emphasis]; see now the standard grammar in English (Holton et al. 1997).
[74] Kriaras 1987: 14–15, 22–3.
[75] The Greek Language Society was founded in 1982; the views of its members, including Babiniotis, Elytis, and the popular composer Dionysis Savvopoulos, appear in volumes published in 1982 and 1986.
[76] Mackridge (1992b) cites no fewer than four books on this theme published between 1987 and 1990. The book *Linguistic Observations* by Dimitris Lypourlis (1990) alludes in its title to Kondos' condemnation of contemporary usage just over a century earlier.

balanced by a no less powerful centrifugal tendency to reject any system of standards actually prescribed. Thus defined, the Greek 'Language Question' merely externalizes a tension that is inbuilt in the nature of all languages. Why it should have been externalized to such an extent in Greek cultural life will be briefly considered in the third section of this chapter.

THE 'LANGUAGE QUESTION' IN PRACTICE: THE LANGUAGE OF LITERATURE

A full examination of the language actually used by poets and writers of fiction in Greek during the last two hundred years would obviously go far beyond the scope of this book. Some comments on the linguistic practice of individual writers have already been made in earlier chapters; here the focus will be mainly on larger trends of linguistic usage throughout the last two centuries, and the description will be kept at a level that is intelligible to the reader who knows little or no Greek (although some points of detail will inevitably be lost in translation). There are two, related questions to be addressed here. First, what effect, if any, did the theoretical debate and the rival prescriptive norms actually have on the language of literature? And secondly, while the debate was going on, how did literary writers in fact go about the business of writing?

If we begin by looking at written usage in the early nineteenth century, we find a range of styles whose extreme ends are far apart, but with a broad area of common ground in the middle. At one end of the spectrum, conservatives like Doukas still tried to retain Ancient Greek as the basis of their usage, although by no means consistently; at the other, Vilaras did his best to represent the idiom of contemporary speech in writing. But underlying both extremes and the written style in which Korais proposed his 'middle way' between them is a common late-eighteenth-century style of rhetorical utterance, little of which would have been comprehensible to an Athenian of the fifth century BC, and all of it fairly remote from what a modern classical scholar would recognize as 'Greek'. Korais was not, as his opponents professed to believe, seeking to impose a new, artificial language on his countrymen. His somewhat heavy-handed principles of 'correction' and 'embellishment' can be seen as no more than an attempt to systematize a process that was going on everywhere around him and in his own writing. By a different route his arch-rival Kodrikas seems to have set himself a very similar goal in his study of 'our own Common Greek Dialect, as used by us nationally at the present day'.[77] Kodrikas' assertion, noted earlier, that this dialect is not the spoken idiom of any one group or region but of the Church[78] seems at first sight contradictory until we look critically at the language in which he himself is writing. If the language in which Kodrikas actually writes has any claim to religious authority, it is not the authority of the scriptures or the liturgy but of *contemporary* ecclesiastical bureaucracy. The dispute between Korais and Kodrikas may be schematically reduced to an underlying conflict between the Church and the Greek-speaking Ottoman civil service on the one side, and the merchant class of the Diaspora with its republican, liberal sympathies, from which Korais came, on the other.

Be that as it may, the language used by the combatants in the debate is, in the following instances, scarcely more different than the sentiments expressed:

Korais (1804): Η γλώσσα είναι το εργαλείον, με το οποίον η ψυχή πλάττει πρώτον ενδιαθέτως, έπειτα προφέρει τους λογισμούς της. Όταν το εργαλείον είναι ανακόνητον, ιωμένον, ή κακά κατασκευασμένον, ατελές εξ ανάγκης μένει και το έργον του τεχνίτου.[79]

Language is a tool, with which the soul at first innately shapes, then utters its thoughts. When the tool is blunt, rusty, or badly made, of necessity the work of the craftsman will be imperfect.

Kodrikas (1818): Η Διάλεκτος προς τον άνθρωπον είναι το υλικόν όργανον, δι' ού η άυλος δύναμις του ενδιαθέτου λόγου υπόστασιν, ως ειπείν, προσλαμβάνουσα υλικήν, και σχήμα, και μορφήν οργανικήν, συνθέτει τον προφορικόν λόγον, δι' ού ο άνθρωπος, όχι μόνον προσλαμβάνει έξωθεν τας ιδέας των πραγμάτων, αλλά και αυτώς καθ' εαυτόν ενδιαθέτως εξηγεί τας εννοίας του, ερμηνεύει τας ενεργείας, τα πάθη, τα αισθήματα της ψυχής του.[80]

Dialect [i.e. language] is to man the material instrument, by means of which the insubstantial power of innate utterance, so to speak, assuming material substance and organic shape and form, creates speech, by means of which man internalizes the ideas of things, but [at the same time] also inwardly explains his meanings to himself, [and] interprets the actions, the passions, and the feelings of his soul.

[77] η καθ' ημάς Κοινή Ελληνική Διάλεκτος, τοιαύτη οία παρ' ημίν εθνικώς εν χρήσει είναι την σήμερον (Daskalakis 1966: 488).
[78] See n. 14.   [79] Korais 1964: A850.   [80] Daskalakis 1966: 485–6.

It was this broadly common linguistic ground, rather than the prescriptive details of Korais' system or any systematic refutation of them, that prevailed with remarkably little debate in the early years of the Greek state and effortlessly became the language of its officialdom and education.[81]

In the spheres of poetry and fiction, the search for a written language has historically been in essence a search for precedents. For the writers who came to Athens from Constantinople and the Danubian principalities in their youth, to establish what became known later as the 'Old Athenian School' of literature, these were the same precedents as had also shaped the written style of Korais, Kodrikas, and their generation, and of course now included the written usage of that generation itself. To these must be added the spoken language of educated Greeks in the Ottoman capital and the cities of the Danubian principalities, to which the best witnesses surviving today are the posthumously published writings of Katartzis, the *Modern Geography* of Philippidis and Konstandas, who followed more cautiously in his footsteps, and the short stories of Constantinopolitan life published anonymously in 1792, *Results of Love*.[82] In poetry, the rural folksongs, of which a collection had for the first time been published in Paris in the mid-1820s,[83] provided yet another precedent, first used by a Phanariot poet in Rangavis' fragmentary poem *Dimos and Eleni* of 1831.

One of the reasons that linguistic homogeneity in Greek literature was so long in coming must be sought in the significantly different cultural history of the Ionian islands. Here, despite the declaration in the constitution of the 'United States' of the islands, of 1817, that the official language was to be 'Greek' (not otherwise defined), the language of officialdom continued to be Italian, which only gradually gave way to Greek (*katharevousa*) on the eve of the islands' cession to Greece in 1864. As a result, there was a far less solid basis in usage in the Ionian islands for the written styles that had emerged at the end of the previous century in Constantinople. (There were, for example, no newspapers in the Ionian islands until 1850, and even the official government *Gazette* was published solely in Italian

---

[81] For examples see the documents of the period assembled by A. Dimaras (1974: vol. i).
[82] See respectively Katartzis 1970; Philippidis and Konstandas 1970; I.K. 1989. For the *Results of Love* see also Ch. 1.
[83] Fauriel 1824–5.

until 1831.) A counterbalance to the Phanariot precedents in written usage was provided in the Ionian islands by the legacy of the Italian Renaissance in Crete, where a literary vernacular, based on the local Greek dialect, had been cultivated to a high degree of sophistication between the fourteenth century and the fall of Crete to the Ottomans in the mid-seventeenth. As we saw in Chapter I, the language and sophisticated literary style of Cretan vernacular poetry, as well as of the folk-songs that had been published in the 1820s, were systematically studied by Solomos as the basis for a new 'national' poetry, and despite the delayed publication of so much of Solomos' work, these precedents had become firmly established among his successors in the Ionian islands by the mid-nineteenth century.[84] Significantly, it is almost exclusively in the Ionian islands that *prose* was published in demotic before the late nineteenth century.[85]

The principal exception to these trends in the Ionian islands can be seen in the poetry of Andreas Kalvos. Educated in Italy but largely self-taught, Kalvos was probably the only poet to try consciously to implement the linguistic programme of his fellow expatriate Korais. Kalvos' language is artificial in a way that the written styles of the Phanariots (however archaic) were not: the language of Kalvos' odes is unusually remote from either spoken or written usage, and therein lies the peculiar fascination that it has exercised for poets and critics of the twentieth century. In his own century, however, Kalvos had no successors either in his native Ionian islands or in Athens.

In Athens itself the trend towards ever-increasing 'purification' of the language and avoidance, in writing, of spoken usage begins probably no earlier than 1840 and reaches its peak in the 1850s and 1860s. Once again there is no evidence that the prescriptive

---

[84] The Cretan legacy is most obviously developed by Markoras, that of folk-poetry by Valaoritis.

[85] Both the spoken register of the educated élite of the islands, and the 'common tongue' are effectively exploited in Andonios Matesis' play *The Basil Plant* (written 1828–30, published 1859; Matesis 1973). In the mid-century Andreas Laskaratos' satires on Cefallonian life were published in demotic, as were the contributions to the 'Language Question' by Solomos, Manousos, and Konemenos. Spyridon Zambelios, on the other hand, wrote his scholarly treatises of the 1850s and his (unsuccessful) novel *Cretan Wedding* (1871) in *katharevousa*. Quantitatively there is much *less* literary prose produced in the Ionian islands than in Athens, and it may be that the absence of a style of written prose that could be used without self-consciousness in both a literary and a non-literary context was an additional factor contributing to the late appearance of prose fiction in these islands (see Ch. 1).

programmes over which Soutsos and Asopios quarrelled were the causes so much as the symptoms of this phenomenon. In 1842 Grigorios Palaiologos' second novel, *The Artist*, includes a scene in which the heroine's backwoods father appears in an Athenian drawing room, and the contrast between his untutored speech (given at length) and the prevailing etiquette has disastrous consequences in the plot.[86] Palaiologos writes in a language that closely reflects, so far as we can tell, the spoken dialect of the Constantinopolitan/ Athenian élite, with its conventional rather than systematic concessions to older written usage. That is to say, his language is the direct descendant of that used in the short stories of the 1790s and also, in its practical rather than theoretical aspects, even by Korais.

Thirteen years later, Pavlos Kalligas, in his novel *Thanos Vlekas* (1855), produced an action plot with a (romanticized) rustic hero. Not only are the narrative parts of his novel much more linguistically self-conscious, with copious imports from Ancient Greek morphology and syntax, but all the characters, regardless of their varied social backgrounds and places of origin, speak in a similar style, with only occasional and sometimes rather awkward concessions to the language of speech.[87] Nor, it seems, is this an accidental blemish. Kalligas was of the party of Panayotis Soutsos (whose *New School of the Written Word* had appeared two years earlier), as is clear from one of the novel's numerous digressions. Here a veteran pupil of the most conservative Phanariot circles at the turn of the century rails in picturesque terms against the monstrosity that results when the modern language is mixed with the ancient according to the compromise formula of Korais. According to this formidable character:

Κατ' εμέ κριτήν, ενός και μόνου έχομεν χρείαν, και άνευ αυτού ουδεμία προκοπή, να εννοώμεν τους αρχαίους.[88]

In my judgement, there is one thing and one thing only that we really need, and without that there can be no advancement: to understand the ancients.

It was in the same spirit that Soutsos himself, as we saw in Chapter 1, revised his early long poem *The Wayfarer* no fewer than

---

[86] Palaiologos 1989b: 176–81
[87] Note the elements of *katharevousa* (underlined) intermixed with spoken forms in the following sample of dialogue from the novel: Εγώ ως άνθρωπος, ο οποίος έφαγα τοσάκις ψωμί και άλας εις το σπήτι σας... (Kalligas 1991: 238).
[88] Kalligas 1991: 47.

three times, transforming its originally vernacular style so as to conform, not so much with his own or anyone else's prescriptive formula, but simply with the increasingly archaic usage of the time. A comparable, although from a literary point of view more interesting, progress can be discerned in the career of his prolific contemporary A. R. Rangavis, from romantic homage to folk-poetry in *Dimos and Eleni* (1831) to sophisticated play upon the conventions of neoclassicism in *The Voyage of Dionysos* (1864).

During the same decades, the annual poetry competitions held under the aegis of the University of Athens became something of a national event, attracting even contributions from the Ionian islands, and often generating heated controversy in the periodical press. The heavy hand of the university was often apparent in the published judgements of these competitions, although the adjudicators themselves were as likely to be poets as academics. In the same year that Soutsos and Asopios published their theoretical treatises, in 1853, 'purity' of language became established as one of the criteria for the prize, and by this was meant a high degree of piecemeal archaizing and imitation of ancient authors.

Most of the contributions in practice were written in a 'mixed' style, which was only to be expected at a time before the later polarization between demotic and *katharevousa* had become established.[89] The judges invariably commented on the language of the contributions, frequently awarding or withholding the prize on grounds more linguistic than, in today's terms, literary. (This happened most blatantly, and for the last time, in 1891 and 1892, when the judgements served to provoke the concerted demoticist backlash of Polylas and Roidis.) But the policy adopted (by different adjudicators) from year to year was neither uniform nor consistently intolerant of the spoken language. Even elements of demotic could be accepted, on the grounds that 'the popular language is necessary to comedy and lyric poetry until such time as the language of books is spoken in the family'. These were the words of no less a person that G. Mistriotis, in the judgement of the 1873 competition, some years before he became one of the most outspoken and inflammatory opponents of demoticism.[90]

Earlier, Rangavis, in his judgement of the competition of 1854, had put forward his own definition of poetic language, in which he

---

[89] On the language of poetry at this time see Gounelas 1980.
[90] Cited (in French translation) by Moullas (1989: 309).

adapted the terms used at the beginning of the century by Korais and Kodrikas to define language in general, and this definition holds good for much of the poetic practice of the mid-nineteenth century in Greece:

we consider language in poetry as the perceptible surface of the poetic work of art, as, so to speak, the external embodiment of innate poetry, as an instrument whose beauty so far contributes to the perfection of the poem as the melody of the voice contributes to the success of the song, as the choice of colours to the beauty of a picture.[91]

In prose, very little seems to have been written in demotic in Athens before the 1880s. The major exception, the *Memoirs* of General Makriyannis, written between 1829 and 1850, only serves to prove the rule. Makriyannis, who on his own admission taught himself to write at the age of 30 in order to record his experiences of the war of independence and his disillusion with the politics that followed, was posthumously (and especially in the 1930s and 1940s) revered as a founding father of demoticism along with Solomos. Although his work is factual rather than literary and his linguistic practice was dictated by need rather than choice, Makriyannis was *necessary* to the later demoticists precisely because there were no other precedents for demotic prose among the founding generation of the Greek state. It was the demoticist G. Vlachoyannis who first published Makriyannis' *Memoirs*, in 1907, when demoticism was at the height of its momentum.[92]

Although the *theoretical* furthest point of archaizing reform in Athens was marked, as we saw, by the publication of Kondos' *Observations* in 1882, in practice the tide had already begun to turn

---

[91] θεωρούμεν την γλώσσαν εν τη ποιήσει ως του ποιητικού καλλιτεχνήματος την αισθητήν έκφρασιν, ως της ενδιαθέτου ποιήσεως [cf. the use of the term ενδιάθετος in the extracts from Korais and Kodrikas cited above] την εξωτερικήν ούτως ειπείν ενσωμάτωσιν, ως όργανον [again, this recalls the terms of the same two passages], ού το κάλλος τοσούτον συμβάλλεται εις του ποιήματος την εντέλειαν, όσον η μελωδία της φωνής συντελεί εις την επιτυχίαν του άσματος, όσον η εκλογή των χρωμάτων εις της εικόνος το κάλλος (Rangavis in the periodical *Pandora*, 4 (1854–5), 30).

[92] Even Makriyannis, self-taught as he was, could hardly escape the conventions of written usage altogether. For a discussion of the place of 'learned' terms and ideas in the *Memoirs* see Holton 1984–5. On Makriyannis' high reputation in the 1930s see e.g. Tziovas 1989a: 40–2; for a critique of his 'sanctification' in the 1930s and 1940s see Gourgouris 1996: 175–200. Makriyannis is also one of only two Greek writers since the 16th century whose work has been the subject of a published computer concordance (Kyriazidis *et al.* 1983).

during the previous decade. In prose fiction the 'high baroqve' of Roidis' *Pope Joan* marked the furthest point of development in that direction, and thereafter the language of fiction begins to put increasing emphasis on the neglected communicative function of language. In prose, this shift is evident in the anonymous *Military Life in Greece* (1870–1) and *Loukis Laras* by Dimitrios Vikelas (1879), relatively factual narratives aimed at a less rarefied readership. At the same time, the poetic experiments of the early 1880s increasingly turn away from *katharevousa* altogether, although this trend continues to find its theoretical justification largely in the appeal to the tradition of oral folk-poetry.

Even before the publication of Psycharis' *Journey*, the language of prose fiction had already jettisoned much of the archaic baggage with which it had been progressively encumbered in the middle years of the century. In the wake of Psycharis' book, some writers, such as Karkavitsas and Xenopoulos, who had previously published in *katharevousa*, turned to demotic. Others, such as Eftaliotis, whose first short story was published in *Estia* in 1889, wrote in demotic from the beginning.[93] Older writers, notably Roidis and Papadiamandis, continued to write as they had done previously. The full range of the written language available to an able writer in the 1890s, as it had not been earlier in the century and would not be again for more than fifty years, can be illustrated by two extracts from a short story by Papadiamandis of 1891.

A description of an allotment-garden is expressly predicated on the double simile in the *Iliad* which sets side by side the waves of the sea and the effects of a wind in a cornfield. The passage from Homer is then quoted in the original, although its content is also paraphrased. The description continues in a lush rhetorical style, appropriate to the subject-matter, and including a high proportion of complex syntax and rare words derived from the ancient language:

Και αύρα ποντιάς εθώπευε μαλθακώς την άσπιλον κυματίζουσαν οθόνην προκαλούσα απείρους χαριέσσας μυρμηκιζούσας, παροδικάς ρυτίδας, ως επί του μετώπου νύμφης βασιλίδος περικαλλούς, επιδεικνυούσης παιδικόν θυμόν και πείσμα, διάλειμμα μεταξύ δύο μειδιαμάτων προκλητικόν, εις το βάθος του οποίου ο βυθός δεν φαίνεται πλέον, και η επιφάνεια παύει ανταυγάζουσα την άπειρον της κτίσεως φαιδρότητα.[94]

---

[93] Interestingly, the editorial columns of *Estia* at this time confined themselves to supporting the cause of demotic in *poetry* (Papakostas 1982: 53–6).
[94] Papadiamandis 1981–8: ii. 154. The Homeric simile occurs at *Iliad* ii. 144–9.

And a sea-breeze would gently caress the immaculate undulating screen [of growing plants], instigating an infinite number of delightful, rippling, fleeting dimples, like those that might appear upon the radiant brow of a royal bride displaying, in the provocative interval between two smiles, the obstinate temper of a child, which while it lasts obscures the depth of the furrow, while the surface ceases to reflect the infinite brightness of creation.

Here the richness of the rhetoric, aided rather than hindered by the obscurity of the syntax, draws on a tradition stretching back to late antiquity. A particular linguistic and stylistic resource, inherent in the older written traditions of the language, is here harnessed for a literary purpose. But Papadiamandis is sparing in his use of such pyrotechnics, which he reserves strictly for descriptive passages. The narrative parts of this story, as is normal with this writer, are couched in the matter-of-fact, 'simple' *katharevousa* also used by Vikelas and Vizyinos among others, and which seems at this time to have been the normal idiom for unadorned written communication. This language, however, is interspersed here and there with demotic words and phrases, typographically marked off, and alternates with dialogue in which characters speak either in demotic or, depending on context and the effect to be achieved, in the dialect of Papadiamandis' native Skiathos:

Ο μικρός, όστις είχεν ιδεί κατά το προλαβόν θέρως κολυμβητάς πηδώντας αφ' ύψους του βράχου τούτου, εξετέλει μιμικήν, ότι τάχα ήθελε να *δώση βουτιά* από τον Μύτικα, ως κάμνουσιν οι έφηβοι και οι ακμαίοι νε ανί σκοι.

...Η μήτηρ οργισθείσα ανέτεινε τον κόπανόν της, δι' ού έτυπτε τα λευκαινόμενα ράκη προς το μέρος του βράχου και τον επέσειεν απειλητικώς προς τον παίδα : "'Εννοια σ', αρέ σκάνταλε, έννοια σ', χάρε μαύρε! Το βράδ', σα 'ρθή ο πατέρας σ' απ' το χωράφ', δώσε λόγο".[95]

The child, who the summer before had seen divers leaping from the top of this rock, executed a mime as though he were about to *take the plunge* [demotic expression; author's emphasis] from [the rock called] Mytika, like the youths and young men in their prime.
...Its mother was furious and held out the stick with which she was beating the bleaching rags and shook it threateningly in the child's direction: 'Just you watch out, you little stinker, just watch it, you'll be the death of me! You just wait till your father gets in from the field' [this in demotic, with some phonetic representation of the local dialect].

With its Homeric quotation and descriptive elaboration on it, in a style which recalls late Hellenistic and Byzantine rhetoric, framed by

[95] Papadiamandis 1981–8: ii. 163.

an unadorned narrative style in *katharevousa* that in its turn alternates with demotic and dialect in the speech of the characters, this
story almost provocatively seeks to reclaim the entire history of the
Greek language up to Papadiamandis' own day. But the linguistic
effects achieved here (and indeed throughout Papadiamandis' stories from 1887 onwards) are far from being either 'museum pieces' of
the past or yoked into some prescriptive programme for the language in future. At the end of the nineteenth century it was possible
to exploit the wide range of linguistic diversity that existed within the
language for literary effects which are neither repeatable nor (inevitably) fully translatable.

If one considers the history of written, and particularly of literary,
Greek in the nineteenth century, from Korais and Solomos to
Papadiamandis, the conventional term 'diglossia' seems more than
ever an unlikely straitjacket. What we see instead is a range of
linguistic styles, mostly determined by precedent rather than by
precept, which coexisted rather than competed, and which afforded
a considerable range of choice to the individual writer. Although
there undoubtedly were constraints on the exercise of that choice,
particularly in the middle decades of the century, linguistic style can
be correlated to some extent with both subject-matter and intended
readership. Diglossia, in practice as well as in theory, begins with the
advent of *demoticism* as opposed to *demotic*; and this development,
whether seen as the backswing of a pendulum against the excesses of
mid-nineteenth-century Athens, or as the result of the reformist
programme of Psycharis and his supporters, had the effect of *redu-
cing* the range of linguistic styles available to writers within a given
context.

The symptoms of diglossia in this sense become apparent in the
work of those writers of the first half of the twentieth century who
also had professional careers. Palamas, from 1897 to 1928, held,
sometimes precariously, the post of Secretary to the University of
Athens, and assiduously composed official minutes in *katharevousa*
by day while writing poetry and criticism in demotic by night.[96] No
trace of the Secretary to the University is detectable in Palamas'
literary writing. Forty-one years his junior, Yorgos Seferiadis was
obliged to use *katharevousa* throughout a highly successful diplomatic career from 1926 to 1962, and at the same time, under the

[96] See the letter of 1901 cited by Fletcher 1984: 76.

name of Seferis, wrote the poetry and essays, in demotic, that would win him the Nobel Prize for Literature in 1963. Although Seferis' demoticism was more professed than rigorously applied in his poetry, there is again no trace, in his literary writings, of the language of Seferiadis the diplomat.

But even during the half-century or so when diglossia prevailed in the written language, not all writers of literature were content to remain behind the demoticist barricades. The most striking exception, in this as in so much else, was Cavafy, with his cosmopolitan Alexandrian background. At a distance from the tumult of Athens in the first years of the century, Cavafy significantly modified the linguistic style of his poetry at about the same time as his Athenian contemporaries, but in a way that was markedly different from theirs. Cavafy's first poems, of the early 1880s, are written in English, French, and the *katharevousa* of Athenian verse of the mid-century. By 1900 he had dropped the elaborate archaisms of the Greek poetry he had grown up with, and had begun to develop the seemingly informal, conversational style for which he has been admired ever since. But the linguistic basis of this style is not demotic, as the term was understood in Greece at the time. Cavafy's language is, *mutatis mutandis*, the mixed language of the 'Phanariot' poetry of the previous two generations in Athens, with its roots in the educated dialect of Constantinople and the Danubian principalities a century before. That is to say, his language is based on the spoken style of an educated urban class that was insulated from rural speech and influenced instead by the written style of daily commerce.[97]

The result is that Cavafy's language does not seem to have impinged on readers, at least after the 1940s, as '*katharevousa*'; on the other hand, by not renouncing its links with the morphology and syntax of older written usage, it is able to exploit for particular effects the full diachronic range of Greek as it had been written and spoken throughout the long history that is also the subject-matter of many of Cavafy's poems. In this Cavafy's language is comparable to that of

[97] Cavafy was publicly reticent on the 'Language Question', although scattered hints of his views after 1900 can be found in book reviews. His clearest overt comment comes in a long review of the second edition of H. Pernot, *Grammaire du Grec Moderne* (1917) commissioned and written the following year but only published posthumously in 1955 (Cavafy 1963: 195–234). I. Sareyannis records the poet's disgust at both sides of the debate, each of which, he declared, was determined to 'throw half our language away' (Sareyannis 1964: 42).

Papadiamandis, although the solutions favoured by the two writers differ greatly in practice. Cavafy is adept at annulling the boundaries between the conversational style of his own place and time and the Greek of (especially) the Hellenistic diaspora of two thousand years before. The poem 'Caesarion', about the son of Cleopatra murdered by Octavian as part of the progress that would establish him as the first emperor of Rome, ends with the word, meaning 'too many Caesars', that had been reported by Plutarch in the first century AD, and is itself a knowing pun on a rare word in Homer. It is part of Cavafy's achievement to provide a context in which this item of linguistic archaeology can be perfectly comprehensible to a modern reader.

The archaeological metaphor is even more appropriate to those poems by Cavafy which deal with tombs and inscriptions, usually commemorating beautiful youths. The most famous of these, 'In the Month of Athyr', enacts the reconstruction of a damaged inscription in the ancient language, in such a way as to convey both the remoteness in time of the young man commemorated and the precarious power of language to convey meaning across such a gap of time. Using a similar device, in one of his posthumously published poems, Cavafy draws on a very different historical manifestation of the Greek language: the dialect of Trebizond. 'Has Fallen' describes the poet's thoughts on reading the laments for the fall of Constantinople in 1453 composed in this dialect, and depends for its effect on the juxtaposition of the poet's own language and the quotations from the folk-song worked into his text.[98]

Another poet, who in his lifetime was often bracketed with Cavafy and, like him, strayed deliberately across the no man's land which now marked off demotic from *katharevousa*, was Karyotakis. A generation younger than Cavafy, Karyotakis served his poetic apprenticeship in Athens, in the (demoticist) circle of the periodical *Noumas*. Like Cavafy, Karyotakis exploits the nuances inherent in adopting elements of the formal, now official linguistic style in a poem, to achieve a real precision in his use of language which simultaneously mocks the pompous and bureaucratic connotations that this kind of language had already acquired.[99] It is likely that both

[98] Καισαρίων (Cavafy 1991: i. 73–4); cf. Ricks 1989: 115–16. Εν τω μηνί Αθύρ (Cavafy 1991: i. 82); Πάρθεν (Cavafy 1993: 108).

[99] On Karyotakis' language see Peri 1972; Hokwerda 1980.

poets drew on their backgrounds and training as relatively lowly civil servants (Cavafy in British-ruled Egypt working in the medium of English; Karyotakis, in the Athenian and provincial bureaucracy, working in the strictly formal Greek of the 1911 Constitution). But Cavafy started out from the *katharevousa* tradition in poetry and sought inclusiveness through allusion to different phases and styles of the Greek language; Karyotakis by contrast moved out from the demoticist camp increasingly to incorporate the language of his official self into his poetry. But Karyotakis only does so in order to pour scorn on the pettiness both of bureaucracy and of a poetry whose corruptibility is demonstrated by this very language. Karyotakis' transgression of the bounds of demotic appears as yet another symptom of the failure of poetry and poetic ideals before the petty triviality of modern life, which is a dominant theme in his work.

With these partial exceptions, demotic came to be accepted as the normal medium for poetry and prose fiction, as also for the theatre, during the last decade of the nineteenth century and the first decade of the twentieth. In theory, this remains the case today, and indeed the slow victory of demoticism is an underlying theme of most post-war histories of Modern Greek literature and of the 'Language Question'.[100] But what such accounts often obscure is the fact that the range of meaning of the term 'demotic' has changed progressively since the time of Psycharis. The strict adherents to the principles and practice of *My Journey*, in the literary sphere, were few, although they included the Marxist poet Kostas Varnalis and the Kazantzakis of the *Odyssey* (1938).[101] The last-named work, deliberately designed to be a repository of the spoken Greek language in all its diversity, also had the effect of demonstrating that demotic, no less than *katharevousa*, if taken to its logical conclusion risked becoming incomprehensible to educated readers: Kazantzakis soon found it necessary to publish a separate glossary of about 2,000 words that he had used in his poem.[102]

But more influential than the rigorous, if elusive, standardization of demotic by Psycharis was the practice of Palamas in poetry, and of

[100] On histories of literature see the Introduction. It is notable that one of the most comprehensive accounts of the linguistic debate in the 20th century (Moschonas 1975: οθ΄) refers to the linguistic practice of the Surrealists, on which see below, as a 'revolt' (ανταρσία).

[101] To these should be added the short-story writer and historian Argyris Eftaliotis (1849–1923) and the translator and essayist Alexandros Pallis (1851–1935).

[102] See Bien 1972: 210–20.

Xenopoulos in prose. Palamas' authority, both as poet and critic, had become firmly established on the Athenian literary scene by 1910. No less staunch a supporter of demotic than Psycharis, Palamas had by this time quarrelled with Psycharis' theory and diverged very considerably from him in practice. Where Psycharis was notoriously insensitive to the claims of existing usage, proposing in effect a clean sweep of the spoken as well as the written language to make it conform to his principles, Palamas was attentive to the literary precedents available to a writer, and particularly to a poet, committed to demotic. To this end he did much to rehabilitate the nineteenth-century poets of the Ionian islands, and chief among them Solomos, as well as even earlier models. Of these, the Cretan romance *Erotokritos* and folk-song had already been available to Solomos; Palamas was the first poet of stature to extend the perspective back even further, to draw on the recently rediscovered narrative poems in the Byzantine vernacular that had been written between the twelfth and the sixteenth centuries. Xenopoulos, although the language of his fiction, after he turned to demotic during the 1890s, and its later influence have been less studied, plays a parallel role to Palamas in prose. Xenopoulos did not, of course, have such distant precedents on which to draw for vernacular prose, but as a native of the Ionian islands he did have immediate access to the tradition of prose in demotic written and published in the islands during the nineteenth century.

By the 1930s, although the theoretical battle lines had hardly been redrawn at all, the literary language was already beginning to change. At the turn of the decade, those writers of fiction who set out to represent recent events in all their shocking vividness were the most rigorous in their use of an oral, and particularly rural, idiom as the basis of their writing. Doukas, Venezis, and especially Myrivilis bring to its logical conclusion a linguistic trajectory that had been launched, as far back as 1896, by Karkavitsas in his novel *The Beggar*. Far beyond merely calling a spade a spade, Karkavitsas, and the writers who later chronicled the First World War and the Asia Minor catastrophe, delve deep into the vocabulary and expressive resources of the rural population, in order to imbue narrated experience with immediacy and even horror.[103]

But by this time the pendulum was already beginning, silently, to swing in the opposite direction. All three of these novelists of the

---

[103] See in particular the chapter by Vitti entitled, Τα όρια της δημοτικιστικής εκζήτησης: Η ζωή εν τάφω (Vitti 1979: 257–67).

342 LITERATURE AND LANGUAGE

early 1930s returned to their work during the next twenty years and in successive editions modified the language of their texts (just as Soutsos had done exactly a century before) to bring it closer to the slowly emerging standard. Most of the poets and writers of fiction who peopled the 'generation of the thirties', which was the subject of Chapter 3, professed adherence to the demoticist cause, but actually allowed some degree of compromise, both with what must be assumed to have been the spoken usage of educated circles at the time, and even with older, non-demotic, written forms of the language.[104]

The most striking exceptions to this broad, and mostly silent, consensus were the Surrealists Embirikos and Engonopoulos. The following passage from Embirikos' *Blast-Furnace* was shocking, when it appeared in 1935, not only in its near unintelligibility, but at least as much for the abrupt juxtaposition of linguistic styles that were considered incompatible. In the following passage, elements of *katharevousa*, not conventionally acceptable in poetry at this time, are underlined:

Ενωρίτερα κι' απ' την αυριανή της <u>συνουσία</u> η <u>δεινοπαθήσασα</u> αιχμή της τελευταίας οροσειράς χαμήλωσε τα βλέφαρα για να δεχτή τα δώρα των <u>αυτομάτων</u> περιστρόφων. Τριάντα μέλη της ερμαφρόδιτης συνομιλίας <u>κατέσχον</u> την ανεπανόρθωτον δενδροστοιχία<u>ν εν</u> <u>χορδαίς και οργάνοις</u> ενώ τα νυμφοπάζαρα έβριθαν με αστακούς κυρίως και με κομψές λεμονάδες του κουτιού....[105]

Previous to her sexual intercourse of the next day, the tip of the last mountain range, having become a serious case, had lowered her eyelids to receive the gifts of the automatic revolvers. Thirty members of the hermaphrodite *conversazione* were occupying the irreparable avenue of trees with stringed instruments and organs [see Psalm 150, v. 4] while the arranged marriages were bristling with lobsters, mainly, and with elegant lemonades done up to a tee....

By mixing elements of *katharevousa* and demotic, of accepted poetic diction with journalese and the language of officialdom, the Surrealists targeted the conventions of diglossia by flagrantly violating them. This practice of juxtaposing linguistic styles conventionally seen as separate is clearly part of the Surrealist programme of

---

[104] Documented by Vitti 1979. For an illustration of Seferis' practice in the 1930s see Beaton 1991: 16–20.
[105] Το Καλώς 'Ηλθατε των πραματευτάδων (Embirikos 1980a: 23).

challenging all artificial and rational constraints on the free operation of the unconscious. There is probably no aspect of Greek Surrealism in the 1930s, and its numerous offshoots in the postwar period, that has been more discussed than its stance on the Greek language. Engonopoulos, in the preface to the second edition of his pre-war poems, in 1966, replied to his critics in these terms:

I have to say, very simply, that this is the language I speak. In any case, isn't it the most important thing for someone to make himself understood by those who really want to understand him? The legitimate language, for us, is the Greek language. All these fanatical opinions about 'mixed', 'katharevousa', 'demotic', are absolutely meaningless. They must be treated with absolute indifference or, if we think it advisable, with the only permissible fanaticism: that which inspires us to make war on every kind of fanaticism.[106]

Engonopoulos goes on to identify Papadiamandis and Cavafy as exemplary precedents for breaking down these barriers and regaining access to the full range of the Greek language.[107]

The Surrealists, of course, were more concerned to shock through their often violent juxtapositions of linguistic styles, than to lay the basis for pragmatic compromise between the rival forms of the written language. On the other hand, a change is detectable even in the later writings of Embirikos and Engonopoulos, and this change is more evident still in the large amount of poetry, and some prose, of the immediate post-war period that admits a debt to Greek Surrealism. In much of the post-war work of Embirikos the linguistic basis seems no longer to be the demotic of the 1930s (on to which elements of katharevousa may be violently grafted), but the 'simple' katharevousa of the late nineteenth century, in which the very instability of the linguistic medium becomes a source of delight rather than embarrassment. In any case the unassimilated juxtaposition of styles seems to have been replaced in the later work of the Surrealists by a highly individual, composite style.

---

[106] Πρέπει να πω πως είναι απλούστατα η γλώσσα που μιλώ. Άλλωστε πρωτεύουσα σημασία δεν έχει το να γίνεται κανείς αντιληπτός από κείνους που επιθυμούν, πραγματικά, να τον καταλάβουν; Νόμιμη γλώσσα, για μας, είναι η γλώσσα η ελληνική. Δεν έχουν κανένα νόημα απολύτως αυτές οι γνώμες οι φανατικές για "μικτή", "καθαρεύουσα", "δημοτική". Πρέπει ν' αντιμετωπίζονται με απόλυτη αδιαφορία ή, αν το θεωρούμε σκόπιμο, μ' αυτόν τον μόνον επιτρεπόμενο φανατισμό: εκείνον που εμπνέει τον πόλεμο εναντίον κάθε είδους φανατισμού (Engonopoulos 1977: i. 154). Cf. the (negative) comments of Moschonas (1975: οθ').

[107] Engonopoulos 1977: i. 155.

In poetry up to the 1960s such a composite style tends to be the hallmark of those writers whose work was described in Chapter 4 as 'hermetic', and who also owe a thematic debt to the Surrealists, while by contrast the 'social' poets tend to stick more closely to the language of speech, associated then as earlier with unmediated experience, as well as with the left-wing affiliation of many of them. But even this is an over-simplification, since the progressive rediscovery of Cavafy by poets, especially of the latter group, injects a strong element of conscious linguistic play and artifice into the 'social' poetry of, particularly, the 1960s.

In fiction too there is a generally discernible move during the same period away from the monolithic use of demotic. In the post-war period pompous characters are likely to use elements of *katharevousa* in their speech, and the language of newspapers and officialdom may be quoted or even parodied. Although these developments were undoubtedly gradual, their effects became spectacularly visible, and much discussed, in a single novel of the early 1960s: *The Third Wedding* by Kostas Tachtsis.[108] The language of this book has been more discussed than any other aspect of it, and in the context of this discussion it is interesting to set *The Third Wedding*, as a comic masterpiece, alongside nineteenth-century achievements in comedy which had taken the 'Language Question' as their butt. In *Korakistika* and *Babel*, humour had been derived from the inappropriate use of *written* style in an oral context. Tachtsis turned this comic equation on its head, to produce a supposedly oral narrative (two middle-class women telling their stories) in which the speech and the narrative mannerisms of the women are steeped in clichés that have filtered through from the official, written language to become an inseparable part of their everyday vocabulary. The point of the joke, in so far as it is a linguistic one, is that these elements of the women's speech, far from being an incongruous imposition, are an essential part both of the world that they perceive and of their highly vivacious, oral response to it. Tachtsis, according to a leading academic critic from the demoticist camp, 'freed the Greek language from the tyranny of demotic'.[109] His novel certainly provided persuasive evidence that real life could not be bound by the

[108] Tachtsis 1974a. On this novel see also Ch. 4.
[109] G. P. Savvidis, cited by Kazazis (1979: 18).

artificial categories of diglossia, as well as a demonstration that narrative fiction need not be either.

The acceptance of 'demotic' as the officially sanctioned language of education, and increasingly, throughout the later 1970s and 1980s, of all state functions, may now be seen more clearly, not as a simple 'victory' for the demoticist movement, but as a recognition of the written, and particularly the literary, usage that had evolved by the time that the Colonels seized power in 1967. With the official abolition of diglossia (that is, of formally recognized, competing *written* styles) many writers have simply followed and extended the path that began hesitantly in the 1930s, gained momentum after the war, and became clearly established in the 1960s: towards recognizing and exploiting the widest possible range of available linguistic styles in their writing. The rural demotic of older 'testimonies' continues to be available to writers, such as Thanasis Valtinos in the 1960s and Chronis Missios in the 1980s, whose work appeals to the immediacy associated with the oral tradition. At the other extreme, we find the *katharevousa* of the late nineteenth century used as the basis (although not as the only linguistic style) of Embirikos' posthumous novel of the 1950s and 1960s, published in the early 1990s, *The Great Eastern*. In between we find a rich diversity of linguistic styles, which writers seem increasingly confident in handling to achieve particular effects. The most recent volume of poetry by Jenny Mastoraki, for example, was praised on its appearance for its rich pickings from older, traditional forms of the language: one reviewer listed just over a hundred non-standard, and mostly historically attested, words in a collection of sixty pages.[110] At the opposite extreme, but surely no less legitimate, is the modern macaronism of this boardroom dialogue from a novel by Philippos Drakondaidis, published in 1984:

——'Έλεγα λοιπόν πως everything is related to the market development.

——Τότε πρέπει να σκεφτούμε το positionning [*sic*] των προιόντων.

——Μη λέμε βλακείες, Ανάργυρε. Το positionning αφορά τον καταναλωτή, εμείς έχουμε προβλήματα πολιτική προς το εμπόριο.

——Στο μεταξύ, οι πωλήσεις πέφτουν. Στα γάλατα έχουμε μείωση κατά 32,2% σε σχέση με τον περσινό Οκτώβριο. Τα τυράκια βρίσκονται 15,73% πίσω σε σχέση με τα forecasts!

---

[110] See Mastoraki 1989 and the review by Savvidis (1989).

——It's incredible!

——Τι να κάνουμε;[111]

'As I was saying, *everything is related to the market development.*'

'Then we've got to think about the *positionning* [*sic*] of the products.'

'Don't let's fool ourselves, Anargyros. The *positionning's* a matter for the consumer, we've got policy problems on the market side.'

'Meantime, sales are falling. Milk is down 32.2% on last October. Cheese is 15.73% behind in relation to the *forecasts!*'

'*It's incredible!*'

'What are we to do?'

For all the unease and uncertainty that this highly varied practice arouses among those who have the unenviable task of devising school curricula and textbooks, this situation surely testifies to the enormous resources potentially available to the writer in Greek, as well as to the vigour and imagination of many of those who draw upon them. From the *Babel* of the 1830s, (written) Greek has evolved towards the polyphony of the 1980s and 1990s. Or, to put it another way, despite the vicissitudes of the theoretical debate and the slow swings of practical usage from one extreme to the other and back to the middle again, the Greek language has lost none of the diversity it had at the beginning of the nineteenth century;[112] what has changed is the attitude of writers and readers to the linguistic resources that they share. And, of course, the number and kind of the available precedents have grown immeasurably.

BEYOND THE 'LANGUAGE QUESTION': WORDS AND THINGS

To discuss the language in which one speaks and writes, and particularly with the vehemence that this has been done in Greece for so long, implies a set of beliefs or attitudes about the nature and function of language itself. And here the overt debate about the Greek language is tantalizingly unhelpful: although current and older theories drawn from the philosophy of language are widely invoked, nowhere in the debate is a distinctive theory of language developed and articulated in support of a particular view on the more immediate issue. There is not even a very consistent adherence by individuals or like-minded groups to any one underlying

[111] Drakondaidis 1984: 155.

[112] For a variety of socio-linguistic approaches to the current diversity of the spoken language, see the essays edited by Joseph (1992).

philosophy of language. The confused eclecticism of the demoticists in the late nineteenth and early twentieth centuries has been well demonstrated;[113] but the same concepts, and the same eclecticism in their use, also underlie the statements of their opponents. Even the distinction between a neoclassical concept of language as the external clothing for ideas, and a Romantic identification between language and the 'spontaneous overflow of powerful feelings', cannot be made to stick convincingly to the respective sides of the debate.[114]

The explanation for the 'Language Question' as a phenomenon is at one level, of course, a practical one. There has been a need to establish an agreed standard for a written language, and since the early nineteenth century this need has been inextricably linked with the demands of national self-identity. But neither of these factors is peculiar to Greece, while the intensity, volume, and centrality of the debate in public life are hard to match elsewhere in Europe. What implicit, and perhaps more fundamental, attitude to language itself can we extrapolate from the existence, and from the conduct, of the debate? What corroboration or extension of these findings can be found elsewhere in Greek culture? And how do these in turn reflect upon literary texts?

Language as Object in the Linguistic Debate. One way to approach this question is by way of the characteristic metaphors for language used by participants in the debate.[115] Two fairly conventional instances have already been cited: language, according to both Korais and Kodrikas, is a 'tool' or 'instrument'. These are examples

[113] See Tziovas 1986, esp. 86–149. Although the overlap with the opposing camp is also documented to some extent by Tziovas, there is as yet no comparably systematic study of the theoretical basis underlying support for *katharevousa* at this period.

[114] C.-D. Gounelas has made a useful start in identifying the philosophical assumptions of earlier participants in the debate (1991), but the distinction that he draws is not in fact clear-cut: 'Polylas and Solomos have their philosophical basis in particular aspects of the philosophy of Hegel. . . . P. Soutsos in parallel has adopted the line of the Port-Royalistes, seeing language as the clothing of thought' (352–3); cf. Gounelas 1995: 151–3. But there is evidence that Solomos, too, thought of language, or at any rate of poetic language, as a form of 'clothing' (implicit in his practice of writing his early drafts of Greek poems in Italian *prose*), while it was Soutsos who declared: 'Let your language be as clear and transparent as translucent springs' (Η γλώσσα υμών έστω καθαρά και διαυγής ως τα διαφανή νάματα..., Panayotopoulos *et al.* 1956: 55).

[115] The conspicuous place of metaphor in the debate had been noticed, as early as 1890, by G. Hatzidakis (1901: 297).

of a tendency, that has been better documented in the opposing demoticist camp, to treat language as an object.[116] Other more colourful metaphors, from both sides in the debate, confirm this same trend. Korais frequently refers to the modern spoken language as the 'mother tongue' of his fellow countrymen, but this language in turn has a 'mother': Ancient Greek.[117] Elsewhere Korais describes the modern language as the '*daughter and heir* of the old and immeasurably rich [Ancient] Greek language', and the metaphor becomes further complicated in a curious statement from late in his life, in which the close bond between language and country is also implicit. So dispirited had he been in his youth at the backward influence of the Turks upon his countrymen, Korais tells us, that he had even been prepared 'to deny my *fatherland*, which I now saw more as a *stepmother* than as a *mother*' (my emphases).[118] The confusion raised by the metaphor of the two mothers, or the mother and the stepmother, is indicative of the central contradiction that Korais' proposals for reform never really resolved, between allegiance to the 'language imbibed with one's mother's milk' and allegiance to 'Mother [Ancient] Greece' with her ancient, 'mother' language.

This kind of metaphorical iconography of language reaches its peak in the nineteenth century in the extended similes of the demoticist Konemenos:

The ancient language is like a great lady, hugely rich and elegantly refined and tall in stature; you can see how beautiful she must have been in her time, but for us today she is a wrinkled old woman. The modern [spoken] language is a humble little girl of the people who hasn't yet grown to her full stature and who needs only a simple change of clothes and a wash for her appealing charms to become apparent.[119]

---

[116] Tziovas 1986: see esp. 108, 110, 113, 129.

[117] Korais 1964: A853.

[118] See respectively Ἄτακτα Α΄ (Korais 1964: A1266) and Βίος Ἀδαμαντίου Κοραῆ, συγγραφείς παρά του ιδίου, 1833 (Korais 1964: Aliii–10).

[119] Η αρχαία γλώσσα είναι σα μια μεγάλη αρχόντισσα, πλουσιώτατα και κομψότατα ευτρεπισμένη και ψηλού αναστήματος δείχνει 'πως να εστάθηκε στον καιρό της ωραία, αλλά για 'μας σήμερα είναι γρηα κ' είναι ζαρωμένη. Η νέα γλώσσα είναι μια ταπεινή παιδούλα του λαού 'πού δεν απόχτησε ακόμα όλο της το ανάστημα κι' οπού έχει χρεία μόνον από ένα απλό άλλασμα κι'από ένα νίψιμο για να φανούν η χάραις και νοστιμάδαις της (Konemenos 1873: 5). A similar comparison had earlier been drawn by Vilaras, in a letter to Psalidas of 1812, although it seems unlikely that Konemenos, admirer of Vilaras though he was, could have known this letter which was first published in 1905 (see Vilaras et al. 1981: 148–9).

In many of the metaphors from this time on, language is seen not only as an object but as a particular kind of object: a living organism.[120] By the end of the nineteenth century the organic metaphor was commonly being invoked by the demoticists. Solomos' comparison of a poem to a plant, dating from even earlier, was influentially taken up and repeated by Seferis a century later.[121] Once again, however, the demoticists do not have a monopoly of this kind of metaphor: Konemenos (a demoticist) unsurprisingly, in addition to the metaphors quoted above, described language as a 'living body'; but from the other side in the debate Vernardakis in 1884 elaborated a complicated metaphor of the spoken language as an overgrown tree in need of careful pruning.[122] So pervasive were such metaphors among twentieth-century demoticists that Greece's military rulers between 1967 and 1974, in the curious pamphlet designed to put the clock back by almost a century, insisted that language is not, after all, an organism but, as the eighteenth-century Enlightenment had had it, a set of clothes.[123]

The complaint of Yanidis, writing in 1908, against the supporters of *katharevousa* applies equally well to almost all the participants in the debate: 'instead of revering literature, we've learnt to bow down before language.'[124] Only Katartzis and Vilaras, early and radical supporters of the spoken language as the basis for writing, use a different kind of metaphor altogether, according to which language is not a thing (whether the product of culture or nature) but a process: both compare the acquisition of linguistic competence to learning to play music.[125] These exceptions are the more striking for their rarity (and both pre-date Greek independence). Throughout the history of the Greek state, the overwhelming tendency in the debate about the language has been to treat language as an object. Tellingly, and frequently, language is described as a *possession*. An invariable preoccupation throughout the debate is the concomitant fear that this prized possession may be either destroyed or taken away.

[120] See Tziovas 1985.
[121] Seferis 1981: i. 121, ii. 173.
[122] Konemenos 1873: 8; Vernardakis 1884: 3.
[123] Armed Forces HQ 1973: 11–12.
[124] Αντί να λατρέψουμε τη φιλολογία, εμάθαμε να προσκυνούμε τη γλώσσα... (Yanidis 1969: 19).
[125] Katartzis 1970: 22–3; Vilaras *et al.* 1981: 128–30 (from the preface to *The Romaic Tongue*).

Language, declared Korais, is the 'common and popular *possession* of all who share a common tongue' (my emphasis);[126] Solomos' 'Dialogue' of 1824 ends with the furious complaint:

our people are shedding their blood under the [banner of] the Cross to set us free, while this man and those like him [an allusion to the supporters of Korais] are fighting as mercenaries *to take away from us our language* [my emphasis].[127]

Almost identical fears can be seen to have motivated the passions on both sides of the debate in the first years of the twentieth century. During the Second World War, in the 'Trial of the Accents', the perceived threat was of an enforced replacement of the orthographic system. In the 1980s the crusade launched by the Greek Language Society, and indeed much that has been written about the language since the late 1970s, was informed by a similar rhetoric. Among many examples of this is the denunciation, by the editor of an economics magazine, of the linguistic practice of a newspaper in which an article of his had appeared in 1984:

I consider *extremely dangerous for the future of our people* the debasement of the Greek language in recent years, and would not wish to be included among those who participate in what is, in my opinion, *a national crime* [my emphases].[128]

Language, in the dominant terms of the linguistic debate in Greece, is, then, a thing rather than a process, and moreover a thing with talismanic properties. Possession of it is a prerequisite for the survival and prosperity of the nation (a view shared most obviously by Korais and Psycharis, but which also underlies most of the overt debate); conversely, as a thing, it is subject to the risks of damage and loss. Such a view of language is not, of course, confined to Greek culture nor, as we saw, are all Greek views on language reducible to it. But the debate itself can now be interpreted as a

---

[126] η γλώσσα είναι κοινόν και δημοτικόν όλων των ομογλώσσων κτήμα (᾽Ατακτα Β᾽, Korais 1964: Α1254).

[127] οι δικοί μας χύνουν το αίμα τους αποκάτου από το Σταυρό για να μας κάμουν ελεύθερους, και τούτος και όσοι του ομοιάζουν πολεμούν γι᾽ ανταμοιβή να τους σηκώσουν τη γλώσσα (Solomos 1986: ii. 27).

[128] θεωρώντας πολύ επικίνδυνο για το μέλλον του λαού μας τον κατήφορο που πήρε η ελληνική γλώσσα τα τελευταία χρόνια, δεν θα ήθελα να περιληφθώ ανάμεσα σ᾽ εκείνους που συμμετέχουν σ᾽ αυτό το, κατά τη γνώμη μου, εθνικό έγκλημα, quoted by G. M. Kalioris, among a number of such denunciations, in Dimosios Dialogos 1988: 40.

symptom of what is often called a 'reification' or 'objectivization' of language, developed to an unusually high degree.

Language as Object in Greek Culture. The consequences of habitually regarding language in this way have not been lost on twentieth-century philosophers of language. Ernst Cassirer, writing in 1930, warned that:

Language is misjudged if it is taken in some way or other as a thinglike being, as a substantial medium which interposes itself between man and the reality surrounding him. However one were then to define this medium more precisely, it always appears nevertheless—while wanting to be the *connecting link* between two worlds—as the barrier which separates the one from the other.[129]

More tendentiously, Michel Foucault, in the book which lends its title to this section, equated the entire growth of modern European literature with a separation, during the nineteenth century, between knowledge and language, between world and word. Foucault attempted to chart historically the growing opacity of language in European culture since the Enlightenment until, as he claimed, in the modern literary text, language has ceased to be a transitive medium at all.[130]

It seems, then, that in a culture where the habit of mind that regards language as an object is highly developed, as has been the case in Greece, the reciprocal links that bind together words and the things they refer to may become loosened or problematic. Psycharis, musing on the glories of the Acropolis of Athens, could declare:

Σας βεβαιώνω που ο Παρθενώνας δε μ' αρέσει όσο μ' αρέσει τόνομά της...[131]

I assure you that the Parthenon does not give me as much pleasure as does its name...

[129] From ' "Geist" und "Leben" in der Philosophie der Gegenwart', quoted by Bruns 1974: 11.

[130] 'The nineteenth century was to dissolve that link [sc. between knowledge and language], and to leave behind it, in confrontation, a knowledge closed in upon itself and a pure language that had become, in nature and function, enigmatic—something that has been called, since that time, *Literature*' (Foucault 1970: 89). Cf. 'literature becomes progressively more differentiated from the discourse of ideas, and encloses itself within a radical intransitivity... it addresses itself to itself as a writing subjectivity, ... and thus all its threads converge upon the ... simple act of writing' (Foucault 1970: 300).

[131] Psycharis 1971: 191.

Demotic is to be upheld, according to Psycharis, not because it more faithfully reflects and transmits an objective reality, but because it is, in itself, superior not only to *katharevousa* but even to the things it names! To conceive of language in this way involves some cost, as Cassirer recognized: attention is diverted from the meanings of words to their substance, and we saw ample evidence of this in the Greek language debate, and especially in the way that it has so often dictated the terms of literary criticism. But there is another, compensatory consequence of this reification and the attendant loosening of the links between words and things. Both sides in the debate invested language-as-thing with extraordinary power: the power to create or destroy the foundations of the state.

In quite everyday contexts in Greek society one can find examples of real power being attributed to language, both in general and in the form of specific utterances. Greece is often cited as still having a predominantly oral culture, but the oral traditions which have held an important position in Greek life and literature well into the twentieth century are themselves very far from being transparent 'mirrors held up to nature'.[132] The signs of 'residual orality' need to be set against a historical background in which writing has been used continuously for nearly three thousand years; in which religious truths are enshrined in 'Scripture', that is, recited and chanted daily in church; and in which, according to the proverbial expressions, 'Fate writes' and 'What is written cannot be unwritten'. Written language possesses especial power, as these last examples testify, and this traditional power has in modern times been inherited by the apparatus of state bureaucracy and the law.[133] In daily parlance, an offender will be 'written down' (i.e. charged) by a policeman, and a rogue taxi driver may be seriously chastened by a threat to 'write down' the number of his cab. In other contexts, notably in the performance of religious rites such as baptism and marriage, and also in popular exorcisms, the uttering of particular words is understood to be itself a powerful form of action.[134] In all of these instances, the power attributed to the word, whether written

---

[132] See Eideneier 1985; Tziovas 1989*b*. For a descriptive account of the oral traditions of Modern Greece see Beaton 1986; on the symbolic rather than referential nature of 'meaning' in oral songs, see Beaton 1980: 110–11, 120–35. It should be noted that ever since the time of Solomos oral poetry has been an influential part of Modern Greek culture in a *written* as well as in a traditional, oral form.

[133] Documented in detail in Herzfeld 1991.

[134] See Stewart 1991, esp. 211–43.

or spoken, lies in whole or in part outside the literal *meanings* of the words used.

Another area of discourse in which a lack of fit has been observed between words and the things or actions to which they refer is the way in which language may be used, in certain circumstances, by parents and close relatives in talking to small children. Renée Hirschon has presented examples, drawn from anthropological field-work in Greece, of enticing promises and bloodcurdling threats made to young children, which rather than signalling action to follow, are apparently uttered as a *substitute* for the action named: a promise of an ice cream is itself a reward, the threat of a beating a punishment. The result, according to Hirschon, is a 'disjunction between words and action', so that 'the relationship between words and actions is much looser' than would be expected in the case of comparable utterances in English.[135] In such exercises of language, it is the (adult) speaker whose power and autonomy are affirmed,[136] but the consequence for the child and even, Hirschon suggests, for the adult that the child eventually becomes, is a symmetrically reduced faith in the reliability of language to represent the world: 'Truth is not to be found in words, nor is it accessible through verbal expression.'[137]

Language as Object in Greek Literature. The perception of language in Greek culture that underlies all of these manifestations has also left its mark upon Greek literature, particularly during the last hundred years. At its simplest, this can be seen in narrated incidents, or in the statements of fictional characters, which tend to corroborate the non-literary evidence just considered. But it is also both reflected and extended in the statements and practice of writers, who have often exploited the power and autonomy of language, so perceived, in order to achieve particular literary ends.

Confirmation of the potentially formative power of language, when used in a way that does not refer directly to things, can be

---

[135] Hirschon 1992: 40, 44.

[136] 'With the freedom to dissociate words from actions in Greek, whether in promises, threats, lies or fantasies, the speaker may retain an inner sense of personal autonomy' (Hirschon 1992: 46); cf. Mackridge 1992b: 113: 'the linguistic sign has tended to be seen by the Greeks as readily separable from the referent and replaceable by another belonging to a different register.'

[137] Hirschon 1992: 51; cf. p. 37: 'this verbal conduct...is...instrumental in the transmission of ontological perceptions relating to the wider cosmology, and thus plays a role in cultural reproduction.'

found in the title story of the collection *Small Change*, first published in 1964, by Kostas Tachtsis. In this story a young boy is taught a harsh lesson not to loiter on the way home from the corner shop with his mother's change. The story begins:

—"Έφτυσα! Αλίμονό σου αν χαζέψεις πάλι στο δρόμο!"
—Δεν έφτυνε ποτέ στ' αλήθεια, μόνο με λόγια, μα το νόημα της απειλής ήταν καθαρό: Έπρεπε νάχεις γυρίσει πίσω *πριν* στεγνώσει το σάλιο.[138]

'I've spat! God help you if you dawdle again in the street!'
She never did spit really, only in words, but the meaning of the threat was plain: you had to be back *before* the spit had time to dry.

The act of spitting, with which this story begins, in fact never took place at all; but it creates a reality for the child in which the 'meaning of the threat' is perfectly clear—a meaning which is still interpreted, in the second paragraph, in terms of this created 'reality' (the length of time taken for the non-existent spit to dry). The 'game' that is being played with words here is only incidentally a literary one: the false narrative statement is the more striking when promoted to be the first word of a fictional text; but the story told, whether true or not, is one of everyday experience. At the end of the story, the mother's strategy is seen, years later, to have been counter-productive. The hero never manages to 'become a man', as his mother had exhorted him to do, and this failure is attributed to the capricious threats with which the story began. In a real sense, although it is not expressed in this way in the story, the 'reality' conjured up by the mother's threat determines the future (deviant) attitude of the grown man to the adult world.

Other fictional characters in recent times are described as being variously affected by a perception of words as entities in their own right, separate from the things to which they refer. In a novel by Vasilis Vasilikos, published in the same year as Tachtsis' story, the young hero's sense of reality is seriously disturbed by the discovery of minor typographical errors in some poems that he has published. The reason for this is given, with a hint of irony:

Ίσως γιατί ο Άγγελος είχε μάθει τη ζωή μόνο με τις λέξεις, με τις εικόνες, ίσως γιατί είχε μάθει να ερμηνεύει τον κόσμο μόνο με τα γράμματα...[139]

[138] Tachtsis 1974*b*: 9.
[139] *Οι φωτογραφίες* (Vasilikos 1987: 282).

Perhaps because Angelos had learned about life only through words,
through pictures, perhaps because he had learned to interpret the world
only through writing...

And, perhaps less negatively, the narrator of the novel *The Chronicle
of an Adultery* by Maro Vamvounaki (1981) declares at one point:

Το είπα και πιο πάνω, οι λέξεις μ' αγγίζουν με την αόριστη αίσθηση που
αποπνέουν, με τον ήχο. Πιο πολύ αυτό μετράει, πιο πολύ κι από την
έννοια.[140]

I said it earlier on, words touch me with an indefinable sensation that they
breathe out with their sound. This is what counts the most, more than their
meaning.

This evidence of the primacy given to the word over the things to
which it should refer, and of the effect of this phenomenon on users
of the language, is not restricted to the second half of the twentieth
century. The play by Neroulos which lampooned Korais and his
proposals for linguistic reform (published in 1813) turns, as we saw,
upon the moment when the principal character *chokes* upon a *word*.
Elsewhere this same character had declared, in a wicked parody of
the style and the ideas of Korais:

η γλώσσα δεν έφθασεν ακόμην εις τον βαθμόν του να επιδέχηται την
ποιητικήν ποικιλίαν και σοβαρότητα· διά τούτο αγωνιζόμεθα να
διορθώσωμεν, και να πλουτίσωμεν πρώτον αυτήν, και ύστερον ν'
αρχίση το Γένος πεζώς και ποιητικώς να συγγράφη· πρώτον είνι η
μορφή, και ύστερον η ύλη. Πρώτον το πώς, και ύστερον το τι. Πρώτον
οι κανόνες της γλώσσας, και ύστερον η γλώσσα.[141]

our language has not yet reached the stage where it can be susceptible of
poetic variety and seriousness; for that we must first fight to correct and
enrich it, and then the Nation can begin to write in prose and verse; first the
form, then the matter. First the how, and then the what. First the rules of the
language, and then the language.

The play itself does not of course endorse this view, but Neroulos is
making comic capital out of (exaggerating) a tendency already latent
in the contemporary linguistic debate. By implication, the *Korakistika* ruefully recognizes (and comically exaggerates) a well-
established habit of mind. Almost identical sentiments, combining
both rueful pride and a sense of loss, were expressed almost two
centuries later when Vasilikos had the final word in a BBC television

[140] Vamvounaki 1981: 51.   [141] Vilaras *et al.* 1981: 31.

programme about modern Greece, broadcast in 1984: 'The Greeks have a word for it,' he said, 'but they don't have *it*.'[142] The situation humorously decried in the *Korakistika* at the beginning of the nineteenth century, and epigrammatically summed up by Vasilikos in the late twentieth, is clearly not universally welcomed by writers. Indeed, much of the Greek literature that is most accessible to the non-Greek reader, and is often the most widely read in Greece itself, seems driven by a powerful desire to break down the barrier between language and the world that these commentators have discerned. We have seen many examples, particularly in fiction, of attempts to 'tell it the way it was', to present an unvarnished testimony through which events could in some sense seem to 'speak for themselves'.[143] The urgency with which so many Greek writers have attempted this is all the more explicable against a cultural background in which the written word possesses great power, but at the same time is a dangerously unreliable instrument for conveying the truth about events and experiences.

This is the background against which we can best understand the phenomenon of General Makriyannis, at the end of the war of independence in the 1820s, teaching himself to write in order to 'record the naked truth without passion', or as he later put it, to 'write down the disasters against fatherland and religion'; to 'write down the causes and the circumstances'; to 'write with great anger against the causes'.[144] There are many examples in Greek fiction of narrators, often not clearly distinguished from the writers themselves, explicitly or implicitly declaring similar aims. Myrivilis' narrator in the 1930 version of the novel *Life in the Tomb*, expresses the whole *raison d'être* of the book like this:

Ἴσως κι ὅλας νὰ τὰ κλείσω στέρεα μέσα σ᾽ἕναν κάλυκα ἀπὸ ὀβίδα καὶ νὰ γράψω χτυπητὰ μ᾽ἕνα καρφὶ πάνου στὸ μπρούντζο: "Ἀληθινὴ ἱστορία

[142] 'The Greeks Have a Word For It', BBC television programme, 1984.
[143] Commenting on Hirschon's paper, cited above, Peter Mackridge notes: 'What requires some explanation, however, is why so much Modern Greek literary *prose* (what in English is traditionally called *fiction*) adheres very closely to experienced *fact*, serving the function of a documentary or apologia: the author's personal testimony and often his or her self-justification' (1992*b*: 113).
[144] From the Introduction (1829) to the *Memoirs*: Θὰ σημειώσω γυμνὴ τὴν ἀλήθεια καὶ χωρὶς πάθος (Makriyannis n.d.: 91). From the Author's Preface (1850): Μπαίνοντας εἰς αὐτὸ τὸ ἔργον καὶ ἀκολουθώντας νὰ γράφω δυστυχήματα ἀναντίον τῆς πατρίδος καὶ θρησκείας...Γράφοντας αὐτὰ τὰ αἴτια καὶ τῆς [sic] περίστασες...γράφω μὲ πολλὴ ἀγανάχτησιν ἀναντίον τῶν αἰτίων (Makriyannis n.d.: 85).

ενούς στρατιώτη". Έτσι, ποιος ξαίρει, μπορεί, σαν περάσει τούτη η παραφροσύνη του πολέμου, που κάνει όσους τον είδανε από κοντά να τον πλαστογραφούνε μέσα στα λογής τυπωμένα χαρτιά, να βγει κάποτε στο φως του ήλιου και μια φωνή που θάχει το κουράγιο να πει την αλήθεια χωρίς να φοβάται την καταδίωξη και τη βρυσιά [sic], γιατί θάνε η φωνή ενούς πεθαμένου.[145]

Perhaps I'll close them [sc. these diaries] in the casing of a shell and write in bold lettering, with a nail on the metal: 'The true story of a soldier'. That way, who knows, it may be that when this madness of war is over that makes all those who've seen it at close range falsify the truth in all kinds of printed papers, a voice will break forth into the light of the sun and have the courage to tell the truth without fear of persecution and insult, because it will be the voice of a dead man.

As we have seen, the means by which these writers fulfilled their aims cannot be separated from the medium of language. Indeed, it is ironic that Makriyannis, whose *Memoirs* were unknown until fifty years after his death, has ever since been valued more highly for his *language* than for his historical testimony. In the cases of Doukas, Myrivilis, and Venezis after the First World War, and Beratis after the Second, we have noted the ways in which these writers cultivated and developed particular written styles in order to enhance the *illusion* or effect of unmediated experience springing directly off the page. This is not to say that these writers fail in their aim: quite the contrary. But the very determination with which they set out to present the 'unvarnished truth' of experience and also, more often than not, to justify their own perspective on events, can in turn be seen as a response to the same kind of linguistic perception that we have been discussing. The very fickleness of language gives urgency and purpose to the writer's mission to overcome it.

It is in this context, I believe, that the moving plea for simplicity and clarity in a poem by Yorgos Seferis, and also the same poet's untiring quest in his essays and diaries to find an 'authentic voice', can best be understood:

Δε θέλω τίποτε άλλο παρά να μιλήσω απλά, να μου δοθεί
ετούτη η χάρη.
Γιατί και το τραγούδι το φορτώσαμε με τόσες μουσικές
που σιγά-σιγά βουλιάζει

[145] Myrivilis 1993: 406–7. The standard edition of 1955 (on which the English translation of the novel is based) has slightly diluted the force of this passage.

κι και την τέχνη μας τη στολίσαμε τόσο πολύ που φαγώθηκε
από τα μαλάματα το πρόσωπο της
κι είναι καιρός να πούμε τα λιγοστά μας λόγια γιατί η
ψυχή μας αύριο κάνει πανιά.[146]

I want nothing other than to speak simply, for this grace
to be given me.
Because we've weighted down our song with so much music
that slowly it is sinking
and we've so adorned our art that the gold leaf has eaten
into its face
and it's time to say the few words we have because tomorrow
our souls set sail.

The voice that speaks here seems only too well aware of the impossibility of what it seeks. In the context of twentieth-century Greek
literature, this is not a naïve statement of belief in a one-to-one
relationship between words and things. Rather it reflects the same
nostalgia, also evident in a different way in the epigrammatic statement of Vasilikos quoted above, for such a relationship, which *in a
Greek context cannot be taken for granted*.[147]

In all the literary examples we have considered so far, the tendency in Greek culture to view language as an object has been viewed
largely negatively: with humour, with resignation, or even with the
determination to overcome its consequences. But it is by no means
always so. Writers in modern times have frequently chosen to
remind themselves and their readers that, according to the Gospel
of St John:

In the beginning was the Word [Logos]. And the Word was with God and
the Word was God. . . . All things were made by him; and without him was
not any thing made that was made.[148]

The Word, in this highly problematic sense, comes to be identified more or less playfully with poetic language, especially in the
decades following 1930. In 1933 the novelist Kosmas Politis put into
the mouth of one of his characters the following declaration:

---

[146] Ένας γέροντας στην ακροποταμιά, 1942 (Seferis 1972: 201).
[147] The 'point' of this passage is not, as has been claimed, that Seferis' 'dream of a
poetry returning to the simplicity and purity of nature' is fatally at odds with the real
nature of the poetic and rhetorical language in which it is expressed (Dimiroulis 1985:
77 and *passim*). Recognition of the 'fatal flaw' inherent in its own linguistic medium is
very much part of the poem.
[148] John I, 1: 3.

Φίλε μου, εν αρχή ην ο λόγος. Το άπαντο είναι η λέξη και το σημείο. Με το
να κάνεις ένα σημείο ή να προφέρεις κάποια λέξη, δημιουργείς ή
προσκαλείς μια δύναμη, ένα ον... Τι έπεται λοιπόν; Έπεται πως τα λόγια
είναι πιο δυνατά κι από τα έργα...¹⁴⁹

My friend, in the beginning was the word. The word and the sign are all. In
making a sign or uttering some word, you create or call down a power, a
being... What follows then? It follows that words are more powerful even
than deeds...

It is characteristic of Politis' often tongue-in-cheek way of handling
large ideas that these words are described in their context as 'chat-
ter', and that they are attributed to a crank. But in invoking the
Gospel text in order to set language above the things to which it
refers, Politis hints at a more serious claim that would be pressed
further by poets and novelists among his contemporaries.

The poet Yorgos Sarandaris, in 1939, used the same starting-point
for an attack upon the philosophy of Kierkegaard. Quoting the
biblical text, Sarandaris asserts: 'Kierkegaard's philosophy is not
based on "In the beginning was the Word"', and he continues,
'Our direct and certain self is for us not sensation, as for Kierkegaard, but the word [logos].'¹⁵⁰ And in less philosophical vein
Seferis could write (at almost exactly the same time as he wrote
the poem quoted above): 'Nowhere more than in poetry is the saying
applicable: "In the beginning was the word."'¹⁵¹

The most explicit extension of this observation into the practice of
literature is again made by Seferis, who as early as 1939 had
declared: 'The final aim of the poet is not to describe things but to
create them by naming them.'¹⁵² In a later essay Seferis developed
this idea further. Echoing his earlier statement, he continues: 'The

¹⁴⁹ K. Politis 1985: 79.
¹⁵⁰ Sarandaris 1987: v. 233–4. Sarandaris goes further, to identify logos as the 'first
link' between man and the undefined primary being of the presocratic philosopher
Parmenides: Ο άμεσος βέβαιος εαυτός μας για μας δεν είναι η αίσθηση, όπως κατά
τον Κίρκεγκωρντ, αλλά ο λόγος. Γιατί εκείνο που μας ενδιαφέρει, εκείνο που
θεωρούμε γόνιμο, είναι η πρώτη σχέση μας με το ον, με το ον του Παρμενίδη,
δηλαδή με το απόλυτο... Implied in this link is no doubt a further link with the Logos
which, in the philosophy of Parmenides' older contemporary Heraclitus, was itself the
governing principle of the universe. Thus the concept of language as a creative
instrument is linked, at least from the 1930s, with the recurrent interest of Greek
poets with the earliest Greek philosophy (see Ch. 4).
¹⁵¹ Seferis 1981: i. 189 (dated '12–21 December 1941'). The poem 'An Old Man on
the Riverbank' is dated '20 June 1942'.
¹⁵² Ο στερνός σκοπός του ποιητή δεν είναι να περιγράψει τα πράγματα αλλά να
τα δημιουργεί ονομάζοντάς τα... (Seferis 1981: i. 139).

extreme point to which the poet tends, is to be able to say "let there be light", and for there to be light.'[153] Just as the *word* of God's commands, in the Book of Genesis, created the real world, so may the word of the poet in some sense create that which he names.

To observe this principle in action we have only to look back at some of the writers and works discussed in Chapters 3 and 4: Pentzikis achieving through words the 'miracle' of resurrecting a dead man (in *The Dead Man and the Resurrection*); Elytis, in his long poem of 1959, *The Axion Esti*, bringing about the triumph of poetic language over the violence and destruction experienced by the Greek people in the 1940s; and the attempt of Embirikos to create a new (albeit unintelligible) language as a necessary stage in his crusade to found a new world. The same principle can also be traced back in practice at least as far as the turn of the century. Towards the end of Palamas' long poem *The Dodecalogue of the Gypsy*, the hero/narrator finds the miraculous violin whose music will enable him to resurrect the fallen idols he had cast down earlier in the poem.[154] Although Palamas is notoriously ambivalent in the status he accords to 'Logos' in his work, and particularly in his critical essays, here at least language and music are united as a power capable of creating the world anew:

Χτύπα, δοξάρι μου, και χτίζε,
ο κόσμος γίνεται από
μέσα στα χέρια μου τα δυο.
Ω γέννα, ω γέννα!...
Βιολί μου, υπάρχεις εσύ μόνο,
και μια είν' η γλώσσα, κι ο ήχος σου είναι,
κ' ένας ο πλάστης, και είμ' εγώ,
κι ο λόγος που θαματουργεί
κι ο λόγος είναι η μουσική![155]

Strike [the strings], my bow, and build,
the world is made through me
within my two hands.
O birth, O birth!...
My violin, only you exist,
there is but language and that's your sound,
and one creator, and that is I,
and the word that works miracles
and the word is music.

[153] Το ακραίο όριο όπου τείνει ο ποιητής, είναι να μπορέσει να πει "γενηθήτω φως" και να γίνει φως (Seferis 1981: ii. 164).
[154] Discussed in Ch. 2.   [155] Palamas n.d.: iii. 405.

In Greek the words for 'birth' and 'becoming' are cognate with the biblical 'Genesis' and the command (in the Greek version of the Old Testament, the Septuagint) 'Let there be...'. A late poem of Sikelianos (published in 1946) draws on the same nexus of terms as Seferis and Palamas had used, to make explicit the way in which Sikelianos conceives of his own poetic language as it had functioned in earlier poems:

Φοβερή στιγμή
πριν απ' τον πρώτο μες στα βάθη της καρδιάς μου
ψίθυρο του "Γενηθήτω"!
Παρουσία απόλυτη τον όντων
από την κορφή ώς τα βάθη,
παρουσία ειδών, μορφών, πλασμάτων,
λαών, εθνών, νεκρών και ζώντων,
παρουσία αιώνων![156]

Terrible moment
before the first whisper in the depths of my heart
of the words 'Let there be'!
Absolute presence of beings
from the heights to the depths,
presence of objects, shapes, creatures,
peoples, nations, the living and the dead,
presence of ages.

But the most extended development of this concept of language is undoubtedly to be found in the poetry of Elytis. *The Axion Esti*, already discussed, begins with an allusion to the biblical Genesis, and its whole first section (called 'Genesis') depicts simultaneously the birth of the individual consciousness and the creation of the world in which the new-born child will live:

Στην αρχή το φως...[157]

In the beginning was the light...

and the world is then created out of syllables and words. The power of a language freed from reference is a recurring, perhaps the dominant, preoccupation in Elytis' poetry, which may also help to account for the bafflement with which it has sometimes been received in translation. A late poem, 'Verb The Obscure', takes

---

[156] Προς την ποίηση-πράξη (Sikelianos 1965: iii. 241).
[157] Elytis 1970: 13.

this potential of language, which Elytis has made very much his own, even further.

The speaker in this poem, meditating on impending death, and frustrated in his desire to communicate directly with 'nature and the earth', which are described as 'locked up', sets about devising a word—a verb—'the way a burglar makes a skeleton key'. The invented word is pronounced with ceremony, *katarkithmevo*, and a new world appears. The poem ends:

Να γιατί καταρκυθμεύω
Που οι βαριές υποχωρούν αμπάρες τρίζοντας κι οι μεγάλες
θύρες ανοίγονται
Στο φως του Ήλιου του κρυπτού μια στιγμούλα, η φύση μας
η τρίτη να φανερωθεί
Έχει συνέχεια. Δε θα την πω. Κανείς δεν πιάνει τα δωρεάν
Στον κακόν αγέρα ή που χάνεσαι ή που επακολουθεί γαλήνη
Αυτά στη γλώσσα τη δική μου. Κι άλλοι άλλα σ' άλλες. Αλλ'
Η αλήθεια μόνον έναντι θανάτου δίδεται.[158]

This is why I *katarkithmevo*
and the heavy bolts draw back creaking and the great
doors open
to the light of the Hidden Sun for an instant, to reveal our
third nature
It goes on. I shan't say it. No one takes a gift for nothing
in the evil air where either you're lost or tranquillity follows
That's what I have to say in my language. Others will have
other things in others. But
truth is given only in exchange for death.

Taken literally, Seferis' statements and the practice of Palamas, Sikelianos, Pentzikis, Embirikos, and Elytis amount to a declaration of the *primacy* of language over the objectively perceptible world. This entails a claim to efficacy, to transitivity (however quixotic we may regard it), that marks off this position from that of the French Symbolists and their twentieth-century successors, according to which the poem constitutes an autonomous world constructed out of language. At the same time it is more than a restatement of the ancient fallacy (usually called 'Cratylism' after the character in Plato's dialogue *Cratylus* who first articulated it) that words possess

[158] Ρήμα το σκοτεινόν (Elytis 1991: 36–7). (See also guide to Translations: Elytis.)

an innate resemblance to the things that they name.[159] Even the modern descendant of Cratylism, the 'Orphism' attributed to writers and thinkers associated, for the most part, with the German Romantic tradition, differs from the poetics of the Greek writers under discussion, in starting out from an equivalence between language and the actual world.[160]

Language, in the work of these Greek writers, is not bound in a reliable or stable relationship to the reality to which it refers. To say this is not at all to deny that language, either in these literary works or in Greek culture at large, can and does refer to the external world of actions and things. Indeed if it did not, the particular effects we have been discussing, as well as most of the practical uses to which language is put in Greece as everywhere else, would be neutralized. It is only if language does refer (however partially and imperfectly) to things, that the relationship between the two can be experienced as unstable or unreliable. In most of the cases we have been considering, the language used or proposed is perfectly intelligible: a word which is admired or deplored *as a word* does not thereby lose its meaning, it simply comes to be seen as detachable from the meaning that it has. The words of a promise or a threat which takes the place of the action it names do not thereby cease to refer to that action: the words 'I've spat' refer to exactly the same action regardless of whether or not it is carried out. They just refer in a different way.[161]

---

[159] Opinions expressed by different speakers in the *Cratylus* had been adduced at various points in the language debate, where they are somewhat indiscriminately attributed to 'divine' Plato (see e.g. Vilaras in Vilaras *et al.* 1981: 130; Kodrikas in Daskalakis 1966: 486); cf. Gounelas 1995: esp. 21–48.

[160] See Bruns 1974, esp. 7: 'it is by virtue of the identity of word and being that the poet is able once more to play his Orphic role, according to which the world itself becomes a kind of ultimate poem, within whose harmonious contours man discovers his true dwelling-place', and the quotation from Heidegger on p. 216: 'Poetry is the establishing of being by means of the word.' In Heidegger's formulation the 'being' of the world is already there; in the Greek examples we have been considering, it is 'made' by the poet.

[161] The disjunction under discussion is not to be equated with the 'splitting of the sign' that plays such a large part in the theoretical approaches to language of e.g. Derrida and Lacan. We do not here have an 'endless chain of signification' in which signifiers, detached from the signifieds that, according to Saussurean terminology, are equally inherent in the linguistic sign, refer only to other signifiers, so 'deferring' meaning indefinitely. What happens in most of the instances that are considered here is that the linguistic sign *as a whole* becomes partially detached from its referent. In theoretical terms, we are dealing with a disruption of the relationship not between signifier and signified, but between *signified* and referent, in other words between the

It may be concluded that Greek writers, particularly during the twentieth century, have explored and exploited the ambiguous relation of words to things in ways that draw not only on European philosophy and poetics but also on indigenous perceptions of the nature and function of language. Alongside a powerful nostalgia for an ideal condition in which words would speak for things and actions would speak for themselves, we have identified a widespread cultural acceptance that this ideal relationship is unattainable. Integrally coupled with this perception is a strong tendency to regard words and utterances as things and actions in their own right, and to attribute value and potency to them.

For the writer, this inbuilt ambivalence of the medium in which he is working may be cause, by turns or according to temperament, for rejoicing or despair. Of the two veteran masters of the Greek language at the end of the 1980s, Elytis in the poem quoted above discovers, on unlocking the door to a new reality with the key of an invented word:

'Ωστε λοιπόν, αυτό που λέγαμε "ουρανός δεν είναι·
"αγάπη" δεν· "αιώνιο" δεν· Δεν
Υπακούουν τα πράγματα στα ονόματά τους.

So then, what we used to call 'sky' is not; 'love' not;
'immortal' not. Things are not
obedient to their names.

It is almost certainly by coincidence that the other, Yannis Ritsos, in one of his last poems, wrote:

Δεν είχαμε πια καμιά δικαιολογία για το σήμερα
ούτε για το αύριο. Τα ονόματα
δεν εφάρμοζαν πια πάνω στα πράγματα.[162]

We'd no excuse any more for today
or for tomorrow either. Names
didn't apply to things any more.

conceptualized representation of the object that inheres in the linguistic sign and the object itself. The only instances where the 'splitting of the sign' comes into play are to be found in the meaningless words of a new language created by Embirikos, and the invented word of Elytis in 'Verb The Obscure'. Here the detachment of the sign from its referent is taken to a further (and unusual) degree, in that 'signs' are created which consist only of signifiers without signifieds. These are best considered as extreme cases of the more widespread disjunction between a fully functioning sign, consisting of signifier and signified, and its referent.

[162] Στάδια κούρασης, dated Jan. 1988 (Ritsos 1991: 171).

The difference, as Ritsos himself might have put it, lies in the one short word that in Greek means 'any more'.

The final part of this chapter has, as promised, been somewhat speculative. I have tried to suggest ways in which the well-known fact of the 'Language Question' in Greece may be connected to fundamental perceptions of the nature and function of language in Greek culture. Following this approach, the 'Language Question' can be seen as just one part of a continuing and complex dialogue between words and things, in which literature, naturally, has an important part to play. The experiences and the achievements of Greek writers over the past two centuries are not, of course, determined by a single, monolithic concept of language which is peculiarly Greek. But language and the written word are themselves part of the experience that constitutes the raw material of literature. In so far as there is a distinct 'Greek experience', made up, among other things, of the consequences of the historical events summarized at the start of Chapters 1–5 in this book, then that experience also includes the experience of language and the varied uses to which, socially and historically, language has been put.

I have not attempted to explore the historical origin of the perception of language discussed here (that is something that needs further study), nor to press too far the implied distinction between 'western' and 'indigenous Greek' concepts. There is obviously no such thing as '*the* Greek perception of language'; on the other hand, within the gamut of European thought about language and its relation to the world since ancient times, particular strands can be seen to be highly developed among modern speakers and writers of Greek. If literature is in some sense a way of experiencing the world through language, then it may be suggested that Greek writers, particularly in the twentieth century, have 'unlocked doors', in Elytis' metaphor, and achieved results that deserve to be better known beyond the bounds of Greece itself and the Greek-speaking community worldwide.

Epilogue (1998)

THIS book has been intended, as was explained in the Introduction, as a contribution to literary history. Since it is written from a perspective (and in a language) at some distance from that of its subject-matter, it should be clear that the literary history in question is not merely that of the Greek nation state with which we began. As was argued in the Introduction, the poetry and fiction written in Greek during the last two centuries are part of a European, not to say 'global', heritage. Their importance, both within and outside Greece, does not, according to this perspective, lie in the fact that their authors have been Greek and express a particular culture. It lies rather in the fact that these writers have drawn on and added to a common European heritage, both ancient and more recent. The achievements of Greek writers, over the last two hundred years, are of importance and interest not just to speakers of the Greek language, or to academic specialists, but to all of us who share the broader heritage in which these writers have worked.

Yorgos Theotokas, on the threshold of the innovative literary decade of the 1930s in Greece, lamented, as we saw in Chapter 3, the lack of influence exerted by Greek writers beyond their country's borders. The language of cultural diplomacy, and certainly of literary study, has moved on since then, and it would be as inappropriate, perhaps, to measure the worth of a culture's production in terms of 'influence' as it would be to adopt the belligerent stance of Psycharis half a century earlier. (Psycharis, as we saw in Chapter 2, had likened the growth of a nation's literature to the expansion of its physical borders.)

How, then, do we measure the status or importance of the writers and works discussed here, in a European or global context? If 'influence' is too crude a term, there is nonetheless plenty of evidence that writers in the 'major' languages, since the time of Theotokas, have creatively been reading (or, in Harold Bloom's term, 'misreading') Modern Greek literature. A list, confined only to English-language writers, and to names that are well-enough known to require no particular justification for being cited, would include, at a minimum: W. H. Auden, D. J. Enright, Lawrence

Durrell, E. M. Forster, John Fowles, Henry Miller, Patrick White, to
say nothing of poets and novelists of more recent generations, who
have not only chosen Greece as a point of reference in their work
(Robert Liddell, Francis King, Barry Unsworth, most recently
Louis de Bernières) but may also have had a formative encounter
with the translated work of Cavafy, Seferis, Kazantzakis, or, more
recently, of Elytis or Ritsos. But even this is only part of the story.
Greek writers also write and achieve success in other languages:
Stratis Haviaras in English, Aris Fakinos in French, for example.
It would be an impossible, and probably not very worthwhile task, to
try to separate the 'Greek' from the 'English' or 'French' strands in
the work of writers such as these. The boundaries of 'national'
literature, such as are implied in a book of this kind, in today's
world are porous, and probably always have been (one need only
think of the bilingualism of Solomos and Kalvos, in the early nineteenth century, or the cosmopolitan linguistic and cultural background of Cavafy or Seferis, among many others, in the twentieth).

Happily, there are signs, throughout Europe, that the place of
Modern Greek literature is increasingly being recognized. In universities from Lisbon to Moscow, from the Baltic to the Mediterranean, the serious study of post-Byzantine Greek literature has
gained an accepted place in the academic curriculum. If translations, particularly into English, still lag behind, there has been an
impressive range of cultural events in the last ten years, throughout
the continent, designed to provide a forum for Greek writers to
present their work and be heard. In Greece itself, such institutions
as the Ministry of Culture, the Foundation for Hellenic Culture
(established 1992), and the Center for the Modern Greek Language
(established 1994) have all been active in promoting Greek literature abroad. In 1995 a European Association of Modern Greek
Studies was formed, with a secretariat in Athens and an international membership, and held its first international conference
in Berlin in the autumn of 1998. Over the same period, in the
English-speaking world, Modern Greek studies have continued to
advance, as witness the large number of specialist studies in English
that have been added to the References for the second edition of this
book.

Modern Greek literature, at the end of the twentieth century, is in
the process of vigorous renewal, both in the active reassessment by
Greek writers and critics of the past of their tradition, and in the

creation of new works and new trends with which to confront the future. The academic study of that literature is now truly an international field. If this book has provided for the English-speaking reader a window, at least, upon the richness of the literary tradition that exists in Modern Greek today, then it will not have failed in its purpose.

Guide to Translations

In this section entries are arranged alphabetically by author. Where the author's name or the title appears in a different form in this book the latter form is given in square brackets following the relevant part of the entry. Citations are limited to works mentioned in the preceding chapters and, for reasons of space, to free-standing volumes. For the many translations from Modern Greek which have appeared in periodicals see Philippides 1990 (currently being updated).

ANAGNOSTAKIS, MANOLIS, *The Target: Selected Poems*, trans. with introduction by Kimon Friar (New York: Pella, 1980). [Parallel text.]

ANGHELAKI-ROOKE, KATERINA, *Beings and Things on their Own*, trans. by the author and Jackie Willcox (Brockport, NY: BOA Editions, 1986). [Short poems of the early 1980s.]

BAKOLAS, NIKOS, *Crossroads [The Great Square]*, trans. Caroline Harbouri (Athens: Kedros 1997).

CAVAFY, C. P., *Collected Poems*, trans. Edmund Keeley and Philip Sherrard, ed. George Savidis [= G. P. Savvidis] (Princeton, NJ: Princeton University Press, revd. edn. 1992).

—— *The Complete Poems of Cavafy*, trans. Rae Dalven, introduction by W. H. Auden (expanded edn.; New York: Harcourt Brace Jovanovich, 1976). [A selection from the 'Unpublished Poems' has been added to the first edition of 1961.]

—— *The Greek Poems of C. P. Cavafy, as Translated by Memas Kolaitis* (2 vols; New Rochelle, NY: Caratzas, 1989). [Vol. 1 contains the 'canon': the poems which Cavafy himself published in later life; vol. 2 the posthumous poems, first published in Greek in 1968, and the 'rejected' poems, first published in Greek in 1983.]

DOUKA, MARO, *Fool's Gold*, trans. Roderick Beaton (Athens: Kedros, 1991).

ELYTIS, ODYSSEUS, *Collected Poems*, trans. Jeffrey Carson and Nikos Sarris. Introduction and notes by Jeffrey Carson (Baltimore, MD: Johns Hopkins University Press, 1997).

—— *The Oxopetra Elegies*, trans. David Connolly (Amsterdam: Harwood Academic Publishers, 1996).

—— *The Axion Esti*, trans. and annotated by Edmund Keeley and George Savidis [= G. P. Savvidis] (Pittsburgh: University of Pittsburgh Press, 1974; London: Anvil Press, 1980). [Includes a useful schema drawn up by Elytis himself and published here for the first time, which helps the reader to elucidate the poem's complex structure. The American edition (only) is in parallel-text format.]

ELYTIS, ODYSSEUS, *Maria Nephele: A Poem in Two Voices* [*Maria Nefeli*], trans. Athan Anagnostopoulos (Boston: Houghton Mifflin, 1981).

—— *Selected Poems*, chosen and introduced by Edmund Keeley and Philip Sherrard, trans. Edmund Keeley *et al.* (New York: Viking Press; London: Anvil Press Poetry, 1982; paperback repr. 1991). [Translations of short poems and sections of longer ones revised from anthologies by Keeley and Sherrard, with excerpts from more recent poems translated by John Stathatos and Nanos Valaoritis.]

—— *The Sovereign Sun: Selected Poems*, trans. with introduction and notes by Kimon Friar (Philadelphia: Temple University Press, 1974; Newcastle upon Tyne: Bloodaxe Books, 1990).

—— *What I Love: Selected Poems*, trans. Olga Broumas, with Translator's Note and Afterword (Port Townsend, Wash.: Copper Canyon Press, 1986). [Parallel text.]

EMBIRIKOS, ANDREAS, *Amour, Amour: Writings or Personal Mythology* [*Amour-Amur*], trans. Nikos Stangos and Alan Ross (London: A. Ross, 1966).

FAKINOU, EUGENIA [EVYENIA], *The Seventh Garment*, trans. Ed Emery (London: Serpent's Tail, 1991).

GALANAKI, RHEA [REA], *The Life of Ismail Ferik Pasha*, trans. Kay Cicellis (London: Peter Owen, 1996).

—— ; MASTORAKI, JENNY: LAINA, MARIA, The Rehearsal of Misunderstanding: Three Collections by Contemporary Greek Women Poets. Bilingual edition, edn., trans. and introduction by Karen van Dyck (Hanover, NH: University Press of New England, 1998).

GATSOS, NIKOS, *Amorgos*, trans. Sally Purcell (London: Other Poetry Editions, 1980; Athens: Zodion Press, 1986).

HATZIS, DIMITRIS, *The End of Our Small Town*, trans. David Vere, edited by Dimitris Tziovas (Birmingham: Centre for Byzantine, Ottoman and Modern Greek Studies, University of Birmingham, 1995).

HEIMONAS, GIORGOS [YORGOS], *The Builders*, trans. Robert Crist (Athens: Kedros, 1991).

IOANNOU, YORGOS, *Good Friday Vigil*, trans. Peter Mackridge and Jackie Willcox (Athens: Kedros, 1995). [The only volume of this writer's stories to be published in translation so far; see Ioannou 1980.]

KARAPANOU, MARGARITA, *Kassandra* [*Cassandra*] *and the Wolf*, trans. N. C. Germanacos (New York: Harcourt Brace Jovanovich, 1976). [Predates the publication of the original Greek by a year.]

KARKAVITSAS, ANDREAS, *The Beggar*, trans. with notes, by William F. Wyatt, Jun., appendix by P. D. Mastrodimítris (New York: Caratzas,

1982). [An abridged version of the editor's introduction to the Greek text, translated, forms an appendix to the English edition.]

KAVADIAS [KAVVADIAS], NIKOS, *The Collected Poems of Nikos Kavadias*, trans. Gail Holst-Warhaft (Amsterdam: Hakkert, 1987). [Parallel text.]

KAZANTZAKIS, NIKOS, *Freedom and Death*, trans. Jonathan Griffin, preface by A. Den Doolaard (London: Faber and Faber, 1966; New York: Simon and Schuster, 1956).

—— *God's Pauper: Saint Francis of Assisi*, trans. Peter Bien (Oxford: Cassirer, 1962; London: Faber and Faber, 1975). Published in the US as *Saint Francis* (New York: Simon and Schuster, 1962).

—— *The Fratricides*, trans. Athena Gianakas Dallas (Oxford: Cassirer, 1967; London: Faber and Faber, 1975; New York: Simon and Schuster, 1964).

—— *Christ Recrucified*, trans. Jonathan Griffin (Oxford: Cassirer, 1954; London: Faber and Faber, 1962). Published in the US as *The Greek Passion* (New York: Simon and Schuster, 1954).

—— *The Last Temptation*, trans. Peter Bien (Oxford: Cassirer, 1960; London: Faber and Faber, 1975). Published in the US as *The Last Temptation of Christ* (New York: Simon and Schuster, 1960).

—— *The Odyssey: A Modern Sequel*, trans., with introduction, synopsis, and notes, by Kimon Friar (London: Secker and Warburg; New York: Simon and Schuster, 1958).

—— *The Saviors of God: Spiritual Exercises*, trans. with introduction by Kimon Friar (New York: Simon and Schuster, 1960).

—— *Zorba the Greek*, trans. Carl Wildman, introduction by Ian Scott-Kilvert (London: J. Lehmann; New York: Simon and Schuster, 1952; London: Faber and Faber, 1961).

KONDOS, YANNIS, *Danger in the Streets*, trans. John Stathatos (London: Oxus Press, 1978). [Selected poems from the 1970s.]

—— *The Bones: Selected Poems 1972–1982*, trans. James Stone (Cleveland and New York: The Globe Press, 1985).

LIBERAKI [LYMBERAKI], MARGARITA *Three Summers* [*Straw Hats*], trans. Karen van Dyck (Athens: Kedros, 1995).

MAKRIYANNIS, GENERAL, *The Memoirs of General Makriyannis, 1797–1864*, ed. and trans. Hal Lidderdale, introduction by C. M. Woodhouse (London: Oxford University Press, 1966). [Abridged translation.]

MOURSELAS, KOSTAS, *Red Dyed Hair*, trans. Fred A. Reed (Athens: Kedros, 1992).

MYRIVILIS, STRATIS, *Life in the Tomb*, trans. Peter Bien (Hanover, NH: University Press of New England, 1977; London: Quartet, 1987). [The now standard 1955 edition, with some restorations from the edition of 1930.]

MYRIVILIS, STRATIS, *The Schoolmistress with the Golden Eyes*, trans. Philip Sherrard (London: Hutchinson, 1964).
—— *Vasilis Arvanitis*, trans. with introduction and notes by Pavlos Andronikos (Armidale, NSW [Australia]: University of New England Publishing Unit, 1983).

PALAMAS, KOSTIS, *The King's Flute* [*The Emperor's Reed-Pipe*], trans. Theodore Ph. Stephanides and George C. Katsimbalis, preface by Charles Diehl, introduction by E. P. Papanoutsos (Athens: Idryma Kosti Palama, 1982). [Parallel text. The preface by the eminent Byzantinist Charles Diehl is reprinted from the French translation by Eugénie Clément (Paris, 1934) and is given in the original French with an English translation.]
—— *The King's Flute* [*The Emperor's Reed-Pipe*], trans. with introduction by Frederic Will (Lincoln, Nebr.: University of Nebraska Press, 1967).
—— *The Twelve Lays of the Gipsy* [*The Dodecalogue of the Gypsy*], trans. with introduction by George Thomson (London: Lawrence and Wishart, 1969).
—— *The Twelve Words of the Gypsy* [*The Dodecalogue of the Gypsy*], trans. Theodore Ph. Stephanides and George C. Katsimbalis (London: The Translators, 1974; Memphis, Tenn.: Memphis State University Press, 1975).

PAPADIAMANDIS, ALEXANDROS, *Tales from a Greek Island*, trans. with introduction and notes by Elizabeth Constantinides (Baltimore and London: Johns Hopkins University Press, 1987). [Selected short stories.]
—— *The Murderess*, trans. Peter Levi (London and New York: Writers and Readers, 1983). [Part of the text has been displaced on pp. 121–4, so that the end of the novel has become garbled.]

PAPATSONIS, TAKIS, *Ursa Minor and Other Poems*, trans. Kimon Friar and Kostas Myrsiades (Nostos Books; Minneapolis: North Central Publishing, 1987).

PREVELAKIS, PANDELIS, *The Cretan*, vol. i trans. Abbot Rick, vols. ii–iii trans. Peter Mackridge (Nostos Books; Minneapolis: North Central Publishing, 1991).
—— *The Tale of a Town* [*The Chronicle of a Town*], trans. Kenneth Johnstone (London and Athens: Doric Publications, 1976).

RITSOS, YANNIS, *Chronicle of Exile*, trans. with introduction by Minas Savvas, Forward [*sic*] by Louis Aragon (San Francisco: Wire Press, 1977). [Selected poems.]
—— *Iconostasis of Anonymous Saints: Ariostos the Observant Recounts Moments of His Life and Sleep, Such Strange Things, With a Nudge of the Elbow*, trans. Amy Mims (Athens: Kedros 1996).

——*Eighteen Short Songs of the Bitter Motherland*, trans. Amy Mims, illus. Yannis Ritsos, ed. with introduction by Theofanis G. Stavrou (Nostos Books, 1; St Paul: North Central Publishing, 1974). [Parallel text.]

——*Exile and Return*, trans. Edmund Keeley (New York: Ecco Press, 1985, 1987; London: Anvil Press, 1989). [Selected poems of the late 1960s and early 1970s.]

——*Gestures and Other Poems, 1968–1970*, trans. Nikos Stangos, illus. by the poet (London: Cape Goliard Press, 1971).

——*Repetitions, Testimonies, Parentheses*, trans. Edmund Keeley (Princeton University Press, 1990). [Representative selection of Ritsos' short poems written between 1946 and 1975.]

——*Selected Poems, 1938–1988*, ed. and trans. Kimon Friar and Kostas Myrsiades [and others] (Brockport, NY: BOA, 1989). [The most substantial translated selection of the work of this prolific poet, running to 486 pp. Includes long essays by the editors.]

——*Selected Poems*, trans. Nikos Stangos, introduction by Peter Bien (Harmondsworth: Penguin Books, 1974). [Short and long poems of the 1960s, sadly out of print.]

——*The Fourth Dimension*, trans. Peter Green and Beverly Bardsley (Princeton: Princeton University Press; London: Anvil Press, 1993). [The complete collection of 17 monologues written between 1956 and 1975.]

ROYIDIS [ROIDIS], EMMANUEL, *Pope Joan*, trans. and adapted by Lawrence Durrell (New York: Dutton, 1960; London: Overlook Press, 1984).

SACHTOURIS [SAHTOURIS], MILTOS, *Selected Poems*, trans. with introduction by Kimon Friar (Old Chatham, NY: Sachem Press, 1982).

SAMARAKIS, ANDONIS, *The Flaw*, trans. Peter Mansfield and Richard Burns (London: Hutchinson, 1969).

——*The Passport and Other Stories*, trans. with introduction by Gavin Betts (Melbourne: Longman Cheshire, 1980).

SEFERIS, GEORGE [YORGOS], *Collected Poems*, trans. and ed. with introduction by Edmund Keeley and Philip Sherrard (expanded edn.; Princeton: Princeton University Press, 1981; London: Anvil Press Poetry, 1982). [Parallel text, with some notes. Includes all but one of the poems published by Seferis in his lifetime.]

——*Complete Poems*, trans. and ed. with introduction by Edmund Keeley and Philip Sherrard (Princeton: Princeton University Press; London: Anvil Press Poetry, 1995). [Updated translations, but without the facing Greek text.]

——*On the Greek Style: Selected Essays in Poetry and Hellenism*, trans. Rex Warner and Th. D. Frangopoulos, introduction by Rex Warner (Boston: Little, Brown, 1966; Athens: Denise Harvey, 1982).

SIKELIANOS, ANGELOS, *Selected Poems*, trans. and introduced by Edmund Keeley and Philip Sherrard (Princeton: Princeton University Press, 1979; London: Allen and Unwin, 1980). [A fairly slim selection from the work of the prolific poet.]

SINOPOULOS, TAKIS, *Landscape of Death: The Selected Poems of Tákis Sinópoulos*, trans. with introduction by Kimon Friar (Columbus, Oh.: Ohio State University Press, 1979). [Parallel text. A substantial selection of poems written between 1944 and 1976.]

—— *Selected Poems*, trans. with introduction by John Stathatos (London: Oxus Press, 1981). [A slimmer selection, including some of the poet's late work and his last poem 'The Grey Light', not included in the collected Greek edition.]

SOTIRIOU, DIDO, *Farewell Anatolia* [*Bloodied Earth*], trans. Fred A. Reed (Athens: Kedros, 1991).

TAKTSIS [TACHTSIS], KOSTAS, *The Third Wedding*, trans. Leslie Finer (London: Alan Ross, 1967; Harmondsworth: Penguin Books, 1969). [Sadly out of print, this remains the only translation of a Modern Greek novel to have been published by Penguin!]

—— *The Third Wedding Wreath*, [*The Third Wedding*], trans. with introduction by John Chioles (Athens: Hermes [= Ermis], 1985).

THEOTOKAS, GIORGOS [YORGOS], *Argo*, trans. E. Margaret Brooke and Ares Tsatsopoulos (London: Methuen, 1951).

—— *Leonis: A Novel*, trans. Donald E. Martin, with a preface by Theofanis G. Stavrou (Minneapolis: Nostos, 1985).

TSIRKAS, STRATIS, *Drifting Cities*, trans. Kay Cicellis (Athens: Kedros 1995). (Translation first publd. New York: Knopf, 1974).

VAKALO, ELENI, *Genealogy*, trans. Paul Merchant (Exeter: Rougemont Press, 1971; rev. edn. Egham, UK: Interim Press, 1977). [Parallel text.]

VASSILIKOS, VASSILIS [VASILIKOS, VASILIS], *The Photographs*, trans. Mike Edwards (London: Secker and Warburg, 1971; Sphere, 1972; New York: Harcourt Brace Jovanovich, 1971).

—— *The Plant; The Well; The Angel: A Trilogy*, trans. Edmund and Mary Keeley (New York: Knopf, 1964).

VENEZIS, ILIAS, *Aeolia* [*Aeolian Earth*], trans. E. D. Scott-Kilvert, preface by Lawrence Durrell (New York: Vanguard Press, 1957).

VIZYENOS, GEORGIOS [VIZYINOS, G. M.], *My Mother's Sin and Other Stories*, trans. William F. Wyatt, Jun., preface by Roderick Beaton (Hanover, NH and London: University Press of New England, 1988). [The six stories published between 1883 and 1895. Each story is prefaced by a brief introduction by the translator.]

VRETTAKOS, NIKIFOROS, *Gifts in Abeyance: Last Poems 1981–91*, trans. David Connolly (Minneapolis: Nostos, 1992).

GUIDE TO TRANSLATIONS 375

YATROMANOLAKIS, YORGI [YORYIS], *History of a Vendetta* [*History*],
trans. Helen Cavanagh (Cambridge: Dedalus; New York: Hippocrene,
1991).
ZEI, ALKI, *Achilles' Fiancée*, trans. Gail Holst-Warhaft (Athens: Kedros,
1991).

References

ALEXANDROU 1974. Αλεξάνδρου, 'Αρης. *Το κιβώτιο* (Athens: Kedros).
—— 1978. *Ποιήματα (1941–1974)* (Athens: Kastaniotis).
ALEXIOU, MARGARET 1982. 'Diglossia in Greece', in W. Haas (ed.), *Standard Languages, Spoken and Written* (Manchester University Press), 156–92.
—— (ed.) 1983. C. P. Cavafy: *Special Double Issue, Journal of the Hellenic Diaspora*, 10/1–2 (New York: Pella).
—— 1993. 'Writing Against Silence: Antithesis and Ekphrasis in the Prose Fiction of Georgios Vizyenos', *Dumbarton Oaks Papers*, 47: 263–86.
—— 1995. 'Why Vizyenos?', *Journal of Modern Greek Studies*, 13/2: 289–98.
—— and LAMBROPOULOS, VASSILIS (eds.) 1985. *The Text and its Margins: Post-Structuralist Approaches to Twentieth-Century Greek Literature* (New York: Pella).
ALEXIOU, S. 1986. Αλεξίου, Στυλιανός. *Σολωμικά, Palimpsisto* (Heraklion, Crete), 3: 11–34.
—— 1990. *Δημοσθένης Βουτηράς*, in *Αφιέρωμα στον* Ι. Μ. *Παναγιωτόπουλο* (Thessaloniki: Malliaris-Paideia), 25–33.
—— 1997. *Σολωμιστές και Σολωμός* (Athens: Stigmi).
ANAGNOSTAKI 1980. Αναγνωστάκη, Νώρα. *Μαγικές εικόνες: 7 δοκίμια 1960–1965* (Athens: Nefeli) (first pub. 1973).
—— *et al.* 1961. *Για τον Σεφέρη: τιμητικό αφιέρωμα στα τριάντα χρόνια της "Στροφής"* (Athens).
ANAGNOSTAKIS 1985. Αναγνωστάκης, Μανόλης. *Τα ποιήματα 1941–1971* (Athens: Stigmi) (first pub. 1971).
—— (ed.) 1990. *Η χαμηλή φωνή · Τα λυρικά μιας περασμένης εποχής στους παλιούς ρυθμούς* (Athens: Nefeli).
ANDREIOMENOS 1993. Ανδρειωμένος, Γ. *Βιβλιογραφία Ανδρέα Κάλβου* (Athens: Elliniko Logotechniko kai Istoriko Archeio (ELIA)).
ANGELOPOULOS *et al.* 1992. Αγγελόπουλος, Λ. κ. ά. *Η αδιάπτωτη μαγεία. Παπαδιαμάντης 1991 - ένα αφιέρωμα* (Athens: Idryma Goulandri-Horn).
ANGELOU 1988*a*. Αγγέλου, 'Αλκης. *Των φώτων* (Νεοελληνικά Μελετήματα, 9; Athens: Ermis).
—— 1988*b*. Giulio Cesare dalla Croce: *Ο Μπερτόλδος και ο Μπερτολδίνος* (Athens: Ermis).
—— 1988*c*. *Η εκκλησία, η Πάπισσα Ιωάννα, ο Ροΐδης*, Introduction, in Roidis 1988*a* (first pub. 1967).
—— 1989. Εισαγωγή, in Palaiologos 1989*a*.

REFERENCES 377

ANGHELAKI-ROOKE 1971. Αγγελάκη-Rooke, Κατερίνα. *Ποιήματα 63–69* (Athens: Ermeias).

ANON. 1977. *Η στρατιωτική ζωή εν Ελλάδι*, ed. M. Vitti (Athens: Ermis).

ANTON, JOHN P. 1995. *The Poetry and Poetics of Constantine P. Cavafy: Aesthetic Visions of Sensual Reality* (Chur, Switzerland: Harwood Academic Publishers).

APOSTOLIDOU 1988. Αποστολίδου, Β. *Η επτανησιακή σχολή στις ιστορίες της νεοελληνικής λογοτεχνίας*, in *Μνήμη Λίνου Πολίτη*. Επιστημονική Επετηρίδα Φιλοσοφικής Σχολής (University of Thessaloniki), 197–208.

—— 1992. *Ο Κωστής Παλαμάς ιστορικός της νεοελληνικής λογοτεχνίας* (Athens: Themelio).

ARGYRIOU 1961. Αργυρίου, Α. Προτάσεις για την "Κίχλη". Μια πρώτη προσέγγιση, in Anagnostaki *et al.* (eds.) 1961: 231–42.

—— (ed.) 1979. *Νεωτερικοί ποιητές του μεσοπολέμου* (Athens: Sokolis).

—— (ed.) 1982. *Η πρώτη μεταπολεμική γενιά* (Athens: Sokolis).

—— 1983. *Διαδοχικές αναγνώσεις ελλήνων υπερρεαλιστών* (Athens: Gnosi).

—— *et al.* 1973. Η νεοελληνική πραγματικότητα και η πεζογραφία μας, *Synecheia*, 4: 172–9.

—————— 1977. Οι Α. Αργυρίου, Α. Ζήρας, Α. Κοτζιάς, Κ. Κουλουφάκος συζητάνε για τη στροφή της ελληνικής πεζογραφίας μετά του πόλεμο, *Diavazo*, 5–6: 62–83.

Armed Forces HQ 1973. Αρχηγείον Ενόπλων Δυνάμεων. *Εθνική γλώσσα* (Athens: Etairia ton Filon tou Laou).

ATHANASOPOULOS 1992. Αθανασόπουλος, Βαγγέλης. *Οι μύθοι της ζωής και του έργου του Γ. Βιζυηνού* (Athens: Kardamitsa).

AXIOTI 1981. Αξιώτη, Μέλπω. *Δύσκολες νύχτες· Άπαντα, Τόμ. Α'*, ed. M. Douka and V. Lambropoulos (Athens: Kedros) (first pub. 1938).

BABINIOTIS, G. 1979*a*. 'A Linguistic Approach to the "Language Question" in Greece', *Byzantine and Modern Greek Studies*, 5: 1–16.

—— 1979*b*. Μπαμπινιώτης, Γεώργιος. *Νεοελληνική κοινή: Πέρα της καθαρευούσης και της δημοτικής* (Athens: Grigoris).

—— and KONDOS 1967.——Κόντος, Π. *Συγχρονική γραμματική της κοινής νέας ελληνικής: Θεωρία, ασκήσεις* (Athens, privately published).

BACOPOULOU-HALLS, ALIKI 1982. *Modern Greek Theater: Roots and Blossoms* (Athens: Diogenis).

BALOUMIS [1990]. Μπαλούμης, Ε. *Ηθογραφικό διήγημα: Κοινωνικοϊστορική προσέγγιση* (Athens: Bouras).

—— 1996. *Πεζογραφία του '20: μεσοπόλεμος* (Athens: Ellinika Grammata).

BANCROFT-MARCUS, ROSEMARY (forthcoming). *Georgios Chortatsis: Plays of the Cretan Renaissance* (Oxford University Press).

BARBEITO, PATRICIA FELISA 1995. 'Altered States: Space, Gender, and the (Un) making of Identity in the Short Stories of Giorgios M. Vizyenos', *Journal of Modern Greek Studies*, 13/2: 299–326.

BEATON, RODERICK 1976. 'Dionysios Solomos: The Tree of Poetry', *Byzantine and Modern Greek Studies*, 2: 161–82.

—— 1980. *Folk Poetry of Modern Greece* (Cambridge University Press).

—— 1982–3. 'Realism and Folklore in Nineteenth- Century Greek Fiction', *Byzantine and Modern Greek Studies*, 8: 103–22.

—— 1983. 'The History Man', in M. Alexiou 1983: 23–44.

—— 1986. 'The Oral Traditions of Modern Greece', *Oral Tradition* (Columbia, Miss.), 1: 110–33.

—— 1987a. 'Cavafy and Proust', *Grand Street* (New York), 6/2: 127–41.

—— 1987b. 'From *Mythos* to *Logos:* The Poetics of George Seferis', *Journal of Modern Greek Studies*, 5/2: 135–52.

—— (ed.) 1988a. *The Greek Novel: AD 1–1985* (London and Sydney: Croom Helm).

—— 1988b. 'Romanticism in Greece', in R. Porter and M. Teich (eds.), *Romanticism in National Context* (Cambridge University Press), 92–108.

—— 1989a. Ο Σολωμός ρομαντικός: Οι διακειμενικές σχέσεις του "Κρητικού" και του "Πόρφυρα", *Ellinika*, 40: 133–47.

—— 1989b. 'The Sea as Metaphorical Space in Modern Greek Literature', *Journal of Modern Greek Studies*, 7/2: 253–72.

—— 1991. *George Seferis* (Studies in Modern Greek; Bristol: Bristol Classical Press, and New Rochelle, NY: Aristide Caratzas).

—— 1992. 'Out of this World with Andreas Embirikos', *Journal of Mediterranean Studies* (Malta), 2/2: 256–70.

—— 1996a. *The Medieval Greek Romance* (revd. and expanded edn. London: Routledge) (1st edn. 1989).

—— 1996b. 'Aphrodite at War: The Wartime Poetry of Embirikos, Kaknavatos, Papatsonis and Seferis', in Mackridge (ed.), 1996: 131–8.

—— 1998. ' "W(h)ither the Neohellenic?": A Commentary', *Journal of Modern Greek Studies*, 16: 171–6.

BEKATOROS and FLORAKIS 1971. Μπεκατώρος, Στέφανος—Φλωράκης, Αλέκος (eds.), *Η νέα γενιά· Ποιητική ανθολογία 65–70* (2nd edn.; Athens: Kedros).

BERATIS 1976. Μπεράτης, Γιάννης. *Οδοιπορικό του 43* (2nd edn.; Athens: Ermis) (first pub. 1946).

—— 1980. *Διασπορά. Στρόβιλος* (Athens: Ermis) (first pub. 1930 and 1961 respectively).

—— 1992. *Το πλατύ ποτάμι* (4th edn.; Athens: Ermis) (first pub. 1946).

BERLIS 1992. Μπερλής, Άρης. Τα αδιέξοδα της σύγχρονης ποίησης, *I Kathimerini*, (15 Dec.): 10.

—— 1993. Και πάλι περί ελευθέρου στίχου, *I Kathimerini* (5 Jan.): 10.

BIEN, PETER 1964. *Constantine Cavafy* (New York and London: Columbia University Press).

—— 1972. *Kazantzakis and the Linguistic Revolution in Greek Literature* (Princeton University Press).

—— 1989a. *Kazantzakis: Politics of the Spirit* (Princeton University Press).

—— 1989b. *Nikos Kazantzakis: Novelist* (Studies in Modern Greek; Bristol: Bristol Classical Press, and New Rochelle, NY: Aristide Caratzas).

—— 1990–1. 'Ritsos's Painterly Technique in Short and Long Poems', *Yofiri* (Sydney), 11: 5–11.

BOUDOURIS, JEANNE 1983. *Stratis Myrivilis, l'écrivain et l'homme: à travers les remaniements et les variantes des sept premières éditions de son roman "He zoe en tapho"* (Athens: Institut Français).

Boukoumanis 1973. *Κατάθεση '73* (Athens: Boukoumanis).

—— 1974. *Κατάθεση '74* (Athens: Boukoumanis).

BROWNING, ROBERT 1983. *Medieval and Modern Greek* (2nd edn.; Cambridge University Press).

BRUNS, GERALD L. 1974. *Modern Poetry and the Idea of Language: A Critical and Historical Study* (New Haven, Conn. and London: Yale University Press).

CALOTYCHOS, VANGELIS 1997. 'Thorns in the Side of Venice? Galanaki's *Pasha* and Pamuk's *White Castle* in the Global Market', in Tziovas (ed.), 1997: 243–60.

CAPRI-KARKA, C. 1982. *Love and the Symbolic Journey in the Poetry of Cavafy, Eliot and Seferis* (New York: Pella).

—— 1985. *War in the Poetry of George Seferis* (New York: Pella).

CARABOTT, PHILIP 1993. 'Politics, Orthodoxy and the Language Question in Greece: The Gospel Riots of November 1901', *Journal of Mediterranean Studies* (Malta), 3/1: 117–38.

—— (ed.) 1997 *Greek Society in the Making, 1863–1913: Realities, Symbols and Visions* (Aldershot: Ashgate/Variorum).

CAVAFY 1963. Καβάφης, Κωνσταντίνος Π. *Ανέκδοτα πεζά κείμενα*, ed. M. Peridis (Athens).

—— 1983. *Τα αποκυρηγμένα: Ποιήματα και μεταφράσεις*, ed. G. P. Savvidis (Athens: Ikaros).

—— 1991. *Τα ποιήματα: νέα έκδοση*, ed. G. P. Savvidis [with revised and expanded editorial material]. 2 vols. Athens: Ikaros (1st edn. 1963).

—— 1993. *Κρυμμένα ποιήματα, 1877; -1923*, ed. G. P. Savvidis (Athens: Ikaros) (1st pub. 1968, with the title *Ανέκδοτα ποιήματα*. New editorial material added).

—— 1994. *Ατελή ποιήματα, 1918–1932*, ed. Renata Lavagnini (Athens: Ikaros).

380 REFERENCES

CHACONAS, S. G. 1968. *Adamantios Korais: A Study in Greek Nationalism* (New York) (first pub. 1942).

CHARALAMBIDOU, NADIA 1997. 'Seferis's *Six Nights on the Acropolis*: A Modernist Tale?', in Tziovas (ed.), 1997: 163–76.

CHRISTIANOPOULOS 1975. Χριστιανόπουλος, Ντίνος. Ποίηση ή μεταποίηση; *Diagonios* (Thessaloniki), 11: 168–73.

CHRISTOMANOS 1988. Χρηστομάνος, Κωνσταντίνος. *Η κερένια κούκλα* (Athens: Nefeli) (first pub. 1911).

CHRISTOPOULOS 1970. Χριστόπουλος, Αθανάσιος. *Λυρικά*, ed. E. Tsantsanoglou (Athens: Ermis) (first edn. 1811).

CHRYSSANTHOPOULOS, MICHALIS, 1988. 'Reality and Imagination: The Use of History in the Short Stories of Yeoryios Viziinos', in Beaton (ed.), 1988*a*: 11–22.

——1994. Χρυσανθόπουλος, Μιχάλης. *Γεώργιος Βιζυηνός: μεταξύ φαντασίας και μνήμης* (Athens: Estia).

——1997. 'Anticipating Modernism: Constructing a Genre, a Past, and a Place', in Tziovas (ed.), 1997: 61–76.

CLOGG, RICHARD 1986. *A Short History of Modern Greece* (2nd edn.; Cambridge University Press) (first edn. 1979).

——1987. *Parties and Elections in Greece: The Search for Legitimacy* (London: C. Hurst).

——1992. *A Concise History of Greece* (Cambridge University Press).

CLOSE, DAVID H. (ed.) 1993. *The Greek Civil War: Studies of Polarization* (London: Routledge, 1993).

——1995. *The Origins of the Greek Civil War* (London: Longman).

CONSTANTINIDES, ELIZABETH 1985. 'Toward a Redefinition of Greek Romanticism', *Journal of Modern Greek Studies*, 3: 121–36.

——1988. 'The Sea in the Work of Alexandros Papadiamantis', *Modern Greek Studies Yearbook*, 4: 99–110.

CONSTANTINIDES, STRATOS (ed.) 1996. *Modern Greek Theater, Special Issue, Journal of Modern Greek Studies*, 14/1: 1–176.

COUTELLE, LOUIS 1990. *Πλαισιώνοντας τον Σολωμό (1965–1989)* (Athens: Nefeli).

DALLAS 1974. Δάλλας, Γιάννης. *Καβάφης και ιστορία: Αισθητικές λειτουργίες* (Athens: Ermis).

——1984. Ο *Καβάφης και η Δεύτερη Σοφιστική* (Athens: Stigmi).

——1990. *Ποιήματα 1948–1988* (Athens: Nefeli).

DASKALAKIS 1966. Δασκαλάκης, Α. *Κοραής και Κοδρικάς: Η μεγάλη φιλολογική διαμάχη των Ελλήνων 1815–1821* (Athens, privately published).

DASKALOPOULOS 1979. Δασκαλόπουλος, Δημήτρης. *Εργογραφία Σεφέρη (1931–1979)* (Athens: Elliniko Logotechniko kai Istoriko Archeio (ELIA)).

—— 1986. Βιβλιογραφικά Σεφέρη (1979–1986), *Diavazo*, 142: 138–47.

—— 1993. *Βιβλιογραφία Οδυσσέα Ελύτη 1971–1992* (Athens: Etaireia Syngrafeon).

DÉBAISIEUX, RENÉE-PAULE 1995. *Le Décadentisme grec dans les oeuvres en prose (1894–1912)* (Paris: L'Harmattan).

DELIOS 1939. Δέλιος, Γ. *Το σύγχρονο μυθιστόρημα* (Thessaloniki, privately published).

Dendro 1991. Το Δέντρο. Νεοελληνική κοινωνία, λογοτεχνική κριτική, πεζογραφία: Αφετηρίες και παρόν (Το "Δ" συνομιλεί με τους Ευγένιο Αρανίτση, Δημοσθένη Κούρτοβικ και Πέτρο Τατσόπουλο), *To Dendro*, 60–1: 3–54.

—— 1992. Το Δέντρο. Γύρω από την πεζογραφία (Το "Δ" συνομιλεί με τους: Αντρέα Φραγκιά, Σπύρο Πλασκοβίτη και Αλέξη Πανσέληνο), *To Dendro*, 66: 7–29.

DENISI 1990. Ντενίση, Σοφία. Για τις αρχές της πεζογραφίας μας, *O Politis*, 109: 55–63.

—— 1992. Οι αρχές του ελληνικού ιστορικού μυθιστορήματος, *Diavazo*, 291: 28–34.

—— 1994. *Το ελληνικό ιστορικό μυθιστόρημα και ο Sir Walter Scott (1830–1880)* (Athens: Kastaniotis).

DIALISMAS 1984. Διαλησμάς, Στέφανος. *Εισαγωγή στην ποίηση του Γιάννη Ρίτσου* (Athens: Epikairotita).

DIKTAIOS 1974. Δικταίος, Άρης. *Τα ποιήματα, 1934–1965* (Athens: Dodoni).

DIMADIS 1991. Δημάδης, Κ. Α. *Δικτατορία – πόλεμος και πεζογραφία 1936–1944* (Athens: Gnosi).

DIMARAS, A. 1974. Δημαράς, Αλέξης. *Η μεταρρύθμιση που δεν έγινε (τεκμήρια ιστορίας)* (2 vols.; Athens: Ermis).

DIMARAS, K. 1974. Dimaras, C. Th., *A History of Modern Greek Literature*, trans. Mary P. Gianos (University of London Press) (first pub. 1948; Eng. trans. first pub. State University of New York Press, 1972).

—— 1975. Δημαράς, Κ. Θ. *Ιστορία της νεοελληνικής λογοτεχνίας· Από τις πρώτες ρίζες ώς την εποχή μας* (6th edn. Athens: Ikaros) (first edn. 1948).

—— 1982. *Ελληνικός ρομαντισμός* (Athens: Ermis).

—— 1983. *Νεοελληνικός διαφωτισμός* (Νεοελληνικά Μελετήματα, 2; 3rd edn., Athens: Ermis) (first edn. 1977).

—— 1989. *Κωστής Παλαμάς. Η πορεία του προς την τέχνη* (3rd edn.; Athens: Nefeli) (first edn. 1943).

DIMIROULIS, DIMITRIS 1985. 'The "Humble Art" and the Exquisite Rhetoric: Tropes in the Manner of George Seferis', in M. Alexiou and Lambropoulos 1985, 59–84.

Dimosios Dialogos 1988. *Ο δημόσιος διάλογος για την γλώσσα* (Athens: Domos).

DIMOULA 1990a. Δημουλά, Κική. *Έρεβος* (Athens: Stigmi).

—— 1990b. *Ερήμην* (Athens: Stigmi).

—— 1990c. *Το λίγο του κόσμου* (3rd edn., Athens: Stigmi).

DIMOULAS 1986. Δημουλάς, 'Αθως. *Τα ποιήματα 1951–85* (Athens: Stigmi).

DORROS 1981. Ντόρρος, Θεόδορος. *Στου γλιτωμού το χάζι*, prologue A. Argyriou (Athens).

DOUKA 1979. Δούκα, Μάρω. *Η αρχαία σκουριά* (Athens: Kedros).

DOUKAS 1980. Δούκας, Στρατής. *Ιστορία ενός αιχμαλώτου* (7th edn.; Athens: Kedros) (first edn. 1929).

DOULIS, THOMAS 1975. *George Theotokas* (Twayne's World Authors Series, 339; Boston: Twayne).

DRAKONDAIDIS 1984. Δρακονταειδής, Φίλιππος. *Το σπίτι της θείας* (Athens: Kedros).

EIDENEIER, H. 1985. Ο προφορικός χαρακτήρας της νεοελληνικής λογοτεχνίας, *Dodoni: Filoloyia* (Ioannina), 14: 39–53.

—— 1996. Ο συγγραφέας του "'Ερωτος αποτελέσματα", *Thesavrismata* (Venice), 24: 282–5.

EKLUND, BO-LENNART 1972. *The Ideal and the Real: A Study of the Ideas in Kostis Palamás' "Ο Δωδεκάλογος του Γύφτου"* (University of Gothenburg, Classical Institute).

ELYTIS 1970. Ελύτης, Οδυσσέας. *Το 'Αξιον εστί* (6th edn.; Athens: Ikaros) (first pub. 1959).

—— 1971. *'Ηλιος ο πρώτος* (4th edn.; Athens: Ikaros) (first pub. 1942/1943).

—— 1978. *Μαρία Νεφέλη* (Athens: Ikaros).

—— 1979. *'Εξι και μία τύψεις για τον ουρανό* (6th edn.; Athens: Ikaros) (first pub. 1960).

—— 1981. *'Ασμα ηρωικό και πένθιμο για τον χαμένο ανθυπολοχαγό της Αλβανίας* (6th edn.; Athens: Ikaros) (first edn. 1945).

—— 1985. *Ο μικρός ναυτίλος* (Athens: Ikaros).

—— [1987]. *Ανοιχτά χαρτιά* (3rd edn.; Athens: Ikaros) (first pub. 1974).

—— 1989. *Η μαγεία του Παπαδιαμάντη*. Athens: Ermeia (1st pub. 1978; reprinted in idem, *Εν λευκώ* (Athens: Ikaros, 1992), 57–106).

—— 1991. *Τα ελεγεία της Οξώπετρας* (Athens: Ikaros).

EMBIRIKOS 1980a. Εμπειρίκος, Ανδρέας. *Υψικάμινος* (Athens: Agra) (first pub. 1935).

—— 1980b. *Ενδοχώρα* (Athens: Agra) (first pub. 1945).

—— 1980c. *Γραπτά, ή προσωπική μυθολογία* (Athens: Agra) (first pub. 1960).

—— 1980d. Αργώ, ή πλους αεροστάτου (Athens: Ypsilon/Vivlia).

—— 1980e. Οκτάνα (Athens: Ikaros).

—— 1984. Αι Γενεαί Πάσαι, ή Η Σήμερον ως αύριον και ως χθες, ed. G. Yatromanolakis (Athens: Agra).

—— 1990–2. Ο Μέγας Ανατολικός, ed. G. Yatromanolakis (8 vols.; Athens: Agra).

ENGONOPOULOS 1977. Εγγονόπουλος, Νίκος. Ποιήματα (2 vols.; Athens: Ikaros).

—— 1981. [Interview], IKON (Athens) 7: 27–32.

EVANGELOU (ed.) 1994. Ευαγγέλου, Ανέστης. Η δεύτερη μεταπολεμική ποιητική γενιά (1950–1970) (introduction G. Arayis) (Thessaloniki: Paratiritis).

FAKINOU 1983. Φακίνου, Ευγενία. Το έβδομο ρούχο (Athens: Kastaniotis).

FARINOU 1977. Φαρίνου, Γεωργία. Γ. Θεοτοκά: Οι Καμπάνες (εξελικτική πορεία, αρχέτυπα, επιδράσεις), Parnassos 19/3: 421–36.

FARINOU-MALAMATARI 1987. Φαρίνου-Μαλαματάρη, Γ. Αφηγηματικές τεχνικές στον Παπαδιαμάντη 1887–1910 (Athens: Kedros).

—— 1988. Farinou-Malamatari, Georgia. 'The Novel of Adolescence Written by a Woman: Margarita Limberáki', in Beaton 1988a, 103–9.

—— 1990. Οι πρόλογοι των πεζών έργων του Γρ. Ξενόπουλου, Filologos, 60: 95–118; 61: 190–200.

—— 1991. "Ελληνικός Ζιλβλάσιος": Ο Πολυπαθής του Γρ. Παλαιολόγου, in Επιστημονική Επετηρίδα της Φιλοσοφικής Σχολής (University of Thessaloniki) i. 297–324.

—— 1994. Γιάννης Μπεράτης: σχεδίασμα βιο-εργογραφίας, Το πλατύ ποτάμι (Athens: Idryma Goulandri-Horn).

FAURIEL, CLAUDE 1824–5. Chants populaires de la Grèce moderne (Paris).

FLETCHER, ROBIN 1984. Kostes Palamas: A Great Modern Greek Poet—His Life, his Work and his Struggle for Demoticism (Athens: Idryma Kosti Palama).

FOKKEMA, DOUWE W. 1984. Literary History, Modernism, and Postmodernism (Amsterdam and Philadelphia: J. Benjamins).

FORSTER, E. M., et al. 1983. The Mind and Art of C. P. Cavafy: Essays on his Life and Work (Athens: Denise Harvey).

FOUCAULT, MICHEL 1970. The Order of Things: An Archaeology of the Human Sciences (London: Tavistock) (first pub. as Les mots et les choses, Paris, 1966).

FRANGIAS 1987. Φραγκιάς, Ανδρέας. Λοιμός (7th edn.; Athens: Kedros) (first edn. 1972).

FRIAR, KIMON 1958. 'Introduction', in N. Kazantzakis, The Odyssey: A Modern Sequel, trans. (London: Secker and Warburg; New York: Simon and Schuster), ix–xxxviii.

FRIAR, KIMON 1989. 'The Short Poems of Yannis Ritsos', in Y. Ritsos, *Selected Poems 1938–1988*, ed. and trans. K. Friar and K. Myrsiades (Brockport, NY: BOA), 407–46.

——1990. 'Introduction', in O. Elytis, *The Sovereign Sun*, trans. (Newcastle: Bloodaxe), 3–44 (first pub. 1974).

GALANAKI 1975. Γαλανάκη, Ρέα. *Πλην εύχαρις* (Athens: Olkos).

——1980. *Το κέικ* (Athens: Kedros).

——1989. *Ο βίος του Ισμαήλ Φερίκ πασά* (Athens: Agra).

GANAS 1989. Γκανάς, Μιχάλης. *Γυάλινα Γιάννενα* (Athens: Kastaniotis).

——1993. *Παραλογή* (Athens: Kastaniotis).

GARANTOUDIS 1992. Γαραντούδης, Ευριπίδης. Η γοητεία του ποιητικού ρετρό, *I Kathimerini*, (29 Dec.): 10.

——1993. Για το σύγχρονο ελληνικό ελεύθερο στίχο, *Piisi*, 1: 105–40.

GATSOS 1987. Γκάτσος, Νίκος. *Αμοργός* (5th edn.; Athens: Ikaros) (first edn. 1943).

——1992. .... *φύσα αεράκι φύσα με, μη χαμηλώνεις ίσαμε* ... (Athens: Ikaros).

GEORGANTA 1993. Γεωργαντά, Αθηνά. *Εμμανουήλ Ροΐδης· η πορεία προς την "Πάπισσα Ιωάννα"* (Athens: Istos).

GERMANACOS, N. C. 1973. 'An Interview with Three Greek Prose Writers (May, 1972): Stratis Tsirkas, Thanassis Valtinos, George Ioannou', *Boundary 2*, 1/2: 266–313.

GIMOSOULIS 1983. Γκιμοσούλης, Κωστής. *Η αγία μελάνη* (Athens: Kedros).

——1986. *Το στόμα κλέφτης* (Athens: Kedros).

GOTSI, GEORGIA 1996a. 'Narratives in Perambulation: Poe's *The Man of the Crowd* and Metsakes' Αυτόχειρ', *Byzantine and Modern Greek Studies*, 20: 35–55.

——1996b. Experiencing the Urban: Athens in Greek Prose Fiction, 1880–1912 (Unpublished PhD thesis, University of London).

GOUNELAS, C. D. 1980. 'Neither Katharevousa nor Demotic: The Language of Greek Poetry in the Nineteenth Century', *Byzantine and Modern Greek Studies*, 6: 81–107.

——1984. Γουνελάς, Χ.-Δ. *Η σοσιαλιστική συνείδηση στην ελληνική λογοτεχνία 1897–1912* (Athens: Kedros).

——1991. Οι φιλοσοφικές θέσεις των Πολυλά, Ροΐδη και Π. Σούτσου, in *Επιστημονική Επετηρίδα Φιλοσοφικής Σχολής* (University of Thessaloniki), i. 325–59.

——1995. *Η φιλοσοφία της γλώσσας και η νεοελληνική ποίηση* (Athens: Delfini).

GOURGOURIS, STATHIS 1996. *Dream Nation: Enlightenment, Colonization and the Institution of Modern Greece* (Stanford University Press).

GRITSI-MILLIEX 1990. Γκρίτση-Μιλλιέξ, Τατιάνα. *Και ιδού ίππος χλωρός* (7th edn.; Athens: Kastaniotis) (first edn. 1963).

GRYPARIS 1967. Γρυπάρης, Ιωάννης. *'Απαντα τα πρωτότυπα με τα μικρά μεταφράσματα*, ed. G. Valetas (2nd edn.; Athens: Dorikos).

HAKKAS 1986. Χάκκας, Μάριος. *'Απαντα* (3rd, expanded, edn.; Athens: Kedros).

HATZIDAKIS, G. 1901. Χατζιδάκις, Γεώργιος. *Γλωσσολογικαί μελέται, Τόμ. Α'* (Athens: Sakellarios).

—— 1907. *La question de la langue écrite néo-grecque* (Athens: Sakellarios).

HATZIDAKIS, M. 1988. Χατζιδάκις, Μάνος. *Ο καθρέφτης και το μαχαίρι* (Athens: Ikaros).

HATZIPATERAS and FAFALIOU 1988. Χατζηπατέρας, Κώστας—Φαφαλιού, Μαρία (eds.), *Μαρτυρίες 40–1* (Athens: Kedros) (first pub. 1982).

HATZIS 1974. Χατζής, Δημήτρης. *Το τέλος της μικρής μας πόλης* (Athens: Pleias) (first pub. 1960).

HATZOPOULOS 1986. Χατζόπουλος, Κωνσταντίνος. *Ο πύργος του ακροπόταμου*, ed. G. Veloudis (Athens: Odysseas).

—— 1990. *Φθινόπωρο*, introduction P. Haris (Athens: Idryma Kosta kai Elenis Ourani).

—— 1992. *Τα ποιήματα*, introduction G. Veloudis (Athens: Idryma Kosta kai Elenis Ourani).

HEIMONAS 1979. Χειμωνάς, Γιώργος. *Οι χτίστες* (Athens: Kedros).

HENDERSON, G. P. 1970. *The Revival of Greek Thought, 1620–1830* (Albany, NY: State University of New York Press).

HERZFELD, MICHAEL 1982. *Ours Once More: Folklore, Ideology, and the Making of Modern Greece* (Austin: University of Texas Press).

—— 1991. *A Place in History: Social and Monumental Time in a Cretan Town* (Princeton University Press).

HESSELING, D. C. 1924. *Histoire de la littérature grecque moderne* (Paris: Les Belles Lettres) (revision of the Dutch original, pub. 1920).

HIONIDES, HARRY 1975. *Yannis Manglis* (Twayne's World Authors Series, 350; Boston: Twayne).

HIRSCHON, RENÉE 1992. 'Greek Adults' Verbal Play, or, How to Train for Caution', in Joseph 1992, 35–56.

HIRST, ANTHONY 1995. 'Philosophical, Historical and Sensual: An Examination of Cavafy's Thematic Collections', *Byzantine and Modern Greek Studies*, 19: 33–93.

—— 1998. 'Two Cheers for Byzantium: Equivocal Attitudes in the Poetry of Palamas and Cavafy', in David Ricks and Paul Magdalino (eds.), *Byzantium and the Modern Greek Identity* (Aldershot: Ashgate/Variorum).

HOKWERDA, HERO 1980. 'Karyotakis and Katharevousa', *Byzantine and Modern Greek Studies*, 6: 109–30.

HOLTON, DAVID 1984-5. 'Ethnic Identity and Patriotic Idealism in the Writings of General Makriyannis', *Byzantine and Modern Greek Studies*, 9: 133-60.

——(ed.) 1988. *Ο Ψυχάρης και το κίνημα του δημοτικισμού*, *Mandatoforos*, 28: 7-99.

——(ed.) 1991. *Literature and Society in Renaissance Crete* (Cambridge University Press).

HOLTON, DAVID; MACKRIDGE, PETER; and PHILIPPAKI-WARBURTON, IRENE 1997. *Greek: A Comprehensive Grammar of the Modern Language* (London: Routledge).

HONDROS, JOHN 1983. *Occupation and Resistance: The Greek Agony, 1941-44* (New York: Pella).

HORROCKS, GEOFFREY 1997. *Greek: A History of the Language and its Speakers* (London: Longman).

HOULIARAS 1979. Χουλιαράς, Νίκος. *Ο Λούσιας* (Athens: Kedros).

HOUSEHOLDER, F. W., Jun. 1962. 'Greek Diglossia', *Georgetown Monographs*, 15: 109-32.

HUET, PIERRE DANIEL 1966. *Traité de l'origine des romans* (facsimile repr., Stuttgart: J. B. Metzler) (first pub. 1670).

HUTCHEON, LINDA 1988. *A Poetics of Postmodernism: History, Theory, Fiction* (New York and London: Routledge).

I.K. 1989. *Έρωτος αποτελέσματα, ιστορίαι ηθικοερωτικαί—1792*, ed. M. Vitti (Athens: Odysseas) (first pub. 1792).

IATROPOULOS 1971. Ιατρόπουλος, Δημήτριος. *Ποιητική αντιανθολογία* (Athens: Giovanis).

ILINSKAYA 1978. Ιλίνσκαγια, Σόνια. *Η ρομαντική ποίηση στην Ελλάδα: ένα σχεδιάγραμμα*, *O Politis*, 20 (June-July): 45-53.

——1983. *Κ. Π. Καβάφης· Οι δρόμοι προς το ρεαλισμό στην ποίηση του εικοστού αιώνα* (Athens: Kedros).

IOANNOU 1973. Ιωάννου, Γιώργος. *Για ένα φιλότιμο* (3rd edn.; Athens: Kedros) (first edn. 1964).

——1974. *Η μόνη κληρονομιά* (Athens: Ermis).

——1980. *Επιτάφιος θρήνος* (Athens: Kedros).

IORDANIDOU 1980. Ιορδανίδου, Μαρία. *Λωξάντρα* (18th edn.; Athens: Estia) (first edn. 1961).

JAUSS, HANS ROBERT 1982. *Toward an Aesthetic of Reception*, trans. T. Bahti, introduction P. de Man (Brighton: Harvester Press).

JENKINS, ROMILLY 1981. *Dionysius Solomòs* (Athens: Denise Harvey) (first pub. Cambridge, 1940).

JOSEPH, BRIAN (ed.) 1992. 'Language, Power and Freedom in Greek Society', *Journal of Modern Greek Studies*, 10: 1-120.

——and WARBURTON, IRENE 1987. *Modern Greek* (Croom Helm Descriptive Grammars Series; London: Croom Helm).

JUSDANIS, GREGORY 1987a. 'Is Postmodernism Possible outside the "West"? The Case of Greece', *Byzantine and Modern Greek Studies*, 11: 69–92.

—— 1987b. *The Poetics of Cavafy: Textuality, Eroticism, History* (Princeton University Press).

—— 1991. *Belated Modernity and Aesthetic Culture: Inventing National Literature* (Theory and History of Literature, 81; Minneapolis: University of Minnesota Press).

—— (ed.) 1997. 'Whither the Neohellenic?', *Journal of Modern Greek Studies*, 15/2: 167–281.

KACHTITSIS 1985. Καχτίτσης, Νίκος. *Ο εξώστης* (2nd edn.; Athens: Stigmi) (first edn. 1964).

KAKAVOULIA, MARIA 1992. *Interior Monologue and its Discursive Formation in Melpo Axioti's Δύσκολες Νύχτες* (Miscellanea Byzantina Monacensia, 3; Munich; Universität München, Institut für Byzantinistik und Neogriechische Philologie).

—— 1997. 'Interior Monologue: Recontextualizing a Modernist Practice in Greece', in Tziovas (ed.), 1997: 135–50.

KAKNAVATOS 1990. Κακναβάτος, ΄Εκτωρ. *Ποιήματα* (2 vols.; Athens: Agra).

KALAS 1977. Κάλας, Νικόλαος. *Οδός Νικήτα Ράντου* (Athens: Ikaros).

—— 1983. *Γραφή και φως* (Athens: Ikaros).

KALLIGAS 1991. Καλλιγάς, Παύλος. *Θάνος Βλέκας*, introduction E. N. Horafas (Athens: Idryma Kosta kai Elenis Ourani).

KALVOS 1981. Κάλβος, Ανδρέας. *Οι Ψαλμοί του Δαβίδ*, introduction and notes G. Dallas (Athens: Keimena).

—— 1988a. *Ωδαί*, ed. F. M. Pontani (Athens: Ikaros) (edn. first pub. 1970).

—— 1988b. *Ωδαί*, ed. S. Dialismas (Athens: Idryma Kosta kai Elenis Ourani).

—— 1988c. *Συναπταί, Επιστολαί και Ευαγγέλια*, ed. G. Andreiomenos (Athens: Exandas).

—— n.d. *Ωδαί* (1–20), ερμηνευτική έκδοση, ed. M. G. Meraklis (Athens: Estia).

KAPSALIS 1982. Καψάλης, Διονύσης. *Βιβλίο πρώτο* (Athens: Agra).

—— 1986. *Ακόμα μια φορά* (Athens: Agra).

KAPSOMENOS 1992. Καψωμένος, Ερατοσθένης. *"Καλή 'ναι η μαύρη πέτρα σου". Ερμηνευτικά κλειδιά στο Σολωμό* (Athens: Estia).

KARAGATSIS 1976. Καραγάτσης, Μ. *Ο συνταγματάρχης Λιάπκιν* (9th edn.; Athens: Estia) (first edn. 1933).

—— 1978. *Ο Γιούγκερμαν και τα στερνά του* (9th edn.; Athens: Estia) (includes *Ο Γιούγκερμαν*, first pub. 1938, and *Τα στερνά του Γιούγκερμαν*, first pub. 1941).

388 REFERENCES

KARAGATSIS 1980. Ο κίτρινος φάκελος (2 vols.; 5th edn.; Athens: Estia) (first edn. 1956).

KARANIKAS, ALEXANDER, and KARANIKAS, HELEN 1969. Elias Venezis (Twayne's World Authors Series, 74; New York: Twayne).

KARAPANOU 1977. Καραπάνου, Μαργαρίτα. Η Κασσάνδρα και ο λύκος (Athens: Ermis).

KARATHANASIS 1978. Καραθανάσης, Α. (ed.), 'Ανθη ευλαβείας (Athens: Ermis) (first edn. 1708).

KARKAVITSAS 1994. Καρκαβίτσας, Α. Η λυγερή, ed. with introduction by P. D. Mastrodimitris (Athens: Idryma Kosta kai Elenis Ourani) (first pub. 1891).

KAROUZOS 1979. Καρούζος, Νίκος. Δυνατότητες και χρήση της ομιλίας (Thessaloniki: Egnatia).

——1981. Νίκος Καρούζος, introd. by E. Aranitsis (Athens: Akmon).

——1986. Συντήρηση ανελκυστήρων (Athens: Kastaniotis).

——1994. Τα ποιήματα (2 vols.) (Athens: Ikaros).

KARYOTAKIS 1972. Καρυωτάκης, Κ. Γ. Ποιήματα και πεζά, ed. G. P. Savvidis (Athens: Ermis).

KASDAGLIS 1985. Κάσδαγλης, Νίκος. Η νευρή (Athens: Kedros).

KASSIS 1983. Κάσσης, Κυριάκος. Το ελληνικό λαϊκό μυθιστόρημα, 1840–1940 (Athens, privately published).

KATARTZIS 1970. Καταρτζής, Δημήτριος. Τα ευρισκόμενα, ed. K. Th. Dimaras (Athens: Ermis).

KAVVADIAS, N. 1987. The Collected Poems of Nikos Kavadias [parallel Greek and English texts], trans. G. Holst-Warhaft (Amsterdam: Hakkert).

KAYALIS 1991. Καγιαλής, Τάκης. "Γλουμυμάουθ": Ο βικτωριανός A. P. Ραγκαβής (Athens: Nefeli).

KAZANTZAKIS 1960. Καζαντζάκης, Νίκος. Οδύσσεια (3rd edn.; Athens: Dorikos) (first edn. 1938).

——1969. Βίος και πολιτεία του Αλέξη Ζορμπά (6th edn.; Athens: Ekdoseis Elenis Kazantzaki) (first edn. 1946).

——1971. Ασκητική—Salvatores Dei (5th edn.; Athens: Ekdoseis Elenis Kazantzaki) (first edn. 1928).

——1981. Ο Χριστός ξανασταυρώνεται (6th edn.; Athens: Ekdoseis Elenis Kazantzaki) (first edn. 1954).

KAZAZIS, KOSTAS 1979. 'Learnedisms in Costas Taktsis's Third Wedding', Byzantine and Modern Greek Studies, 5: 17–27.

KEDROS 1970. Δεκαοχτώ κείμενα (Athens: Kedros).

——1972. Νέα κείμενα 2 (Athens: Kedros).

KEELEY, EDMUND 1983. Modern Greek Poetry: Voice and Myth (Princeton University Press).

—— 1996a. *Cavafy's Alexandria: Study of a Myth in Progress* (Princeton University Press) (first pub. Cambridge, Mass.: Harvard University Press, 1976).

—— 1996b. 'Nostos and the Poet's Vision in Seferis and Ritsos', in Mackridge (ed.), 1996: 81–96.

KEFALAS 1989. Κεφάλας, Ηλίας. *Ανθολογία σύγχρονης ελληνικής ποίησης· η δεκαετία του 1980 (ιδιωτικό όραμα)* (Athens: Nea Synora).

KEHAYOGLOU 1979. Κεχαγιόγλου, Γιώργος. Προτάσεις για τον "Πόρφυρα" του Σολωμού, in *Αφιέρωμα στον καθηγητή Λίνο Πολίτη* (Thessaloniki: Nikolaidis), pp. 153–84.

—— 1980. Οι ιστορίες της νεοελληνικής λογοτεχνίας, *Mandatoforos*, 15: 5–66.

—— 1984. *Ο έρωτας στα χιόνια του Αλέξανδρου Παπαδιαμάντη: μιά ανάγνωση* (Thessaloniki: Polytypo).

—— 1987. *Ανδρέας Εμπειρίκος: "Αι λέξεις". Μορφολογία του μύθου* (Thessaloniki: University Studio Press).

—— 1991a. 1790–1800: γέννηση, αναβίωση, ανατροφοδότηση ή επανεκτίμηση της ελληνικής ερωτικής πλασματικής πεζογραφίας; *Σύγκριση / Comparaison* (Athens), 2–3: 53–62.

—— 1991b. Νεοελληνικά λογοτεχνικά λαϊκά βιβλία: προκαταρκτικά γραμματολογικά-ειδολογικά και βιβλιογραφικά ζητήματα. *Επιστημονική Επετηρίδα Φιλοσοφικής Σχολής Πανεπιστημίου Θεσσαλονίκης, (Τμήμα Φιλολογίας)* (University of Thessaloniki, i 249–60).

—— 1991c. Προτάσεις για την "Έγκωμη" του Σεφέρη, in *Πρακτικά Συμποσίου Σεφέρη (Αγία Νάπα, 14–16 Απριλίου 1988)* (Nicosia), 253–72.

—— 1995. Ένα ανέκδοτο υπόμνημα του Ελύτη για το 'Αξιον Εστί, *Piisi* (Athens), 5: 27–65.

KITROEFF, ALEXANDER 1983. 'The Alexandria we have Lost', in M. Alexiou 1983: 11–21.

KITROMILIDES, PASCHALIS 1992. *Enlightenment as Social Criticism: Iosipos Moisiodax and Greek Culture in the Eighteenth Century* (Princeton University Press).

KODRIKAS 1991. Κοδρικάς, Παναγιώτης. *Εφημερίδες*, ed. A. Angelou (Athens: Ermis).

KOHLER, DENIS 1985. *L'aviron d'Ulysse. L'itinéraire de Georges Séféris* (Paris: Les Belles Lettres).

KOKORIS 1991. Κόκορης, Δημήτρης. Η πορεία του Γιάννη Ρίτσου προς τον ελεύθερο στίχο, *Ta Potamoploia* (Thessaloniki), 4: 139–59.

KOLYVAS 1991. Κολυβάς, Ι.-Κ. *Λογική της αφήγησης και ηθική του λόγου: μελετήματα του Παπαδιαμάντη* (Athens: Nefeli).

KONDOGLOU 1967. Κόντογλου, Φώτης. *Έργα* (6 vols.; Athens: Astir).

KONDOS, G. 1982. Κοντός, Γιάννης. *Τα οστά* (Athens: Kedros).

—— 1983. *Το χρονόμετρο* (4th edn.; Athens: Kedros) (first edn. 1972).

—— 1985. *Ανωνύμου μοναχού* (Athens: Kedros).

KONDOS, K. 1882. Κόντος, Κωνσταντίνος Σ. *Γλωσσικαί παρατηρήσεις αναφερόμεναι εις την νέαν ελληνικήν γλώσσαν* (Athens: A. Koromilas).

KONDYLAKIS 1980. Κονδυλάκης, Ιωάννης. *Οι άθλιοι των Αθηνών* (Athens: Dorikos) (first pub. 1894).

KONEMENOS 1873. Κονεμένος, Νικόλαος. *Το ζήτημα της γλώσσας* (Corfu: Karayannis).

—— 1875. *Και πάλε περί γλώσσας* (Corfu: Kadmos).

KORAIS 1964. Κοραής, Αδαμάντιος. *Άπαντα τα πρωτότυπα έργα*, ed. G. Valetas (4 vols., numbered A1–2, B1–2; Athens: Dorikos).

—— 1978. *Ο Παπατρέχας*, ed. A. Angelou (Athens: Ermis) (first edn. 1842).

KORFIS 1985. Κόρφης, Τάσος. *Ναπολέων Λαπαθιώτης: Συμβολή στη μελέτη της ζωής και του έργου του* (Athens: Prosperos).

—— 1988. *Βιογραφία Στρατή Δούκα, από 1895 ως 1936* (Athens: Prosperos).

—— 1991. *Νίκος Καββαδίας· συμβολή στη μελέτη της ζωής και του έργου του* (Athens: Prosperos).

—— 1992. *Ρώμος Φιλύρας· Συμβολή στη μελέτη της ζωής και του έργου του* (Athens: Prosperos).

KORNAROS 1980. Κορνάρος, Βιτσέντζος. *Ερωτόκριτος*, ed. S. Alexiou (Athens: Ermis).

—— 1988. *Ερωτόκριτος*, ed. S. Alexiou (rev. edn. (in small format); Athens: Ermis).

KOSTIOU (ed.) 1994. Κωστίου, Κατερίνα. *Για τον Σκαρίμπα* (Nicosia: Aigaion).

KOTZIAS 1979. Κοτζιάς, Αλέξανδρος. *Αντιποίησις αρχής* (Athens: Kedros).

—— 1992. *Τα Αθηναϊκά διηγήματα*, in Angelopoulos et al. (eds.) 1992: 103–121.

—— et al. 1989. Γλώσσα και νεοελληνική έκφραση, *To Dendro*, 42–3: 3–38.

KOUMANDAREAS 1982. Κουμανταρέας, Μένης. *Ο ωραίος λοχαγός* (Athens: Kedros).

—— 1986. *Τα μηχανάκια* (9th edn.; Athens: Kedros) (first edn. 1962).

KOUMANOUDIS 1980. Κουμανούδης, Στέφανος. *Συναγωγή νέων λέξεων*, introd. by K. Th. Dimaras (Νεοελληνικά Μελετήματα, 4; Athens: Ermis) (first edn. 1900).

KRANAKI 1982. Κρανάκη, Μιμίκα. *Contre-Temps* (3rd edn.; Athens: Estia) (first edn. 1947).

KRIARAS 1987. Κριαράς, Εμμανουήλ. Το θέμα της γλώσσας μας σήμερα και τα ιστορικά αίτια που οδήγησαν στη σημερινή γλωσσική κακοδαιμονία, in Λόγιοι και δημοτικισμός (Athens: Ekdotiki Athinon), 9–26 (first pub. 1985).

KRIKOS-DAVIS, KATERINA 1994. *Kolokes: A Study of George Seferis' Logbook III (1953-1955)* (Amsterdam: Hakkert).

KYRIAKIDOU-NESTOROS 1978. Κυριακίδου-Νέστορος, 'Αλκη. Η θεωρία της ελληνικής λαογραφίας: Κριτική ανάλυση (Athens: Etairia Spoudon).

KYRIAZIDIS *et al.* 1983. Το λεξιλόγιο του Μακρυγιάννη ή πώς μιλούσαν οι Έλληνες προτού βιαστεί η γλώσσα μας από την καθαρεύουσα. Ιδέα : Γενική επιμέλεια Ν.Ι. Κυριαζίδης, Γλωσσική επεξεργασία: Ι.Ν. Καζάζης, Προγράμματα κομπιούτερ: J. Bréhier (3 vols.; Athens).

LAINA 1985. Λαϊνά, Μαρία. Δικό της (Athens: Keimena).

—— 1993. Ρόδινος φόβος (Athens: Stigmi).

LAMBROPOULOS, VASSILIS 1988. *Literature as National Institution: Studies in the Politics of Modern Greek Criticism* (Princeton University Press).

—— 1989. 'Modern Greek Studies at the Crossroads: The Paradigm Shift from Empiricism to Skepticism', *Journal of Modern Greek Studies*, 7/1: 1–39.

LANDSMAN, DAVID 1989. 'The Greeks' Sense of Language and the 1976 Linguistic Reforms: Illusions and Disappointments', *Byzantine and Modern Greek Studies*, 13: 159–82.

LASKARATOS 1981. Λασκαράτος, Ανδρέας. Ποιήματα, ed. E. I. Moschonas (Athens: Odysseas).

—— 1982. Τα μυστήρια της Κεφαλονιάς, ed. V. Makis (Athens: Epikairotita).

—— 1987. Ιδού ο άνθρωπος, ed. G. G. Alisandratos (Athens: Ermis).

LASKARIS 1938. Λάσκαρης, Νικόλαος. Ιστορία του νεοελληνικού θεάτρου (2 vols.) (Athens: M. Vasiliou).

LAYIOS *et al.* 1991. Λάγιος, Ηλίας – Καψάλης, Διονύσης – Κοροπούλης, Γιώργος, Ανθοδέσμη (Athens: Agra).

—— 1993. Λάγιος, Ηλίας – Καψάλης, Διονύσης – Κοροπούλης, Γιώργος – Γκανάς, Μιχάλης. Ανθοδέσμη (Athens: Agra).

LAYOUN, MARY N. (ed.) 1990. *Travels of a Genre: The Modern Novel and Ideology* (Princeton University Press).

LIAKOS 1993. Λιάκος, Αντώνης. Εργασία και πολιτική στην Ελλάδα του μεσοπολέμου (Athens: Emboriki Trapeza, Idryma Erevnas kai Paideias).

LIDDELL, ROBERT 1974. *Cavafy: A Critical Biography* (London: Duckworth).

LIGNADIS 1983. Λιγνάδης, Τάσος. Διπλή επισκόπηση σε μια ηλικία και σ' έναν ποιητή : Ένα βιβλίο για τον Νίκο Γκάτσο (Athens: Gnosi).

LIVADITIS 1978, 1987, 1988. Λειβαδίτης, Τάσος, Ποίηση (3 vols.) (Athens: Kedros).

LORENTZATOS 1961. Λορεντζάτος, Ζήσιμος. Το χαμένο κέντρο, in Anagnostaki et al. (eds.) 1961: 86–146.

——1986. Δίπτυχο (Athens: Domos).

LYKOURGOU 1993. Λυκούργου, Νίκη. Επίμετρο, in Myrivilis 1993: 539–643.

LYMBERAKI 1974. Λυμπεράκη, Μαργαρίτα. Τα ψάθινα καπέλα (4th edn.; Athens: Kedros) (first edn. 1946).

——1976. Το μυστήριο (Athens: Kedros).

——1979. Ο άλλος Αλέξανδρος (3rd edn.; Athens: Ermis) (first edn. 1950).

——1994. Τα δέντρα (6th edn., Athens: Kastaniotis) (1st pub. 1945 under the name of Margarita Karapanou).

MCDONALD, ROBERT 1982. Pillar and Tinderbox: The Greek Press under Dictatorship (Boston: Marion Boyars).

MACKRIDGE, PETER 1985a. 'European Influences on the Greek Novel during the 1930s', Journal of Modern Greek Studies, 3: 1–20.

——1985b. The Modern Greek Language: A Descriptive Analysis of Standard Modern Greek (Oxford University Press).

——1988. 'Testimony and Fiction in Greek Narrative Prose, 1944–1967', in Beaton 1988a, 90–102.

——1989. Dionysios Solomos (Studies in Modern Greek; Bristol: Bristol Classical Press, and New Rochelle, NY: Aristide Caratzas).

——1991. 'The Protean Self of Costas Tahtsis', The European Gay Review, 6/7: 172–98.

——1992a. 'The Textualization of Place in Greek Fiction, 1883–1903', Journal of Mediterranean Studies (Malta), 2/2: 148–68.

——1992b. 'Games of Power and Solidarity—Commentary', in Joseph 1992, 111–20.

——1994. 'Dionisio Salamon / Διονύσιος Σολωμός: poetry as a dialogue between languages', Dialogos: Hellenic Studies Review (London: Frank Cass), 1: 59–76.

——(ed.) 1996 Ancient Myth in Modern Greek Poetry: Essays in Memory of C. A. Trypanis (London: Frank Cass).

——1997. 'Cultivating New Lands: The Consolidation of Territorial Gains in Greek Macedonia through Literature, 1912–1940', in Peter Mackridge and Eleni Yannakaki (eds.), Ourselves and Others: The Development of a Greek Macedonian Cultural Identity since 1912 (Oxford: Berg), 175–86.

MAKRIYANNIS n.d. Μακρυγιάννη, Στρατηγού. Απομνημονεύματα (Athens: Byron).

MAKRYNIKOLA 1993. Μακρυνικόλα, Αικατερίνη. Βιβλιογραφία Γιάννη Ρίτσου 1924–1989 (Athens: Etairia Spoudon).

MALANOS 1933. Μαλάνος, Τίμος. Ο ποιητής Κ. Π. Καβάφης: Ο άνθρωπος και το έργο του (Athens: Govostis).

MANOUSOS 1969. Μανούσος, Αντώνιος. Τραγούδια εθνικά, photographic repr. of the 1850 edn. (Athens: Ilias Rizos).

MARKORAS 1988. Μαρκοράς, Γεράσιμος. Ποιήματα, ed. P. D. Mastrodimitris (Athens: Idryma Kosta kai Elenis Ourani).

MARONITIS 1976. Μαρωνίτης, Δ Ν. Ποιητική και πολιτική ηθική : Πρώτη μεταπολεμική γενιά : Αλεξάνδρου—Αναγνωστάκης—Πατρίκιος (Athens: Kedros).

—— 1980. Όροι του λυρισμού στον Οδυσσέα Ελύτη (Athens: Kedros).

—— 1986. Η πεζογραφία του Γιώργου Χειμωνά : αφηρημένο και συγκεκριμένο (Athens: Lotos).

—— 1987. Μέτρια και μικρά : Περιοδικά και εφήμερα (Athens: Kedros).

—— 1992. Διαλέξεις (Athens: Stigmi).

MASKALERIS, THANASSIS 1972. Kostis Palamas (Twayne's World Authors Series, 197; New York: Twayne).

MASTORAKI 1972. Μαστοράκη, Τζένη. Διόδια (Athens: Kedros).

—— 1983. Ιστορίες για τα βαθιά (Athens: Kedros).

—— 1989. Μ' ένα στεφάνι φως (Athens: Kedros).

MASTRODIMITRIS (ed.) 1980. Μαστροδημήτρης, Π.Δ. "Ο Ζητιάνος" του Καρκαβίτσα : Εισαγωγή—κείμενο—γλωσσάριο (Athens: Kardamitsa).

—— 1997. Εισαγωγή στη νεοελληνική φιλολογία (6th edn.; Athens: Domos).

MATESIS 1973. Μάτεσης, Αντώνιος. Ο Βασιλικός, introduction by A. Terzakis (Athens: Ermis) (first pub. Zakynthos, 1859).

MAVILIS 1990. Μαβίλης, Λορέντζος. Τα ποιήματα, ed. G. G. Alisandratos (Athens: Idryma Kosta kai Elenis Ourani).

MAZOWER, MARK 1991. Greece and the Inter-War Economic Crisis (Oxford: Clarendon Press).

—— 1993. Inside Hitler's Greece: The Experience of Occupation, 1941–44 (New Haven and London: Yale University Press).

MERAKLIS 1987. Μερακλής, Μ. Σύγχρονη ελληνική λογοτεχνία 1945–1980. Μέρος πρώτο: Ποίηση (Athens: Patakis).

MIKE and GANA 1988. Μικέ, Μαίρη—Γκανά, Λένα. Δημήτρης Μεντζέλος "Ο Εσωτερικός Μονόλογος" (1933), in Μνήμη Λίνου Πολίτη, Επιστημονική Επετηρίδα Φιλοσοφικής Σχολής (University of Thessaloniki), 293–304.

MILIONIS 1992. Μιλιώνης, Χριστόφορος. Παπαδιαμάντης και ηθογραφία, ή, ηθογραφίας αναίρεσις, Grammata kai Technes, Jan. 1992: 5–22.

MISSIOS 1985. Μίσσιος, Χρόνης…. καλά, εσύ σκοτώθηκες νωρίς (Athens: Grammata).

MITROPOULOS 1993. Μητρόπουλος, Δημήτρης. "'Ενα παιχνίδι με μάσκες": μοντερνισμός, μεταμοντερνισμός και αδιέξοδα στο έργο του Κώστα Ταχτσή, in Tachtsis, Kostas, Συγγνώμην, εσείς δεν είσθε ο κύριος Ταχτσής; (Th. Niarchos and K. Stamatis eds.) (Athens: Patakis), 11–24.

MITSAKIS 1985. Μητσάκης, Κ. Η ελληνική λογοτεχνία στον εικοστό αιώνα : Συνοπτικό διάγραμμα (Athens: Filippotis).

Moderno-Metamoderno 1988. Μοντέρνο—μεταμοντέρνο (Athens: Smili).

MOSCHONAS 1975. Μοσχονάς, Ε. 'Ενας αιώνας δημοτικισμού: Κοινωνικές και πολιτικές προσεγγίσεις [Introduction], in A. Pallis, Μπρουσός (Athens: Ermis).

—— 1981. Εισαγωγή: Αγώνας για μια χαμένη υπόθεση, in Vilaras et al. 1981.

MOSCHOS 1984. Μόσχος, Μιχάλης. Δομή και ύφος στον "Παπατρέχα", in Πρακτικά Συνεδρίου : "Κοραής και Χίος" (Athens: Omireion Pnevmatikon Kentron), i. 169–86.

MOTSIOS (ed.) 1990. Μότσιος, Γιάννης. Ελληνική πεζογραφία 1600–1821 (Athens: Grigoris).

MOULLAS 1974. Μουλλάς, Π. Το διήγημα, αυτοβιογραφία του Παπαδιαμάντη, Introduction in Papadiamandis 1974.

—— 1980. Το νεοελληνικό διήγημα και ο Γ. Μ. Βιζυηνός, Introduction in Vizyinos 1980.

—— 1989. Moullas, P., Les Concours Poétiques de l'Université d'Athènes 1851–1877 (Athens: Archives Historiques de la Jeunesse Grecque).

—— 1997. 'Ενας γνωστός άγνωστος: ο συγγραφέας της Στρατιωτικής Ζωής εν Ελλάδι, in Vayenas (ed.), 1997: 267–77.

MOURELOS (ed.) 1980–2. Μουρέλος, Γιάννης, Η έξοδος (2 vols.; Athens: Kentro Mikrasiatikon Spoudon).

MOUTZAN-MARTINENGOU 1956. Μουτζάν-Μαρτινέγκου, Ελισάβετ. Αυτοβιογραφία, ed. Κ. Porfyris (Athens) (first pub. 1881).

MYRIVILIS 1955. Μυριβήλης, Στράτης. Η ζωή εν τάφω (7th edn.; Athens: Estia)

—— 1956. Η δασκάλα με τα χρυσά μάτια (Athens: Estia) (first pub. 1933).

—— 1971. Ο Βασίλης ο Αρβανίτης, ed. M. Vitti (Athens: Ermis) (first pub. 1943).

—— 1991. Η ζωή εν τάφω. 'Εκδοση Μυτιλήνης 1924 (Athens: Estia).

—— 1993. Η ζωή εν τάφω : ιστορίες του πολέμου. Ανατύπωση της β' έκδοσης (Αθήνα 1930) (Athens: Estia).

MYRSIADES, KOSTAS 1974. Takis Papatsonis (Twayne's World Authors Series, 313; New York: Twayne).

NEROULOS 1870. Νερουλός, Ιάκωβος Ρίζος. Ιστορία των γραμμάτων παρά τοις νεωτέροις 'Ελλησι (Thessaloniki: Abbot) (first pub. Geneva, 1827).

PALAIOLOGOS 1989a. Παλαιολόγος, Γρηγόριος. Ο πολυπαθής, ed. A. Angelou (Athens: Ermis).

——1989b. Ο ζωγράφος, introduction by A. Angelou (Athens: Idryma Kosta kai Elenis Ourani).

PALAMAS 1970. Παλαμάς, Κωστής. Διονύσιος Σολωμός, ed. M. Hatziyakoumis (Athens: Ermis).

——n.d. 'Απαντα (16 vols.; Athens: Biris/Idryma Kosti Palama).

——1984. 'Απαντα, vol. 17. Τα ευρητήρια, ed. G. P. Savvidis and G. Kehayoglou (Athens: Idryma Kosti Palama).

PANAYOTAKIS, N. M. (ed.) 1993. Origini della letteratura neogreca (Αρχές της νεοελληνικής λογοτεχνίας) (2 vols.; Venice: Istituto Ellenico di Studi Neoellenici e Postbizantini).

PANAYOTOPOULOS et al. 1956. Παναγιωτόπουλος, Ι. Μ. κ.ά. Νεοελληνική κριτική (Βασική Βιβλιοθήκη, 42; Athens: Zacharopoulos).

PANAYOTOU 1979. Παναγιώτου Γ. Α. Γενιά του '70. Εισαγωγή. Ανθολόγηση (2 vols.; Athens: Sisifos).

PAPADEMETRIOU 1975–9. Παπαδημητρίου, 'Ελλη (ed.), Ο κοινός λόγος : Αφηγήματα (4 vols.; 2nd edn.; Athens: Kedros) (first edn. 1964–72).

PAPADIAMANDIS 1974. Παπαδιαμάντης, Αλέξανδρος. Αυτοβιογραφούμενος, ed. P. Moullas (Athens: Ermis).

——1981–8. 'Απαντα, ed. N. D. Triandafyllopoulos (5 vols.; Athens: Domos).

——1988. Η φόνισσα (Athens: Nefeli) (first pub. 1903).

PAPADITSAS 1974. Παπαδίτσας, Δ. Π. Ποίηση, 2 (Athens: Oi Ekdoseis ton Filon).

——1978. Ποίηση, 1 (2nd edn.; Athens: Proti Yli) (first edn. 1964).

PAPAKOSTAS 1982. Παπακώστας, Γιάννης. Το περιοδικό Εστία και το διήγημα (Athens: Ekpaidefteria Kostea- Geitona).

——1985. Το περιοδικό Εστία (1876–1895) και το διήγημα: μια θέση και μια αντίθεση (Athens: Kodikas).

PAPATSONIS 1962. Παπατσώνης, Τ. Κ. Εκλογή, i: Ursa Minor (2nd edn.; Athens: Ikaros).

PAPAYEORYIOU 1989. Παπαγεωργίου, Κώστας Γ. Η γενιά του '70. Ιστορία, ποιητικές διαδρομές (Athens: Kedros).

PAPAZOGLOU, C. 1991. ' "Démotique": Δημοτική (γλώσσα) et Δημοτικά (τραγούδια)', Molyvdo-Kondylo-Pelekitis, 3: 15–29.

PARORITIS 1982. Παρορίτης, Κ. Διηγήματα, ed. Stelios Fokos (Athens: Odysseas).

PATRIKIOS 1990. Πατρίκιος, Τίτος. Ποιήματα, i: 1948–1954 (3rd edn.; Athens: Themelio) (first edn. 1954).

PECKHAM, R. SHANNAN 1995. 'Memory and Homelands: Vizyinos, Papadiamantis and Geographical Imagination', Kambos: Cambridge

Papers in Modern Greek (University of Cambridge, Faculty of Modern and Medieval Languages), 3: 95–123.

PECKHAM, R. SHANNAN 1996. 'Between East and West: the Border Writing of Yeoryios Vizyinos', *Ecumene* 3/2: 167–80.

PENTZIKIS 1977. Πεντζίκης, Ν. Γ. *Αντρέας Δημακούδης και άλλες μαρτυριές χαμού και δεύτερης πανοπλίας* (Thessaloniki: ASE).

——1987. *Ο πεθαμένος και η ανάσταση* (3rd edn.; Athens: Agra) (first edn. 1944).

——1992. *Το μυθιστόρημα της κυρίας 'Ερσης* (4th edn. Athens: Agra) (first pub. 1966).

PERI, MASSIMO 1972. *Il linguaggio di Kariotakis* (Padua).

——1994. *Δοκίμια αφηγηματολογίας*, ed. S. N. Philippides (Heraklion: Crete University Press).

PERKINS, DAVID (ed.) 1991. *Theoretical Issues in Literary History* (Cambridge, Mass. and London: Harvard University Press).

PERYSINAKIS 1985. Περυσινάκης, Ι. Ν. Η ωδή *Εις Μούσας* του A. Κάλβου, *Dodoni: Filologia* (Ioannina), 14: 1–37.

PHILIPPIDES, DIA M. L. 1990. *CENSUS of Modern Greek Literature: Check-List of English-Language Sources Useful in the Study of Modern Greek Literature (1824–1987)* (Occasional Papers, 2; New Haven, Conn.: Modern Greek Studies Association).

PHILIPPIDIS and KONSTANDAS 1970. Φιλιππίδης, Δανιήλ–Κωνσταντάς, Γρηγόριος. *Γεωγραφία νεωτερική Περί της Ελλάδος*, ed. A. Koumarianou (Athens: Ermis).

PHILOKYPROU, ELLI 1991. 'Greek Post-Symbolist Poetics' (D.Phil. thesis, University of Oxford).

——1996. Φιλοκύπρου, 'Ελλη. *Λόγια και ιστορίες από το χωριό των ποδηλάτων* (Athens: Diavlos).

PIERIS 1992. Πιερής, Μιχάλης. *Χώρος, φως και λόγος: η διαλεκτική του "μέσα-έξω" στην ποίηση του Καβάφη* (Athens: Kastaniotis).

PIKRAMENOU-VARFI 1986. Πικραμένου – Βάρφη, Δήμητρα. Θανάσης *Πετσάλης-Διομήδης· Η "πνευματική οδοιπορία" του και "Οι Μαυρόλυκοι"* (Athens: Elliniko Logotechniko kai Istoriko Archeio).

PIKROS 1979. Πικρός, Πέτρος. *Τουμπεκί* (Athens: Kaktos) (first pub. 1927).

PILIDIS 1991. Πηλείδης, Τέρπος. *Ο ποιητής Νίκος Καρούζος· Κριτικά σημειώματα* (Athens: Estia).

PITSIPIOS 1995a. Πιτζιπίος, Ι. Η *Ορφανή της Χίου. Ο Πίθηκος Ξουθ*, ed. D. Tziovas (Athens: Idryma Kosta kai Elenis Ourani).

——1995b. Πιτσιπίος, Ι. *Ο πίθηκος Ξουθ*, ed. N. Vayenas (Athens: Nefeli).

PLASKOVITIS 1976. Πλασκοβίτης, Σπύρος. *Το συρματόπλεγμα* (2nd edn.; Athens: Kedros) (first edn. 1975).

——1977. *Το φράγμα* (3rd edn.; Athens: Kedros) (first edn. 1961).

POLITI 1981. Πολίτη, Τζίνα. Η μυθιστορηματική κατεργασία της ιδεολογίας: Ανάλυση της Λυγερής του Ανδρέα Καρκαβίτσα, *Επιστημονική Επετηρίδα Φιλοσοφικής Σχολής*, 20 (University of Thessaloniki), 317–51.

—— 1988. Politi, Jina, 'The Tongue and the Pen: A Reading of Karkavítsas' *O Arheológos*', in Beaton 1988a, 42–53.

POLITIS, A. 1993. Πολίτης, Αλέξης. *Ρομαντικά χρόνια: ιδεολογίες και νοοτροπίες στην Ελλάδα του 1830–1880* (Athens: E.M.N.E.-Mnemon).

POLITIS, K. 1982. Πολίτης, Κοσμάς. *Eroica*, ed. and introduction by P. Mackridge (Athens: Ermis) (first pub. 1937; in book form, 1938).

—— 1985. *Εκάτη* (Athens: Ermis) (first pub. 1933).

—— 1988. *Στου Χατζηφράγκου· Τα σαραντάχρονα μιας χαμένης πολιτείας*, ed. and introduction P. Mackridge (Athens: Ermis) (first pub. 1962; in book form, 1963).

POLITIS, L. 1966. Πολίτης, Λίνος. Τρίτη ή ενιαία δημοτική; *Epohes*, 44: 528–31.

—— 1973. Politis, Linos, *A History of Modern Greek Literature* (Oxford: Clarendon Press).

—— 1980. *Ποιητική ανθολογία* (*8* vols.; 3rd edn., Athens: Dodoni) (first edn. 1969).

—— 1985. *Γύρω στον Σολωμό* (expanded edn.; Athens: Ethniki Trapeza tis Ellados).

POLITOU-MARMARINOU 1979. Πολίτου – Μαρμαρινού, Ελένη. Η εφημερίδα Ραμπαγάς (1878–89) και η συμβολή της στην ανανέωση της νεοελληνικής λογοτεχνίας, *Parnassos*, 21/2: 235–57.

—— 1985. Το περιοδικό Εστία (1876–1895) και το διήγημα, *Parousia* (University of Athens, School of Philosophy), 3: 123–52.

POLYLAS 1959. Πολυλάς, Ιάκωβος. *'Απαντα*, ed. G. Valetas (Athens).

—— 1988. *Διηγήματα* (Athens: Nefeli).

POULIOS 1982. Πούλιος, Λευτέρης. *Ποιήματα: Επιλογή 1969–1978* (2nd edn.; Athens: Kedros).

PREVELAKIS 1976. Πρεβελάκης, Παντελής. *Το χρονικό μιας πολιτείας* (7th edn.; Athens: Estia) (first edn. 1938).

—— 1981. *Ο ποιητής Γιάννης Ρίτσος* (Athens: Kedros).

—— n.d. *Ο ήλιος του θανάτου* (Athens: Estia) (first pub. 1959).

PSYCHARIS 1971. Ψυχάρης. *Το ταξίδι μου*, ed. A. Angelou (Athens: Ermis) (first pub. 1888).

PUCHNER, WALTER 1984. *Ιστορικά νεοελληνικού θεάτρου: έξι μελετήματα* (Athens: Pairides).

—— 1992. *Το θέατρο στην Ελλάδα: μορφολογικές επισημάνσεις* (Athens: Pairides.)

RAIZIS, M. BYRON 1972. *Dionysios Solomos* (Twayne's World Authors Series, 193; New York: Twayne).

RANGAVIS 1874–89. Ραγκαβής, Αλέξανδρος Ρίζος. 'Απαντα τα φιλολογικά (19 vols.; Athens).

—— 1877. Rangabé, A. R., *Précis d'une histoire de la littérature néo-hellénique* (2 vols.; Berlin: S. Calvary).

—— 1988. Διηγήματα, ed. K. Kafandaris (Athens: Odysseas).

—— 1989. Ο αυθέντης τον Μορέως, introduction by A. Sachinis (Athens: Idryma Kosta kai Elenis Ourani) (first pub. 1850).

—— 1991. Ο συμβολαιογράφος (Athens: Nefeli) (first pub. 1851).

RICKS, DAVID 1987. 'A. R. Rangavis: *The Voyage of Dionysus*', *Ellinika*, 38: 89–97.

—— 1988. 'A Greek Poet's Tribute to Keats', *Keats–Shelley Journal*, 37: 35–42.

—— 1989. *The Shade of Homer: A Study in Modern Greek Poetry* (Cambridge University Press).

—— 1990. 'Translating Palamas', *Journal of Modern Greek Studies*, 8/2: 275–90.

—— 1992. 'Papadiamandis, Paganism and the Sanctity of Place', *Journal of Mediterranean Studies* (Malta), 2/2: 169–82.

—— 1995–6. ' "The Best Wall to Hide Our Face Behind": An Introduction to the Poetry of Manolis Anagnostakis', *Journal of Modern Hellenism*, 12–13: 1–26.

—— 1996. 'Titos Patrikios and the Legacy of the Greek Civil War', *Kambos: Cambridge Papers in Modern Greek* (University of Cambridge, Faculty of Modern and Medieval Languages), 4: 81–104.

—— 1997. 'Tradition and the Individual Talent: Remarks on the Poetry of Michael Ganas', *Byzantine and Modern Greek Studies*, 21: 132–53.

RIGAS 1971a. Ρήγας ("Φερραίος"). Η ελληνική δημοκρατία (Athens: Pythia) (first pub. Vienna, 1797).

—— 1971b. Σχολείον των ντελικάτων εραστών, ed. P. S. Pistas (Athens: Ermis).

RITSOS 1983. Ρίτσος, Γιάννης. Αρίοστος ο προσεχτικός αφηγείται στιγμές του βίου του και του ύπνου του (2nd edn.; Athens: Kedros) (first edn. 1982).

—— 1989–90. Ποιήματα (10 vols.; Athens: Kedros, vol. 11, 1993; vol. 12, 1997).

—— 1991. Αργά, πολύ αργά μέσα στη νύχτα (Athens: Kedros).

ROBINSON, CHRISTOPHER 1988. *C. P. Cavafy* (Studies in Modern Greek; Bristol: Bristol Classical Press, and New Rochelle, NY: Aristide Caratzas).

—— 1989. 'Greece', in M. Arkin and B. Sholler (eds.), *Longman Anthology of World Literature by Women (1875–1975)* (New York: Longman), 1127–33.

—— 1997*a*. 'Social, Sexual and Textual Transgression: Kostas Tahtsis and Michel Tremblay, A Comparison', in Tziovas (ed.), 1997: 205–14.

—— 1997*b*. 'Gender, Sexuality and Narration in Kostas Tachtsis: A Reading of *Τα ρέστα*', *Kambos: Cambridge Papers in Modern Greek* (University of Cambridge, Faculty of Modern and Medieval Languages), 5: 63–80.

ROIDIS 1971. Ροΐδης, Εμμανουήλ. *Η Πάπισσα Ιωάννα, μεσαιωνική μελέτη*, ed. T. Vournas (Athens: Tolidis) (first pub. 1866).

—— 1978. *'Απαντα*, ed. A. Angelou (5 vols.; Athens: Ermis).

—— 1986. *Σκαλαθύρματα*, ed. A. Angelou (Athens: Ermis).

—— 1988*a*. *Η Πάπισσα Ιωάννα*, ed. A. Angelou (Athens: Ermis) (first pub. 1866).

—— 1988*b*. *Αφηγήματα* (Athens: Nefeli).

SACHINIS 1975. Σαχίνης, Απόστολος. *Το νεοελληνικό μυθιστόρημα* (4th edn.; Athens).

—— 1981. *Το ιστορικό μυθιστόρημα* (Athens) (first pub. 1957).

—— 1982. *Παλαιότεροι πεζογράφοι* (Athens: Estia) (first pub. 1973).

SAHTOURIS 1977. Σαχτούρης, Μίλτος. *Ποιήματα (1945–1971)* (Athens: Kedros).

—— 1980. *Χρωμοτραύματα* (Athens: Gnosi).

—— 1986. *Εκτοπλάσματα* (Athens: Stigmi).

—— 1990. *Καταβύθιση* (Athens: Kedros).

SAMARAKIS 1970. Σαμαράκης, Αντώνης. *Το λάθος* (3rd edn.; Athens: Estia) (first edn. 1965).

—— 1973. *Το διαβατήριο* (Athens: Eleftheroudakis).

SARANDARIS 1987. Σαραντάρης, Γιώργος. *Ποιήματα*, ed. G. Marinakis (5 vols.; Athens: Gutenberg).

SAREYANNIS 1964. Σαρεγιάννης, Ι. Α. *Σχόλια στον Καβάφη* (Athens: Ikaros).

SAVVIDIS 1961. Σαββίδης, Γ. Π. Μια περιδιάβαση, in Anagnostaki *et al.* (eds.) 1961: 304–408.

—— 1966. *Οι καβαφικές εκδόσεις, 1891–1932* (Athens: Tachydromos).

—— 1980. Savidis, George P., *Odysseus Elytis: Roes, Esa, Nus, Miroltamity* (Athens: Leschi; rep. in Savvidis 1994: 77–95).

—— 1981*a*. Ελληνικός ρομαντισμός 1830–1880. Σχεδίασμα για ένα χρονολόγιο, *Nea Estia*, 110/1307: 279–329.

—— 1981*b*. Ο Σικελιανός και οι άγγλοι ποιητές, *Nea Estia*, 110/1307: 92–108.

—— 1985; 1987. *Μικρά καβαφικά* (2 vols.; Athens: Ermis).

—— 1989. [Review of Mastoraki 1989], *To Vima*, 26 Nov., 59.

—— 1990. *Μεταμορφώσεις του Ελπήνορα (από τον Πάουντ στον Σινόπουλο)* (Athens: Ermis 1st edn. 1981).

—— 1993. Πότε άραγες αρχίζει η Νεότερη Ελληνική Λογοτεχνία; in Panayotakis (ed.), 1993: 37–41, reprinted in Savvidis 1994: 312–16.

SAVVIDIS 1994. *Τράπεζα Πνευματική* (Athens: Poreia).

SAVVOPOULOS 1983. Σαββόπουλος, Διονύσης. *Τα λόγια από τα τραγούδια (1965–75)* (Athens: Ikaros).

SEFERIS 1972. Σεφέρης, Γιώργος. *Ποιήματα* (8th edn. [with additions and line numbering]; Athens: Ikaros).

—— 1973. Ιγνάτης Τρελός [= Γιώργος Σεφέρης]. *Οι ώρες της "Κυρίας Έρσης"*, ed. G. P. Eftychidis [= G. P. Savvidis] (Athens: Ermis) (first pub. 1967; repr. in Seferis 1992).

—— 1974. *Έξι νύχτες στην Ακρόπολη*, ed. G. P. Savvidis (Athens: Ermis).

—— 1976. *Τετράδιο γυμνασμάτων Β'*, ed G. P. Savvidis (Athens: Ikaros).

—— 1981. *Δοκιμές* (2 vols.; 4th edn., corrected; Athens: Ikaros).

—— 1992. *Δοκιμές, τρίτος τόμος: παραλειπόμενα (1932–1971)*, ed. D. Daskalopoulos (Athens: Ikaros).

SHERMAN, JON 1988. 'Psycharis and the Εκπαιδευτικός Όμιλος', in Holton 1988: 87–94.

SHERRARD, PHILIP 1975. 'Andreas Kalvos and the Eighteenth-Century Ethos', *Byzantine and Modern Greek Studies*, 1: 175–206.

—— 1982. *The Marble Threshing Floor: Studies in Modern Greek Poetry* (Athens: Denise Harvey) (first pub. London, 1956).

SIAFLEKIS 1988. Σιαφλέκης, Z. I. *Συγκριτισμός και ιστορία της λογοτεχνίας* (Athens: Epikairotita).

SIDERIS 1953. Σιδέρης, Γιάννης. *Νεοελληνικό θέατρο, 1795–1929* (Βασική Βιβλιοθήκη, 40; Athens: Aetos).

SIKELIANOS 1965. Σικελιανός, Άγγελος. *Λυρικός βίος*, ed. G. P. Savvidis (7 vols.; Athens: Ikaros).

—— 1983. *Πεζός λόγος*, ed. G. P. Savvidis (4 vols., Athens: Ikaros).

SINOPOULOS 1976, 1980. Σινόπουλος, Τάκης. *Συλλογή* (2 vols.) (Athens: Ermis).

Six Poets 1971. *Έξι ποιητές: Κατερίνα Αγγελάκη-Ρουκ, Τάσος Δενέγρης, Νανά Ησαΐα, Δημήτρης Ποταμίτης, Λεφτέρης Πούλιος, Βασίλης Στεριάδης* (Athens).

SKARIMBAS 1992a. Σκαρίμπας, Γιάννης. *Μαριάμπας*, ed. K. Kostiou (Athens: Nefeli) (first pub. 1935).

—— 1992b. *Το σόλο του Φίγκαρω*, ed. K. Kostiou (Athens: Nefeli) (first pub. 1938).

—— 1993. *Το θείο τραγί*, ed. K. Kostiou (Athens: Nefeli) (first pub. 1933).

SKARTSIS 1982. Σκαρτσής, Σωκράτης (ed.), *Πρακτικά πρώτου συμποσίου νεοελληνικής ποίησης* (Athens: Gnosi).

SKOPETEA 1988. Σκοπετέα, Έλλη. *Το πρότυπο βασίλειο και η Μεγάλη Ιδέα: όψεις του εθνικού προβλήματος στην Ελλάδα (1830–1880)* (Athens: Polytypo).

Sokolis 1988–90. *Η μεταπολεμική πεζογραφία· Από τον πόλεμο του '40 ώς τη δικτατορία του '67* (8 vols.; Athens: Sokolis).

—— 1993. *Η μεσοπολεμική πεζογραφία: από τον πρώτο ως τον δεύτερο παγκόσμιο πόλεμο (1914-1939)*, introduction P. Moullas (8 vols.) (Athens: Sokolis).

—— 1996–7. *Η παλαιότερη πεζογραφία μας. Από τις αρχές της ως τον πρώτο παγκόσμιο πόλεμο* (8 vols.) (Athens: Sokolis).

SOLOMOS 1964. Σολωμός, Διονύσιος. *Αυτόγραφα έργα*, ed. L. Politis (2 vols.; University of Thessaloniki).

—— 1986. *Άπαντα*, ed. L. Politis (2 vols.; Athens: Ikaros) (first edn. 1948/ 55).

—— 1991. *Η Γύναικα της Ζάκυθος. Όραμα του Διονυσίου Ιερομονάχου, εγκατοίκου εις ξωκλήσι Ζακύνθου*, ed. E. Tsantsanoglou (Heraklion, Crete: Vikelaia Dimotiki Vivliothiki).

—— 1994. *Ποιήματα και πεζά*, ed. Stylianos Alexiou (Athens: Stigmi).

SOTIRIOU 1983. Σωτηρίου, Διδώ. *Ματωμένα χώματα* (26th edn. (reset); Athens: Kedros) (first edn. 1962).

SOURBATI, ATHANASSIA 1992. 'Reading the Subversive in Contemporary Greek Women's Fiction' (Ph.D. thesis, University of London).

SOUTSOS, A. 1994. Σούτσος, Αλέξανδρος. *Ο εξόριστος του 1831*, ed. with introduction by L. Droulia (Athens: Idryma Kosta kai Elenis Ourani).

—— 1996. *Ο εξόριστος του 1831*, ed. with introduction by Nasos Vayenas. (Athens: Nefeli).

SOUTSOS, P. 1915. Σούτσος, Παναγιώτης. *Ποιήματα*, prologue by I. Zervos (Athens: Fexis).

—— 1996. *Ο Λέανδρος*, ed. Alexandra Samouil (Athens: Nefeli).

STAVRIDI-PATRIKIOU 1976. Σταυρίδη-Πατρικίου, Ρένα (ed.), *Δημοτικισμός και κοινωνικό πρόβλημα* (Athens: Ermis).

STAVROPOULOU 1987. Σταυροπούλου, Ερασμία-Λουίζα. *Παναγιώτης Πανάς (1832-1896): Ένας ριζοσπαστικός ρομαντικός* (Athens).

STERYOPOULOS 1967. Στεργιόπουλος, Κώστας. *Από τον συμβολισμό στην "νέα ποίηση"* (Athens: Bakon).

—— 1988; 1992. *Τα ποιήματα I: 1944-1965. II : 1965-1983* (Athens: Nefeli).

STEWART, CHARLES 1991. *Demons and the Devil: Moral Imagination in Modern Greek Culture* (Princeton University Press).

SVORONOS 1976. Σβορώνος, Ν. *Επισκόπηση της νεοελληνικής ιστορίας* (Athens: Themelio).

SYRIMIS, GEORGE 1995. 'Gender, Narrative Modes, and the Procreative Cycle: The Pregnant Word in Vizyenos', *Journal of Modern Greek Studies*, 13/2: 327–49.

TACHTSIS 1974a. Ταχτσής, Κώστας. *Το τρίτο στεφάνι* (4th edn.; Athens: Ermis) (first edn. 1962).

—— 1974b. *Τα ρέστα* (Athens: Ermis) (first pub. 1972).

TANNEN, DEBORAH 1983. *Lilika Nakos* (Twayne's World Authors Series, 677; Boston: Twayne).

402 REFERENCES

TATSOPOULOS 1988. Τατσόπουλος, Πέτρος. *Η καρδιά του κτήνους* (Athens: Ermis).

TERZAKIS 1985. Τερζάκης, 'Αγγελος. *Ταξίδι με τον 'Εσπερο* (5th edn.; Athens: Estia) (first edn. 1946).

——1989. *Δίχως θεό* (8th edn.; Athens: Estia) (first edn. 1951).

THALASSIS, ALEXANDRA 1991. 'Incarnations of Greekness in the Greek Novel of World War II' (Ph.D. thesis, University of London).

THALASSIS, G. 1992. Θαλάσσης, Γιώργος. *Η άρνηση του Λόγου στο ελληνικό μυθιστόρημα μετά το 1974* (Athens: Gnosi).

THANIEL, GEORGE 1977. 'George Seferis's "Thrush": A Modern Descent', *Canadian Review of Comparative Literature*, 4: 89–102.

——1981. Δανιήλ, Γιώργος. *Ο λεπιδόπτερος της αγωνίας: Νίκος Καχτίτσης* (Athens: Nefeli).

——1983. *Homage to Byzantium: The Life and Work of Nikos Gabriel Pentzikis* (Minneapolis: Nostos).

THEMELIS 1969–70. Θέμελης, Γιώργος. *Ποιήματα* (2 vols.; Thessaloniki).

——1978. *Η νεώτερη ποίησή μας*, i. (Thessaloniki: Konstandinidis) (first pub. 1963).

THEODORAKIS 1987. Θεοδωράκης, Μίκης. *'Ολα τα τραγούδια* (Athens: Kaktos).

THEOTOKAS 1967. Θεοτοκάς, Γιώργος. *Ασθενείς και οδοιπόροι* (2 vols.; 5th edn.; Athens: Estia) (vol. i (*Ιερά οδός*), first edn. 1950; first complete edn. 1964).

——1973. *Ελεύθερο πνεύμα*, ed. K. Th. Dimaras (Athens: Ermis) (first pub. 1929).

——1985. *Σημαίες στον ήλιο*, ed. G. P. Savvidis and M. Pieris (Athens: Ermis).

——n.d. (1). *Αργώ* (2 vols.; Athens: Estia) (first pub. 1933; 1936).

——n.d. (2). *Οι καμπάνες* (Athens: Estia) (first pub. 1966).

THEOTOKIS 1978. Θεοτόκης, Κωνσταντίνος. *Η τιμή και το χρήμα* (Athens: Keimena) (first pub. 1912).

——1979. *Κατάδικος*, ed. G. Dallas (Athens: Keimena) (first pub. 1919).

——1981. *Οι σκλάβοι στα δεσμά τους*, introduction by G. Dallas (Athens: Keimena) (first pub. 1922).

——1990. *Η ζωή και ο θάνατος του Καραβέλα* (Athens: Nefeli) (first pub. 1920).

THOMSON, GEORGE 1969. 'Introduction', in K. Palamas, *The Twelve Lays of the Gipsy* (London: Lawrence and Wishart).

TONNET, HENRI 1994. 'Roman grec ancien, roman grec moderne. Le cas de l'*Orpheline de Chio* (Η ορφανή της Χίου) de J. Pitsipios (1839)', *Revue des Etudes Néo-Helléniques*, 3/1: 23–39.

——1996. *Histoire du roman grec (des origines à 1960)* (Paris: L'Harmattan).

TRIANDAFYLLIDIS 1938. Τριανταφυλλίδης, Μανόλης. *Νεοελληνική γραμματική, πρώτος τόμος: Ιστορική εισαγωγή* (Athens: Dimitrakos).

TRIANTAFYLLOPOULOS 1981. Τριανταφυλλόπουλος, Ν. Δ. (ed.) *Φώτα ολόφωτα – ένα αφιέρωμα στον Παπαδιαμάντη και τον κόσμο του* (Athens: Elliniko Logotechniko kai Istoriko Archeio (ELIA)).

TRIVIZAS 1996. Τριβίζας, Σωτήρης. *Το σουρρεαλιστικό σκάνδαλο: χρονικό της υποδοχής του υπερρεαλιστικού κινήματος στην Ελλάδα* (Athens: Kastaniotis).

TROVAS 1984. Τροβάς, Διονύσιος. *Ξενόπουλος, η ζωή και το έργο του* (Athens: I. G. Vasiliou).

TSAKONAS 1981. Τσάκωνας, Δ. *Ιστορία της νεοελληνικής λογοτεχνίας* (3 vols.; Athens: Ladias).

—— 1988. *Ο ελληνικός υπερρεαλισμός* (Athens: Kaktos).

—— 1989. *Η γενιά του 30: Τα πριν και τα μετά* (Athens: Kaktos).

—— 1992. *Ιστορία της νεοελληνικής λογοτεχνίας και πολιτικής κοινωνίας* (9 vols.) (Athens: Sofron).

TSIRKAS 1958. Τσίρκας, Στρατής. *Ο Καβάφης και η εποχή του* (Athens: Kedros).

—— 1971. *Ο πολιτικός Καβάφης* (Athens: Kedros).

—— 1980–1. *Ακυβέρνητες πολιτείες* (3 vols.; 13th edn.; Athens: Kedros) (first pub. 1960; 1962; 1965).

TSOPANAKIS 1966. Τσοπανάκης, Α. Γ. Η τρίτη δημοτική, *Epohes*, 39: 8–17; 40: 148–53.

TZIOVAS, DIMITRIS 1985. 'The Organic Discourse of Nationistic Demoticism: A Tropological Approach', in M. Alexiou and Lambropoulos 1985: 253–77.

—— 1986. *The Nationism of the Demoticists and its Impact on their Literary Theory (1888–1930)* (Amsterdam: Hakkert).

—— 1987. Τζιόβας, Δημήτρης. *Μετά την αισθητική* (Athens: Gnosi).

—— 1988*a*. 'Re-reading Theotokas's *Argo*: The Mythical Journey and the Crisis of Greek Identity', *Modern Greek Studies Yearbook*, 4: 83–97.

—— 1988*b*. *Η ώρα της πεζογραφίας ή η εξάντληση της ποίησης*, *Porfyras*, 47: 68–71.

—— 1989*a*. *Οι μεταμορφώσεις του εθνισμού και το ιδεολόγημα της ελληνικότητας στο μεσοπόλεμο* (Athens: Odysseas).

—— 1989*b*. 'Residual Orality and Belated Textuality in Greek Literature and Culture', *Journal of Modern Greek Studies*, 7/2: 321–35.

—— 1993*a*. Τζιόβας, Δημήτρης. *Το παλίμψηστο της ελληνικής αφήγησης: από την αφηγηματολογία στη διαλογικότητα* (Athens: Odysseas).

—— 1993*b*. 'Dialogism and Interpretation: Reading Papadiamantis' *A Dream among the Waters*', *Byzantine and Modern Greek Studies*, 17: 141–60.

TZIOVAS, DIMITRIS 1994. 'A Telling Absence: The Novel in the Ionian Islands', *Journal of Mediterranean Studies* (Malta), 4/1: 73–82.

——(ed.) 1997. *Greek Modernism and Beyond*. Essays in Honor of Peter Bien (Lanham, Maryland: Rowman & Littlefield).

University of Thessaloniki 1994. *Ζητήματα ιστορίας των νεοελληνικών γραμμάτων* (Thessaloniki: Paratiritis).

VAFOPOULOS 1990. Βαφόπουλος, Γ.Θ. *Άπαντα τα ποιητικά*, ed. G. Kehayoglou (Thessaloniki: Paratiritis).

VAKALO 1990. Βακαλό, Ελένη. *Γενεαλογία. Του κόσμου* (2nd edn.; Athens: Ypsilon/Vivlia) (first pub. 1971 and 1978 respectively).

——1995. *Το άλλο του πράγματος: ποίηση 1954–1994* (Athens: Nefeli).

VALAORITIS, A. 1970. Βαλαωρίτης, Αριστοτέλης. *Ο Φωτεινός*, ed. G. P. Savvidis (Athens: Ermis) (first pub. 1879).

——1981. *Ποιήματα και πεζά*, ed. G. P. Savvidis and E. Tsantsanoglou (Athens: Ikaros).

VALAORITIS, N. 1981. Βαλαωρίτης, Νάνος. *Ο διαμαντένιος γαληνευτής* (Athens: Ypsilon).

——1983. *Ποιήματα, i.: 1944–1964* (Athens: Ypsilon).

VALETAS 1983. Βαλέτας, Γ. *Το ελληνικό διήγημα, η θεωρία και η ιστορία του* (rev. edn.; Athens: Filippotis).

VALTINOS 1984. Βαλτινός, Θανάσης. *Η κάθοδος των εννιά* (3rd edn.; Athens: Agra) (first edn. 1963).

VAMVOUNAKI 1981. Βαμβουνάκη, Μαρώ. *Το χρονικό μιας μοιχείας* (Athens: Estia).

VAN DYCK, KAREN 1996. 'Bruised Necks and Crumpled Petticoats: What's Left of Myth in Contemporary Greek Women's Poetry', in Mackridge (ed.), 1996: 121–30.

——1997. *Kassandra and the Censors: Greek Poetry Since 1967* (Ithaca, NY: Cornell University Press).

VARNALIS 1988. Βάρναλης, Κώστας. *Προσκυνητής*, ed. G. P. Savvidis (Athens: Kedros) (first pub. 1919).

——1989. *Το φως που καίει* (17th edn.; Athens: Kedros) (first pub. 1922; rev. edn. 1933).

——1990. *Σκλάβοι πολιορκημένοι*, ed. G. Dallas (Athens: Kedros) (first pub. 1927).

VASILIKOS 1987. Βασιλικός, Βασίλης. *Η τριλογία (Το φύλλο, Το πηγάδι, Τ' αγγέλιασμα)* (Athens: Gnosi).

——1994. *Το φύλλο, Το πηγάδι, Τ' αγγέλιασμα* (Athens: Nea Synora) (1st edn. 1961).

VAYENAS 1974. Βαγενάς, Νάσος. *Πεδίον Άρεως (Ποιήματα 1970–1974)* (Athens: Diogenes).

—— 1979a. Vayenas, Nasos, 'The Language of Irony (Towards a Definition of the Poetry of Cavafy)', *Byzantine and Modern Greek Studies*, 5: 43–56.

—— 1979b. *Ο ποιητής και ο χορευτής· Μια εξέταση της ποιητικής και της ποίησης του Σεφέρη* (Athens: Kedros).

—— 1982. *Ο λαβύρινθος της σιωπής : Δοκίμιο για την ποίηση* (Athens: Kedros).

—— 1984. *Για έναν ορισμό του μοντέρνου στην ποίηση* (Athens: Stigmi).

—— 1989. *Ποίηση και μετάφραση* (Athens: Stigmi).

—— (ed.) 1991. *Νεοελληνικά μετρικά* (Heraklion: Crete University Press).

—— (ed.) 1992a. *Οι Ωδές του Κάλβου· επιλογή κριτικών κειμένων* (Heraklion: Crete University Press).

—— 1992b. *Βάρβαρες Ωδές* (Athens: Kedros).

—— 1994. *Η ειρωνική γλώσσα· κριτικές μελέτες για τη νεοελληνική γραμματεία* (Athens: Stigmi).

—— (ed.) 1996. *Η ελευθέρωση των μορφών: η ελληνική ποίηση από τον έμμετρο στον ελεύθερο στίχο (1880–1940)* (Heraklion: Crete University Press).

—— (ed.) 1997. *Από τον Λέανδρο στον Λουκή Λάρα : μελέτες για την πεζογραφία της περιόδου 1830–1880* (Heraklion: Crete University Press).

VELOUDIS 1989. Βελουδής, Γ. Δ. *Σολωμός: Ρομαντική ποίηση και ποιητική: Οι γερμανικές πηγές* (Athens: Gnosi).

VENEZIS 1969. Βενέζης, Ηλίας. *Αιολική γη* (8th edn.; Athens: Estia) (first pub. 1943).

—— 1971. *Γαλήνη* (Athens: Estia) (first pub. 1939).

—— n.d. *Το νούμερο 31328* (12th edn.; Athens: Estia) (first pub. 1924; revised 1931).

VERNARDAKIS 1884. [Βερναρδάκης, Δ.]. *Ψευδαττικισμού έλεγχος, ήτοι Κ. Σ. Κόντου γλωσσικών παρατηρήσεων εις την νέαν ελληνικήν γλώσσαν ανασκευή* (Trieste: Lloyd).

VIKELAS 1991. Βικέλας, Δ. *Λουκής Λάρας*, ed. M. Ditsa (Athens: Ermis).

VILARAS 1995. Βηλαράς, Ιωάννης. *Τα ποιήματα*, ed. G. Andreiomenos (Athens: Idryma Kosta kai Elenis Ourani).

—— et al. 1981. Βηλαράς, Ψαλίδας, Χριστόπουλος κ.ά. *Η δημοτικιστική αντίθεση στην κοραϊκή "μέση οδό"*, ed. E. Moschonas (Athens: Odysseas).

VITTI, MARIO 1960. *A. Kalvos e i suoi scritti in italiano* (Naples: Istituto Universitario Orientale).

—— 1977. *Οδυσσέας Ελύτης: βιβλιογραφία 1935–1971* (with Angeliki Gabatha) (Athens: Ikaros).

—— 1979. *Η γενιά του τριάντα: Ιδεολογία και μορφή* (2nd (rev.) edn.; Athens: Ermis).

—— [1980]. Σημείωμα στο "Διονύσου πλους" του Ραγκαβή: Επίμετρο Β',
in Ιδεολογική λειτουργία της ελληνικής ηθογραφίας, 2nd edn. (Athens:
Kedros), 141–52 (omitted from 3rd edn., see Vitti 1991).

—— 1984. Οδυσσέας Ελύτης: Κριτική μελέτη (Athens: Ermis).

—— 1987. Ιστορία της νεοελληνικής λογοτεχνίας (rev. edn., Athens:
Odysseas) (first Italian edn. 1971; first Greek edn. 1978).

—— 1988. 'The Inadequate Tradition: Prose Narrative during the First
Half of the Nineteenth Century', in Beaton 1988a, 3–10.

—— 1989. Φθορά και λόγος· εισαγωγή στην ποίηση του Γιώργου Σεφέρη
(new edn., revd.) (Athens: Estia) (1st edn. 1974).

—— 1991. Ιδεολογική λειτουργία της ελληνικής ηθογραφίας (3rd
(expanded) edn., Athens: Kedros) (first edn. 1974).

—— 1995. Ο Κάλβος και η εποχή του (Athens: Stigmi).

VIZYINOS 1980. Βιζυηνός, Γ. Μ. Νεοελληνικά διηγήματα, ed. P. Moullas (Athens: Ermis).

—— 1991. Τα διηγήματα, introduction by Vangelis Athanasopoulos
(Athens: Idryma Kosta kai Elenis Ourani).

VLACHOS 1967. Βλάχος, Α. Νεοελληνικά, Epohes, 46: 126–8.

VLAVIANOS 1991. Βλαβιανός, Χάρης, Η νοσταλγία των ουρανών
(Athens: Nefeli).

VOULGARI, SOPHIA 1997. 'Playing with Genre(s): The "Prose Poems" of
Nanos Valaoritis', in Tziovas 1997: 229–42.

VOUTIERIDIS 1924, 1927. Βουτιερίδης, Ηλίας. Ιστορία της νεοελληνικής
λογοτεχνίας από των μέσων του ΧV αιώνος μέχρι των νεοτάτων
χρόνων (2 vols) (Athens: Zekakis).

VOUTOURIS 1995. Βουτουρής, Παντελής. Ως εις καθρέπτην...
Προτάσεις και υποθέσεις για την ελληνική πεζογραφία του 19ου
αιώνα (Athens: Nefeli).

VOUTYRAS 1994–5. Βουτυράς, Δημοσθένης. Άπαντα, ed. Vasias Tsoko-
poulos (3 vols) (Athens: Delfini).

VRETTAKOS 1981. Βρεττάκος, Ν. Τα ποιήματα (2 vols.; Athens: Tria Fylla).

VYZANDIOS 1972. Βυζάντιος, Δ. Κ. Η Βαβυλωνία, α' και β' έκδοση, ed.
S. Evangelatos (Athens: Ermis) (first pub. 1836; rev. edn. 1840).

WILSON, SAMUEL SHERIDAN 1990. Το παλληκάριον, introduction by
D. Polemis (Athens: Idryma Kosta kai Elenis Ourani) (first pub. Malta
1835).

WOODHOUSE, C. M. 1985. The Rise and Fall of the Greek Colonels (London:
Granada).

—— 1991. The Story of Modern Greece (London 1991) (first pub. 1964).

WYATT, WILLIAM F., Jun., 1985. 'Andreas Karkavitsas's The Beggar and
The Archaeologist', Modern Greek Studies Yearbook, I: 115–30.

—— 1988. 'Nature and Point of View in A. Karkavitsas' The Beggar', in
Beaton 1988a, 31–41.

XENOPOULOS 1958–71. Ξενόπουλος, Γρηγόριος. 'Απαντα (11 vols.; Athens: Biris).

YANIDIS 1969. Γιανίδης, Ελισαίος. *Γλώσσα και ζωή: Αναλυτική μελέτη του γλωσσικού ζητήματος* (Athens: Kalvos) (first pub. 1908).

YANNAKAKI, ELENI 1990. Yannakakis, Helen. 'Narcissus in the Novel: A Study of Self-Referentiality in the Greek Novel 1930–1945' (Ph.D. thesis, University of London).

——1991. Γιαννακάκη, Ελένη. Ο θάνατος και η ανάσταση του Ναρκίσσου: *Ο πεθαμένος και η ανάσταση* του Ν. Γ. Πεντζίκη, *Palimpsisto* (Heraklion, Crete), 11: 101–25.

——1994. 'History as Fiction in Rea Galanaki's *The Life of Ismail Ferik Pasha*', *Kambos: Cambridge Papers in Modern Greek* (University of Cambridge, Faculty of Modern and Medieval Languages), 2: 121–41.

YATROMANOLAKIS 1982. Γιατρομανωλάκης, Γιώργης. *Ιστορία* (Athens: Kedros).

——1983. *Ανδρέας Εμπειρίκος: Ο ποιητής του έρωτα και του νόστου* (Athens: Kedros).

——1990. Επίμετρο, in Embirikos 1990–2: i. 285–322.

——*et al.* 1987. Ιδεολογία και μορφή της νεοελληνικής λογοτεχνίας την τελευταία εικοσαετία, in *Ανοιχτές Συζητήσεις* (Athens: Ypourgeio Politismou).

ZACHARIADIS 1945. Ζαχαριάδης, Νίκος. *Ο αληθινός Παλαμάς* (Athens, privately published).

ZAMAROU 1993. Ζαμάρου, Ρένα. *Ο ποιητής Νίκος Εγγονόπουλος: επίσκεψη τόπων και προσώπων* (Athens: Kardamitsa).

ZAMBELIOS 1989. Ζαμπέλιος, Σπυρίδων. *Οι κρητικοί γάμοι* (Athens: Idryma Kosta kai Elenis Ourani) (first pub. Turin, 1871).

ZATELLI 1993. Ζατέλλη, Ζυράννα. *Και με το φως του λύκου επανέρχονται* (Athens: Kastaniotis).

ZIRAS 1979. Ζήρας, Αλέξης. *Νεώτερη ελληνική ποίηση 1965–1980* (Athens: Grafi).

Index